A New Response to Youth Crime

A New Response to Youth Crime

Edited by
David J. Smith

WILLAN
PUBLISHING

Published by

Willan Publishing
Culmcott House
Mill Street, Uffculme
Cullompton, Devon
EX15 3AT, UK
Tel: +44(0)1884 840337
Fax: +44(0)1884 840251
e-mail: info@willanpublishing.co.uk
Website: www.willanpublishing.co.uk

Published simultaneously in the USA and Canada by

Willan Publishing
c/o ISBS, 920 NE 58th Ave, Suite 300,
Portland, Oregon 97213-3786, USA
Tel: +001(0)503 287 3093
Fax: +001(0)503 280 8832
e-mail: info@isbs.com
Website: www.isbs.com

First published 2010

ISBN   978-1-84392-754-9 paperback
       978-1-84392-755-6 hardback

British Library Cataloguing-in-Publication Data

A catalogue record for this book is available from the British Library

FSC
Mixed Sources
Product group from well-managed
forests and other controlled sources

Cert no. SGS-COC-2482
www.fsc.org
© 1996 Forest Stewardship Council

Project managed by Deer Park Productions, Tavistock, Devon
Typeset by TW Typesetting, Plymouth, Devon
Printed and bound by T.J. International Ltd, Padstow, Cornwall

Contents

List of figures and tables

Figures

Tables

List of acronyms and abbreviations

ABC	acceptable behaviour contract
ADD	attention deficit disorder
ADHD	attention deficit hyperactivity disorder
ASBO	anti-social behaviour order
BBBS	Big Brothers Big Sisters
BCS	British Crime Survey
CaPE	Care Placement Evaluation
CDA	Crime and Disorder Act
CDRP	Crime and Disorder Reduction Partnership
CJIA	Criminal Justice and Immigration Act
CJPO	Criminal Justice and Public Order Act
CMDs	common mental disorders
CME	coordinated market economy
CPC	Child-Parent Center
CrASBO	criminal anti-social behaviour order
CSP	Community Safety Partnership
CTC	Communities That Care
CYDS	Community Youth Development Study
DARE	Drug Abuse Resistance Education
DCSF	Department for Children, Schools and Families
DCSO	deferred custody and supervision order
DTO	detention and training order
ECHR	European Convention on Human Rights
EEG	electroencephalogram
ESPAD	European School Survey Project on Alcohol and Other Drugs
EU	European Union
FCG	family group conference
FIP	family intervention programme
FPN	fixed-penalty notice

FTE	first-time entrant
FFT	Functional Family Therapy
GASBO	gang-related anti-social behaviour order
GDP	Gross Domestic Product
Hansard	House of Commons Daily Debates
IPTW	inverse probability of treatment weighting
IRCS	intensive rehabilitative custody and supervision order
IRL	in real life
ISO	individual support order
ISSP	Intensive Supervision and Surveillance Programme
IVF	*in vitro* fertilization
LME	liberal market economy
MoJ	Ministry of Justice
MST	multisystemic therapy
MTFC	Multidimensional Treatment Foster Care
MTO	Moving to Opportunity
NAO	National Audit Office
NEET	not in employment, education or training
NFP	Nurse Family Partnership
NHS	National Health Service
NICE	National Institution for Health and Clinical Excellence
OBTJ	offences brought to justice
OCJS	Offending, Crime and Justice Survey
OECD	Organisation for Economic Co-operation and Development
PALS	Participate and Learn Skills
PATHE	Positive Action Through Holistic Education
PATHS	Promoting Alternative Thinking Strategies
PAYP	Positive Activities for Young People
PND	penalty notice for disorder
PR	proportional representation
PSA	public service agreement
RAF	Royal Air Force
RDS	Home Office Research, Development and Statistics Directorate
SPACE1	The Council of Europe Annual Penal Statistics
STATUS	Student Training Through Urban Strategies
STC	Secure Training Centre
STO	Secure Training Order
Triple P	Positive Parenting Programme
UNCRC	United Nations Convention on the Rights of the Child
WHO	World Health Organization

Notes on contributors

Nicholas Bala has been a professor at the Faculty of Law at Queen's University, in Kingston, Canada since 1980. His primary area of teaching and research interest is family and children's law, focusing on such issues as juvenile justice, child witnesses, and domestic violence. Much of his work is interdisciplinary, and he has collaborated with criminologists, psychologists and other professionals to better understand and improve the effectiveness of the justice system in responding to the problems of children and families. He has co-authored or written 15 books and over 140 articles and book chapters, and his work is frequently cited by Canadian courts.

Peter Carrington is Professor of Sociology at the University of Waterloo, Ontario. He combines his long-standing interests in social network analysis and crime and delinquency in his current research, the *Canadian Criminal Careers and Criminal Networks Study*. Other research interests include police discretion and the impact of the Canadian Youth Criminal Justice Act. His article 'Co-offending and the development of the delinquent career' recently appeared in *Criminology*. With John Scott he is editing the *Sage Handbook of Social Network Analysis* (forthcoming), and with John Scott and Stanley Wasserman he edited *Models and Methods in Social Network Analysis* (Cambridge 2005).

Frances Gardner is Professor of Child and Family Psychology, Department of Social Policy and Social Work, University of Oxford, and Fellow of Wolfson College, and is a clinical psychologist. She has been director and deputy director of the graduate programme in Evidence-Based Social Intervention since 2003, and co-director of the Centre for Evidence-Based Intervention. Her research focuses on the development of antisocial behaviour in young people, particularly how early parenting style influences child mental health. She conducts randomized trials of commu-nity-based parenting programmes in UK and US, including the NIH-funded 'Early Steps' trial; systematic reviews, and longitudinal studies of the development of mental health problems, including longitudinal studies of risk and resilience in orphans and vulnerable children in South Africa; and UK cohort studies of time trends in parenting and antisocial behaviour.

John Graham is currently Director of the Police Foundation. Prior to this, he was an associate director at the Audit Commission, deputy director of strategic policy in the Home Office and senior research and policy adviser in the Social Exclusion Unit. He has also been a consultant to the United Nations and a scientific advisor to the Council of Europe and is currently a visiting professor at the Centre for Crime and Social Change at the University of Bedfordshire. He has published widely in the field of youth crime and youth justice, including the entry for England and Wales in the *International Handbook of Juvenile Justice* and the Audit Commission's assessment of youth justice reforms implemented since 1997.

J. David Hawkins, PhD is Endowed Professor of Prevention and Founding Director of the Social Development Research Group, School of Social Work, University of Washington, Seattle. His research focuses on understanding and preventing child and adolescent health and behaviour problems. He develops and tests prevention strategies which seek to reduce risk through the enhancement of strengths and protective factors in families, schools, and communities. He has authored numerous articles and several books as well as prevention programmes for parents and families, including *Guiding Good Choices*, *Parents Who Care*, and *Supporting School Success*. His prevention work is guided by the social development model, his theory of human behaviour.

Trevor Jones is Reader in Criminology, and Deputy Director of the Centre for Crime, Law and Justice at Cardiff University. He has published research on a range of subjects, including police accountability, policing and ethnic minorities, the growth of private security, policy transfer in crime control, and the politics of crime and punishment. Recent books include *Plural Policing: A Comparative Perspective* (Routledge 2006); *Policy Transfer and Criminal Justice* (Open University Press 2007) both with Tim Newburn; and *Tourism and Crime: Key Themes* (Goodfellow Publishing 2010 forthcoming) with David Botterill.

Barbara Maughan is Professor of Developmental Epidemiology at King's College London Institute of Psychiatry, and a member of MRC External Scientific Staff. Her research centres on risk factors for mental health problems in childhood; time trends in child and adolescent mental health; and the long-term implications of disorder in childhood for psychosocial functioning in adult life.

Lesley McAra holds the Chair of Penology in the School of Law at the University of Edinburgh and is co-director of the *Edinburgh Study of Youth Transitions and Crime*. Prior to joining the university, she worked in the Central Research Unit of the (then) Scottish Office. She has acted as a specialist advisor on youth justice to the Justice 2 Committee of the Scottish Parliament and is currently an academic advisor to the Scottish Government's Scotstat, Crime and Justice Committee. Recent publications include a series of articles (with Susan McVie) exploring the impact of contact with youth justice agencies on patterns of desistance from offending. She is co-editor (with Sarah Armstrong) of *Perspectives on Punishment: the Contours of Control* (Oxford University Press 2006).

Larissa Pople is currently Senior Researcher for the Independent Commission on Youth Crime and Antisocial Behaviour. She has worked for a number of years on a range of issues affecting children and their families, initially with an international perspective (at the UNICEF Innocenti Research Centre and in London) and latterly with a UK perspective on The Children's Society's *Good Childhood Inquiry* and, most recently, on youth crime and youth justice.

Julian V. Roberts is Professor of Criminology in the Faculty of Law, University of Oxford. He is editor in chief of the *European Journal of Criminology* and associate editor of the *Canadian Journal of Criminology and Criminal Justice*. He has been a visiting scholar in the Department of Justice Canada, a visiting professor at the University of Toronto, the School of Law, King's College and the Catholic University of Leuven.

Michael Rutter, MD, FRS, FMed.Sci, FBA is Professor of Developmental Psychopathology at the Institute of Psychiatry, King's College, London. His research interests include antisocial behaviour (*Antisocial Behaviour by Young People*, Rutter, Griller and Hagell 1998); the testing of hypotheses about environmental mediation (*Identifying the Environmental Causes of Disease*, Academy of Medical Sciences 2007); the interface between science and policy (*Social Sciences and Family Policies*, British Academy 2010) and gene-environment interdependence (*Genetic Effects on Environmental Vulnerability to Disease*, Rutter, M. ed. 2008).

David J. Smith is Honorary Professor of Criminology at the University of Edinburgh, and Visiting Professor at the London School of Economics. In earlier years he headed the Social Justice and Social Order group at the Policy Studies Institute. He was founding editor of the *European Journal of Criminology*. His interests include policing and legitimacy (*Transformations of Policing*, 2007, edited with Alistair Henry), ethnic and religious discrimination and disadvantage, time trends in youth problems (*Psychosocial Disorders in Young People*, 1995, edited with Michael Rutter), links between victimization and offending, and the effectiveness of the youth justice system. With Lesley McAra, he established *The Edinburgh Study of Youth Transitions and Crime* in 1998.

David Utting is Secretary to the Independent Commission on Youth Crime and Antisocial Behaviour and a former deputy director of the Policy Research Bureau. His authored and co-authored publications include *Crime and the Family* (Family Policy Studies Centre 1993); *Family and Parenthood* (Joseph Rowntree Foundation 1995); *Reducing Criminality Among Young People* (Home Office 1996); *What Works With Young Offenders in the Community?* (Barnardos 2000); *Support from the Start* (DfES 2004); *Risk and Protective Factors* (Youth Justice Board 2005); and *Interventions for Children at Risk of Antisocial Personality Disorders* (Policy Research Bureau 2007).

Brandon C. Welsh, Ph.D. is Associate Professor of Criminology at Northeastern University in Boston, Mass., and a senior research fellow at the Netherlands Institute for the Study of Crime and Law Enforcement at Free University, Amsterdam. He is an author or editor of seven books, including *Saving Children from a Life of Crime: Early Risk Factors and Effective Interventions* (Oxford University Press 2007) and *Preventing Crime: What Works for Children, Offenders, Victims, and Places* (Springer 2006).

Preface and acknowledgements

The Independent Commission on Youth Crime and Antisocial Behaviour was established in 2008 under the auspices of the Police Foundation with funding from the Nuffield Foundation. Its purpose is to provide a blueprint for an effective, humane and sustainable approach to youth crime and antisocial behaviour that is based on clear principles and on sound evidence. The Commission's analysis and proposals are set out in its Report. This book presents the more detailed analysis and evidence that forms the background to the Commission's proposals. The aim is to provide an authoritative review by leading experts of the relevant social science and socio-legal analysis.

The editor is a member of the Independent Commission, although other authors (with the exception of John Graham and David Utting) have no particular connection with it. The views expressed here are those of the authors and do not necessarily coincide with those of the Commission.

I am grateful to the Commission's Chair, Anthony Salz, and to its other members, for asking some of the questions that have powered this project, and to John Graham and David Utting for help, comments and suggestions at various stages. I owe a debt that will be hard to repay to the Commission's Senior Researcher, Larissa Pople, who not only stepped in to write one chapter and two-thirds of another, but also checked all of the references and helped with the myriad smaller tasks entailed in publishing a complex volume of this kind.

Chapter I

The need for a fresh start

David J. Smith

We need a fresh start in responding to youth crime because of intractable and deep-rooted problems that current systems cannot resolve. The task of the Independent Commission on Youth Crime and Antisocial Behaviour is to draw up a blueprint for reform, and the purpose of this book is to provide a framework of evidence and analysis to support the work of the Commission. Evidence of the failings of the present system is not hard to find. It is far more difficult to design workable and durable reforms that will attract widespread support. Although the following chapters highlight ways in which the current arrangements in England and Wales are wasteful, ineffective, and damaging, their more important purpose is to support the effort of designing something better.

The problems are intractable because of underlying tensions – in some respects, contradictions – between different objectives. The clearest opposition is the one characterized by David Garland (1985) as the clash between punishment and welfare. Even within the youth justice system in England and Wales – and still more in the adult system – punishment and retribution are essential elements, and they are leading themes of popular narratives of famous cases such as the killing of James Bulger by two ten-year-old boys in 1993. Yet punishment of young offenders conflicts with the need to help them to change, with the requirement to take account of their immaturity, and with the duty to promote their welfare. This tension between punishment and welfare is not a contest between the needs of the offender and the rights of the victim (and by extension, of the wider public). Punishment in fact does little to help or satisfy victims: it plays to a wider audience. Equally important, care of the young offender, more plausibly than retributive punishment, can be seen as a way of reducing the chances of reoffending. But irrespective of their outcomes, punishment and welfare both retain symbolic power, and the claims of these opposing symbols have not been reconciled within the present youth justice system, as later chapters will show.

A second unresolved tension is the clash between two conceptions of crime prevention. On one account, young people commit crimes because they can, and the central task of the youth justice system is to deter the majority from offending by a well-dramatized threat of punishment, backed up by effective action. On a very different account, the youth justice system is only the backstop in dealing with antisocial and criminal behaviour. A functioning youth justice system is a minimal condition for maintaining order, but effective deterrence is not the main driver of levels of youth crime. Instead, the causes of crime are deficits in individual development from childhood to adulthood and features of the social settings in which adolescents move. Crime prevention therefore means programmes that aim to make good those deficits and to change the social settings in productive ways. That conception is in tension with crime prevention viewed as deterrence through the youth justice system.

Because contradictions and tensions like these have not been resolved, the response to youth crime lacks integrity and conviction. As youth crime has become the stuff of politics, the real tensions within the system have been exaggerated by political rhetoric. As a result, whichever of the conflicting objectives are for the moment emphasized by the political class or the general public, in key respects the youth justice system fails to deliver.

The general backdrop to the evolution of policy is the tenfold rise in police-recorded crime that occurred in the 40 years from 1950. As detailed in Chapter 3, this certainly corresponded to a very substantial increase in crime in the real world (as well as the world of government statistics) although the actual rise may have been less than tenfold, because more of the incidents that happened were ending up in police records. A fair proportion of the increasing volume of crime was committed by young offenders, although the exact share depends on definitions (how young is 'young'?) and on methods of measurement. As crime became more of a problem, so cross-party consensus broke down and criminal justice policies began to appear in party manifestos and became the stuff of party political contest. In 1994, at a time when a Conservative administration was presenting itself as tough on crime with the slogan 'prison works', the long upward trend in crime reversed, and crime began to go down according to both the recorded crime statistics and the British Crime Survey. Since then both property crime and violent crime, as measured by the British Crime Survey, have continuously declined to reach levels about 40 per cent below their peak. In the current landscape, crime is a much bigger problem than 50 years ago, but it has declined considerably over the past 15 years.

Crime trends have been similar in other developed countries: with the exception of Japan, they all experienced a major rise in the post-war period followed by a decline from some point in the 1990s or before. However, the UK spends proportionately more on 'law and order' than any other country in the Organisation for Economic Co-operation and Development (OECD) (Prime Minister's Strategy Unit 2006). As a whole, expenditure on public order and safety[1] amounted to £24.6 billion in 2008/9, about the same as expenditure on children and families (see Chapter 12). As also explained in Chapter 12, a rough estimate of the cost of criminal justice services in response to youth crime is of the order of £4 billion. Moreover, spending on youth crime through the Youth Justice Board and Youth Offending Teams rose by 45 per cent in real terms between 2000 and 2006/7 (Solomon and Garside 2008). What was the performance of the youth justice system for this large and greatly increased expenditure?

As detailed in Chapter 4, the proportion of young offenders who are reconvicted within a year hovers just under 40 per cent, having declined very slightly between 2000 and 2008.[2] There was a more substantial decline in the number and seriousness of further offences committed. On the latest figures, three quarters of young offenders sentenced to custody are reconvicted within a year of release, a pattern that has changed very little (Ministry of Justice 2009a). This rate for young offenders leaving custody is about 50 per cent worse than for adults. Of course, young people sentenced to custody are far more likely to be serious and persistent offenders than those given other sentences, so in most cases they already have a proven propensity to reoffend. It is not surprising to find that their reconviction rate is higher than for young offenders given community sentences or fines. Nevertheless, this 75 per cent rate of reconviction within a year is shockingly high. It is a clear indication that custody, viewed as a method of changing lives, is simply not working.

Despite the fall in crime, youth justice continued until recently to draw about the same number of people into the system – in 2007/8, 146,526 young people – and to dispose of about the same number of offences – 277,896 in the same year (Youth Justice Board 2009). Research in Scotland, where the youth justice system is less avowedly punitive than in England and Wales, has shown that whereas most young offenders are not captured, the system tends to target the poor, the disadvantaged, those living in disordered neighbourhoods, and those who have been in trouble with the police before. In fact, after controlling for self-reported offending and other factors, the odds of being warned or charged were raised 5.1 times if the young person had had earlier adversarial contact with the police (McAra and McVie 2005).

The way the system targets 'the usual suspects' again highlights underlying tensions between different objectives. If we are thinking in a constructive way about the welfare of offenders, about ways of helping them to overcome disadvantages and difficulties, about giving them more opportunities to change their lives, then it makes sense to sort young offenders according to the pattern of their behaviour (how serious, how persistent) and the depth and breadth of their deficits and difficulties, and to focus resources on the most needy whose behaviour is most difficult to change. That is exactly what the youth justice system tries to do through the assessment tool known as 'Asset'. Since 2000, this instrument has been used to evaluate the criminal histories, education, health, family environments and attitudes of young people in contact with the youth justice system and to calculate their likelihood of reoffending. The Youth Justice Board's 'Scaled Approach', which came into effect in late 2009, matches the intensity and duration of interventions to a young offender's 'Asset' score. If we think of the Youth Rehabilitation Order as a suite of interventions aiming to repair deficits in education and personal development and an opportunity and inducement to change behaviour, then this is an intelligent way of channelling resources to the young people who need them most. Also, it applies a flat rather than a steeply rising tariff to reoffenders, looking to find a more appropriate and effective intervention rather than a more severe one. If, on the other hand, we think of the Youth Rehabilitation Order as part of a system that retains the aim of punishing young offenders, then it looks like a way of stigmatizing the same young people again and again. This second interpretation cannot be entirely avoided, because the system still retains some of the symbolism of punishment. After allowing for their actual levels of offending, it is those with disadvantages and difficulties and those already known to the police who tend to be caught and convicted, and on conviction, those with disadvantages and difficulties, through the application of the 'Scaled Approach', tend to be given longer and more intensive interventions.

Young people from specific ethnic groups (African–Caribbean, African, and mixed) are more likely than others to be captured by the system, and in particular are more likely to receive custodial sentences. Earlier reviews of the wider evidence, most of it relating to the adult system, suggested that specific ethnic groups are over-represented partly because of discrimination in policing and youth justice, partly because features of the system (such as the criteria that determine whether suspects are held in custody awaiting trial) can work to the disadvantage of certain ethnic groups, and partly because of elevated rates of offending among such groups (Smith 1997). Two recent studies of the processing of cases through the youth justice system confirm that there may be some discrimination against ethnic minorities (Hood and Feilzer 2004; May et al. 2010: for more detail, see Chapter 3).

According to United Nations figures, England and Wales has the highest rate of youth custody in Europe (Hazel 2008: 60). There are great difficulties in making exact comparisons, because the nature of the institutions varies so much, and because what are secure units in one country may be called mental health centres in another. Also, most available figures are out of date.[3] Still, it is clear enough that there are gross disparities between England and Wales and most other countries.[4] On Hazel's figures (2008: table 8.1) the rate of imprisonment of youths under the age of 18 per 100,000 population in the 2000s was 46.8 in England and Wales compared with 18.6 in France, 23.1 in Germany and 11.1 in Italy. The rates were very much lower still in the Scandinavian countries,[5] although this may partly reflect difficulties in identifying 'custody' within their systems. A different problem with systems in some continental European countries is that young people are held in non-penal facilities for indefinite periods, a practice that may contravene international norms and standards.

As detailed in Chapter 4, the numbers of young people[6] sentenced to custody fell from nearly 8,000 in 1981 to under 2,000 in 1990, then rose again steeply to about 7,500 in 1999, declining after that to around 6,000. The high level of imprisonment of young people is therefore a long-established feature of the system in England and Wales, except for a dramatic diversionary interlude in the 1980s. A new feature over the ten years up to 2008 is that the lengths of custodial sentences handed out to young offenders have doubled, on average; this applies to every type of offence, so it is not explained by a shift to more serious offences (Ministry of Justice 2009b; table 2.16). Around one in five young people in custody are on remand awaiting trial, yet three quarters are subsequently acquitted or given a community sentence (Gibbs and Hickson 2009). A preliminary count shows that the population of young offenders in custody in early 2010 was down to about 2,200, well below the peak of about 3,100 that was reached in 2002. This is probably because of a reduction in the number of first-time entrants to the youth justice system following the introduction of a target to reduce it. Even after the recent fall, the numbers in custody remain very high compared with other European countries.

The large majority (85 per cent) of young people in custody are held in young offender institutions (YOIs) run by the Prison Service. Male YOIs are large, typically holding between 100 and 400 young men on dedicated or split sites, with one staff member to every 10 or 15 young people. Here bullying and violence are widespread, and a substantial minority of inmates have felt unsafe (Parke 2009). Around a quarter of boys and half of girls in custody are held over 50 miles away from their home (Youth Justice Board 2007) and only a third of young prisoners think it is easy for their families to visit. Huntercombe, for example, is a converted RAF base that was deliberately located in a remote spot for reasons entirely unconnected with the needs of a youth justice unit. Most young people in custody have diagnosable mental health problems (Lader *et al.* 2000) and around a third have been in local authority care (Parke 2009). Nearly half have literacy and numeracy levels below those of the average 11-year-old, and over a quarter equivalent to those of the average 7-year-old or younger (ECOTEC 2001). The Youth Justice Board has targets for improving literacy and numeracy, which has improved in secure children's homes and youth offender institutions, although not in secure training centres (STCs). Education provision was recently cut back from 25 hours to 15 hours a week. Conditions are more favourable at STCs and secure children's homes, which are much smaller units with much higher staff to young people ratios, but this kind of accommodation, which houses only a small minority of young people in custody, is being cut back because of its relatively high cost (see Chapter 4).

In short, England and Wales sustain a very high level of youth custody – much higher than in France, Germany, or Scandinavia – producing a very high rate of reconviction at a heavy financial cost without offering education, training or resettlement services that are anywhere near sufficient to meet the needs of young offenders. Maintaining these services absorbs a substantial proportion of the youth justice budget when, as set out in later chapters, more effective programmes are available both to prevent young people from embarking on a criminal career and to deal with young offenders upon conviction.

Alongside the youth justice system, the New Labour reforms have set up a parallel and competing system for dealing with 'antisocial behaviour'. Sometimes this is criminal behaviour under another name; sometimes nuisance behaviour and harassment that can be seriously disturbing when it is common in a neighbourhood or repeated against the same victims. Although young people were not originally intended to be the targets of enforcement, they account for about half of the Anti-Social Behaviour Orders issued. ASBOs make use of civil procedures with their lower procedural safeguards, but breaching them is a criminal offence. Since around half of ASBOs are breached (Solanki et al. 2006), this is an important new gateway to the criminal justice system, one that can lead to a custodial sentence.

When, 40 years ago, youth court procedures were replaced in Scotland by children's hearings, one of the objectives was to create a tribunal that young people and their families could understand and in which they could fully participate. In England and Wales, there is still a need for a fresh start in the youth courts in order to achieve similar objectives, although not necessarily in the same ways. The form and structure of the process in the youth courts is singularly ill-adapted to the needs of young participants. Young defendants say they often do not understand the legal proceedings or language, feel patronized, intimidated and isolated in the courtroom, and often have events explained to them only after they have left (Hazel et al. 2002). Magistrates cannot have a sense of involvement with young offenders, because they seldom see the same one twice, they have no say in the detailed working out of community sentences, and no means of following through on how they are applied. The disconnected nature of the court experience is closely related to its punitive orientation. Attempts to reintegrate offenders would require continuous involvement and accountability, for example a return to court after a community sentence to report on how it had been discharged.

Overall, then, the returns from greatly increased expenditure on youth justice are poor. These poor outcomes do not arise from detailed technical faults in the systems. Instead, the failings spring from underlying tensions between punishment and welfare, and between deterrence and prevention. The way forward, as discussed in the final chapter, is to replace these oppositions with a new objective of delivering justice to individual young offenders and victims in a way that is appropriate to their maturity and needs. Justice for young offenders means insisting that they accept responsibility – consistent with their level of maturity – for what they have done, but it also means abandoning punishment as an aim. Does abandoning punishment run the risk of encouraging a crime wave as young people recognize that the criminal justice system no longer has teeth? To set the context for this book, and for the Commission's proposals, the next section takes a brief tour of the research on the deterrent effects of criminal justice.

Deterring crime through criminal justice: the evidence

No one seriously doubts that the existence of a functioning criminal justice system deters offending. At times when the police or criminal justice system ceases to function, for example in Norway at the end of the Second World War, crime soars and order tends to break down. But given a functioning criminal justice system, the important question is whether marginal changes in the likelihood or severity of sanctions, or changes in the nature of sanctions, will lead to changes in the level of crime.

In principle, criminal justice can control crime in three ways: by taking offenders out of circulation through imprisonment or electronic tagging (incapacitation); by demonstrating to the law-abiding majority that offenders are punished (general deterrence); and by changing the behaviour of those offenders who are caught (specific deterrence). The distinction between these three processes is important, even though it may be hard to quantify their separate effects.

In the eighteenth century, criminal justice in European countries was brutally punitive with widespread use of death penalties and torture, but it was also haphazard and poorly resourced, so that only a tiny minority of offences resulted in a sanction. Beccaria in Italy and Bentham in England argued that effective deterrence depended far more on certainty than on severity of sanction, so that an enlightened policy would be to improve the efficiency of the police and courts while making sanctions more humane. Assessing the importance of the likelihood of being caught versus the sanctions that follow a conviction continues to be an important issue for research and policy.

Serious attempts to measure the effects of criminal justice on the level of crime only began in the 1960s, but by now there is a considerable volume of research evidence. Major reviews of the evidence have been published at intervals over the past 30 years (Blumstein *et al.* 1978; Cook 1980; Nagin 1998; von Hirsch *et al.* 1999; Doob and Webster 2003; Pratt *et al.* 2006; Levitt and Miles 2007; Tonry 2008; Nagin *et al.* 2009). On the whole, the evidence that changes in the amount or severity of criminal justice sanctions cause changes in the level of crime is surprisingly weak, although economists have thought the evidence stronger than specialists in criminology or criminal justice. It turns out that the linkage between crime and punishment is more complex and indirect than might at first appear; for that and other reasons, there are profound difficulties in providing reliable quantitative estimates.

In controlling unwanted behaviour, criminal justice is essentially the backstop that is used when other methods have failed. Particularly in the case of young people, social pressure by peers, parents, schools and minor authority figures are much the most important controls. In seeking to explain the tenfold rise in crime between 1950 and 1994 and the subsequent reversal of the long upward trend, it is likely that a range of societal transformations are more important than the activity of the criminal justice system (Smith 1999: for more detail, see Chapter 2).

Any economic model assumes that people act in such a way as to maximize their chances of achieving the goals they value, although they have to make choices based only on the limited information available to them about links between actions and outcomes. Any economic model therefore predicts that an increase in the likelihood or severity of sanctions will reduce crime, because this makes it less likely that people can achieve their valued objectives by offending. However, there are several reasons why the connection might become tenuous. As already pointed out, other factors that feed into powerful informal control mechanisms may be more important. Also, the perceptions and knowledge of the potential offender have to be considered. People have limited knowledge and awareness of changes in penalties or the chances of being caught. Offenders pay more attention to cues in the immediate situation that indicate which properties or individuals are most vulnerable. Finally, formal sanctions depend for their effect on informal mechanisms and interact with them. Conventional sanctions, such as imprisonment, are a form of drama intended to degrade and stigmatize the offender, who is meant to feel shame as a result. If that were not so, then (as Andrew von Hirsch has observed) a term of imprisonment would be no different from a spell on the crew of a submarine. If the rate of imprisonment is greatly increased so that having a spell in prison becomes commonplace (as now for young African American males in poor neighbourhoods) then rejection, stigma and shame are greatly reduced. The informal mechanisms are needed to deliver the force of the formal sanctions, but when formal sanctions are increased stigma and shame may no longer result (Nagin 1998).

Just as the linkages between criminal justice and crime rates are indirect and complex, so it is also difficult to measure the effects of sanctions on levels of crime. To start with, it is even difficult to measure how much crime is prevented by keeping offenders out of circulation, in prison. This is not the simple problem that it looks. Because the frequency and seriousness of offending changes over the individual's offending career, much depends on whether the offender happens to be in prison at the time when his offending would have peaked, or (as is more likely) at some time after, when his offending would have been declining anyhow. Nevertheless, one approach towards assessing the effects of incapacitation is to analyse statistics on lifetime patterns of offending, and then calculate how much offending would be prevented by putting a higher proportion of offenders in prison for longer. Thirty years ago, when Home Office researchers did this for adult offenders, they found that reducing the length of prison sentences would produce very small increases in the number of offences leading to a conviction: for example, if the time served by each offender were reduced by four months, convictions would increase by 1.6 per cent. If, instead, mandatory sentences of 18 months were handed out to all offenders at that time receiving sentences of less than 18 months, which would mean increasing sentence lengths sevenfold on average, then convictions would be reduced by about 17 to 25 per cent (Brody and Tarling 1980). This suggests that only drastic and wholly impracticable sentencing policies could (in theory) yield a substantial dividend in terms of incapacitation.

In political debate, keeping people in prison is usually represented as a sure-fire way of protecting the public from dangerous criminals, so it is surprising to find that the yield from incapacitation is actually quite modest. On reflection, the reasons for this are simple and obvious. Most active offenders are not in prison, and this would remain true even if unjust and draconian policies were adopted. Offenders typically commit a large number of offences before they are caught, and within any thinkable system, most offenders cannot be sent to prison on their first conviction. Moreover, even if sentence lengths are increased, most offenders will be released by the time they have spent a couple of years in prison; most reoffend, and any offences they commit after release cannot be prevented by incapacitation. Thus in a more recent study Spelman (1994) estimated that the adult US criminal justice system incarcerated around 8 per cent of offenders at any given time – bearing in mind that the US imprisonment rate per head of population was about five times that in England and Wales. Spelman estimated that the very high level of incarceration in the US reduced the aggregate crime rate by around 20 per cent, meaning that a 1 per cent increase in imprisonment would reduce crime by about 0.15 per cent. Even then, Spelman's estimates, and Brody and Tarling's, probably overstate the yield from incapacitation, because crimes that prisoners would have committed had they been at large are not always prevented by locking them up. Someone else may step in to commit the crime instead, especially where opportunities are very compelling, for example in a well-developed illicit market where demand is very insistent. If drug dealers are imprisoned, other people will step in to handle the distribution, and the supply will probably only be temporarily interrupted.

When it comes to assessing the deterrent effects of sanctions, the difficulties are far greater. The point can be illustrated by considering a key article by David Farrington and Patrick Langan (1992) which compared crime trends in England and the US in the 1980s. The starting point for these comparisons was the contrast in crime trends between the US and England after 1980. As in England there was an explosive growth of crime in America in the golden era of economic growth between 1950 and 1973. However, in the US, the reversal came much earlier than in England. Most categories of crime in the US declined substantially from around 1980. At the same time, from the 1970s onwards, America began its imprisonment binge, which quadrupled its prison population in 20 years. The reversal of the crime trend coincided with the expansion of imprisonment and an increase in the number of convictions. By contrast, in England, crime continued to rise steeply throughout the 1980s, whereas convictions fell because of a turn in policy towards diversion from criminal justice (see Chapter 4). In their analysis, Farrington and Langan used crime survey data to estimate trends in the total amount of crime. They combined these data with criminal justice statistics to estimate the probability of conviction, given an offence; the probability of imprisonment, given an offence; and the average length of prison sentences. They repeated the analyses for four specific offences that could be closely compared between the two countries: burglary, assault, motor vehicle theft, and robbery. Broadly, these comparisons showed that as the probability of being caught and punished rose in the US, each category of crime went down, whereas as the probability of being caught and punished fell in England, each category of crime went up. Farrington and Langan considered that the associations with length of prison sentence were much less clear-cut. As such, the findings were consistent with the hypothesis that an increase in the certainty of punishment deterred offenders, but not an increase in severity.

However, as I argued in an article published some years later (Smith 1999), it is perfectly possible to come up with an alternative explanation. Farrington and Langan's study describes an association between crime rates and probability of punishment, but it does not establish a causal relationship. The question is whether changes in the probability of punishment drive the crime rate, or changes in the crime rate drive changes in the probability of punishment. The example of Japan will help to make the point. There the resources devoted to law enforcement – the number of police per head of population, for example – are broadly similar to those in European countries. The crime rate in Japan, however, is very much lower. Not surprisingly, the police are much more successful than in Europe in catching the very much smaller number of criminals. Clearly, the low crime rate leads to a much higher probability of sanction than in Europe. Equally, the higher probability of sanction presumably helps to maintain the low crime rate. Thus the causal arrows point both ways. It then becomes extremely difficult to devise statistical models to estimate the strength of the effects in each direction. It is perfectly possible that in the US crime levelled off and fell for reasons unconnected with sanctions, and this fall in crime then led to an increase in the effectiveness of law enforcement: in that case, the main causal arrow points from the crime rate to sanctions, not from sanctions to the crime rate.

There is a considerable body of studies that analyse the relationships over time between prison populations and crime rates, mostly in different US states. The outstanding problem with these studies is how to build a model that correctly identifies the effect of prison population on crime rates and the effect of crime rates on prison population when these two effects have to be estimated simultaneously. Most of the reviewers (referred to earlier) have concluded that this problem has not been solved in a satisfactory way. Levitt (1996) hit on the idea of focusing on twelve states that were forced to reduce their prison population because of legislation on prison overcrowding, comparing them with other states. The essential point is that here we know that the changes in the prison population, being an immediate response to regulation, were not a reaction to changes in the crime rate. The results appear to suggest that imprisonment yields a considerable reduction in crime (through a combination of deterrence and incapacitation) but most commentators (e.g. Nagin 1998) believe that this does not help us to understand the effects of real-life policies. Levitt's study shows what happens when a broad range of prisoners are suddenly released early and not, for example, what happens if penalties are increased or reduced for certain specific offences.

As outlined by Tonry (2008) there is some conflict between the reviews by economists (e.g. Levitt and Miles 2007) and criminologists (e.g. Pratt *et al*. 2006), with the economists drawing stronger conclusions about the effects of marginal changes in sanctions. Although some of the non-economists (e.g. Nagin 1998) believe that there is enough evidence to show that marginal changes in sanctions lead to at least some change in crime rates, others (e.g. Pratt *et al*. 2006; Tonry 2008) believe there is not enough consistent evidence to support even this conclusion. Whereas the economists focus on the aggregate relationships between sanctions and crime rates, the non-economists emphasize the need to understand the perceptions and behaviour of different kinds of offender – depending on context, motive, and offending history, some offenders will be influenced nctions, whereas others will not.

Although the distinction between certainty and severity of sanctions is important in principle, most empirical studies of deterrence cannot reliably distinguish between them, and most cannot distinguish between deterrence and incapacitation, either. The evidence, such as it is, relates the quantity of punishment to the quantity of crime. However, in one of the major reviews, Doob and Webster (2003) focused on sentence severity, and argued strongly that the null hypothesis – that sentence severity has no influence on the crime rate – should be accepted.

Studies that track relationships in the aggregate between the quantity of sanctions and the quantity of crime obscure one important aspect of what is going on: the effect of the sanction on the individual offender who is punished. The plausible argument for specific deterrence is that offenders learn from being caught and punished that the game is not worth the candle. There are equally plausible arguments that punishment is criminogenic – that it makes reoffending more likely – and these are particularly powerful in the case of young offenders. Prisons, in particular, can be seen as a learning environment in which people absorb a criminal culture, including the attitudes, ways, means, and social contacts needed to offend successfully in future. More generally, public sanctions, and prisons especially, label people as bad and deviant. If offenders respond by thinking 'You call me a crook, I may as well *be* a crook' then the label becomes an essential part of their identity and they turn into the kind of person that police, judges and prison officers say they are. Moreover, a spell in prison removes them from family, social ties, and legitimate friends, and makes it harder for them to find a job, housing and a law-abiding way of life.

Nagin *et al.* (2009) have recently reviewed the evidence from the relatively few well-conducted studies on the effects of imprisonment on reoffending. Five studies randomly assigned offenders to custodial and non-custodial sentences. Nagin *et al.* (2009: 145) concluded that 'Taken as a whole, it is our judgement that [these] experimental studies point more toward a criminogenic than preventive effect of custodial sanctions'. There were eleven further studies that compared offenders given custodial sentences with similar offenders, matched on a range of other characteristics, given non-custodial sentences. Nagin *et al.* (2009: 153) concluded that 'Overall across both types of matching studies,[7] the evidence points to a criminogenic effect of the experience of incarceration'.

Supposing that imprisonment does reduce crime to some extent, by taking offenders out of circulation, and by deterring the majority of the population from offending, these latest findings pose a dilemma. They mean that locking people up increases offending among those who are punished, and worsens their life chances in many other ways, while possibly reducing the level of crime in society at large. Happily, the dilemma is not acute, because, as we have seen, any benefits from increasing the quantity of sanctions are extremely uncertain.

Setting the context for a new youth justice

As set out earlier, the Commission's task is to set out the framework for a new response to youth crime, with the aim of delivering justice to individual victims and young offenders in a way that is appropriate to their maturity and needs. The meaning of justice goes beyond the oppositions between punishment and welfare, and between deterrence and prevention. The research evidence summarized above about the effects of sanctions on the level of crime nearly all concerns adults, but the conclusions probably apply to young offenders with redoubled force, because the harmful effects of custody are probably most marked in vulnerable young people who are negotiating a critical turning point in life. If, as seems to be the case, the severity of sanctions is unrelated to the level of crime, then there is plenty of scope for fundamentally redesigning the consequences that follow a juvenile conviction. The broad principle is that these consequences must be seen to be just, and that does not mean that they have to constitute punishment. For example, restorative justice practices may demand more of offenders than conventional sentences, they may do more to hold offenders to account and make them recognize the harm they have done, they may be satisfying to victims, yet unlike punishments they do not set out to humiliate or harm offenders. From the evidence reviewed, it is unlikely that a fundamental shift in the nature of sentences towards justice and away from punishment would lead to a rise in youth crime.

That conclusion is reinforced by comparative research on the effects of juvenile justice systems. A close comparison between contrasting systems in Bremen and Denver has shown that a far more punitive system in Denver produced a similar level of juvenile delinquency to a more lenient system in Bremen. Neither arrest nor severity of sanctions was associated with a reduction in future delinquency among young people in either city. At the same time, the results of this comparative study were consistent with the theory that some form of prompt response to offending was a minimum condition for controlling youth crime (Huizinga *et al.* 2003; Smith 2005).

There is wide scope, then, for creating a more just and constructive system of youth justice, which can be at least as successful as the present one in controlling youth crime. This book aims to fill out the context of evidence and analysis for designing that system.

Notes

1 Not including expenditure on fire services and immigration, which are included in the Treasury's published figures.
2 In more detail, the reconviction rate declined very slightly after controlling for the nature of the offence, previous offending histories, and offenders'

backgrounds. The method of controlling for such factors is to compare the predicted reconviction rate (after taking account of these factors) with the actual rate.

3 The Council of Europe Annual Penal Statistics (SPACE1) provide the best available data on numbers of young people in prison (latest year 2007) and these confirm that *numbers* in England and Wales are higher than in other countries in Europe, but they do not provide a comparison in terms of *rates* per 100,000 population in the relevant age group.

4 Other countries with high rates similar to that in England and Wales were the Netherlands, New Zealand and South Africa. In the US, the rate of youth imprisonment was about seven times as high as in England and Wales.

5 But Pitts and Kuula (2005) argue that comparing like with like, Finland actually 'incarcerates children and young people who offend at a slightly higher rate than the system in England and Wales'.

6 The age group was 10–16 up to 1991, but 10–17 from 1992.

7 One type of matching is on individual variables, e.g. a male offender aged 19 convicted of armed robbery is matched with another male aged 19 convicted of armed robbery. The other type of matching is by propensity scores, that is a score calculated from a range of variables to reflect the likelihood that someone will reoffend.

References

Blumstein, A., Cohen, J. and Nagin, D. (1978) *Deterrence and Incapacitation: Estimating the Effects of Criminal Sanction on Crime Rates* (Washington, D.C.: National Academy Press).

Brody, S. and Tarling, R. (1980) *Taking Offenders out of Circulation*, Home Office Research Study no. 64 (London: Home Office).

Cook, P. J. (1980) 'Research in Criminal Deterrence: Laying the Groundwork for the Second Decade' in N. Morris and M. Tonry (eds), *Crime and Justice: An Annual Review of Research*, vol. 2, pp. 211–68 (Chicago: University of Chicago Press).

Doob, A. N. and Webster, C. M. (2003) 'Sentence Severity and Crime: Accepting the Null Hypothesis' in M. Tonry (ed.) *Crime and Justice: A Review of Research* vol. 30, pp. 143–95 (Chicago: University of Chicago Press).

ECOTEC (2001) *An Audit of Education Provision Within the Juvenile Secure Estate* (London: Youth Justice Board).

Farrington, D. P. and Langan, P. A. (1992) 'Changes in Crime and Punishment in England and America in the 1980s', *Justice Quarterly* 9.1, pp. 5–46.

Garland, D. (1985) *Punishment and Welfare* (Aldershot: Gower).

Gibbs, P. and Hickson, S. (2009) *Children: Innocent Until Proven Guilty* (London: Prison Reform Trust).

Hazel, N. (2008) *Cross-National Comparison of Youth Justice* (London: Youth Justice Board).

Hazel, N., Hagell, A. and Brazier, L. (2002) *Young Offenders' Perceptions of their Experiences in the Criminal Justice System* (London: Policy Research Bureau).

Hood, R. and Feilzer, M. (2004) *Differences or Discrimination?* (London: Youth Justice Board).

Huizinga, D., Schumann, K., Ehret, B. and Elliott, A. (2003) *The Effect of Juvenile System Processing on Subsequent Delinquent and Criminal Behavior: A Cross-National Study* (Washington, DC: Final Report to the National Institute of Justice).

Lader, D, Singleton, N. and Meltzer, H. (2000) *Psychiatric Morbidity among Young Offenders in England and Wales* (London: Office for National Statistics).

Levitt, S. (1996) 'The Effect of Prison Population Size on Crime Rates: Evidence from Prison Overcrowding Litigation', *Quarterly Journal of Economics* vol. 111, pp. 319–52.

Levitt, S. D. and Miles, T. J. (2007) 'Empirical Study of Criminal Punishment' in A. M. Polinsky and S. Shavell (eds) *Handbook of Law and Economics* vol. 1, pp. 455–95.

May, T., Gyateng, T. and Hough, M. (2010) *Differential Treatment in the Youth Justice System* (London: Equality and Human Rights Commission).

McAra, L. and McVie, S. (2005) 'The Usual Suspects? Street Life, Young People and the Police', *Criminal Justice* 5, 1, pp. 5–36.

Ministry of Justice (2009a) *Reoffending of Juveniles: Results from the 2007 Cohort, England and Wales* (London: Ministry of Justice).

Ministry of Justice (2009b) *Sentencing Statistics England and Wales 2008* (London: Ministry of Justice).

Nagin, D. (1998) 'Criminal Deterrence Research at the Outset of the Twenty-first Century' in M. Tonry (ed.) *Crime and Justice: A Review of Research* vol. 23, pp. 1–42 (Chicago: University of Chicago Press).

Nagin, D., Cullen, F. T. and Jonson, C. L. (2009) 'Imprisonment and Reoffending' in M. Tonry (ed.) *Crime and Justice: A Review of Research* vol. 38, pp. 115–200 (Chicago: University of Chicago Press).

Parke, S. (2009) *Children and Young People in Custody 2006–2008: An Analysis of the Experiences of 15–18-Year-Olds in Prison* (London: HM Inspectorate of Prisons and Youth Justice Board).

Pitts, J. and Kuula, T. (2005) 'Incarcerating Young People: An Anglo-Finnish Comparison', *Youth Justice* 5, pp. 147–64.

Pratt, T. C., Cullen, F. T., Blevins, K. R., Daigle, L. H. and Madensen, T. D. (2006) 'The Empirical Status of Deterrence Theory: A Meta-Analysis' in F. T. Cullen, J. P. Wrightand K. R. Blevins (eds) *Taking Stock: The Status of Criminological Theory*, pp. 367–96 (New Brunswick, NJ: Transaction).

Prime Minister's Strategy Unit (2006) *Strategic Priorities for the UK: The Policy Review* (London: Cabinet Office).

Smith, D. J. (1997) 'Ethnic Origins, Crime, and Criminal Justice' in M. Maguire, R. Morgan and R. Reiner (eds) *The Oxford Handbook of Criminology* 2nd edn., pp. 703–59.

Smith, D. J. (1999) 'Less Crime Without More Punishment', *Edinburgh Law Review* 3, pp. 294–316.

Smith, D. J. (2005) 'The Effectiveness of the Juvenile Justice System', *Criminal Justice* 5.2, pp. 181–95.

Solanki, A., Bateman, T., Boswell, G. and Hill, E. (2006) *Anti-Social Behaviour Orders* (London: Youth Justice Board).

Solomon, E. and Garside, R. (2008) *Ten Years of Labour's Youth Justice Reforms: An Independent Audit* (London: Centre for Crime and Justice Studies, King's College).

Spelman, W. (1994) *Criminal Incapacitation* (New York and London: Plenum Press).

Tonry, M. (2008) 'Learning from the Limitations of Deterrence Research' in M. Tonry (ed.) *Crime and Justice: A Review of Research* vol. 37, pp. 279–311 (Chicago: University of Chicago Press).

von Hirsch, A., Bottoms, A. E., Burney, E. and Wikström, P.-O. (1999) *Criminal Deterrence and Sentence Severity: An Analysis of Recent Research* (Oxford: Hart).

Youth Justice Board (2007) *Youth Justice Annual Statistics 2005/06* (London: Youth Justice Board).

Youth Justice Board (2009) *Youth Justice Annual Workload Data 2007/08* (London: YJB).

Chapter 2

Changing patterns of youth

David J. Smith

The juvenile justice system exists at a point of collision between competing principles. Mature adults are treated as moral beings who make choices. Children, on the other hand, are regarded as a force of nature, and not as independent moral agents. Juvenile justice is the site of conflict between these two principles. There is no well-defined rite of passage from the status of incompetent, supervised child to that of autonomous and morally responsible adult. Instead, there is the ambiguous status of youth, or adolescence. This ambiguity is central to the whole of criminal justice, because many kinds of offending peak in adolescence. We are uncertain whether to treat young offenders as morally responsible agents who are fully culpable and therefore deserve to be punished. Since around 1900, and particularly since the 1950s, new patterning of transitions from childhood to adulthood has transformed youth into something more conspicuous and at the same time more ambiguous. Because of the vast expansion of education and training, youth has become a considerably longer part of the life course. Typical adolescents have always been mature in some ways but not in others, since various transitions are negotiated at different times, but the order and timing of transitions has changed, maybe leading to increased tensions. Whereas the transition to work now comes much later than at earlier periods, first sexual experiences come much earlier. Delayed economic independence (and its implications for accessing independent housing and breaking away from parental dependency) is at odds with an increasing stress on the autonomy and distinctiveness of young people.

Since the 1950s, when the word 'teenager' first came to be widely used, there has been growing recognition of adolescence as a distinct stage of development and of youth as a unique status. It can be argued that people tend to live in a 'youth ghetto' for a longer and longer period of their lives. Whereas towards the beginning of the twentieth century most people belonged to mixed-age workgroups from the age of 12 or 13, towards the beginning of the twenty-first century most people spend most of their time at schools, colleges and universities mainly with others of their own age group until they reach the age of 18 at least and in many cases up to the age of 23 or so. Age segregation may help to explain the development of spectacular youth cultures from the 1950s onwards, expressed in language, music, clothes, and other forms of consumption. These have been given a hefty boost by consumer marketing which identifies youth as a key segment, not only because of its new purchasing power, but still more because of the leadership role assigned to the young in pioneering new products and associated ways of life.

The transition from childhood to adulthood has always involved the loosening of primary social bonds and the formation of new ones. But instead of being a short phase of life in which there is dynamic change, a lengthened process of transition may perhaps evolve into a period of drifting and weakened attachments. This combines with a softening of rigid hierarchies and the rejection of deferential relationships between young and old, along with a growing emphasis, instead, on a democratic ethic and the expectation that conflicts will be resolved through negotiation. At the same time, the growth of education, the mass media, foreign travel, and the internet have expanded the horizons of young people beyond recognition compared with the period before the Second World War. With this growth of awareness comes a new emphasis on the capacity of the individual to make choices from a vast array of possibilities, whereas at earlier periods most young people were shunted directly from school into a simple manual job with one of a few large local employers. Yet, as argued by Furlong and Cartmel (2007), despite the widening of horizons and the emphasis on the individual's capacity to 'make it happen', social structures still lock many young people into places where very few options are available to them. There is a high level of youth unemployment and employment instability in certain strata – especially among educational drop-outs – which makes a substantial minority of young people look and feel out of place in a fundamentally rich and consumption-driven society. It has been argued that, whereas the majority now make slow-track transitions, youths from disadvantaged backgrounds 'tend to take a "fast-track" route to adulthood which includes finishing education at or before the minimum age, unemployment or insecure badly-paid work and early parenthood, with all the attendant risks these combinations bring' (Devitt et al. 2009: 2).

Between 1950 and 1994, these changes in the patterns of youth transitions coincided in England and Wales with a tenfold increase in the rate of recorded crime, much of it committed by young people – and there were similar increases in other developed countries, with the exception of Japan. With the development of crime surveys from the 1970s onwards, substantial increases were also demonstrated in the number of offences recalled by the victims, so it was no longer plausible to argue – as many criminologists had done – that the rise in police-recorded crime was just a reflection of crime control activity. Over the same period, there were also substantial increases in other psychosocial problems that tend to rise or peak in frequency during the teenage years, including abuse of alcohol and psychoactive drugs, suicide and suicidal behaviours, and depression (Smith and Rutter 1995).

It is tempting to suggest that these far-reaching changes in the lives of young people amount to an explanation for the tenfold rise in recorded crime that happened between 1950 and 1994, but the research and analysis needed to establish a causal explanation has not been done. A key challenge for any theory explaining the rise in youth crime is to explain why a historic reversal of the long-term upward trend occurred in 1994, since when the general trend has been down (see Chapter 3). This cautions against any account which suggests that youth transitions have become more difficult in every respect and continue to do so. Nevertheless, a factual account of changes in the lives of young people is a necessary background to policy on responding to youth crime and antisocial behaviour. After considering the extent of these changes, it becomes obvious that what the youth justice system does, although important, is not the leading influence on youth behaviour problems.

Population

With the long-term increase in life expectancy, there is a trend for young people to become a considerably smaller proportion of the population. For example, people aged 10–19 accounted for 21 per cent of the population of Great Britain in 1821, but for only 13 per cent in 2005 (Office for National Statistics: *Social Trends* 2007: fig. 1.3). Just how many young people there are of course depends on the exact definition. According to the official estimates for England and Wales, young people aged 10–24 accounted for 19.5 per cent of the total population, divided almost evenly between the three age groups 10–14, 15–19, and 20–24. Thus youth are a small but substantial minority, amounting to one-fifth of the whole population at most.

The ethnic diversity of the population as a consequence of immigration from 1947 onwards is particularly marked among young people, because ethnic minorities have a relatively young age profile. As shown in Table 2.1, young people aged 10–24 accounted for 25.7 per cent of the ethnic minority population in England in 2007, compared with 18.5 per cent of the white population. All ethnic minorities (including those describing themselves as being of mixed descent) accounted for 15.6 per cent of the youth population aged 10–24, and since the minorities are distributed very unevenly over the country, they accounted for much higher proportions in many areas. The further detail in Table 2.1 shows the wide range of

Table 2.1 Ethnic group of the youth population: England, 2007

	All ages (thousands)	Aged 10–24 as % of all ages	Ethnic group as % of those aged 10–24
White	45,032.8	18.5	84.4
Mixed white and black	397.2	36.9	1.5
Mixed white and Asian	260.9	30.6	0.8
Other mixed	212.0	29.7	0.6
Indian	1,316.0	22.6	3.0
Pakistani	905.7	28.4	2.6
Bangladeshi	353.9	30.0	1.1
Other Asian	339.2	22.3	0.8
Black Caribbean	599.7	19.6	1.2
Black African or other black	848.2	25.8	2.2
Chinese or other	776.4	23.8	1.9
All ethnic groups	51,092.0	19.4	100.0

Source: Office for National Statistics, *Population Estimates by Ethnic Group mid 2007 – Experimental*

ethnic minority groups, the substantial proportion originating from the Indian subcontinent (7.5 per cent of young people), and the considerable proportion describing their origins as mixed (2.9 per cent). As mentioned in Chapter 3, young people of mixed ethnic origins are substantially over-represented in the youth justice system, and there is evidence that the system discriminates against them.

Education and employment

Until the late nineteenth century, education in England and Wales was largely restricted to a small minority who could afford to pay for it. Parliament first voted to pay for the construction of schools for poor people in 1833, but the numbers of children who attended them remained small. It was the Elementary Education Act 1870 that first created schools for the general population, but it was only ten years later with the Elementary Education Act 1880 that the state insisted that children aged 5–10 should attend school. School Attendance Officers enforced the policy and children employed under the age of 13 had to have a certificate to show that they had reached the required educational standard. Even though there were important exceptions (such as to allow children to work on farms) these were the beginnings of universal education, but restricted to children well below the age of puberty. In 1893 the school leaving age was raised to 11, while the Education Act 1918 made education compulsory up to the age of 14. Until the end of the Second

World War, most attended elementary schools up to that age, and only a small minority attended the grammar schools which offered a more advanced curriculum. R. A. Butler's Education Act 1944 made a split between primary (ages 5–11) and secondary education, the latter being divided between grammar schools for about 20 per cent of children who passed the 11+ exam (earlier known as the scholarship exam), and secondary modern schools for the rest.[1] After the war, the school leaving age was raised to 15, then in 1973 to 16, and there are current plans to raise it again to 18 as from 2013 (Gillard 2009).

It was not until the nineteenth century that the system of university education in England began to expand beyond the two ancient universities of Oxford and Cambridge. University College and Kings College, London, were established in the early part of the century, along with Durham University. Between 1900 and 1909 six civic ('redbrick') universities were founded in Birmingham, Liverpool, Sheffield, Leeds, Bristol and Manchester. It was 50 years before the next major expansion in the 1960s, when 20 new universities were created in England. The post-war period also saw the creation of many higher education institutions called polytechnics, many of them evolving from earlier technical colleges and before that from Victorian mechanics institutes. In 1992, 35 polytechnics were converted into new universities. Also, 29 further new universities – ones that had not been formerly designated polytechnics – were created in the UK after 1992. At the same time, there was a rapid growth of colleges providing post-school education, often vocational in character. Thus the cautious expansion of tertiary education in the nineteenth century turned into rapidly accelerating growth after the Second World War.

The recent trends in this long-term process of expansion are illustrated in Figures 2.1 and 2.2. The first figure shows, for example, that the proportion of 18-year-olds in full-time education rose from 17 per cent in 1985 to 44 per cent in 2008. Also, by 2008, 82 per cent of 16-year-olds were in full-time education even though they were free to leave school on reaching their sixteenth birthday. The second figure illustrates the explosive growth of numbers in both further education colleges and universities since 1970, but particularly from 1990 onwards. As further education expanded, work-based learning and employer-funded training declined – essentially a switch from apprenticeships to learning in a college environment. In combination, these changes meant that by 2008, 63 per cent of 18-year-olds were in full-time education or training of some sort. Today, nearly half of young people continue in full-time education into their twenties. Among the rest there is a substantial group who continue learning in an educational environment up to the age of 18 or so, whereas previously they would have been in a work environment where training and education might also be provided. In the post-war years, therefore, the period of the life-course spent in education and training and mostly among people of a similar age has greatly increased. Those who

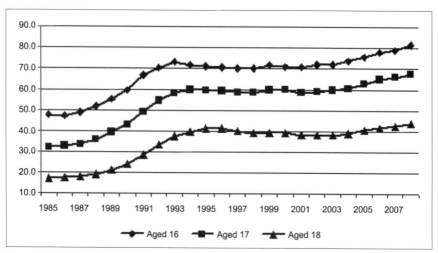

Figure 2.1 Percentage of 16–18-year-olds participating in full-time education: England 1985–2008

Source: DCSF, *Participation in Education, Training and Employment by 16–18-year-olds in England.*

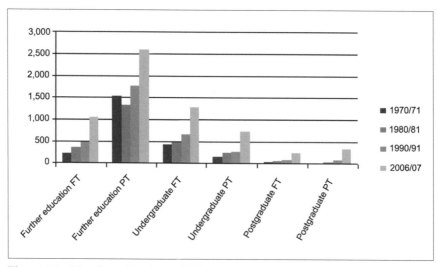

Figure 2.2 Number of students (full-time and part-time) in further and higher education: UK

Source: Social Trends vol. 39 (2009).

drop out of school and fail to gain access to further education or training begin to look like a deviant group rather than the natural candidates for straightforward manual jobs.

Access to higher education is strongly related to social class, income, and neighbourhood characteristics. In 1940, the proportion of young people entering higher education was 8.4 per cent for those from families of professional and non-manual workers, compared with 1.5 per cent for those from families of manual workers (a ratio of 5.6). Over the 60 years up to 2000, the gap narrowed considerably: the participation rate grew to 41 per cent among those from non-manual families, and to 22 per cent among those from manual families, although the growing number of entrants from manual backgrounds went largely to the newer institutions having lower academic and social standing (Sutton Trust 2008: 12–14). It is unclear whether this narrowing of the gap continued after 2000 because comparisons are clouded by a change in the definitions of social classes.

As education has lengthened and higher education has expanded, so have young people without qualifications become a smaller and smaller minority: they accounted for 15.1 per cent of the 16–24 age group in 1997, falling to 9.9 per cent in 2007 (see Figure 2.3). The proportion of this age group who are not in employment, education or training (NEET in the jargon) is more substantial (18.5 per cent in 1997 falling to 17.6 per cent in 2007). NEETs having no qualifications were 4 per cent of the 16–24 age group in 2007, a slight fall from 5.4 per cent ten years earlier. On this measure, the proportion of young people in a highly disadvantaged position has if anything fallen slightly, but as the general level of qualifications rises it may be that this group becomes more acutely disadvantaged and more obviously deviant from the norm. On a longer time scale, the proportion of NEETs fell between 1985 and 1999, but then

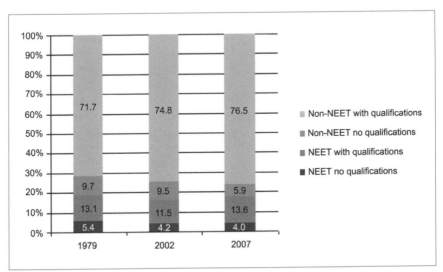

Figure 2.3 Young people aged 16–24 by qualifications and whether 'not in employment, education or training' (NEET): UK

Source: Labour Force Survey (tables supplied by Institute of Employment Studies).
Note: with qualifications means at level 1 or above in the National Qualifications Framework.

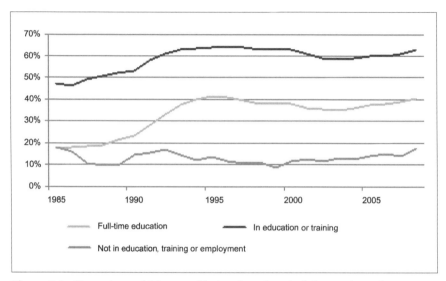

Figure 2.4 Percentage of 18-year-olds in education, training and employment, England

Source: DCSF (2009), *Participation in Education, Training and Employment by 16–18-year-olds in England.*

rose again, as illustrated for 18-year-olds in Figure 2.4. On the other hand, as also illustrated by Figure 2.4, there has been a major increase over the long term in the proportion of 18-year-olds in education or training. This reflects the lengthening transition from childhood to work and economic independence.

The main stages of the life course are illustrated in Figure 2.5. Among males aged 16–19, 43.1 per cent are already working, rising to 71.1 per cent among those aged 20–24 and to 87.8 per cent for the prime age group 25–54. Among females the timing is essentially the same, but the proportion who ever enter the labour market is smaller. Unemployment is at its highest for the youngest age group and at its lowest for the prime age group, showing that the labour market is relatively difficult and precarious for young people. Nevertheless, youth labour markets in Britain have been more favourable than in many European countries over the past 25 years or so. In 2007, youth unemployment in the UK was below the average for the 15 EU countries in 2007, and substantially lower for example than in Italy, France, Spain and Sweden (Coleman and Brooks 2009: fig. 2.20, using Eurostat statistics).

The first oil shock of 1973 set in motion an interconnected set of structural changes, including global competition, the decline of manufacturing, the decline of trade union power, the growth of service industries, privatization of state-owned industries, and sub-contracting of government services; at the same time, the increasing pace of technological change led to staff redundancies and to re-training and re-deployment of

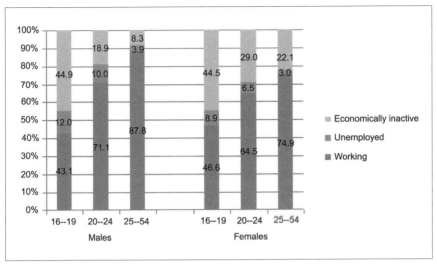

Figure 2.5 Economic activity, UK 2006
Source: *Social Trends* 37 (Labour Force Survey).

existing staff. The standard view among most commentators is that because of such changes work has become precarious and career paths fragmented. As Mortimer (2009: 150) puts it:

> workers can no longer expect to choose a single line of work and follow a recognizable 'career path' within the same field during a lifetime of employment. Instead, workers are increasingly likely to experience multiple job and occupational changes, with need for 're-tooling', additional certification, degrees, or continuing education … Instead of following preordained, scripted career paths, the individual must construct his or her own trajectory.

Even before such changes, young people tended to go through a phase of fragmented and insecure employment before settling into a steady job, but the new structures raise their insecurities to a new level, according to many authors, and place far more onus on the individual to pick out a path instead of accepting factory or labouring work as a preordained fate. Many writers (e.g. Furlong and Cartmel 2007) connect the growth of flexible, precarious employment with Ulrich Beck's (1992) vision of a 'risk society'. On this view, a general proliferation of risk overtakes earlier structural divisions so that instead of fitting into a pre-formed slot, each individual must plot a course through hazards and obstacles. As Furlong and Cartmel (2007) point out, however, risks are still distributed very unevenly between those from different social strata: for example, the risk of youth unemployment varies widely according to social class origins and educational attainment. Thus, in the UK in 2007, among those aged 15–24 the unemployment rate was 26.4 per cent for those with 'lower secondary' qualifications, 11.3 per cent for those with 'upper secondary' qualifications, and 6.4 per cent for those with tertiary qualifications (Eurostat 2009), and there are similar contrasts in other European countries. As noted earlier, educational qualifications are in turn strongly related to social class origins. Also, longitudinal studies show that in Britain, young people from working class origins are much more likely to enter the labour market early and to experience fragmented transitions to work than those from more advantaged backgrounds (Furlong and Cartmel 2007: 45). Although youth has become far more extended on average, more than 40 per cent of 16–19-year-olds in the UK are already working (Figure 2.5) and the bulk of these early entrants to the labour market are from working class origins.

Inequality, poverty and family background

Since the Second World War, the lives of most young people, as of the majority of the whole population, have been transformed by the huge increase in material prosperity both in Britain and in other developed countries. There has been a large increase in the total value of goods produced and consumed, as captured by Gross Domestic Product (GDP), a large increase in government expenditure, and a large increase in government expenditure on social objects – both as a proportion of GDP and (still more) in absolute terms (Smith 1995: 217–30). The main categories of social expenditure that have vastly increased are income maintenance, education, health, social services, and housing. Obvious examples of increased consumption are on cars, labour-saving machines, housing (bathrooms, central heating), holidays, wider range of food, eating out, fashion, telephones (first fixed line, then mobile), information and entertainment (radio and television, cinema, vastly increased numbers of magazines and books, and latterly the internet). It is clear that economic growth has profoundly affected all or nearly all of the population: for example, it has changed the number of years they can expect to live, the kinds of jobs they do, the kind of accommodation they live in, the way they travel about, how they do their shopping, the kind of medical attention available to them, and the way they obtain information and entertainment. On the other hand, it is equally clear that substantial inequalities remain in developed countries, to the extent that a substantial minority are excluded from products and pursuits that have become the stuff of everyday life for the majority and an integral part of the social fabric. Such inequalities could have key importance in understanding youth crime and how societies respond to it.

Throughout most of the process of economic development from the industrial revolution onwards, societies tended to become more equal, and this is reflected in international comparisons today, with the least developed economies showing the most unequal income distributions. As first argued by Lydall (1968) this is because the spread of education and the switch from agriculture to industry lead to more equality. A vivid illustration of this principle is Japan, where rapid industrialization in the 1950s was accompanied by rapid reduction in income inequality. At the beginning of the twentieth century, the distribution of income in Britain was more equal than a century before but was almost certainly far more unequal than today. Analysis of income tax records has shown that the share going to the top 10 per cent (and to smaller groups such as the top 1 per cent and the top 0.5 per cent) declined continuously and substantially up to 1969, remained stable for ten years, then began to increase from 1979 onwards (Hills 2004: 27). Of course, far more comprehensive data are available for the period since the Second World War. Individual incomes are measured by government surveys and adjusted to take account of household composition.[2] Results are expressed both before and after deducting housing costs. In a telling analysis, Hills (2004) divided UK households into deciles, from the poorest to the richest, and considered the change (after allowing for inflation) in the real incomes of each decile over two periods: (a) 1961–79; (b) 1979–94/95. Over the earlier period, the incomes of the poorest decile increased most, whereas increases for the remaining deciles were similar. By contrast, between 1979 and 1994/5, the increase was least for the poorest decile and greatest for the richest decile, with steadily increasing gradations for the deciles in between. Hills also calculated that 'for every £100 in additional net real income over the 23-year period [1979–2003] for the population as a whole, £40 of this went to the richest tenth' (2004: 24). A measure of the overall dispersion of UK incomes remained rather steady in the early part of the post-war period, declined sharply throughout the 1970s, then rose strongly and consistently up to the early 1990s, declining somewhat subsequently, with the result that incomes are much more unequally distributed now than in the immediate post-war period (Hills 2004: fig. 2.9).[3] The income distribution has also become more unequal in a number of other countries, including the USA, Canada, and Norway, but this is not a consistent pattern, and there is no doubt that the increase in the UK is exceptional (Atkinson 2003).

Bringing the analysis up to date, the latest results show that in the ten years from 1996/7, the period of growth in income inequality had come to an end. There were some fluctuations, but over this ten-year period UK incomes became rather more equally distributed (Sefton et al. 2009: 25). Against this trend, those at the very top of the income distribution experienced the fastest growth. For example, 'the total earnings of FTSE 100 CEOs grew by more than 11% per annum in real terms between 1999 and 2006, compared with 1.4% for the median of all full-time employees' (Sefton et al. 2009: 26).

Of course, certain groups are much more likely to be poor than others, and generally groups that are poor in material resources are those that are stigmatized and likely to be involved in crime both as victims and as offenders. Groups at high risk of being in the lowest fifth of households by income are those who are unemployed or workless, lone parents, those in local authority housing, and certain ethnic minorities (particularly Pakistanis and Bangladeshis). Most ordinary crime is very local, so it is highly significant that housing tenures have become far more polarized by income since 1979.

> As the proportion of the population living in social housing has declined, so it has become increasingly concentrated in the poorest groups ... By 2001–02, only 19 per cent of the population were living in social housing [compared with 42 per cent in 1979] but 73 per cent of these were in the poorest two-fifths. Only 2 per cent of those living in social housing were in the top fifth, compared with 13 per cent in 1979. (Hills 2004: 14–15)

Thus increasing inequality has combined with a concentration of the poor in the rump of council housing that could not be sold to tenants.

So far this discussion has focused on inequality rather than poverty. Defining poverty raises a complex set of issues. Many approaches have been tried. Most have their uses, and no single definition is adequate. Measures based on relative incomes are now most widely used in Britain and across Europe. They have the advantage that they give robust indications of trends over time, and there is evidence that they come closest to the way most people think about poverty. Based on a relative measure (below half of median income), roughly 10 per cent of households were in poverty in the 1960s, falling to a low-point of 6 per cent in 1977. The proportion then rose sharply, peaking at 21 per cent in 1991/92, before stabilizing at around 18 per cent in the early 2000s (Hills 2004: 48). The Labour government elected in 1997 made reduction of child poverty a high priority, and over the following decade there were significant reductions in the proportion of children and also of pensioners in poor households on a relative measure (Sefton et al. 2009: table 2.2). The risk of poverty has fallen most among lone-parent families. Despite these improvements, Britain was still at the bottom of the class in Europe in 2006 (along with Spain and Italy) in terms of the proportion of children in poverty (24 per cent below 60 per cent of median income, compared with 9 per cent in Finland at the top of the class) (Stewart 2009b: table 13.1).

Bearing in mind that children soon become adolescents, who account for a high proportion of criminal offending, it is worth looking at trends in child poverty in rather more detail. The measure used by Stewart (2009a) – the best up-to-date source – is the proportion of children in households with (equivalent) income below 60 per cent of the median, after housing costs. On that measure, the proportion of children in poverty rose from 14 per cent in 1979 to 33 per cent in 1991, remained around that level until 1998, then declined to around 27 per cent in 2004 before starting to rise again slightly. This modest reduction may understate progress, since there is also evidence of a large decline in persistent poverty, measured as the percentage of children below the poverty line in three successive years (down from 17 per cent to 11 per cent between the 1990s and the 2000s) (Stewart 2009a: 55). The proportion of children in poverty varies widely between family types. In 1996/7, 67 per cent of children in lone-parent families were in poverty (falling to 52 per cent in 2006/7), and 86 per cent of those in lone-parent families without work were in poverty in 1996/7 (falling to 77 per cent in 2006/7). Levels of child poverty were also very high in couple families where parents either did not work or worked only part-time (Stewart 2009a: table 3.3).

Income inequalities have tangible and persistent effects on the development of young people because of their influence on education and health. Data about educational outcomes in relation to family income are not available, so analysis must be based instead on social class – which is of course closely related to income. In 1989, the proportion of year 11 pupils who attained at least five GCSE grades A*–C was 4.3 times as high among those from managerial or professional families as among those from unskilled manual families (52 per cent compared with 12 per cent). By 2004 this gap had reduced to 2.3 times (Lupton et al. 2009: table 4.1). There is also a large gap between state schools in the most and least deprived neighbourhoods. In 2007, 68 per cent of school leavers in the least deprived decile of neighbourhoods left school with at least five A*–C GCSEs including English and mathematics, compared with 25 per cent of those in the most deprived decile, a ratio of 2.7 (Lupton et al. 2009: table 4.3). As noted in the last section, participation in tertiary education and especially access to elite universities are strongly related to social class origins. The latest figures, which are for 2006, show that the proportion of 18–20-year-olds participating in education was 40 per cent for those from families in the managerial, professional and intermediate classes, compared with 19 per cent for those from other classes (Lupton et al. 2009: table 4.4).

In 1972–6, there was a gap of about five years in life expectancy between social classes I and V. For women, this gap had increased markedly, to seven years, in the period 2002–5. For men, it had increased earlier, in the 1980s, to reach nine years in 1992–6, but then reduced to seven years in 2002–5 (Sassi 2009: fig. 7.2). Both life expectancy and healthy life expectancy are strongly related to neighbourhood deprivation (Sassi 2009: 143). Inequality in life expectancy between neighbourhoods increased steadily between 1992 and 2002, but then remained level up to 2005. This illustrates the increasing concentration of health problems in deprived areas, in parallel with the increasing concentration of poor people in specific neighbourhoods and in local authority housing – all developments that have important implications for youth crime. At the same time, there has been a striking increase in differences between social classes in people's assessments of their own health. Comparing the top and bottom groups in a fivefold set of social class categories, 3 per cent of the top group compared with 6 per cent of the bottom group assessed their own health as poor in 1991, compared with 6 per cent of the top group and 17 per cent of the bottom group in 2005 (Sassi 2009: fig. 7.5).[4] In a similar fashion, rates of cardiovascular disease among different social classes have moved further apart: they have declined for the top social class while increasing for the bottom one (Sassi 2009: fig. 7.7).

Although an increasing proportion of young people go on to tertiary education, still a substantial proportion do not, and these tend very strongly to come from a working-class background. Among this group, youth unemployment is a very important source of inequality. Over the period since 1992, the number of unemployed 16- and 17-year-olds has fluctuated between 150,000 and 200,000. Within this age group, the rate of unemployment (as a proportion of the economically active) sharply increased from 20 per cent in 1997 to a high of 29 per cent towards the middle of 2007, although it began to fall thereafter. The increased rate results both from a rise in the number of unemployed 16- and 17-year-olds, and from a decline in the number who are economically active, as more enter tertiary education (McKnight 2009: 104). Among the next age group (18–24), the unemployment rate among young men peaked at 22 per cent in 1993 (14 per cent for young women) then fell to around 10 per cent in 2000 before rising to around 12 per cent towards the beginning of 2008. It is the continuing high unemployment rate among the youngest age group (16–17) that seems particularly significant for the development of youth offending.

Material inequality may be important not only for the deprived but also for society as a whole, and this strengthens the argument that inequality is important in explaining youth offending. For the past 30 years, Richard Wilkinson has developed a considerable body of evidence and analysis in support of the idea that inequality produces bad outcomes for privileged as well as under-privileged groups. This starts from the observation that economic growth is associated with increases in life expectancy up to a certain point, but beyond that point improvements level off, and further increases in material prosperity produce diminishing – indeed vanishing – benefits. Once basic needs have been met, Wilkinson argues, getting richer no longer increases health and happiness. In their recent book, Wilkinson and Pickett (2009) produced analyses to show that among rich nations, life expectancy is unrelated to prosperity (national income per person) whereas within each nation, life expectancy is of course strongly related to income or social class, as noted above. Their explanation of this paradox is that income acts as an indicator of relative social standing, and that those who are low in the social scale are stressed by the lack of respect and autonomy that goes with that position. Differences in income inequality among rich nations and among US states are strongly related to an index of nine health and social problems. More detailed analyses show, in particular, that inequality at the level of the nation or US state is related to levels of trust, mental illness, alcohol and drug abuse, life expectancy, obesity, children's educational performance, teenage births, homicide, and imprisonment rates. Only health and social problems that are more common further down the social hierarchy are more common in unequal societies, and the steeper the social gradient a problem has within a society, the more strongly it will be related to inequality at the societal level. Health problems such as breast cancer that are *not* usually more common among the less well off are unrelated to societal differences in inequality. But health problems such as obesity in women that *are* strongly related to income are much more common in unequal societies, affecting the rich as well as the poor, so that well-off women in the US (a rich but highly unequal society) are much more likely to be obese than well-off women in Japan (a rich but far more equal society). Wilkinson and Pickett (2009) argue that people experience more challenges to their self-worth in late modern societies than at earlier periods, leading to an increase in anxiety and stress which is now well-documented for young people in the US. A part of their response is an increase in insecure narcissism – an unfounded assertion of their own importance and value – leading to a touchy demand for respect. The wider the differences in social status in a society (as reflected and indexed by differences in income) the more stressed young people are by any challenges from people close to them in the hierarchy. Although these interpretations are somewhat speculative, the analyses of associations at the societal level between inequality and social problems (including crime) are robust. This provides an important framework for policy on the response to youth crime.

Major changes in family structure have swept across all developed countries since the mid twentieth century, coming earliest in the northern and Protestant countries, including the UK, and latest in the southern and Catholic countries. They are of course closely connected with the movement towards female liberation, new control over fertility, and the sexual revolution. The consequences of these changes for family functioning and child development are discussed in Chapter 8. Here it is important to note that changes in the family are one of the main influences on the structure of inequality. The proportion of families with dependent children that are headed by a lone parent in Britain increased from 8 per cent in 1971 to a peak of 27 per cent in 2002 before falling back slightly to 25 per cent in 2006 (Coleman and Brooks 2009: fig. 1.5). The main components within this rise are the growth in never-married lone parents (10 per cent of mothers with dependent children in 2006) and in divorced lone parents (7 per cent). The main problem with single parenthood is that it places a substantial proportion of families in poverty. A major reason is that it is very hard for single parents, especially those without skills or qualifications, to hold down a job that pays more than the cost of child care. Consequently, many single-parent households are workless. In 2007, the proportion of children in workless households was 6.5 per cent where the household comprised a couple, compared with 48 per cent where there was a single parent (Stewart 2009a: table 3.4). The proportion of children in relative poverty (below 60 per cent of equivalized median income after housing costs) was dramatically higher for lone-parent than for couple households. Despite progress over the years of New Labour government since 1997, 52 per cent of children in lone-parent households and 77 per cent of those in workless lone-parent households were below this poverty line in 2006/7, compared with 23 per cent of those in couple households.[5] Lone parenthood also leads to a concentration of poverty in certain ethnic groups. In 2004, the proportion of 5–16-year-olds living in lone parent households was 57 per cent for African Caribbeans, 44 per cent for Black Africans, and 41 per cent for those of mixed heritage, compared with 23 per cent for White British children and considerably smaller proportions for those originating from the Indian subcontinent (Coleman and Brooks 2009: fig. 1.8). The increase in single parenthood forms an important background to understanding youth crime, but it should not be assumed that outcomes for young people in single-parent families are necessarily poor. A recent meta-analysis by the OECD of data from 122 studies found that outcomes in five domains (including conduct) were on average only slightly worse for children in single-parent families than for those in two-parent families, despite the fact that single-parent families tend to be much poorer in material resources (OECD 2009: ch. 5).

Sexual maturity, sexual activity, pregnancy

Perhaps the single most significant transition to be negotiated by young people is from childhood ignorance of sex through the physical transformations of puberty to sexual activity and conceiving or giving birth to children. The period of youth has become extended over the past hundred years not only because of the growth of education, which postpones entry into full-time work, but also because puberty has tended to come earlier: in these ways the beginning of adolescence has moved back, whereas the end of adolescence has moved forward.

Puberty brings about striking changes, including a sudden increase in height, as well as menstruation and breast development (in girls) and voice deepening and growth of facial and body hair (in boys). In both sexes, the sudden increase in height is accompanied by marked changes in physique, but the pattern of changes differs between the sexes. Girls increase in hip width, with substantial accumulation of fat as their growth in height slows down. By contrast, boys show an increase in shoulder breadth and a greater increase in muscle than girls, and most boys tend to lose fat. The net result is that most boys in Western societies are pleased by the physical changes of adolescence, whereas many girls are unhappy with the changes in their bodies, especially with becoming fatter. These visible changes are accompanied by major internal changes in hormone secretion.

Adolescents in Western countries today (and also in Japan) reach puberty earlier than 100 years ago. Also, they grow taller, weigh more, and look more physically mature than in previous generations. In Western Europe, the average age of first menstruation dropped from about 17 in 1800 to about 12 or 13 in the 1990s (Leffert and Petersen 1995). Recently this fall in the age of menarche has either levelled off or stopped. In boys, the average age of voice deepening has probably decreased from about 18 in 1800 to about 14 today. The fall in the age of puberty is paralleled by the increase in average height, and both are probably caused by improvement in diet and lessening of disease.

The hormonal changes in adolescence are of course related to increasing sexual drive, with the result that interest in sex now begins at an earlier age than in the past. Figure 2.6 shows that in Britain the proportion of girls who said their first sexual intercourse happened before the age of 16 rose from 5 per cent in 1964 to 37 per cent in 2002, although this long rising trend reversed between 2002 and 2006. There was a similar rising trend

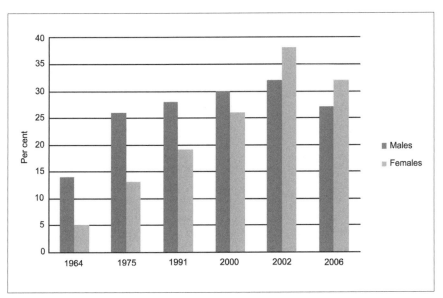

Figure 2.6 Reported first sexual intercourse before age 16, Great Britain 1964–2006

Sources: Schofield (1965); Farrell (1978); Johnson *et al.* (1994); Wellings *et al.* (2001); Currie *et al.* (2004); Currie *et al.* (2008).

for boys, but whereas early intercourse was more common in boys than girls between 1960 and 2000, since 2000 it has become more common in girls than boys. Probably sociocultural factors are more important than biological factors in bringing about earlier sexual experience. In the United States, early sexual intercourse is considerably more common among African Americans than among white people, and it is associated with poverty, disadvantage, and family disorganization (Leffert and Petersen 1995). In Britain, too, early sexual intercourse is far more common among African British boys (although not girls) than among any other group. It is particularly uncommon among Asians (Coleman and Schofield 2007: fig. 4.3). Coinciding with the reversal in the long-term trend of increase in the rate of early intercourse, the rate of conception among girls aged 15–17 in England and Wales declined from 47.1 per thousand in 1998 to 40.9 in 2006. However, the proportion of these pregnancies leading to abortion increased from 42 to 48 per cent over the same period (*source*: Office for National Statistics and Teenage Pregnancy Unit). The rate of pregnancies brought to term and of abortions among women aged 15–19 is higher in the United Kingdom than in all other European countries with the exception of Romania and Bulgaria (World Health Organization 2009: table 4.4.2).

Family formation, living arrangements, homelessness

In modern conditions, young people nearly always leave the parental home at some stage, and this is seen as an essential step towards becoming an independent adult. Leaving home is linked with other key transitions such as going to university, living with someone as a couple, getting married, having children, and finding a job. Yet these linkages are not straightforward. For example, a substantial proportion of young people in Britain (and higher proportions in other countries like France and Germany) study at university while still living with their parents; many young people stay at home after finding full-time employment; and some young women live with their parents after becoming mothers. One or more of these other transitions is often the reason for leaving home: some young people leave to get married or live with someone as a couple, some to take up a job or a place in higher education elsewhere, others to gain independence from their parents, to escape from conflict in the parental home, or to join the military (Mulder 2009). Cross-nationally, trends in the timing of leaving home have changed direction over the period since the Second World War. In the USA, for example, between 1940 and 1960 there was a trend towards leaving home at an earlier age, but after a decade of stability, the trend reversed between 1970 and 1995 with a movement towards leaving home at a later age. There were similar trends in most European countries. The decline then rise in the proportion of young people staying at home was partly driven by a similar fall then rise in the age of marriage and unmarried cohabitation. However, the picture was complicated by the new phenomenon of living alone or with room-mates, which pushed down the age of leaving home in recent years (Mulder 2009).

The contemporary patterns of living arrangements among young people in the UK are illustrated in Figure 2.7. More than six out of ten young men aged 20–21 are still living with their parents, shrinking to one-quarter of

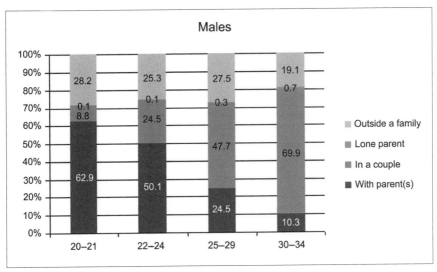

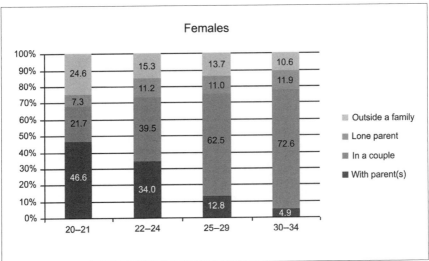

Figure 2.7 Living arrangements of young men and women by age group, UK 2008

Source: Berrington *et al.* (2009) tables 1 and 2.

those aged 25–29 and to one-tenth of those aged 30–34. Young women tend to leave home considerably earlier than men, primarily because they tend to become part of a couple at an earlier age. For example, among those aged 22–24, 40 per cent of women compared with 25 per cent of men are living in a couple. Between 1991 and 2005 the proportion both of men and women in their twenties who were living with their parents consistently increased (*Social Trends* 36, 2006: table 2.5), possibly reflecting the trend towards later marriage and childbearing. The main reasons that young people give for living with their parents are that they can't afford to move out and that there is no affordable housing available. Lack of affordable housing was mentioned in the UK much more often than in other European countries (*Social Trends* 39, 2009: table 2.9).

The number of marriages registered in England and Wales peaked in 1972 and by 2006 had fallen to 56 per cent of the 1972 figure. Not only is marriage becoming less popular, but also people are getting married at a later age. This trend has continued for about 50 years. In 1966 the average age at first marriage was 24.9 for men and 22.5 for women. In 2006 it was 31.8 for men and 29.7 for women. Over the same period, cohabitation became much more common. Figure 2.8 compares three cohorts born between 1966 and 1980 at three different ages. For all three cohorts, cohabitation was unusual between the ages of 15 and 19. Once they reached their twenties, members of each succeeding cohort were much more likely to cohabit than members of the preceding one. Among the most recent cohort (born 1976–1980) nearly three out of ten were

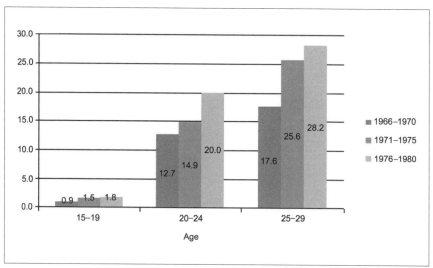

Figure 2.8 Proportion of individuals cohabiting, by year of birth and age at survey, Great Britain 2006

Source: Social Trends 39 (2009), fig. 2.16.

cohabiting between the ages of 25 and 29. The results of the British Social Attitudes Survey show that even though traditional attitudes have changed, and even though two-thirds of people in 2006 thought that there was little social difference between being married and living together, three in ten people felt that married couples make better parents than unmarried ones, and two-thirds thought marriage was financially more secure than cohabitation (*Social Trends* 39, 2009: table 2.14).

As people have tended to form couples at a later age than in the past, so childbearing has also tended to shift to a later point in the life cycle. Other reasons for this shift are women's increasing emphasis on their careers (meaning that they need to establish a career path before taking time off to raise children) and pressure to establish financial security before starting a family. The average age of women in England and Wales at the birth of their first child was 27.5 years in 2007 compared with 26.1 years in 1997 and 23.7 years in 1971 (*Social Trends* 39, 2009: 22). Along with the general trend towards later childbirth, there has also been some reduction in births to teenage mothers, from 9.5 per cent of all births in 1977 to 7 per cent in 2004 (Coleman and Brooks 2009: fig. 5.15). Nevertheless, teenage births are at a considerably higher level in the UK than in other European countries (Coleman and Brooks 2009: fig. 5.14) although still lower than in the US (Furstenberg 2009). Earlier studies tended to suggest that giving birth as a teenager tended to have long-term adverse consequences for a range of outcomes, including involvement in crime. Many of these analyses did not adequately allow for the fact that it is girls with various disadvantages who tend to become teenage mothers. More recent analyses of longitudinal studies that use more adequate statistical techniques have found that the effects of early childbearing on later outcomes are modest, at most (Furstenberg 2009).

A substantial minority of young people when they leave the parental home become homeless. The main trigger for homelessness in young people is a breakdown in relationships, usually with parents or step-parents, often after long-term conflict in the home, and often involving violence. Depression and other mental health problems are prevalent among homeless young people, along with abuse of alcohol and illicit drugs, and homelessness probably makes these problems worse. There is strong evidence that it makes it harder for young people to get work and to participate in education and training (Quilgars *et al.* 2008: 36).

Estimating the numbers of homeless young people is inherently difficult, because of problems of definition and patchiness of data, but well-founded estimates are provided in the recent report for the Joseph Rowntree Foundation. According to these estimates, about 75,000 young people aged 16–24 experience homelessness in a year, suggesting that 1 out of every 24 young people experiences some form of homelessness annually. This total includes people accepted as statutorily homeless (the largest sub-group) together with non-statutorily homeless people who make use of Supporting People services or who are re-housed by housing associations, together with several hundred who experience rough sleeping at some time in a year. Over the ten years up to 2008, the numbers of statutorily homeless young people (i.e. those officially designated homeless) reduced in England, but this may be because some were diverted to be dealt with under other heads within different preventive programmes. The numbers of non-statutorily homeless young people did not decline, but there was certainly a substantial reduction in the numbers sleeping rough (Quilgars *et al.* 2008). Affecting as it does a fairly small minority of young people who tend to suffer from a range of other disadvantages, deficits, and difficulties, homelessness is an important part of the context for certain kinds of youth crime.

Youth culture and markets

From the 1950s onwards, youth became a more distinct and identifiable group. There was not one but an increasing number of partly overlapping youth subcultures distinguished by style, clothing, music and language. Youth cultures continuously evolved, with important influences from various ethnic minorities that were becoming a considerable proportion of the youth population. Also these youth cultures became an important influence on the development of popular tastes across all age groups. As the mass marketing of the inter-war years gave way in the 1950s to the concept of market segmentation, manufacturers and advertisers began to target products and marketing at specific population groups defined first in terms of demographic characteristics and later in terms of interests and aspirations (e.g. teenagers 'with attitude', aspiring young couples). Young people were seen as having key importance for marketing, because they had rapidly increasing disposable incomes, because they were innovators who could kick-start new products and markets, and because the new products and habits they adopted would spread through the whole of society as they grew older (whereas the habits of older consumers would simply die with them).

The growth of youth cultures and youth markets in the post-war period are two inseparable aspects of the same phenomenon. Indisputably this constitutes a massive social change, although it is one that is hard or impossible to quantify. Although there is extensive information, it was mostly obtained for commercial purposes and is not publicly available, it has not been organized so as to provide consistent measures of long-term trends, and it does not consistently identify the youth component within specific markets. Nevertheless it is clear enough that there has been huge growth in youth markets for products such as recorded music, clothes, cosmetics, live events, dance clubs, and holidays. Young people have been pioneers in the use of mobile phones and constitute almost all of the huge and still growing market for computer games and games consoles.

One interpretation of these developments, arising from the ideas of the Frankfurt School, is that under capitalism the large corporations and their allies use consumer goods to pacify young people and to distract them from the injustices that prevent them from fulfilling themselves in contemporary societies. Contrasting interpretations emphasize that young people make choices and that they selectively use the products of capitalism (e.g. clothes, music) to establish an identity and to send out messages about what they want to achieve (Best 2009). On some interpretations, spectacular youth cultures (Mods, Rockers, Skinheads, Goths) enact 'rituals of resistance' against the roles assigned to them in the social order (Hebdige 1979). Focusing on more recent developments, a different interpretation is that young people, lacking a sense of where they belong in the class or social structure, use consumer products as symbols to construct a new idea of who they are and where they are heading (Baumann 2000; Best 2009).

Some of these points can be illustrated by taking the example of alcoholic drinks that are sold to young people specifically and that young people use as a way of defining themselves. In the words of a recent report for the Joseph Rowntree Foundation:

> alcohol marketing and promotion involves enormous and ever-increasing financial budgets, a trend that looks set to continue ... In the UK more than £200 million was spent on alcohol advertising in 2004, with a 2.5% annual increase ... Additional promotional and marketing budgets are estimated to be worth more than three times that figure; for example, drinks are being increasingly promoted through sponsorship of sports and music events, many of which have a strong youth appeal. (Velleman 2009: 31)

Powerful analyses of longitudinal studies have shown that advertising and marketing of alcohol are significant factors in the rise of alcohol consumption by young people. For example, Snyder et al. (2006) showed that for each additional alcohol advertisement viewed each month, there followed a 1 per cent rise in the number of drinks consumed, and that young drinkers in US regions with greater alcohol advertising expenditures drank more than those in regions with less expenditure. 'Content analysis ... suggests that drinking is portrayed as being an important part of sociability, physical attractiveness, masculinity and femininity, romance, relaxation and adventure. Many alcohol advertisements use rock music, animation, image appeals and celebrity endorsers, which increase their popularity with underage television viewers' (Velleman 2009: 32). There are also many indirect forms of advertising, via representations in films and television programmes, mentions on popular records and on the internet, sports promotions and sponsorships, all of which tend to target the young. Use of these indirect methods is closely allied to the growing influence of the 'brand' as the dominant force in contemporary marketing. Brand affiliation has come to assume central importance in the construction of youth identity. Indirect marketing activities 'are designed to embed brand names and products in the everyday activities of the target audience' (Velleman 2009: 32). Drinking, getting intoxicated or 'high' are very frequently mentioned in popular music. One study found that product placements or brand names occurred in 30 per cent of songs with reference to alcohol, and were particularly common in rap music (Roberts *et al.* 1999). Placement of brands of alcoholic drinks is also very frequent in television programmes. The alcohol industry has been successful in linking its names to many sports, including football (Carling Cup) and rugby (Heineken Cup) in the UK. 'Alcohol sponsorship . . . has expanded across the world in all the key areas of youth culture: music, sport, dance, film and television' (Velleman 2009: 33). Sponsorship can avoid regulation of direct advertising, it can target youth markets cheaply and effectively, and it bypasses critical audience responses to direct advertising.

At the same time, it is obvious that young people are not just the passive recipients of marketing messages. They consume alcohol in a huge variety of specific settings that are expressions of particular youth subcultures, and it is certainly not the drinks manufacturers who have created the traditions of punk or rap or bhangra within which mentions of their brands are embedded. Moreover, advertisers constantly try to catch hints about what is 'hot', what is 'cool', and what is on the wane among young people, and tune their messages and new product launches accordingly. Sticking with the example of drinks, the 'alcopops' story serves to illustrate the point. These sweet, fizzy, fairly low-strength alcoholic drinks were launched in 1995 with very young drinkers (who tend to dislike the taste of traditional alcoholic drinks) clearly the target, despite the denials of manufacturers. For several years, until 2003, they showed exceptional growth and yielded substantial profits for the producers. By 2004, the tide had turned. According to a BBC report in February of that year,

> drinks giant Diageo . . . has unveiled a slump in alcopops consumption . . . One big problem . . . has been the Treasury's decision to levy Excise Tax. Alcopops drinkers, usually price-conscious 18–25-year-olds, have turned away in droves . . . But the reverse is also a sign that the market has matured and that alcopops are possibly not as fashionable as they were. According to some estimates, younger British drinkers are shifting their allegiance back to traditional spirits and beer. (BBC News Channel 19 February 2004)

In this as in every other youth market the producers and consumers engage in a complex dance in which each makes use of the other. If the producer tries to amplify and manipulate desires, the young consumer chooses from available products and deploys them to convey messages both about group solidarity and about a fresh and unique personal identity.

These developments are important as a background to understanding youth offending in at least two ways. First, because youth cultures – often signified by patterns of consumption – have become so much more important, young people have become a more distinctive and identifiable group which is regularly stigmatized as being associated with crime and disorder. Most discussions of this topic come up with quotations from medieval or even Babylonian times to show that youth has always been regarded as dangerous and out of control. But there is a good case for arguing that consumerism and distinctive youth cultures since the Second World War have created a genuinely new situation. Second, if often expensive brands are an indispensable source of identity for at least a part of the youth population, then deprivation of the means to acquire these products can be disorienting even if basic needs for food, shelter, and clothing are met.

Media and widening horizons

Perhaps the most striking change in the lives of young people over the past 60 years has been a widening of horizons leading to a greater awareness of the world beyond their immediate social circle and physical surroundings. Here the expansion of education and cheap foreign travel are important factors, along with the growth of the traditional mass media – radio, cinema and television – and the later explosion of the new media – mobile phones, computer games, the internet, and multiple digital television channels. These changes are so large, complex and new that they are hard to describe, especially since they are qualitative as well as quantitative: people not only consume far more information, but they also engage with the new media in different ways and often more actively than in the past. There is extensive research about the exposure of young people to the media and how they make use of the internet and mobile phones, but no substantive research on how the new flood of information and interaction frames the developmental tasks of becoming an adult. There is a danger that it may make these tasks more forbidding. Most young people 60 years ago had limited awareness of any options available to them other than working in a manual job for one of a few employers in their home town. Most young people today must have awareness of wider possibilities that exist in a world beyond their immediate social and physical zone, although they may have no useful or realistic information and may not know how to step outside their immediate environment. Thinking about the consequences of the information revolution for the development of young people, we can imagine both a progressive and a regressive scenario. In the progressive scenario, widening horizons encourage young people to explore more possible futures and a good proportion of these new ambitions are realized. Also, the explosion of information is a democratizing force: possibilities that only elites used to know about can now be realized by a broader section of youth. In the regressive scenario, most young people become aware of a vast range of possibilities that remain out of reach, so that widening horizons open up the gap between imagined and real futures.

The growth of the new media has been explosive, and for the most part use of new media has not replaced older media, but has added another layer, so that total time spent engaging with media has increased. For example, in 1995 boys aged 11–16 spent an average of 3.3 hours per day watching television, and this remained much the same (3.0 hours) in 2008. Over the same period, time spent by the same group on the internet grew from virtually nil to an average of 2.0 hours a day (Childwise 2009), so there was a very substantial growth in television plus internet time overall. Over the same period, of course, there was a rapid growth in use of mobile phones among young people, and as mobile phone technology developed, these devices were used for more and more tasks, and to engage with more sources of information. Equally, there was rapid growth in ownership and usage of games consoles. We do not have data on hours of usage for 1995, but by 2008, 11–16-year-old boys were spending 2.0 hours a week on average playing with a games console. Although hours spent watching television did not increase over the same period, the proportion of 11–16-year-old boys having access to multi-channel television increased from 48 to 88 per cent over the slightly shorter period from 1997 to 2008, and the proportion who had watched non-terrestrial television in the past week increased from 56 to 99 per cent, signalling substantial change in the variety of programmes available and watched. The one information-gathering activity that may have declined among young people over a similar period is reading, although the findings from the Childwise surveys suggest a rise from 1999 to 2005 followed by a drop over the next three years, and this drop (in terms of time spent) is small compared with the rise in the total time spent on all of these activities.

An important feature of these developments is that young people now often engage with audio-visual media individually and privately rather than communally with the rest of the family, or with friends. By 2008, 70 per cent of boys and 68 per cent of girls aged 11–16 had a personal computer in their own room; 53 per cent of boys and 43 per cent of girls accessed the internet in their own room; 90 per cent of boys and 61 per cent of girls had a games console in their own room; 87 per cent of boys and 80 per cent of girls had a television set in their own room; and 81 per cent of boys and 75 per cent of girls had a DVD player in their own room (Childwise 2009). These different media of course merge into one another: for example, many young people use the internet to download audio and audiovisual material and for playing games. Much of the use of these media is interactive and inventive, rather than purely passive (Livingstone 2005, 2008). For example, among those who use the internet (the great majority of those aged 11 +) substantial proportions of young people have profiles on one or more social networking sites (Childwise 2009). Children and young people living with their parents use the new media as a means of establishing a space of their own, largely away from the direct control of parents, where they can begin to find out who they are and what they want to become (Livingstone 2005, 2008).

An older tradition of research was concerned with the effects of watching television – especially portrayals of violence – on young people's behaviour. Much of the evidence is weak, either because it deals with short exposure to material in unrealistic 'laboratory' conditions, or because it does not take account of how young people interact with and interpret what they see, or because the influence of watching television is not evaluated in the context of other influences and compared with them. A further – crucial – problem is that some material may be harmless for most young people, but have serious adverse effects on small, vulnerable groups. A recent re-evaluation of the evidence (Livingstone 2008) concludes that although there is evidence for short-term effects of exposure to violent imagery, there is little evidence that this translates into long-term effects, probably because research on short-term effects does not take account of context and the way that young people use and interact with the media. The more recent tradition of use on media harm is concerned with the whole range of risks associated with young people using the new media, including for example online bullying, unexpected exposure to violent or sexual images, and attacks by sexual abusers. The question is how to minimize such risks and how to balance them against the benefits to young people of going online. Findings suggest that parents often have little real knowledge of what their children are doing online, partly because the children are using the web to build a private space. With increasing understanding on the part of parents as their own use of the internet grows, the balance is likely to shift, with some reduction of risk to young people without gross invasion of their privacy (Livingstone and Haddon 2009). Looking more broadly at perceptions of risk, parents today tend to think the streets are far more dangerous than parents did in earlier generations, for a variety of reasons including the radical change in traffic conditions, and the 'moral panics' about violent crime and about paedophiles. Hence more children are ferried to school, and fewer go on foot or on bicycles. In this and other ways, children and young people live less independent lives than in earlier generations because adults are anxious to protect them from risks. Parents are much happier for their child to be interacting with audiovisual media in their bedroom than to be out on the streets, and are willing to trade a loss of control over what they do in their bedrooms to achieve this. Young people, having lost a large chunk of independence on the streets, have managed to regain it in the virtual worlds of television, computer games, and MySpace.

Thus, although there are risks associated with use of the media, there is not much evidence that audiovisual material has had a major effect on youth behaviour, for example through young people imitating violence depicted on television. What the research shows, however, is that young people spend far more time engaging with a virtual world through audiovisual media than in the past, and that their involvement is often active and intense. The true significance of these changes is that they provide young people with ways of exploring and imagining the world that were not available to earlier generations. This creates new opportunities but also new tensions and bruises when young people bump up against objects, people, organizations and limited opportunities IRL 'in real life'.

Social bonds, social capital, authority

The lives of young people are strongly influenced by long-term changes in the patterns of bonding between members of society. There are associated changes in the ways that social norms are defined and understood. A starting point for thinking about these changes is social control theory as it was proposed more than a generation ago (Hirschi 1969). On this perspective, people are restrained from breaking social norms by their bonds with other individuals, groups, and institutions. Social bonds are defined as reciprocal relationships, for example between husband and wife or between employee and employer. The stronger and the denser their relationships with others, the more people are constrained from breaking accepted norms of behaviour, because these others put pressure on them to conform, because the expectations of their closest associates become a part of their own identity and system of beliefs, and because people calculate that they could lose relationships and associated advantages if they do not conform. This makes it look as though social bonds are a negative force that prevents people from satisfying their desires in a direct and natural way. In fact they are in many ways a positive force, because man or woman is an essentially social animal: an infant cannot become a person having speech and a sense of self except through relationships with other people. Hence, as well as imposing constraints, social bonds are also a resource through which people can get things done: those with a great deal of power and freedom also have many reciprocal social relationships.

From this reasoning, we would expect individuals to conform to the law and to more informal social norms to the extent that they have formed multiple strong social bonds, and a large tradition of research broadly confirms this expectation. A more recent body of work broadens the analysis by introducing the concept of social capital. If we focus on the individual, as social control theory does, then we can characterize each individual by describing the set of linkages radiating outwards from that person to other persons, organizations and institutions. If we focus instead on a whole society, or some section of it, then what we have is a whole network of social connections. Just as we expect an individual to be regulated, powerful and free to the extent that he or she is 'well-connected', so we would expect a country, a town, or a neighbourhood to be safe and prosperous to the extent that there are dense and strong connections among the individuals within it. Since the 1980s, social commentators have been describing this quality of 'connectedness' which facilitates all kinds of enterprises as 'social capital' – the key original thinkers being James Coleman (1988) and Robert Putnam (2000). Halpern (2005: 10, emphasis in original) suggests that social capital is composed of three components: 'a *network*; a cluster of *norms, values and expectancies* that are shared by group members; and *sanctions* – punishments and rewards – that help to maintain the norms and network'. Social capital is necessary to make the world go round – as is financial and physical capital – but it may not benefit everyone. For example, Old Etonians have a great deal of social capital arising from their bonds with other Old Etonians, which is greatly to their benefit but not necessarily to the benefit of the rest of society, and the same can be said for members of the Mafia. Not all bonds or networks are similar. Early agricultural societies are characterized by very strong bonds among people belonging to the same family or village, but weak linkages between one family or village and another, or between different levels of a social hierarchy. In such a system, strangers will be treated with suspicion and hostility, and local groups will act strongly to defend their own interest with little concern for the interests of the wider collectivity. Advanced societies are characterized by weaker primary ties to family and neighbours but many more, relatively weak, ties to more distant people and institutions. In that kind of society, people are more concerned with maintaining standards of civility and good conduct that are common to the wider community, and less concerned with blind loyalty to their nearest and dearest.

After more than two decades of research, there is good evidence that both levels and patterns of social capital are related to economic performance, health, educational performance and crime (Halpern 2005). These relationships hold at various levels. Individuals who are 'well-connected' are thereby more likely to be prosperous and healthy, to perform well at school, and to avoid criminal offending, but the same also applies to communities, to institutions (such as schools or businesses) and to countries.

Putnam (2000) used a range of measures to describe participation and involvement in clubs, associations and activities in the US and found there had been a major decline over the years from 1960. Halpern (2005: 216) concluded that 'Britain has witnessed a significant decline in social capital over the last few decades, though not as universally or simply as the USA'. There were, for example, declines in trade union membership, voting, church membership and participation, membership of Women's Institutes, and charitable giving. This is offset to an extent by a rise in membership of the National Trust, the Royal Society for the Protection of Birds, and a bundle of environmental organizations, but Halpern argued that these organizations have grown on the back of 'chequebook' and 'ticket' memberships that involve visiting an attraction or receiving information about a cause, but never meeting other members. Comparisons of cohort studies show a marked decline in membership of associations. 'When those born in 1946 were in their thirties, around 60 per cent of men and 50 per cent of women belonged to at least one organization . . . For those born in 1970, when in their thirties, only 10 and 15 per cent respectively belonged to at least one organization' (Halpern 2005: 213). The proportion of young people volunteering, and the amount of time young volunteers give, fell over the 1990s (although not among older people). An important feature of the pattern of change in Britain is a divergence of trends between social classes. Levels of social capital, on several measures, have declined substantially among people from un-skilled and semi-skilled households, whereas they have remained the same for people from middle-class households (Halpern 2005: 215). It was suggested in an earlier section that over a period when inequality has grown and qualification levels have increased, the group without qualifi-cations begin to look deviant. It now seems that a similar group may be socially disconnected as well.

These declines in participation and involvement are not seen in every country: notable exceptions are Sweden, the Netherlands and Japan. Nevertheless, they are reflected in many of the countries that have so far been studied, and this suggests that they are part of a more general set of transformations in late modern societies, ones that are particularly clear in the US and, to a lesser extent, in Britain. These transformations can best be described as a move towards individualism and away from being defined and constrained by the given social background such as immedi-ate family and neighbourhood. The spread-out American suburbs and the development of the mass media and the internet allow most people to meet their needs in private spaces without the compromises involved in group activities. This growing individualism is paralleled by a growing belief in abstract principles of justice and human rights, and a growing reliance on formal as opposed to informal methods of regulation. Formal control and regulation have in fact increased over the past 50 years, as evidenced by the exponential growth of national and European legisla-tion, the new emphasis on human rights, the proliferation of regulatory bodies, the establishment of databases for control of crime and credit, the spread of television and electronic surveillance, and the expansion of police and private security personnel, among many other examples.

Analysis of attitude surveys reveals a pattern of complex change in moral concepts and values, but broadly there is evidence of increasing faith in formal, rule-based control systems (Halpern 1995). Some (such as Reiner 2007) believe that this has been accompanied by a decline in informal controls. It can be argued that as formal regulation advances into the private sphere it tends to weaken the capacity for local communities, schools and families to control themselves. The policy of placing police officers in schools is a possible example. There is evidence that where school-based officers avoid resort to law enforcement, their presence is welcomed and makes pupils and teachers feel more secure. However, it remains to be seen whether, several years later, reliance on these police officers has tended to erode the informal controls on which the whole order maintenance project ultimately rests.

What is new, then, about the present generation of young people is that whereas their bonds with people in the immediate social sphere are weaker than for earlier generations, their 'thin' connections to a wider range of contacts are more extensive, and they are far more open to information from a range of media about the wider world. Their lives are more individualistic and atomized than in the past in some ways, but they place more emphasis on abstract rules, ideals of justice, and formal regulation. These trends create new tensions, because formal regulation ultimately rests on informal social controls, which are weakened because of declining participation and involvement of young people in active local groups and organizations.

There are related changes in attitudes towards authority that may be important in understanding the development of young people. In the way that people talk, particularly about the family and the school, there has been a move from justifying authority 'because it's there' towards authority proving its legitimacy through reasoned argument and debate. This is, of course, a counterpart of the move from emphasis on the unquestionable primacy of familial social bonds towards greater emphasis on the individual, on the individual's connections to the wider society and on associated ideals of justice and democracy. In a variety of ways, many forms of authority have become challengeable where they were not before. Examples include strengthened systems of appeal at every level of the legal system; a stronger and more independent system for dealing with complaints against the police; systems for handling allegations of physical and sexual abuse of children which, it is claimed, undermine the authority of teachers; the response of the churches to allegations of child abuse by priests and ministers; newspaper columns, television and radio programmes that take up and investigate complaints against businesses and against local and central government; and the proliferation of ombudsmen and regulators in every institutional sphere. These changes certainly mean that authority has to be justified and exercised differently, but do they mean that people are less obedient to authority?

Some light is shed on the question by a recent limited replication of one of Stanley Milgram's famous experiments on obedience to authority that were carried out in the 1960s (Milgram 1963, 1965, 1974). In the original experiments, subjects were told by an authoritative white-coated figure to press a switch to administer apparently painful electric shocks to someone in the adjoining room. A high proportion pressed the switch apparently delivering shocks of up to 400 volts despite hearing what they thought were cries of agony. Until recently the experiments have not been replicated because of ethical constraints (although the subjects in the original experiments were interviewed afterwards, and none regretted having taken part). Forty-five years after the original experiments, Burger (2009) succeeded in carrying out a partial replication that was approved by the relevant committee of ethics. The main restriction was that the shock went up to an apparent 150 (rather than 400) volts. Interpretation is aided because in the original experiments, nearly all of those who complied up to 150 volts continued to comply up to 400. The results suggest that there has been some decline in obedience to authority, although opinions vary as to the exact interpretation. Twenge (2009) suggested that allowing for halting the experiment at 150 volts and for a change in the ethnic composition of the sample, the true drop may be greater than shown. Nevertheless, given the widespread changes in social bonds, moral concepts and values, and the wider social context that have been discussed in this chapter, the change in obedience to authority was less striking than expected.

Conclusion

In the period since the Second World War, the developmental path leading from childhood to adulthood has become much longer because puberty and sexual activity come earlier, whereas education and training continue for longer; joining the labour force comes later, leaving the parental home is often postponed, cohabitation and marriage come at a later age, and even though there is still a substantial minority of teenage mothers, most women start to bear children at a later age. These changes are so significant that some writers describe a phase of 'emerging adulthood' (more popularly, 'kidulthood') between adolescence and maturity when there is a moratorium on social roles and commitments (Tanner and Arnett 2009). Changes in societal structures that frame these developmental processes have been both profound and wide-ranging. Britain became a strikingly more unequal society both at the top and at the bottom end of the income distribution. A group of unqualified young people became more conspicuously different from the increasing majority with some sort of qualification, and the social ties and social capital of this group declined steeply. Although not yet confirmed by quantitative research, it is likely that young people came to spend a much longer period of their lives in a 'youth ghetto' mixing mainly with others in their own age group, where previously they tended to work in mixed-age work groups from an early age. Because of the extended period of youth and the intensive interaction among people of a similar age, young people became a more conspicuous and identifiable group, and distinctive, sometimes spectacular youth cultures took shape. These were given added impetus by the development of youth markets for products that were then used as markers of identity, with the result that young people needed to buy and consume in order to 'be someone'. The extraordinary expansion of audiovisual media meant that young people had far more exposure than earlier generations to images, stories and hard information about the world beyond their bedrooms. This, along with the explosion of cheap foreign travel, widened horizons so that most young people now had a vague awareness of a vast range of possible lives that they would never, in fact, be able to live. Finally, young people became less rooted in local attachments to family and neighbourhood, and more connected through weak links to a wider range of people and organizations all over the place. In parallel, they became more individualistic, and placed more value on formal and wide-ranging values such as human rights or protecting the environment, and less on loyalty to family and close associates.

As explained in the next chapter, there was a large increase in crime, including youth crime, between 1950 and 1994, followed by a decline in property crime and a plateau in violent crime. A convincing explanation for these crime trends cannot yet be put forward. Nevertheless, the changes discussed in this chapter provide a framework for understanding crime trends, and an eventual explanation will certainly involve the societal transformations discussed here. These changes in youth transitions and in the societal structures that frame them will probably be far more important in explaining youth crime than the workings of the youth justice system.

Notes

1 The Act also provided for a third type – technical schools – but few of these were ever built.
2 Results are expressed as 'equivalent household income' to adjust for differences in the cost of maintaining a given standard of living depending on the size and composition of the household. Data are from the Family Expenditure Survey (1979–1994/5) and from the Family Resources Survey (since 1994/5).
3 The statistic used is the Gini coefficient. Three different series of data (covering different periods) are used, as described in Hills (2004).
4 After controlling for several other factors in a multivariate analysis.

5 An equally high proportion (77 per cent) of children in workless couple households were below the poverty line, but workless couple households were much less numerous than workless lone-parent households. The point is that lone parenthood and worklessness tend very strongly to go together.

References

Atkinson, A. B. (2003) 'Income Inequality in OECD Countries: Data and Explanations', *CSInfo Economic Studies*, 49: 479–513.

Baumann, Z. (2000) *Liquid Modernity* (New York: Polity Press).

Beck, U. (1992) *Risk Society* (London: Sage).

Berrington, A., Stone, J. and Falkingham, J. (2009) 'The Changing Living Arrangements of Young Adults in the UK', *Population Trends* 138 (Winter 2009), pp. 27–37.

Best, A. L. (2009) 'Young People and Consumption' in A. Furlong (ed.) *Handbook of Youth and Young Adulthood* (Abingdon: Routledge) pp. 255–62.

Burger, J. M. (2009) 'Replicating Milgram: Would People Still Obey Today?' *American Psychologist* 64.1, pp. 1–11.

Childwise (2009) *The Monitor Trends Report 2009: Trends Data from the Childwise Monitor Report 1994–2008* (Norwich: Childwise).

Coleman, J. (1988) 'Social Capital in the Creation of Human Capital', *American Journal of Sociology* 94 Supplement, S95-S120.

Coleman, J. and Brooks, F. (2009) *Key Data on Adolescence* (Brighton: Young People in Focus).

Coleman, J. and Schofield, J. (2007) *Key Data on Adolescence* (Brighton: Trust for the Study of Adolescence).

Currie, C., Roberts, C., Morgan, A., Smith, R., Settertobulte, W., Samdal, O. and Rasmussen, V. B. (2004) *Young People's Health in Context: Health Behaviour in School-Age Children (HBSC) Study: International Report from the 2001/2 Survey* (Geneva: World Health Organization).

Currie, C., Nic Gabhainn, S., Godeau, E., Roberts, C., Smith, R., Currie, D., Picket, W., Richter, M., Morgan, A. and Barnekow, V. (2008) *Inequalities in Young People's Health: HBSC International Report from the 2005/6 Survey* (Edinburgh: University of Edinburgh Child and Adolescent Health Research Unit, for World Health Organization) at www.education.ac.uk/cahru

Department for Children, Schools and Families (2009) *Participation in Education, Training and Employment by 16–18 Year-Olds in England*, Statistical First Release (London: Department for Children, Schools and Families).

Devitt, K., Knighton, L., and Lowe, K. (2009) *Young Adults Today: Key Data on 16–25 Year-Olds, Transitions, Disadvantage and Crime* (Brighton: Young People in Focus).

Eurostat (2009) *Youth in Europe: A Statistical Portrait* (Luxembourg: Eurostat).

Farrell, C. (1978) *My Mother Said . . .* (London: Routledge).

Furlong, A. and Cartmel, F. (2007) *Young People and Social Change*, 2nd edition (Maidenhead: Open University Press).

Furstenberg, F. Jr. (2009) 'Early Childbearing in the New Era of Delayed Adulthood', in A. Furlong (ed.) *Handbook of Youth and Young Adulthood* (Abingdon: Routledge) pp. 226–31.

Gillard, D. (2009) *Education in England* available at: http://www.dg.dial.pipex. com/history/timeline.shtml

Halpern, D. S. (1995) 'Values, Morals and Modernity: The Values, Constraints and Norms of European Youth', in M. Rutter and D. J. Smith (eds) *Psychosocial Disorders in Young People: Time Trends and Their Causes* (Chichester: Wiley) pp. 324–88.

Halpern, D. S. (2005) *Social Capital* (Cambridge: Polity Press).

Hebdige, D. (1979) *Subculture: The Meaning of Style* (London: Routledge).

Hills, J. (2004) *Inequality and the State* (Oxford: Oxford University Press).

Hirschi, T. (1969) *Causes of Delinquency* (Berkeley: University of California Press).

Johnson, A. (1994) *Sexual Attitudes and Lifestyles* (Oxford: Blackwell Scientific).

Leffert, N. and Petersen, A. (1995) 'Patterns of Development During Adolescence', in M. Rutter and D. J. Smith (eds), *Psychosocial Disorders in Young People: Time Trends and their Causes* (Chichester: Wiley) pp. 67–103.

Livingstone, S. (2005) 'Mediating the Public/Private Boundary at Home: Children's Use of the Internet for Privacy and Participation', *Journal of Media Practice* 6.1, pp. 41–51, available at: http://eprints.lse.ac.uk/archive/00000506

Livingstone, S. (2008) 'Drawing Conclusions from New Media Research: Reflexions and Puzzles Regarding Children's Experiences of the Internet', *The Information Society* 22.4, pp. 219–30, available at: http://eprints.lse.ac.uk/1015/.

Livingstone, S. and Haddon, L. (2009) *EU Kids Online: Final Report* (London: LSE, EU Kids Online).

Lupton, R., Heath, N. and Salter, E. (2009) 'Education: New Labour's Top Priority', in J. Hills, T. Sefton and K. Stewart, *Towards a More Equal Society? Poverty, Inequality and Social Policy Since 1997* (Bristol: The Policy Press), pp. 71–90.

Lydall, H. (1968) *The Structure of Earnings* (Oxford: Clarendon Press).

Milgram, S. (1963) 'Behavioral Study of Obedience', *Journal of Abnormal and Social Psychology* 67, 371–8.

Milgram, S. (1965) 'Some Conditions of Obedience and Disobedience to Authority', *Human Relations* 18, 57–76.

Milgram, S. (1974) *Obedience to Authority: An Experimental View* (New York: Harper & Row).

McKnight, A. (2009) 'More Equal Working Lives? An Assessment of New Labour Policies', in J. Hills, T. Sefton and K. Stewart, *Towards a More Equal Society? Poverty, Inequality and Social Policy Since 1997* (Bristol: The Policy Press), pp. 91–114.

Mortimer, J. T. (2009) 'Changing Experiences of Work', in A. Furlong (ed.) *Handbook of Youth and Young Adulthood* (Abingdon: Routledge) pp. 149–56.

Mulder, C. H. (2009) 'Leaving the Parental Home in Young Adulthood', in A. Furlong (ed.) *Handbook of Youth and Young Adulthood* (Abingdon: Routledge) pp. 203–10.

Organisation for Economic Co-operation and Development (2009) *Doing Better for Children* (Paris: Organisation for Economic Co-operation and Development) at *www.oecd.org/els/social/childwellbeing*

Office for National Statistics, *Population Estimates by Ethnic Group Mid-2007 – Experimental*, at: http://www.statistics.gov.uk/statbase/product.asp?vlnk= 14238

Office for National Statistics, *Social Trends* annual series (Basingstoke: Palgrave Macmillan).

Putnam, R. D. (2000) *Bowling Alone: The Collapse and Revival of American Community* (New York: Simon and Schuster).

Quilgars, D., Johnsen, S. and Pleace, N (2008) *Youth Homelessness in the UK: A Decade of Progress?* (York: Joseph Rowntree Foundation) available at: http://www.jrf.org.uk/sites/files/jrf/2220-homelessness-young-people.pdf

Reiner, R. (2007) *Law and Order: An Honest Citizen's Guide to Crime and Control* (Cambridge: Polity Press).

Roberts, D. F., Henriksen, L. and Christensen, P. G. (1999) *Substance Use in Popular Movies and Music* (Washington, DC: Office of National Drug Control Policy, available at: http://www.eric.ed.gov/ERICDOCS/data/ericdocs2sql/content_storage_01/0000019b/80/16/d0/04.pdf)

Sassi, F. (2009) 'Health Inequalities: A Persistent Problem', in J. Hills, T. Sefton and K. Stewart, *Towards a More Equal Society? Poverty, Inequality and Social Policy Since 1997* (Bristol: The Policy Press), pp. 135–56.

Schofield, M. (1965) *The Sexual Behaviour of Young People* (London: Longmans).

Sefton, T, Hills, J. and Sutherland, H. (2009) 'Poverty, Inequality and Redistribution', in J. Hills, T. Sefton and K. Stewart, *Towards a More Equal Society? Poverty, Inequality and Social Policy Since 1997* (Bristol: The Policy Press) pp. 21–46.

Smith, D. J. (1995) 'Living Conditions in the Twentieth Century', in M. Rutter and D. J. Smith (eds) *Psychosocial Disorders in Young People: Time Trends and Their Causes* (Chichester: Wiley) pp. 194–295.

Smith, D. J. and Rutter, M. (1995) 'Time Trends in Psychosocial Disorders of Youth', in M. Rutter and D. J. Smith (eds) *Psychosocial Disorders in Young People: Time Trends and Their Causes* (Chichester: Wiley) pp. 763–81.

Snyder, L., Milici, F., Slater, M., Sun, H. and Strizhakova, Y. (2006) 'Effects of Alcohol Advertising Exposure on Drinking among Youth', *Archives of Pediatrics and Adolescent Medicine*, 160, 18–24.

Stewart, K. (2009a) '"A Scar on the Soul of Britain": Child Poverty and Disadvantage Under New Labour', in J. Hills, T. Sefton and K. Stewart, *Towards a More Equal Society? Poverty, Inequality and Social Policy Since 1997* (Bristol: The Policy Press), pp. 47–70.

Stewart, K. (2009b) 'Poverty, Inequality and Child Well-being in International Context: Still Bottom of the Pack?', in J. Hills, T. Sefton and K. Stewart, *Towards a More Equal Society? Poverty, Inequality and Social Policy Since 1997* (Bristol: The Policy Press) pp. 267–90.

Sutton Trust (2008) *Increasing Higher Education Participation among Disadvantaged People in Poor Communities*, available at: http://www.suttontrust.com/reports

Tanner, J. L. and Arnett, J. J. (2009) 'The Emergence of "Emerging Adulthood": The New Life Stage between Adolescence and Young Adulthood', in A. Furlong (ed.) *Handbook of Youth and Young Adulthood* (Abingdon: Routledge) pp. 39–45.

Twenge, J. M. (2009) 'Change Over Time in Disobedience: The Jury's Still Out, But It Might Be Decreasing', *American Psychologist* 64.1, pp. 28–31.

Velleman, R. (2009) *Influences on How Children and Young People Learn About and Behave Towards Alcohol: A Review of the Literature for the Joseph Rowntree Foundation (Part One)* (York: Joseph Rowntree Foundation) available at: http://www.jrf.org.uk/sites/files/jrf/children-alcohol-use-partone.pdf

Wellings, K., Nanchahal, K., Mcdowall, W., McManus, S., Erens, B, Mercer, C. H., Johnson, A. M., Copas, A. J., Korovessis, C., Fenton, K. A. and Field, J. (2001)

'Sexual Behaviour in Britain: Early Heterosexual Experience', *The Lancet* vol. 358, issue 9296, pp. 1843–50.

Wilkinson, R. G. and Pickett, K. E. (2009) *The Spirit Level: Why More Equal Societies Almost Always Do Better* (London: Allen Lane).

World Health Organization (2009) *A Snapshot of the Health of Young People in Europe* (Geneva: World Health Organization).

Chapter 3

Time trends in youth crime and in justice system responses

Larissa Pople and David J. Smith

In political debate and everyday conversation it is widely assumed that crime is rising, that crimes committed by young people, being a large part of the problem, are also rising, and that offensive but often non-criminal conduct among the young – dubbed 'antisocial behaviour' by politicians – is also on the increase. That there is solid and detailed evidence which flatly contradicts these assumptions seems to make little impact either on politicians or on the general public. It is true that recorded crime in England and Wales increased tenfold between 1950 and 1994, and crime surveys confirm a strong rise from the first year they covered (1981) up to the mid 1990s. There is no doubt that young offenders played a major role in this large, even spectacular, post-war rise in crime. Equally remarkable, however, is the reversal of the upward trend, established for half a century or more, that occurred around 1994. Since then all crime, however measured, has declined substantially, whereas violent crime has either levelled off or declined, depending on whether recorded crime statistics or survey-based measures are used. Within that overall picture, there has also been a substantial decline in offences committed by young people. Antisocial behaviour also seems to have decreased. What has remained high during this period is 'noise' about youth crime, with high levels of public anxiety, media scrutiny, and political debate. It is hard to disentangle this 'noise' and the activity generated by the system response from objective measures. To an important extent, therefore, political debate about youth crime has created the problem it tries to address.

Measuring youth crime

There are various ways to measure crime, such as counting incidents recorded by the police, or those reported either by victims or else by offenders in surveys. Each of these methods provides a different perspective on crime, each adds to the information provided by the others, but each method on its own has important shortcomings. An independent review of crime statistics carried out for the Home Office in 2006 observed that there can never be a measure of 'total' crime as 'there will always be crimes not adequately captured in the statistics and a single total number would bring together a very wide range of acts and degrees of seriousness in a not very meaningful way' (Smith 2006: 9). An added problem in attempting to gauge trends in *youth* crime is that the main sources – police records and the British Crime Survey – tell us little about the age of offenders. It is only when crimes are cleared up or survey respondents answer questions about their own offending that the age of offenders becomes known. By looking at various sources of data alongside one another, however, and being clear about their relative strengths and weaknesses, we can build a good picture of the incidence of different types of crime and map trends in youth offending and antisocial behaviour over time.

The age-crime curve

Official figures for cautions and convictions, as well as self-report and longitudinal studies, show that offending rises steeply from the age of criminal responsibility (which is 10 in England and Wales) to a peak in the mid to late teenage years, followed by a gradual decline into old age. The 'age-crime curve' is a well-established phenomenon that has been shown to apply in different places and time periods, notwithstanding variations in steepness and peak ages. For example, a comparative study of youth crime in England and Wales, Spain and the Netherlands found similar curves in each country (Barbaret *et al.* 2004). The age-crime curve in England and Wales was also much the same in the mid nineteenth century as at the start of the twentieth century, and in 1965 (Gottfredson and Hirschi 1990). Figure 3.1 compares the age-crime curves generated by official data in England for 1892 and 2008, showing much the same pattern, although the peak between the ages of 16 and 20 became even more marked over this period of 115 years.

Offending varies with age in much the same way for males and females, although the rate of offending is much lower for females at every age. Criminal involvement peaks somewhere between 14 and 18 years, with a lower age for girls and a higher age for boys. Different sources specify slightly different ages (see Table 3.1).

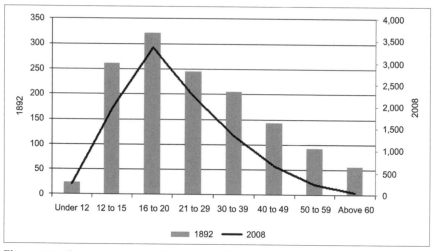

Figure 3.1 Persons found guilty of an indictable offence per 100,000 population: 1892 and 2008

Sources: Home Office (1993) *Home Office Statistical Findings: Criminal Justice Statistics 1882–1892*, table 4; and Ministry of Justice (2010) *Criminal Statistics 2008*, table 15.

Table 3.1 Peak age of offending

	Boys	*Girls*
Cautions/convictions for indictable offences, Ministry of Justice (2007)	17	15
Offending, Crime and Justice Survey (2006)	14–17	
Offending, Crime and Justice Survey (2006) – antisocial behaviour	14–15	
Youth Lifestyles Survey (1995)	18	14
MORI/YJB (2008)	15–16	

Although the basic shape of the age-crime curve appears to have wide application, it also masks some complexity. For example, the peak age of offending varies considerably according to the type of offence, with younger age distributions for offences like burglary, robbery, theft and criminal damage, and somewhat older peaks for fraud and forgery, violence, drug offences and sexual offences (see for example, Smith 2007 and Ministry of Justice 2008).

A number of researchers have investigated whether the high volume of incidents involving teenagers is due to prevalence (a larger proportion of young people who offend) or frequency (young offenders are more prolific). The balance of evidence would seem to suggest the former rather than the latter, with the sharp rise in crime in the teenage years reflecting the offending debut of those with an inclination to crime, and the subsequent fall reflecting the desistance of many and a low number of new recruits (McVie 2005).

Recorded crime

Until the latter part of the twentieth century, the only source of data that could be used to gauge trends in crime was official figures of recorded crime compiled from returns from the police and courts. The benefits of recorded crime figures are that they are available as far back as the mid nineteenth century, and they cover the full range of offences dealt with by the criminal justice system. However, they face a major shortcoming in being dependent on crimes being reported to, and then recorded by, the police.

Levels of crime probably rose in the first half of the nineteenth century but started to fall from the mid 1850s (Gatrell 1980). This decline continued up to the Great Depression of the 1930s, when, after an initial spike, recorded crime began to rise gently. It was not until after the Second World War that this gentle increase gathered pace. Recorded crime rose tenfold in the years between 1950 and 1992, and certain crimes – such as robbery – rose at a much faster rate still. The tide turned in 1993, when all three major categories of recorded crime began to fall: property crime (accounting for the bulk of recorded crimes), vehicle crime, and violent crime. After 1998, trends in recorded crime are clouded because of two separate changes in recording practices, each of which substantially increased the counts. In 1998, new counting rules were introduced meaning that a number of summary offences were included for the first time. The effect of this change can be clearly seen in Figure 3.2 which allows comparison between the numbers for 1998/9 on the old and new basis. Later, in 2002, the National Crime Recording Standard was launched to improve the integrity and consistency of police recording practices. This required police to adopt a prima facie approach and record a crime if a victim reported it as such, unless they had evidence to disbelieve them. This was intended to make the recording of crimes more complete and must certainly have increased the number recorded, but since the implementation occurred over an extended period between 1999 and 2004, the effects of the change cannot be accurately quantified (Maguire 2007). These two changes have considerably inflated recorded crime statistics from 1998 onwards, making comparisons difficult.

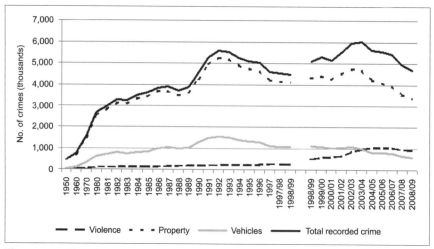

Figure 3.2 Trends in recorded crime, England and Wales

Source: Walker *et al.* (2009) *Crime in England and Wales 2008/09*, table 2.05.

Note: Break in series in 1998/99 to show the old and new counting methods.

The British Crime Survey

In the 1970s rising levels of recorded crime became the focus of much public and political interest, and different ways to measure crime were devised to address the limitations of police records. The main alternative source of data (introduced in 1982 and describing victimization over the previous 12 months) is the British Crime Survey (BCS), which asks a large sample of the public about crimes committed against them. The British Crime Survey is considered by informed commentators to be a reliable measure of the offences that it covers, being unaffected by changes in definitions, and counting incidents regardless of whether they are reported to the police and recorded by them. Although the crime survey measure is generally more inclusive than the recorded crime statistics, it is more limited in some respects: important omissions are crime experienced by under 16s or those not living in 'normal households',[1] and 'victimless' crimes, including those where the victim cannot be interviewed, such as possession of drugs, shoplifting and murder.

For comparable offences[2] the British Crime Survey suggests crime rates to be three to four times higher than those generated by police records. However, this varies considerably according to the nature of the crime so that, for example, 85 per cent of vehicle thefts reported in the British Crime Survey are also recorded, while this is the case for only 19 per cent of reports of common assault (Maguire 2007).

Despite these differences, the trends suggested by the British Crime

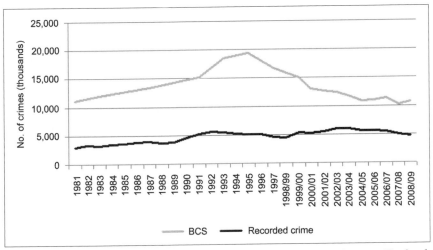

Figure 3.3 Overall trends in British Crime Survey and recorded crime, England and Wales

Source: Walker *et al.* (2009) *Crime in England and Wales 2008/09*, tables 2.01 and 2.05.

Survey and recorded crime statistics are broadly the same, showing a rise in the 1980s and early 1990s, a peak in the mid 1990s (1992 for recorded crime; 1995 for BCS crime) and then a downward trend thereafter (see Figure 3.3 and 3.5). Nonetheless, there are some notable divergences between the two sources. Initially, crime trends measured by the British Crime Survey increased at a slower rate than those shown by recorded crime because of an increase in the reporting of crime by the public (see Figure 3.4). However, recorded crime rose more slowly than BCS crime between 1991 and 1995, as a decreasing proportion of incidents reported to the police were being recorded by them. This situation reversed between 1995 and 2005, gradually at first and then sharply, following the introduction of the National Crime Recording Standard in 2002. Since 2005 the two trends have tracked each other well.

Overall, total British Crime Survey crime has fallen by 45 per cent since 1995, with parallel drops in property and violent crime.

Violent crime

Violent crime figures have generated heated discussion in recent years because the two official sources of data – police records and the British Crime Survey – have produced trends that move in opposite directions. The former shows violent crime to have increased continuously from 1950 to 2005/06, while the latter indicates a downward trend since 1995 (see Figures 3.6 and 3.7).

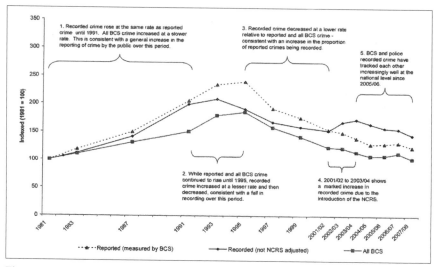

Figure 3.4 Comparing trends in British Crime Survey and recorded crime, England and Wales: indexed (1981 = 100)

Source: Walker *et al.* (2009) *Crime in England and Wales 2008/09.*

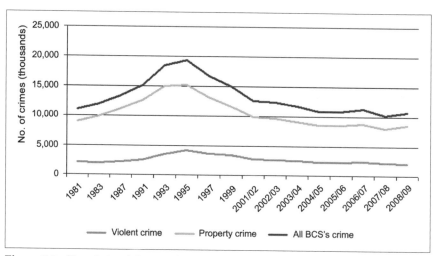

Figure 3.5 Trends in violent and property crime: British Crime Survey, England and Wales

Source: Walker *et al.* (2009) *Crime in England and Wales 2008/09*, table 2.01.

The counting rules change mentioned earlier explains part of this anomaly. From 1998 onwards, recorded crime included summary offences such as common assault, harassment, and assault on a constable. As a result, half of all 'violent crime' (47 per cent of BCS and 53 per cent of recorded violence) now involves no injury to the victim (Walker *et al.*

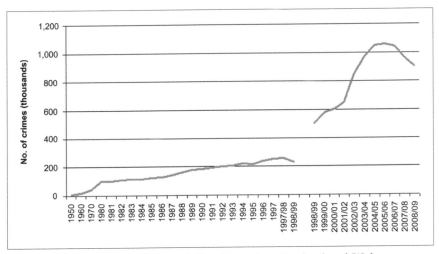

Figure 3.6 Trend in police-recorded violent crime, England and Wales
Source: Walker *et al.* (2009) *Crime in England and Wales 2008/09*, table 2.05.

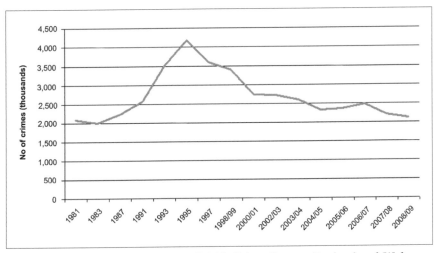

Figure 3.7 Trend in violent crime, British Crime Survey, England and Wales
Source: Walker *et al.* (2009) *Crime in England and Wales 2008/09*, table 2.01.

2009) and 250,000 extra offences were immediately added to the category (Maguire 2007). The National Crime Recording Standard compounded the problem by further inflating the recording of violent crime. These changes, leading to divergent trends, have caused considerable confusion and scepticism amongst commentators. The Home Office has argued that the increase in recorded violent crime is entirely an artefact of the new recording practices, and that the BCS trend is the correct one (Allen and Ruparel 2006). Others, especially in the popular press, have used the recorded crime statistics to back up the claim that violent crime is soaring – and by providing two different measures while changing the counting and recording principles underlying one of them, government has certainly handed free ammunition to alarmists. On a sober assessment, however, there is no valid reason to doubt the trend shown by the results of the consistently administered British Crime Survey.

A longer-term view tells a different story. A number of historians have expanded our knowledge of the incidence of violent crime and the administration of justice in earlier periods by examining judicial archives in different parts of Western Europe.[3] Based on over 90 such studies with 390 estimates of homicide rates, Eisner (2003) assembled a database to track trends in violent crime over several centuries. Notwithstanding methodological questions about the validity of extrapolating trends from a wide range of pre-modern records, a clear and consistent picture emerges: a long-term decline in homicide across Western Europe from around 1500 to the mid twentieth century. Eisner estimated that five hundred years ago the level of homicide was at least 50 times higher than it is today.

Proportion of all crime attributed to young people

As unsolved crimes and victim reports cannot reliably identify the age of offenders, recorded crime figures and the British Crime Survey are not very helpful in providing estimates of the proportion of offences commit-ted by young people. It is only when offences result in convictions that the age of the offender becomes known, and this is comparatively rare. Farrington and Joliffe (2005) estimated the probability of a burglary leading to a conviction to be 1 in 136.

The Ministry of Justice's *Criminal Statistics* show that in 2007, 21 per cent of all those convicted or cautioned for indictable offences were aged under 18; 36 per cent were aged under 21; and 50 per cent were aged under 25. These proportions have changed little since 1998, although they decreased considerably during the 15 years before that (see Figure 3.8). Historical data from the end of the nineteenth century, however, are more comparable to present-day figures. A Home Office report commemorating 100 years of collecting criminal statistics revealed that in 1892, 41 per cent of persons convicted of indictable offences were aged under 21 (Home Office 1993). From 1892, the proportion of offenders who are young first rose, then after 1980 gradually fell back to roughly the 1892 figure. When the recent statistics are broken down into smaller age groups, we can see that the overall downward trend masks a recent increase in the share of cautions and convictions given to 12–17-year-olds.

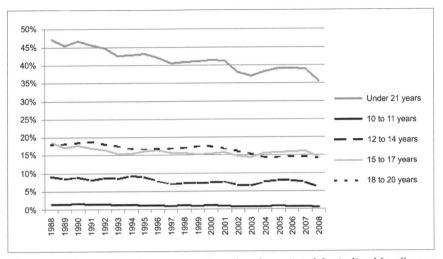

Figure 3.8 Proportion of persons cautioned and convicted for indictable offences that are under 21 years, England and Wales

Sources: Home Office, *Cautions, Court Proceedings and Sentencing*, table 5 (for 1987 to 2000); Home Office, *Criminal Statistics*, table 2.23 (for 2001 to 2006); and Ministry of Justice (2009) *Criminal Statistics*, table 3.24 (for 2007); and Ministry of Justice (2010) *Criminal Statistics*, table 14 (for 2008).

Self-reported crime

Self-report surveys are in principle a useful method of measuring youth crime levels, and can reveal a fuller picture of crime than official records. A number of studies have tested the validity of self-reports against official records (Farrington 1973; Huizinga and Elliott 1986; Huizinga 1991). Such evidence suggests that self-reports can generally be believed, although there may be some systematic biases (e.g. specific ethnic groups may tend to understate their offending, according to research by Junger 1989). An important shortcoming is that serious and persistent offenders, who account for a large proportion of offences, are likely to be under-sampled (e.g. because they are in custody). Although the self-report method is widely used in studies concerned with the causes and correlates of offending, self-report studies have not been repeated with enough consistency and regularity to establish clear trends over time in offending among the general population of young people in England and Wales. The Home Office carried out just two waves of the Youth Lifestyles Survey in the 1990s and four waves of the Offending, Crime and Justice Survey in the 2000s. The Youth Justice Board (YJB) also commissioned six waves of the MORI Youth Survey between 2000 and 2008, using a sketchy questioning method.[4] These three sets of surveys are not directly comparable.

Nonetheless, what they show is that offending by young people is common. In the 1992/3 Youth Lifestyles Survey, 55 per cent of males and 31 per cent of females aged 14 to 25 admitted having committed one or more offences in their lifetimes (Graham and Bowling 1995). In the latest Offending, Crime and Justice Survey of young people aged 10 to 25, just over a fifth (22 per cent) reported offending in the previous year (Roe and Ashe 2008). A similar proportion (23 per cent) of 11 to 16-year-olds in mainstream schools said the same in the latest MORI Youth Survey (YJB 2009b). Among young people attending Pupil Referral Units after being excluded from school, however, the proportion offending in the past 12 months was almost three times as high at 64 per cent (YJB 2009c).

The 1992/3 and 1998/9 waves of the Youth Lifestyles Survey suggested some changes over time, with a significant increase (9.5 per cent) in the prevalence of offending amongst 14 to 17-year-olds and a significant decrease (-5.5 per cent) amongst 18 to 25-year-olds (Flood-Page et al. 2000).

In the 2000s, four successive waves of the Offending, Crime and Justice Survey found no significant change in offending between 2003 and 2006. Inspite of its use of a different questioning method, this is broadly consistent with seven waves of the MORI Youth Survey, which saw a gradual increase in offending amongst young people in mainstream schools between 2000 and 2005, followed by a drop in 2008 to earlier levels (see Figure 3.9). There were some apparent ups and downs in offending among samples of young people excluded from school, but these changes are probably not statistically significant.

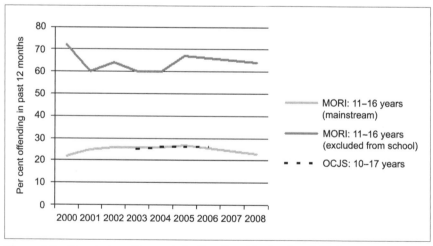

Figure 3.9   Trends in self-reported offending, England and Wales

Sources: Youth Justice Board (2009) *Youth Survey 2008: Young people in mainstream education*, figure 2.1; Youth Justice Board (2009) *MORI Youth Survey 2008: Young people in pupil referral units*, figure 2.1; and Roe and Ashe (2008) *Young people and crime: findings from the 2006 Offending, Crime and Justice Survey*, table 2.6.

The 2008 MORI Youth Survey of 11- to 16-year-olds found clear gender differences in offending, with 1.5 times as many boys (27 per cent) as girls (18 per cent) saying that they had committed an offence in the previous year. This ratio remained broadly the same between 2001 and 2008 (YJB 2009b). The Youth Lifestyles Survey shows that young women 'grow out of crime' at an earlier age than young men: at age 12 to 13, the male to female ratio was only 1.25 to 1; at 14 to 17 it was almost 2 to 1; and by 18 to 21 it was 2.3 to 1 (Flood-Page *et al.* 2000). The ratio of males to females among convicted offenders is more lopsided at every age than among self-reported offenders. Edinburgh Study findings show that this is partly because males tend to commit more serious offences (which are therefore more likely to be prosecuted) but also because law enforcement tends to target young males (McAra and McVie 2005).

The MORI Youth Survey reveals some differences in offending by ethnicity, with considerably more African Caribbean young people (36 per cent in 2005) admitting offending than white (27 per cent) and Asian (18 per cent) young people. These differences were present in all five waves of the survey between 2001 and 2005.[5]

Most of the offences reported in self-report surveys are minor or even trivial: typical examples are fare-dodging, shoplifting (mostly low-value items), assault without injury, criminal damage, and graffiti. More serious offences are reported too, but the repeated surveys cited above have not been used, and probably cannot be used, to describe trends in individual, more serious offences, or in more serious offences as a group. Also they do not attempt to measure frequency of offending among those who offend at all. For these and other reasons, they are of very limited use in assessing trends over time in the pattern of youth offending. The best they can do is give some indication of changes in the proportion of young people who offend at all. They suggest there has been little or no change in the prevalence of youth offending over the past 20 years.

Public perceptions of youth crime and anti-social behaviour

As well as measuring the public's experience of crime as victims, the British Crime Survey gauges feelings of safety, worry about crime, and perceptions of crime levels. Since its inception respondents have been asked 'how safe do you feel walking alone in this area after dark?' The proportion of people who reported feeling 'very unsafe' remained fairly constant during this period at around 10–13 per cent (Jansson 2007), whereas crime victimization from the same survey increased from 1981 to 1995, then declined substantially. Since 1984, however, further questions were added to the British Crime Survey to measure fear of different types of crime, and here responses mirror more closely the trends in crime.

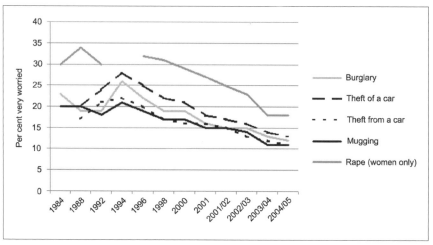

Figure 3.10 Worry about different crimes, England and Wales
Source: Jansson (2007) *British Crime Survey: Measuring crime for 25 years.*

Worry about mugging, burglary and vehicle-related theft peaked in the mid 1990s, declining steadily thereafter (see Figure 3.10).

Since 1997, questions about different crimes have been combined to form three summary measures of worry (about violent crime, vehicle crime and burglary) and these have all followed a downward trend. People who read national tabloids are much more likely than readers of national broadsheets to worry about every type of crime: in 2008/09 *Sun* and *Mirror* readers were two to five times more likely than *Guardian, Times* and *Telegraph* readers to worry about burglary, and two to three times more likely to worry about violent crime. Women were almost three times as likely as men to worry about violent crime (Walker *et al.* 2009).

Perceptions of crime trends do not match actual crime trends as described by the same series of surveys. In 2008/09, around three quarters of respondents (75 per cent) thought that crime had risen 'a little' or 'a lot' across the country in the previous two years, despite the downward trend in crime victimization among these same respondents, and also in the statistics of recorded crime. Fewer (36 per cent) thought that crime had risen in their local area, illustrating a general tendency for people to assume that bad things they see reported in the media are happening in neighbourhoods other than their own.[6] Again, tabloid readers were more likely than broadsheet readers to think that the national crime rate had increased: 81–82 per cent of *Sun* and *Mirror* readers thought so compared with 52 per cent of *Guardian* readers (Walker *et al.* 2009).

Perceptions of antisocial behaviour are considered in more detail in Chapter 5, but it is worth summarizing time trends in the context of the present analysis of crime trends. Because preoccupation with antisocial

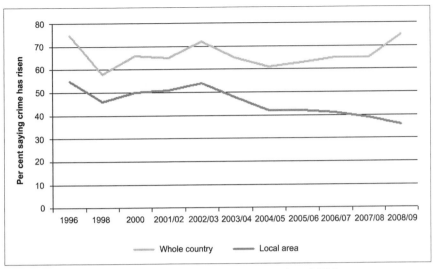

Figure 3.11 Perceptions of increasing crime, England and Wales
Source: Walker *et al.* (2009) *Crime in England and Wales 2008/09*, figure 5.1.

behaviour is a recent phenomenon, the British Crime Survey measures began only in 1992. They show rising perceptions of antisocial behaviours as a problem in the neighbourhood between 1992 and 2000,[7] with especially large increases for 'teenagers hanging around' and 'people using or dealing drugs'. Since then, there has been little significant change for all but one of the indicators, and decreasing concern about 'abandoned and burnt-out cars'. Since 2004, 'teenagers hanging around' has been the problem eliciting most concern (Walker *et al.* 2009: see ch. 5: fig. 5.4). Because 'hanging around' is not self-evidently offensive in itself – and is certainly not criminal – this finding illustrates the build-up of anxiety associated with political debate and media interest, combined with the increasing separateness of young people, their visibility and distinctiveness, and their potential as a focus of feelings of hostility and threat (see Chapter 2).

Perceptions of anti-social behaviour are most common among lower socio-economic groups, among those living in the most deprived areas and those in social housing. They are also highest amongst the youngest age group (16 to 24) and among those that have been a victim or witness of crime in the previous year (Walker *et al.* 2009).

Gangs

Gangs, weapons and violent crime have collided in the popular imagination and are often discussed in the same breath. Yet the widely-held belief that youth gangs are responsible for a large proportion of violent crime is hard to prove or disprove because of a lack of data on gang-related crime. When teenagers offend, it is usually in a group rather than on their own. For example, the MORI survey carried out for the Youth Justice Board in 2008 showed that of young people who had committed an offence in the past 12 months, two-thirds said they had offended with others, usually friends, whereas only one-fifth said they had offended on their own (YJB 2009b). Whereas co-offending, rather than lone offending, is certainly the norm among teenage offenders,[8] whether youth gangs are an important factor is a different question. To begin to provide an answer, the first issue that has to be tackled is how to define a gang.

The most important feature of a gang is probably its involvement in criminal activity as a group, yet this does not seem to be enough on its own to define what is meant by a gang: as stated, when they offend, teenagers usually offend in a group, but we do not want to call all of these small groups of offenders gangs. Another complication is that some young people will say that they are in a 'gang' when they are referring to a friendship group that does not normally commit crimes, whereas others will say that they are not in a 'gang' but will admit to relatively serious group-related offending. For these definitional reasons and others, including a scarcity of useful data on the subject, some are in favour of abandoning the term altogether and instead focusing on specific issues such as 'serious group offending' (YJB 2007). Others, like the Eurogang network of international researchers (Decker and Weerman 2005), have persevered and come up with the following definition:

> A youth gang, or troublesome youth group, is a durable, street-oriented youth group whose involvement in illegal activity is part of their group identity.[9]

A similar description was used by the government's Offending, Crime and Justice Survey (OCJS), which is one of only a few sources of UK data on the issue. The researchers decided against using the term 'gang', and opted instead for 'delinquent youth groups' to describe groups of three or more young people that:

- spend a lot of time in public places [i.e. 'street-oriented'];

- have existed for three months or more [i.e. 'durable'];

- have engaged in delinquent or criminal behaviour together in the last 12 months;

- have at least one structural feature, either a name, an area, a leader, or rules.

On the basis of this set of criteria, the OCJS 2004 found that 6 per cent of 10 to 19-year-olds belonged to a delinquent youth group, rising to 12 per cent among 14 and 15-year-olds, which was the peak age for membership.[10] Based on their own self-definitions, however, one in ten youths aged 10 to 19 described themselves as gang members (Roe and Ashe 2008).

The Edinburgh Study of Youth Transitions and Crime asked a cohort of young people of secondary school age whether they considered the group of friends that they hang around with to be a gang: approximately 20 per cent did at age 13, but by the time they were 17 this figure had fallen to just 5 per cent. The proportion saying that their gang had both a name and a special sign or saying, however, remained fairly steady at 2 per cent at age 13, 4 per cent at age 16 and 3 per cent at age 17. The young people were not asked whether the gang was involved in criminal activity, which distinguishes these findings from the OCJS (Smith and Bradshaw 2005).[11]

Contrary to the popular notion that gangs mainly involve young people of African Caribbean origin, the ethnicity of gangs tends to reflect the population living in the area: the OCJS found that 60 per cent of gangs were white only, 31 per cent were ethnically mixed, 5 per cent were Asian only and 3 per cent were African Caribbean only. The factors most strongly associated with gang membership were having friends in trouble with the police, having run away from home, commitment to 'deviant' friends (i.e. who get them into trouble at home or with the police), having been expelled or suspended from school, and being frequently drunk (Roe and Ashe 2008).

Predictably, perhaps, given the definition of a gang, there is a clear relationship between gang membership and offending. In the OCJS, 63 per cent of gang members reported offending in the last year, compared with only 26 per cent of non-gang members, and 43 per cent of non-gang members who had delinquent friends. Gang members were also over three times more likely (13 per cent) than non-members (4 per cent) to have carried a knife with them in the previous year. Only a minority had committed a serious offence (34 per cent) or committed six or more offences in the last year (28 per cent), but these figures were three to four times higher than those for non-gang members (13 per cent and 7 per cent respectively) (Roe and Ashe 2008).

The OCJS also found that three times as many gang members had taken drugs in the previous year as non-members (45 compared with 15 per cent). After drug-taking, the most common illegal activity carried out together in a gang was 'threatening or frightening people' (40 per cent), graffiti (36 per cent), criminal damage (31 per cent) and 'using force or violence on people' (29 per cent). Contrary to the popular stereotype, selling drugs was fairly uncommon among gang members: only 12 per cent had done so, although this compares with just 2 per cent of non-gang members (Roe and Ashe 2008).

Given all the definitional issues that exist in relation to gangs, it is not surprising that there are no reliable data with which to establish gang trends over time, and nothing to shed light on the proportion of violent offences that are gang-related. Consequently, the oft-repeated assertion that the UK is experiencing 'an increase in gang culture and associated violence' (Centre for Social Justice 2009) remains unsubstantiated, although this is clearly what many people perceive to be the case. We do know that gang members as defined by the OCJS are three times more likely than non-gang members to carry a weapon, and so it may be reasonable to assume that they are responsible for a disproportionate number of incidents in which weapons are used. Survey results suggest that weapon carrying among young people is mainly motivated by fear: 85 per cent of those who reported carrying a knife said it was for protection, while just 4 per cent had used it to threaten someone, and 1 per cent to injure someone (Roe and Ashe 2008). Of course, this may understate aggressive intentions, since respondents may prefer to justify carrying a weapon by saying it is for self-protection, and in any case, if a weapon is being carried for whatever reason, it may end up being used.

Although there is no evidence on whether gang membership has increased in Britain in recent years, or on whether the activities of gangs have become more serious and violent, there is good evidence that gang membership is a causal factor leading to offending. Two American studies in the early 1990s showed that individuals offended more frequently during periods when they were members of gangs than when they were not (Esbensen and Huizinga 1993; Thornberry et al. 1993). In Britain, Smith and Bradshaw (2005) analysed six annual sweeps of data on a cohort of more than 4,000 teenagers in the City of Edinburgh. Three findings jointly constitute strong evidence that gang membership increases offending, and the evidence is particularly strong in this case because gangs were defined without reference to involvement in criminal offending (see above). First, offending was up to five times as high among gang members as among non-members. Second, offending of the same individuals was considerably higher than expected during years of gang membership and lower during years of non-membership. Third, gang membership at age 13 and again at age 16 was associated with higher offending after allowing for the effects of many other explanatory variables, and this was on top of the effect of having friends who were involved in offending. Taken together these findings show that gangs are an important factor in explaining youth offending, but there is no evidence to show whether youth gangs and the associated problems are becoming more or less common in Britain.

Serious youth violence

Young people's involvement in violent crime as victims and offenders – especially in 'grave' crimes such as murder, manslaughter, grievous bodily harm, robbery and sexual offences – often captures the headlines

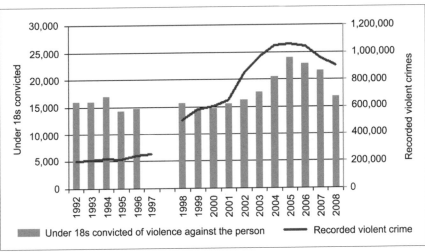

Figure 3.12 Under 18s convicted of violence against the person, and all recorded violent crimes, England and Wales

Sources: Home Office, *Cautions, Court Proceedings and Sentencing*, table 5 (for 1992 to 2000); Home Office, *Criminal Statistics*, table 2.10 (for 2001 to 2006); Ministry of Justice (2010) *Criminal Statistics*, table 3 (for 2007); and Walker *et al.* (2009) *Crime in England and Wales 2008/09*, table 2.05.

and the attention of politicians and the public. Media stories give the impression that 'things have got much worse' in recent years.[12] However, official statistics and surveys suggest a much more complex picture.

Trends in convictions of under 18-year-olds for violence against the person are similar to those for all recorded violent crime, showing a sharp increase in the early 2000s and a peak in 2005/6 (see Figure 3.12). As we have seen, these increases in all recorded violent crimes are at odds with the British Crime Survey, which finds violent crime to have decreased continuously since 1995. The discrepancy is either partly or fully accounted for by changes in counting rules in 1998 and the introduction of the National Crime Reporting Standard in 2002, both of which inflated the number of violent crimes recorded. If the continuous downward trend in violent crime shown by the British Crime Survey is correct – the most likely possibility – then the increase in youth convictions for violence must indicate either a *rise* in youth violence in the context of a general *decline* in violence, or a rise in police and court activity targeting young people, or both.

Interestingly, trends in other violent offences (e.g. sexual offences and robbery) moved in different directions (see Figure 3.13). Youth convictions for sexual offences fell during the 1990s and then remained level during the 2000s, whereas youth convictions for robbery have followed an upward trajectory to the present day.

Recent trends in the use of weapons are also mixed. According to the British Crime Survey, weapons were used in a fifth (21 per cent) of violent

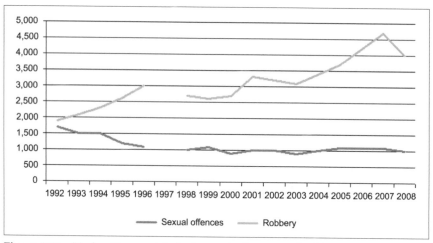

Figure 3.13 Under 18s convicted of sexual offences and robbery, England and Wales

Sources: Home Office, *Cautions, Court Proceedings and Sentencing*, table 5 (for 1992 to 2000); Home Office, *Criminal Statistics*, table 2.10 (for 2001 to 2006); and Ministry of Justice (2010) *Criminal Statistics*, table 3 (for 2007).

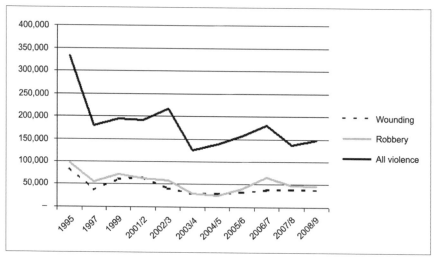

Figure 3.14 Violence with a knife: British Crime Survey, number of incidents, England and Wales

Source: Walker *et al.* (2009) *Crime in England and Wales 2008/09*.

crimes in 2008/9, a figure that has been stable over the past decade, but that is a stable proportion of a declining number of violent crimes.[13] Hence, the total *number* of violent offences involving a knife has fallen quite considerably since the mid 1990s (see Figure 3.14).

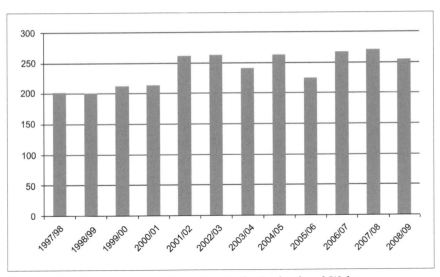

Figure 3.15 Recorded homicides with a knife, England and Wales

Sources: Povey *et al.* (2009) *Homicides, Firearm Offences and Intimate Violence 2007/08*, table 1.03 (for 1997/8); Smith *et al.* (2010) *Homicides, Firearm Offences and Intimate Violence 2008/09*, table 1.03 (for 1998/99 to 2008/09).

In July 2008, police forces started to publish data on the most serious offences involving a knife,[14] of which there were 22,151 in 2007/08, including 270 fatalities. The number of fatal stabbings recorded in 2007/8 was the highest since the Homicide Index began in 1977, although Figure 3.15 shows that this number has hovered around 260–70 since 2001/2. The latest statistics show a subsequent fall to 252 in 2008/9 alongside a rise in the number of attempted murders involving a knife, up from 245 to 271 offences (Walker *et al.* 2009). A knife is the most common method of killing, accounting for 35 per cent of homicides (Povey *et al.* 2009).

Guns are used less frequently and cause fewer casualties. In 2008/9 firearms (excluding air weapons) were reported to have been used in 9,865 recorded crimes, with 320 serious injuries and 38 fatalities. Figure 3.16 shows that gun homicides have been following a downward trend since 2001/2.

Just as offending generally, and violent offending in particular, is most common among young men, so also young men are the group most likely to be victims of violent crime. According to the British Crime Survey, 13 per cent of young men aged 16–24 were victims of violent crime in the past 12 months, higher than for any other group (Walker *et al.* 2009). This pattern arises because people tend to commit offences on others within their own social circle, and the tendency is particularly strong for assaults, which mostly emerge out of personal interactions. The pattern is also an example of a more general tendency for the same people to be victims and offenders at different times. One study showed that 15-year-olds who

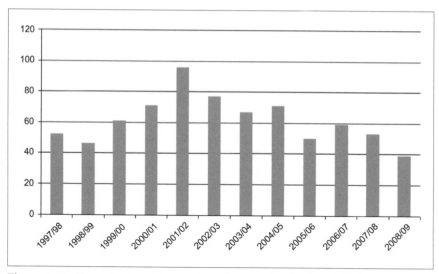

Figure 3.16   Recorded homicides with a firearm, England and Wales

Sources: Povey *et al.* (2009) *Homicides, Firearm Offences and Intimate Violence 2007/08*, table 1.03 (for 1997/8); Smith *et al.* (2010) *Homicides, Firearm Offences and Intimate Violence 2008/09*, table 1.03 (for 1998/99 to 2008/09).

were victims of five types of crime were seven times more likely to have offended than those who had not been victims, and 14 times more likely to have offended 'seriously' (Smith 2005). Young men are also the group most likely to be victims of homicide, except that the highest rate of all is for infants under the age of one. Thus the rate of homicide victimization for men aged 16–29 in 2008/9 was 32 per million, compared with 9 for women aged 16–29, 22 for men aged 30–49, and 14 for men aged 50–70 (Smith and Flatley 2009: table 1.07).

Behavioural and psychosocial problems

Here we consider a number of other behavioural and psychosocial problems that are related to youth offending in various ways. Some – like difficult behaviour at school, leading to exclusion, or attention deficit disorder – are often precursors of offending. Others, like early alcohol and drug abuse, are often part of the same pattern of behaviour as teenage offending. Others again – such as self-harming, suicide, or depression – are very different responses from criminal offending to the stresses of growing up. These other youth problems can be considered only briefly here, especially since limited information about time trends is available. Nevertheless, a brief discussion helps to sketch the wider context for understanding trends in youth offending.

Conduct disorders and hyperkinetic disorders

Whereas the starting point for the measurement of crime is the definition of criminal acts in law, child psychiatrists adopt a broader perspective: their diagnoses are based on behavioural assessments of children from a young age when their problem behaviour cannot be construed as criminal. Conduct disorders and Attention Deficit Hyperactivity Disorders (ADHD) describe syndromes of chronic persistent behaviour problems. Conduct disorders are characterized by defiance, irritability, anger, aggression and cruelty, destructiveness, lying and stealing. ADHD, which often overlaps with conduct disorders, relates to excessive, age-inappropriate levels of motor activity, inattention and impulsiveness (Earls and Mezzacapa 2002; Schachar and Tannock 2002).

According to a national survey carried out in 2004, conduct disorders affect 7.5 per cent of boys and 3.9 per cent of girls aged 5 to 16 (Green et al. 2005). Conduct disorders at a young age have been consistently linked with criminality during adolescence. In one study, 90 per cent of adolescents convicted of crime were found to have had conduct disorders in childhood (Scott et al. 2001). In a longitudinal study in New Zealand, children with conduct problems aged between seven and nine years were several times more likely than those without to be involved in crime, to have mental health problems, and to be drug or alcohol dependent as adults (Fergusson et al. 2005).[15] Forty per cent of children with the most severe conduct problems in childhood (the most disturbed 5 per cent of the cohort) were frequent offenders when they were 18, while 35 per cent were committing violent offences at age 25 (see Table 3.2).

Evidence suggests that there has been a substantial post-war increase in conduct problems (Rutter and Smith 1995), although time trends are difficult to establish since diagnostic criteria and assessment methods have changed during this period as have levels of awareness and attitudes (Goodman and Scott 2005). The most convincing evidence comes from three large-scale surveys carried out in 1974, 1986 and 1999 in which

Table 3.2 Later histories of children with and without conduct disorders

	Diagnosis at age 7–9	
	Most disturbed 5%	Least disturbed 5%
Frequent offenders at age 18	40	7
Violent offenders at age 25	35	3
Imprisoned by age 25	14	0.2
Dependent on drugs [query age]	29	8
Dependent on alcohol	24	16

Source: Fergusson et al. 2005

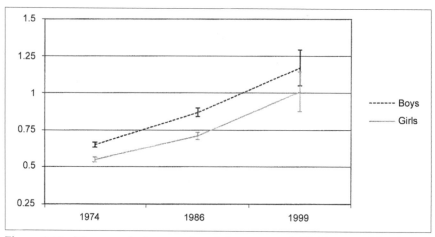

Figure 3.17 Mean conduct scores for adolescents aged 15–16 as rated by their parents

Source: Collishaw *et al.* (2004) 'Time trends in adolescent mental health', *Journal of Child Psychology and Psychiatry*, 45: 8.

parents were asked to rate the behaviour of their 15–16-year-old children.[16] Figure 3.17 shows that conduct scores more than doubled between 1974 and 1999 for both boys and girls, affecting all social classes and family types. These changes were clearly statistically significant. The same study also found increases in adolescent emotional problems between 1986 and 1999 (Collishaw *et al.* 2004).

ADHD, which describes children who are inattentive, disruptive, over-active and impulsive, affects 2.6 per cent of boys and 0.4 per cent of girls aged 5–16, according to the survey by the Office of National Statistics that was mentioned earlier (Green *et al.* 2005). Evidence from the 1974, 1986 and 1999 surveys did not support the idea that ADHD had become more common (see Figure 3.18). In fact, there was a decrease for boys between 1974 and 1986 followed by an increase in 1999, and no significant change for girls over this 25-year period (Collishaw *et al.* 2004).

The more recent evidence from the Office for National Statistics shows no change in the prevalence of conduct disorders or ADHD between 1999 and 2004, confirming that things have not got worse in recent years but neither have they improved (Green *et al.* 2005).

Exclusion from school

Exclusion is one of the main strategies used by schools – ideally as a last resort – to control unruly pupils. In principle, excluded pupils are required to receive alternative provision, most often in Pupil Referral Units, but considerable numbers probably slip through the net. There is

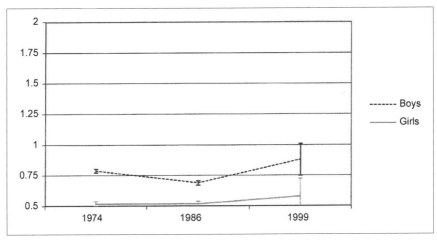

Figure 3.18 Mean ADHD scores for adolescents aged 15–16 as rated by their parents

Source: Collishaw *et al.* (2004) 'Time trends in adolescent mental health', *Journal of Child Psychology and Psychiatry*, 45: 8.

certainly the danger that school exclusions may create a pool of unsupervised teenagers who have little opportunity or incentive to develop along a conventional path and plenty of opportunity to commit offences during school hours. It is not surprising to find that excluded pupils have higher levels of offending than others. For example, analysis of the Edinburgh Study, which follows a complete age cohort of more than 4,000 young people in the City of Edinburgh, has shown that at age 15 those who had ever been excluded from secondary school had committed an average 25.7 acts of delinquency over the previous 12 months, compared with 11.6 for those who had not been excluded (Smith 2006). A more detailed analysis made use of pupils' self-reports of their own bad behaviour at school, along with other information. Bad behaviour at school was clearly associated with exclusion after controlling for other factors, but delinquency and truancy were only weakly related to exclusion. Even though bad behaviour at school – as reported by pupils themselves – was clearly related to exclusion, it was not nearly enough to explain why some were excluded whereas others were not. Instead, there was a tendency for schools to target certain social groups for exclusion. After controlling for the effects of the young person's behaviour in school and for other factors, boys and those from manual or unemployed households were substantially more likely to be excluded than girls or those from middle-class households (Smith 2006). In a comprehensive analysis of the factors explaining offending at age 15, exclusion from school was found to have a significant effect after controlling for the effects of 23 other factors (McAra and Smith forthcoming). Taken together, these findings strongly suggest that although young people who offend are somewhat more likely than others to be excluded from school, exclusion also leads to more offending.

Official statistics on the numbers of exclusions are available in England from 1997/98, when there were 10,190 permanent exclusions from local authority maintained secondary schools (Department for Children, Schools and Families 2009). The numbers of permanent exclusions fell below 7,000 two years later, then after a gentle rise around 2003/4, fell back to 7,000 in 2007/8, the latest year for which statistics are available. Permanent exclusions account for about 0.24 per cent of the secondary school population, and that figure has remained almost constant. Data on exclusions for a fixed period are available only from 2003/4. Numbers have fluctuated somewhat, but there were 324,180 fixed period exclusions from state-funded secondary schools in 2007/8. The most common duration of these fixed-term exclusions was 1, 2, 3 or 5 days, and the average duration was 2.7 days. The peak age for exclusion was 14, and exclusion at that age was common: pupils excluded one or more times accounted for 10.9 per cent of 14-year-old boys and for 5.4 per cent of 14-year-old girls. The official statistics confirm the Edinburgh Study analysis in showing that disadvantaged pupils are far more likely to be excluded than others. Secondary school pupils with special educational needs are nine times more likely to be permanently excluded than those without. Secondary school pupils eligible for free school meals are three times more likely to be permanently excluded than those not eligible. Exclusion is also strongly related to ethnic group. For example, the proportion of the whole school population (primary and secondary) that was excluded in 2007/8 was 0.53 per cent of African Caribbean boys, 0.18 per cent of White British boys, and 0.05 per cent of Indian boys.

These findings suggest that there is potential for reducing youth crime by persuading schools to use exclusion more sparingly, and to take more responsibility for their unruly pupils. A particularly strong argument for this policy is that even after allowing for their actual behaviour, exclusion tends to target the disadvantaged. The findings also draw attention to the need for well-resourced specialist programmes for the small number of teenagers who will have to be educated separately within any system.

Use of alcohol and illegal drugs

There is overwhelming evidence of a strong association between use of alcohol and aggression, including violent crime; and between use of various illicit drugs and a wide range of delinquent and criminal activity (Fagan 1990; Chaiken and Chaiken 1990). The nature of the relationship goes well beyond the direct psychoactive effect of the substances: any satisfactory explanation has to take account of perceptions, expectations, cultural beliefs, social controls, and the way these factors interact.

Although the link between alcohol and aggression is certainly not straightforward, there is good evidence from time series analyses of data for Scandinavian countries (Wiklund and Lidberg 1990) and Australia (Smith 1990) that changes in the total consumption of alcohol are associated with changes in the level of recorded violent crime. Estimates from the British Medical Association suggest that the offender or victim had been drinking in 65 per cent of murders, 75 per cent of stabbings, 70 per cent of beatings, and 50 per cent of fights or domestic assaults (*The Lancet* 1999). A survey of 16 to 20-year-olds in custody revealed that 70 per cent of sentenced young men, 62 per cent of young men on remand and 51 per cent of sentenced young women were drinking hazardously in the year before coming to prison (Lader *et al.* 2000) compared with 45 per cent of young men and 32 per cent of young women of this age group in the general population (Singleton *et al.* 2001).

There is a large body of evidence, most of it from the US, that offenders who persistently and frequently use large amounts of multiple types of drugs commit more offences, and more serious ones, than less drug-involved offenders, and go on offending for longer (Chaiken and Chaiken 1990). This group probably accounts for a considerable proportion of all crime, but it is an unusual one. The relation between drugs and crime for the great majority of offenders and drug users is entirely different. Most drug users do not have serious criminal careers. From American evidence, about half of delinquent youngsters are delinquent before they start using drugs, while the remaining half start concurrently or after (Chaiken and Chaiken 1990). From British evidence, the age of starting to offend is considerably younger on average than the age of starting to use drugs (Pudney 2002). This suggests that preventing delinquency is likely to be a better approach than preventing drug use among adolescents. Whatever the chain of causation, drug use is very common among young offenders. An official survey of 16 to 20-year-olds in custody found that 58 per cent of sentenced young women, 57 per cent of young men on remand and 52 per cent of sentenced young men were drug dependent in the year before prison compared with 6 per cent of young women and 13 per cent of young men in the general population. Urine testing of arrested people in 16 sites across England and Wales found that 71 per cent of those aged 17 to 24 tested positive for at least one illegal drug, and 32 per cent for opiates and/or cocaine or crack (Holloway and Bennett 2004: calculated from table 2.1b).

Alcohol and illegal drugs are used as symbolic markers in youth culture. Drinking and consuming drugs in some contexts indicates that someone belongs to a particular youth clique and not to the general body of the population, and starting to drink and/or consume drugs indicates that someone has passed a milestone in development from childhood to youth-hood. As discussed in Chapter 2, drinks producers have tried to cultivate youth markets by manipulating and amplifying these symbolic meanings.

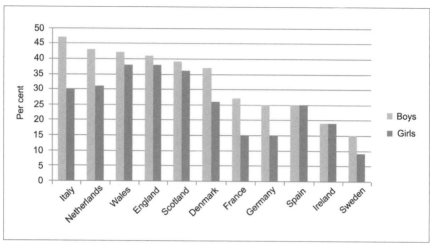

Figure 3.19 Percentage of 15-year-olds who drink alcohol at least once a week, various European countries, 2005/6

Source: Currie *et al.* (2008) *Inequalities in Young People's Health*, p. 125.

Consumption of both alcohol and (what are now) illegal drugs was at a relatively low level in the first half of the twentieth century, but in both Europe and North America there was a very substantial increase from the 1950s to the 1980s. Overall levels of alcohol consumption rose and a substantial minority of young people came to engage in at least occasional recreational use of illegal drugs (Silbereisen *et al.* 1995). From the 1990s, these rising trends have levelled off – and it is notable that the rising trend in crime levelled off or reversed at around the same time.

Europeans are more likely to drink than their counterparts elsewhere in the world and drinking is more common among young people in England than in other European countries. A survey carried out for the World Health Organization (WHO) in 2005/6 showed that the proportion of 15-year-olds drinking alcohol at least once a week was highest in Italy, the Netherlands, Wales and England, with Scotland not far behind (see Figure 3.19). The proportion of girls drinking at least once a week was higher in Britain than in any other country.

In another international survey – the European School Survey Project on Alcohol and Other Drugs (ESPAD) – British 15–16-year-olds reported some of the highest rates of 'binge drinking' in Europe. Again this was most conspicuous among British girls, 55 per cent of whom admitted drinking five or more drinks on one occasion during the last month. Only girls from the Isle of Man reported higher levels of 'binge drinking' (Hibbell *et al.* 2008).

Four waves of the WHO survey show that regular drinking amongst 15-year-olds in England and Wales increased during the latter half of the

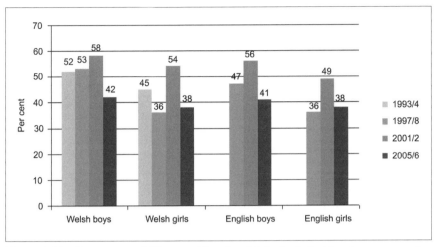

Figure 3.20 Percentage of 15-year-olds who drink alcohol at least once a week, England and Wales

Sources: WHO (1996) *The Health of Youth*, figure 2.5 (for 1993/4); WHO (2000) *Health and Health Behaviour among Young People*, figure 9.5 (for 1997/8); WHO (2004) *Young People's Health in Context*, figure 3.8 (for 2001/2); WHO (2008) *Inequalities in Young People's Health*, p. 125 (for 2005/6).

1990s but has declined since the turn of the millennium (see Figure 3.20). 'Binge drinking' has also come down since 1999 for boys, and since 2003 for girls (Hibbell *et al.* 2008).

These trends are consistent with the findings of a survey of drinking in England that is carried out each year for the NHS Information Centre. Apart from a dip in the late 1990s, there was a generally upward trend in the proportion of 15-year-olds that 'drank last week' between 1988 and 2001, and a downward trend since then (Figure 3.21).

The same survey also shows that although fewer 11 to 15-year-olds drink regularly, those that do are drinking more heavily. The number of units consumed by those who 'drank last week' more than doubled between 1990 and 2006.[17]

Drug use among young people has also followed a downward trend since the 1980s. Cannabis is by far the most popular drug among young people (and the general population), with 21.8 per cent of 15-year-olds reporting in 2008 that they had used it in the previous year. Solvents are the most common drug taken by 11 to 13-year-olds. Other drugs – stimulants, hallucinogens and opiates – are used by only a small proportion of young people, with individual drugs rising and falling in popularity at different time points. Use of any drug, and consumption of every individual drug but cocaine, decreased or remained constant over the whole period from 2001 to 2008 (Figure 3.23).

In short, there was a large increase in use of alcohol and illegal drugs among young people over the period of 40 years following the Second

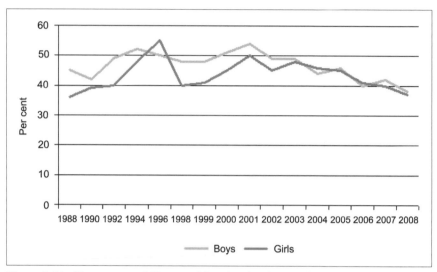

Figure 3.21 Percentage of 15-year-olds who drank any alcohol in the last week, England

Source: Fuller (2009) *Smoking, Drinking and Drug Use Among Young People in England in 2008*, table 3.5.

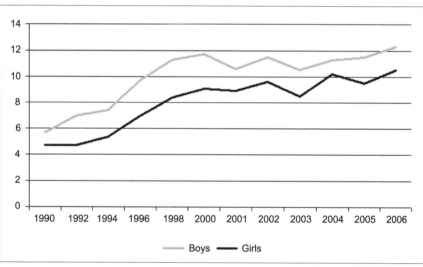

Figure 3.22 Mean units consumed by 11–15-year-olds who drank any alcohol in the last week, England

Source: Fuller (2009) *Smoking, Drinking and Drug Use Among Young People in England in 2008*, table 3.12a.

World War, and this coincided with a rapid growth in prosperity and in crime, with the emergence of young people as an increasingly separate and distinct group and with the development of youth cultures in which

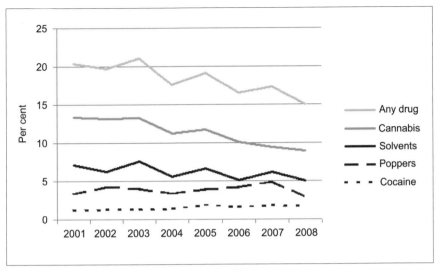

Figure 3.23 Percentage of 11 to 15-year-olds that have taken drugs in the last year, England

Source: Fuller (2009) *Smoking, Drinking and Drug Use Among Young People in England in 2008*, table 4.6c.

alcohol and drugs had a part to play. Regular drinking and binge drinking among teenagers is higher in England and Wales than for nearly every other country for which data are available. Although there are important and complex linkages between use of alcohol and drugs and criminal offending, the great majority of young people who use alcohol or drugs are not serious offenders. The proportion of regular users of alcohol and drugs in England and Wales seems to have peaked in the 1990s and declined since, but the amount of alcohol consumed by young regular drinkers has continued to increase. Apart from its linkages with criminal offending, youthful use of alcohol and drugs of course causes significant harms to physical and mental health.

Suicide, self-harm, common mental disorders

Suicide is very rare in children, becomes far more common in the teenage years, then gradually increases in frequency in succeeding age groups. It is considerably more common in males than females. These patterns are similar across different cultures, although overall rates of suicide vary widely between countries. The rate of suicide in the UK is rather low compared with other countries: the latest figure (as at 2009) for males in the UK (per 100,000 population) is 10.1 compared with 17.7 in the US, 17.9 in Germany, 25.5 in France, 26.8 in Poland, 42.3 in Hungary, and 53.9 in the Russian Federation (WHO 2009). Suicide is one of the psychosocial disorders in young people that substantially increased in frequency over

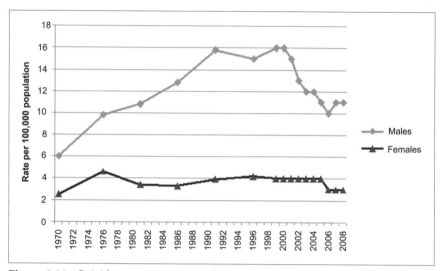

Figure 3.24 Suicide rates among people aged 15–24, UK

Sources: Social Trends 34, table 7.21; Diekstra *et al.* (1995), figure 13.7c; Samaritans *Suicide Statistics* 1999–2008, table G.

a period of 40 years or so from 1950 across a wide range of countries, although this increase was much more marked in males than in females (Diekstra *et al.* 1995). In the UK, however, this rising trend levelled off from around 1990, then reversed from 2000. As shown by Figure 3.24, the male suicide rate among young men aged 15–24 declined steeply between 2000 and 2006. Although the timing was a little later in the case of suicide, this is strikingly similar to the reversal in the rising trend of crime.

Whereas suicide is more common among males than females, the opposite is true of self-harming. A survey of teenagers, mainly aged 15 and 16, in 41 schools in the Midlands (England) in 2000/1 found that 11.2 per cent of girls and 3.2 per cent of boys had deliberately harmed themselves in the previous year, in most cases by cutting or poisoning (taking an overdose) (Hawton *et al.* 2002). This survey was part of a seven-country study which found that the 12-month prevalence of self-harming among girls was about the same in Australia, Belgium, England and Norway, but markedly lower in Hungary, Ireland and (lowest of all) the Netherlands (Madge *et al.* 2008). Patterns of self-harming and suicide are entirely different, since Hungary has an exceptionally high rate of suicide, but a low rate of self-harming, at least among teenagers. It is not possible to track long-term trends in self-harming behaviour, but the government's Adult Psychiatric Morbidity Survey supports a comparison between 2000 and 2007 of the proportion that have deliberately harmed themselves at any time in their lives. Over this period, lifetime prevalence of self-harming rose from 6.5 per cent to

11.7 per cent among women aged 16–24 and from 4.2 per cent to 6.3 per cent among men in the same age group, both changes being clearly statistically significant (McManus *et al.* 2009: table 4.2). Over this period, by contrast, rates of suicide declined steeply among young men, and remained constant among young women. The estimates of self-harming from the seven-country survey and two British surveys are not closely comparable, because of differences in questioning method and in the age group for which findings can be quoted, but both indicate that self-harming among young women is fairly common in England, and the government survey shows that its prevalence rapidly increased in the 2000s.

Depressive disorders are uncommon in childhood, but become rapidly more common between the ages of 10 and 15, and remain common throughout adult life. From the available evidence, it is hard to distinguish change over the life course from historic or 'secular' change from one generation to another, but Fombonne (1995: 567) concluded after an exhaustive review that 'the evidence strongly suggests that there has been a true increase in depressive conditions in the most recent cohorts'. The government's psychiatric morbidity survey covered a range of 'common mental disorders' (CMDs) including depression, anxiety, phobias, panics, and obsessive compulsive disorder. In 2007 it found that 8.2 per cent of young men aged 16–24 and 12.3 per cent of young women had experienced mixed anxiety and depressive disorder in the past week, and that 1.5 per cent of young men and 2.9 per cent of young women had experienced a depressive episode in the past week. Altogether 13.0 per cent of young men aged 16–24 and 22.2 per cent of young women had experienced any common mental disorder in the past week, and these proportions were slightly higher for those aged 25–34 (McManus *et al.* 2009: table 2.3). Prevalence of these disorders increased slightly from 1993 to 2007: for example, the proportion of young women aged 16–34 who had experienced any CMD in the past week was 20.0 per cent in 1993, 21.2 per cent in 2000, and 22.6 per cent in 2007 (McManus *et al.* 2009: table 2.4).

Trends in responses to youth crime

As mentioned earlier, the typical response to youth crime is no response at all. Farrington and Joliffe (2005) estimated the probability of a conviction for an offence of burglary in 1999 to be one in 136, and since only 60 per cent of convictions resulted in custodial sentences in that year a young offender might expect to commit 200 burglaries before ending up in custody. Although individual offences usually provoke no formal response from the system, young people who commit many offences and who continue over a long period are likely to be captured eventually. This process can be studied in some detail through analysis of the Edinburgh

Table 3.3 Police warnings and charges by level of self-reported serious offending: Edinburgh Study cohort at age 15

	Volume of serious offending in past 12 months (%)				Total (%)
	0	*1–4*	*5–9*	*10–77*	
Warned or charged in past 12 months	6.5	26.8	37.0	46.1	14.8
	93.5	73.2	63.0	53.9	85.2
N (base for percentages)	2,824	537	216	395	3,972
	100.0	100.0	100.0	100.0	100.0

Source: previously unpublished analyses of the Edinburgh Study of Youth Transitions and Crime

Study of Youth Transitions and Crime, which has followed a cohort of more than 4,000 young people since 1998. Table 3.3 divides the cohort into four groups according to their level of self-reported serious offending[18] over the previous 12 months at the age of 15. It shows the proportion of each group who said they had been warned or charged by the police over the same period. As expected, police warnings and charges are strongly related to the level of offending. For example, 46.1 per cent of the high-offending group had been warned or charged, compared with only 6.5 per cent of the zero-offending group. Nevertheless, the glass is half-empty as well as half-full: more than half even of the high-offending group (10+ self-reported offending incidents over the 12-month period) had not been warned or charged. If we lump together all offenders (one or more serious offences in the past 12 months) then 64.6 per cent of self-reported offenders had not been warned or charged over the same period.

This analysis shows that most young people who have committed one or more offences are not captured. Who, then, are the ones that are? From analysis of the same data, McAra and McVie (2005) have shown that holding self-reported offending constant, 15-year-olds who have had recent adversarial contact with the police are more likely than others to be male, to come from manual and from single-parent households and from deprived neighbourhoods, and to be users of alcohol and drugs. They are also more visible because they are more often hanging about on the street, more often truanting from school, and less subject to parental supervision. However, the strongest predictor of adversarial police contact, alongside self-reported offending, is 'previous form': contact with the police one to three years earlier. After controlling for self-reported offending and other factors, the odds of being warned or charged were raised 5.1 times if the young person had had earlier adversarial contact with the police. In short, the initial suspects tend to come from a deprived or dysfunctional background: subsequently the system tends to focus on 'the usual suspects' who are already on its books.

The Youth Justice Board counts the number of offences committed by young people under 18 resulting in a disposal (that is, a pre-court or a court judgment). In 2008/9 young people committed 244,543 offences resulting in a disposal; this was a drop to 81 per cent of the peak number reached in 2005/6. These offences were committed by 237,917 young people, with an average of two offences each (MoJ 2010b). A longer-term view of cautions and convictions for indictable offences[19] shows a gradual downward trend for all age groups from the late 1980s to 2003, a subsequent rise in 2007, and a recent fall in 2008 (see Figure 3.25). These trends suggest rather small changes over the past 20 years in the total volume of behaviour to which the youth justice system is responding in some way or other.

As shown in Figure 3.26, the most common offences resulting in a disposal were theft and violence, with criminal damage some way behind. There has been a dramatic fall in motoring offences and a considerable rise in violent offences dealt with over the period.

Figure 3.27 divides disposals into four broad categories as follows.

Pre-court: Police reprimand, final warning without intervention, final warning with intervention.

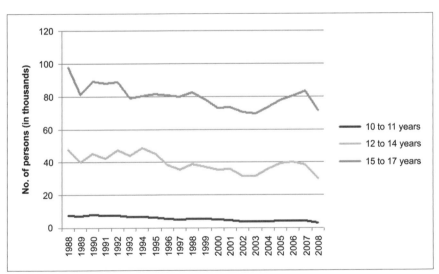

Figure 3.25 Number of young offenders found guilty or cautioned for indictable offences, England and Wales

Sources: Home Office, *Cautions, Court Proceedings and Sentencing*, table 5 (for 1988 to 2000); Home Office, *Criminal Statistics*, table 2.23 (for 2001 to 2006); and Ministry of Justice (2009) *Criminal Statistics*, table 3.24 (for 2007).

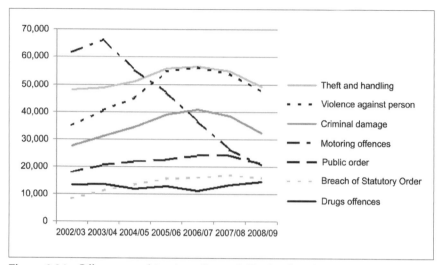

Figure 3.26 Offences resulting in a disposal, England and Wales

Sources: Youth Justice Board (2004 and 2005) *Youth Justice Annual Statistics,* p. 5 (for 2002/3 and 2003/4); and Ministry of Justice (2010) *Youth Justice Annual Workload Data 2008/09,* table 1.4 (for 2004/5 to 2008/9).

First-tier: Absolute discharge, bind over, compensation order, conditional discharge, fine, referral order, reparation order, sentence deferred.

Community: Action plan order, attendance centre order, community punishment and rehabilitation order, community punishment order, community rehabilitation order, community rehabilitation order and

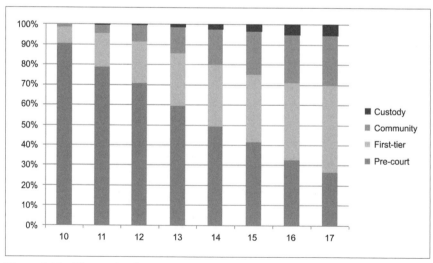

Figure 3.27 Disposals of young offenders, England and Wales, 2008/09

Source: Ministry of Justice (2010) *Youth Justice Annual Workload Data 2008/09,* table 3.1.

conditions, curfew order, drug treatment and testing order, supervision order, supervision order and conditions.

Custody: Detention and training order (4 months), detention and training order (4 months plus to 2 years), s. 90/91, s. 226 (detention for life), s. 226 (detention for public protection), s. 228.

Of the 184,850 disposals that were given to young people in 2008/09, 41 per cent were pre-court (reprimands and final warnings), 35 per cent were first-tier, 21 per cent were community and 4 per cent were custodial sentences. The proportion of pre-court disposals is very high for the youngest age group and falls with age, whereas the proportions of first-tier and community disposals rise with age.

Confusingly, the counts of offenders, offences, and disposals are all different, because the same offender may be dealt with for one or several offences, and also a single disposal may cover one or several offences. As stated above, the count of offences dealt with rose from 2002/3 to a peak in 2005/6, then fell. The number of disposals rose and fell in a broadly similar pattern, but the rise in disposals was greater, and the fall was less marked, so there were more disposals in 2008/9 than six years earlier, even though at the later date the system was dealing with fewer offences than before. The explanation is that the system is moving towards disposing separately of different offences by the same individual instead of dealing with several offences by means of the same disposal. Despite the net rise in the number of disposals over the six years, the pattern has changed only slightly: community sentences have increased from 17 per cent in 2002/3 to 21 per cent in 2008/9, whereas pre-court disposals have declined by a similar amount, and custody continues to account for 4 per cent of the total. Statistics compiled on a slightly different basis show that over the longer period between 1998 and 2007 there was little or no change in the share of cautions as a proportion of offenders cautioned or convicted, and this remains true for young offenders within each age group (Criminal Statistics 2007: table 3.4). Overall these findings show a constant number of offences by young people being dealt with and an unchanging division between pre-court and court disposals.

In 1999, anti-social behaviour orders (ASBOs) were introduced to help protect the public from behaviour 'that causes or is likely to cause harassment, alarm or distress' (Crime and Disorder Act 1998). These are civil orders that, if breached, can incur criminal sanctions. Between June 2000 and December 2007, 6,028 ASBOs were issued to young people aged 10 to 17, which is 40 per cent of the total number issued. The number of ASBOs issued to this age group has grown considerably since they were first introduced, with almost five times as many young recipients in 2007 as there were in 2001, the first full year in which age data was made

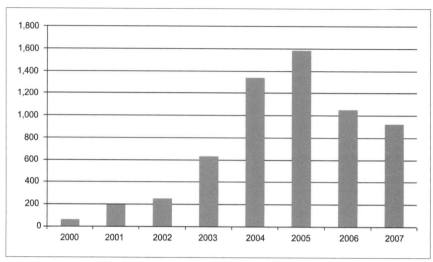

Figure 3.28   Anti-social behaviour orders issued to 10–17-year-olds: 2000 to 2007
Source: OCJR Evidence and Analysis Unit, see www.crimereduction.homeoffice.gov.uk

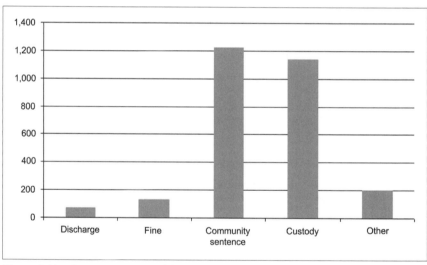

Figure 3.29   Sentences received for breach of an ASBO by 10 to 17-year-olds: 2000 to 2007

Source: OCJR Evidence and Analysis Unit, see www.crimereduction.homeoffice.gov.uk

available (Figure 3.28). The breach rate is high, especially for under 18s, 64 per cent of whom are known to have breached their ASBOs. Between June 2000 and December 2007, 1,142 young people aged 10 to 17 received a custodial sentence for breaching their ASBO, with an average sentence of 6.5 months (see Figure 3.29). This happened on 3,248 occasions, suggesting, presumably, that each young person in custody for this reason received on average 2.8 custodial sentences.[21] (For more detail about the response to antisocial behaviour, see Chapter 5.)

Ethnicity and youth crime

It is hard to disentangle ethnicity from the range of socio-demographic factors that increase the likelihood that an individual will be a victim of crime or an offender. The age structures, economic circumstances and neighbourhoods typical of different ethnic groups explain many of the differences in their involvement in crime. For example, it has consistently been shown that being a victim and a perpetrator of violence is strongly associated with being young and male; but while only 14 per cent of white men are aged 16 to 24, almost three times as many men from mixed ethnic backgrounds (38 per cent) fall into this age group (Jansson 2007).

In 1988 the British Crime Survey included a booster sample of African Caribbean and Asian respondents to explore their experiences of crime. Both groups had a heightened risk of being victims of certain crimes: burglary, theft, assault and robbery for African Caribbean respondents, and vandalism, vehicle crime, threats and robbery for Asian respondents (Mayhew et al. 1989). Later, these findings were confirmed by an analysis of combined samples from the 1988 and 1992 BCS. However, African Caribbean and Asian respondents were more likely than whites to live in higher-risk, inner-city areas and in social housing, to be unemployed, and to have lower household incomes. After controlling for such factors in a multivariate analysis, the difference in victimization between ethnic minorities and whites became less or in some cases disappeared (Fitz-Gerald and Hale 1996). Twenty years on, respondents from mixed ethnic backgrounds were most at risk of being victims of crime (36 per cent compared with 24–27 per cent of other ethnic groups[22]) but further analysis shows that this is likely to reflect their young age profile (Jansson 2007).

The British Crime Survey shows clear ethnic differences in perceptions and fear of crime. Non-white ethnic groups are considerably more likely than white respondents to worry about crime and to think that crime has a high or moderate impact on their quality of life.[23] They are also more likely to think that antisocial behaviour is a problem in their area.[24] On the other hand, they have generally higher levels of confidence in the local police and the criminal justice system (Walker et al. 2009).

It is well known that compared with their numbers in the population, certain ethnic groups (especially African Caribbean and mixed) are greatly over-represented at every stage of the criminal justice system. For example, in 2007/08 African Caribbean people were nearly eight times (7.6) and Asians more than twice (2.3) as likely as white people to be stopped and searched, although similar proportions were arrested as a

Table 3.4 Ethnic group of young people aged 10–17 cautioned or convicted

Ethnicity	% of young people cautioned or convicted in 2007/08	% of general population aged 10 and over (based on 2001 Census)
Asian	3.6	4.4
African Caribbean	6.1	2.2
Mixed	3.7	1.3
White	84.2	91.3
Other	0.4	0.9
Not known	1.9	n/a

Sources: YJB 2009a; Riley *et al.* 2009.

result: 12 per cent of 'stop and searches' of white and African Caribbean people led to an arrest, while for Asians it was 10 per cent. At the terminus of the criminal justice process, African Caribbean people were more than five times as likely as white people to be in prison, while those of mixed ethnic backgrounds were almost three times as likely (Riley *et al.* 2009).

Table 3.4 shows the ethnic background of those captured by the youth justice system, compared with their proportions in the general population. There is a clear over-representation of African Caribbean and mixed young people and an under-representation of white and Asian young people.

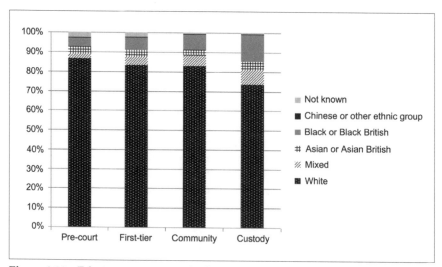

Figure 3.30 Ethnic composition of offenders given various disposals: England and Wales 2008/9

Source: Ministry of Justice (2010) *Youth Justice Annual Workload Data 2008/09*, table 3.2.

This contrast is even more pronounced in relation to custody (see Figure 3.30). In contrast to white young people, of those of African Caribbean and mixed heritage account for only 6.1 per cent and 3.7 per cent of cautions and convictions overall, whereas they receive twice as great a share of custodial sentences (13.7 per cent and 6.9 per cent respectively). However, it is hard to know whether these differences arise from unfair differential treatment since the decision to impose a particular sentence on a young person is influenced by a number of factors including their offending history, the seriousness of the offence, and other mitigating factors. It might be that stiffer sentences for young offenders of African Caribbean and mixed ethnic backgrounds are explained by more serious offences and more prolific offending histories. Nearly 20 years ago, a powerful analysis of sentencing in adult courts concluded that there was evidence of bias against ethnic minorities (Hood 1992) and a broader review concluded that there was evidence of bias at each stage of criminal process (Smith 1997). More recently, Feilzer and Hood (2004) undertook an analysis of more than 17,000 files in juvenile cases in eight chosen Youth Offending Team (YOT) areas. The study found differences in outcome according to ethnic group at various points in the process. For the most part, these differences were largely or entirely explained by relevant characteristics of the case (such as the nature of the offence or the offending history) yet after controlling for case characteristics a number of differences remained that were consistent with discriminatory treatment. For example, black males and those of mixed race were more likely than others to be prosecuted; black and Asian males were more likely than others to be remanded in custody before sentence; and black males convicted in the Crown Court were much more likely than others to be given long sentences of custody (more than 12 months). Another, still more recent, study came up with broadly similar findings (May et al. 2010).

Self-report studies can be useful for describing the characteristics of offenders, although they may be unreliable when it comes to ethnicity because of differences in the extent to which ethnic groups conceal or exaggerate their offending (see Junger 1989; Sampson and Lauritsen 1997) and because of sampling biases.[25] Nonetheless, what they show is generally higher offending rates among African Caribbean young people, generally lower rates among Asian young people, and an inconsistent picture for white young people. For example, the 1992/93 Youth Lifestyles Survey found similar rates of offending among African Caribbean and white young people, and substantially lower rates among Asians (of Indian, Pakistani and Bangladeshi origin). The 2005 MORI Youth Survey, however, found higher rates among African Caribbean young people (36 per cent) than white (27 per cent) and Asian (18 per cent) young people (see Phillips and Chamberlain 2006).[26]

Analysis of Youth Justice Board figures shows that certain types of crime are associated with different ethnic groups. Although white young people accounted for 84.3 per cent of all offences resulting in a disposal in 2008/09, they accounted for a higher proportion of arson cases (90.6 per cent), and a much lower proportion of robbery cases (47.7 per cent), the majority of which were carried out by other ethnic groups (27.8 per cent by African Caribbean, 10.5 per cent by mixed, and 10.7 per cent of Asian young people). A similar pattern exists for drugs offences, which were less common amongst white young people (74.5 per cent), and more typical of African Caribbean (12.5 per cent), Asian (6.3 per cent) and mixed (4.9 per cent) young people. These differences with respect to drugs do not correspond to similar differences in the prevalence of drug use between ethnic groups, so it is plausible that they reflect the pattern of policing in a field where police discretion is exceptionally wide.[27] These ethnic differences in respect of arson, robbery and drugs offences are found for every year since 2002/03.

There has been much heated debate as to whether the striking differences in outcomes for different ethnic groups in the criminal justice system are a consequence of different rates of offending; of rules and procedures that work to the disadvantage of ethnic minorities; or of discriminatory application of rules and procedures. The answer is probably all three.

Conclusions

For a period of at least 30 years after the Second World War, the main political parties adopted a bipartisan approach to policy on crime and criminal justice, but that came to an end when the Conservative party made 'law and order' a central plank of its campaign in the 1979 General Election. Since then, the parties have highlighted the problems of crime and antisocial behaviour and have competed to come up with solutions. Although this may be a way of getting up steam to power effective action, it carries with it the danger of making the problem worse. Effective crime prevention depends on confidence and trust, which tend to be eroded by competitive political debate about the crime problem. Politicians may end up making people feel more anxious even when things are actually getting better. In fact, public opinions on crime and antisocial behaviour are multi-layered and complex, but there is evidence that at some of these levels political debate has indeed had such an effect. Three-quarters of respondents in the latest British Crime Survey thought that crime had risen in the past two years – despite the fact that victimization of those same respondents in that very survey had actually declined! There is strong evidence that these paradoxical views are fed by the national political debate filtered through popular newspapers and other mass media. Tabloid readers were far more likely than broadsheet readers to think the crime rate had increased. Illustrating the multi-layered structure of public opinion, respondents were far less likely to think that crime had increased in their own neighbourhood than nationally. This of course confirms that general views are based on politics refracted through the media, and not on personal experience. Further confirmation comes from the findings on anxiety about crime, which has steadily declined for the last 12 years. This may seem to conflict with the same respondents' predominant view that crime has increased, but these two opinions relate to different cognitive levels. When asked to make a judgement as to whether crime has increased, most people say it has. When asked at one point in time if they are worried about specific kinds of crime (violent crime, vehicle crime, burglary) the proportion saying they are worried declines over time. These findings show how trends in actual experience of victimization and in feelings about crime run counter to cognitive judgements about the direction of change. It is mainly these cognitive judgements that are influenced by the political debate.

It is easy to influence people's judgements, because measuring crime is inherently difficult and complex. If experts can sometimes disagree about trends and patterns of crime it is hardly surprising that the public can sometimes hold unreasonable views on the subject. From the best of motives, government has muddied the waters by providing two different measures of crime while changing definitions and counting procedures used by one of them. The police-recorded crime statistics are the long-established measure, providing useful information on trends going back to the nineteenth century. They will always miss out a considerable proportion of crime, however, because there are many incidents that people do not choose to report to the authorities, judging that nothing much would be achieved by doing so. As confidence in the police increases, a larger proportion of incidents are reported, inflating the count of recorded crimes. In an effort to make the statistics more complete, between 1998 and 2004 government changed counting rules and definitions and encouraged police officers to accept descriptions of incidents at their face value rather than form their own judgements as to whether or not they constitute crimes. This considerably inflated the counts of certain crimes, especially minor assaults. Consequently, the statistics of recorded crime have become more complete, at the cost of losing consistency over a lengthy transitional period. From 1981 onwards, the British Crime Survey provides a more consistent and a more complete measure, although it leaves some notable gaps (crimes against children, crimes against corporations, major frauds, victimless crimes such as possession of drugs).

Combining the evidence from the recorded crime statistics up to 1997 with the British Crime Survey results from 1981 onwards, trends in crime are reasonably clear. There was a sustained, strong rise in crime from 1950 to 1994, a reversal of this long-term trend in the mid 1990s, and a fall in crime thereafter. Violent crime as a whole has fallen at a slower rate than property crime. Serious violent crimes have also probably declined in the 2000s. The total number of knife crimes has fallen considerably since the mid 1990s (from Crime Survey data). Police data show a decline in gun homicides, but a rise up to 2007/8 in fatal stabbings (which of course form a tiny proportion of all knife crimes).

Probably trends in youth crime are much the same as trends in overall crime. However, there was an upward trend in convictions of young people for violence, reaching a peak in 2005/6. We cannot be sure about the reasons for this, but the most likely explanation is that the system became more active in targeting and prosecuting violent young offenders. Public perceptions of antisocial behaviour increased from 1992 to 2000, but have not increased since. Gangs are an important factor in youth offending, but there is no reliable evidence on whether or not they are becoming more common in Britain.

Most offences do not result in a penalty from the youth justice system. Holding constant young people's actual level of offending, the system tends to target certain groups: males, those from manual and single-parent households and from deprived neighbourhoods, and users of alcohol and drugs. Also, it targets young people who are visible because they are hanging about on the street, truanting from school, and less subject to parental supervision. Further, it targets those who have already come into conflict with the police. The initial suspects tend to come from a deprived or dysfunctional background, and subsequently the system tends to focus on 'the usual suspects' who are already on its books. These patterns probably emerge from deep structural features that are common to nearly all youth justice systems, so the only way to reduce the problem is to use the system more sparingly and deal with fewer young offenders in a punitive way.

Exclusion from school is quite strongly related to youth offending, and may well be a causal factor. There is potential for reducing youth crime by insisting that schools take more responsibility for their unruly pupils rather than allowing them to be segregated from the mainstream. A particularly strong argument for this policy is that exclusion tends to target the disadvantaged. This also draws attention to the need for well-resourced specialist programmes for the small number of teenagers who will despite all efforts have to be educated separately.

There is robust evidence of an increase in conduct disorders and emotional problems in young people from the 1970s to the 1990s, which has levelled off since. The evidence suggests that there has been no increase in attention deficit and hyperactive disorder (ADHD). There was a strong upward trend in suicides among young men over the post-war period, but like the crime trend this reversed in the mid 1990s. Consumption of alcohol and illegal drugs among young people is high in Britain, and higher than in most countries in Europe or, probably, elsewhere in the world. Consumption of both alcohol and illegal drugs increased substantially over the post-war period, although recent trends have been downward, reversing a very long upward trend. Both alcohol and drugs are intertwined with youth offending in complex ways, although offending often comes first as people grow up. In very broad terms, there are a number of psychosocial disorders in young people that increased substantially over a period of 30 or 40 years following the Second World War, but in several instances these earlier increases have levelled off or gone into reverse. Trends in crime have to be understood primarily in this broader context, and not primarily as responses to the activities of the youth justice system.

Notes

1 The Crime Statistics Independent Review recommended that the sample be extended to include under 16s and those in group residences such as student halls and old people's homes. This came into effect in January 2009.

2 Comparable offences are those that can be strictly compared between the crime survey and the recorded crime statistics. They include vandalism, theft from the person, burglary, robbery, vehicle-related theft, common assault, bicycle theft, and wounding.

3 Namely England, the Netherlands, Belgium, Sweden, Finland, Germany, Switzerland and Italy.

4 The vast body of studies in the criminological literature, many of them following the same individuals over several years, ask questions about a long list of specific behaviours, such as shoplifting, stealing from home, breaking into cars, or robbery with violence or threats of violence. The MORI survey (commissioned by the Youth Justice Board) instead starts by asking whether respondents have done anything criminal, leaving them to decide what that might include. This is a weak method compared with serious studies, and will lead to quite different results.

5 The 2008 survey combined Asian and African Caribbean young people into a single BME category, making comparisons with earlier years meaningless.

6 Thus, respondents in the British Social Attitudes Survey were far more likely to think people treat each other with respect and consideration in their own neighbourhood than in Britain as a whole (Clery and Stockdale 2009: table 9.4a) among innumerable other examples.

7 Between 1992 and 2000 respondents were asked about five indicators of antisocial behaviour: noisy neighbours, rubbish or litter, people using or dealing drugs, vandalism and graffiti, and teenagers hanging around. Since 2000 two more items have been added: abandoned or burnt-out cars, and people being drunk or rowdy in public.

8 For a review of earlier US research on co-offending, see Reiss (1988).

9 See http://www.umsl.edu/ccj/eurogang/euroganghome.htm

10 When the item 'the group considers it ok to do illegal things' was added to the list above, membership fell to 2 per cent, and when this item was included but the 'structural feature' item was omitted (this is the official Eurogang definition) membership was 3 per cent.

11 They were asked about their own offending, which was fairly strongly related to gang membership (see below).

12 In a recent example from 19 October 2009: *The Metro* newspaper (which has an estimated daily readership of over 3.3 million) printed an article entitled *Teenage gun crime 'fuelled by punishment shootings'*, the opening sentence of which claimed that 'The Met has seized more than 1,000 guns as "extreme" youth violence in London soars'.

13 Knives were used in 7 per cent of violent incidents, glasses or bottles in 5 per cent, 'hitting implements' in 4 per cent and firearms in 1 per cent.

14 These are attempted murder, wounding causing grievous bodily harm with or without intent, and robbery.

15 This was found to be the case even after controlling for confounding factors such as social, family and educational disadvantages.

16 This was in response to identical questions, thus allowing direct comparisons between these three time points.

17 Because the method used to estimate the number of units consumed by pupils changed in the 2007 survey, the data from 2007 and 2008 are not included in the figure.

18 Serious offending includes driving or riding in a stolen car, breaking into a car, carrying a weapon, housebreaking, robbery, fire-setting, and assaults/fighting where there were five or more such incidents over 12 months. The measure is a count of the number of incidents of serious offending in the previous 12 months.

19 The summary offences left out of Figure 3.25, which are of course less serious than indictable offences, accounted for 48 per cent of cautions and convictions of 10–17-year-olds in 2007. Note that the Youth Justice Board statistics for offences resulting in a disposal, quoted earlier in this paragraph, include summary as well as indictable offences.

20 From this point the commentary reverts to the Youth Justice Board statistics which relate to summary as well as indictable offences.

21 OCJR court proceedings database http://www.crimereduction.homeoffice.gov.uk/asbos/asbos2.htm

22 The risk of being a victim of any BCS crime was 27 per cent for African Caribbean respondents, 25 per cent for Asian respondents, 25 per cent for Chinese and 'other' respondents and 24 per cent for white respondents.

23 For example, in the 2008/09 British Crime Survey 37 per cent of Chinese/Other, 30 per cent of African Caribbean, 26 per cent of Asian and 26 per cent of mixed respondents had high levels of worry about violent crime, compared with just 12 per cent of white respondents.

24 For example, in the 2008/09 British Crime Survey 24 per cent of Chinese/Other, 22 per cent of African Caribbean, 26 per cent of Asian and 29 per cent of mixed respondents perceived there to be high levels of antisocial behaviour in their local area, compared with just 16 per cent of white respondents.

25 Response rates tend to be low in inner-city neighbourhoods, interviewers are mostly white, and prolific offenders are unlikely to be interviewed because they will often be in custody or out on the street.

26 These differences were present in every wave of the survey between 2001 and 2005.

27 In general, it is very easy for the police to find young people in possession of illegal drugs if they wish to do so, and they have plenty of choice about where and how to find them.

References

Allen, J. and Ruparel, C (2006) 'Reporting and Recording Crime', in A. Walker, C. Kershaw and S. Nicholas (eds) *Crime in England and Wales 2005/06* (London: Home Office).

Barberet, R., Bowling, B., Junger-Tas, J., Rechea-Alberola, C., van Kesteren, J. and Zurawan, A. (2004) *Self-Reported Juvenile Delinquency in England and Wales, The Netherlands and Spain* (Helsinki: HEUNI).

Centre for Social Justice (2009) *Dying to Belong: An In-depth Review of Street Gangs in Britain* (London: Centre for Social Justice).

Chaiken, J. M. and Chaiken, M. R. (1990) 'Drugs and Predatory Crime' in M. Tonry and J. Q. Wilson (eds) *Drugs and Crime: Crime and Justice, A Review of Research* 13 (Chicago: University of Chicago Press), pp. 203–40.

Collishaw, S., Maughan, B., Goodman, R. and Pickles, A. (2004) 'Time Trends in Adolescent Mental Health', *Journal of Child Psychology and Psychiatry*, 45: 8, pp. 1350–62.

Currie, C., Nic Gabhainn, S., Godeau, E., Roberts, C., Smith, R., Currie, D., Picket, W., Richter, M., Morgan, A. and Barnekow, V. (2008) *Inequalities in Young People's Health: HBSC International Report from the 2005/6 Survey* (Edinburgh: University of Edinburgh Child and Adolescence Health Research Unit, for World Health Organization). Available at www.education.ac.uk/cahru

Currie, C., Hurrelmann, K., Settertobulte, B., Smith, R. and Todd, J. (2000) *Health and Health Behaviour Among Young People* (Geneva: World Health Organization). Available at http://www.hbsc.org/downloads/Int_Report_00.pdf

Decker, S. H. and Weerman, F. M. (eds) (2005) *European Street Gangs and Troublesome Youth Groups* (Walnut Creek: Altamira Press).

Department for Children, Schools and Families (2009) *Permanent and Fixed Period Exclusions from Schools and Exclusion Appeals in England, 2007/8: Statistical First Release 18/2009* (London: DCSF).

Diekstra, R. F. W., Kienhorst, C. W. M., and de Wilde, E. J. (1995) 'Suicide and Suicidal Behaviour Among Adolescents' in M. Rutter and D. J. Smith (eds) *Psychosocial Disorders in Young People: Time Trends and Their Causes* (Chichester: Wiley), pp. 686–761.

Earls, F. and Mezzacapa, E. (2002) 'Conduct and Oppositional Disorders', in M. Rutter and E. Taylor (eds) *Child and Adolescent Psychiatry*, 4th edition (Oxford: Blackwell).

Eisner, M. (2003) 'Long-Term Historical Trends in Violent Crime', in M. Tonry (ed.) *Crime and Justice. A Review of Research*, 30 (Chicago and London: University of Chicago Press), pp. 84–142.

Esbensen, F.-A. and Huizinga, D. (1993) 'Gangs, Drugs, and Delinquency in a Survey of Urban Youth', *Criminology* 31:4, pp. 565–87.

Fagan, J. (1990) 'Intoxication and Aggresson', in M. Tonry and J. Q. Wilson (eds) *Drugs and Crime: Crime and Justice, A Review of Research* 13 (Chicago: University of Chicago Press), pp. 241–320.

Farrington, D. P. (1973) 'Self-Reports of Deviant Behaviour: Predictive and Stable?', *Journal of Criminal Law and Criminology*, 64, pp. 99–110.

Farrington, D. P. and Joliffe, D. (2005) 'Crime and Punishment in England and Wales, 1981–1999', in M. Tonry and D. P. Farrington (eds) *Crime and Punishment in Western countries*, 33 (Chicago and London: University of Chicago Press), pp. 41–81.

Feilzer, M. and Hood, R. (2004) *Differences or Discrimination?* (London: Youth Justice Board).

Fergusson, D., Horwood, J. and Ridder, E. (2005) 'Show Me the Child at Seven: The consequences of conduct problems in childhood for psychosocial functioning in adulthood', *Journal of Child Psychology and Psychiatry*, 46, pp. 837–49.

FitzGerald, M. and Hale, C. (1996) *Ethnic Minorities, Victimization and Racial Harassment: Findings from the 1988 and 1992 British Crime Surveys*, Home Office Research Study no. 154 (London: Home Office).

Flood-Page, C., Campbell, S., Harrington, V. and Miller, J. (2000) *Youth Crime: Findings from the 1998/99 Youth Lifestyles Survey* (London: Home Office).

Fombonne, E. (1995) 'Depressive Disorders: Time Trends and Possible Explanatory Factors', in M. Rutter and D. J. Smith (eds) *Psychosocial Disorders in Young People: Time Trends and Their Causes* (Chichester: Wiley), pp. 544–615.

Fuller, E. (2009) *Smoking, Drinking and Drug Use Among Young People in England in 2008* (London: NHS Information Centre for Health and Social Care).

Gatrell, V.A.C. (1980) 'The Decline of Theft and Violence in Victorian and Edwardian England and Wales', in V.A.C. Gatrell, B. Lenman, and G. Parker (eds) *Crime and the Law: the Social History of Crime in Western Europe since 1500* (London: Europa), pp. 238–370.

Goodman, R. and Scott, S. (2005) *Child Psychiatry*, 2nd edition (Oxford: Blackwell).

Gottfredson, M. and Hirschi, T. (1990) *A General Theory of Crime* (Stanford: Stanford University Press).

Graham, J. and Bowling, B. (1995) *Young People and Crime* (London: Home Office).

Green, H., McGinnity, A., Meltzer, H., Ford, T. and Goodman, R. (2005) *Mental Health of Children and Young People in Great Britain* (London: Office for National Statistics).

Hawton, K., Rodham, K., Evans, E. and Weatherall, R. (2002) 'Deliberate Self Harm in Adolescents: Self Report Survey in Schools in England', *British Medical Journal*, 325, pp. 1207–11.

Hibbel, B., Guttormsson, U., Ahlström, S. Balakireva, O., Bjarnason, T., Kokkeri, A. and Kraus, L. (2009) *The 2007 ESPAD Report – Substance Use Among Students in 35 European Countries* (Stockholm: The Swedish Council for Information on Alcohol and Other Drugs (CAN)).

Holloway, K. and Bennett, T. (2004) *The Results of the First Two Years of the NEW-ADAM Programme* Home Office Online Report 19/04 (London: Home Office).

Home Office (1992 to 2000) *Cautions, Court Proceedings and Sentencing* (London: Home Office).

Home Office (1993) *Home Office Statistical Findings: Criminal Justice Statistics 1882–1892* (London: Home Office).

Home Office (2000 to 2005) *Criminal Statistics* (London: Home Office).

Hood, R. (1992) *Race and Sentencing* (Oxford: Oxford University Press).

Huizinga, D. (1991) 'Assessing Violent Behavior with Self-Reports', in J. S. Milner (ed.) *Neuropsychology of Aggression* (Boston: Kluwer), pp. 47–66.

Huizinga, D. and Elliott, D. S. (1986) 'Reasserting the Reliability and Validity of Self-Report Delinquency Measures', *Journal of Quantitative Criminology*, 2:4, pp. 293–327.

Jansson, K. (2007) *British Crime Survey: Measuring Crime for 25 years* (London: Home Office).

Junger, M. (1989) 'Discrepancies Between Police and Self-Report Data for Dutch Racial Minorities', *British Journal of Criminology*, 29, pp. 273–84.

Kershaw, C., Nicholas, S. and Walker, A. (2008) *Crime in England and Wales 2007/08* (London: Home Office).

Lader, D., Singleton, N. and Meltzer, H. (2000) *Psychiatric Morbidity among Young Offenders in England and Wales* (London: Office for National Statistics).

Lancet, The (1999) 'Alcohol and Violence', *The Lancet* 326, pp. 1223–24, 17 November.

Madge, N., Hewitt, A., Hawton, K., de Wilde, E. J., Corcoran, P., Fekete, S., van Heeringen, K., De Leo, D. and Ystgaard, M. (2008) 'Deliberate Self-Harm Within an International Community Sample of Young People: Comparative Findings from the Child & Adolescent Self-Harm in Europe (CASE) Study', *Journal of Child Psychology and Psychiatry*, 49:6, pp. 667–77.

McManus, S., Meltzer, H., Brugha, T., Bebbington, P. and Jenkins, R. (eds) (2009) *Adult Psychiatric Morbidity in England, 2007* (London: Office for National Statistics, NHS Information Centre).

Maguire, M. (2007) 'Crime Data and Statistics', in M. Maguire, R. Reiner and R. Morgan (eds) *The Oxford Handbook of Criminology*, 4th edition (Oxford: Oxford University Press).

May, T., Gyateng, T. and Hough, M. (2010) *Differential Treatment in the Youth Justice System* (London: Equality and Human Rights Commission).

Mayhew, P., Elliott, D. and Dowds, L. (1989) *The 1988 British Crime Survey* (London: Home Office).

McAra, L. and McVie, S. (2005) 'The Usual Suspects? Street Life, Young People and the Police', *Criminal Justice* 5:1, pp. 5–36.

McAra, L. and Smith, D. J. (forthcoming) 'How Different are Girls? Testing the Need for Gendered Explanations of Criminal Offending'.

McVie, S. (2005) 'Patterns of Deviance underlying the Age-Crime Curve: The Long Term Evidence', *British Society of Criminology E-Journal*, 7.

Ministry of Justice (2008) *Criminal Statistics 2007* (London: Ministry of Justice).

Ministry of Justice (2010a) *Criminal Statistics* (London: Ministry of Justice).

Ministry of Justice (2010b) *Youth Justice Annual Workload Data 2008/9* (London: Ministry of Justice).

Phillips, A. and Chamberlain, V. (2006) *MORI Five-Year Report: An Analysis of Youth Survey Data* (London: Youth Justice Board).

Povey, D (ed.) Coleman, K., Kaiza, P. and Roe, S. (2009) *Homicides, Firearm Offences and Intimate Violence 2007/08*, Supplementary Volume 2 to Crime in England and Wales 2007/08 (London: Home Office).

Pudney, S. (2002) *The Road to Ruin? Sequences of Initiation into Drug Use and Offending by Young People in Britain* HORS 253 (London: Home Office).

Reiss, A. L. Jr. (1988) 'Co-offending and Criminal Careers', in M. Tonry and N. Morris (eds) *Crime and Justice: A Review of Research*, volume 10 (Chicago: University of Chicago Press), pp. 117–70.

Riley, J., Cassidy, D. and Becker, J. (2009) *Statistics on Race and the Criminal Justice System 2007/8* (London: Ministry of Justice).

Roe, S. and Ashe, J. (2008) *Young People and Crime: Findings from the 2006 Offending, Crime and Justice Survey* (London: Home Office).

Rutter, M. and Smith, D. J. (1995) *Psychosocial Disorders in Young People: Time Trends and Their Causes* (Chichester: Wiley).

Sampson, R. J. and Lauritsen, J. L. (1997) 'Criminal Behavior, Criminal Justice: On Racial and Ethnic Disparities in the United States', in M. Tonry (ed.) *Ethnicity, Crime and Immigration: Comparative and Cross-National Perspectives* (Chicago and London: University of Chicago Press).

Schachar, R. and Tannock, R. (2002) 'Syndromes of Hyperactivity and Attention Deficit', in M. Rutter and E. Taylor (eds) *Child and Adolescent Psychiatry*, 4th edition (Oxford: Blackwell).

Scott, S., Knapp, M., Henderson, J. and Maughan, B. (2001) 'Financial Cost of Social Exclusion: Follow up Study of Antisocial Children into Adulthood', *British Medical Journal*, 323, pp. 191–4.

Silbereisen, R. K., Robins, L. and Rutter, M. (1995) 'Secular Trends in Substance Use: Concepts and Data on the Impact of Social Change on Alcohol and Drug Abuse', in M. Rutter and D. J. Smith (eds) *Psychosocial Disorders in Young People: Time Trends and Their Causes* (Chichester: Wiley), pp. 490–543.

Singleton, N., Bumpstead, R., O'Brien, M., Lee, A. and Meltzer, H. (2001) *Psychiatric Morbidity among Adults Living in Private Households 2000* (London: Office for National Statistics).

Smith, A. (2006) *Crime Statistics: An independent review carried out for the Secretary of State for the Home Department* (London: Home Office).

Smith, D. J. (1997) 'Ethnic Origins, Crime, and Criminal Justice', in M. Maguire, R. Morgan and R. Reiner (eds) *The Oxford Handbook of Criminology*, 2nd edition, pp. 703–59.

Smith, D.J. (2007) 'Crime and the Life Course', in Maguire, M., Morgan, R. and Reiner, R. (eds) *The Oxford Handbook of Criminology*, 4th edition (Oxford: Oxford University Press).

Smith, D.J. (2005) *The Links Between Victimization and Offending* (University of Edinburgh: Centre for Law and Society). Available at: http://www.law.ed.ac.uk/cls/esytc

Smith, D. J. (2006) *School Experience and Delinquency at Ages 13 to 16* (University of Edinburgh: Centre for Law and Society). Available at: www.law.ed.ac.uk/cls/esytc

Smith, D.J. and Bradshaw, P. (2005) *Gang Membership and Teenage Offending* (University of Edinburgh: Centre for Law and Society). Available at: http://www.law.ed.ac.uk/cls/esytc

Smith, I. (1990) 'Alcohol and Crime: The Problem in Australia', in R. Bluglass and P. Bowden (eds) *Principles and Practice of Forensic Psychiatry* (Edinburgh: Churchill Livingstone), pp. 947–51.

Smith, K. and Flatley, J. (eds) (2009) *Homicide, Firearm Offences and Intimate Violence, 2008/9*, Supplementary Volume 2 to Crime in England and Wales (London: Home Office).

Smith, K. (ed.), Flatley, J. (ed.), Coleman, K., Osborne, S., Kaiza, P. and Roe, S. (2010) *Homicide Offences, Firearms and Intimate Violence, 2008/9: Supplementary volume 2 to Crime in England and Wales 2008/9* (London: Home Office).

Thornberry, T. P., Krohn, M. D., Lizotte, A. J. and Chard-Wierschem, D. (1993) 'The Role of Juvenile Gangs in Facilitating Delinquent Behavior', *Journal of Research in Crime and Delinquency* 30:1, pp. 55–87.

Walker, A., Flatley, J., Kershaw, C. and Moon, D. (2009) *Crime in England and Wales 2008/09* (London: Home Office).

Wiklund, N. and Lidberg, L (1990) 'Alcohol as a Causal Crimingenic Factor: The Scandinavian Experience', in R. Bluglass and P. Bowden (eds) *Principles and Practice of Forensic Psychiatry* (Edinburgh: Churchill Livingstone), pp. 941–5.

World Health Organization (2000) *Health and Health Behaviour among Young People* (Copenhagen: WHO Regional Office for Europe).

World Health Organization (2009) *Suicide Rates*. Available at: http://www.who.int/mental_health/prevention/suicide_rates/en/index.html

Youth Justice Board (2007) *Groups, Gangs and Weapons* (London: Youth Justice Board).

Youth Justice Board (2009a) *Youth Justice Annual Workload Data 2007/08* (London: Youth Justice Board).

Youth Justice Board (2009b) *Youth Survey 2008: Young People in Mainstream Education* (London: Youth Justice Board).

Youth Justice Board (2009c) *MORI Youth Survey 2008: Young People in Pupil Referral Units* (London: Youth Justice Board).

Chapter 4

Responding to youth crime

John Graham

Towards the end of the twentieth century, there was a brief moment in the history of youth justice when ideology and political self-interest were subordinated to a more rational and evidence-based response to the age-old problem of youth crime. During this brief period, the notion that arresting, prosecuting, convicting and incarcerating young offenders was the answer to youth crime was turned on its head leaving the juvenile courts (as they were then called) and prisons half empty. A consensus emerged between practitioners, policy makers and academics as politicians took a back seat. Savings to the exchequer were considerable, but the moment was, in historic terms, fleeting. By the beginning of the twenty-first century, the seeds of change had already been sown and, following a single, tragic event that shook the nation's sense of itself to the core, the political status quo was restored.

This chapter relates how, in recent times, the youth justice policy agenda in England and Wales has been effectively hijacked by the interests of party politics at the expense of those caught up in the system. It starts by tracing the historical unfolding of events over the last 30 years that led up to and followed on from this brief interlude before presenting a careful assessment of the current arrangements for responding to youth crime. In so doing, it cites where possible evidence gleaned from research that either supports or undermines the wisdom of such arrangements. It then assesses the government's reforms against a range of additional criteria beyond the targets it set for itself. There is much to be valued in what currently passes for youth justice policy and practice, but there is also much that cries out to be changed.

Youth justice policy during the last 30 years can be roughly divided into three distinctive eras. During the 1980s, policy and practice was dominated by the notion that prosecution and incarceration were measures of last resort and should be avoided where possible. During the early and mid 1990s, the doctrine of diversion was reversed as the courts and the prisons filled up in response to a surge in populist punitivism. Following a change of government in 1997, youth justice policy and practice underwent possibly the greatest upheaval in its relatively brief history. More difficult to caricature than previous eras, it has nevertheless been dubbed by some the era of managerialism. The development of policy and practice in each of these periods is described in turn.

The era of diversion

Thirty years ago, the prevailing view about how best to respond to juvenile crime was dominated by the orthodoxy that criminal justice interventions had little or no impact on future offending behaviour (and could even be counter-productive) and that juvenile justice policy should, as far as possible, focus on diverting young offenders from the criminal justice system (see, for example, Morris and Giller 1987). During this period, the number of juvenile offenders aged 10–16[1] who were prosecuted, convicted and imprisoned fell dramatically (see Allen 1991). This shift in policy and practice was based on the premise that most young people commit relatively minor crimes over a relatively short period of time and that prosecuting and incarcerating them tended to exacerbate rather than reduce their chances of further involvement in crime.[2]

Young offenders, with the exception of those who committed serious crimes, were therefore diverted from court and informally warned or cautioned rather than prosecuted. Between 1980 and 1990, the proportion of 14–16-year-old boys cautioned for indictable offences doubled and for girls it increased by 50 per cent. By 1990, two-thirds of 14–16-year-old boys and nearly 9 out of 10 girls were being cautioned. During the same period, the known juvenile offending rate (i.e. recorded offences per 100,000 of the population) declined by 16 per cent, although much if not all of this was probably due to the increase in the use of informal cautions.[3]

Although the impact of diversion on juvenile offending was contested – in the absence of self-report data it is not possible to know whether juvenile offending actually fell or not – it was argued that young people who are cautioned rather than prosecuted are less likely to be re-convicted and acquire a deviant identity and so this constituted a success. Practitioners favoured multiple cautioning for repeat offenders which led, inevitably, to a marked increase in the cautioning rate, particularly for younger and female offenders (see Bottoms and Dignan 2004). This was later supported by the Audit Commission, which presented evidence – albeit somewhat anecdotal – to suggest that cautioning up to and including a third caution was still effective in reducing the risk of further offending (Audit Commission 1996). But at the same time, concern was expressed about the potential for exerting pressure on young people to

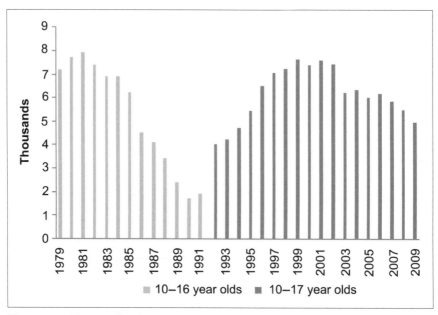

Figure 4.1   Young offenders sentenced to custody, England and Wales

Note: In 1991, a change in legislation resulted in 17-year-olds being brought into the Youth Court. Sentences cover detention in a young offender institution (abolished in April 2000), secure training orders, detention and training orders and long term detention.

admit to offences they had not committed simply to avoid a criminal trial. This, it was suggested, could amount to a breach of Article 6 (the right to a fair trial) of the European Convention on Human Rights.[4] Nevertheless, reflecting what was happening in practice,[5] Home Office guidance issued in 1985 confirmed cautioning as the principal response to juvenile offending with prosecution reserved as a last resort. Soon after, this guidance was incorporated into the first Crown Prosecutor's Code of Practice and two years later extended to adults (Home Office 1988).

The concern of practitioners over the efficacy of formal prosecution was matched by an equal if not greater concern over the efficacy of custody. Diversion from custody became as central to policy and practice as diversion from court and by the end of the decade, the number of juvenile offenders sentenced to immediate custody had fallen by over 400 per cent (see Figure 4.1).

The reasons for the dramatic decline in custody during the 1980s are not simple to discern, but include:

- a fall in the population of young people in this age group;
- a favourable political climate in which the government was keen to cut public spending (custody is expensive) and successive Home Secretaries taking a consistently liberal approach to juvenile justice;

- a growing belief among practitioners that in all but the most serious cases, formal interventions were likely to do more harm than good;

- the discrediting of the 'short, sharp, shock', a new regime for young offenders in juvenile detention centres based on short periods of tough, military-style discipline,[6] followed by legislation[7] that set out new criteria for restricting the use of custody for juvenile offenders, reduced the minimum length of a detention centre sentence, abolished indeterminate custodial sentences (i.e. Borstal) and introduced community based alternatives to custody;[8]

- an increase in the proportion of juveniles represented by legal aid, which more than doubled during the decade;

- the introduction in 1983 of 105 alternative to custody projects managed through the voluntary sector;

- the big rise in the diversion of cases from prosecution and the accompanying fall in the total juvenile court case load.

The last of these is particularly salient since during the first half of the decade, the proportion of juvenile offenders sentenced to immediate custody remained almost unchanged at about 12 per cent. With fewer young offenders appearing in court but the same proportion being sentenced to custody, this automatically meant that fewer of them ended up in prison. However, during the second half of the decade, the proportion sentenced to custody almost halved to 7 per cent, which suggests that diversion from prosecution can only account for part of the decline in custody. Since the custody rate declined despite courts being faced with a relatively older and more serious caseload, it seems likely that there must also have been a real change in sentencing practice.

Demographics account for some of the change – there were simply fewer 10–16-year-olds around – but this cannot explain the fall in the proportion of those convicted being sentenced to custody during the latter half of the decade. It seems likely therefore that the impact of diversion from prosecution was compounded by changes in sentencing practice that resulted from a combination of political, legal and cultural factors, as outlined above. It is, however, pertinent that in Canada a series of legislative changes, including the introduction of strict criteria for sentencing young offenders to custody, has produced very similar outcomes – a substantial decline in the use of prosecution and custody – but with the added bonus of being able to demonstrate no rise in youth crime (see Chapter 10).

The response to youth crime during the 1980s, which has been described as 'remarkable' and even 'revolutionary' (see for example, Newburn 2002), is important primarily because it provides evidence to support the notion that radical changes to the way society responds to youth crime can be introduced with little interference from politicians. This is not to suggest a return to these reforms – there is no unequivocal evidence to show whether or not they reduced juvenile crime and society is different today – but it illustrates that such reforms are not only possible but, taking account of the evidence from Canada, also encouraging.

Somewhat paradoxically, this orthodoxy coincided with a steep rise in overall crime (but not necessarily juvenile crime) and led some commentators to conclude that if the number of young people involved in offending is relatively stable, then perhaps at least part of this rise must be due to a small number of them committing a large and disproportionate amount of crime. Thus the 'persistent juvenile offender' was born.

The era of populist punitivism

The end of the decade was marked by two significant Acts of Parliament, both of which had long term, far-reaching but entirely unintended effects. The first, the Children Act 1989, led to the complete separation of proceedings for children in need of care and protection from those accused of committing crimes. The former were to be dealt with in Family Proceedings Courts and the latter in the Juvenile Court, which stands in contrast to Scotland where both categories are dealt with together in Children's Hearings. The rationale for this separation was based on the notion that those in need of care and protection should not be contaminated by being processed alongside those who have broken the law. In practice, they are often one and the same children,[9] but to this day there is no mechanism for referring cases from one court to the other. Thus children and young people sentenced for criminal offences with complex welfare needs cannot have their cases transferred to the Family Proceedings Court, where family issues such as abuse, neglect and other parenting deficits could be addressed. Since these are often not just part of the problem but part of the solution, this constitutes a serious limitation on the capacity of the youth justice system to tackle the underlying causes of offending behaviour.

Furthermore, and perhaps more importantly, this inadvertently confirmed a simple but potentially misleading distinction between those young people who are responsible for their behaviour and need to be sanctioned and those who are victims and need to be helped. Research shows that the distinction between young offenders and young victims is by no means clear cut. Self-reported offending by 12–15-year-olds is one of the strongest predictors of criminal victimization, especially assault, thefts from the person and harassment (Aye-Maung 1995), and research in Scotland shows that at age 15, delinquency is seven times higher among those who have been victims of five types of crime compared with those who have not been victims at all (Smith 2004).

This crude but ultimately misleading distinction was later dramatized by politicians eager to be seen to be protecting the victim (the innocent) while punishing the offender (the guilty). The notion of 'protecting the public' was soon to become the key aim of the criminal justice system (as opposed to delivering justice), but this failed to acknowledge the fact that offenders are also members of the public and that they too need protecting. Young men aged 16 to 24 are more likely to be victimized than any other group: more than 1 in 8 (13.4 per cent) was a victim of violent crime in 2007/08 (Kershaw *et al.* 2008) and in a recent survey of 800 young people under the age of 24, 29 per cent said they had been affected by gun and knife crime and 1 in 5 (20 per cent) felt they were sometimes or often in danger (Action for Children 2009).

The second Act of Parliament was the 1991 Criminal Justice Act, which attempted to consolidate the principle of diversion from court and custody and move a step closer towards taking 10–13-year-olds out of the jurisdiction of the courts altogether. It succeeded in bringing 17-year-olds into the jurisdiction of a newly defined Youth Court, reflecting the Government's ratification in the same year of the UN Convention on the Rights of the Child, and abolished custody for 14-year-old boys. However, its emphasis on proportional justice led to the courts focusing almost exclusively on the seriousness of the offence committed, with little or no consideration of a defendant's personal circumstances or prior criminal record. This attracted criticism from magistrates, who were concerned that their sentencing powers were being fettered by an exclusive focus on offence seriousness at the expense of persistence.

In October 1992, a new Home Secretary, eager to make his mark, raised the public profile of the persistent juvenile offender, setting in motion a more populist approach to youth crime. In a speech to the Metropolitan Police Federation he stated: in the case of 'a very small number of children who are offending frequently and are out of control, we need increased court powers to lock up, educate and train those children in their own interests and everyone else's' (reported in *The Independent*, 15 October 1992). A year later, the 1993 Criminal Justice Act reinstated the power of the courts to take account of a young offender's previous record and in response to heightened public concern the House of Commons Home Affairs Committee announced that it would be looking into the problem of persistent juvenile offenders and the apparent inability of the criminal justice system to deal adequately with them (Home Affairs Select Committee 1993).

The Home Secretary continued to focus on persistent young offenders in spite of the findings of research commissioned by his own Department (Hagell and Newburn 1994) which drew attention to three key issues. Firstly, it found that persistent young offenders committed the same kinds of offences as less prolific offenders, but committed them more often and started to commit them earlier. Secondly, it showed that persistent young offenders tended to have much more complex backgrounds, with high levels of educational disaffection, family disruption and developmental deficits. And thirdly it highlighted the difficulties of accurately defining[10] and therefore identifying persistent young offenders and the implications of this for the delivery of equity in law.[11] The first of these findings helped to lay the foundations for intervening earlier, which became one of the main planks of the next government's reforms in 1998. But the rest were ignored, missing a clear opportunity to address the underlying causes in many of these cases by amending the Children Act 1989 to enable transfers to the Family Proceedings Court.

Meanwhile, a new shadow Home Secretary, drawing on the successful political campaign of President Bill Clinton in the US, shifted the opposition party's line on the issue of law and order to one which resembled much more closely that of the government's. Both of the major political parties raised the stakes in terms of who could promise the toughest measures on crime as the sound bite 'tough on crime, tough on the causes of crime' was born. The increasing politicization of criminal justice meant that the route towards a more rational, humane and evidence-based response to youth crime became more distant and has remained so ever since.

The new politics of law and order were reflected in the national press, which published articles highlighting the exploits of individual young offenders, referring to 'one-boy crime waves' (*Daily Mail*) and 'mini-gangsters beyond our control' (*Daily Express*). These were followed by calls for tougher measures to deal with 'crooks in short trousers' and 'a truly frightening explosion of kiddie crime' (*Daily Star*). But it was the tragic events of February 1993 and their highly publicized aftermath that tilted public concern into public panic. The abduction and murder of a young child, James Bulger, by two 10-year-old boys, shocked the nation and confirmed to public and politicians alike that action was needed 'to curb the delinquent tendencies of the new generation of ever-younger and increasingly persistent offenders' (Graham and Moore 2006). Three days after the murder of James Bulger, the public's thirst for retribution was captured by the then prime minister who said: 'Society needs to condemn a little more and understand a little less'.

In March 1993, just a month after the murder of James Bulger and against a backdrop of heightened public anxiety, the government announced the introduction of Secure Training Centres (STCs) for '. . . that comparatively small group of very persistent juvenile offenders whose repeated offending made them a menace to the community' (Hansard, 2 March 1993). The new STCs would cater for 12–14-year-old offenders who had been convicted of at least three imprisonable offences and who had failed to comply with the requirements of supervision in the community while on remand or under sentence. A year later, with the passing of the

1994 Criminal Justice and Public Order Act (CJPO), deterrence and retribution were placed at the heart of youth justice policy.

The 1994 CJPO Act reintroduced custody not only for 14-year-old boys (which had only just been abolished – see above), but also for all children aged 12–14, both males and females. It achieved this by introducing the new secure training order (STO) for persistent young offenders aged 12–14, who would serve sentences of up to two years of which half would be in custody and half under supervision in the community. It also doubled the maximum custodial sentence for 15–17-year-olds to 24 months, lowered the age for secure remands from 15 to 12 and extended the powers of the courts to impose long-term detention for grave crimes down to 10-year-olds. During the 1990s, the number of sentences imposed by the Youth Court for grave crimes increased by more than 700 per cent, which is highly unlikely to simply reflect a proportional increase in the number of young people committing such offences.

In the same year, Home Office Circular 18/94 ended the practice of repeat cautioning, handing the decision to caution to the police. Together, these sealed the fate of the diversion movement and led to a steep rise in the prosecution and incarceration of young offenders. Between 1993 and 1998, the number of imprisoned 15–17-year-olds almost doubled; the number of imprisoned 15–17-year-old boys as a proportion of the total prison population more than doubled; and for girls of the same age, it trebled (Social Exclusion Unit 2002). It was at this time that Michael Howard, the new Home Secretary, countered the opposition's 'tough on crime' sound bite with his own – 'prison works' – confirming once and for all that reducing or even containing the prison population was no longer a government priority.

In response to a populist campaign led by the tabloid press, the Home Secretary used his discretionary powers under section 35 of the Criminal Justice Act 1991 to demonstrate his populist credentials. He extended the minimum period of detention to be served by the two 10-year-old boys convicted of murdering James Bulger from 10 years to 15 years, citing the high level of public concern. This was subsequently reduced on appeal to 12 years by the House of Lords which held that the Secretary of State's decision was unlawful, primarily because it was grounded in a direct response to demands made by the public for a more punitive (and in fact adult equivalent) sentence. A number of years later, the European Court of Human Rights held that the trial itself was unlawful.

In contrast to the previous decade, the first half of the 1990s witnessed the beginning of a move towards a much more punitive and less tolerant approach towards young offenders, particularly persistent young offenders. The focus on frequency and not just severity exaggerated the degree to which persistent young offenders were perceived as a threat to society which in turn helped to legitimize a more punitive response to their behaviour (Weitekamp *et al.* 1996). With each party competing to occupy the same ground by out-toughing its rival, the following years witnessed a steep rise in the prison population and spiralling costs.

The era of managerialism

In the mid 1990s, while politicians were busy competing for the 'who can be the toughest' high ground, the growth of state-aided legal aid, the introduction of new rules on the disclosure of evidence and the flooding of the youth courts with more suspects following the inclusion of 17-year-olds, began to increase delays as well as costs. This raised concerns about efficiency and effectiveness and in 1996 the Audit Commission, an independent body, published their detailed assessment of the youth justice system.

In their report *Misspent Youth* the Commission criticized the cost-effectiveness of the youth justice system and the services that supported it (Audit Commission 1996). It concluded that the time taken from arrest to sentence – four months on average – was unsupportable; that most of the £1 billion per annum spent on young offenders is taken up by processing and administration costs with virtually no money being used to address their offending behaviour; that the management of the youth justice system was largely uncoordinated, inconsistent, unsystematic and inefficient; and that too little was undertaken to prevent children and young people from becoming offenders in the first place. By pulling together the evidence on interventions with young offenders,[12] the Audit Commission finally put to bed the notion that efforts to rehabilitate offenders had no appreciable effect on recidivism.[13]

In 1997, the new government immediately began consulting on a series of reforms they had developed while in opposition that drew heavily on the findings and recommendations of the Audit Commission. Reducing costs and improving performance were very soon to become the driving forces behind a new managerialism, with an emphasis on devising plans, setting targets, measuring performance and reviewing progress. Within a year, it passed the 1998 Crime and Disorder Act (CDA), which fundamentally altered the youth justice landscape.

The new youth justice system

The new reforms brought in by the CDA 1998 can be broadly categorized into five themes:

A. Widening criminal responsibility
B. Introducing restorative justice
C. Deploying strategic management

D. Investing in early intervention and prevention
E. Extending containment and control

A. Widening criminal responsibility

The new reforms widened criminal responsibility in three main ways: through the abolition of *doli incapax*; by increasing the extent to which parents are held responsible for the offending behaviour of their children; and by introducing a new civil order to tackle antisocial behaviour.

Doli incapax

Prior to the introduction of the CDA in 1998, the prosecution had to show that where a child aged 10–13 was convicted of an offence, he/she not only intended to commit the offence but also appreciated that it constituted a serious wrongdoing. If the court decided that the offender was not able to distinguish right from wrong, then he/she was deemed *doli incapax*. The idea behind this principle is that it allows for the fact that a child's understanding, knowledge and ability to reason is not the same as that of a fully grown adult. The CDA 1998 abolished this principle on the grounds that it is extremely difficult to provide the necessary evidence to support it, but an additional consideration was that its abolition would reduce delays and help to ensure the child received an intervention to prevent any further offending. Since the majority of children who appear before the Youth Court plead guilty, the issue of *doli incapax* rarely arises in practice, but its abolition sent out a powerful message about the government's intention to hold children as young as 10 personally responsible for their offending behaviour. This stands in stark contrast to most other European countries where children between 10 and 13 years of age are not held criminally responsible, let alone deemed to be as culpable as adults.

Parenting orders

The CDA 1998 also cemented in legislation a growing trend towards placing greater responsibility for children's offending behaviour on their parents. It introduced the parenting order, whereby a court can require an offender's parent(s) to attend regular parenting classes for a specified period or comply with other requirements to help them control their children, such as ensuring they attend school or are at home at certain hours of the day. For young offenders aged 10–15, a parenting order is now a statutory requirement if the court considers it will help to prevent further offending. This reflects to a large degree the accumulation of research evidence that shows the importance of the family and parenting in the aetiology of crime (see Chapter 8). In practice, parents almost unanimously welcome the help that comes with a parenting order, whether participating on a voluntary or a compulsory basis (Ghate and Ramella 2002), but the issue of compulsion remains controversial. The Council of Europe recommends voluntary as opposed to compulsory parenting orders on the grounds that a parent should not be held criminally liable for the offending behaviour of a third party (Council of Europe 2003).[14]

Antisocial behaviour orders

The third way in which the 1998 CDA widens criminal responsibility is through the introduction of a parallel system for tackling antisocial behaviour and introducing in particular the anti-social behaviour order (ASBO). These are civil orders[15] that prohibit an individual from engaging in specific behaviour, such as entering a particular location or associating with a particular individual. Originally intended for adults, they are now used as often for under-18s. Breach of the order constitutes a criminal offence that can attract a custodial sentence of up to two years.[16] Antisocial behaviour and in particular ASBOs are covered in more detail in Chapter 5.

B. Introducing restorative justice

Reflecting the government's concern that the interests of victims were all too often overridden by those of offenders, the CDA 1998 initiated the introduction of restorative justice – mediation, reconciliation and repar-ation – into the youth justice system (YJS). The first mechanism for achieving this was the introduction of the reparation order, which requires young offenders to make reparation to the individual victim of his/her crime where the victim desires this, or to the community that has been harmed. A year later, the government passed the Youth Justice and Criminal Evidence Act 1999, which built on this by introducing the more radical but also more controversial referral order. The vast majority of young offenders who appear before the court for the first time and plead guilty are referred to a Youth Offender Panel (YOP)[17] run by volunteers. The panel brings victims, offenders and their families together to agree a contract that addresses the victims' needs and ensures offenders face up to the consequences of their behaviour. Contracts last for up to a year. If contracts are broken, offenders are brought back to court where they may be sentenced for the original offence. Other interventions and orders can require offenders to make amends, such as final warnings (see below) and supervision orders.

YOPs, although not as well developed as in some other European countries, constitute an important move towards a more informal, less adversarial and more community-based approach to dealing with youth offending. The theme of ensuring young offenders (and their parents) take greater responsibility for their offending behaviour and make amends was reinforced by the government in its strategy on restorative justice in 2003 (Home Office 2003).

C. Deploying strategic management

Reducing costs and driving up performance through strategic management lies at the heart of the government's approach to the delivery of all public services, including youth justice. All local authorities are required by statute to provide youth justice services through multi-agency partnerships, commonly referred to as Youth Offending Teams (YOTs). The legislation also introduced a new statutory aim: to prevent offending and reoffending. It set up the Youth Justice Board (YJB) to monitor performance, to set standards and to oversee the operation of the youth justice system; and it introduced measures to reduce the time taken from arrest to sentence for persistent young offenders.

A key but also controversial tool in any system of performance management is the use of performance targets. The YJB introduced a range of targets for Youth Offending Teams that cover a wide range of inputs and outcomes. They include reducing specific crimes (e.g. burglary and street robbery), reducing reconvictions, reducing the use of secure remands, increasing victim and parental satisfaction, reducing court delays, providing a better service to the courts and improving offender assessment, supervision and support. An assessment of performance against the main targets follows below.

D. Investing in prevention and early intervention

In its report, the Audit Commission identified a number of ways in which considerable savings could be made by intervening earlier and shifting resources from processing suspects through the courts to preventing children from becoming offenders in the first place. The CDA 1998 reflected the intuitive appeal of prevention through its introduction of a statutory aim for the YJS – the prevention of offending and reoffending – and a range of measures for intervening earlier. The new reforms were accompanied by considerable additional investment in youth crime prevention programmes, such as Youth Inclusion Programmes that target the most at-risk young people in deprived, high-crime neighbourhoods and Youth Inclusion and Support Panels, which help 8–13-year-olds at risk of offending and antisocial behaviour access mainstream services. Alongside these measures, considerable resources were made available to fund major public investment programmes to enhance pre-school education, tackle social exclusion and improve the lives of those living in the most deprived neighbourhoods, with £250m specifically set aside to fund a new crime reduction strategy.[18] After a modest start, YJB expenditure on youth crime prevention today amounts to over £36m.

The CDA 1998 also replaced the old non-statutory cautioning system with a new statutory final warning scheme, which allows young offenders no more than two chances – a reprimand and a final warning – before they are automatically referred to court. YOTs were expected to provide intervention programmes for all young people receiving final warnings. Reprimands are usually used for first-time offenders who have committed relatively minor offences, whereas final warnings usually trigger the YOT to prepare a programme of interventions to address the young person's offending behaviour and prevent further offending. The introduction of the reprimand and final warning led to an increase in the number of young offenders appearing in court and a decline in the number cautioned, but it soon became evident that too many minor offences were taking up valuable court time as the number of absolute discharges rose steeply (Audit Commission 2004). The idea of 'nipping offending in the bud' by ensuring that more young offenders received interventions early on conflicted with the requirement for greater efficiency and cost-effectiveness.

E. Extending containment and control

While the previous government had already done much to increase the powers of the courts to impose custodial sentences, the legislation which accompanied the reform of the YJS continued in the same vein. The White Paper which preceded the CDA 1998 explicitly underlined the importance of punishment as an appropriate response to children who break the law (Home Office 1997). Notwithstanding the expansion of electronic monitoring[19] and the rapid spread of surveillance cameras (House of Lords Constitution Committee 2009), the legislation which followed also:

- extended remands to custody to 12–14-year-olds (CDA 1998);

- abolished the offsetting of time served in custody from time spent on remand (Powers of Criminal Courts (Sentencing) Act 2000);

- extended the maximum sentence lengths for violent and sexual offences (Powers of Criminal Courts (Sentencing) Act 2000);

- introduced powers to impose secure remands on young offenders who repeatedly committed offences on bail (Criminal Justice and Police Act 2001);

- introduced special provisions for remanding young street robbers in custody rather than on bail (Criminal Justice Act 2003); and

- brought in two new custodial sentences for young offenders deemed to be 'dangerous', one of which is for a minimum of 12 months and the other which is indeterminate (Criminal Justice Act 2003).

In 2000, the government introduced the detention and training order (DTO) for 12–17-year-olds, a custodial sentence of no less than four months and no more than 24 months. The first half of a DTO is served in custody and the second under supervision in the community. The most common length of a DTO when first introduced was also the shortest one: four months in total, two months of which was spent in custody. This reflected (despite evidence to the contrary) magistrates' enduring belief in the deterrent effect of the 'short, sharp, shock' and their attraction to a sentence which mixed custodial and community provision. As a result, the numbers of young people in custody rose by approximately 8 per cent in the first year after its introduction. In practice, the short DTO was replacing community penalties and pushing up the juvenile prison population in the process.

In response to the rising prison population the YJB recommended the replacement of the short DTO with a new, high-tariff community programme, the intensive supervision and surveillance programme (ISSP). ISSPs combine intensive supervision, electronic monitoring and rigorous enforcement and were sold to the public as tough alternatives to custody that would reduce the juvenile prison population by a third (*The Independent*, 27 January 2003). The fact that it didn't (see Figure 4.1) suggests that it tended instead to add to the already substantial range of intensive and restrictive court orders, with high breach rates further fuelling the custodial population (Audit Commission 2004).[20]

It is difficult to reconcile the ratcheting-up of penal policy with the introduction of targets to reduce the number of young offenders remanded and sentenced to custody, which in turn is difficult to reconcile with the 25 per cent increase in expenditure on custody between 2000/01 and 2005/06 (Solomon and Garside 2008). Such contradictions are arguably the product of a government intent on convincing a punitive-minded public of their tough credentials while at the same time attempting to deliver a rational, more evidence-based policy.

Before going on to assess the effectiveness of the new reforms it is necessary to briefly describe the system today and in particular some very recent changes which have begun to shift the system back towards one that more closely resembles what it replaced.

The current youth justice system

Figure 4.2 summarizes the different stages of the youth justice system and what happens to a young person at each stage.[21]

Broadly speaking, the delivery infrastructure that accompanied the introduction of the new reforms in 1998 has remained largely in place. The Youth Justice Board continues to oversee the operation of the youth justice system and manage the secure estate, while 157 multi-agency Youth

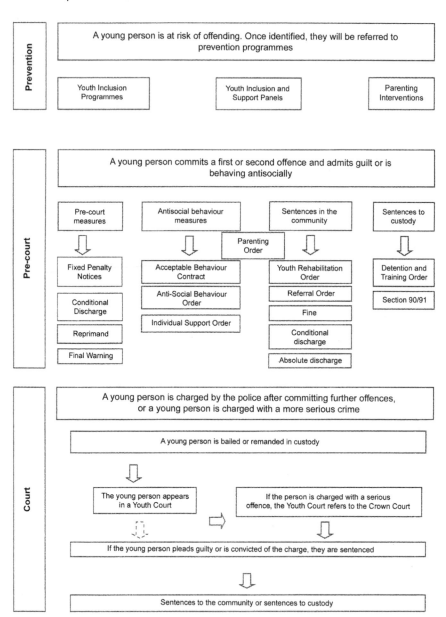

Figure 4.2 The stages of the youth justice system in England and Wales (adapted from YJB website)

Offending Teams continue to deliver services on the ground. However, in the last three years, there have been a number of important changes that have begun to alter the youth justice landscape once again.

The first of these came in 2007 when the Home Office split into two departments and responsibility for youth justice policy shifted to the Department for Children, Schools and Families (DCSF) and the newly formed Ministry of Justice (MoJ). Youth justice policy was coordinated by a joint Youth Justice Unit located in the DCSF and aligned with the wider policy agenda for children's services. Children and young people who come into contact with the youth justice system were to be helped to achieve the five outcomes set out in 'Every Child Matters'.[22] This helped to bring youth justice policy closer to policy relating to children's services, but in May 2010, following a change of government, responsibility for youth justice policy shifted again, this time to the Ministry of Justice, which is now the single lead department. The attempt to embed youth justice policy within the wider policy context of child welfare lasted less than three years.

The second came a year later with the passing of the Criminal Justice and Immigration Act 2008 (CJIA). The most significant aspect of the CJIA is the introduction of the youth conditional caution (YCC) and the youth rehabilitation order (YRO). The former, which is based on the adult conditional caution, effectively reverses the abolition of cautions by the CDA 1998 and acknowledges the potential benefits of expanding opportunities to prevent the criminalization of young offenders by diverting them from prosecution. There are resonances here of the diversion movement of the 1980s.

The latter – the YRO – is a generic community sentence with a menu of requirements from which the court can select and attach to the order. Requirements include, for example, supervision, unpaid work, curfews, residence with a specified person or at a specified place, or the provision of treatment for mental health, drug and alcohol problems. The main idea behind the YRO, which can run for up to three years, is to provide a flexible, more tailored approach to the needs and problems of individual young offenders. It was implemented in November 2009 alongside the roll-out of the YJB's Scaled Approach, which aims to reduce reoffending by tailoring the intensity of interventions to a young offender's assessed risks and needs.

On average, young people on community orders receive just over one hour a week of contact time with a member of their YOT (Audit Commission 2004). This is little time in which to build a trusting relationship with a young person and address the problems in their lives that contribute to their offending. In their length and intensity, most community orders have tended in the past to focus on time frames that fulfil sentencing objectives rather than trying to solve the problems in young people's lives. It is possible that the introduction of the YRO may help to mitigate this.

The YRO is designed to be used on more than one occasion with new requirements being selected where previous ones have not been as effective as intended or where changed circumstances warrant them. This could help to flatten the sentencing tariff (see Audit Commission 2004) and reduce the numbers being sentenced to custody. A YRO with Intensive Supervision and Surveillance or Intensive Fostering is explicitly intended as an alternative to custody and if not imposed, sentencers are required to state why, which may also contribute to reducing the custodial population. Again, there are resonances here of the 1980s diversion movement.

The third change came with the publication in 2008 of the Youth Crime Action Plan (YCAP). It is based on a triple-track approach to youth crime: 'enforcement and punishment where behaviour is unacceptable, non-negotiable support and challenge where it is most needed, and better and earlier prevention' (HM Government 2008b). It announced new funding for prevention and post-sentence interventions, including resettlement, greater support for young victims, a new target to reduce the number of first-time entrants and the piloting of a triage system for diverting young offenders from prosecution. The latter consists of placing a YOT worker in police stations to provide early advice to the police and the CPS as to whether the young person is known to the YOT or children's services and whether they could be more suitably dealt with through a restorative or preventative intervention.

Countersigned by not two but three government departments – the Home Office, the Department for Children Schools and Families and the Ministry of Justice – the YCAP reflects the different approaches to children and young people who get into trouble by the three departments. The language is often punitive – the word 'punish' (or derivatives thereof) is used ten times and 'enforcement' 15 times, whereas the term 'welfare' appears just once – while many of the proposals reflect in substance the best interests of the child. The YCAP exemplifies the government's ambiguity towards children and young people who offend and in particular whether they should be considered offenders first and children second or the other way around.

But it is not just a matter of language. One of the main criticisms of the YJB's Scaled Approach is that the most vulnerable young offenders sentenced to the new YRO will be subject to the most demanding requirements; but since they are also the least able to comply with such requirements, they are most at risk of breaching the order and ending up in custody (Standing Committee for Youth Justice 2008). The Scaled Approach is still firmly driven by an assessment tool that focuses on estimating the future risk of reoffending, which at worst conflicts with the principle of proportionality in sentencing, as enshrined most recently in the 2008 CJIA.

In contrast to the political (and populist) tone of the YCAP, the fourth and most encouraging change has been the recent publication of the Sentencing Guidelines Council's overarching principles for the sentencing of young offenders (Sentencing Guidelines Council 2009). Grounded in evidence and professional expertise rather than political self-interest, these principles place the child and his/her developmental status at the heart of their guidance. They start by referring to the existing statutory requirements to:

- ensure that the sentence reflects the seriousness of the offence and in so doing considers the offender's culpability and the harm caused by the offence (CJA 2003);

- prevent offending and reoffending (CDA 1998); and

- ensure the welfare of the offender (Children and Young Persons' Act 1933).

But more significantly they contain many other clauses which, if followed, could substantially alter the sentencing of young offenders and potentially the ethos of the youth justice system.

In setting out the purposes of sentencing, the guidelines deliberately avoid some of the adult purposes of sentencing – punishment, protection of the public, deterrence – and instead emphasize the importance of treating children and young people differently from adults. They explicitly caution against the undue criminalization of children and young people and the need to consider their developing maturity, not just their chronological age. In so doing, they draw on the research evidence that shows that young people are particularly susceptible to peer pressure and that care should be taken to avoid undue stigmatization as most of them grow out of crime. The guidelines acknowledge that some interventions with young offenders can even be counter-productive and the emphasis throughout is on individually tailored sentences that promote reintegration rather than deliver retribution. However, although the Sentencing Guidelines Council state that the statutory aim to prevent offending overrides the purposes of sentencing, it does not go so far as to offer guidance on which of the new purposes should be prioritized.

Have the new reforms achieved their objectives?

The first independent assessment of the new reforms was undertaken by the Audit Commission in 2004. Its findings were mixed. On the one hand, it found that young offenders were more likely to be dealt with more quickly, receive an intervention and make amends for their wrongdoing. It also found the new arrangements for monitoring, coordinating and delivering the reforms were an improvement on those they replaced. But on the other hand the Commission was critical of the low level of public confidence in the youth justice system, the high number of minor offences that were taking up valuable court time, the (still) minimal amount of contact time young offenders on supervision orders received, the failure to meet the wider needs of some young offenders and the consistently high use of custody, especially for black and mixed race young people. Most significantly, it was equivocal about whether the reforms had actually reduced reconvictions, arguably the most important measure of the government's new policies, and argued strongly for reducing the expensive and all-too-often ineffective use of custody.

On the basis of this assessment, it made a number of recommendations, some of which have since been taken up by government. Chief among these was the need to free up more court time and resources in order to focus more effectively on the most persistent and serious offenders by ensuring minor offences were dealt with outside the court. It also recommended reducing the use of custody by improving the quality of alternatives, raising public awareness about its limitations and creating a less-steep sentencing tariff, which the new YRO may help to bring about.

A detailed analysis undertaken of how children and young people are consistently failed long before they end up in the youth justice system produced the most compelling recommendation. Using a real case study, the Commission calculated that if effective interventions were provided at the right time and in the right place throughout a young offender's childhood, huge savings could be made. They went on to recommend that mainstream agencies (as opposed to YOTs) should take much greater responsibility for preventing offending, but this is yet to be endorsed by a government that continues to fund prevention through ad hoc projects and initiatives.

When the Commission published its assessment in 2004, some of the reforms had only been in place for a relatively short period of time so that, potentially at least, their success (or otherwise) was still to emerge. It is now more than ten years since the new reforms were implemented and Table 4.1 summarizes the government's performance against the targets it has set itself.

It presents a rather mixed picture of performance since the beginning of the decade when the reforms were introduced. Early attempts to measure performance against trends in self-reported offending proved to be misguided and were abandoned in 2005. There are many influences on youth crime and it is questionable whether changes to any youth justice system can have anything other than a marginal impact on overall youth offending rates; only a small proportion of offences end up in court and only three offences out of every 100 end up in a conviction. Self-reported offending in England and Wales has remained more-or-less stable ever since it was first measured in 1993.

Perhaps unsurprisingly, the reforms have delivered efficiency improvements. So, for example, the government's pledge to halve the time from arrest to sentence for persistent young offenders has been honoured and court delays have been reduced. The main underlying principle here is not

Table 4.1 Youth justice reforms: targets and performance

Target	Progress	Comments
Reduce percentage who self-report offending over two year period.	*Not met, although self-report offending did not increase during period.*	Originally set in 2002/03, all these targets were discontinued in 2005.
Reduce convictions for vehicle crime, domestic burglary and robbery over two year period.	*All targets were easily exceeded, but convictions are a poor measure of changes in offending.*	Reduction reflects overall decline in recorded vehicle crime and burglary, a long-term trend that predates new reforms.
Reduce number of first time entrants[1] to YJS by 5% between 2005 and 2008.	*Met. If PNDs[2] included, number of FTEs fell by 5.2%, but if excluded fell by 6.6%.*	Prior to setting of target, number of FTEs had been steadily rising. YJB reported 10% fall in 2007/08,[3] but had to be revised. In 2008/09 number of FTEs fell considerably following new target set by Youth Crime Action Plan.[4]
Halve average time from arrest to sentence from 142 days to 71 days for persistent young offenders by 2002.	*Achieved with six months to spare.*	Unequivocal success in achieving manifesto pledge.
Reduce average time from arrest to sentence to 61 days – later revised to 51 days – for all young offenders by 2004.	*Revised target not met by 2003, when target dropped.*	
Reduce number remanded to custody by 15% and those sentenced to custody by 10% between 2001 and 2005. Latterly, to reduce number of secure remands to 30% of all remand decisions (or 9% including conditional bail).	*None of these targets has been met.*	Increasing use of electronic monitoring has created a steady decline in the use of secure remands, but remand population has still increased.

Table 4.1 *Continued*

Target	Progress	Comments
Reduce number sent to custody by 10% between 2002 and 2005, subsequently revised to between 2003 and 2006 and then again to between 2005 and 2008. Latterly, to reduce number of custodial sentences to 6% (and a year later 5%) of all court disposals.	*First target on numbers sent to custody was met, but the next two were not met. More recent target was met in 05/06 but subsequent years not yet met.*	Custodial population has recently begun to fall, but targets have rarely been met. 05/06 target probably met because of hike in custodial population the year before following street crime initiative. The extension of ISSPs in 2003, an alternative to custody, had little impact on the custodial population (YJB 2004), but recent fall in first time entrants may account for recent sharp drop in numbers in custody.
Reduce reoffending by 5% [5] between 2001 and 2004, revised to between 2000 and 2006 and latterly to between 2002 and 2008. A new PSA target to reduce reoffending by 10% between 2005 and 2011 was introduced in 2008.	*The early targets were not met, but some progress in the right direction was made. Performance against the most recent target looks promising.*	Early claims that the first target had been exceeded were subsequently retracted. Steady reductions in the frequency and seriousness of reoffending since 2000.
Provide suitable accommodation for those subject to community penalties or released from custody.	*Not met. Good early progress not maintained.*	Poor target. YOTs can't affect availability of accommodation and doesn't measure whether accommodation sustained.
Ensure at least 90% of young offenders supervised by YOTs are in suitable full time education, training or employment by 2004.	*Not met. Target date dropped in YJB's 2005/06 Business Plan.*	YOTs can't easily provide access to education, training and employment and target doesn't measure whether placements sustained.

90% of those in custody to receive 25 hours (30 in STCs and SCHs) of education, training and personal development activity.	*Target met for YOIs and STCs, but not SCHs.*	Success in YOIs partly offset by failure to achieve numeracy and literacy targets, in contrast to SCHs and STCs.
Ensure all substance misusers are screened, assessed and access treatment in timely manner.	*Not met, although target very demanding. Good progress made.*	No measure of quality and continuity of interventions, which are crucial for success. Also no measure of numbers entering and completing treatment.
Timely assessment of those with mental health needs.	*Targets not met, but some improvement, especially early on.*	Targets measure inputs, not outcomes such as entering and completing mental health treatment or proportion who report improvement in their mental health.

[1] First time entrants are defined as children and young people who have received a reprimand, a final warning or a court disposal.
[2] Penalty Notices for Disorder.
[3] See: Youth Justice Annual Workload Data 2007/08.
[4] See: DCSF 2009.
[5] Defined as an offence resulting in a conviction or an out-of-court disposal.

just to achieve efficiency gains, but also to help establish a better link in the young person's mind between the crime and the punishment. It is however questionable whether 71 days is any better than 142 days in establishing such a link; research in fact suggests that in practice, fast-tracking has little if any effect on offending behaviour (Crow and Stubbing 1999).

The introduction in 2005 of a target to reduce the number of first-time entrants needs some explanation. Prior to its introduction, the government was concerned to increase the number of offenders brought to justice. A Public Service Agreement (PSA) target to this effect was announced in 2002, but it led to some perverse and unintended effects. In practice, the target pushed the police towards focusing their efforts on so-called 'low-hanging fruit' – principally children and young people whose offences are typically minor in nature and who are easy to apprehend and charge. This led to extensive net-widening as children and young people were drawn into the criminal justice system: between 2002/03 and 2006/07, the number of pre-court and court disposals rose by 28 per cent (Morgan 2008).

Within two years, the YJB claimed that the number of first-time entrants had fallen by over 10 per cent. This was subsequently revised once it had been pointed out that this failed to include the steep rise in the number of penalty notices for disorder (PNDs) issued to young people – some 20,000 in 2007/08 alone (Morgan 2008). Following a recalculation, it would seem that the target has still not been met, but the very fact that such a target has been introduced illustrates again the ambiguity that lies at the heart of youth justice policy – to intervene or not to intervene, that seems now to be the question.

Performance in terms of reducing reoffending, which is arguably the most important outcome measure, is mixed.[23] While targets may have been missed, there are some encouraging signs. Between 2000 and 2007, the proportion of young offenders who reoffended within a year fell by 4 per cent once the characteristics of offenders are taken into account (Ministry of Justice 2010). Both the frequency and seriousness of reoffending improved too. However, the reoffending rate of those in custody has not changed and although those released from custody seem to be committing fewer offences, the evidence on seriousness is less promising.[24]

The introduction of YOTs seems to have had some impact, with some progress being made in identifying and responding to the multiple needs of young offenders (education, training, employment, mental health, accommodation and substance misuse). However, none of the targets has been met and performance has particularly deteriorated in the last two years. Recent data from the YJB shows furthermore that most risk of offending measures (asset scores) after a final warning, community disposal or custodial sentence remain largely unchanged and most YOTs struggle to make a significant impact on reconviction rates (YJB 2009a). One might, however, argue that since the capacity of YOTs to influence the life chances of those with whom they work is decidedly limited, they have performed quite well. It is the targets themselves which are questionable since they overestimate the capacity of YOTs to resolve the complex issues faced by vulnerable young people caught up in the youth justice system.

On the slightly brighter side, there has been a reduction in the use of secure remands as courts have increasingly kept young offenders in the community with the assistance of electronic monitoring. Secure remands (including court-ordered secure remands) have fallen by 24 per cent in the last five years while the use of electronic monitoring has more than doubled (YJB 2009a). However, the number of secure remands as a proportion of all remands (16 per cent) remains well above the target (9 per cent) (YJB 2009a) and the secure remand population has actually increased in the last five years by 5 per cent (Gibbs and Hickson 2009).

At present, one in five young people in custody is on remand awaiting trial, which equates to around 600 young people at any one time, yet three-quarters are subsequently acquitted (24 per cent) or given a community sentence (51 per cent) (Ministry of Justice 2010).[25] Children on remand typically spend a short period of time in custody (on average, just over a month), which means little can be provided in terms of education, training or other interventions to meet their needs.

Performance in relation to custodial sentences is more encouraging, but largely because of a recent relatively steep decline in the custodial population. The average population in 2007/08 was little different from in 2000/01, but since November 2008 it has declined by 15 per cent. The total population in November 2009 stood at 2,464, which is lower than at any time since 2000 (YJB custody figures).[26] The reasons for this sharp drop are not entirely clear, but are almost certainly related to:

- the recent drop in first time entrants, which followed the introduction of a target to reduce first time entrants and a change in the 'offenders brought to justice' target towards focusing only on serious offences;

- the introduction of early assessment, support and diversion from arrest at the police station by YOT workers (known as 'triage') in some 69 YOTs; and

- the expansion of pre-court summary measures such as fixed penalty notices and penalty notices for disorder as well as the piloting of the new Youth Restorative Disposal (YRD).

This assessment suggests that in terms of its own targets, the government's performance is at best mixed (albeit with some encouraging signs of improvement in the last year or so). This reflects the findings of an 'independent audit' of the youth justice reforms carried out in 2007, which assessed the government's achievements against a 45 per cent real-terms increase in spending between 1997 and 2007 (Solomon and Garside 2008).[27] Like the Audit Commission three years earlier, it commended the government for establishing locally accountable multi-agency youth offending teams that provide a more integrated approach than elsewhere in the criminal justice system, but criticized it for siphoning off resources from other agencies which could otherwise have been put to better use in supporting young people at risk and preventing future offending. It concluded that the government had overstated its claims of success, especially given the substantial real-terms increase in investment, and criticized the wisdom of investing in the machinery of youth justice as a means of addressing the problem of youth crime.

But assessing the government's reforms simply in terms of the targets it set for itself ignores a range of alternative criteria against which the new reforms could have been assessed. Have they led to a more just and humane response to offending by children and young people? Do they protect the vulnerable and avoid discrimination against minorities? Do they ensure children and young people fully understand and participate in proceedings? How well disposed are the public to the new reforms? Do they more closely align with our obligations under international law? The final part of this chapter examines how well the new youth justice system matches up to these alternative criteria.

How well do the reforms meet broader objectives?

The substance (as opposed to the rhetoric) of the new reforms was heavily influenced by the Audit Commission's assessment of the youth justice system undertaken in the mid 1990s (Audit Commission 1996). The Audit Commission aims to reduce costs and increase efficiency and effectiveness in the delivery of public services and unsurprisingly its recommendations reflected these principles – quicker proceedings, more efficient and effective administrative arrangements and better targeting of resources. What it did not do is frame its assessment and the recommendations that flowed from it within the wider context set by a different set of questions. Does the youth justice system express values of fairness and equality? Does it comply with our international obligations? Does it deliver social justice? There is certainly evidence to suggest that these wider criteria have not been met.

The new reforms have increasingly targeted *younger* children, not only through the abolition of *doli incapax*, but through lowering the age at which secure remands and custodial disposals can be applied (see above). Detention and training orders should, according to the Powers and Criminal Courts (Sentencing) Act 2000, only be used for 12–14-year-olds who have committed a serious offence and are persistent offenders. Research shows, however, that more than a third (35 per cent) of this age group who are incarcerated do not meet these criteria, with more than a fifth (22 per cent) being locked up for breach of a community order or an ASBO (Glover and Hibbert 2009).

The system has also become relatively more punitive towards girls and those from specific ethnic minority backgrounds. Between 2002 and 2008, the number of known young female offenders increased from just under 42,000 to nearly 58,000, a rise of 38 per cent (YJB 2009b), despite no evidence of any change in self-reported rates of offending (Phillips and Chamberlain 2006).[28] Girls are also being convicted at a younger age even though the average age at which girls start to commit offences has remained constant (Phillips and Chamberlain 2006) and they are increasingly likely to be remanded in custody; the numbers doubled between 2000 and 2005 (YJB 2009b). In 1990, the number of girls being sent to custody was sufficiently low (less than 100) for the government to consider abolishing secure facilities for all but those convicted of grave crimes (Home Office 1990), but by 2008 some 446 girls were sentenced to custody.

As early as 2004, the Audit Commission drew attention to the increasingly disproportionate use of high tariff community and custodial sentences for young people who are black or of mixed race (Audit Commission 2004). Three years later, the House of Commons Home Affairs Committee confirmed that young people from specific ethnic groups (African Caribbean, African, and mixed) were over-represented among those processed by the youth justice system, and in particular among those given custodial sentences (House of Commons Home Affairs Committee 2007). This, they concluded, was partly because of discrimination in policing[29] and the youth justice system, partly because features of the system work to the disadvantage of ethnic minorities, and partly because of elevated rates of offending among certain ethnic groups.[30] With evidence to show that over-representation remains even after seriousness of offending is taken into account (Feilzer and Hood 2004), the Committee concluded that there is both direct and indirect discrimination in policing and the youth justice system.[31]

The government conceded in its response to the House of Commons report that discrimination exists ('racial disparities which cannot be explained or objectively justified') and has developed a strategy to reduce it. YOTs now have to address over-representation at each stage of the YJS, from first time entrants into the system to the remanding and sentencing of young people to custody (HM Government 2008a). However, so far this appears to have had little impact. Between 2004/05 and 2007/08, the proportion of young black people remanded in custody increased from 9.0 per cent to 9.9 per cent and for mixed raced young people the proportion increased from 3.4 per cent to 5 per cent, even though the overall numbers remanded to custody fell by 33 per cent (YJB 2009a). The picture for custodial sentences is no better. For black children and young people the proportion also increased, but more worryingly the proportion of mixed race young people sentenced to custody increased by nearly 50 per cent between 2004/05 and 2007/08 (YJB 2009a).

Young defendants say that they often do not understand legal proceedings feel patronized, intimidated and isolated in the courtroom with events often only explained to them after they have left (Hazel et al. 2002). But little if anything has been done to address the criticisms of court proceedings, which were also raised by the Audit Commission in 2004. It found that young offenders and their parents were not sufficiently engaged with court processes and that magistrates lacked the specialist knowledge required to work effectively with them (Audit Commission 2004). There is no flexibility in the system to accommodate the needs of young people at different stages in their development (except that which is afforded by their chronological age), and within the framework of a lay system, magistrates are rarely able to see the same young person twice, which undermines any continuity of relationship that could otherwise be developed. Furthermore, they are not held to account for their decisions and, thus, have no incentive to adopt a problem-solving approach or take any account of the potential resource implications of their decisions.

One of the most damning criticisms of the current system is its inappropriate overuse of custodial provision for a highly vulnerable population of children and young people. Although the number of young people in custody is slightly lower now than when the new reforms were introduced in 2000, it is still much higher than it was at the beginning of the 1990s and considerably higher than in other European countries. In 1990, approximately 1,800 young people were sentenced to custody, whereas in 2008, the equivalent figure was about three times as many (see Figure 4.1). Children and young people also receive longer custodial sentences than they did in the early 1990s. In 1993, the average custodial sentence was 6.9 months rising to 11.4 months in 2008 (see Figure 4.3).

Crucially, the increase in average sentence lengths did not reflect a simple change in offence seriousness (Ministry of Justice 2008). Average custodial sentences lengthened in every offence category, including for motoring offences, which more than doubled. According to Hagell (2005), trends in penal custody do not reflect changes in the prevalence and frequency of youth crime or the outcome of custodial interventions, but rather, she suggests, shifts in political imperatives. But it is not just the numbers in custody that matter, but who ends up in custody and what happens to them when they get there.

Most young people who are sentenced to custody are highly vulnerable in one way or another. Most have experienced a catalogue of personal difficulties in childhood, such as abuse, bereavement, poverty, homeless-

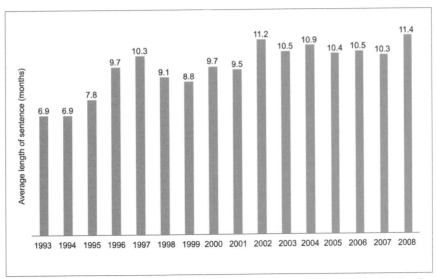

Figure 4.3 Average length of custodial sentences for 10–17-year-olds, England and Wales

ness, exclusion from school and mental health problems. Antisocial personality disorders are near universal among young men in prison (81 per cent), while emotional disorders such as anxiety or depression are very common amongst young female prisoners (68 per cent) (Lader *et al.* 2000). Around a third of young people in custody have been in care, about four out of five have been excluded from school at some point and around a third were under the age of 14 when they last went to school (Parke 2009). And during the early years of the new reforms, the number of children and young people in the secure estate assessed on entry as 'vulnerable' soared:[32] between 2000/01 and 2003/04, the number increased from 432 to 3,337 (Hansard, 7 June 2004).

Placing large numbers of vulnerable young people together in an environment that is almost entirely antithetical to their health and well-being let alone their future life chances is one of the most distressing aspects of any youth justice system. That is why all the international conventions relating to youth crime underline the importance of ensuring that custody is only used as a last resort and for the shortest possible period of time. Custody should be restricted to those who commit serious, violent crimes and pose a real threat to their community. But in England and Wales, that is not the case; more children are imprisoned for breaching a community order than for burglary (Prison Reform Trust 2008).

The large majority (85 per cent) of under-18-year-olds in the secure estate are held in young offender institutions (YOIs) run by the Prison Service. Male YOIs are large, typically holding between 100 and 400 young men, with one staff member to every 10 to 15 young people (National Audit Office 2004).[33] Bullying, self-harm and violence are not uncommon: in 2007 there were 1,007 incidents of self-harm in YOIs and 78 imprisoned children received hospital treatment for the damage done by restraint, assault or self-harm (Prison Reform Trust 2008). Around a quarter of boys and half of girls in custody are held over 50 miles away from their home (YJB 2007) and over half say they are hardly ever, or never, visited by friends and family (Parke 2009).

Research for the YJB has shown that nearly half of young people in custody of school age had literacy and numeracy levels below those of the average 11-year-old and over a quarter equivalent to those of the average 7-year-old or younger (ECOTEC 2001). Until recently, secure institutions were required to provide 25 hours a week of education or training, but this has now been cut back to just 15 hours. This is difficult to comprehend when it is known that most young offenders in custody are completely detached from education, employment and training.

Research suggests that securing good quality, stable employment is one of the most effective means of helping offenders to desist from crime. Resettlement services for young people leaving custody are, however, one of the most under-resourced areas of the youth justice system. The job prospects of all young offenders are further undermined by having a criminal record, which provides a barrier to one of the most effective means of preventing further offending. The only significant item on their CV may be their criminal record. A review of the Rehabilitation of Offenders Act 1974, carried out by the Home Office in 2002, recommended that the majority of criminal records of those young offenders who have committed minor offences should be wiped clean for the purposes of employment at age 18 (Home Office 2002). The government, however, did not have the political courage to implement the review's findings.

The single most important failure of the youth justice reforms was to reverse the steep rise in the number of young offenders being sentenced to custody during the mid 1990s and ensure compliance with the principle of *ultima ratio* (last resort). This has been compounded by placing too many young people in custody who should not be there, failing to provide the right kind of regimes for those who are there and failing to ensure they are effectively reintegrated into a law-abiding, healthy, and rewarding lifestyle on their release.

Our position at the top of the European youth custody league table is a reflection of a wider disdain for European and other international norms and standards. The UK is a signatory to the European Convention on Human Rights (ECHR), the UN Convention on the Rights of the Child (UNCRC) and other international agreements governing the administration of youth justice.[34] Yet a number of features of the youth justice system in England and Wales go against the spirit as well as the letter of these agreements.

The ECHR, which is monitored by the European Court of Human Rights, is especially important since its judgments on member states are binding. Key provisions such as the right to a fair trial (Article 6) and to liberty and security (Article 5) were invoked in the case of 10-year-olds Robert Thompson and Jon Venables, who were convicted of the murder of James Bulger.[35] The ECHR judgment was critical of the fact that their trial took place in an adult court (the Crown Court) making it difficult for the young defendants to participate effectively in the proceedings. In 1999, the Lord Chancellor, the Home Secretary and the Attorney General appointed Lord Justice Auld to undertake a review into the workings of the criminal courts in England and Wales. Two years later, Lord Justice Auld recommended that all young defendants committed to the Crown Court for trial should in future be dealt with in the Youth Court (Auld 2001). Again, the government displayed its lack of political courage and ignored his recommendation. Last year 3,600 under-18s appeared at the Crown Court for trial (Ministry of Justice 2008).

In 2008, as a member of the Council of Europe, the UK adopted the 'European Rules for juvenile offenders subject to sanctions or measures', which recognized the need for common action to develop a *'child-friendly justice system'* Council of Europe (2008). The European Rules make a number of statements about children in custody including that life in an institution should *'approximate as closely as possible the positive aspects of life in the community'*. This means that institutions should be small enough *'to enable individualized care'* and be located in places that families can easily access. Institutions should also be *'established and integrated into the social, economic and cultural environment of the community'*. Young prisoners should also *'be allowed regular periods of leave, either escorted or alone'*. Some of these provisions are sorely lacking from the typical custodial regime in England and Wales.

The high number of children in custody, the application of ASBOs to children, and the age of criminal responsibility are other elements of the youth justice system that have been singled out for rebuke by the United Nations (UN Committee on the Rights of the Child 2008). There are still others. The criteria for refusing bail to under-18s are the same as they are for adults, with no recognition of their lesser maturity and greater vulnerability, and 17-year-olds are still treated as adults for remand purposes, a strange anomaly that has never been addressed. This conflicts with the UNCRC (all under-18s should be treated as children) and the UN Standard Minimum Rules for the Administration of Juvenile Justice (detention pending trial shall be replaced by alternative measures, such as close supervision, intensive care or placement with a family or in an educational setting or home). The failure to use arrest, custody and restraint as a last resort and the publicizing of the names of convicted children, are also breaches of the UN Convention on the Rights of the Child and all have been drawn to the attention of the government by the

UN Committee on the Rights of the Child. The failure of the new reforms to comply with the government's own international obligations might be simply remedied by incorporating the UNCRC into UK law, but there are no signs that this is imminent.

As well as its failure to satisfy the norms and standards set out in international treaties and conventions, the reforms do not seem to have satisfied the public. Despite the tough rhetoric, public confidence in the criminal justice system is lowest regarding its capacity to 'deal with young people accused of crime'.[36] Only one in nine people believe that the youth justice system is doing a good job (Hough and Roberts 2004). This is mainly because people know little about it and believe that sentences are more lenient than they actually are. A 'tough' approach to youth crime is correctly assumed to be what the public wants: 71 per cent think that the youth justice system is 'too soft' on young offenders (Hough and Roberts 2004). However, most people are ill-informed about both youth crime and the youth justice system. A large proportion (42 per cent) believe that half of all crimes are committed by young people (they are not) while three-quarters (75 per cent) believe that youth crime is getting worse (it is not). Almost two-thirds (64 per cent) admitted that the media informed their views, but when people are given information about the offender's history or evidence of their remorse, they become a lot less punitive (Hough and Roberts 2004). In its assessment of the reforms, the Audit Commission (2004) recommended that the government should extend the recommendation made in its own Review of Sentencing (Home Office 2001) – to increase public knowledge about the effectiveness of sentencing and how it works – to young offenders, but this has not been heeded. Without a more informed and involved public, it is difficult to see how public opinion will not continue to be primarily influenced (and therefore easily manipulated) by the national media.

Conclusion

This chapter has traced the history of youth justice policy and practice over the last 30 years and provided an assessment of a major transformation of the youth justice system introduced in 1998 by a new government, eager to make its mark. It has shown that in its own terms, the new reforms have delivered mixed results, but that measured against wider criteria, the current system fails in many respects. Between 2000/01 and 2006/07, government funding for the YJB nearly doubled in real terms from £234m to £457m (Hansard, 26 February 2010), which must lead one to ask just how so much activity and investment could have delivered at best only marginal benefit.

The word 'justice' is not for nothing at the centre of the phase which describes the system for dealing with breaches of the criminal law. The rule of law is one of the central planks of a healthy, modern democracy and the criminal courts play an essential and exclusive role in upholding the rule of law. In doing so, it has regard to a number of important legal principles that have become enshrined in our legal system. The presumption of innocence, the right to trial by jury, the principle of proportionality and many other legal norms and safeguards are not only embedded in our own CJS, but also in international law to which we ourselves are signatories. In adopting a managerial approach to youth justice, these profound and widely accepted principles have been undermined.

The Audit Commission's 2004 review of the youth justice reforms omitted to assess a number of important issues that do not fit within their remit of auditing public services in terms of their efficiency, effectiveness and economy. In short, the Audit Commission's two reports, which together have had a profound influence on the evolution of current practice, focused predominantly on the efficacy of the system, not on whether it delivers justice. They did not examine the fairness and equity of the processes of arresting, charging, bailing, prosecuting and sentencing young offenders or the appropriateness or otherwise of the rights and safeguards available to defendants, victims and witnesses. And they did not look at the extent to which youth justice policy and practice complies with our international obligations. Perhaps if they had, their conclusions might have been very different.

At the beginning of this chapter, it was suggested that in recent times, youth justice policy (and consequently practice) has been hijacked by party politics and hence determined primarily by political self-interest. The last 20 years have been notable for all the 'noise' about youth crime, characterized by heated political debate, intense media scrutiny and public anxiety. Politicians on all sides have exploited youth crime for their own ends, and have become locked in a 'law and order' contest that neither can win. This has made the government reactive to headline-grabbing events, and vulnerable to political whim. As Lord Justice Auld noted almost a decade ago:

> ... the criminal justice system and the public's confidence in it are damaged if ... insufficiently considered legislative reforms are hurried through in seeming response to political pressures or for quick political advantage. (Auld 2001)

As a consequence, there are now a series of complex tensions and contradictions that lie at the heart of the government's strategy on youth crime. It wants to *reduce* the number of young offenders who are re-convicted, but at the same time it wants to *increase* the number of young people who are convicted (the phrase used is 'brought to justice'). It wants to *reduce* the number of first-time entrants into the youth justice system but at the same time *increase* the rate at which young offenders are processed through the courts. The government, by trying to be both populist and effective, seems unable to decide whether the youth justice system is part of the solution or part of the problem. Sounding and being tough may help to secure votes, but it does little to reduce crime. A recent report by the House of Commons Justice Committee candidly acknowledges the problem:

> Wider factors, such as the media, public opinion and political rhetoric, contribute to risk averse court, probation and parole decisions and hence play a role in unnecessary system expansion. If Ministers wish the system to become sustainable within existing resources, they must recognize the distorting effect which these pressures have on the pursuit of a rational strategy.

It goes on to say:

> We do not contest that crime and responses to it are important political issues but we believe that the extreme politicization of criminal justice policy is counterproductive, undermines rational policy-making, and conceals the consensus that does exist around the future direction for the criminal justice system. (House of Commons Justice Committee 2009)

Between 1997 and mid 2006, some 3,200 new criminal offences were created and some 60 crime-related Bills were passed (Crawford 2009). It would seem that the time is long overdue to stop governing through crime and create instead a political space for a rational, humane and effective response to the problem of youth crime to emerge.

Notes

1 Up to the 1991 Criminal Justice Act, young offenders were aged 10–16 and were called juveniles.

2 Recent research carried out in Scotland now provides robust empirical evidence for the criminogenic effects of formal proceedings (see McAra and McVie 2007).

3 ACPO, in its evidence to the Home Affairs Select Committee (1993), argued that there had actually been an increase in the number of offences committed by young people between 1980 and 1990 since the increase in the use of informal cautions hid the real number of offences.

4 This was raised as an objection to diversion from court even though diversion was endorsed by the United Nations Convention on the Rights of the Child and the United Nations Standard Minimum Rules for the Administration of Juvenile Justice (also known as the Beijing Rules).

5 The Juvenile Liaison Bureaux in Northamptonshire pioneered diversionary practice and with some considerable success (see Home Affairs Select Committee 1993).

6 The short sharp shock regime, first mooted in a speech by the Home Secretary, William Whitelaw in 1983, was subsequently evaluated by the Home Office and found to be no more effective than the regimes it replaced (Home Office 1984).

7 Criminal Justice Act 1982.

8 According to Allen (1991), some 3,400 places were made available on Intermediate Treatment schemes, an alternative to custody, between 1983 and 1987. Also, Haines and Drakeford (1998) report that community-based supervision increased from 15 per cent to 20 per cent during this period.

9 There is a very high correlation between early experiences of serious and persistent abuse (physical, emotional and sexual) and later antisocial, violent and delinquent behaviour (see for example, Boswell 1996).

10 The authors tried three different definitions of persistence, each of which produced different populations who, over time, moved in and out of the defined category according to changes in their circumstances.

11 A more recent study of persistent young offenders in Scotland reached similar conclusions and cautioned against generalizations about the nature of their offending and the kinds of remedies that might be used in response (McNeill and Batchelor 2002). The authors similarly identified the chaotic lives of persistent young offenders, but went on to point out how responses to this chaos seemed to be based on containment rather than behavioural change.

12 Large scale meta-analyses of interventions with young offenders showed that re-offending rates could be reduced, albeit with mostly moderate improvements (see for example, Lipsey 1992 and 1995; Lipsey and Wilson 1998; and McGuire and Priestly 1995).

13 A meta-analysis undertaken in the US concluded that rehabilitation had no appreciable impact on reoffending rates (see Lipton *et al.* 1975). This led to headlines in the press that 'Nothing works', which became a slogan of the times. Robert Martinson, one of the co-authors of the study, retreated from his earlier position that 'nothing worked'.

14 It has also been suggested that exerting coercion on dysfunctional, uncooperative or lone parent families may increase the risk of abuse, neglect and family breakdown and that in the event of breach (for which parents can be fined), the additional financial pressure on families that may already be struggling to make ends meet would be counter-productive, but there is little empirical evidence to support this.

15 ASBOs can now also be used in criminal proceedings in addition to any sentence the court may pass – these are commonly referred to as CrASBOs.

16 Since February 2009 there has been a legal requirement for ASBOs on young people under 17 to be reviewed after the first year.

17 Exceptions are where the court intends to impose a custodial sentence, a hospital order or an absolute discharge.

18 See: http://www.crimereduction.homeoffice.gov.uk/crsdoc.htm.

19 The use of electronic monitoring increased by 49 per cent between 2003/04 and 2007/08 (see: YJB 2009a).

20 There is some evidence to suggest that 12 (as opposed to 6) month ISSPs are more likely to act as an alternative to custody (Sutherland *et al.* 2007).

21 For further details of these different stages and the disposals available at each stage see: www.yjb.gov.uk/en-gb/yjs/TheSystem.

22 These are: be healthy, stay safe, enjoy and achieve, make a positive contribution and achieve economic well-being. For further detail, see: http://www.dcsf.gov.uk/everychildmatters.

23 The measure of reoffending – an offence resulting in conviction or an out-of-court disposal – does not include offences which are not detected.

24 The number of severe offences per 100 reoffenders has fluctuated since 2000, but since the numbers are small, they should be treated with caution (Ministry of Justice 2010).

25 In 2003, these figures were 34 per cent and 42 per cent respectively.

26 At the time of going to press, the population had fallen to 2,209 (March 2010).

27 This does not include expenditure by the police, the CPS and the courts but only includes spending by the YJB and the contributions of statutory agencies to YOTs.

28 This is based on trend data for the five year period from 2001 to 2005.

29 Research on street robbery, for example, has shown that the increased use of police search powers in London was disproportionately experienced by ethnic minority groups (FitzGerald *et al.* 2003).

30 According to self-report survey data, more African Caribbean young people (36 per cent in 2005) reported offending than white (27 per cent) and Asian (18 per cent) young people. These differences were present in the five waves of the YJB's MORI survey carried out between 2001 and 2005 (Phillips and Chamberlain 2006).

31 More recent research confirms that once offence and criminal history are taken into account, young black and mixed race young offenders are more likely than whites to be remanded in custody than white defendants, although young black defendants are more likely to be acquitted than whites. Young mixed race offenders were more likely than whites to be prosecuted and given a community sentence rather than a penalty such as a referral order or a fine (May *et al.* 2010).

32 Vulnerability was defined as including bullying, abuse, neglect, separation, loss, change of care, substance misuse, self-harm and suicide concerns.

33 This compares with two members of staff for every three young people in secure children's homes and three staff for every eight young people in secure training centres.

34 For example, the UN Standard Minimum Rules for the Administration of Juvenile Justice ('The Beijing Rules') and the UN Guidelines for the Prevention of Juvenile Delinquency (The Riyadh Guidelines).

35 The court judged that these two articles had indeed been violated because Thompson and Venables had been unable to participate effectively in the proceedings, had their tariffs set by the Home Secretary rather than by an 'independent' tribunal and were subject to an indeterminate detention.

36 In the 2007/08 British Crime Survey, 25 per cent were fairly or very confident in this aspect, compared with 44 per cent who thought it was 'effective in bringing people who commit crimes to justice' (Kershaw *et al.* 2008).

References

Allen, R. (1991) 'Out of Jail: The Reduction in the Use of Penal Custody for Male Juveniles 1981–1988', *Howard Journal*, 30:1, pp. 30–52.

Audit Commission, (1996) *Misspent Youth: Young People and Crime* (London: Audit Commission).

Audit Commission (2004) *Youth Justice 2004: A review of the reformed youth justice system* (London: Audit Commission).

Auld, L. J. (2001) *Review of the Criminal Courts of England and Wales* (London: The Stationery Office).

Aye-Maung, N. (1995) *Young People, Victimisation and the Police: British Crime Survey findings on experiences and attitudes of 12–15 year olds* (Home Office Research Study, No. 140 (London: HMSO).

Boswell, G. (1996) *Young and Dangerous: The backgrounds and careers of section 53 offenders* (Aldershot: Avebury).

Bottoms, A.E. and Dignan, J. (2004) 'Youth Justice in Great Britain', in M. Tonry, and A.N. Doob (eds) *Youth Crime and Youth Justice: Comparative and Cross-National Perspectives. Crime and Justice: A Review of Research*, vol. 31, pp. 21–184 (Chicago: University of Chicago Press).

Council of Europe (2003) *New Ways of Dealing with Juvenile Delinquency and the Role of Juvenile Justice*, Recommendation R, 2003, 20 (Strasbourg: Council of Europe).

Council of Europe (2008) 'Recommendation CM/Rec (2008) 11 of the Committee of Ministers to number states on the European Rules for juvenile offenders subject to sanctions or measures' (Strasbourg: Council of Europe).

Crawford, A. (2009) 'Governing through Anti-social Behaviour: Regulatory Challenges to Criminal Justice', *British Journal of Criminology*, 49, pp. 810–31.

Crow, I. and Stubbing, T. (1999) 'Fast-Tracking Persistent Young Offenders: To What Effect'? *Liverpool Law Review*, 21, pp. 169–96.

Department for Children, Schools and Families (2009) *Youth Crime: Young people aged 10–17 receiving their first reprimand, warning or conviction, England and Wales, 2000–01 to 2008–09* (London: Department for Children, Schools and Families).

ECOTEC (2001) *An Audit of Education Provision within the Juvenile Secure Estate* (London: Youth Justice Board).

Feilzer, M. and Hood, R. (2004) *Difference or Discrimination? Minority Ethnic People in the Youth Justice System* (London: Youth Justice Board).

FitzGerald, M., Stockdale, J.E. and Hale, C. (2003) *Young People and Street Crime: Research into Young People's Involvement in Street Crime* (London: Youth Justice Board).

Ghate, D. and Ramella, M. (2002) *Positive Parenting: The National Evaluation of the Youth Justice Board's Parenting Programme* (London: Youth Justice Board).

Gibbs, P. and Hickson, S. (2009) *Children: Innocent Until Proven Guilty? A report on the overuse of remand for children in England and Wales and how it can be addressed* (London: Prison Reform Trust), available at: http://www.prisonreform trust.org.uk/uploads/documents/Outoftroublereport(1).pdf

Glover, J. and Hibbert, P. (2009) *Locking Up or Giving Up: Why custody thresholds for teenagers aged 12, 13 and 14 need to be raised* (Ilford: Barnardo's), available at: http://www.barnardos.org.uk/locking_up_or_giving_up_august_2009.pdf

Graham, J. and Moore, C. (2006) 'Beyond Welfare Versus Justice: Juvenile Justice in England and Wales', in Junger-Tas, J. and Decker, S. H. (eds) *International Handbook of Juvenile Justice* (Dordrecht: Springer).

Hagell, A. (2005) 'The Use of Custody for Children and Young People', in T. Bateman and J. Pitts (eds) *Russell House Companion to Youth Justice* (Lyme Regis, Dorset: Russell House Publishing Ltd).

Hagell, A. and Newburn, T. (1994) *Persistent Young Offenders* (London: Policy Studies Institute).

Haines, K. and Drakeford, M. (1998) *Young People and Youth Justice* (Basingstoke: Macmillan).

Hazel, N., Hagell, A. and Brazier, L. (2002) *Young Offenders' Perceptions of their Experiences in the Criminal Justice System* (London: Policy Research Bureau).

HM Government (2008a) *Home Affairs Select Committee Inquiry: Young Black People and the Criminal Justice System*, First Annual report (London: HM Government).

HM Government (2008b) *Youth Crime Action Plan 2008* (London: HM Government), available at: http://www.homeoffice.gov.uk/documents/youth-crime-action-plan/youth-crime-action-plan-082835.pdf?view=Binary

Home Affairs Select Committee (1993) *Juvenile Offenders*, Sixth Report, HAC 441–I (London: HMSO).

Home Office (1988) *Tougher Regimes in Detention Centres: Report of an Evaluation by the Young Offender Psychology Unit* (London: HMSO).

Home Office (1988) *Punishment, Custody and the Community*, Cm 424 (London: Home Office).

Home Office (1990) *Crime, Justice and Protecting the Public* (London: The Stationery Office).

Home Office (1997) *No More Excuses: A New Approach to Tackling Youth Crime in England and Wales*, Cn 3809 (London: HMSO), available at: http://www.homeoffice.gov.uk/documents/jou-no-more-excuses?view=html

Home Office (2001) *Making Punishments Work: Report of a Review of the Sentencing Framework for England and Wales* (London: Home Office), available at: http://www.homeoffice.gov.uk/documents/halliday-report-sppu/chap-1-2-halliday2835.pdf?view=Binary

Home Office (2002) *A Review of the Rehabilitation of Offenders Act 1974* (London: Home Office), available at: http://www.homeoffice.gov.uk/documents/cons-2001-rehab-offendersa8cf.html?view=html

Home Office (2003) *Restorative Justice: The Government's Strategy* (London: Home Office), available at: http://www.crimereduction.homeoffice.gov.uk/workingoffenders/workingoffenders42.htm

Home Office (2005) *Sentencing Statistics 2003, England and Wales*, Home Office Statistical Bulletin (London: Home Office).

Hough, M. and Roberts, J. (2004) *Youth Crime and Youth Justice: Public opinion in England and Wales* (Bristol: Policy Press).

House of Commons Home Affairs Committee (2007) *Young Black People and the Criminal Justice System: Second Report of Session 2006–07* (London: The Stationery Office), available at: http://www.publications.parliament.uk/pa/cm200607/cmselect/cmhaff/181/18102.htm

House of Commons Justice Committee (2009) *Cutting Crime: the Case for Justice Reinvestment* (London: The Stationery Office), available at: http://www.publications.parliament.uk/pa/cm200910/cmselect/cmjust/94/9402.htm

House of Lords Constitution Committee (2009) *Surveillance: Citizens and the State*, available at: http://www.publications.parliament.uk/pa/ld200809/ldselect/ldconst/18/1802.htm

Kershaw, C., Nicholas, S. and Walker, A. (2008) *Crime in England and Wales 2007/08* (London: Home Office).

Lader, D., Singleton, N. and Meltzer, H. (2000) *Psychiatric Morbidity among Young Offenders in England and Wales* (London: Office for National Statistics).

Lipsey, M. W. (1992) 'Juvenile Delinquency Treatment: A Meta-Analytic Inquiry into the Variability of Effects', in D. Cook, H. Cooper, D.S. Cordray, H. Hartmann, L.V. Hedges, R.J. Light, T. A. Louis and F. Mosteller (eds) *Meta-Analysis for Explanation: A Casebook, pp 83–127* (New York: Russell Sage Foundation).

Lipsey, M.W. (1995) 'What Do We Learn from 400 Research Studies on the Effectiveness of Treatment with Juvenile Delinquents?', in J. McGuire (ed.) *What Works: Reducing Re-offending* (Thousand Oaks, CA: Sage Publications), pp. 313–45.

Lipsey, M.W. and Wilson, D.B. (1998) 'Effective Interventions with Serious Juvenile Offenders', in R.E. Loeber and D. Farrington (eds) *Serious and Violent Juvenile Offenders* (London: Sage).

Lipton, D., Martinson, R. and Wilks, J. (1975) *The Effectiveness of Correctional Treatment: a survey of treatment evaluation studies* (New York: Praeger).

May, T., Gyateng, T. and Hough, M. (2010) *Differential Treatment in the Youth Justice System*, Equality and Human Rights Commission Research report no. 50 (Manchester: Equality and Human Rights Commission).

McAra, L. and McVie, S. (2007). 'Youth Justice? The impact of system contact on patterns of desistance from offending', *European Journal of Criminology*, 4, pp. 315–45.

McGuire, J. and Priestly, P. (1995) *What Works: Reducing Re-offending: Guidelines from Research and Practice* (Chichester: Wiley).

McNeill, F. and Batchelor, S. (2002) 'Chaos, Containment and Change: Responding to Persistent Offending by Young People', *Youth Justice*, 2:1, pp. 27–43.

Ministry of Justice (2008) *Criminal Statistics: England and Wales 2007* (London: Ministry of Justice).

Ministry of Justice (2010) *Sentencing Statistics, England and Wales, 2008* (London: Ministry of Justice).

Morgan, R. (2008) *Summary Justice: Fast but Fair?* (London: Centre for Crime and Justice Studies, Kings College).

Morris, A. and Giller, H. (1987) *Understanding Juvenile Justice* (London: Croom Helm).

National Audit Office (2004) *Youth Offending: The delivery of community and custodial sentences* (London: The Stationery Office).

Newburn, T. (2002) 'Young People, Crime and Youth Justice', in M. Maguire, R. Morgan and R. Reiner (eds) *The Oxford Handbook of Criminology* (Oxford: Oxford University Press).

Parke, S. (2009) *Children and Young People in Custody 2006–2008: An analysis of the experiences of 15–18-year-olds in prison* (London: HM Inspectorate of Prisons and Youth Justice Board).

Phillips, C. and Chamberlain, V. (2006) *MORI Five Year Report: an analysis of youth justice data* (London: YJB).

Prison Reform Trust (2008) *Criminal Damage: Why we should lock up fewer children* (London: Prison Reform Trust), available at: http://www.prisonrefor-mtrust.org.uk/uploads/documents/Criminal%20Damage.pdf

Sentencing Guidelines Council (2009) *Overarching Principles – Sentencing Youths: Definitive Guideline*, available at: http://www.sentencing-guidelines.gov.uk/docs/overarching_principles_sentencing_youths.pdf

Smith, D. (2004) *The Links Between Victimisation and Offending*, Occasional paper no. 5 (Edinburgh: Edinburgh Study of Youth Transitions and Crime).

Social Exclusion Unit (2002) *Reducing Re-offending by Ex-prisoners* (London: Office of the Deputy Prime Minister), available at: http://www.cabinetoffice.gov.uk/media/cabinetoffice/social_exclusion_task_force/assets/publications_1997_to_2006/reducing_summary.pdf

Solomon, E. and Garside, R. (2008) *Ten Years of Labour's Youth Justice Reforms: an Independent Audit* (London: Centre for Crime and Justice Studies, Kings College), available at: http://www.crimeandjustice.org.uk/opus647/youthjusticeaudit.pdf

Standing Committee for Youth Justice (2008) *Response to Youth Crime Action Plan*, available at: http://www.scyj.org.uk/files/SCYJ_YCAP_RESPONSE_FINAL.pdf

Sutherland, A., Taylor, E., Gray, E., Merrington, S. and Robertsm C. (2007) *Twelve-Month ISSP: Evaluation and Research Findings* (London: Youth Justice Board).

UN Committee on the Rights of the Child (2008) *Concluding Observations: United Kingdom of Great Britain and Northern Ireland*, Forty-ninth session (Geneva: UN Committee on the Rights of the Child).

Weitekamp, E., Kerner, H.J., Schubert, A. and Schindler, V. (1996) 'Multiple and Habitual Offending among Young Males: Criminology and criminal policy lessons from re-analysis of the Philadelphia Birth Cohort Studies', *International Annals of Criminology* 12, pp. 9–52.

Youth Justice Board (2007) *Youth Justice Annual Statistics 2005/06* (London: Youth Justice Board), available at: http://www.yjb.gov.uk/Publications/Resources/Downloads/Youth%20Justice%20Annual%20Statistics%202005-06.pdf

Youth Justice Board (2009a) *Annual Statistics and Annual Workload Data, 2003 to 2007/08* (London: Youth Justice Board). http://www.yjb.gov.uk/publications/Resources/Downloads/Youth%20Justice%20Annual%20Workload%20Data%20200708.pdf

Youth Justice Board (2009b) *Girls and Offending – Patterns, Perceptions and Interventions* (London: Youth Justice Board), available at: http://www.yjb.gov.uk/Publications/Resources/Downloads/Girls_offending_fullreport.pdf

Chapter 5

Responding to antisocial behaviour

Larissa Pople

In October 2007, after years of alleged harassment by a group of young people, Fiona Pilkington set light to the car that contained herself and her disabled daughter. An inquest into their deaths heard that the police had been called 33 times over a period of seven years about the harassment, which reportedly involved a group of young people hanging around outside her home in Leicestershire, hurling stones and other objects at the house, and taunting the family. We have no way of knowing what drove Fiona Pilkington to take the lives of herself and her daughter,[1] but if this repeated harassment played a role (which is plausible) then it would justify the suggestion made by journalists and politicians that antisocial behaviour was to blame for their deaths, at least in part.

Part of the problem with the term 'antisocial behaviour' is its breadth, including, as it does, any behaviour causing 'harassment, alarm or distress'. Using this definition, the repeated harassment of the Pilkington family would certainly qualify as antisocial behaviour. On the other hand, most would agree that the reported behaviour was more serious than antisocial behaviour and could have been dealt with by the criminal law. According to public surveys and qualitative research, a more typical experience of antisocial behaviour is likely to comprise damage caused to property and the environment, or the boisterous and rowdy behaviour of young people congregating in groups (Walker *et al.* 2009; Millie *et al.* 2005). Antisocial behaviour of this kind is reported to be a problem for a significant minority of the population.

Antisocial behaviour has become a major political priority over the last 15 years and the focus of a panoply of new laws and policies. Politicians on all sides have tried to outdo each other in their 'tough' stance on antisocial behaviour. The sentiments that they are trading on are ones of anger and indignation at a perceived moral decline that has caused everyday nuisance behaviour, amongst young people in particular, to go unchecked. Given the strength of public feeling on this issue, it is perhaps no surprise that policies of enforcing standards of behaviour have been popular. Yet antisocial behaviour was almost unheard of in a public enforcement context before the 1990s, and nuisance behaviour is clearly not a phenomenon that is peculiar to the last two decades. Which begs the question: to what extent is it a problem created by politicians?

Background and concepts

It is important to distinguish between two distinct concepts of antisocial behaviour: the psychological usage that has occupied researchers since the 1960s, and the more recent political and legal usage that is referred to in the introduction. These two concepts are only loosely related, although the political discourse borrows from the psychological research. In the 1960s, psychologists identified a trait in some children and adults that was characterized by antisocial acts, a disregard for others and a 'gross, repetitive failure to conform to societal norms in many areas of life' (Robins 1966). Psychologists were not primarily concerned with how such behaviour was sanctioned by society and whether or not it was against the law. They were, however, interested in its stability over the life-course, and whether its presence in childhood predicted problems later on in life (see Chapter 6, this volume). In children, a 'repetitive and persistent pattern' of antisocial behaviour will usually result in a diagnosis of conduct disorder. Qualifying behaviours include aggression and cruelty to people and animals, destruction of property, deceitfulness, theft, and violation of rules, for example, by staying out at night, running away and playing truant (American Psychiatric Association 1994). Some of these activities are lawbreaking, but this is only of tangential importance to the diagnosis.

Politicians, on the other hand, were interested in a 'catch-all' term that could be used to sanction incivilities and offensive behaviour that might not reach the criminal threshold, and thus could not be dealt with by the criminal law. In the 1990s the term began to be used in relation to public order enforcement, and then with increasing vigour. One commentator recently observed that antisocial behaviour has become such a focus of media debate in current times that it is strange to discover that the term was rarely mentioned before the 1990s. In just one month in 2006 (January), over 1,500 articles in British newspapers were written on the subject, equating to around 17,000 articles in one year (Waiton 2007).

It was a Conservative government that first referred to antisocial behaviour in legislation (in the Housing Act 1996) but the Labour Party made sure it was firmly planted in the public consciousness. Tackling antisocial behaviour became a central plank of their campaign to be 'tough on crime and the causes of crime', and was a priority for action when they came to power in 1997 (Labour Party Manifesto 1997). The focus on antisocial behaviour arose from an acknowledgement that for many people, particularly those living in poor neighbourhoods, everyday experiences of bad behaviour and minor forms of criminality had a major impact on fear of crime. Interestingly, these low-level issues seemed to be disproportionately important in shaping people's sense of insecurity in comparison with more serious crime or crime rates in general. Innes and Fielding (2002) argued that this was because visible low-level crime and disorder acted as 'warning signals' about potential threats to people's safety.[2] During the 1990s, the British Crime Survey showed a rise in the proportion of people that considered a range of low-level issues to be a problem in their area. (This is discussed in more detail later.)

Coupled with this appreciation of the importance of low-level crime and disorder to the public was the sense that the police were over-stretched and unable to deal with such problems effectively. Antisocial behaviour was unlikely to be a priority for police forces when perform-ance targets provided incentives to focus on crime control (Hough 2004). As a result, there was an 'enforcement deficit' that needed to be addressed (see Squires and Stephen 2005). Furthermore, whilst the criminal justice system had always been plagued by the knowledge that only a small minority of known offences are 'brought to justice', antisocial behaviour had the added problem of including within its ambit acts that are not criminal offences, and indeed singly are not suitable for criminalization. It is in aggregate and through repetition that they derive their harmful impact. A new approach could bring greater powers to bear on those guilty of a course of conduct with a cumulative effect on the quality of life of individuals and communities.

Definitions

In the Crime and Disorder Act 1998, acting in an 'antisocial manner' was defined as 'in a manner that caused or was likely to cause harassment, alarm or distress to one or more persons not of the same household as himself'. This broad description, which focuses on the consequences of antisocial behaviour rather than on its specific form, is the most widely used definition. A central problem (or a great advantage depending on one's standpoint) since the early days of antisocial behaviour legislation, then, has been one of precision.

The government has always acknowledged that antisocial behaviour can take many forms, and indeed the examples given vary from one place to another. Thus, according to the Home Office website, antisocial behaviour can include 'rowdy, noisy and yobbish behaviour'; 'vandalism, graffiti and fly-posting'; 'dealing or buying drugs on the street'; 'fly-tipping'; 'aggressive begging'; 'street drinking'; and 'setting off fireworks late at night'.[3] Meanwhile the government's dedicated antisocial behaviour website (previously the Respect website) adds to this list 'nuisance neighbours'; 'intimidating groups taking over public spaces'; 'abandoned cars'; and 'the reckless driving of mini-motorbikes',[4] while the Respect Action Plan (2006) and the Youth Justice Board's Guidance on antisocial behaviour (2005) contribute a whole host of other activities, including 'playing loud music in the early hours'; 'offensive and threatening remarks'; 'smoking and drinking alcohol under-age'; 'prostitution'; and 'assault'.

This assortment of examples shows that behaviours that are deemed antisocial range from those that are simply a nuisance, through those that damage property to those that are harmful to others (Whitehead *et al.* 2003). Thus, some activities are non-criminal (e.g. rowdy, noisy and yobbish behaviour) while others involve relatively serious crimes for which the criminal law is already available (e.g. dealing drugs).

These descriptions are careful not to label antisocial behaviour a 'youth' problem, but the implication is clear, and there is no doubt that for many adults antisocial behaviour is synonymous with youth. Most problematic from the perspective of children's rights is the inclusion of activities such as 'intimidating groups taking over public spaces' and 'rowdy, noisy and yobbish behaviour', which people commonly associate with young people. In the British Crime Survey the association is made unequivocally clear as 'teenagers hanging around' constitutes a measure of antisocial behaviour. Whether young people 'hanging around', 'being rowdy or noisy', or 'taking over public space' is experienced as a nuisance, however, depends very much on the attitudes of the individual. This links with material contained in Chapter 2, which shows that in many ways, and to a greater extent than in the past, young people are a distinct and stigmatized group.

In an attempt to capture the whole range of activities that might fall under the umbrella of 'antisocial behaviour', the Home Office Research Development and Statistics Directorate (RDS) drew up a typology of behaviours 'that are widely accepted to be antisocial' (see Table 5.1).

This typology confirms that the definition of antisocial behaviour is wide-ranging and open to interpretation. Factors such as context, location, levels of community tolerance and expectations for quality of life will make a difference to what people consider antisocial (Nixon *et al.* 2003). Crucially, 'what may be considered antisocial behaviour to one person can be seen as acceptable behaviour to another' (Home Office 2004). Indeed, local areas are encouraged to come up with a working definition of antisocial behaviour themselves based on their local experiences and circumstances. The problem with this approach (as we shall see later) is that it can lead to a 'postcode lottery' in the types of behaviour that are

Table 5.1 Home Office typology of antisocial behaviour

Misuse of public space	Disregard for community/ personal well-being	Acts directed at people	Environmental damage
Drug/substance misuse and dealing: • Taking drugs • Sniffing volatile substances • Discarding needles/drug paraphernalia • Crack houses • Presence of dealers or users *Street drinking* *Begging* *Prostitution:* • Soliciting • Cards in phone boxes • Discarded condoms	*Noise:* • Noisy neighbours • Noisy cars/motorbikes • Loud music • Alarms (persistent ringing/ malfunction) • Noise from pubs/clubs • Noise from business/ industry *Rowdy behaviour:* • Shouting and swearing • Fighting • Drunken behaviour • Hooliganism/loutish behaviour	*Intimidation/harassment:* • Groups or individuals making threats • Verbal abuse • Bullying • Following people • Pestering people • Voyeurism • Sending nasty/offensive letters • Obscene/nuisance phone calls • Menacing gestures *Can be on the grounds of:* • Race • Sexual orientation • Gender • Religion • Disability • Age	*Criminal damage/ vandalism:* • Graffiti • Damage to bus shelters • Damage to phone kiosks • Damage to street furniture • Damage to buildings • Damage to trees/plants/ hedges *Litter/rubbish:* • Dropping litter • Dumping rubbish • Fly-tipping • Fly-posting

Table 5.1 *Continued*

Misuse of public space	Disregard for community/personal well-being	Acts directed at people	Environmental damage
Kerb crawling: • Loitering • Pestering residents	*Hoax calls:* • False calls to emergency services		
Sexual acts: • Inappropriate sexual conduct • Indecent exposure	*Animal-related problems:* • Uncontrolled animals		
Abandoned cars **Vehicle-related nuisance and inappropriate vehicle use:** • Inconvenient/illegal parking • Car repairs on the street/in gardens • Setting vehicles alight • Joyriding • Racing cars • Off-road motorcycling • Cycling/skateboarding in pedestrian areas/footpaths	*Nuisance behaviour:* • Urinating in public • Setting fires (not directed at specific persons or property) • Inappropriate use of fireworks • Throwing missiles • Climbing on buildings • Impeding access to communal areas • Games in restricted/inappropriate areas • Misuse of air guns • Letting down tyres		

Source: Home Office (2004) *Defining and Measuring Anti-Social Behaviour*

targeted and the responses that are used. There are clear implications for fairness if one area cracks down on behaviours that another tolerates, and enforcement measures are applied according to local preferences.

Extent and time trends

There is an implication in official pronouncements on the subject that anyone of good sense can recognize antisocial behaviour (Millie *et al.* 2005). But clearly defining the nature of the 'problem' is not just an academic exercise. Without so doing, its true scale cannot be known, changes over time cannot be discerned, and assessing the effectiveness of different interventions is fraught with difficulty.

As we have seen, individual attitudes are key to the concept of antisocial behaviour. So it is fitting, and perhaps inevitable, that the main indicator of changes over time relates to people's perceptions. The British Crime Survey has been measuring perceptions of antisocial behaviour since 1992 and has found that antisocial behaviour is a problem for a significant minority of people. Between 1992 and 2000[5] the proportion of people perceiving a fairly or very big problem in their area rose, with especially large increases for 'teenagers hanging around' and 'people using or dealing drugs'. Since then, however, there has been little significant change for all but one of the indicators, and decreasing concern about 'abandoned and burnt-out cars' (Walker *et al.* 2009).

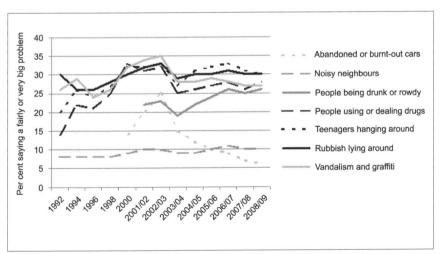

Figure 5.1 Public perceptions of various indicators of antisocial behaviour being a problem in their area, England and Wales

Source: Walker *et al.* (2009) *Crime in England and Wales 2008/09*, table 5.10.

149

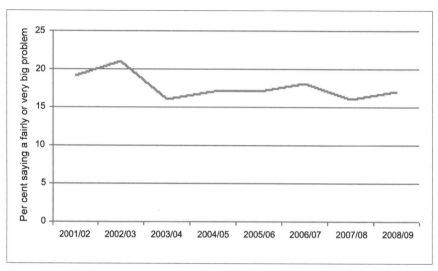

Figure 5.2   Public perceptions of antisocial behaviour as a problem in their area: composite measure from 7 items

Source: Walker *et al.* (2009) *Crime in England and Wales 2008/09*, table 5.10.

When all seven indicators are combined into one composite measure, the British Crime Survey shows an overall marginal decrease in the proportion of people perceiving anti-social behaviour to be a fairly or very big problem in their area, from 19 per cent in 2001/2 to 17 per cent in 2008/9.

There is considerable variation across socio-economic groups in respect of this composite measure of antisocial behaviour. A much larger proportion of respondents living in the most deprived areas (31 per cent) and in social housing (29 per cent) perceived antisocial behaviour to be a fairly or very big problem in their area in comparison with those living in the least deprived areas (7 per cent) and their own homes (13 per cent). In addition, according to a new Output Area Classification devised by the Office for National Statistics, respondents living in an area classified as 'multicultural' were more likely to perceive antisocial behaviour as a problem in their area (29 per cent) than those living in other areas, notably in the 'countryside' (5 per cent) or 'prospering suburbs' (7 per cent).[6] Perceptions of antisocial behaviour also varied with age and experience of crime. Antisocial behaviour was more problematic for younger age groups (24 per cent of 16 to 24-year-olds compared with 4 per cent of people aged 75 years and over) and those that had been a victim in the previous year (29 per cent of victims compared with 13 per cent of non-victims) (Walker *et al.* 2009).

Despite not being a lawbreaking activity in itself, it is interesting to note that 'teenagers hanging around' has been the item eliciting most concern since 2004, with a large rise between 1992 and 2002/3 in the proportion perceiving this to be a fairly or very big problem in their area (from 20 per cent to 33 per cent). In 2008/9 the British Crime Survey introduced further questions to explore the issue in more detail. Of the 30 per cent of people that perceived 'teenagers hanging around' to be a problem in their area, the large majority (81 per cent) said that the young people were behaving in an antisocial manner and identified specific acts of antisocial behaviour associated with them (Moon *et al.* 2009). This provides a clearer picture of what people found objectionable. The behaviours cited are set out in the table below.

Audit Commission (2009) research with young people confirms that they were also concerned about, and were victims of, antisocial behaviour. However, in contrast to adults, young people saw 'hanging around' as normal behaviour. Eighty per cent said that they 'hang around' themselves, and only 2 per cent considered this to be antisocial behaviour, seeing it instead as an opportunity to socialize with friends and enjoy some freedom away from the supervision of adults. Young people also acknowledged that they derive a sense of safety from being in a group. This finding is supported by research with young people living in four

Table 5.2 Perceived behaviours of teenagers 'hanging around', British Crime Survey: England and Wales 2008/9

Observed behaviour	% of respondents who had seen 'teenagers hanging around'
Swearing/using bad language	80
Being loud, rowdy or noisy	78
Drinking alcohol	77
Just being a general nuisance	72
Littering (e.g. spitting gum on the street)	63
Blocking the pavement	52
Being abusive/harassing or insulting people	50
Fighting with each other	38
Taking drugs	37
Intimidating or threatening people	36
Blocking the entrance to shops	34
Damaging property or cars	33
Writing graffiti	27
Carrying knives	12
Physically assaulting people	11
Mugging or robbing people	10
Other behaviours	2
Not doing anything in particular	<1%

Source: Moon *et al.* (2009) *Perceptions of crime and antisocial behaviour: Findings from the 2008/09 British Crime Survey.*

disadvantaged areas of Glasgow, who saw their friendships as having a positive role in providing 'safety in numbers', something that was overlooked by the parents (Seaman *et al.* 2006).

The 2008/9 British Crime Survey also gave special attention to the issue of drugs, and people being drunk or rowdy. An interesting issue in relation to the former is that of all the individual strands of antisocial behaviour, perceptions of drug use or dealing were least commonly formed through personal experience. Thus of the 28 per cent who perceived a problem with 'drug use or dealing', only two-thirds (61 per cent) had actually seen drug use in their area, while only 54 per cent had seen drug dealing. A much larger majority (86 per cent) of those perceiving a problem with 'people being drunk and rowdy' had borne witness to this. The main problems associated with drunken and rowdy behaviour were 'noise from people in the streets', 'cans and bottle left on the streets or thrown into gardens', 'young people drinking', and 'people being abusive' (Moon *et al.* 2009).

The British Crime Survey provides a useful gauge of what people are most concerned about in relation to antisocial behaviour. However, since there is no objective measure of 'actual' antisocial behaviour with which to make a comparison, it is difficult to discern the accuracy of their concerns. As Crawford and Lister (2007) have pointed out, 'there is no simple correspondence between perceptions of risk and actual levels of victimization'. No doubt with this in mind, the Home Office Anti-Social Behaviour Unit carried out its own 'snapshot' of recorded incidents of antisocial behaviour by arranging for more than 1,500 public service and local government organizations that receive first-hand reports of antisocial behaviour to count all the incidents reported to them during one day (10 September 2003). The one-day count took place in every Crime and Disorder Reduction Partnership area in England and every Community Safety Partnership area in Wales. In total 66,000 reports of antisocial behaviour were made to participating organizations, at an estimated cost of £13.5 million. Multiplying this figure by 250 working days produced an estimate for the annual cost of responding to antisocial behaviour of £3.4 billion (Home Office 2003).

The one-day count faced a number of methodological shortcomings in that it undoubtedly suffered from underreporting in some areas and double counting in others. Furthermore, since it has never been repeated there is no way of knowing whether this particular methodology produces changes over time. Nonetheless it gives an interesting insight into the kinds of issues that are being reported to public services on a daily basis, and some indication of the scale of the problem (see Table 5.3).

Another indication can be drawn from analysis of antisocial behaviour interventions. The National Audit Office (NAO) reviewed the case files of 893 people who received antisocial behaviour interventions in six areas of England and discovered that the main behaviour against which action

Table 5.3 Results of the one-day count of antisocial behaviour: England and Wales 2003

	Reports	Estimated cost to agencies per day	Estimated cost to agencies per year
Litter	10,686	£1.87m	£466m
Criminal damage/vandalism	7,855	£2.67m	£667m
Vehicle-related nuisance and inappropriate vehicle use	7,782	£1.36m	£340m
Nuisance behaviour	7,660	£1.42m	£355m
Intimidation and harassment	5,415	£1.98m	£496m
Noise	5,374	£994,000	£249m
Rowdy behaviour	5,339	£995,000	£249m
Abandoned vehicles	4,994	£360,000	£90m
Street drinking and begging	3,239	£504,000	£126m
Drug/substance misuse and drug dealing	2,920	£527,000	£132m
Animal-related problems	2,546	£458,000	£114m
Hoax calls	1,286	£198,000	£49m
Prostitution, kerb crawling and other sexual acts	1,011	£167,000	£42m
Total	66,107	£13.5m	£3.4bn

Source: Home Office (2003) *The One-day Count of Anti-Social Behaviour*

was taken was 'nuisance behaviour'. The next most common behaviours resulting in a response were 'intimidation/harassment'; 'criminal damage/vandalism'; 'street drinking'; 'rowdy behaviour'; and 'noise'. The study showed that individuals of all ages received an official response for their involvement in antisocial behaviour (see Table 5.4). However, the largest group was young men aged under 18, who accounted for more than a third (34.9 per cent) of the sample (National Audit Office 2006).

Responses to antisocial behaviour

There has been a great deal of political activity to deal with antisocial behaviour since 1998, and a raft of legislation and policy developments. The Labour government's high-profile campaign reached its apogee in 2006 with the publication of the Respect Action Plan.

> ... there are still intractable problems with the behaviour of some individuals and families, behaviour which can make life a misery for others, particularly in the most disadvantaged communities. What

Table 5.4 Age and gender of 893 people receiving an antisocial behaviour intervention: England 2006

	Global percentages	
Age	*Male*	*Female*
18 or under	34.9	9.6
19–24	20.0	4.7
25 and over	21.9	8.8
Total	76.8	23.2

Source: National Audit Office (2006) *The Home Office: Tackling Anti-social Behaviour*

lies at the heart of this behaviour is a lack of respect for values that almost everyone in this country shares – consideration for others, a recognition that we all have responsibilities as well as rights, civility and good manners. (from Tony Blair's preface to the *Respect Action Plan*, January 2006)

It is hard to know to what extent the data on trends in antisocial behaviour discussed in the last section have been affected by the government's numerous and vocal attempts to deal with the problem. The activity in this area may have lessened people's fears by reassuring them that 'something is being done'; or it may have led to a heightened awareness of the problem. As cautioned by Michael Tonry (2004):

By making antisocial behaviour into a major social policy problem, and by giving it sustained high-visibility attention, Labour has made a small problem larger, thereby making people more aware of it and less satisfied with their lives and their government. (p. 57)

The next sections look at the main antisocial behaviour interventions targeting young people (set out in Table 5.5) and, where relevant, what is known about their effectiveness. As a general point, however, it is worth highlighting that little systematic evidence is available regarding the impact of antisocial behaviour-related interventions on different groups in the population (as noted, for example, in Isal 2006; National Audit Office 2006; Youth Justice Board 2006; The House of Commons Committee of Public Accounts 2007).

Antisocial Behaviour Orders (ASBOs)

The year after Labour came to power, the Crime and Disorder Act came into effect. The 1998 Act created a statutory requirement for local

Table 5.5 Main antisocial behaviour interventions of relevance to young people, England and Wales

Intervention	Legislative basis
1998	
Anti-Social Behaviour Orders (ASBOs)	Introduced by Crime and Disorder Act 1998
Parenting Orders	Introduced by the Crime and Disorder Act 1998
2003	
Acceptable Behaviour Contracts (ABC)	A voluntary agreement, introduced in 2003
Individual Support Orders	Criminal Justice Act 2003 (as amended by the Criminal Justice and Immigration Act 2008)
Dispersal Orders	Introduced by the Anti-Social Behaviour Act 2003
Parenting Contracts	A voluntary agreement, introduced by the Anti-Social Behaviour Act 2003
Penalty Notices for Disorder	Introduced by the Criminal Justice and Police Act 2001 for adults, and for 16 and 17-year olds by the 2003 Anti-Social Behaviour Act
2006	
Family Intervention Programmes	Introduced by the Respect Action Plan in 2006

authorities, police and other responsible authorities in the community to formulate a strategy for addressing crime and antisocial behaviour at a local level. It also introduced weighty civil enforcement measures to tackle antisocial behaviour, namely ASBOs and Parenting Orders.

The 1998 Act made it possible for a relevant authority to apply for an ASBO when an individual over the age of 10 had acted in an 'antisocial manner' and where such an order was necessary to protect the public from further such behaviour. This 'stand-alone' ASBO, which has been available since 1999, was complemented in 2002 by three further variants set out in the Police Reform Act:

- Orders made on conviction in criminal proceedings, also known as 'CrASBOs'. These are issued as a supplement to any sentence the court may impose, and now account for the majority of ASBOs issued.

- Interim orders that can be imposed before a full court hearing, and which can carry the same prohibitions and breach penalties as a full order.

- Orders made in county court proceedings. These are rarely used with young people.

ASBOs run for a minimum of two years and can last indefinitely. However, since February 2009 there has been a legal requirement for orders issued to young people under 17 to be reviewed after the first year (Criminal Justice and Immigration Act 2008).

Public support for the use of ASBOs is high at 82 per cent. In a survey by Ipsos MORI (2005) 59 per cent of adults agreed that ASBOs were a good way of dealing with teenagers responsible for antisocial behaviour, while 53 per cent saw them as an effective means of demonstrating that something is being done. Yet a similar proportion (55 per cent) admitted that they knew just a little or nothing about them, while a further 8 per cent had never heard of them.

ASBO usage reached its peak in 2005 when 4,122 were issued overall. This figure has dropped by almost half since then to 2,299 in 2007. Young people aged under 18 were not originally intended to be the target of ASBOs, yet between June 2000 and December 2007 they were the recipients of 6,028 orders and 41 per cent of all orders made. Enthusiasm for the use of ASBOs with young people seems to have waned a little more recently. In 2001 and 2002, more than half of all orders were issued to under-18s (56 per cent and 60 per cent respectively where the age is known), but since 2004 this figure has hovered around 39–40 per cent.

One issue that has provoked a great deal of discussion is the wide geographical variation in usage. For example, between 2000 and 2007,

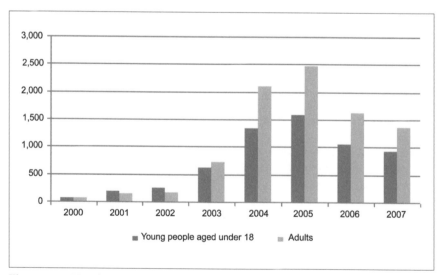

Figure 5.3 Number of ASBOs issued to under-18s and adults, England and Wales

Source: OCJR Evidence and Analysis Unit, see www.crimereduction.homeoffice.gov.uk

Table 5.6 ASBO usage in Manchester, London and Dyfed Powys

CJS area	Estimated population (ONS 2007)	No of ASBOs issued to under 18s: 2000–2007	No of stand-alone ASBOs issued per 10,000 population: 1999 to 2007	No of CrASBOs issued per 10,000 population: 2003 to 2007
Greater Manchester	2,562,200	819	2.88	3.53
Greater London	7,556,600	568	0.91	1.48
Dyfed Powys	507,200	11	0.14*	0.87

*Incomplete data.
Note: Only the third column (the number of ASBOs issued between 2000 and 2007) relates to young people aged under 18; the rates per population are for all age groups.
Source: CDRP/CSP survey, see www.asbhomeoffice.gov.uk.

Greater Manchester issued 819 ASBOs to under-18s, while Dyfed Powys issued only 11. Even when the size of the population is taken into account, the contrast between these two areas is stark, as is shown in Table 5.6. It is highly unlikely that these figures reflect differences in the underlying behaviour of young people to the same magnitude.

Although originally planned as a measure of last resort, Home Office guidance in 1999 stated that an ASBO application could generally be made:

> either when other methods to prevent further misbehaviour have failed or when such methods have been considered but have been deemed either to be inappropriate in the circumstances or to be less effective than an order. (Home Office 1999)

Yet, in a study for the Youth Justice Board, Solanki and colleagues (2006) found that most magistrates and District Judges did not appear to systematically address whether an order was necessary. Many appeared to assume that ASBO proceedings were being used after other remedies had failed.

ASBOs involve a two-step process: an initial civil stage, in which the order is issued and its prohibitions set out, and a criminal stage to prosecute breaches of those prohibitions if and when they occur. This 'hybrid' nature and blurring of the boundaries between the civil and criminal law has created a number of thorny issues for jurisprudence, and attracted criticism from various quarters (see for example, Gardner *et al.* 1998; Gask 2004; Simester and von Hirsch 2006; and Ashworth, forthcoming).

The main criticism of the two-step process is that the civil stage lacks the procedural safeguards that are contained in the criminal law (such as stringent evidential requirements), yet the criminal stage allows for substantial penalties to be imposed for breach of the order and, further-more, the triggering conduct itself may be neither criminal nor harmful to others. Indeed, the purpose of the legal structure of the ASBO is to avoid the protections bestowed by the criminal law and the fact that these make criminal prosecution difficult. For example, in the civil process of applying for an ASBO, hearsay evidence is admissible, including that given by 'professional' witnesses (for example, a housing officer's account of what tenants too frightened to give evidence themselves have alleged). Thus, the civil courts can be used to 'get round the due process protections of the criminal law' (Ashworth *et al.* 1998).

A House of Lords judgement in 2002 (see *R on behalf of McCann* v *Crown Court at Manchester*)[7] dismissed this argument, maintaining that the two stages in the ASBO are distinct, and each complies with the necessary procedural safeguards. The judgement did concede, however, that the standard of proof in the civil proceedings should be equivalent to that required by the criminal law i.e. beyond reasonable doubt. Ashworth (forthcoming) has observed that this concession undermines the assertion that the two stages are separate by giving some acknowledgement that the reverse is true. Thus he argues that all of the safeguards of the criminal law, including the right to confront witnesses, should be available during the initial civil proceedings.

In its most recent report to the UK, the UN Committee on the Rights of the Child questioned whether ASBOs are in the best interests of children or simply facilitate their entry into the criminal justice system. The Committee also criticized the public 'naming and shaming' of children subject to ASBOs (made possible by the Antisocial Behaviour Act 2003, which lifted reporting restrictions). Child recipients of an ASBO could have (and in practice have had) their identity and the terms of their order widely publicized in the press. This is in contravention of the rights to privacy contained in the UN Convention of the Rights of the Child, and 'almost certainly' violates the European Convention on Human Rights (Gil-Robles 2005). For these reasons and others, the UN Committee called for an independent review of ASBOs, with a view to abolishing their application to children (United Nations Committee on the Rights of the Child 2008).

Criticism has also been levelled at ASBOs for allowing a substantial delegation of power to the civil courts. The court can prohibit the defendant from doing 'anything described in the order' unless that person can prove that there was 'reasonable' excuse for doing it. Thus, prohib-itions can, and do, go well beyond the scope of the antisocial behaviour that elicited them. Although the prohibitions should be 'necessary to protect other people from antisocial acts', this principle has not always been upheld (see Ramsay 2004).

Some of the prohibitions that have been imposed on young people have been criticized for being unreasonable, 'undoable' or so long in duration that breach is almost inevitable. Some of the more extreme or unusual prohibitions that have been placed on young people include being banned from wearing a baseball cap or hooded top, being in any street in the local area except their own, being in any vehicle, showing their tattoos, and using the front door of their own home.[8] A study for the Youth Justice Board found that young people subject to an ASBO often had no clear understanding of the detail of their orders, and often breached prohibitions concerning particular places or association with friends (Solanki *et al.* 2006). Yet these kinds of prohibitions are common. There is also a human rights dimension to imposing restrictions on people's freedom of movement and peaceful assembly, the enjoyment of which is essential for children's development and should be subject to very limited restrictions (UN Committee on the Rights of the Child 2008).

The definitions used in antisocial behaviour legislation also make it possible for behaviour deemed 'antisocial' to be penalized even if that harassment, alarm or distress is unjustified. Indeed ASBOs have been imposed on young people with mental health problems or disabilities because their behaviour has frightened others.[9] One widely cited example is a profoundly deaf girl who was given an ASBO for spitting. When the girl breached her order she was held in custody on remand.

The Judicial Studies Board has developed guidance on ASBOs to limit the scope of prohibitions to those that are precise, capable of being understood, tailored to the defendant, proportionate, necessary, and not so numerous as to impede compliance (Judicial Studies Board 2007). Nonetheless, there is no requirement that the subject of a prohibition itself 'cause or is likely to cause harassment, alarm or distress'. This has been criticized for allowing a circumvention of the principle of generality in which everyone has equal standing before the law. The ASBO allows for *ex ante* prohibitions on future activities that would otherwise be lawful, with the consequence that there is one rule for the ASBO bearer, and one rule for everyone else (Simester and von Hirsch 2006). For the European Commissioner for Human Rights such individualized restrictions look like 'personalized penal codes' (Gil-Robles 2005). Another source of concern is that the sanctions that are available under an ASBO are just as severe, and sometimes more severe, than those offered via the criminal law. The maximum penalty available for breaching an ASBO is five years' imprisonment, while the maximum penalty for assault, for example, is only six months. Ashworth (forthcoming) has commented that the order, which is 'ostensibly preventive in purpose', has 'a ferocious sting in the tail' when it is breached, which is most of the time in the case of young people aged under 18. The Court of Appeal has ruled that it is not admissible for the court to impose an ASBO merely to increase the sentence of the criminal offence (see *R* v *Kirby* 2005),[10] except in 'exceptional circumstances' if the ASBO breach can be said to go 'beyond that offence' (see *R* v *Morrison* 2006).[11] However, this logic was criticized in another Court of Appeal case on the grounds that it 'appears to ignore the impact of antisocial behaviour on the wider public which was the purpose of the legislation in the first place' (*R v Lamb* 2005).[12]

Almost half (47 per cent) of all ASBOs are shown in court to have been breached. This proportion is markedly higher for under-18s, 64 per cent of whom are known to have breached their ASBO. Since these figures reflect only breaches that are known to the authorities, however, the real rates are likely to be higher. Like rates of usage, breach rates for this age group vary considerably across England and Wales with a low of 42 per cent in Suffolk and a high of 85 per cent in Lincolnshire. Between June 2000 and December 2007, 1,142 young people aged 10 to 17 received a custodial sentence for breaching an ASBO, and custody accounted for 41.3 per cent of all sentences for breach (see Table 5.7 below). The average custodial sentence was 6.5 months, and custody was given on 3,248 occasions, suggesting, presumably, that each young person in custody for this reason received on average 2.8 custodial sentences (OCJR court proceedings database). It would be interesting to know how many young people, who otherwise have no convictions, have ended up in custody for breaching an ASBO issued by the civil courts. However, this information is not publicly available.

The latest addition to the armoury of civil preventive orders is an injunction to prevent gang-related violence, introduced by the Policing and Crime Act 2009. This power is not intended to be used as a response to antisocial behaviour but in other respects it is so similar to an ASBO that it may have a similar application. An injunction can be imposed for up to two years by a county court, on application by the police or a local authority, if the court is satisfied on the balance of probabilities that the respondent has engaged in, or has encouraged or assisted, gang-related violence; and considers that an injunction is necessary to prevent the respondent from engaging in, or encouraging or assisting, gang related-violence, or to protect the respondent from gang-related violence. 'Gang-related violence' is defined as violence or a threat of violence relating to the activities of a group that consists of at least three people; uses a name, emblem or colour or has any other characteristic that enables its members to be identified as a group; and is associated with a particular area.

Table 5.7 Sentences received for breach of an ASBO by 10 to 17-year-olds between 1 June 2000 and 31 December 2007, England and Wales

	Discharge	Fine	Community sentence	Custody	Other	Total
No of ASBOs breached	68	130	1,227	1,142	201	2,768
% of ASBOs breached	2.5%	4.7%	44.3%	41.3%	7.3%	

Source: OCJR court proceedings database.

Like an ASBO, the injunction enables the court to impose prohibitions on an individual, but also to make positive requirements, such as to take part in particular activities. Breach is not in itself a criminal offence, but can lead to the subject being prosecuted for contempt of court (which can result in custody for up to one month if the offender is 18 or over, or a fine up to £2,500, or both).

The Crime and Security Act, which was passed by Parliament in April 2010, extended the injunction to children and young people over the age of 14, and introduced new powers of breach for 14 to 17-year-olds to include a Supervision Order and a Detention Order (both of which are no longer available in criminal proceedings). At the time of writing the Crime and Security Act was still in its early days. As would be expected, the prospect of this injunction being applied to 14 to 17-year-olds has caused great concern amongst those promoting the interests of this age group. Many of the arguments detailed above in relation to ASBOs apply equally to these 'GASBO's, in particular that they require only a civil standard of proof. There are also fears that the powers could result in groups of young people being targeted even if they are not involved in gang-related violence, especially given the poor quality of intelligence on 'gangs' (Standing Committee on Youth Justice 2010). This has obvious implications for the treatment of young people involved in antisocial behaviour.

Individual support orders

Individual support orders (ISOs) were introduced by the Criminal Justice Act 2003, and have been available since May 2004. They are civil orders for young people aged between 10 and 17 years that are intended to supplement the prohibitions contained in ASBOs with positive requirements to 'tackle the underlying causes that led to the ASBO being made' (YJB/ACPO/Home Office 2009). ISOs last for up to six months and can require a young person to comply with educational requirements and take part in specified activities that are delivered by YOTs through existing prevention programmes or dedicated ISO schemes (depending on local provision). Breach of an ISO is a criminal offence, which may be punished by way of a financial penalty of up to £1,000, or £250 for children under the age of 14. In evidence to the Home Affairs Committee, it was reported that an ISO costs £1,500.

Magistrates who impose an ASBO in civil proceedings on young people have a duty to consider imposing an ISO. The Criminal Justice and Immigration Act 2008 expanded ISOs to allow them to be made more than once, as well as subsequent to the original ASBO, and attached to a CrASBO. However, a study conducted for the Youth Justice Board found that little use has been made of ISOs, and the majority of sentencers were unaware of their existence (Solanki et al. 2006). Home Office figures confirm that uptake was initially very slow but that ISO usage has been increasing every year since 2004. In response to a Parliamentary Question, the Home Office revealed that 7 ISOs were issued to young people in 2004 rising to 42 in 2005, and 75 in 2006. These figures equate to 2 per cent of relevant ASBOs in 2004, 7 per cent in 2005 and 18 per cent in 2006. Unfortunately, there is no available data as to whether ISOs are effective in helping young people to desist from antisocial behaviour, or whether young people with an ISO are more or less likely to breach their ASBO.

Parenting orders and contracts

The Crime and Disorder Act 1998 signalled a new and controversial direction by underlining the responsibilities of parents and establishing parenting orders. Interestingly, this emphasis on parental responsibility in the 1998 Act was accompanied by the abolition of *doli incapax*, which had hitherto had tended to protect children under 14 from prosecution, thus making clear the government's desire to hold both children *and* their parents to greater account for their actions.

Under the 1998 Act, the civil and criminal courts are required to make a parenting order when a young person under the age of 16 has been made subject to an ASBO or convicted of an offence, unless he or she is a first-time offender who can be given a referral order, or the court deems a parenting order unnecessary. The order requires parents to attend a parenting programme for up to three months and to obey other requirements for preventing their child's further offending for up to a year (such as ensuring school attendance or that their child is home during certain hours). Breach of the order is a criminal offence carrying a maximum fine of £1,000.

Parenting orders were expanded by the Anti-Social Behaviour Act 2003, which created powers for courts to impose stand-alone orders without the need for children to be convicted of a criminal offence and regardless of the child's age. The 2003 Act also allowed a residential requirement to be included in an order in support of the Family Intervention Programme (which is discussed in more detail in a later section).

The 2003 Act also introduced a statutory power to make parenting contracts, which are voluntary agreements between the parents of young people aged up to 17 years old, who agree to comply with requirements for a specified period (e.g. to attend a parenting programme and exercise control over their child's behaviour) and the applicant agency, who agree to support the parents through this process. If an acceptable behaviour contract (ABC) is being considered for a young person, a parenting contract should also be considered. In addition, the 2003 Act gave schools and local education authorities the power to make a parenting contract or apply for a parenting order when children were persistently absent or had been excluded from school for disciplinary reasons. The Police and Justice

Act 2006 further expanded these powers to local authorities and registered social landlords.

A national evaluation of parenting programmes completed in 2002 found – perhaps surprisingly – that parents reported high levels of satisfaction and nine out of ten would recommend the course to other parents in their situation. This was true irrespective of whether they had been referred voluntarily (the majority of those taking part) or compulsorily via parenting orders. The vast majority of the 800 parents who took part in the research (81 per cent) were mothers, most (60 per cent) were parents of younger children aged 14 and under, and half (49 per cent) were lone parents (Ghate and Ramella 2002). Those on parenting orders were more negative in their expectations before taking part, but afterwards there was no difference in the level of derived benefit that they reported. The improvements they mentioned included:

- better communication with their child;

- improved supervision and monitoring;

- less conflict with their child, and better approaches to handling conflict when it arose;

- better relationships, including less use of criticism and more use of praise;

- greater influence over their child's behaviour;

- more confidence to cope with parenting in general. (Ghate and Ramella 2002)

The research also found that in the year following the parenting course, the reconviction rate among the young people was 61.5 per cent compared with 89 per cent in the year before referral. The average number of offences committed in the follow-up year was 2.1 per offender, compared with 4.4 per offender in the year before the parenting course. The researchers described these results as 'very positive' but – in the absence of any control group – warned against ascribing the drop in offending to the parenting programme, or to the parenting programme alone. They pointed out that the course was relatively short in duration and came at a comparatively late stage in the young people's lives when problems were likely to be well established. The fall in offending might be due to the young people's behaviour having reached a peak just before the parenting order was imposed, in which case it would have declined irrespective of the intervention (Ghate and Ramella 2002).

In response to a Parliamentary Question posed on 8 December 2009, the Home Office revealed that 10,561 parenting orders were made between 2000/01 and 2007/08, of which 7,094 were issued in relation to crime and

Table 5.8 Parenting orders issued in England and Wales, by legal basis[13]

	2000–1	2001–2	2002–3	2003–4	2004–5	2005–6	2006–7	2007–8	Total
In relation to crime or ASB	725	807	765	686	979	1,069	1,014	1,049	7,094
In relation to education	96	276	209	215	237	213	166	230	1,642
In relation to other	158	129	202	197					686
In conjunction with a referral order					176	183	227	295	881
In conjunction with an ASBO					36	33	64	46	179
Free standing, issued by YOT					7	7	16	8	38
Free standing, issued by LEA					0	0	18	21	39

			2003	2004	2005	2006	2007	Total
Defendants proven in court to have breached a parenting order			11	20	22	25	31	109

Source: Hansard, December 2009.
Note: Notes accompanying the Home Office data acknowledge that the figures for 'education' and 'free-standing LEA' orders may not be complete as YOTs are not always informed of these orders.

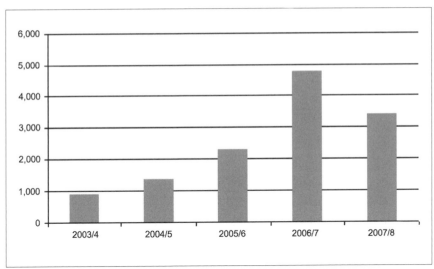

Figure 5.4 Number of parenting contracts issued, England and Wales
Source: Home Office CDRP/CSP Survey, see www.asb.homeoffice.gov.uk

antisocial behaviour, 179 were attached to an ASBO, and 881 were attached to a referral order. In response to the same Parliamentary Question, it was revealed that 109 parenting orders were proven in court to have been breached between 2003 and 2007, which suggests a low breach rate overall (see Table 5.8).

According to a Home Office survey of Crime and Disorder Reduction Partnerships and Community Safety Partnerships (in Wales), at least 12,679 parenting contracts were issued in the five-year period from 2003/4 to 2007/8 (see Figure 5.4). The accompanying notes explain that this figure excludes missing responses and therefore equates to the minimum number issued.

Acceptable behaviour contracts (ABCs) and warning letters

Warning letters and ABCs are often described as a way of 'nipping antisocial behaviour in the bud' without resorting to an ASBO application (Home Office 2007). ABCs run for a renewable six months and, although they are not legally binding, breach can trigger a decision to seek an ASBO or eviction proceedings. This threat of sanctions has led Crawford (2009) to question whether they constitute a genuine 'contract'. Alongside warning letters (the first response for most reported incidents of antisocial behaviour, ABCs are by far the most common form of antisocial behaviour intervention. The government does not have definitive figures on the use of ABCs as they are informal voluntary agreements. However, the Home Office survey of Crime and Disorder Reduction Partnerships (CDRPs) and

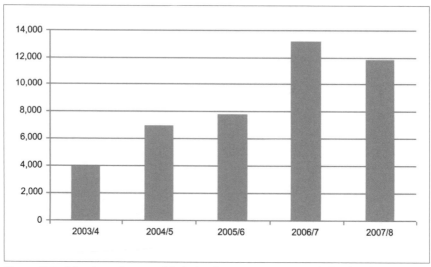

Figure 5.5 Number of acceptable behaviour contracts issued, England and Wales
Source: Home Office CDRP/CSP Survey, see www.asb.homeoffice.gov.uk

Community Safety Partnerships (CSPs) mentioned above suggests that 43,789 ABCs were issued between 2003/4 and 2007/8 (see Figure 5.5).

The National Audit Office study of the use of antisocial behaviour interventions mentioned earlier found that warning letters were both 'effective' and 'cost effective' (as is shown in Table 5.9). ABCs were effective overall, but not with young people: almost two-thirds (61 per cent) of under-18s subject to an ABC went on to receive a further antisocial behaviour intervention during the period studied (i.e. a warning letter, ABC, ASBO or other intervention, or were found to have breached the conditions of their ASBO). These findings came with various caveats. For example, without a control group it is not possible to know whether other interventions would have achieved the same or a better result, and whether desistance from antisocial behaviour was due to other factors such as a change in family or personal circumstances. In a similar vein, like criminal justice system responses in general, different interventions are not directly comparable as they reflect differences in the seriousness and persistence of the underlying behaviour.

Although ABCs are often seen as a cheap, flexible, less formal and more consensual way of tackling antisocial behaviour, interviews with young people in the National Audit Office study showed that they were not always engaged in the process of setting the conditions of their ABCs and sometimes agreed conditions that were very difficult to achieve (National Audit Office 2006). Another study found that contracts were negatively drafted, with few positive statements, opportunities or support services conferred. About half the contracts studied concerned young people with

Table 5.9 Reconviction rates for 893 people subject to different antisocial behaviour interventions

Intervention	% receiving furtherASB interventions	Median time to further intervention	% of under 18s receiving further ASB interventions	Cost of intervention
Warning letter	37	73 days	38	£66
ABC	35	155 days	61	£230
ASBO	55	296 days	Data not given	£3,100

Source: NAO (2006) *The Home Office: Tackling Anti-social Behaviour.*

diagnosed personality disorders, who were offered little social support (Squires and Stephen 2005).

Dispersal orders

The dispersal order is the most prominent of the area-based restrictions introduced by the Labour Government. It was reportedly created in frustration over the failure of local authorities to use the curfew powers that were introduced in the Crime and Disorder Act 1998 for children under 10 in designated areas (not one local authority sought to use these powers), which were extended to the police for use with children up to the age of 16 via the Criminal Justice and Police Act 2001.

The Anti-Social Behaviour Act 2003 created dispersal orders, which gave police officers and community support officers the power to disperse groups of two or more people within a designated area for up to 24 hours (although the dispersal zone itself may be designated for six months) if they have reasonable grounds to believe that their behaviour has resulted or is likely to result 'in any members of the public being intimidated, harassed, alarmed or distressed'. Refusal to cooperate can lead to arrest and a summary charge of failing to comply, punishable by a fine of up to £5,000. In addition, anyone under 16 found unsupervised in a designated area between 9pm and 6am can be taken home by the police, unless they believe this is likely to result in significant harm to the young person concerned.

Researchers have observed that dispersal orders highlight a central problem concerning antisocial behaviour enforcement as to whether it should target *potential* nuisance by dispersing young people who look as though they might cause trouble, or confine responses to *actual* behaviour (Crawford and Lister 2007; Millie 2008). Legal arguments over whether police removing young people under 16 from the streets at night can use 'reasonable force' have led to a Court of Appeal ruling that they are not empowered to take arbitrary action, and that their attention should

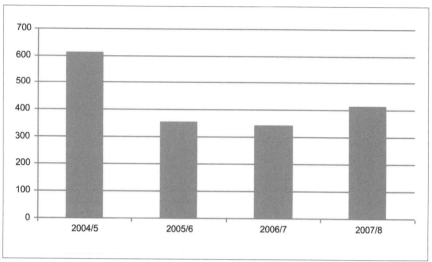

Figure 5.6 Number of dispersal orders issued, England and Wales
Source: Home Office CDRP/CSP Survey, see www.asb.homeoffice.gov.uk

be limited to those 'at risk' of committing antisocial behaviour or an offence.

Although police forces have made limited use of the powers to take home unsupervised under-16s, there has been comparatively widespread use of the main dispersal powers, especially on estates and town centres (Crawford and Lister 2007). Nevertheless, Home Office figures show that after an initial surge of activity, with 610 dispersal orders issued in 2004/5, their use declined, with about 300 to 400 issued each year since.

As seems to be the pattern with antisocial behaviour interventions, there is considerable regional variation in usage. According to the CDRP/CSP survey, four areas[14] made one or two dispersal orders between January 2004 and 2007/8, while the West Midlands made 157, Hampshire made 106 and Northamptonshire made 95.

Crawford and Lister (2007) found dispersal orders to be used most commonly in relation to perceived problems with groups of young people. Where antisocial behaviour is a significant and persistent problem, they concluded that these measures can provide 'a brief period of respite' and a window of opportunity to address the underlying problems. However, they found their value to be as much in the process of authorization, which presented opportunities for engagement between the police, young people, the community and other agencies, as in the powers per se. Police reportedly used the dispersal powers sparingly and informally to facilitate dialogue with young people. However, when the powers were used, the study found evidence of displacement effects, with crime and antisocial behaviour shifting from the designated zone to nearby areas. In one neighbouring 'displacement zone', crime rose by 148 per cent on the previous six months and 83 per cent on the previous year. As such, they concluded that the orders were no more than a 'sticking plaster', invariably failing to address the wider causes of the identified problems.

Another example of area-based restrictions is the Designated Public Place Order, in force since 2006, which gives local authorities the power to restrict antisocial drinking in defined areas. Police can enforce the orders by confiscating alcohol and imposition of fixed-penalty fines of £50.

On-the-spot fines (FPNs AND PNDs)

Fixed-penalty notices (FPNs) have been translated from traffic regulation to tackling antisocial behaviour to deliver 'simple, speedy, summary justice' (Home Office *et al.* 2006). The offences that they cover include antisocial acts like littering, fly posting, graffiti, noise nuisance and dog fouling. FPNs – usually for £75 – can be issued to anyone over 10 years old by the police, Community Support Officers, local authority staff and other 'accredited' officials.

The Criminal Justice and Police Act 2001 introduced penalty notices for disorder (PNDs) for more serious but still low-level antisocial behaviour. Initially only for adults, their use was extended to 16 and 17-year-olds under the Anti-Social Behaviour Act 2003. Offences were divided between an upper tier,[15] carrying an £80 fine and a lower tier[16] with a £50 penalty. In 2004, the use of PNDs was extended again to 10 to 15-year-olds in six areas.[17] PNDs could be issued to children for 24 offences[18] with the liability to pay the fines – of either £40 or £30 – falling on their parents (Amadi 2008).

FPNs and PNDs do not carry a criminal record. They, nevertheless, count towards the government's target for Offences Brought to Justice (OBTJ) and failure to pay may result in higher fines, or imprisonment. Commentators have noted how they blur the distinction between criminal and non-criminal behaviour, for example, by treating littering and theft in the same way. They also reverse the normal presumption of innocence until proven guilty (Millie 2008). However, the additional safeguards available under the criminal law are preserved by the opportunity to refuse the penalty and insist on the matter being heard in court. That said, there may be powerful pressures to accept the penalty (Ashworth, forthcoming).

PNDs, in particular, appear popular with many police forces. In 2007 – the most recent figures available – 207,544 PNDs were issued in England and Wales. Of these 19,246 were issued to 16 and 17-year-olds, with use varying between police force areas. PNDs were most commonly issued to under-18s for 'harassment, alarm or distress' (37 per cent) and theft (23 per cent). The payment rate without enforcement action among 16 and

17-year-olds was 58 per cent, compared with 51 per cent for those aged 18 and over (Amadi 2008).

In the pilot scheme for issuing PNDs to 10 to 15-year-olds, there were considerable variations between the seven participating police forces. Although a total of 4,434 notices were issued between July 2005 and June 2006, two police areas were responsible for 90 per cent of the PNDs and one force issued only four during the whole year. About a third (32 per cent) were for 'destroying or damaging property', followed by 'harassment alarm or distress' (29 per cent) and shoplifting (26 per cent). PNDs were issued to relatively few 10-year-olds (2.3 per cent) with 14 and 15-year-olds accounting for two out of three notices. Unlike adults, about as many girls as boys were penalized. Payment rates (by parents) without further enforcement increased with the age of the child from 53 per cent for 10-year-olds to just under 70 per cent for 15-year-olds (Amadi 2008).

An evaluation of the pilot scheme found that police officers felt that PNDs were a better deterrent than reprimands or final warnings and less time-consuming for the officers involved. Young people, parents and YOTs were less enthusiastic, with concerns expressed about the unfairness of penalizing parents and that poorer parents were dispro-portionately punished. It emerged that the pilot areas were using PNDs at different stages in the 'offending lifecycle'. For example, one only imposed them after a final warning while another used them between the reprimand and final warning stages. Difficulties were also apparent in the ability of police to check young people's background and offending records before issuing PNDs 'on the street'; repeat offenders could consequently receive more than one notice, against the intention of the scheme (Amadi 2008).

Both this evaluation and that of PNDs for over-16s (Halligan-Davies and Spicer 2004) identified a significant 'net-widening' effect. Individuals were being brought into the formal, criminal justice system who would otherwise have been dealt with informally. In the pilot with 10–15-year-olds, over 70 per cent of 'harassment, alarm and distress' penalties were considered to be 'new business' that would not previously have had a formal consequence. Amadi (2008) noted that the increase in the number of individuals being drawn into the system was likely to impact on any efficiency savings made.

We might expect to see this net-widening effect in the number of new entrants to the youth justice system. Until recently, statistics published by the Youth Justice Board in relation to first-time entrants (FTEs) excluded PNDs. However, in November 2009 the government updated their figures to include PNDs, and surprisingly, this had no effect on the overall reduction of FTEs (of 10 per cent between 2005 and 2008). PNDs issued to 16 and 17-year-olds increased from 3,793 in 2004/5 to a high of 19,598 in 2006/7, followed by a marginal decrease to 19,246 in 2007/8. However, the increase in use of these out-of-court penalties appears to have been counteracted by other changes in the youth justice system that have resulted in fewer new entrants overall.

Family Intervention Project (FIP)

The Respect Action Plan, which was strongly focused on young people and their families, had a number of different strands, of which intensive family support for the most antisocial and challenging families was one. This led to the setting up of a network of 53 Family Intervention Projects (FIPs), whose primary objective was to help support families reduce their problematic behaviour in order to prevent the associated cycles of eviction and homelessness. The action plan said it would consider imposing financial or housing benefit penalties on families that 'refuse to take up offers of help'.

Family Intervention Projects take a 'whole family' approach to assess the underlying problems driving the antisocial behaviour. The support provided by the projects varies from family to family but commonly comprises intensive '11th hour' multi-agency services in relation to: 'practical assistance in the home, provision of advice, liaison and advocacy support, sign-posting to other relevant services, help in managing finances and claiming benefits, personal skills development, anger management, parenting skills training, and behaviour management' (Nixon et al. 2008).

The intervention can be delivered in three distinct ways:

- Intensive outreach to families in their own homes to help them stay in their existing accommodation.

- Intensive outreach to families that have been moved into accommodation with a non-secure tenancy.

- Intensive support to families in supervised accommodation with 24-hour support from staff, with the aim of moving them into one of two other types of programme.

FIPs are modelled on The Dundee Project run by the charity Action for Children (formerly NCH), which a Glasgow University evaluation showed to have helped families make good progress (although many continued to have serious problems with parenting). Cost estimates suggested that the project was, at worst, no more expensive than conventional methods of dealing with highly antisocial tenants (Dillane et al. 2001).

A two-year evaluation by Sheffield Hallam University of six Family Intervention Projects in the north of England found that the three most common reasons for referral were youth nuisance (70 per cent), neighbour conflict (54 per cent) and property damage (43 per cent). However, they also discovered that six out of ten families were 'victims' of antisocial behaviour as well as perpetrators – supporting a conclusion reached by other studies that the two are often not easily distinguished (see also Jones *et al.* 2006). High levels of family violence were also identified with partner or intergenerational violence an issue in almost half the referred families (47 per cent).

Typical families referred to the projects were large (62 per cent had three or more children). Four out of ten families were assessed as being at risk of family breakdown, while one in five had at least one child on the child protection register. In addition, 20 per cent of the children had attention-deficit disorders (ADD), which compares with an estimated 1.5 per cent of children in the general population (Green *et al.* 2004). At the time of referral 14 per cent were statutorily homeless or at imminent risk of becoming so, while the vast majority (89 per cent) had their tenancy under threat.

The study concluded that the broad, multi-disciplinary nature of the projects enabled families to achieve an impressive degree of change. More than eight out of ten (85 per cent) left the programmes at a point where complaints about their antisocial behaviour had ceased or been reduced to a level where their tenancy was no longer under threat. Project workers assessed that in 80 per cent of cases, families' tenancies had been stabilized with an associated reduction in their risk of homelessness. The optimum referral point for families was judged to be just before the start of legal action. The researchers also calculated an average cost for the projects for each closed case of between £27,214 and £36,580 in 2004/5. They contrasted this with estimated costs to the Exchequer of between £250,000 and £330,000 in a year for large families that are evicted because of antisocial behaviour, creating a need for custodial, residential and foster care placements (Nixon *et al.* 2006)

A follow-up evaluation looking at the longer-term changes found that for almost three-quarters of the families (i.e. 20 out of 28) positive change had been sustained and no significant further complaints about antisocial behaviour had been received. For these families, the risk of homelessness had been significantly reduced and the family home was secure. However, over half of the families (16 out of 28) had moved home since finishing the project and some had exchanged secure tenancies for less secure accommodation.

Recreational activities

A common complaint by both adults and teenagers is that there is not enough for young people to do in their area, and that the ensuing boredom can lead to involvement in antisocial behaviour (4Children 2007). To address concerns such as these, the Education and Inspections

Act 2006 imposed a statutory duty on councils to provide access to recreational and educational activities for young people. This duty was accompanied by a ten-year strategy for positive activities, 'Aiming High for Young People', which committed £679 million for youth initiatives and £190 million for new and improved youth facilities over the 2008–11 funding period.

Sports and other leisure activities can be used as a 'hook' to engage young people who are at risk of antisocial behaviour and offending, but even though they may offer short-term diversionary benefits, they are not likely to be enough to achieve lasting behaviour change (Audit Commission 2009). It is in combination with developmental components that these activities have been found to be most effective, for example, by reducing impulsiveness and risk-taking behaviour, improving cognitive and social skills, raising self-esteem and self-confidence and improving education and employment prospects (Utting 1996). Yet structured provision that contains elements such as these tends to hold little appeal to those most at risk of engaging in antisocial behaviour (Feinstein *et al.* 2005). This challenge seems not to have been creatively addressed, and young people are rarely consulted when new projects or activities are planned.

One structured project that has combined recreational activities with learning a skill is the Participate and Learn Skills (PALS) programme for 5 to 15-year-olds living on a socially disadvantaged estate in Ontario. An evaluation found a 75 per cent decrease in juvenile arrests by police compared with a 67 per cent increase on a similar control estate (Jones and Offord 1989).

In 2003, the government launched Positive Activities for Young People (PAYP), a targeted programme of diversionary and developmental activities including sport, arts, music, educational, recreational, and outdoor activities. These were aimed at reducing crime and antisocial behaviour amongst 8 to 19-year-olds 'at risk' of social exclusion and offending. An evaluation of the programme concluded that PAYP was successful in delivering a targeted programme to a 'hard to engage' client group and achieving a range of positive outcomes for participating young people, including reductions in crime and antisocial behaviour and supporting young people back into education. Without an appropriate comparison group, however, the impact of PAYP could not be isolated from the raft of other initiatives that were in place at the same time (CRG Research 2006).

Conclusions

Over the last two decades, antisocial behaviour has been the subject of a catalogue of laws, policies and interventions, and a lot of 'tough talk'. Just as with youth crime (see Chapter 3) a quick look at the headlines would give the impression that antisocial behaviour has become an increasing problem in recent years. However, it is hard to assess the accuracy of this contention because, objectively speaking, the scale of antisocial behaviour is not known. This is because official definitions of antisocial behaviour relate to its consequences rather than its form, placing it firmly 'in the eye of the beholder'. Thus, we do not know, and may never know, whether antisocial behaviour as it is understood by the government is going up or down. In addition, and equally importantly, there is a general lack of systematic evidence to shed light on the effectiveness of the interventions that have been introduced to address antisocial behaviour.

The only source of consistent data over time is the British Crime Survey, which has been measuring perceptions of antisocial behaviour since 1992. This showed a rise in a composite measure of perceived antisocial behaviour between 1992 and 2000, followed by a small decrease between 2001/2 and 2008/9. There is considerable variation across demographic groups, however, which reveals that antisocial behaviour is primarily a problem for younger age groups, those living in deprived areas, and those that have been a victim of crime.

A central problem for those concerned with children's rights and interests is that for many adults, antisocial behaviour is synonymous with youth. A key measure of antisocial behaviour – indeed the one that concerns adults the most according to the BCS – is 'teenagers hanging around'. Associated activities range from those that are illegal (drug-taking, underage drinking, damage to property), to those that cause harm or offence to others (harassing, insulting, intimidating and threatening people) and those that are simply a nuisance (swearing, being rowdy/noisy, blocking the pavement). This highlights the subjective nature of antisocial behaviour, since for many young people 'hanging around' is a normal activity from which they derive pleasure and a sense of 'safety in numbers'.

There has been a raft of antisocial behaviour-related legislation since 1998 and a growing armoury of responses. By far the most commonly used elements of this armoury are ABCs and PNDs, which are intended to serve a preventive purpose and/or deliver out-of-court 'summary justice'. It is ASBOs, however, that have captured the limelight. Their 'hybrid' fusion of the civil and criminal law has made these orders highly controversial. Disliked by defenders of human rights and legal philos-ophers for the lack of procedural safeguards and severe penalties for breach, and liked by enforcement enthusiasts and the general public for much the same reasons, these preventive orders were never intended for use with young people. But used in large numbers they were – between 2000 and 2007, over 6,000 ASBOs were issued to 10 to 17-year-olds. Very high breach rates for this age group (64 per cent) caused critics to argue that these orders were simply 'setting them up to fail'.

Enthusiasm for ASBOs has waned in recent years, and there has been an increasing emphasis on 'preventive' agreements such as ABCs and 'supportive' interventions such as ISOs and FIPs, which seek to address the causes of antisocial behaviour. Family-based interventions such as FIPs and parenting programmes enjoy high levels of satisfaction, and are associated with a number of successful outcomes including reductions in antisocial behaviour. Without control groups, though, these findings are not conclusive.

Patterns of low-level crime and disorder that have a cumulative impact on individuals and neighbourhoods clearly exist, especially in the most deprived neighbourhoods. Politicians seem to feel that they need a new word and a new campaign to kickstart action in a particular area, and antisocial behaviour seems to be a prime example of this. However, a more sensible approach would be to take these problems seriously while avoiding a moral panic. Based on the evidence set out in this chapter we might reasonably conclude that the most promising measures are those that address the underlying reasons why young people commit antisocial behaviour and offer practical assistance to help them change their behaviour.

Notes

1 Doubtless Fiona Pilkington had a difficult life as she was raising two disabled children alone. In a profile published on 29 September 2009, *The Guardian* reported that she suffered from anxiety and depression, and couldn't work because her daughter Francecca's severe learning difficulties required her mother's constant supervision. Her son, Anthony, also had learning difficulties but they were milder.

2 Linked to this idea is the 'broken windows' thesis, which became influential in the US in the 1980s. The thesis, which was originally put forward by J.Q. Wilson and G. Kelling in 1982, posited that dealing with early signs of neighbourhood disorder, insecurity and decay, such as 'broken windows' left unrepaired, helps to avoid a spiral of decline into more serious problems, especially crime and fear of crime. Thus visible policing that deals with minor disorder can increase the sense of security in communities and prevent more serious crime from taking hold. The theory and its empirical foundations have been subjected to strong criticism, but nonetheless it still exerts influence on the government's approach to antisocial behaviour. See the Labour Party's report *A Quiet Life*, which was published in 1995, and the Home Office's website, which (in 2010) stated that 'Antisocial behaviour doesn't just make life unpleasant. It holds back the regeneration of disadvantaged areas and creates an environment where more serious crime can take hold.' www.asb.homeoffice.gov.uk.

3 See http://homeoffice.gov.uk/anti-social-behaviour/what-is-asb/index.html.

4 See http://www.asb.homeoffice.gov.uk/article.aspx?id=9066.

5 Between 1992 and 2000 respondents were asked about five indicators of antisocial behaviour: noisy neighbours, rubbish or litter, people using or

dealing drugs, vandalism and graffiti, teenagers hanging around. Since 2000 two more items have been added: abandoned or burnt-out cars and people being drunk or rowdy in public.

6   The full range of categories and results were: 5 per cent for 'countryside', 7 per cent for 'prospering suburbs', 16 per cent for 'typical traits', 17 per cent for 'city living', 25 per cent for 'constrained by circumstances', 25 per cent for 'blue collar communities' and 29 per cent for 'multicultural'.

7   *R (McCann and Others) v Crown Court at Manchester and Another* [2003] 1 AC 787, Lord Steyn at [808], Lord Hope at [821], Lord Hutton at [830].

8   See ASBOwatch http://www.statewatch.org/asbo/ASBOwatch.html.

9   See 'Children with Autism the Target of ASBOs' *Observer* 22 May 2005, and ASBOwatch for other examples http://www.statewatch.org/asbo/asbowatch-children.htm.

10 *R v Kirby* [2005] EWCA Crim 1228 at [6].

11 *R v Morrison* [2006] 1 Cr App R (S) 85.

12 *R v Lamb* [2005] All ER (D) 132 at [16]

13 In addition to the figures contained in this table, one parenting order was issued in conjunction with a sex offences prevention order, and one was issued in conjunction with a child safety order, both in 2006/07.

14 Gloucestershire (1), Cumbria (2), Dyfed-Powys (2) and South Wales (2).

15 These were: wasting police time or giving false report; using public telecommunications system for sending false messages; knowingly giving a false alarm to a fire brigade; causing harassment, alarm or distress; throwing fireworks in a thoroughfare; being drunk and disorderly; selling alcohol to/purchasing alcohol for/delivering alcohol to a person under 18; destroying/damaging property (under £500); theft (retail under £200); breach of fireworks curfew; possessing Category 4 firework; possessing adult firework by person under 18.

16 These were: trespassing on a railway; throwing stones etc. at trains or other things on railways; being drunk in a highway, other public place or licensed premises; consuming alcohol in designated public place; depositing and leaving litter; consuming alcohol by person under 18 in licensed premises; allowing consumption of alcohol by person under 18 in licensed premises.

17 These were: Essex, Lancashire, Nottinghamshire, Merseyside, West Midlands including the local British Transport Police, and the Kingston division of the Metropolitan Police.

18 These were the same offences as listed in notes 15 and 16, with the additional offences of: selling alcohol to a drunken person and buying or attempting to buy alcohol by a person under 18. However, in the pilot, PNDs were not issued for four offences: breach of fireworks curfew, selling alcohol to a drunken person, consumption of alcohol by a person aged under 18 in licensed premises, and allowing consumption of alcohol by a person aged under 18 in a bar in licensed premises.

References

4Children (2007) *Makespace Youth Review: Transforming the Offer for Young People in the UK* (London: 4Children).

Amadi, J. (2008) *Piloting Penalty Notices for Disorder on 10- to 15-year-olds: results from a one year pilot*, Ministry of Justice Research Series 19/08 (London: Ministry of Justice).

American Psychiatric Association (1994) *Diagnostic and Statistical Manual of Mental Health Disorders*, 4th edition (Arlington: American Psychiatric Association).

Ashworth (forthcoming) 'Civil preventive orders' in *Sentencing and Criminal Justice*, 5th edition (Cambridge: Cambridge University Press).

Ashworth, A., Gardner, J., Morgan, R., Smith, A., von Hirsch, A. and Wasik, M. (1998) 'Neighbouring on the Oppressive: the Government's 'Anti-Social Behaviour Order' proposals', *Criminal Justice*, 16:1, pp. 7–14.

Audit Commission (2009) *Tired of Hanging Around: Using sport and leisure activities to prevent anti-social behaviour by young people* (London: Audit Commission).

CRG Research (2006) *Positive Activities For Young People: National evaluation final report* (London: Department for Education and Skills).

Crawford, A. (2009) 'Governing Through Anti-Social Behaviour: Regulatory Challenges to Criminal Justice', *British Journal of Criminology*, Advance Access published on 1 July 2009.

Crawford, A. and Lister, S. (2007) *The Use and Impact of Dispersal Orders: Sticking plasters and wake-up calls* (Bristol: Policy Press).

Dillane, J., Hill, M., Bannister, J., and Scott, S. (2001) *Evaluation of the Dundee Families Project* (Glasgow: University of Glasgow).

Feinstein, L., Bynner, J. and Duckworth, K. (2005) *Leisure Contexts in Adolescence and their Effects on Adult Outcomes* (London: Centre for Research on the Wider Benefits of Learning).

Gardner, J., von Hirsch, A., Smith, A. T. H., Morgan, R., Ashworth, A. and Wasik, N. (1998) 'Clause 1 – The Hybrid Law from Hell?', *Criminal Justice Matters*, 31: 25.

Gask, A. (2004) *Anti-Social Behaviour Orders and Human Rights* (London: Liberty).

Ghate, D. and Ramella, M. (2002) *Positive Parenting: The National Evaluation of the Youth Justice Board's Parenting Programme* (London: Youth Justice Board)

Gil-Robles, A. (2005) *Report by Mr Alvaro Gil-Robles, Commissioner for Human Rights, on his visit to the United Kingdom, 4th–12th November 2004* (Strasbourg: Council of Europe).

Green, H., McGinnity, A., Meltzer, H., Ford, T., and Goodman, R. (2005) *Mental Health of Children and Young People in Great Britain* (London: Office of National Statistics).

Halligan-Davies, G. and Spicer, K. (2004) Piloting 'On the Spot Penalties' for Disorder: final results from a one-year pilot, *Home Office Findings 257* (London: Home Office).

Home Office (1999) *A Guide to Anti-Social Behaviour Orders* (London: Home Office).

Home Office (2003) *The One-day Count of Anti-Social Behaviour, September 2003* (London: Home Office).

Home Office (2004) *Defining and Measuring Anti-Social Behaviour* (London: Home Office).

Home Office (2006) *Respect Action Plan* (London: Home Office).

Home Office (2007) *Acceptable Behaviour Contracts and Agreements* (London: Home Office).

Home Office, Department for Constitutional Affairs and the Attorney General's Office (2006) *Delivering Simple, Speedy, Summary Justice* (London: Dept for Constitutional Affairs).

Hough, M. (2004) 'Modernisation, Scientific Rationalism and the Crime Reduction Programme', *Criminal Justice*, 4:3, pp. 239–53.

House of Commons Committee of Public Accounts (2007) *Tackling Anti–Social Behaviour: Forty–fourth Report of Session 2006–07* (London: The Stationery Office).

House of Commons Home Affairs Committee (2005) *Anti–Social Behaviour: Fifth Report of Session 2004–05* (London: The Stationery Office).

Innes, M. and Fielding, N. (2002) 'From Community to Communicative Policing: "Signal Crimes" and the Problem of Public Reassurance', *Sociological Research Online*, 7:2.

Ipsos MORI (2005) *Public Concern About ASB and Support For ASBOs*, available at: www.ipsos-mori.com.

Isal, S. (2006) *Equal Respect – ASBOs and Race Equality* (London: Runnymede Trust).

Jones, A., Pleace, N., Quilgars, D., (2006) 'Addressing Antisocial Behaviour: An independent evaluation of Shelter Inclusion Project' *London: Shelter*

Jones, M. B. and Offord, D.R. (1989) 'Reduction of Anti-social Behavior in Poor Children by Nonschool Skill Development', *Journal of Child Psychology and Psychiatry and Allied Disciplines*, 30, pp. 737–50.

Judicial Studies Board (2007) *Anti-social Behaviour Orders: A Guide for the Judiciary*, 3rd edition (London: Judicial Studies Board).

Millie, A. (2008) *Anti-Social Behaviour* (Maidenhead: Open University Press).

Millie, A., Jacobson, J., McDonald, E. and Hough, M. (2005) *Anti-Social Behaviour Strategies: Finding a Balance* (Bristol: Policy Press).

Moon, D. (ed.), Walker, A., (ed.), Murphy, R., Flatley, J., Parfrement-Hopkins, J. and Hall, P. (2009) *Perceptions of Crime and Anti-social Behaviour: Findings from the 2008/09 British Crime Survey*, Home Office Statistical Bulletin 17/09 (London: Home Office).

National Audit Office (2006) *The Home Office: Tackling Anti-Social Behaviour* (London: The Stationery Office).

Nixon, J., Blandy, S., Hunter, C., Reeve, K. and Jones, A. (2003) *Tackling Anti-social Behaviour in Mixed Tenure Areas* (London: Office of the Deputy Prime Minister).

Nixon, J., Hunter, C., Parr, S., Myers, S., Whittle, S. and Sanderson, D. (2006) '*Anti-social Behaviour Intensive Family Support Projects: An evaluation of six pioneering projects'* (London: Department for Communities and Local Government).

Nixon, J., Parr, S., Hunter, C., Sanderson, D. and Whittle, S. (2008) '*The Longer-term Outcomes Associated with Families who had Worked with Intensive Family Support Projects'* (London: Department for Communities and Local Government).

Ramsay, P. (2004) 'What is Anti-Social Behaviour?', *Criminal Law Review*, 908.

Robins, L.N. (1966) *Deviant Children Grown Up: A Sociological and Psychiatric Study of Sociopathic Personality* (Baltimore: The Williams and Wilkins Co).

Seaman, P., Turner, K., Hill, M., Stafford, A. and Walker, M. (2006) *Parenting and Children's Resilience in Disadvantaged Communities* (London: Joseph Rowntree Foundation).

Simester, A. P. and von Hirsch, A. (2006) 'Regulating Offensive Conduct through Two-Step Prohibitions', in A. von Hirsch and A.P. Simester (eds) *Incivilities: Regulating Offensive Behaviour* (Oxford: Hart).

Squires, P. and Stephen, D.E. (2005) *Rougher Justice: Anti-social Behaviour and Young People* (Cullompton: Willan Publishing).

Solanki, A., Bateman, T., Boswell, G. and Hill, H. (2006) *Anti-Social Behaviour Orders* (London: Youth Justice Board)

Standing Committee for Youth Justice (2010) *Briefing on the Crime and Security Bill: House of Commons Second Reading*, 18 January 2010.

Tonry, M., (2004) *Punishment and Politics: Evidence and Emulation in the Making of English Crime Control Policy* (Cullompton: Willan Publishing).

United Nations Committee on the Rights of the Child (2008) *49th session: Concluding Observations: United Kingdom of Great Britain and Northern Ireland* CRC/C/GBR/CO/4 (Geneva: OCHR).

Utting, D. (1996) *Reducing Criminality Among Young People: A Sample of Relevant Programmes in the United Kingdom*, Home Office Research Study 161 (London: Home Office).

Waiton, S. (2007) *The Politics of Antisocial Behaviour: Amoral Panics* (New York: Routledge).

Walker, A., Flatley, J., Kershaw, C. and Moon, D. (2009) *Crime in England and Wales 2008/09* (London: Home Office).

Whitehead, C.M.E., Stockdale, J.E. and Razzu, G. (2003) *The Economic and Social Costs of Anti-Social Behaviour: A Review* (London: London School of Economics).

Wilson, J.Q and Kelling, G.L. (1982) 'Broken Windows: The Police and Neighborhood Safety', *The Atlantic Monthly*, March 1982.

Youth Justice Board/ACPO/Home Office (2005) *Anti-social Behaviour Guidance: A guide to the role of youth offending teams in dealing with anti-social behaviour* (London: Youth Justice Board).

Youth Justice Board/ACPO/Home Office (2009) *A Guide to Reviewing Anti-Social Behaviour Orders Given to Young People and Individual Support Orders* (London: Home Office).

Chapter 6

Causes of offending and antisocial behaviour[1]

Michael Rutter

Concept of 'cause'

Before discussing the evidence on causes, it is necessary to clarify several key issues (see Academy of Medical Sciences 2007). First, even with the most straightforward situation, it is very rare to find examples of a one-to-one all-encompassing causal effect. Rothman and Greenland (1998) illustrated the point with the example of turning on a light by flicking a switch. A person need do nothing else except flick the switch to cause the light to go on – surely that must constitute a simple, straightforward, direct causal effect? It does not, however, because the light will not go on unless the bulb is functional, the electric circuit is intact, the required voltage is available and so forth. Even with the simplest situations, it is usual for there to be a 'web of causations' as MacMahon *et al.* (1960) put it. With multifactorial traits or disorders (such as represented by antisocial behaviour) the situation is further complicated by five other considerations. First, the very term 'multifactorial' makes it clear that there will never be a single necessary and sufficient cause, because multiple causal influences are operative, each of which plays a part in contributing to the causal process. Second, it is common for there to be several different causal pathways, each leading to the same end-point (Rutter 1997). Third, each causal starting point is also the end of a prior causal process. The Academy of Medical Sciences (2007) report used the example of smoking and lung cancer. Heavy smoking is likely to involve a genetic susceptibility, the availability of cigarettes and the operation of social pressures. Moreover, the fact that the smoking habit persists will also be influenced by the heavily addictive effects of nicotine. All of this means that the causal background to smoking must be taken into account in assessing the effects of smoking on the risk for lung cancer. Nevertheless, none of this means that a specific causal effect of smoking on lung cancer cannot be identified. It is obvious that similar considerations, with respect to possible sequential causal pathways, apply to antisocial behaviour. Rothman and Greenland (2002) specified that a cause is an antecedent event, condition or characteristic that was necessary (given that other conditions were fixed) for the occurrence of the outcome being studied at the moment it occurred. Without that causal influence, the outcome would not have developed or would have done so at some later time. That is the central point of what is meant by a 'cause'. The implication, of course, is that changing a causal factor will actually reduce the populations' burden either by reducing the overall number of cases or by making the outcomes occur later than they would have done otherwise (Robins and Greenland 1989). It is that consideration that makes the identification of causes so important in terms of implications for prevention or intervention.

Fourth, as exemplified by gene-environment interactions (see Rutter 2008), environmental causes may be operative only when combined with a specific type of genetic susceptibility. Alternatively they may operate only in particular age groups or when some other causal factor is present. Fifth, two-way causal effects are common (see Kendler *et al.* 2008 for their example of deviant peers and conduct disorder). That means that the identification of causes involves a series of quite substantial challenges. It also means that attempts to provide overall, testable models of causation of antisocial behaviour are necessarily going to be constrained by a focus on just some aspects of causation and not others (see Lahey *et al.* 2003).

Different aspects of causation

Much of the literature on the causes of antisocial behaviour focuses on individual differences in the liability to engage in antisocial behaviour. Obviously, that is a very important issue but, particularly when considering offending, there are other aspects of causation that have to be put into the equation. Rutter *et al.* (1998) and Rutter *et al.* (1997) outlined a causal scheme that put together all the various aspects of causation (see Figure 6.1). Situational 'presses' and emotional provocation will include elements inhibiting and elements disinhibiting antisocial behaviour. The former, for example, will include positive societal values, empathy for others, availability of non-delinquent rewards; and disinhibiting effects will include drugs and alcohol, the models provided by previous antisocial acts, peer group models and social group influences. It should be noted that both of these span external and internal domains of quite diverse kinds. Whether or not an individual antisocial liability is translated into a delinquent act will also depend on opportunity features (see Figure 6.2) and perception of cost (see Figure 6.3).

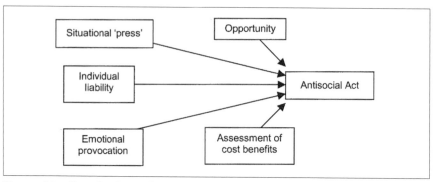

Figure 6.1 Causal scheme for processes leading to crime

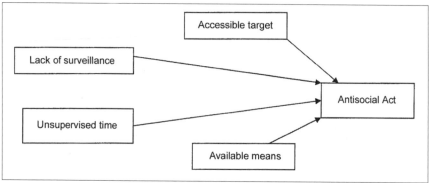

Figure 6.2 Opportunity features

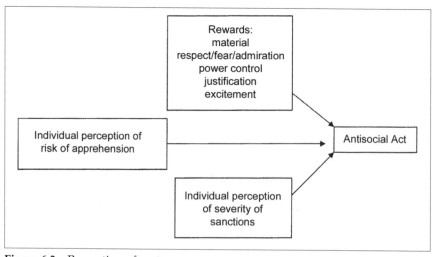

Figure 6.3 Perception of cost

Heterogeneity of antisocial behaviour

For many years there were umpteen fruitless attempts to subdivide antisocial behaviour according to types of crime. These proved unhelpful because most offenders engage in quite a wide range of antisocial acts. The situation was transformed in 1993 when Moffitt proposed that antisocial behaviour should be subdivided into two categories: life-course persistent and adolescence-limited. The former is characterized by early onset and association with overactivity, cognitive limitations, and a difficult temperament. This variety tended to persist into adult life. By contrast, adolescence-limited antisocial behaviour only arose during the adolescent age period and was not associated with the same risk factors. Not only did this concept receive empirical support but it led to much profitable research (see Moffitt 1993; Moffitt et al. 2008). However, although a distinction between two categories of antisocial behaviour has received much empirical support, several modifications have been needed and several queries remain. Thus, follow-up studies have shown that adolescence-limited antisocial behaviour persists into adult life more than originally envisaged. Also, it remains uncertain whether this group differs qualitatively from life-course persistent antisocial behaviour with respect to causal factors, or, rather, differs quantitatively in terms of risk influences. Second, trajectory analyses applied to longitudinal data have shown that it is also necessary to have a category for childhood-limited antisocial behaviour (Odgers et al. 2007b). The evidence from the Dunedin study suggests that this is quite a sizeable group meaning importantly that the *majority* of cases beginning in childhood do not go on to show life-course persistence. Third, it remains uncertain whether the key predictive feature (with respect to life-course persistence) derives from an unusually early age of onset or, rather, from either the presence of hyperactivity/inattention or a heavy genetic loading, or both (Rutter 2009a). The finding that life-course persistence is strongly associated with hyperactivity, cognitive impairments, and temperamental difficulty, strongly suggests that these features may be the key, and not the age of onset as such (Odgers et al. 2007a, 2007b). Also the finding that life-course persistence is associated with a strong family history of antisocial behaviour suggests the possible importance of genetic liability. I pointed out some time ago (Rutter 1989) that there must be caution before assuming that age is itself the driving force. That is because it indexes so many different features and it may be simply a marker of some other feature that provides the true element.

More recently evidence has accumulated to show that antisocial behaviour that is associated with psychopathic traits is meaningfully different (Blair and Viding 2008). Thus, genetic influences are stronger in the case of antisocial behaviour associated with psychopathy than with antisocial behaviour not so associated (Viding *et al.* 2005; Viding *et al.* 2009). There is also evidence that children with callous unemotional traits show a specific neurocognitive profile as manifested by insensitivity to punishment and distress cues (Dadds *et al.* 2006). In addition, it seems that their response to treatment is also different (Dadds and Rhodes 2009).

It has generally been found that it is quite unusual for antisocial behaviour to begin for the first time in adult life, without antisocial behaviour of some kind during childhood. Nevertheless, there are circumstances in which antisocial behaviour does begin in adult life. Elander *et al.* (2000) showed that this was most likely when either a serious adult mental disorder or substance abuse problems began in adult life. Thus, it has been found that schizophrenia is associated with a substantial increase in the risk for violent crime (Hodgins 2009).

None of these categories (and there are others – see Rutter *et al.* 1998) has clear-cut boundaries. The findings certainly do show that there is substantial, meaningful heterogeneity in antisocial behaviour. Accordingly, causal models will have to be explicit with respect to what type of antisocial behaviour they are seeking to explain. Yet one more distinction must be made with respect to causation. Up to this point, all of the discussion has focused on variations that apply at any one point in time. However, in addition, there has been an interest in the causes of changes in rates of antisocial behaviour over time (see Rutter and Smith 1995; Collishaw *et al.* 2004). It might be supposed that the same causes that influence changes over time will also influence individual differences at any one point in time. Nevertheless, the evidence runs counter to that assumption. Sometimes the causes may be similar but quite often they are different.

The last consideration is the need to differentiate between immediate and distant causal influences. Immediate influences are the ones that are more or less directly involved in the causal process. Distant causes are ones that play no part in immediate causation but which influence the immediate causes. A good example concerns the effects of poverty. Poverty is not an immediate cause of antisocial behaviour but it does make good family functioning more difficult and therefore makes the immediate causes of antisocial behaviour more likely (see, for example, Conger *et al.* 1992, 1993; Conger *et al.* 1995).

Testing for causation

Most of the research about possible causes of antisocial behaviour is about associations or correlations, although lip-service is often paid to the need to be cautious about moving from observed correlation to inferred causation. In the past little attempt has been made to determine the steps that need to be taken to test the causal inference. All of that has begun to change (Rutter 2009b, 2007). It is often assumed that statistical controls for possible confounding variables deals with the need satisfactorily, but it does not. This was shown, for example, by Rice *et al.* (2009) using the novel design of *in vitro* fertilization (IVF) to differentiate between mothers who are genetically related to their child and those who are not (see also Thapar *et al.*, in press). What this showed is that exposure to the mother's smoking in pregnancy did not have a causal effect on the child's antisocial behaviour or on hyperkinetic behaviour: instead shared genetic features explained the association between the mother's smoking and the child's antisocial behaviour. This means, for example, that Brennan *et al.* (2003) discussion of a causal model of prenatal influences on conduct disorder is based on a wrong assumption. In general, making the distinction between genetic influences on antisocial behaviour and the influences coming from the home environment turns out to be extremely important. As discussed by Rutter (2007) there is a considerable range of natural experiments that can be used to test causal inferences. None of them provides a totally satisfactory solution but, taken together, they can build up a powerful case for or against causation (Rutter 2009c). That is because each of the different strategies has a different set of strengths and limitations.

There are some half dozen natural experiments that focus particularly on the need to differentiate between genetic and environmental effects. The IVF example illustrated this in showing that it was unlikely that prenatal smoking itself, as opposed to an underlying genetic factor, had an effect on children's antisocial behaviour. Multivariate twin analyses can also pull apart genetic and environmental effects. For example, Jaffee *et al.* (2004) used this approach, with findings that were striking in showing that the main association between corporal punishment and children's antisocial behaviour arises because of shared genetic factors that influence both the child's behaviour and the way the parent responds to it – the same genetic factors that make the child prone to antisocial behaviour also make the parent prone to respond to it with corporal punishment. By contrast, maltreatment had genuine (bad) environmentally mediated effects that did not reflect shared inheritance between parent and child. The corporal punishment finding also reflects the two-way interactions between parent and child. Corporal punishment tends to be used in *response* to children's disruptive behaviour, rather than being a cause of it. Conversely, maltreatment is less affected by children's behaviour and mainly functions as a cause and not just a response. Discordant twin pairs have shown that sexual abuse of children separately from genetic inheritance has a substantial environmentally mediated effect on the risk of later alcoholism and drug use (Kendler and Prescott 2006). The effects on antisocial behaviour were not studied, but the findings probably apply. Studying the children of twins is a way of separating the effects of genetic inheritance from the effects of the social environment, because the children of monozygotic ('identical') twins are genetically like half-brothers or sisters, whereas they are more distant socially, like cousins. Using this method, it was found that harsh forms of physical punishment had a genuine influence on both disruptive behaviour and drug or alcohol use (Lynch *et al.* 2006).

Other natural experiments have been designed to avoid the problem that the causal influence usually operates on a particular group of people who are different from the rest (selection bias). More generally, the environments that increase the risk of antisocial behaviour and that protect people from that risk are not randomly distributed – they are more common for some kinds of people than for others. People's actions play a substantial role in the shaping and selection of environments. This problem of selection bias can be overcome in circumstances where the causal factor under discussion applies to everyone in the population. For example, Costello *et al.* (2003) examined the effects of setting up a casino on an American Indian reservation on the children's psychopathological outcomes. The experiment comes about because by federal law in the United States, a particular proportion of the profits from the casino had to be distributed to all living on the reservation but without any actions by the individuals. The results showed that the relief of poverty was associated with a significant reduction in disruptive behaviour, and more detailed analyses indicated that the benefits were probably brought about through changes in the family. The study illustrates the need to differentiate between immediate and more distant causes.

A further strategy is to compare the timing of within-individual change with the timing of some possible causal influence. Thus, numerous studies have shown that gang members tend to commit many serious and violent offences. Is that because individuals with a greater antisocial liability are likely to join a gang or because being in a gang influences them to engage in delinquent activities? Thornberry *et al.* (1993) used longitudinal data to make this comparison. The findings showed that crime rates were higher during the period of gang membership and hence the social experience facilitated crime (see also Nagin *et al.* 2008). Similarly, researchers have repeatedly found that married men are less likely than unmarried men to engage in crime. Sampson *et al.* (2006) used longitudinal data to compare individual changes in antisocial behaviour during periods of marriage and periods of not being married. They found an average reduction of about 35 per cent associated with marriage. That is to say, people's level of antisocial behaviour tended to vary over time according to whether or not they were married at that time. The rate of crime went up during periods when they were not married and down when they were married.[2]

It should be noted that these examples illustrate that natural experiments can be used, not only to examine effects on individual differences in the liability to commit antisocial behaviour but also individual differences in the course over time of antisocial behaviour. Given the evidence that antisocial behaviour tends to diminish in adult life in many individuals, but persists at a high level in others, the study of effects on developmental course are crucially important.

The environmental mediation of effects associated with particular environments or experiences

Plomin and Bergeman (1991) drew attention to the fact that the presence of gene-environment correlations meant that experiences defined in terms of environments might, nevertheless, involve genetic mediation. Subsequent research has confirmed the presence of important gene-environment correlations (Kendler and Baker 2007) and multivariate twin analyses have, indeed, shown that part of the effects of risk environments involves genetic mediation (see for example, Pike *et al.* 1996). It is not that the genes as such influence environments; rather, the behaviours of individuals serve to shape and select environments and such behaviour will be open to genetic influences. Thus, adoptee studies have shown how children's disruptive behaviour may serve to elicit negative parenting by their adoptive mothers (Ge *et al.* 1996; O'Connor *et al.* 1998). As discussed above, this appreciation has led to the development of a range of 'natural experiments' that can test for environmental mediation (Moffitt and Scott 2008). The results have shown that there are truly causal effects that stem from child maltreatment (Dodge *et al.* 1995; Jaffee *et al.* 2004), family poverty (D'Onofrio *et al.* 2009; Costello *et al.* 2003), being a member of a delinquent gang (Dishion *et al.* 1999; Thornberry *et al.* 1993), being the victim of bullying (Arseneault *et al.* 2006) and experiencing impaired parenting by depressed mothers (Kim-Cohen *et al.* 2005). On the other hand, natural experiments of various kinds have cast doubt on the claims that prenatal exposure to mothers' smoking causes antisocial behaviour (Rice *et al.* 2009; D'Onofrio *et al.* 2008). Also, the evidence as a whole suggests that the risk from witnessing violence is quite small unless victimization is involved (Wilson *et al.* 2009).

Proposed causal models

Before trying to summarize what is known on the causes of antisocial behaviour and offending, it is useful to turn to various different causal models that have been put forward. These were usefully brought together in *Causes of Conduct Disorder and Juvenile Delinquency* edited by Lahey *et al.* (2003). Snyder *et al.* (2003) argued that antisocial development is driven by two core causal processes. First, there are the social and material contingencies that are engendered by aggressive, oppositional and stealthy behaviour. Second, there is the selection of environmental niches that strongly influences the experiences and contingencies to which the children are exposed and the manner in which adults manage such exposure via monitoring. Coercive experiences are seen as particularly critical with respect to the first core function and peer-deviance training as crucial for the second. This research group have used a range of well thought through research strategies involving interventions that can test the postulated mediating function. There is a good deal of supporting evidence for this social learning approach, although the findings raise various queries.

What the theory does not deal with so satisfactorily is the importance of individual differences, although their importance is clearly acknowledged. Thus, Snyder *et al.* (2003) hypothesized that girls show lower rates of antisocial behaviour because they are less frequently involved in coercive parent–child interaction. The careful study of sex differences undertaken by Moffitt *et al.* (2001) casts doubt on this explanation: the findings suggested that the key difference lay in the lower rate of neurodevelopmental problems in girls. A further questionable feature concerns the emphasis on the protective effect of parental monitoring of young people's activities. Stattin and Kerr (2000) persuasively argued from their findings that associations mainly reflected what young people told parents about their activities rather than the efficiency of parental supervision and monitoring (Kerr *et al.* 2010). Nevertheless, Lahey *et al.* (2008) showed that parental knowledge was a meaningful predictor of delinquency and not just a spurious association. Also, there was an independent effect of supervision that was not fully accounted for by parental knowledge.

Developmental distinction between life-course persistence and adolescent-limited antisocial behaviour

As already noted, Moffitt (2003) proposed a development taxonomy in which life-course antisocial behaviour had its origins in neurodevelopmental processes that operated from early childhood; and adolescence-limited antisocial behaviour that began in adolescence and had its origins in social processes. Although Moffitt emphasized the early neurodevelopmental origins of life-course persistent antisocial behaviour, she also noted the empirical findings showing the importance of both family adversity and peer rejection. So far, Moffitt has not articulated the particular ways in which brain development is influenced by genes or parenting, nor has she described the pathway from faulty brain development to antisocial behaviour. Empirical findings from the Dunedin study (Caspi *et al.* 2002) have taken things further in showing the importance of gene-environment interactions (see below). Aguilar *et al.* (2000), on the basis of a longitudinal study of a socially disadvantaged sample, queried Moffitt's claim that deficits in brain development played a crucial role in the biological origins of antisocial behaviour, but the weight of evidence certainly supports Moffitt's claims and Moffitt has put forward reasons why the Minnesota Study findings appeared different. The least tested part of Moffitt's theory is the claim that adolescence-limited antisocial behaviour happens because young people try to demonstrate their maturity by imitating the behaviour of life-course persistent delinquents. Moffitt is unusual among theorists in focusing explicitly on why antisocial behaviour is so much more frequent in males than females (Moffitt et al. 2001). The Dunedin study findings clearly indicated that the key difference lay in the much lower rate of neurodevelopmental abnormalities in females. The theory is said to apply across ethnic and cultural groups, but there has not been an explicit focus on the reasons why antisocial behaviour is more frequent in some groups than in others.

Developmental propensity model

Lahey and Waldman (2003) put forward what they have called a developmental propensity model. This differs from the Moffitt model mainly in arguing that age of onset and the patterns of causal features vary along a continuum, rather than defining distinct categories. They proposed that there is a propensity to antisocial behaviour defined by three aspects of temperament: a tendency to negative (e.g. aggressive) emotions, a lack of prosocial qualities (i.e. lack of ability to cooperate harmoniously) and a high level of daring. Also these aspects of temperament were said to be accompanied by lower cognitive ability and slow language development. They argued that conduct problems starting at an early age, attention deficit hyperactivity disorder (ADHD) and oppositional defiant disorder reflected the same underlying temperamental and cognitive deficits. Like Moffitt, they emphasized the importance of genetic influences but argued that the genes do not directly influence antisocial behaviour, but influence temperament which in turn influences antisocial behaviour. Moreover, they proposed that genes influence both children's disruptive behaviour and the way parents respond to it, and that the children's disruptive behaviour then evokes negative parenting: the upshot is a strong correlation between negative parenting and children's disruptive behaviour that arises from a complex interaction between genetic and environmental influences. This is an effect supported by the findings of both Ge et al. (1996) and O'Connor et al. (1998). There is substantial empirical support for the associations that have given rise to this concept but, again, much is still to be learned about the way in which the causal pathway is mediated.

Social control theories and social context model

A generation ago, Hirschi (1969) proposed that delinquent acts resulted when an individual's bond to society was weak or broken. The key elements in that bond were *attachment* to other people, *commitment* to an organized society, *involvement* in conventional activities, and *belief* in a common value system (see Rutter and Giller 1983). There is consistent evidence in support of many of the key postulates but the theory fails to account for the strong evidence that parents' criminality and delinquent peer groups have an influence on antisocial behaviour. The social control theory assumes that everyone has some potential to commit delinquent acts but it sidesteps the crucial issue of why there are large individual differences in this liability. Few researchers any longer believe that, even with additional considerations (see for example, Johnson 1979; Elliott *et al.* 1979), social control postulates provide an overall explanation of the causes of crime. The modern concept that living in a community showing collective efficacy protects whereas living in a disorganized community damages (Sampson *et al.* 1997) constitutes the sequel to the original concept of social control theory. It differs fundamentally, however, in its focus on community influences and the implications for preventive intervention (see Wikström and Sampson 2003). Crucially this concept suggests not so much that noxious community influences foster antisocial behaviour but, rather, that social disorganization and a lack of collective efficacy fail to inhibit it.

Over- and under-arousal model

Keenan and Shaw (2003) emphasized the role of early individual differences in behavioural style. They suggested that either over-arousal or under-arousal to stress would constitute a pathway to antisocial behaviour: over-arousal being important with respect to reactive aggression; and under-arousal to proactive antisocial behaviour. They noted the evidence that the biological basis of these types of responses were rather different. The model has the advantage of focusing on a possible mediating psychological mechanism. There is empirical support for the observed features but their causal role remains to be tested.

Tremblay's 'learning how not to physically aggress' model

Tremblay's (2003) model, like that of others, incorporates a wide range of both individual features and environmental influences. First, he has emphasized the need to differentiate physical aggression from other forms of disruptive behaviour – a proposition for which there is a good deal of empirical support. Second, physical aggression is at its peak between two and four years of age, as shown by several studies. This points to the need to put the origins of antisocial behaviour early in the pre-school years, and not in adolescence when juvenile delinquency reaches a peak. Following from these two points, he has argued that, instead of focusing on personal characteristics and experiences that cause children to learn to physically aggress, attention should shift to qualities and experiences that help children to learn *not* to physically aggress. Specifically, Tremblay has argued that playfighting during early childhood has a significant impact on learning to regulate physical aggression. Second, the development of executive function (planning and thinking ahead) during early childhood has a significant impact on learning to regulate physical aggression. On this basis he has urged that prevention programmes might usefully concentrate on training in play-fighting games and training in executive function games. In other words, both play-fighting and understanding the consequences of violence are seen as crucial mechanisms in learning not to aggress. The focus on mediation as a way of testing the causal inference is an undoubted strength. On the other hand, the growth trajectories for antisocial behaviour from early childhood to adolescence show that the fall-off in physical aggression, although it occurs, accounts for less of the variation than the major individual differences in the initial level of physical aggression during the preschool period.

Neuropsychological vulnerability model

Nigg and Huang-Pollock (2003), like Lahey and Waldman (2003) brought together three neuropsychological vulnerabilities: difficulty in learning language, an over-emotional response to frustration and lack of ability to think and plan ahead (deficit in executive control). A key element in this model is that the vulnerabilities do not lead to antisocial behaviour directly. Instead it is suggested that they are important because they make it harder for people to adapt to hostile environments or challenging experiences. Research findings provide ample support for the associations with lower verbal IQ, executive function deficits and emotional disregulation. But what is lacking is a rigorous test of the hypothesis that these elements are the key mediators and, moreover, that they primarily operate in terms of making the child vulnerable to high-risk environments.

Maturation of the brain

Both post-mortem studies (Huttenlocher 1979) and prospective brain imaging studies (Gogtay *et al.* 2004) provide definitive evidence of substantial, important brain changes during the period of adolescence and early adult life. It is not that the brain gets larger, rather there is a differential neuronal pruning that in many respects parallels the same 'fine tuning' that takes place in early childhood. Could these brain alterations underlie the changes in crime during the same age period? Whilst it is unlikely that such changes that are a part of normal development constitute a direct cause of crime, it is possible that they could increase vulnerability to drugs or to other physical hazards. Three features complicate possible causal inferences. First, the timing of the brain changes varies across different brain regions. Second, there are substantial individual differences in timing. Third, although it is obvious that the functioning of the brain provides the substrate for the workings of the mind, we remain ignorant on the precise nature of the links between the two (Johnson *et al.* 2009).

Social information-processing model

Dodge's (2003) social information-processing model is distinctive in focusing on how early experiences such as child abuse or peer rejection do or do not lead to later antisocial behaviour. A major strength of Dodge's approach is that it builds on the extensive evidence that experiences do not impinge on a passive organism. Right from early childhood, children actively process their experiences, developing concepts and models of what is happening to them. Thus, if someone is pushed getting off a bus, the recipient of the push may interpret it as an aggressive or hostile act, or they may assume that it was just an accident resulting from the crush of people. Dodge suggested that the bias towards one interpretation or the other may build up (or inhibit) a tendency to attribute hostile intentions to others and thereby to assume that their own aggressive behaviour is justified. There is empirical support for both the idea that social information-processing patterns predict future aggressive behaviour and that such patterns grow out of early adverse experiences. The limitation, however, is that these patterns account for a relatively small part of the variations between individuals in antisocial behaviour. It is not clear, at the moment, how far these relatively weak effects reflect measurement problems and how far they stem from the key causal variables being of a rather different kind.

Prefrontal damage model

Ishikawa and Raine (2003) argued that prefrontal damage is a key factor predisposing to antisocial behaviour. Brain imaging studies in adults provide some empirical support for this notion but there is less evidence available in childhood. A key weakness of the model is that the supposed environmental causes of the postulated brain damage are very questionable. Thus, the evidence on the role of pregnancy complications is unconvincing (see Rutter *et al.* 1998). There is good evidence of the association between minor congenital anomalies and antisocial behaviour but there is a lack of evidence on claims that these are environmentally caused. Also, claims that prenatal smoking causes antisocial behaviour are based on studies that lack adequate control for genetic mediation (Rice *et al.* 2009).

Serotonin functioning and impulsive violence

There is a substantial human and animal literature demonstrating links between serotonin functioning and impulsive violence (see Coccaro 1989; Kruesi and Jacobson 1997; Moffitt *et al.* 1998). Suomi's (2003) research group has also shown associations between deficits in serotonin metabolism and impulsive, aggressive behaviour in rhesus monkeys. They demonstrated that peer rearing (an adverse socialization experience) was associated with reduced serotonin metabolism and that this effect applied to monkeys with the 'short' allele version of the 5-HTT gene. This represented a gene–environment interaction because this polymorphism did not have the same outcome in individuals that experienced the usual maternal rearing.

Mass media

There is a considerable body of evidence, from both naturalistic and experimental studies, into the effects of violence in the media as a possible influence on aggressive or antisocial behaviour. The findings suggest that viewing violence may, in certain circumstances, play a contributory, potentiating role in fostering aggressive behaviour, although the effects are relatively weak. Probably, this comes about through three mechanisms. First, because viewing violence can be exciting, it can serve to disinhibit and therefore release aggressive tendencies. Second, the regular viewing of violence may serve to de-sensitize people to violence. Third, the regular viewing of violence may become incorporated into people's 'mental maps' about how challenges or difficulties should be dealt with (see Rutter *et al.* 1998). Although the evidence on individual differences is limited, it seems likely that these potentiating effects largely apply to individuals already showing an aggressive or antisocial propensity.

Drugs and alcohol

The association between antisocial behaviour and heavy alcohol drinking has been well demonstrated, but the association is likely to reflect two rather different causal processes. On the one hand, the liability to one is closely associated with the liability to the other (McGue and Iacono 2005). The propensity involves an impulsive, reckless, aggressive lifestyle that incorporates both heavy drinking and antisocial behaviour. On the other hand, there is also evidence that alcohol leads to disinhibition (Ito *et al.* 1996) that is associated with disorderly conduct offences and with driving offences, as well as occasionally with violent crime (Collins 1986; Mott 1990). Illicit drugs tend to be viewed by the media as important risk factors for crime, but the drug most associated with crime is alcohol. Nevertheless, regular users of heroin may steal in order to purchase their drugs and also drug trafficking sometimes involves groups that use violence and firearms to control the drug market. It is certainly possible that the growth in the use of drugs and the increase in alcohol consumption are contributory causal influences in explaining the increase in crime over the last half century (Rutter and Smith 1995).

Economic inequalities in society

Wilkinson and Pickett (2009) put together an extensive range of evidence showing that countries with major economic inequalities tend to have a higher rate of a broad range of health problems than countries where these inequalities are much less marked. Curiously, suicide is the exception to this pattern. They have not focused particularly on associations with antisocial behaviour but it is necessary to consider whether between-country variations in rates of crime are associated with parallel variations in income inequality, or whether changes over time in crime rates can be a function of changes in rates of inequality.

The associations are strong for homicide and violent assaults but less so for robbery and rape. They are particularly strong with respect to variations in rates of imprisonment. Similar associations are found among US states that vary in income inequality. All of these data are cross-sectional but secular trends show a broadly comparable picture. That finding makes the causal inference somewhat more justifiable. It should be noted, however, that the associations apply to a wide range of health outcomes and not just to antisocial behaviour. On the other hand, suicide is a surprising exception to this general association with income inequality. The mechanisms involved remain poorly understood but it does seem likely that high levels of income inequality in the society predisposes to antisocial behaviour and offending. The available findings suggest that these effects are not confined to the poor or disadvantaged – rather, they apply across societies. The hypothesized causal effect of income inequalities cannot, however, explain the fact that in the UK there was a marked rise in crime during the several decades following the Second World War despite the fact that income inequalities (and absolute levels of poverty) were diminishing during this time period (Rutter and Smith 1995). Moreover, during the later years of the twentieth century when income inequalities were markedly widening, this seemed to have no effect on the secular trend of antisocial behaviour. So far as the UK is concerned, income inequality over the last decade has remained high, although there have been minor changes for the better in some respects (Hills *et al.* 2009).

Ethnic variations

There is substantial evidence of large ethnic variations in rates of crime and antisocial behaviour (Rutter and Tienda 2005). Because these variations are at their most marked with respect to imprisonment and least marked with respect to self-report, there has been a good deal of discussion of the extent to which the variations reflect true variations in antisocial behaviour or, rather, discriminatory variations in the response of police and courts to antisocial behaviour, according to which ethnic group is involved. Reverse record checks (i.e. evaluation of the validity of self-reports, by matching police and court records to self-reporting by the same individuals), has shown that African Americans are less likely than Whites to report crimes for which they have been convicted (Morenoff 2005). On the other hand, there is evidence that bias accounts for some part of the elevated rates of arrest, conviction and imprisonment among black people as has been shown by studies in the UK (Smith 2005). The reasons for the ethnic variations in crime remain ill-understood but the evidence is clear that neither racial discrimination nor poverty provide anything like the complete explanation. For example, crime rates tend to be low among Asians although they are subjected to discrimination and although some of them (particularly those originally from Bangladesh) have high rates of poverty and disadvantage. Although the topic is politically sensitive, it is important to investigate the possible reasons for ethnic variations in antisocial behaviour and to do so without prejudicial assumptions that the explanation must lie in some form of individual propensity.

In that connection, a re-evaluation of the 1965 Moynihan report (Massey and Sampson 2009) is illuminating. Moynihan's core argument was that whenever any population subgroup lacked widespread access to reliable jobs, decent earnings and key forms of socially rewarded status, it may be expected that single parenthood will increase, with negative effects on both mothers and children. Family instability was seen as a a consequence of external social conditions. Since the Moynihan report, there has been a crisis in black male unemployment in the USA, which deepened greatly in the 1970s and 1980s – accompanied by an unprecedented increase in the prison population – a rise that continued even after a general decline in crime rates. Currently, a third of non-college black men end up in prison by their mid 30s. As Wilson (1996) noted, when work is unavailable there tends to be disengagement from society and the growth of an oppositional culture. In the USA, this is exacerbated by the deep racial divide in housing, and its very high temporal stability (Sampson and Sharkey 2008). With men out of work or in prison, there tends to be partnership instability and multi-partnered fertility leads to cycles of family disadvantage (McLanahan 2009). Whilst it is difficult to be sure about the nature of the causal pathways, the evidence points to the damaging effects of chronic unemployment and also the effects of prison in making it more difficult to get work. Not surprisingly, all of this is likely to have consequent negative effects on family functioning.

Crime in females

The research literature on antisocial behaviour in females is much more limited than that for males, but the relevant findings have been brought together and evaluated by Fontaine et al. (2009). They concluded that the developmental trajectories took a broadly similar form in the two sexes (see for example, Lahey et al. 2006; Odgers et al. 2008) but that an early-onset lifecourse-persistence pattern was much less common in females (as shown previously by Moffitt et al. 2001). Also, an adolescent delayed onset (meaning an onset in adolescence but with a background of childhood risk factors) might be more characteristic of females than males. It is also noteworthy that Dadds *et al.* (2009) found that severe deficits in empathy with other people's feelings were associated with psychopathy in males but not in females. Although, on the whole, crime in males and females involves similar causal pathways, there may be important differences that require study.

Neurobiology

Until very recently, the study of antisocial behaviour and of offending suffered considerably from a divide between basic laboratory neuroscience and clinical or epidemiological research. However, during the last decade or so there have been important attempts to bridge this divide (Hodgins *et al.* 2009). In considering the neurobiology of antisocial behaviour it is necessary to recognize that, on the one hand, there are substantial connections between the causes of antisocial behaviour, substance abuse and risk-taking behaviour (Krueger *et al.* 2007) and, on the other hand, that the features of brain functions associated with responding aggressively differ sharply from those associated with psychopathy (which is usually connected both with responding aggressively and with using aggression as a means to an end). Also, the bulk of the research has concerned adult offenders rather than juveniles. Nevertheless, although there are some inconsistent findings, the weight of evidence indicates that reactive aggression tends to be associated with reduced cortisol and autonomic functioning, and an increased neuroendocrine response to stress (van Goozen and Fairchild 2009; Patrick and Bernat 2009). The electroencephalogram (EEG) pattern responses give rise to much the same picture. Functional imaging studies have shown that adults with psychopathy show specific impairments in fearful expression processing and associated reduced amygdala responses, as well as reduced functional connectivity between the amygdala and the ventromedial prefrontal cortex. There is an extensive literature on executive functions in individuals showing antisocial behaviour (De Brito and Hodgins 2009) and the evidence suggests that response inhibition does tend to be impaired, but the wide-range of other executive functions are not. Almost all the research is cross-sectional in nature, making it very uncertain whether the findings are a cause or a consequence of antisocial behaviour. Also, most studies have not differentiated participants according to the presence or absence of psychopathic features. Davidson *et al.* (2000) has suggested that dysfunction in the neural circuitry of emotion regulation is a possible prelude to violence – and that remains a hypothesis well worth testing – but firm conclusions on causation would be premature.

There are several animal models for attention deficit hyperactivity disorder (ADHD) but it is not clear how far they have been informative for the neurobiology of ADHD in humans (Plessen and Peterson 2009). Functional brain imaging has shown that individuals with ADHD have widespread, lower than normal activation of the brain when performing tasks requiring them to hold back from responding immediately (Aron and Poldrack 2005). The reduced activity of the anterior cingulate cortex has been thought to be particularly important. However, there was increased activation in medial frontal and right paracentral regions. Structural brain imaging has usually shown a reduction in overall brain volume (Castellanos *et al.* 2002; Valera *et al.* 2007). The evidence that this can be seen early in life suggests that it is likely to be involved in causal processes but precisely how is unknown. Despite a substantial body of research, the meaning of these findings for causal mechanisms remains unclear. The implications for antisocial behaviour are even more uncertain despite the prominence of impulsivity as a feature. Pennington (2002) suggested that whereas ADHD may involve dysfunction in a prefrontal-striatal circuit, antisocial behaviour is more related to the orbito-frontal cortex-limited systems.

The higher rate of antisocial behaviour in males than females, together with the peak in offending during adolescence has long led to speculations about the possible causal role of androgens. Nevertheless, individual differences in testosterone levels show only weak, inconsistent associations with either antisocial behaviour generally or violence in particular (van Goozen and Fairchild 2009). Possibly prenatal testosterone levels may play a somewhat greater role.

Genetic influences

There is extensive evidence that there is a concentration of crime in families and also that genetic factors account for some 50 per cent of the variance in the individual liability to engage in antisocial behaviour (Moffitt 2005; Rhee and Waldman 2002). It is important to note, however, that the degree of heritability may vary with the level of environmental adversity. Thus, Hicks *et al.* (2009) using the Minnesota Twin Study data, found that when such adversity was more severe, the strength of the genetic influence was also greater. The findings imply some form of gene-environment interplay.

Twin studies have shown that ADHD and antisocial behaviour involve a genetic liability, which is shared to a considerable degree, and that antisocial behaviour associated with ADHD has a higher heritability than that which is not (Silberg *et al.* 1996; Thapar *et al.* 2001). Viding *et al.* (2005, 2009) have shown that antisocial behaviour associated with the presence of callous unemotional traits is much more strongly heritable than antisocial behaviour without such traits. Moreover, this high heritability has been shown to be independent of whether ADHD is also present. Care needs to be taken, however, before assuming that genetic factors fully account for the association between antisocial behaviour in parents and antisocial behaviour in their offspring. Thornberry's (2009) careful analysis of intergenerational data (across three generations) indicates that the *social* environment is also a key mediator.

Molecular genetic studies (i.e. those that identify specific genes with allelic variations particularly associated with antisocial behaviour) highlight certain key features. Thus, Caspi *et al.* (2008) reported replicated findings that the Val variant of the COMT gene was associated with antisocial behaviour in individuals with ADHD whilst not showing a significant association with either antisocial behaviour or ADHD on their own. The finding emphasizes that it should not be expected that genetic influences will operate in relation to either clinical or judicial categories.

The innovative studies undertaken by Meyer-Lindenberg and his colleagues (Meyer-Lindenberg *et al.* 2006; Buckholtz and Meyer-Lindenberg 2009) have taken forward in a major way the understanding of the causal mechanisms and the biological pathways involved. They used an intermediate phenotype (namely, response to emotional threat) that has the means to shape the neural responses as shown by structural and functional brain imaging. The gene studied was the one involved in the control of MAOA. Deliberately, they used a sample that was free of psychopathology in order to determine whether the risks applied just to disorder or whether they concern dimensions present in the general population as a whole. The findings were striking in four key respects. First, there were marked neural differences (both structural and functional) associated with allelic variations in the MAOA gene. This immediately indicated that a portion of the genetic liability must operate via influences on environment susceptibility (because the genetic effect was evident only in the presence of an environmental challenge). Second, this neural effect applied in individuals without neuropathology and hence must apply to dimensions that do not directly cause antisocial behaviour, although they play a part in a causal pathway to it. Third, the GxE neural findings applied to males but not to females. Fourth, the impaired functional connectivity during the facial emotion processing task between the amygdala and the ventromedial prefrontal cortex was shown by a mediation path analysis to account for the MAOA genetic effect. This body of research clearly indicates the high potential of functional neurobiological studies to delineate causal mechanisms. In this case it seemed that the effects were primarily on impulsive or reactive aggression rather than instrumental aggression as seen with psychopathy. It should be noted, however, that the allelic variation, despite its dramatic effects on neural functioning, accounts for only a small amount of the variation. There will not be a single biological mechanism that accounts for the whole of antisocial behaviour.

Conclusions

It is all too obvious that no succinct, and simple, conclusions on the causes of antisocial behaviour and offending are possible. Nevertheless, there has been considerable progress in unravelling the causal pathways.

1. It is clear that serious family discord and hostility, and the experience of abuse, are an important part of the causal nexus.

2. An involvement in delinquent gangs increases the likelihood of violence offences.

3. Although definitive studies are lacking, a lack of employment opportunities and the negative effects of imprisonment are likely to be important risk factors.

4. Although not primary causes, both media influences and the effects of alcohol (and illicit drugs) probably potentiate the risks.

5. Whereas poverty probably constitutes a weak immediate causal factor, it may be much more important as a distant factor making positive family functioning more difficult. Probably, too, marked income inequalities in any society constitute additional risk factors.

6. Genetic influences on individual difference in the liability to engage in antisocial behaviour are very important – probably especially so for crime associated with either inattention/hyperactivity or psychopathy. However, almost certainly, there is no gene for crime; rather genetic effects operate indirectly via effects on environmental susceptibility on impulsivity, on substance use and on pathways that operate within the general population.

7. There is good evidence that antisocial behaviour is associated with identifiable differences in neural functioning; what remains uncertain is the relative importance of causal influences and of the reverse effects of antisocial behaviour on the brain.

8. There is good evidence that cognitive differences play a role in the propensity to engage in antisocial behaviour but much remains to be learned on the specifics.

9. There is good evidence on the heterogeneity of antisocial behaviour. This is best demonstrated in terms of associations with psychopathy, with inattention/overactivity, and with schizophrenia.

10. Ethnic variations and sex differences are known to be very important but knowledge is lacking on the implications for causal mechanisms.

11. Although little has been said here (because research on the topic has gone out of fashion), situational factors were shown to be important

years ago (Clarke 1983) and there is no reason to doubt their relevance today.

12. It is apparent that not only are there several causal pathways leading to antisocial behaviour, but also there are substantial individual differences in people's response to all causal features.

Notes

1 This review excludes the numerous serious crimes (including genocide) committed by governments and by terrorists around the world, because their consideration involves a range of issues that go well beyond the causes of offending and antisocial behaviour shown by individuals. The review also excludes crimes committed by police officers because the evidence is usually kept secret and rarely leads to prosecution. Accordingly, there is no way of determining whether the features that are associated with antisocial behaviour or offending in the general population also apply to the police.

2 A wide range of features were used to test selection into marriage and an inverse probability of treatment weighting (IPTW) method was used to create, in effect, a pseudo-population of weighted replicas that allowed the comparison of married and unmarried status without the need for making distributional assumptions.

References

Academy of Medical Sciences (2007) *Identifying the Environmental Causes of Disease: How should we decide what to believe and when to take action?* (London: Academy of Medical Sciences).

Aguilar, B., Sroufe, L.A., Egeland, B. and Carlson, E. (2000) 'Distinguishing the early-onset/persistent and adolescence-onset antisocial behavior types: from birth to 16 years', *Development and Psychopathology*, 12, pp. 109–32.

Aron, A.R. and Poldrack, R.A. (2005) 'The cognitive neuroscience of response inhibition: relevance for genetic research in attention-deficit/hyperactivity disorder', *Biological Psychiatry*, 57, pp. 1285–92.

Arseneault, L., Walsh, E., Trzesniewski, K., Newcombe, R., Caspi, A. and Moffitt, T.E. (2006) 'Bullying victimization uniquely contributes to adjustment problems in young children: a nationally representative cohort study' *Pediatrics*, 118, pp. 130–8.

Blair, R.J.R. and Viding, E. (2008) 'Psychopathy', in M. Rutter, D. Bishop, D. Pine, S. Scott, J. Stevenson, E. Taylor and A. Thapar (eds) *Rutter's Child and Adolescent Psychiatry*, 5th edition (Oxford: Blackwell), pp. 852–63.

Brennan, P.A., Grekin, E.R. and Mednick, S.A. (2003) 'Prenatal and perinatal influences on conduct disorder and serious delinquency', in B.B. Lahey, T.E. Moffitt and A. Caspi (eds) *Causes of Conduct Disorder and Juvenile Delinquency* (New York and London: Guilford Press), pp. 319–41.

Buckholtz, J.W. and Meyer-Lindenberg, A. (2009) 'Gene-brain associations: the example of MAOA', in S. Hodgins, E. Viding and A. Plodowski (eds) *The Neurobiological Basis of Violence: Science and rehabilitation* (Oxford: Oxford University Press), pp. 265–85.

Caspi, A., Langley, K., Milne, B., Moffitt, T., O'Donovan, M., Owen, M., Polo-Tomas, M., Poulton, R., Rutter, M., Taylor, A., Williams, B. and Thapar, T. (2008) 'A replicated molecular genetic basis for subtyping antisocial behaviour in children with attention-deficit/hyperactivity disorder', *Archives of General Psychiatry*, 65, pp. 203–10.

Caspi, A., McClay, J., Moffitt, T. E., Mill, J., Martin, J., Craig, I. W., Taylor, A. and Poulton, R. (2002) 'Role of genotype in the cycle of violence in maltreated children', *Science*, 297, pp. 851–4.

Castellanos, F.X., Lee, P.P., Sharp, W., Jeffries, N.O., Greenstein, D.K., Clasen, L.S., Blumenthal, J.D., James, R.S., Ebens, C.L., Walter, J.M., Zijdenbos, A., Evens, A.C., Giedd, J.N. and Rapoport, J.L. (2002) 'Developmental trajectories of brain volume abnormalities in children and adolescents with attention-deficit/hyperactivity disorder', *Journal of the American Medical Association*, 288, pp. 1740–8.

Clarke, R.V. (1983) 'Situational crime prevention: its theoretical basis and practical scope', *Crime and Justice*, 4, pp. 225–56.

Coccaro, E.F. (1989) 'Central serotonin and impulsive aggression', *British Journal of Psychiatry*, 155 (supplement 8), pp. 52–62.

Collins, J.J. (1986) 'The relationship of problem drinking to individual offending sequences', in A. Blumstein, J. Cohen, J.A. Roth and C.AS. Visher (eds) *Criminal Careers and Career Criminals* (Washington, DC: National Academy Press), pp. 89–120.

Collishaw, S., Maughan, B., Goodman, R. and Pickles, A. (2004) 'Time trends in adolescent mental health', *Journal of Child Psychology and Psychiatry*, 45, pp. 1350–62.

Conger, R.D., Conger, K.J., Elder, G.H., Lorenz, F.O., Simons, R.L. and Whitbeck, L.B. (1992) 'A family process model of economic hardship and adjustment of early adolescent boys', *Child Development*, 63, pp. 526–41.

Conger, R.D., Conger, K.J., Elder, G.H. and Lorenz, F.O. (1993) 'Family economic stress and adjustment of early adolescent girls', *Developmental Psychology*, 29, pp. 206–19.

Conger, R.D., Patterson, G.R. and Ge, X. (1995) 'It takes two to replicate: a mediational model for the impact of parent's stress on adolescent adjustment', *Child Development*, 66, pp. 80–97.

Costello, E. J., Compton, S. N., Keeler, S. N. and Angold, A. (2003) 'Relationships between poverty and psychopathology: a natural experiment', *Journal of the American Medical Association*, 290, pp. 2023–9.

Dadds, M.R., Perry, Y., Hawes, D.J,. Merz, S., Riddell, A.C., Haines, D.J., Solak, E. and Abeygunawardane, A.I. (2006) 'Attention to the eyes and fear-recognition deficits in child psychopathy', *British Journal of Psychiatry*, 189, pp. 280–1.

Dadds, M.R. and Rhodes, T. (2009) 'Aggression in young children with concurrent callous-unemotional traits: can the neurosciences inform progress and innovation in treatment approaches?', in S. Hodgins, E. Viding and A. Plodowski (eds) *The Neurobiological Basis of Violence: Science and rehabilitation* (Oxford: Oxford University Press), pp. 85–99.

Davidson, R.J., Putnam, K.M. and Larson, C.L. (2000) 'Dysfunction in the neural circuitry of emotion regulation – a possible prelude to violence', *Science*, 289, pp. 591–4.

De Brito S.A. and Hodgins, S. (2009) 'Executive functions of persistent violent offenders: a critical review of the literature', in S. Hodgins, E. Viding and A. Plodowski (eds) *The Neurobiological Basis of Violence: Science and rehabilitation* (Oxford: Oxford University Press), pp. 167–99.

Dishion, T.J., McCord, J. and Poulin, F. (1999) 'When interventions harm: peer groups and problem behavior', *American Psychologist*, 54, pp. 755–64.

Dodge, K.A. (2003) 'Do social information-processing patterns mediate aggressive behavior?' in B.B. Lahey, T.E. Moffitt and A. Caspi (eds) (2003) *Causes of Conduct Disorder and Juvenile Delinquency* (New York and London: Guilford Press), pp. 254–74.

Dodge, K.A., Pettit, G.S., Bates, J. and Valente, E. (1995) 'Social information: processing patterns partially mediate the effect of early physical abuse on later conduct problems', *Journal of Abnormal Psychology*, 104, pp. 632–43.

D'Onofrio, B.M., Van Hulle, C.A., Waldman, I.D., Rodgers, J.L., Harden, K.P., Rathouz, P.J. and Lahey, B.B. (2008) 'Smoking during pregnancy and offspring externalizing problems: an exploration of genetic and environmental confounds', *Development and Psychopathology*, 20, pp. 139–64.

D'Onofrio, B.M., Goodnight, J.A., Van Julle, C.A., Rodgers, J.L., Rathouz, P.J., Waldman, I.D. and Lahey, B.B. (2009) 'A quasi-experimental analysis of the association between family income and offspring conduct problems', *Journal of Abnormal Child Psychology*, 37, pp. 415–29.

Elander, J., Simonoff, E., Pickles, A., Holmshaw, J. and Rutter, M. (2000) 'Londitudinal study of adolescent and adult conviction rates among children referred to psychiatric services for behavioural or emotional problems', *Criminal Behaviour and Mental Health*, 10, pp. 40–59.

Elliott, D.S., Ageton, S.S. and Canter, R.J. (1979) 'An integrated theoretical perspective on delinquent behaviour', *Journal of Research in Crime and Delinquency*, 16, pp. 3–27.

Fontaine, N., Carbonneau, R., Vitaro, F., Barker, E.D. and Tremblay, R.E. (2009) 'Research review: a critical review of studies on the developmental trajectories of antisocial behavior in females', *Journal of Child Psychology and Psychiatry*, 50, pp. 363–85.

Ge, X., Conger, R.D., Cadoret, R.J., Neiderhiser, J.M., Yates, W., Troughton, E. and Stewart, M.A. (1996) 'The developmental interface between nature and nurture: a mutual influence model of child antisocial behavior and parent behaviors', *Developmental Psychology*, 32, pp. 574–89.

Gogtay, N., Giedd, J.N., Lusk, L., Hayashi, K.M., Greenstein, D., Vaituzis, A.C., Nugent, T.F.3rd, Herman, D.H., Clasen, L.S., Toga, A.W., Rapoport, J.L. and Thompson, P.M. (2004) 'Dynamic mapping of human cortical development during childhood through early adulthood', *Proceedings of the National Academy of Science of the USA*, 101, pp. 8174–9.

Hicks, B. M., South, S.C., Dirago, A.D., Krueger, R. F., Iacono, W.G. and McGue, M. (2009) 'Environmental adversity and increasing genetic risk for externalizing disorders', *Archives of General Psychiatry*, 66, pp. 640–8.

Hills, J., Sefton, T. and Stewart, K. (2009) (eds) *Towards a More Equal Society? Poverty, inequality and policy since 1997* (Bristol: The Policy Press).

Hirschi, T. (1969) *Causes of Delinquency* (Berkeley: University of California Press).

Hodgins, S. (2009) 'Violent behaviour among people with schizophrenia: a framework for investigations of causes, effective treatment, and prevention', in S. Hodgins, E. Viding and A. Plodowski (eds) *The Neurobiological Basis of Violence: Science and rehabilitation* (Oxford: Oxford University Press), pp. 43–64.

Hodgins, S., Viding, E. and Plodowski A. (eds) (2009) *The Neurobiological Basis of Violence: Science and rehabilitation*, (Oxford: Oxford University Press).

Huttenlocher, P.R. (1979) 'Synaptic density in human frontal cortex: developmental changes and effects of aging', *Brain Research*, 163, pp. 195–205.

Ishikawa, S.S. and Raine, A. (2003) 'Prefrontal deficits and antisocial behavior: a causal model', in B.B. Lahey, T.E. Moffitt and A. Caspi (eds) *Causes of Conduct Disorder and Juvenile Delinquency* (New York and London: Guilford Press), pp. 277–304.

Ito, T., Miller, N. and Pollock, V.E. (1996) 'Alcohol and aggression: a meta-analysis on the moderating effects of inhibitory cues, triggering events, and self-focused attention', *Psychological Bulletin*, 120, pp. 60–82.

Jaffee, S.R., Caspi, A., Moffitt, T.E., Polo-Tomas, M., Price, T.S. and Taylor A. (2004) 'The limits of child effects: Evidence for genetically mediated child effects on corporal punishment but not on physical maltreatment', *Developmental Psychology*, 40, pp. 1047–58.

Johnson, R.E. (1979) *Juvenile Delinquency and its Origins* (Cambridge: Cambridge University Press).

Johnson, S.B., Blum, R.W. and Giedd, J.N. (2009) 'Adolescent maturity and the brain: the promise and pitfalls of neuroscience research in adolescent health policy', *Journal of Adolescent Health*, 45, pp. 216–21.

Keenan, K. and Shaw, D.S. (2003) 'Starting at the beginning: exploring the etiology of antisocial behavior in the first years of life', in B.B. Lahey, T.E. Moffitt and A. Caspi (eds) *Causes of Conduct Disorder and Juvenile Delinquency* (New York and London: Guilford Press), pp. 153–81.

Kendler, K.S. and Baker J.H. (2007) 'Genetic influences on measures of the environment: a systematic review', *Psychological Medicine*, 37, pp. 615–26.

Kendler, K.S., Jacobson, K., Myers J. M. and Eaves L. J. (2008) 'A genetically informative developmental study of the relationship between conduct disorder and peer deviance in males', *Psychological Medicine*, 38, pp. 1001–11.

Kendler, K.S. and Prescott, C.A. (2006) *Genes, Environment, and Psychopathology: Understanding the causes of psychiatric and substance use disorders* (New York: Guilford Press).

Kerr, M., Stattin, H. and Burk, W. J. (2010) A reinterpretation of parental monitoring in longitudinal perspective. *Journal of Research on Adolescence*, 20, pp. 39–64.

Kim-Cohen, J., Moffitt, T.E., Taylor, A., Pawlby, S.J. and Caspi, A. (2005) 'Maternal depression and child antisocial behavior: nature and nurture effects', *Archives of General Psychiatry*, 60, pp. 709–17.

Krueger, R.F., Markon, K.E., Patrick, C.J., Benning, S.D. and Kramer, M. (2007) 'Linking antisocial behavior, substance use and personality: an integrative quantitative model of the adult externalizing spectrum', *Journal of Abnormal Psychology*, 111, pp. 411–24.

Kruesi, M.J.P. and Jacobson, T. (1997) 'Serotonin and human violence: Do environmental mediators exist?', in A. Raine, P.A. Brennan and S.A. Mednick (eds) *Biosocial Bases of Violence* (New York: Plenum), pp. 189–205.

Lahey, B.B., Moffitt, T.E. and Caspi, A. (eds) (2003) *Causes of Conduct Disorder and Juvenile Delinquency* (New York and London: Guilford Press).

Lahey, B. and Waldman, I.D. (2003) 'A developmental propensity model of the origins of conduct problems during childhood and adolescence', in B.B. Lahey, T.E. Moffitt and A. Caspi (eds) *Causes of Conduct Disorder and Juvenile Delinquency* (New York and London: Guilford Press), pp. 76–117.

Lahey, B.B., van Hulle, C.A., Waldman, I.D., Rodgers, J.L., D'Onofrio, B.M., Pedlow, S., Rathouz. P. J. and Keenan, K. (2006) 'Testing descriptive hypotheses regarding sex differences in the development of conduct problems and delinquency', *Journal of Abnormal Child Psychology*, 34, pp. 737–55.

Lahey, B.B., Van Hulle, C.A., D'Onofrio, B.M., Rodgers, J.L. and Waldman, I.D. (2008) 'Is parental knowledge of their adolescent offspring's whereabouts and peer associations spuriously associated with offspring delinquency?' *Journal of Abnormal Child Psychology*, 36, pp. 807–23.

Lynch, S.K., Turkheimer, E., D'Onofrio, B.M., Mendle, J. and Emery, R.E. (2006) 'A genetically informed study of the association between harsh punishment and offspring behavioural problems', *Journal of Family Psychology*, 20, pp. 190–8.

MacMahon, B., Pugh, T.F. and Ipsen, J. (1960) *Epidemiologic Methods* (Boston: Little, Brown and Company).

Massey, D.S. and Sampson, R.J. (2009) 'The Moynihan Report revisited: lessons and reflections after four decades', *Annals of the American Academy of Political and Social Science*, 621.

McGue M. and Iacono W.G. (2005) 'The association of early adolescent problem behavior with adult psychopathology', *American Journal of Psychiatry*, 162, pp. 1118–24.

McLanahan, S. (2009) 'Fragile families and the reproduction of poverty', *The Annals of the American Academy of Political and Social Science*, 621, pp. 111–31.

Meyer-Lindenberg, A., Buckholtz, J.W., Kolachana, B., Hariri, A.R., Pezawas, L., Blasi, G., Wabnitz, A., Honea, R., Verchinski, B., Callicott, J.H., Egan, M., Mattay, V. and Weinberger, D.R. (2006) 'Neural mechanisms of genetic risk for impulsivity and violence in humans', *Proceedings of the National Academy of Sciences of the USA*, 103, pp. 6269–74.

Moffitt, T.E. (1993) '"Life-course-persistent" and "adolescence-limited" antisocial behavior: a developmental taxonomy', *Psychological Review*, 100, pp. 674–701.

Moffitt, T.E. (2003) 'Life-course-persistent and adolescence-limited antisocial behavior: a 10-year research review and a research agenda', in B.B. Lahey, T.E. Moffitt and A. Caspi (eds) *Causes of Conduct Disorder and Juvenile Delinquency* (New York and London: Guilford Press), pp. 49–75.

Moffitt, T.E. (2005) 'The new look of behavioral genetics in developmental psychpathology: gene-environment interplay in antisocial behaviors', *Psychological Bulletin*, 131, pp. 533–54.

Moffitt, T. E., Arseneault, L., Jaffee, S. R., Kim-Cohen, J., Koenen, K. C., Odgers, C. L., Slutske, W. S. and Viding, E. (2008) 'Research Review: DSM-V conduct disorder: research needs for an evidence base', *Journal of Child Psychology and Psychiatry*, 49:1, pp. 3–33.

Moffitt, T.E., Brammer, G.L., Caspi, A., Fawcett, J.P., Raleigh, M., Yuwiler, A. and Silva, P. (1998) 'Whole blood-serotonin relates to violence in an epidemiological study', *Biological Psychiatry*, 43, pp. 446–57.

Moffitt, T.E, Caspi, A., Rutter, M. and Silva, P.A. (2001) *Sex differences in antisocial behaviour: conduct disorder, delinquency and violence in the Dunedin longitudinal study* (Cambridge: Cambridge University Press).

Moffitt, T.E. and Scott, S. (2008) 'Conduct disorders of childhood and adolescence', in M. Rutter, D. Bishop, D. Pine, S. Scott, J. Stevenson, E. Taylor and A. Thapar (eds) *Rutter's Child and Adolescent Psychiatry*, 5th edition (Oxford: Blackwell), pp. 543–64.

Morenoff, J.D. (2005) 'Racial and ethnic disparities in crime and delinquency in the United States', in M. Rutter and M. Tienda (eds) *Ethnicity and Causal Mechanisms* (New York: Cambridge University Press), pp. 139–73.

Mott, J. (1990) 'Young people, alcohol and crime', *Home Office Research Bulletin*, 28, pp. 24–8.

Nagin, D.S., Barker, T., Lacourse, E. and Tremblay, R.E. (2008) 'The interrelationship of temporally distinct risk markers and the transit from childhood physical aggression to adolescent violent delinquency', in P. Cohen (ed.) *Applied Data Analytic Techniques for Turning Points Research* (New York: Routledge), pp. 17–36.

Nigg, J.T. and Huang-Pollock, C.L. (2003) 'An early-onset model of the role of executive functions and intelligence in conduct disorder/delinquency', in B.B. Lahey, T.E. Moffitt and A. Caspi (eds) *Causes of Conduct Disorder and Juvenile Delinquency* (New York and London: Guilford Press), pp. 227–53.

O'Connor, T.G., Deater-Deckard, K., Fulker, D., Rutter, M. and Plomin, R. (1998) 'Genotype-environment correlations in late childhood and early adolescence: antisocial behavioral problems and coercive parenting', *Developmental Psychology*, 34, pp. 970–81.

Odgers, C.L., Milne, B.J., Caspi, A., Crump, R., Poulton, R. and Moffitt, T.E. (2007a) 'Predicting prognosis for the conduct-problem boy: can family history help?' *Journal of the American Academy of Child and Adolescent Psychiatry*, 46, pp. 1240–9.

Odgers, C.L., Caspi, A., Broadbent, J.M., Dickson, N., Hancox, R.J., Harrington, H-L., Poulton, R., Sears, M.R., Thomson, W.M. and Moffitt, T.E. (2007b) 'Prediction of differential adult health burden by conduct problem subtypes in males', *Archives of General Psychiatry*, 64, pp. 476–84.

Odgers, C.L., Moffitt, T.E., Broadbent, J.M., Dickson, N.P., Hancox, R.J., Harrington, H., Poulton, R., Sears, M.R., Thompson, W.M. and Caspi, A. (2008) 'Female and male antisocial trajectories: from childhood origins to adult outcomes', *Development and Psychopathology*, 20, pp. 673–716.

Patrick, C.J. and Bernat, E.M. (2009) 'From markers to mechanisms: using psychophysiological measures to elucidate basic processes underlying aggressive externalizing behaviour', in S. Hodgins, E. Viding and A. Plodowski (eds) *The Neurobiological Basis of Violence: Science and Rehabilitation* (Oxford: Oxford University Press), pp. 223–50.

Pennington, B.F. (2002) *The Development of Psychopathology: Nature and Nurture* (New York: Guilford Press).

Pike, A., McGuire, S., Hetherington, E.M., Reiss, D. and Plomin, R. (1996) 'Family environment and adolescent depression and antisocial behavior: a multivariate genetic analysis', *Developmental Psychology*, 32, pp. 590–603.

Plessen, K.J. and Peterson, B.S. (2009) 'The neurobiology of impulsivity and self-regulatory control in children with attention-deficit/hyperactivity disorder', in D.S. Charney and E.J. Nestler (eds) *Neurobiology of Mental Illness*, 3rd edition, (Oxford: Oxford University Press), pp. 1129–52.

Plomin, R. and Bergeman, C. S. (1991) 'The nature of nurture: genetic influence on "environmental" measures', *Behavioral and Brain Sciences*, 14, pp. 373–86.

Rhee, S.H. and Waldman, I.D. (2002) 'Genetic and environmental influences on antisocial behaviour: a meta-analysis of twin and adoption studies', *Psychological Bulletin*, 128, pp. 490–529.

Rice, F., Harold, G., Boivin, J., Hay, D., van den Bree, M. and Thapar, A. (2009) 'Disentangling prenatal and inherited influences in humans with an experimental design', *Proceedings of the National Academy of Sciences of the USA*, 106, pp. 2464–7.

Robins, J.M. and Greenland, S. (1989) 'Identification of causal effects using instrumental variables: Comment', *Journal of the American Statistical Association*, 91, pp. 456–8.

Rothman K.J. and Greenland S. (1998) *Modern Epidemiology*, 2nd edition (Philadelphia: Lippincott-Raven).

Rothman, K.J. and Greenland, S. (2002) 'Causation and causal inference', in R. Detels, J. McEwen, R. Beaglehole and H. Tanaka (eds) *Oxford Textbook of Public Health*, 4th edition (Oxford: Oxford University Press), pp. 641–53.

Rutter, M. (1989) 'Age as an ambiguous variable in developmental research: some epidemiological considerations from developmental psychopathology', *International Journal of Behavioral Development*, 12, pp. 1–34.

Rutter, M. (1997) 'Comorbidity: concepts, claims and choices', *Criminal Behaviour and Mental Health*, 7, pp. 265–86.

Rutter, M. (2007) 'Proceeding from observed correlations to causal inference: the use of natural experiments', *Perspectives in Psychological Science*, 2, pp. 377–95.

Rutter, M. (2008) 'Biological implications of gene-environment interaction', *Journal of Abnormal Child Psychology*, 36, pp. 969–75.

Rutter, M. (2009a) 'Introduction: The two-way interplay between neuroscience and clinical practice in the understanding of violence and of its remediation', in S. Hodgins, E. Viding and A. Plodowski (eds) *The Neurobiological Basis of Violence: Science and Rehabilitation* (Oxford: Oxford University Press).

Rutter, M. (2009b) 'Understanding and testing risk mechanisms for mental disorders', *Journal of Child Psychology and Psychiatry*, 50, pp. 44–52.

Rutter, M. (2009c) 'Epidemiological methods to tackle causal questions', *International Journal of Epidemiology*, 38, pp. 3–6.

Rutter, M. and Giller, H. (1983) *Juvenile Delinquency: Trends and Perspectives* (Harmondsworth: Penguin).

Rutter, M., Giller, H. and Hagell, A. (1998) *Antisocial Behaviour by Young People* (New York and Cambridge: Cambridge University Press).

Rutter, M., Maughan, B., Meyer, J., Pickles, A., Silberg, J., Simonoff, E. and Taylor, E. (1997) 'Heterogeneity of antisocial behavior: causes, continuities and consequences' in R. Dienstbier (Series Editor) and D.W. Osgood (Volume Editor) *Nebraska Symposium on Motivation: Vol.44: Motivation and Delinquency* (Lincoln: University of Nebraska Press), pp. 45–118.

Rutter, M. and Smith, D. (eds) (1995) *Psychosocial Disorders in Young People: Time Trends and Their Causes* (Chichester: Wiley).

Rutter, M. and Tienda, M. (2005) 'The multiple facets of ethnicity', in M. Rutter and M. Tienda (eds) *Ethnicity and Causal Mechanisms* (New York: Cambridge University Press), pp. 50–79.

Sampson, R.J., Raudenbush, S.W. and Earls, F.W. (1997) 'Neighbourhoods and violent crime: a multilevel study of collective efficacy', *Science*, 27, pp. 918–24.

Sampson, R.J. and Sharkey, P. (2008) 'Neighborhood selection and the social reproduction of concentrated racial inequality', *Demography*, 45, pp. 1–29.

Sampson, R.J., Laub, J.H. and Wimer, C. (2006) 'Does marriage reduce crime? A counterfactual approach to within-individual causal effects', *Criminology*, 44, pp. 465–508.

Silberg, J., Meyer, J., Pickles, A., Simonoff, E., Eaves, L., Hewitt, J., Maes, H. and Rutter, M. (1996) 'Heterogeneity among juvenile antisocial behaviours: findings from the Virginia Twin study of Adolescent Behavioural Development', in G.R. Bock and J.A. Goode (eds) *Genetics of Criminal and Antisocial Behavior*, Ciba Foundation Symposium, 194 (Chichester: Wiley), pp. 76–98.

Smith, D.J. (2005) 'Explaining ethnic variations in crime and antisocial behaviour in the United Kingdom', in M. Rutter and M. Tienda (eds) *Ethnicity and Causal Mechanisms* (New York: Cambridge University Press), pp. 174–203.

Snyder, J., Reid, R. and Patterson, G. (2003) 'A social learning model of child and adolescent antisocial behavior', in B.B. Lahey, T.E. Moffitt and A. Caspi (eds) *Causes of Conduct Disorder and Juvenile Delinquency* (New York and London: Guilford Press), pp. 27–48.

Stattin, H. and Kerr, M. (2000) 'Parental monitoring: a reinterpretation', *Child Development*, 71, pp. 1072–85.

Suomi, S. J. (2003) 'Social and biological mechanisms underlying impulsive aggressiveness in rhesus monkeys', in B.B. Lahey, T.E. Moffitt and A. Caspi (eds) *Causes of Conduct Disorder and Juvenile Delinquency* (New York and London: Guilford Press), pp. 345–62.

Thapar, A., Rice, F., Hay, D., Bolvin, J., Langley, K., Van den Bree, M., Rutter, M., and Harold, G. (2009) 'Prenatal smoking may not cause ADHD: evidence from a novel design', *Biological Psychiatry*, 66, pp. 722–7.

Thapar, A., Harrington, R. and McGuffin, P. (2001) 'Examining the comorbidity of ADHD-related behaviours and conduct problems using a twin study design', *British Journal of Psychiatry*, 179, pp. 224–9.

Thornberry, T.P., Krohn, M.D., Lizotte, A.J. and Chard-Wiershem, D. (1993) 'The role of juvenile gangs in facilitating delinquent behavior', *Journal of Research in Crime and Delinquency*, 30, pp. 55–87.

Thornberry, T.P., Freeman-Gallant, and Lovegrove, P.J. (2009) 'Intergenerational linkages in antisocial behaviour', *Criminal Behaviour and Mental Health*, 19, pp. 80–93.

Trembaly, R.E. (2003) Why socialization fails: the case of chronic physical aggression. In B.B. Lahey, T.E. Moffitt and A. Caspi (eds) *Cause of Conduct Disorder and Juvenile Delinquency* (New York and London: Guilford Press), pp. 182–224.

Valera, E.M., Faraone, S.V., Murray, K.E. and Seidman, L.J. (2007) 'Meta-analysis of structural imaging findings in attention-deficit/hyperactivity disorder', *Biological Psychiatry*, 61, pp. 1361–9.

van Goozen, S.H.M. and Fairchild, G. (2009) 'The neuroendocrinology of antisocial behaviour', in S. Hodgins, E. Viding and A. Plodowski (eds) *The Neurobiological Basis of Violence: Science and Rehabilitation* (Oxford University Press), pp. 201–21.

Viding, E., Larsson, H. and Jones, A.P. (2009) 'Quantitative genetic studies of antisocial behaviour', in S. Hodgins, E. Viding and A. Plodowski (eds) *The Neurobiological Basis of Violence: Science and Rehabilitation* (Oxford: Oxford University Press), pp. 251–64.

Viding, E., Blair, R.J.R., Moffitt, T.E. and Plomin, R. (2005) 'Evidence for substantial genetic risk for psychopathy in 7-year-olds', *Journal of Child Psychology and Psychiatry*, 46, pp. 592–7.

Wikström, P.-O. and Sampson, R.J. (2003) 'Social mechanisms of community influences on crime and pathways in criminality' in B.B. Lahey, T.E. Moffitt and A. Caspi (eds) *Causes of Conduct Disorder and Juvenile Delinquency* (New York and London: Guilford Press), pp. 118–48.

Wilkinson, R. and Pickett, K. (2009) *The Spirit Level: Why More Equal Societies Almost Always Do Better* (London: Allen Lane).

Wilson, W.J. (1996) *When Work Disappears: The World of the New Urban Poor* (New York: Vintage).

Wilson, H.W., Stover, C.S. and Berkowitz, S.J. (2009) 'Research review: the relationship between childhood violence exposure and juvenile antisocial behavior: a meta-analytic review', *Journal of Child Psychology and Psychiatry*, 50, pp. 769–79.

Chapter 7

Preventing youth crime: evidence and opportunities

J. David Hawkins, Brandon C. Welsh and David Utting

Before 1980 there was little evidence that delinquency could be prevented. Thirty years ago a review of all the delinquency experiments then conducted in the United States identified nine well-controlled trials. None had been effective in preventing youth crime (Berleman 1980). Perhaps the most notable failure was the Cambridge-Somerville Youth Study, a programme of wrap-around services for 'high risk' boys. Its instigators in the 1930s believed that the intervention of a friendly, socialized adult with a vulnerable boy when the child was still young might lead the child to a normal non-delinquent life. Over ten years they employed community-based counsellors who worked with boys in an economically disadvantaged community. Services were individualized for each boy and his parents. The evaluation of this intervention showed that the programme had no effects on police contacts for delinquency or commitments to state institutions. In fact, a long-term follow-up (McCord 1978) found that youths exposed to the programme were more likely than their control group peers to have developed serious behaviour problems, alcoholism, mental health problems and stress-related diseases over their lives. McCord suggested that one reason for this negative effect was participation in a summer camp component of the programme where delinquent boys had unsupervised opportunities to influence other boys toward delinquent behaviour (McCord 2003).

The Cambridge-Somerville project is a salutary reminder that even well-intended, plausible ideas for preventing youth crime can do harm. Thirty years ago we really did not know how to prevent delinquency. But today this has changed. The development of the field of prevention science has led to the creation and identification of an increasing number of tested and effective interventions for preventing youth crime before it happens.

209

Prevention science is based on the premise that to prevent crime, it is necessary to identify and reduce factors that predict future criminal behaviour, called risk factors, and to identify and strengthen factors that predict future non-criminality. These latter factors are sometimes called *promotive* factors because they promote non-criminal behaviour or *protective* factors because they inhibit criminal behaviour even in the presence of risk or risk exposure. Longitudinal studies by criminologists in the United Kingdom, New Zealand, and the US have consistently identified malleable predictors – risk factors, protective factors, and promotive factors – of a wide range of youth health and behaviour problems including delinquent behaviour. They have found factors in neighbourhoods and communities, families, schools, and peer groups, as well as characteristics of individuals themselves, that increase the probability of delinquency. They have also demonstrated that many of the same factors predict substance abuse, teenage pregnancy, dropping out of school, and other behaviour problems during adolescence and young adulthood (Howell 2009; Rutter *et al.* 1998). Because they predict future criminal behaviour among those not yet involved in crime, risk factors are potential targets for preventive interventions. Though not all risk factors have been proven to be 'causes' of crime, a number of risk factors have been targeted and reduced by prevention programmes and, as a result, later delinquent and criminal behaviours have been prevented. When specific risk factors are changed and later criminal offending is prevented, it indicates that these factors are, in fact, causes of crime. No less important, longitudinal studies have also identified protective and promotive factors that inhibit the development of criminal behaviour, the misuse of drugs, and other risky behaviours of adolescents and young adults (Catalano *et al.* 1996; Catalano *et al.* 2005; Huang *et al.* 2001; Lonczak *et al.* 2001).

Prevention scientists have used this evolving knowledge to design new preventive interventions that seek to reduce identified risk factors predictive of later offending and to increase known protective and promotive factors predictive of later non-offending. They have developed effective crime prevention strategies at different levels of targeting – universal, selective, and indicated – and subjected these preventive interventions to scrupulous evaluation, using randomized controlled trials or rigorous quasi-experimental comparison group studies to assess their effects on antisocial and criminal behaviour.

Diverse preventive interventions, focused on a wide range of risk factors, protective factors, and promotive factors in different developmental phases and domains of children's lives – family, school and community – have been tested and found to be effective in preventing youth crime (Farrington and Welsh 2007). Moreover, rigorous economic analyses of the costs of these interventions compared with the benefits to participants and society in the form of reduced victimization and lower criminal justice expenditure have shown that many delinquency prevention interventions produce benefits that far exceed their costs (Aos *et al.* 2004; Drake *et al.* 2009). In the US State of Washington, these analyses of the benefit-to-cost ratios of tested and effective crime prevention strategies have proven so influential that legislators were recently persuaded to cancel plans for the construction of a new prison and to invest, instead, in a portfolio of cost-saving crime prevention strategies. Yet the Washington state legislature's decision is an exception. Generally speaking, tested and effective strategies for preventing youth crime have not been consistently considered or applied when designing crime reduction approaches in either the US or the UK.

This chapter reviews progress in the development and testing of effective strategies for preventing youth crime. It identifies opportunities that, despite a growing fund of evidence, remain seriously under-used for preventing crime through universal approaches, through early intervention and through intensive efforts focused on those at greatest risk for future criminal behaviour. It concludes with a presentation of recent evidence concerning an effective operating system that guides community-wide efforts to prevent youth crime by choosing and using tested and effective prevention actions capable of yielding population-wide reductions in crime.

The evidence

This section summarizes international scientific evidence on effective methods for preventing criminality across the major institutional domains and life-course stages before criminal behaviour occurs. The scope of prevention includes individual, family, school, peer, community, and labour market programmes. It focuses on universal, selective, and indicated prevention approaches:

- *Universal* interventions seek to reduce risk and enhance promotion and protection in the whole population.

- *Selective* interventions seek to reduce risk and enhance protection in groups at high risk for later crime initiation who have not yet committed crimes, but who are at risk because of exposure to high levels of specific or multiple risk factors.

- *Indicated* preventive interventions target those who have shown early signs of behaviour likely to become criminal with development: oppositional behaviour, defiant behaviour, and aggressive behaviour. As interpreted in this chapter, 'indicated' chiefly describes responses to children and young people who have not already committed or been apprehended for offences.[1]

This review of youth crime prevention programmes focuses on the highest quality research studies. Results discussed are from experiments and rigorous quasi-experiments – with before and after measures of offending among youths exposed to the intervention and those in comparable control conditions who did not receive the programme being tested. Results from systematic and meta-analytic reviews of high-quality studies are also included to ensure that conclusions are based on the best available evidence. Systematic reviews use rigorous methods for locating, appraising, and synthesizing evidence from prior evaluation studies. Meta-analyses involve the statistical or quantitative analysis of results from existing evaluations of preventive interventions (Lipsey and Wilson 2001). These analyses can be important in helping to determine the average effect of a particular type of prevention programme or intervention. This review is organized by the social domain on which the prevention programme focuses: individual, family, school, peers, community, or labour markets. In each of these domains, programmes may focus on universal, selective, or indicated populations. The review identifies the focus of each programme mentioned.

Individual-focused prevention

The most important risk factors for delinquency and later offending at the individual level are low intelligence and attainment, low empathy, impulsivity, attention deficits, and hyperactivity. Relevant prevention programmes may be focused on children's early development through to adolescence. Two main types of individual-focused programmes have been found to be effective in preventing delinquency and later criminal offending: preschool intellectual enrichment and child and adolescent skills training.

Enriched preschool programmes are designed to provide 'economically disadvantaged children with cognitively stimulating and enriching experiences that their parents are unlikely to provide at home' (Duncan and Magnuson 2004: 105). Their main goals are improved cognitive skills, school readiness, and social and emotional development (Currie 2001). A meta-analysis of four such preschool programmes – three evaluated with randomized experimental designs – found that this type of early prevention produced a significant 12 per cent reduction on average in delinquency and offending, from 50 per cent in a control group to 38 per cent in an experimental group (Farrington and Welsh 2007).

The best known preschool intellectual enrichment programme is the High/Scope Perry Preschool project carried out in Ypsilanti, Michigan (Schweinhart and Weikart 1980). In the mid 1960s, a sample of 123 children from a disadvantaged neighbourhood was allocated approximately at random to experimental and control groups. The experimental children attended a daily preschool programme, supported by weekly home visits, usually lasting two years when children were aged three to four. The aim of the 'plan-do-review' curriculum was to provide intellectual stimulation, to increase thinking and reasoning abilities, and to increase later school achievement. Longitudinal research over more than 40 years has shown that the programme produced long-term benefits. For example, Berrueta-Clement and colleagues (1984) found that, at age 19, the experimental group was more likely to be employed, more likely to have graduated from high school, more likely to have received college or vocational training, and less likely to have been arrested. By age 27, the experimental group had accumulated only half as many arrests as the controls – an average of 2.3 compared to 4.6 arrests (Schweinhart *et al.* 1993). They were more likely to have graduated from high school, had significantly higher earnings, and were more likely to be home owners.

The most recent follow-up of this programme, at age 40 (which included 91 per cent of the original sample) found that, compared with the control group, participants in the original preschool programme had significantly fewer lifetime arrests for violent crimes (32 per cent vs. 48 per cent), property crimes (36 per cent vs. 58 per cent), and drug crimes (14 per cent vs. 34 per cent), and were significantly less likely to have been arrested five or more times (36 per cent vs. 55 per cent). Significantly higher levels of schooling (77 per cent vs. 60 per cent graduating from high school), better records of employment (76 per cent vs. 62 per cent), and higher annual incomes also were found at age 40 among preschool participants compared to the controls. A cost-benefit analysis attributed more than \$17 of benefit per dollar of cost to the programme in real terms, with 76 per cent of this being returned to the general public in the form of savings in criminal justice, education, welfare costs, and increased tax revenue, and 24 per cent benefiting the individual participants (Schweinhart *et al.* 2005). Training for preschool practitioners using the High/Scope curriculum has been available in the UK for more than 20 years. Some 17,000 UK practitioners are estimated to be using the approach with around 250,000 children in Sure Start centres, nurseries, infant schools and other early years settings (High/Scope UK 2009).

The Child-Parent Center (CPC) programme in Chicago (Reynolds *et al.* 2001) also provided disadvantaged children, aged three to four, with a high-quality, active learning preschool supplemented with family support. In addition, it provided the children with the educational enrichment component into elementary school, up to age nine. A rigorous quasi-experimental design was used to evaluate the programme with a sample of more than 1,500 children. This found that by the time they were 18, participants who received the programme were significantly less likely to have been arrested for any offence (17 per cent vs 25 per cent), multiple offences (10 per cent vs 13 per cent), and violent offences (9 per cent vs 15 per cent) compared with the control group. Participants also achieved a significantly higher rate of high school completion (50 per cent vs 39 per cent). A cost-benefit analysis measuring crime at age 18 and some outcomes up to age 21 found that for every dollar spent on the programme more than $7 had been saved in the form of averted government expenditure on remedial education and criminal justice, as well as increased economic well-being among participants (Reynolds *et al.* 2003: 645).

Child and adolescent skills training programmes are designed to 'directly teach children social, emotional, and cognitive competence by addressing appropriate social skills, effective problem-solving, anger management, and emotion language' (Webster-Stratton and Taylor 2001: 178). A systematic review and meta-analysis of skills training by Lösel and Beelmann (2003, 2006) found consistent and positive effects in preventing delinquency based on four randomized experiments. Looking at outcomes two months after treatment ended, the meta-analysis found a significant 9 per cent reduction in delinquency in experimental groups compared with control groups, increasing to an average 10 per cent three months or more after treatment ended. The meta-analysis also found that the most effective skills training programmes used cognitive-behavioural approaches and were those implemented with children aged 13 and over. Skills training with indicated populations who were already exhibiting some behavioural problems was shown to be especially effective in preventing delinquency.

An individual example of an effective skills training programme for adolescents aged 12 to 14 is Life Skills Training which teaches skills to children entering adolescence that include how to make good decisions, coping with shyness and anxiety, social communication, assertiveness, and self-management. These are combined with specific information on the consequences of substance use, abuse rates, and the process of becoming dependent on drugs. It is offered in the United States as a universal programme involving a series of 30 lessons spread over the three years of middle or junior high school. It is taught using discussion, demonstration of skills, guided practice and other interactive teaching strategies that have been found to be effective when behavioural change is the goal.

Life Skills Training has been found to prevent violent behaviour and delinquent behaviour in a randomized controlled trial involving 41 schools randomly assigned to receive the programme or to a control condition (Botvin and Griffin 2004). The programme included material focusing on violence and the media, anger management and conflict resolution skills. Survey data from 4,858 students followed-up three months after the programme ended showed significant reductions of up to 50 per cent in self-reported violence, including verbal and physical aggression and fighting, and delinquent behaviour. The strongest effects were found for those adolescents who received at least half of the programme (Botvin *et al.* 2006).

Another example of a universal skills training programme is Participate and Learn Skills or PALS, which was implemented and evaluated in Ottawa, Canada (Jones and Offord 1989). This used constructive leisure pursuits in sport (e.g. swimming, ice hockey) and the arts (e.g. guitar, ballet) to enable children to learn new skills, while diverting them from potential involvement in antisocial behaviour and crime. Implemented in a public housing estate, the programme recruited low-income children (ages 5 to 15) to take part during after-school hours. A comparable estate that did not receive the programme served as the control condition. In the first year, the rate of participation in at least one activity reached almost three-quarters (71 per cent) of the 417 children and young people eligible for the programme. In the second and third years, participation rates fell to 60 per cent and 49 per cent, respectively, largely due to a smaller number of activities being offered.

The programme's largest impact was on delinquency. During the 32 months of the programme, the monthly average number of young people in the relevant age-range who were charged by the police at the experimental site was 80 per cent lower than at the control site (0.2 vs 1.0). This statistically significant effect was diminished somewhat in the 16 months following the intervention period when 0.5 juveniles were charged per month at the experimental site compared to 1.1 at the control site. Complaints to police by residents also declined. Gains were observed in skill acquisition, integration in the wider community, and self-esteem, though not in reduced behaviour problems at school or in the home. A cost-benefit analysis of the programme, which included the post-intervention period (48 months in total), found that for every dollar spent on the programme about $2.60 was saved, with the city housing authority reaping the largest share of benefits (84 per cent) due to reduced demand for private security services (Jones and Offord 1989).

Family-focused prevention

Family-focused prevention programmes target risk factors for delinquency and later offending in the family such as family management problems (including failure to set clear expectations for behaviour, poor supervision or monitoring, and inconsistent or harsh discipline), favourable parental attitudes toward criminal behaviour, and high levels of family conflict. Two main types of family-focused programmes have been found to be effective in preventing delinquency and later criminal offending: general parent education, especially in the context of home visiting by a public health nurse, and parent management training. Parenting programmes in Britain, Australia, the United States and elsewhere have also demonstrated effectiveness in preventing childhood conduct disorders associated with a heightened risk of antisocial, violent and criminal behaviour in adolescence and adulthood. A number of therapeutic programmes focused on the family have also achieved positive, preventive outcomes. While many evaluations of family-based programmes have worked with on young offenders, positive outcomes have also been achieved through universal preventive interventions for parents of children entering adolescence and through selective preventive interventions with families of children and young people 'at risk' (Utting *et al.* 2007).

Home visiting with new parents, especially mothers, is an important family-based intervention. The objectives include educating parents to improve the life chances of children from a very young age, often beginning at birth or the final trimester of pregnancy. Other goals include the prevention of preterm or low weight births, the promotion of healthy child development or school readiness, and the prevention of child abuse and neglect (Gomby *et al.* 1999: 4). Home visits also seek to improve parental well-being, linking parents to community resources to help with employment, education, or addiction recovery. However, while many home visiting programmes have been developed, only those conducted by public health nurses or other health professionals with diverse skills in working with families have been found effective in preventing future crime (Alper 2002; Olds 2002). For example, a meta-analysis that included four randomized controlled experiments of home visiting by public health nurses found that this form of early family intervention was effective in preventing antisocial behaviour and delinquency, corresponding to a significant 12 per cent reduction (e.g. from 50 per cent in a control group to 38 per cent in an experimental group) (Farrington and Welsh 2007).

The best known home visiting programme, and the only one with a direct measure of effects on youth crime, is the Nurse-Family Partnership (NFP) initially carried out in Elmira, New York, by David Olds and his colleagues (1998). The programme was designed to improve the outcomes of pregnancy, to improve the quality of care that mothers provided to their infants, and to improve the women's own personal development through completing education, finding work and planning future pregnancies (Olds *et al.* 1993: 158). The programme enrolled 400 women during pregnancy who had no previous live births and who had at least one characteristic thought to increase risk for health and developmental problems in their babies: being aged under 19, unmarried, or poor. The women were randomly assigned to receive home visits from nurses during pregnancy, or to receive visits both during pregnancy and during the first two years of life, or to a control group who received no visits. Visits lasting more than an hour took place on average every two weeks. The home visitors gave advice about prenatal and post-natal care of the child, about infant development, and about the importance of proper nutrition and avoiding smoking and drinking during pregnancy.

The evaluation showed that the programme caused a significant decrease in recorded physical abuse and neglect of children during the first two years of life, especially by poor, unmarried, teenage mothers; 4 per cent of visited versus 19 per cent of non-visited mothers of this type were guilty of child abuse or neglect (Olds *et al.* 1986). This last result is important, not least because children who are physically abused or neglected have an enhanced likelihood of becoming violent offenders later in life (Widom 1989). In a 15-year follow-up, which included 330 mothers and 315 children, significantly fewer experimental compared with control group mothers were identified as perpetrators of child abuse and neglect (29 per cent versus 54 per cent) and, for the higher risk sample only, significantly fewer treatment mothers had alcohol or substance abuse problems or were arrested (Olds *et al.* 1997). Moreover, by the age of 15, the children of the higher risk mothers who received prenatal or post-natal home visits or both had incurred significantly fewer arrests than their control counterparts (20 as opposed to 45 per 100 children (Olds *et al.* 1998)).

Several cost-benefit analyses show that the benefits of this programme outweighed its costs for the higher risk mothers. Greenwood and colleagues (2001) measured benefits to the government or taxpayer (welfare, education, employment, and criminal justice). Aos and colleagues (2004) measured a somewhat different range of benefits to the government (education, public assistance, substance abuse, teen pregnancy, child abuse and neglect, and criminal justice), as well as tangible benefits to crime victims. Both reported that benefits were about three to four times every dollar spent on the programme; $4.06 according to Greenwood *et al.* and $2.88 according to Aos *et al.*

These and other promising results from trials in the United States persuaded the British government to pilot the programme in ten English locations in 2006, followed by a further wave of 20 test sites in 2008. Re-labelled the Family Nurse Partnership, the programme is being offered to first-time mothers up to the age of 24, but mostly aged under 20. The nurses who visit come mainly from health visiting or midwifery backgrounds. Reporting on the second year of implementation in the first ten pilot sites, evaluators from Birkbeck College in the University of London have found the objectives for the number of visits during infancy were being met, albeit with substantial differences between locations. Retention of families in the programme was also running at target level, subject to some variation between sites. Mothers had given overwhelmingly positive ratings to their Family Nurse visitors, and there had been some success in engaging fathers (51 per cent present during at least one pregnancy visit and 43 per cent during at least one infancy visit). The estimated cost per client has been comparable to the United States at £3,000 per year (Barnes *et al.* 2009). However, robust evidence concerning the impact of the programme in England will depend on the results of a randomized controlled trial initiated during 2009 in most of the pilot sites and ten of the second-wave sites.

Many parent management training programmes have been used to prevent child externalizing behaviour problems and delinquency (Wasserman and Miller 1998). Parent management training refers to 'treatment procedures in which parents are trained to alter their child's behaviour at home' (Kazdin 1997: 1349). Patterson (1982) developed behavioural parent management training. His careful observations of parent-child interaction showed that parents of antisocial children often failed to tell their children how they were expected to behave, failed to monitor their behaviour to ensure that it was desirable, and failed to enforce rules promptly and unambiguously with appropriate rewards and penalties. The parents of antisocial children used more punishment (such as scolding, shouting, or threatening), but failed to make it contingent on the child's behaviour. Patterson attempted to train these parents in effective child rearing methods, namely, noticing what a child is doing, monitoring behaviour over long periods, clearly stating house rules, making rewards and punishments contingent on behaviour, and negotiating disagreements so that conflicts and crises did not escalate.

A meta-analysis of ten high-quality evaluations of parent management training programmes found that this type of early intervention produced a significant 20 per cent reduction in antisocial behaviour and delinquency (e.g. from 50 per cent in a control group to 30 per cent in an experimental group) (Farrington and Welsh 2003, 2007). Each of the ten parent management training programmes included in this meta-analysis aimed to teach parents to use rewards and punishments consistently and contingently in child rearing. The programmes were usually delivered in guided group meetings of parents, including role-playing and modelling exercises, and three of the programmes were delivered by videotape. Piquero and his colleagues (2009) also carried out a broad systematic review and meta-analysis of parent training and found it to be effective in reducing child behaviour problems, including antisocial behaviour and delinquency. The review, which included 55 randomized controlled experiments, investigated the full range of early/family parent training programmes for children up to age 5 years, including home visiting, parent education plus daycare, and parent management training.

Included in these reviews of the effectiveness of parent management training were evaluations carried out in Britain as well as the United States of The Incredible Years, a programme whose aims are to prevent and treat children's aggression and conduct problems, while promoting parental competence and family relationships. A key component of the original ('BASIC') programme is 'videotape modelling' where parents discuss film clips showing everyday interactions between parents and children. An additional ('ADVANCE') programme focuses on adult relationships and problem-solving skills, while related programmes have been introduced to train teachers in classroom management skills and for children themselves ('Dina-Dinosaur'), teaching conflict management and other personal relationship skills. Randomized controlled trials in the United States (Webster-Stratton 1984) and England (Scott *et al.* 2001) have shown The Incredible Years to be effective with conduct-disordered children in clinical settings. Trials involving parents of preschool children in the community have also achieved positive outcomes on both sides of the Atlantic (e.g. Gardner *et al.* 2006; Scott *et al.* 2006; Webster-Stratton 1998), including use of the BASIC course in Welsh Sure Start Centres (Hutchings *et al.* 2007).

Another tested parent management training approach that has been increasingly used and piloted in Britain is Triple P (the Positive Parenting Programme). Developed in Australia by Sanders and colleagues, it offers five different levels of intervention, ranging from universal – intended to be useful to any parent – to an intensive clinical intervention, designed for families of children and young people whose multiple behaviour problems are especially serious and persistent (Sanders 1999). Triple P emphasises the importance of developing parents' resilience and capacity for self-regulation as part of a programme that helps them acquire skills to become self-sufficient and self-confident in their parenting (Sanders *et al.* 2003). Implementation methods have ranged from training through television and other media at the universal level, to the use of home visiting, clinical observations, group work and self-directed learning. The programme has been evaluated at all five levels in both clinical and community settings. A randomized controlled trial by the programme originators (Sanders *et al.* 2000) compared three different versions of Triple P – standard, self-directed and enhanced – with a waiting list control group of disruptive 3-year-olds thought to be at high risk of developing conduct problems. At one-year follow-up the children in all three Triple P groups had achieved clinically reliable improvements in their behaviour compared with the control group. Evaluations of both Triple P and The Incredible Years were taking place in Birmingham at the time of writing, using a randomized-controlled design (The Social Research Unit 2009).

Universal parent management training also has been found to be effective in preventing delinquent behaviour when provided to parents of young people entering adolescence. Mason and colleagues (2003) evaluated the effectiveness of a universal parent management training programme for parents of children aged 10 through 14 called Guiding Good Choices (formerly called Preparing for the Drug Free Years.). The programme involves five weekly parenting sessions each lasting two hours. Children attend the third session with their parents to learn 'refusal skills' together. The programme teaches parents about the risk and protective factors that predict substance abuse and delinquent behaviour; helps them to develop skills for establishing and communicating clear behavioural expectations, monitoring their children's behaviour and consistently enforcing family rules; provides training in skills to manage and reduce family conflict; and encourages parents to find developmentally appropriate ways for their adolescent children to contribute to family life, thereby maintaining strong family bonds even as adolescents explore new roles (Mason *et al.* 2003). In a randomized trial of Guiding Good Choices involving parents of 429 11-year-old children, three and a half years after the five-week programme ended, adolescents whose parents were assigned to Guiding Good Choices had significantly lower rates of delinquent behaviour and substance use than controls. A cost-benefit analysis found that this brief ten-hour programme for parents produced substantial benefits for society in reduced costs of crime, resulting in net benefits of $11.07 for every dollar spent on the programme (Aos *et al.* 2004).

Three family-focused programmes for families of children with behavioural difficulties that originated in the US are being piloted and trialled in the UK: Multi-dimensional Treatment Foster Care (Chamberlain 2003), Functional Family Therapy (Sexton and Alexander 2003), and Multisystemic Therapy (Henggeler 1998). All three were developed, in the first instance, as interventions for children and young people already in trouble with the law, including persistent, serious and violent young offenders. However, they have also been adapted and applied in 'preventive' contexts. For example, Multidimensional Treatment Foster Care (MTFC) provides intensive support for children and young people with serious behaviour problems to be placed in short-term foster homes, while therapeutic work takes place with them and their own families. Evaluations by its originators at the Oregon Social Learning Center produced positive results in terms of lower rates of self-reported reoffending, including fewer serious and violent crimes, and fewer jail sentences compared with young people placed in group homes and other community programmes (Chamberlain 2003; Eddy *et al.* 2004). However, MTFC has also been adapted to support conventional foster care with preschool children and 6- to 12-year-olds. A randomized controlled trial of this adaptation of MTFC in San Diego, California, among 700 foster and kinship parents of 5- to 12-year-olds found that the MTFC support programme achieved significantly larger reductions in child behaviour problems than did control foster families who received caseworker support 'as usual' (Chamberlain *et al.* 2008). In England, a pilot MTFC research project is being funded by the Department for Children, Schools and Families in 15 areas working with young people aged 10 to 16 who are looked after by local authorities. A randomized controlled trial being conducted as part of this Care Placement Evaluation (CaPE) is comparing outcomes for young people placed in Treatment Foster Care with those placed in conventional fostering for young people with complex needs (Roberts 2007). Cost-effectiveness calculations by Aos and colleagues (2004) based on American evaluations comparing it with group care indicated that MFTC saved as much as $10.88 for every dollar of cost.

Functional Family Therapy (FFT), developed as a multisystemic intervention programme with the families of young people aged 11 to 18, has been used preventively to work with young people at risk of criminal involvement as well as young offenders. Its aim is to improve behaviour by helping family members to understand how their behaviour affects relationships and influences each other's behaviour. From a first phase that uses 'reframing' methods to tackle ingrained negative perceptions, the programme guides each family towards implementing its own plan for changing behaviour. Families are then encouraged to apply skills they have learned through programme components (such as conflict management and parenting) in other problem areas (Sexton and Alexander 2003). FFT's promise was first demonstrated more than 30 years ago in a randomized trial where court-referred young offenders whose families took part in a 10-week course were significantly less likely to reoffend than their controls (Alexander and Parsons 1973). Younger siblings in the FFT families were also found to have a lower rate of subsequent court referral than those in the control group (Klein *et al.* 1977). Aos and others (2004), using figures from an evaluation of FFT in the state of Washington, estimated a benefit to society of $7.69 for every dollar of cost. Their estimate of benefit of FFT based on the results from evaluations elsewhere in the US is $13.25. In England, FFT has been used by a number of Youth Offending Teams to work with families subject to parenting orders. It is also being evaluated with young offenders and their families in West Sussex in clinical trials overseen by the National Academy for Parenting Practitioners (2009).

The intensive intervention known as Multisystemic Therapy (MST) is also, at the time of writing, being piloted and evaluated in England in ten pilot sites funded by the former Department for Children, Schools and Families and the Department of Health. Developed in the US, it combines family and cognitive-behavioural therapies with a range of support services that are tailored to the needs of individual families. In targeting multiple factors contributing to serious, chronic, behaviour problems, MST views school, employment, peers and the surrounding community as interconnected influences on young people and their families. The delivery of MST is largely home-based and requires intensive support from trained therapists who are on call 24 hours a day. Treatment ingredients typically include parent management and communication skills training and work on establishing collaborative home–school links (Henggeler 1998). Originally tested in the US with young offenders ordered by the courts to take part, MST has been found to reduce aggression, offending and other antisocial behaviour and lead to lower rearrest rates and time in custody compared with alternative treatments and services (Curtis *et al.* 2004). Not all evaluations have yielded positive results, including replications of the programme in Canada (Cunningham 2002; Littell *et al.* 2005) and Sweden where it appeared no better at improving the behaviour of conduct disordered youths than standard state psychiatric services (Sundell 2009; Sundell *et al.* 2008). However, other replications in the United States (Timmons-Mitchell *et al.* 2006), and with 'seriously antisocial' youths in Norway (Ogden and Hagen 2006) found positive effects on behaviour up to two years after treatment. According to the cost-effectiveness calculations published in 2004 by Aos and colleagues, MST had saved $2.64 per dollar invested on the basis of the evidence then available. In England, the pilot MST programmes are working with young people referred by both children's social care services and youth offending teams (Cabinet Office 2009).

School-focused prevention

Schools are a potential social context for youth crime prevention efforts throughout children's education (Elliott *et al.* 1998). Both academic failure beginning in late elementary grades and low commitment to education are risk factors for later crime. This means that schools should be able to prevent delinquency by using methods of instruction and classroom management and organization that promote interest in learning and academic achievement. Put another way, schools that help children to succeed and learn and to love learning also reduce risk for delinquent behaviour. There have been a number of comprehensive reviews that have investigated the effectiveness of school-based programmes to prevent antisocial behaviour and youth crime. Wilson and colleagues (Gottfredson *et al.* 2006; Wilson *et al.* 2001) conducted a meta-analysis that included 165 randomized and quasi-experimental studies with 216 experimental–control group comparisons. They identified four types of school-based programmes as effective in preventing delinquency:

- school and discipline management;

- classroom and instructional management;

- reorganization of grades or classes; and

- fostering self-control or social competency using cognitive behavioural or behavioural instructional methods.

The last type involves methods similar to those used in child and adolescent skills training described earlier. Examples of the effective approaches are described below. Reorganization of grades or classes was calculated to have the largest mean effect size ($d = .34$), corresponding to a significant 17 per cent reduction in delinquency. Three of these four effective types of school-based programmes (other than school and discipline management) were also effective in preventing alcohol and drug use.

One example of an effective programme that used school and discipline management to improve the school environment to prevent delinquent and criminal behaviour is Project PATHE (Positive Action Through Holistic Education) (Gottfredson 1986), which was implemented in middle schools and high schools in South Carolina. The main elements included increasing shared decision-making in schools, increasing the competence of teachers, increasing the academic competence of students (e.g., through teaching study skills), and improving the school climate (e.g., through a school pride campaign). An evaluation of the programme in seven schools (compared with two control schools) found that it produced a significant 16 per cent reduction in crime, as well as a significant reduction in alcohol or other drug use (17 per cent) and antisocial behaviour (8 per cent) (Gottfredson *et al.* 2006: 75).

An example of an effective programme that used improved classroom management and instructional methods is the Seattle Social Development Project (Hawkins *et al.* 2007). This was a multi-component programme combining parent management training, teacher training, and skills training for children. About 500 first-grade children (aged 6) in 21 classrooms were randomly assigned to be in experimental or control classes in the original study. The parents and teachers of children in the experimental classes received instruction in methods of child management and instruction, which were designed to increase children's attachment to their parents and their bonding to school, based on evidence that such strong social bonds are protective against delinquent behaviour. The children also were trained in interpersonal cognitive problem-solving. Their parents were trained to notice and reinforce socially desirable behaviour in a programme called 'Catch Them Being Good'; to support their children's successful involvement in school through a programme called 'Preparing for School Success'; and to prevent the initiation of drug use and delinquent behaviour through the 'Guiding Good Choices' parenting programme described earlier. Their teachers were trained in classroom management, for example, to establish rules and routines at the beginning of the school year, to provide clear instructions and expectations to children, to reward children for participation in desired behaviour, to use methods least disruptive to instruction to maintain order in the classroom, and to teach children socially desirable methods of solving problems. In a follow-up at age 18, Hawkins and his colleagues (1999) found that the full intervention group who received the intervention from grades 1–6 reported significantly less violence, less alcohol abuse, and fewer sexual partners than controls. A cost-benefit analysis of the programme by Aos *et al.* (2004) found that for every dollar spent on the programme $3.14 was saved to government and crime victims.

An example of an effective programme that used the reorganization of grades or classes to improve the school environment to prevent problem behaviours is Student Training Through Urban Strategies or STATUS, which was evaluated by Gottfredson (1990). The main component of the programme was referred to as 'school-within-a-school' scheduling, whereby high-risk students were brought together for a two-hour block each day to receive an 'integrated social studies and English programme which involved a law-related education curriculum and used instructional methods emphasizing active student participation' (Gottfredson *et al.* 2006: 92). The programme was implemented for a year in one junior and one senior high school (Grades 7 to 9) in Pasadena, California. Pooled results of the evaluations of the programme in the two schools showed that the experimental students, compared with their control counterparts, had significantly lower rates of criminal activity (18 per cent) and alcohol or other drug use (20 per cent), as well as somewhat, but non-significantly, lower rates of school dropout or truancy (12 per cent) and antisocial behaviour (12 per cent) (Gottfredson *et al.* 2006: 95).

An example of a school-based approach applying cognitive-behavioural methods is the PATHS (Promoting Alternative Thinking Strategies) programme. Originally designed as an intervention for children with impaired hearing, it seeks to prevent violence and other behavioural problems by promoting social competence and self-control. A structured curriculum uses pictures, dialogue, role-play and modelling to propose strategies for self-control, emotional understanding and problem solving. The aim is to enhance the thinking skills and increase children's engagement and concentration by reducing potential distractions from learning. A randomized trial in the US comparing elementary and special educational needs classes using PATHS with control schools found positive effects in children's reasoning skills and ability to recognize and name feelings (Greenberg *et al.* 1995). A further trial with randomization at school level found immediate improvements in children's emotional understanding and problem solving skills compared with those in control schools and fewer conduct problems after two years (Greenberg and Kusche 2002). In Britain, the PATHS curriculum has been used by primary schools in England, Scotland and Wales. PATHS has recently been introduced into primary schools in Birmingham, UK with a planned randomized controlled trial evaluation involving 60 schools (The Social Research Unit 2009).

Peer-focused prevention

Peer-focused programmes recognize that association with friends who engage in delinquent behaviour or drug use is one of the strongest risk factors for delinquency and drug use. Their ostensible aims are to reduce the influence of delinquent friends and increase the influence of prosocial friends. Teaching children to resist peer influences that encourage delinquent activities usually takes place through skills training. Skills for resisting opportunities to get into trouble while still keeping friends and 'having a good time' are modelled by skilled peers or teachers and learned through guided practice.

Unfortunately, the literature on peer-focused delinquency prevention programmes is relatively sparse, with some scholars concluding that this approach is, as yet, of unknown effectiveness (e.g., McCord *et al.* 2001; van Lier *et al.* 2007; Farrington and Welsh 2007). More is known about the effects of these programmes on substance use. For example, a meta-analysis of 143 substance use prevention programmes by Tobler (1986) concluded that programmes using peer leaders to teach skills to resist influences to use drugs were the most effective in reducing smoking, drinking, and drug use. Tobler *et al.* (1999) also concluded that using high-status conventional peers to teach children ways of resisting peer pressure was effective in reducing drug use.

A danger has been identified in peer-focused strategies that bring together groups of children or young people with behaviour problems in 'Guided Group Interaction' or other group counselling sessions. Creating groups of delinquent or 'at risk' youths for group counselling or discussion sessions creates opportunities for 'deviance' training in which youths express positive opinions of the law-violating exploits of others shared during or, informally, before or after sessions. Consequently the programmes can cause rather than prevent offending (Dishion *et al.* 1999).

An example of an approach that positively affected peer associations and reduced delinquent behaviour is Children at Risk (Harrell *et al.* 1999), a selective prevention programme which targeted high-risk adolescents (average age 12) in poor neighbourhoods of five cities across the US. The programme differed in each neighbourhood, and included case management and family counselling, family skills training, tutoring, mentoring, after-school activities, and community policing. Initial results from a randomized controlled trial were disappointing (Harrell *et al.* 1997), but a one-year follow-up showed that, according to self-reports, experimental youths were less likely to have committed violent crimes and used or sold drugs (Harrell *et al.* 1999). The process evaluation showed that the greatest change was in peer risk factors. Experimental youths associated less often with delinquent peers, felt less peer pressure to engage in delinquency, and had more positive peer support (Harrell *et al.* 1997: 87).

Community-based prevention

Numerous theories have been advanced over the years to explain community-level influences on crime (Bennett 1998). Community-based efforts to prevent crime are often conceptualized as a combination of developmental prevention, focused on reducing early risk factors for offending, and situational prevention, with a focus on reducing opportunities for crime. But there is little agreement in the literature on the definition of community prevention and the types of programmes that fall within it. Tim Hope's (1995) definition that community crime prevention involves actions designed to change the social conditions and institutions that influence offending in residential communities is among the more informative. It not only distinguishes community crime prevention from developmental and situational prevention, but also speaks to the strength of the community to address the social problems that lead to crime and violence.

Historically, reviews of community preventive interventions (for example, Hope 1995; Rosenbaum 1988) reported that many were of unknown effectiveness in preventing crime because they had not been adequately evaluated. This has changed in recent years through rigorous evaluations of community-based mentoring programmes and of community coalition based efforts to prevent youth crime and substance abuse.

Mentoring usually involves non-professional adult volunteers spending time with young people who are at risk of delinquency, dropping out of school, school failure, and other social problems. Mentors behave in a 'supportive, non-judgmental manner while acting as role models' (Howell 1995: 90). Care is taken in matching the mentor and the young person. Most often, youths are selected to participate in the mentoring programmes through referrals by school officials or community programmes working with families. Mentoring has been found to be an effective prevention approach to preventing youth crime in some community contexts. For example, the average results across evaluations of 18 mentoring programmes analysed by Jolliffe and Farrington (2008) corresponded to a significant 10 per cent reduction in offending. The authors also found that mentoring was more effective in reducing offending when the average duration of each contact between mentor and mentee was greater, in smaller scale studies, and when mentoring was combined with other interventions.

Big Brothers Big Sisters (BBBS) of America is a national youth mentoring organization that is committed to improving the life chances of at-risk children and teens. One BBBS programme brought together unrelated pairs of adult volunteers and youths aged 10 to 16. Rather than trying to address particular problems facing a youth, the programme focused on providing a youth with an adult friend. The mentors met with youths on average three or four times a month, for three to four hours each time, for at least one year. An evaluation, by Grossman and Tierney (1998), took place at eight sites across the US and involved randomly assigning more than 1,100 youths to the programme or a control group that did not receive mentoring. At programme completion, it was found that those youths who received the programme were significantly less likely to have hit someone (32 per cent less), initiated illegal drug use (46 per cent less), initiated alcohol use (27 per cent less), or truanted from school (30 per cent less). A cost-benefit analysis of the programme by Aos *et al.* (2004) found that for every dollar spent on the programme more than $3 was saved to the government and crime victims.

Mentoring has also been a popular intervention in the UK, although robust evidence concerning its effectiveness has been scarce. A 'Mentoring Plus' programme in ten areas that combined one-to-one mentoring by volunteers with educational, training and social support was evaluated by comparing outcomes among participants (aged 12 to 19) with those for young people referred to the programme who did not take part. The results after a 10–12-month programme that started with a residential weekend pointed to a higher level of engagement in education, training and work among the young people who were mentored. However, there was no clear evidence of an impact on offending or substance use. The researchers called for more realistic expectations of what mentoring might achieve in relation to offending (Shiner *et al.* 2004).

Coalitions of diverse stakeholders representing a variety of agencies and organizations concerned with the development of young people have been advocated as infrastructures for advancing prevention in communities. Coalitions have been a popular mechanism for community-wide efforts seeking to prevent substance use and other problems (Roussos and Fawcett 2000).

Unfortunately, many prior efforts to activate coalitions of stakeholders to prevent youth problems have been unsuccessful. Several well-intentioned community-based coalition efforts have failed to make any significant difference in the lives of young people. Scientific evaluations of coalitions focused on preventing problems ranging from drug abuse to teen pregnancy have found no positive effects on these outcomes (Collins *et al.* 2007; Flewelling *et al.* 2005; Hallfors *et al.* 2002; Roussos and Fawcett 2000; Wandersman and Florin 2003; Yin *et al.* 1997; Zakocs and Edwards 2006).

However, a new generation of community coalition-based approaches has emerged with a dual focus on both community mobilization and the use of scientific evidence regarded as essential for the success of community-based prevention. When stakeholders from diverse organizations come together to achieve clear and common goals, use scientific advances regarding what works to prevent problem behaviours, and monitor their activities for quality assurance, positive outcomes can be achieved. By pooling information and resources and selecting tested and effective policies and programmes that address local needs, community coalitions can ensure the adoption of tested and effective prevention activities, enhance community buy-in for these initiatives, and increase the likelihood of their sustainability.

There is now evidence that coalition-based efforts that meet these conditions can produce positive community-wide benefits including the prevention of delinquency. Recent evaluations of the Communities That

Care coalition-driven model (Hawkins *et al.* 1992, 2002) have demonstrated effectiveness. In the Communities That Care system, the community coalition is composed of key leaders and stakeholders from all sectors of the community, including schools, law enforcement, health and human service agencies, youth-serving agencies, local government, business, religious groups, youth, parents and neighbourhood residents. The coalition identifies local prevention needs by conducting a school-based survey of the community's youth and a review of ongoing community prevention services. The coalition then selects prevention activities from a menu of tested and effective preventive interventions to fill gaps in prevention services, implements and tracks these activities and their outcomes, and makes implementation changes as needed to ensure results.

The Communities That Care (CTC) system has been evaluated in two studies, one conducted by the Prevention Research Center at The Pennsylvania State University (Feinberg *et al.* 2007) and one conducted by the Social Development Research Group at the University of Washington (Hawkins *et al.* 2008). The Pennsylvania project involved 120 communities funded to create CTC coalitions that enacted tested and effective prevention programmes, and a group of comparison communities in which CTC was not enacted. CTC communities experienced significant reductions in community-wide delinquent behaviours, and alcohol and cigarette use compared with controls (Feinberg and Greenberg, in press; Feinberg *et al.* 2007).

The most recent CTC evaluation, the Community Youth Development Study (CYDS), involved 24 matched communities across seven states, which were randomly assigned to either implement the CTC system or to conduct prevention services as usual. In a panel of over 4,400 young people in CTC and control communities followed from Grade 5 through Grade 8, young people in CTC communities were 25 per cent less likely to have initiated delinquent behaviour than controls and 31 per cent less likely to have engaged in a variety of delinquent acts. Significant reductions in alcohol and tobacco use were also observed in CTC communities compared with controls. An analysis conducted in collaboration with Steve Aos at the Washington State Institute for Public Policy has estimated that CTC produces $5.30 in benefits to society for every dollar spent, primarily through reduced costs associated with crime.

CTC was introduced to the UK by the Joseph Rowntree Foundation (Crow *et al.* 2004) and has been made available in recent years through the Catch 22 crime prevention organization. In the UK, CTC has encountered implementation issues. All three sites in England and Wales that were chosen to demonstrate the approach were able to complete their risk and protection profiles and produce action plans that included evidenced, promising interventions. Yet only one of these achieved substantial implementation of their plan, while one managed partial implementation, and implementation in the third site largely failed. Not surprisingly, the best evidence from repeated school surveys of progress in reducing the incidence of risk factors for youth crime and promotion of protective factors came from the community that had implemented most of its plan (Crow *et al.* 2004). The reasons for implementation difficulties in the other communities included political and administrative problems, such as failures to identify the budgets needed to sustain interventions or to replace key staff and programme 'champions' after they moved on. The creation of local 'experts' using risk profile evidence to advocate for more resources for their neighbourhood has also, on occasion, proved uncomfortable for managers and political leaders at local authority level (France and Crow 2001). Problems also included resistance among some professionals to evidence-based programming, not least where it might have threatened the continued use of existing, unevaluated interventions with which they were familiar. Not uniquely, CTC in the UK has been subject to the vagaries of short-term local funding for voluntary (non-profit) sector initiatives.

Labour markets and prevention

Growing up in poverty and living in a socially disadvantaged and disorganized neighbourhood are important socio-economic risk factors for youth crime (Farrington and Welsh 2007; Howell 1995). Some prevention programmes aim to address this by increasing the employment of individuals or populations at risk of offending. For example, Bushway and Reuter (2006) found intensive, residential training programmes to be an especially effective selective prevention programme for preventing offending. The best-known and largest of these residential training programmes across the US is Job Corps which operates in 120 centres across the country, and annually provides services to more than 60,000 young people at a cost of over $1 billion.

The programme seeks to improve the employability of at-risk young people (aged 16 to 24) by offering a comprehensive set of services, including vocational training, basic education (the ability to obtain a high school education), and health care. While Job Corps differs greatly from mainstream education – largely because of its vocational emphasis – the basics are provided, enough so that many youths can also go on to college or university. Most of the young people enrolled in the programme are at high risk for delinquency, substance abuse, and social assistance dependency (LaLonde 2003). Almost all Job Corps centres require the participants to live there while taking the programme.

In a long-term follow-up of a large-scale randomized experiment involving 15,400 young people, Schochet *et al.* (2008) found that participation in Job Corps resulted in significant reductions in criminal activity, improvements in educational attainment, and greater earnings for several years after young people took part. An analysis of tax data showed that these earnings gains were being sustained up to eight years after participating.

Another key focus is on programmes that aim to improve the conditions of families living in deprived areas. Here, housing dispersal and mobility programmes have had some success. Kling *et al.* (2005) evaluated the impact of the large-scale Moving to Opportunity (MTO) programme, which gave vouchers to low socio-economic status families to enable them to move to better areas. The authors investigated the impact of moving on children's offending and found that there was little effect on the prevalence of arrests overall. There were, however, desirable effects on the number of arrests of girls for violent and property crimes and undesirable effects on the number of arrests of boys for property crimes. The authors speculated that girls might have reacted to their more affluent neighbourhoods and schoolmates by trying harder in school, while boys reacted with resentment, stealing from classmates.

What does not work?

The Cambridge-Somerville Youth Study described at the start of this chapter is an important example of a crime prevention initiative not only proving ineffective, but actually causing harm. Unfortunately, there are other examples of this sort from more recent times. One example is Drug Abuse Resistance Education or DARE. This programme brings uniformed law-enforcement officers into elementary schools to educate children about the dangers of drug use and the skills needed to resist peer pressure to use drugs. Large-scale evaluations (many of which employed randomized experimental designs) and independent reviews have consistently found that the programme has no effect on substance use or delinquency (see Gottfredson *et al.* 2006; US General Accountability Office 2003). These results have since led hundreds of school districts throughout the US to discontinue its use, as well as its removal from the 'List of Exemplary and Promising Prevention Programs' administered by the US Department of Education's Safe and Drug-Free Schools programme (Weiss *et al.* 2008).

Two other examples of ineffective programmes, which share a punitive orientation, are Scared Straight and juvenile boot camps. Scared Straight is a popular version of a prison tour programme that exposes juvenile offenders, sometimes minor delinquents, to the horrors of prison life, including lectures from rapists, murderers, and other serious adult offenders. This exposure is meant to deter them from engaging in further delinquent behaviour or more serious criminality. A systematic review and meta-analysis of Scared Straight by Petrosino *et al.* (2006), which included nine randomized experiments, found that juveniles who went through the programme were more likely to engage in criminal activity compared with their control group counterparts. The authors summed up their findings this way: 'doing nothing would have been better than exposing juveniles to the programme' (Petrosino *et al.* 2006: 98).

Results from evaluations of juvenile boot camps have not produced positive results. Boot camps or military-style correctional programming that emphasizes discipline emerged on the scene as part of the more recent 'get-tough' approach to juvenile crime in the US. In theory, a successful boot camp programme should rehabilitate juvenile offenders, reduce the number of beds needed in secure facilities, and thus reduce the overall cost of care. A systematic review and meta-analysis of correctional boot camps by Wilson and MacKenzie (2006), which included 17 high-quality evaluations focused on juveniles, found no overall difference in recidivism between boot camp participants and their control group counterparts. A possible reason for their failure to reduce reoffending is that they provide little in the way of therapy or treatment to correct offending behaviour.

The identification of these ineffective programmes emphasizes the importance of subjecting ideas for reducing crime that appear logical and 'good common sense' to rigorous controlled evaluations to determine their actual effects in reducing youth crime. Public policy should be based on evidence that planned policies and programmes can actually work to achieve the desired outcome of reduced crime.

Prevention strategies

Accumulated knowledge about the potential for effective prevention across child, adolescent, and early adult development means that policy makers and the communities they serve are better placed than ever to assess where preventive services are most needed and which interventions are most likely to prove effective. The available menu of tried and tested approaches, as outlined in this review, includes examples of universal, selective, and indicated prevention programmes. Although they operate in different domains of children and young people's lives and intervene at different stages in their development, all are capable of preventing crime before it happens.

Importantly, however, the effectiveness of many of these interventions is not limited to the prevention of youth crime. Robust results have been found for impacts on other life-course outcomes, such as educational attainment, reduced dependence on state welfare, increased employment and income, and decreased substance abuse. These results occur because these prevention programmes address and reduce shared risk factors for these diverse outcomes. Cumulatively, these effects can translate into

231

substantial financial savings for governments and for taxpayers. In Britain, for example, the Sainsbury Centre for Mental Health (2009) has contrasted estimates of the high costs of crime attributable to young people with persistent conduct disorders with evidence concerning the cost-effectiveness of early intervention programmes amassed by Steve Aos and his colleagues (Aos *et al.* 2004; Drake *et al.* 2009). As the authors point out, programmes aimed at preventing or reducing childhood conduct problems do not need to achieve particularly high levels of effectiveness in reducing offending to remain good value. The costs per head of parenting programmes and other early interventions are typically quite low, but the potential benefits in preventing crime are exceptionally high (Sainsbury Centre for Mental Health 2009).

Never too early, never too late

As this review has noted, very early intervention is cost-effective in preventing later crime. For example, public health nurses trained in the Nurse Family Partnership (NFP) programme visited low income unmarried women about to have their first babies during pregnancy and the first two years of the infant's life. Thirteen years after the visits ended, the children whose mothers were visited reported significantly lower rates of arrests and convictions than those in the control group that did not get a nurse home visitor (Olds 2007). Analyses of the programme have suggested financial benefits of the order of three to four times what it costs to run. Yet at the other end of the developmental continuum, there are examples of programmes working with adolescents and young adults that have also demonstrated an ability to prevent offending. Job Corps, in the US, is an example of an effective programme for older adolescents that does not require the participants to have offended before it intervenes. One recent cost-benefit analysis concluded that Job Corps was a worthwhile investment of public resources, saving society $2 for each dollar spent on the programme (Schochet *et al.* 2008). Meanwhile, in the middle range of childhood there is also evidence that school-based programmes implemented in primary and secondary grades are similarly effective.

Even so, prevention strategies in the early years of life that combine effective individual and family focused approaches appear especially promising. This makes theoretical as well as practical sense. As Duncan and Magnuson (2004: 101) note:

> Principles of developmental science suggest that although beneficial changes are possible at any point in life, interventions early on may be more effective at promoting well being and competencies compared with interventions undertaken later in life.

Intervention dosage

When considering how effective programmes can successfully be replicated, it is crucial to take account of not only their key 'active' ingredients, but also 'dosage': the quantity that was administered over time and its intensity. As Tremblay and Craig (1995) found in their review of developmental crime prevention, the evidence today confirms that most youth crime prevention programmes that are effective last for a sufficient duration, usually one or more years. Olds' (2007) NFP is an example of an evidence-based programme that offers a sizeable dose of intervention services over an extended time. In the trial, women who were randomly assigned to the experimental group received home visits during pregnancy and the first two years of their baby's life. Each visit lasted about one and one-quarter hours and the mothers were visited on average every two weeks. The home visitors gave advice about prenatal and post-natal care of the child, about infant development, and about the importance of proper nutrition and avoiding smoking and drinking during pregnancy. Subsequent replication trials in Memphis, Tennessee, and Denver, Colorado, used the same dosage of intervention, which is recommended for other communities that adopt the programme.

Dosage in the Life Skills Training programme involved a total of 30 hour-long lessons for students spread over three academic years. The Guiding Good Choices family focused prevention programme reviewed above involved only five weekly two-hour sessions, but produced effects in reducing delinquency that lasted for years. What is important to note here is that none of these effective prevention programmes used one-time only lectures or assemblies or classroom visits by police officers. The programmes addressed identified risk and protective factors for later delinquent behaviour to bring about positive and sustained change in behaviour.

Universal versus targeted prevention

As discussed above, prevention methods can be classified as universal, selected, or indicated. Universal and targeted (selective or indicated) prevention approaches have advantages and disadvantages, and implementing one over another can be thought of as making trade-offs (Offord et al. 1998). Proponents of universal prevention argue that the whole population stands to benefit rather than just one group. In contrast, proponents of targeted prevention argue that the greatest yield can be gained by focusing on those with the highest levels of risk exposure or on those already manifesting behavioural problems. However, one of the considerations with targeted prevention is the shame or stigma that may be felt by some children and parents for accepting services that others view as indicating that they are somehow deficient. In many circumstances, this may be chiefly a question of ensuring that the intervention responds to the needs of children and their families in the 'here and now' aside from any desirable longer-term impact on offending. For example, parents may be happy to accept specialist help with their child's disruptive behaviour, but less eager to have him labelled a potential criminal (Sutton *et al.* 2004).

Special efforts need to be taken to avoid stigmatization in mounting selective or indicated preventive programmes. An innovative approach was used by the Fast Track prevention programme (Conduct Problems Prevention Research Group 1999). Children who required intensive social skills training were accompanied in training sessions by prosocial peers from the same classroom. This made the Fast Track children feel special, not picked on, when they went to special sessions with their prosocial peer to learn skills for behavioural self-management.

Some youth crime prevention programmes reserve scarce public resources for children and families in greatest need, and these inevitably tend to be the high-risk children and families (Farrington and Welsh 2007; Greenwood 2006). Yet there are a number of evidence-based universal prevention programmes that have prevented youth crime. Examples include Life Skills Training (Botvin *et al.* 2006), Guiding Good Choices (Mason *et al.* 2003), and the Seattle Social Development Project (Hawkins *et al.* 2007), reviewed above.

The good news is that there are many options for communities. Ultimately, communities are in the best position to decide which set of tested and effective programmes will work best given their population, their particular profile of risk and protective factors, and the resources available.

Comprehensive prevention

One of the recurring themes in the evidence base on effective methods of preventing youth crime and antisocial behaviour is the need for programmes to be comprehensive. Children and young people often face multiple risk factors, and it may be insufficient to address just one of these in hopes of preventing youth crime. Several of the effective prevention programmes reviewed above addressed multiple risk factors with multimodal interventions. Tremblay and Craig (1995) identified this as an important component of effective programmes in their review of developmental crime prevention, and Catalano *et al.* (1998), in a review of community crime prevention, found that multiple prevention strategies crossing multiple domains that are mutually reinforcing and that are maintained for several years produce the greatest impact.

The targeting of risk factors in multiple domains is especially important. For example, individual-based early prevention programmes often involve other components that are targeted at parents or other caregivers. The Perry Preschool programme of Schweinhart *et al.* (2005) is a case in point. While the main focus of the programme was the child – via enriched preschool delivered by professional teachers – the parents of the preschoolers were visited weekly by the teachers in order to provide the parents with educational information and encourage them to take an active role in their child's early education.

Community prevention planning and action

Given the weight of evidence now available, it is hard to believe that before 1980 virtually no tested and effective programmes for preventing delinquency had been identified. The problem now facing policymakers, practitioners and researchers is to decide which effective interventions can most usefully be applied in their communities and how they can best be implemented to replicate success. A important starting point is to understand that different communities are likely to have different profiles of risk and protection. Cities, districts and neighbourhoods cannot meet their local needs by simply copying each other's use of the same, standard interventions. A community-wide strategy is needed to guide appropriate decisions at community level regarding developmental foci, the risk and protective factors to be targeted, and the preventive interventions to be included.

As noted earlier, Communities That Care has emerged in the United States as a well-developed, tested, and effective example of a community prevention operating system. Findings from a large-scale randomized controlled trial involving 24 communities in seven states in the US and more than 4,400 school students aged 10 to 14 show that CTC was able to reduce targeted risk factors and delinquent behaviour at a community-wide 'population' level (Hawkins *et al.* 2008, 2009).

CTC is based on a theory called the social development model, which organizes knowledge of risk and protective factors into a strategy for strengthening protection in any social unit. It is modelled after large-scale community-wide public health programmes designed to reduce illnesses such as coronary heart disease by tackling key risk factors in the community (Farquhar *et al.* 1985; Perry *et al.* 1989). Consistent with health promotion approaches (Kaplan 2000; O'Connell *et al.* 2009), there is great emphasis on enhancing protective factors and building strengths. The community could be a city, a local authority area, a small town, or even a neighbourhood or a public housing estate. Antisocial behaviour and later offending are prevented by enabling communities to assess levels of risk and protection faced by the community's young people and then to choose and implement prevention strategies that have demonstrated effectiveness in reducing the community's elevated risk factors and enhancing protective factors that need to be strengthened.

CTC begins with community mobilization, including steps to secure the involvement of residents and the active commitment of key local leaders. Risk and protective factor profiling involves the use of police, school, social, and census records, as well as surveys of secondary school students using a validated questionnaire. Having identified priority risk and protective factors, the community board overseeing the strategy assesses existing resources and develops a plan of prevention and early intervention strategies using tried and tested programmes. As a risk-focused, evidence-based prevention system, CTC is used in several hundred communities in the US (Harachi *et al.* 2003). It has also been implemented in more than 30 sites in England, Scotland, and Wales, and in Australia, Canada, and the Netherlands (Flynn 2008; France and Crow 2005; Utting and Langman 2005).

Conclusion

One of the most important challenges facing the implementation of preventive interventions concerns the scaling-up or rolling-out of tested and effective prevention programmes for wider public use. If a programme works for a sample of the population, then there should be value added to replicating it widely. This view is strengthened when the programme in question has been rigorously evaluated and replicated in different settings (Dodge 2001; Flay *et al.* 2005). The main risk is that desirable effects on antisocial behaviour and youth crime from preventive intervention trials will attenuate once they are scaled-up for wider public use (Dodge 2001; Karoly *et al.* 1998).

Threats to effectiveness in disseminating tested preventive interventions may arise from several sources, for example:

- The scaled-up programme will no longer be provided to the children or families that need it, thus decreasing the potential yield of crimes reduced.

- The programme is offered to a more heterogeneous population than that served in the experimental trial.

- Insufficient service infrastructure is provided.

- The available resources are inadequate – from trained service providers to public funds for personnel and capital.

- Loss of programme fidelity is another important threat. When the programme is expanded and no longer under the control of its developers and well-trained staff, it is essential that the programme be delivered with fidelity if positive results are to be achieved (Welsh *et al.* 2010).

If attenuation of effects of prevention trials is a plausible threat, then the issue for policymakers is how to preserve or even enhance effects in broad-scale dissemination. Although clearly not immune to the implementation difficulties that it seeks to overcome, Communities That Care has the capacity to ensure that due attention is paid to many of the problems that contribute to the attenuation of programme effects; and, thereby, to maintain the expected level of crime reduction and associated economic benefits. Its emphasis on the ownership role of communities in making prevention fit local needs means that it places a potentially powerful tool in the hands of policymakers wanting to base their budgeting decisions on evidence. It also provides the tools the board needs to ensure that the programmes selected are implemented fully and with fidelity so that they achieve their promised effects. The challenge in the specific context of England and Wales may be to ensure a better fit between its scale of operation and the work of increasingly important and inclusive partnerships responsible for planning and commissioning services, such as Children's Trusts.

Prevention represents a sustainable solution to youth crime. Sustainability requires producing beneficial results today, but not at the expense of burdening society in future years. The world is rife with examples of unsustainable approaches to social, economic, health, and other problems that have, in many cases, exacerbated the very problems that they set out to remedy. In the case of youth crime, the approach that is taken has important implications for a sustainable society. A society that relies solely on incarcerating its young people who have come in conflict with the law cannot be said to be contributing to a sustainable future for its young people or the wider population. The evidence shows that incarceration of juveniles does not result in lower reoffending rates, causes some juvenile offenders to become more violent, and exacerbates emotional trauma (e.g., depression from past abuse) often suffered by youthful offenders (McCord et al. 2001). As the evidence reviewed above demonstrates, there are many preventive interventions effective in reducing youth crime that, at the same time, produce favourable and robust impacts on other life-course outcomes, including educational attainment and employment. The growing availability of promising, robustly evaluated interventions, and evidenced operating systems for applying prevention science – notably Communities That Care – is a heartening development of the past 20 years. It is now possible for communities, whatever their proportions, to become self-correcting environments that prevent youth crime – before it happens.

Note

1   Though interventions initiated in response to delinquent or criminal behaviour, including treatment, punishment, and incapacitation, may seek to prevent

future crimes by those who are already delinquents or criminals, they are not truly prevention programmes, as discussed here, because they require identification and apprehension of those who have already committed crimes.

References

Alexander, J. F. and Parsons, B. V. (1973) 'Short-term behavioral intervention with delinquent families: Impact on family process and recidivism', *Journal of Abnormal Psychology*, 81:3, pp. 219–25.

Alper, J. (2002) 'The nurse home visitation program', in S. L. Isaacs and J. R. Knickman (eds) *To improve health and health care: Volume V: The Robert Wood Johnson Anthology* (San Francisco: Jossey-Bass).

Aos, S., Lieb, R., Mayfield, J., Miller, M. and Pennucci, A. (2004) *Benefits and Costs of Prevention and Early Intervention Programs for Youth* (Olympia, WA: Washington State Institute for Public Policy).

Barnes, J., Ball, M., Meadows, P. and Belsky, J. (2009) *Nurse-Family Partnership Programme. Second year pilot sites implementation in England. The infancy period* (London Department for Children, Schools and Families, Department of Health).

Bennett, T. H. (1998) 'Crime prevention', in M. Tonry (ed.) *The Handbook of Crime and Punishment* (New York: Oxford University Press).

Berleman, W. C. (1980) *Reports of the National Juvenile Justice Assessment Centers. Juvenile delinquency prevention experiments: A review and analysis* (Washington, DC: U.S. Department of Justice, Law Enforcement Assistance Administration, Office of Juvenile Justice and Delinquency Prevention).

Berrueta Clement, J. R., Schweinhart, L. J., Barnett, W. S., Epstein, A. S. and Weikart, D. P. (1984) *Changed Lives: The effects of the Perry Preschool Program on youths through age 19. Monographs of the High/Scope Educational Research Foundation, Number Eight* (Ypsilanti, MI: High/Scope Educational Research Foundation).

Botvin, G. J. and Griffin, K. W. (2004) 'Life skills training: empirical findings and future directions', *The Journal of Primary Prevention*, 25:2, pp. 211–32.

Botvin, G. J., Griffin, K. W. and Nichols, T. D. (2006) 'Preventing youth violence and delinquency through a universal school-based prevention approach', *Prevention Science*, 7:4, pp. 403–8.

Bushway, S. D. and Reuter, P. (2006) 'Labor markets and crime risk factors', in L. W. Sherman, D. P. Farrington, B. C. Welsh and D. L. MacKenzie (eds) *Evidence-based Crime Prevention*, revised edition (New York: Routledge).

Cabinet Office (2009) *Multisystemic Therapy*, available at: www.cabinet-office.gov.uk/social_exclusion_task_force/multi_systemic.aspx [accessed on 23 November 2009].

Catalano, R. F., Arthur, M. W., Hawkins, J. D., Berglund, L. and Olson, J. J. (1998) 'Comprehensive community and school based interventions to prevent antisocial behavior', in R. Loeber and D. P. Farrington (eds) *Serious and Violent Juvenile Offenders: Risk factors and successful interventions* (Thousand Oaks, CA: Sage).

Catalano, R. F., Kosterman, R., Hawkins, J. D., Newcomb, M. D. and Abbott, R. D. (1996) Modeling the etiology of adolescent substance use: A test of the social development model, *Journal of Drug Issues*, 26:2, pp. 429–55.

Catalano, R. F., Park, J., Harachi, T. W., Haggerty, K. P., Abbott, R. D., and Hawkins, J. D. (2005) 'Mediating the effects of poverty, gender, individual characteristics, and external constraints on antisocial behavior: A test of the social development model and implications for developmental life-course theory', in D. P. Farrington (ed.) *Advances in Criminological Theory: Vol. 14. Integrated Developmental and Life-course Theories of Offending* (New Brunswick, NJ: Transaction).

Chamberlain, P. (2003) *Treating Chronic Juvenile Offenders. Advances Made through the Oregon Multidimensional Treatment Foster Care model* (Washington, DC: American Psychological Association).

Chamberlain, P., Price, J., Leve, L. D., Laurent, H., Landsverk, J. A. and Reid, J. B. (2008) 'Prevention of behavior problems for children in foster care: outcomes and mediation effects', *Prevention Science*, 9:1, pp. 17–27.

Collins, D., Johnson, K. and Becker, B. J. (2007) 'A meta-analysis of direct and mediating effects of community coalitions that implemented science-based substance abuse prevention interventions', *Substance Use and Misuse*, 42:6, pp. 985–1007.

Conduct Problems Prevention Research Group (1999) 'Initial impact of the Fast Track Prevention Trial for Conduct Problems: II. Classroom effects', *Journal of Consulting and Clinical Psychology*, 67:5, pp. 648–57.

Crow, I., France, A., Hacking, S. and Hart, M. (2004) *Does Communities That Care Work? The Evaluation of Three Communities That Care Demonstation Projects* (York: Joseph Rowntree Foundation).

Cunningham, A. (2002) *One Step Forward. Lessons learned from a randomized study of multisystemic therapy in Canada* (London, Ontario: Centre for Children and Families in the Justice System).

Currie, J. (2001) 'Early childhood education programs', *The Journal of Economic Perspectives*, 15:1, pp. 213–38.

Curtis, N. M., Ronan, K. R. and Borduin, C. M. (2004) 'Multisystemic treatment: a meta-analysis of outcome studies', *Journal of Family Psychology*, 18:3, pp. 411–19.

Dishion, T. J., McCord, J. and Poulin, F. (1999) 'When interventions harm: Peer groups and problem behavior', *American Psychologist*, 54:9, pp. 755–64.

Dodge, K. A. (2001) 'The science of youth violence prevention. Progressing from developmental epidemiology to efficacy to effectiveness to public policy', *American Journal of Preventive Medicine*, 20: 1 Supplement, pp. 63–70.

Drake, E. K., Aos, S. and Miller, M. G. (2009) 'Evidence-based policy options to reduce crime and criminal justice costs: Implications in Washington State', *Victims and Offenders*, 4, pp. 170–96.

Duncan, G. J. and Magnuson, K. (2004) 'Individual and parent-based intervention strategies for promoting human capital and positive behavior', in P. L. Chase-Lansdale, K. Kiernan and R. J. Friedman (eds) *Human Development Across Lives and Generations: The Potential for Change* (New York: Cambridge University Press).

Eddy, J. M., Whaley, R. B. and Chamberlain, P. (2004) 'The prevention of violent behavior by chronic and serious male juvenile offenders: A 2-year follow-up of a randomized clinical trial', *Journal of Emotional and Behavioral Disorders*, 12:1, pp. 2–8.

Elliott, D. S., Hamburg, B. A. and Williams, K. R. (1998) 'Violence in American schools: An overview', in D. S. Elliott, B. A. Hamburg and K. R. Williams (eds)

Violence in American Schools: A New Perspective (New York: Cambridge University Press).

Farquhar, J. W., Fortmann, S. P., Maccoby, N., Haskell, W. L., Williams, P. T., Flora, J. A., Taylor C.B., Brown, B.W., Solomon, D.S. and Hulley, S.B. (1985) 'The Stanford Five-City Project: design and methods', *American Journal of Epidemiology*, 122:2, pp. 323–34.

Farrington, D. P. and Welsh, B. C. (2003) 'Family-based prevention of offending. A meta-analysis', *Australian and New Zealand Journal of Criminology*, 36, pp. 127–51.

Farrington, D. P. and Welsh, B. C. (2007) *Saving Children from a Life of Crime: Early risk factors and effective interventions* (New York: Oxford University Press).

Feinberg, M. E. and Greenberg, M. (in press) 'Preliminary report: CTC impact in Pennsylvania. Findings from the 2001 and 2003 PA Youth Survey', *Prevention Science*.

Feinberg, M. E., Greenberg, M. T., Osgood, D., Sartorius, J. and Bontempo, D. (2007) 'Effects of the Communities That Care model in Pennsylvania on youth risk and problem behaviors', *Prevention Science*, 8:4, pp. 261–70.

Flay, B. R., Biglan, A., Boruch, R. F., Castro, F. G., Gottfredson, D., Kellam, S., Mościcki, E. K., Schinke, S., Valentine, J. C. and Ji, P. (2005) 'Standards of evidence: Criteria for efficacy, effectiveness and dissemination', *Prevention Science*, 6:3, pp. 151–75.

Flewelling, R. L., Austin, D., Hale, K., LoPlante, M., Liebig, M., Piasecki, L. and Uerz, L. (2005) 'Implementing research-based substance abuse prevention in communities: Effects of a coalition-based prevention initiative in Vermont', *Journal of Community Psychology*, 33:3, pp. 333–53.

Flynn, R. J. (2008) 'Communities That Care: A comprehensive system for youth prevention and promotion, and Canadian applications to date', in R. Hastings and M. Bania (eds) *Towards More Comprehensive Approaches to Prevention and Safety. IPC Review*, Vol. 2 (Ottawa, Ontario, Canada: Institute for the Prevention of Crime, University of Ottawa).

France, A. and Crow, I. (2001) *The Story So Far. An Interim Evaluation of Communities That Care* (York: Joseph Rowntree Foundation).

France, A. and Crow, I. (2005) 'Using the 'risk factor paradigm' in prevention: Lessons from the evaluation of Communities That Care', *Children and Society*, 19:2, pp. 172–84.

Gardner, F., Burton, J. and Klimes, I. (2006) 'Randomised controlled trial of a parenting intervention in the voluntary sector for reducing child conduct problems: outcomes and mechanisms of change', *Journal of Child Psychology and Psychiatry and Allied Disciplines*, 47:11, pp. 1123–32.

Gomby, D. S., Culross, P. L. and Behrman, R. E. (1999) 'Home visiting: Recent program evaluations: Analysis and recommendations', *The Future of Children*, 9:1, pp. 4–6.

Gottfredson, D. C. (1986) 'An empirical test of school-based environmental and individual interventions to reduce the risk of delinquent behavior', *Criminology*, 24, pp. 705–731.

Gottfredson, D. C. (1990) 'Changing school structures to benefit high-risk youths', in P. E. Leone (ed.) *Understanding Troubled and Troubling Youth* (Newbury Park, CA: Sage).

Gottfredson, D. C., Wilson, D. B. and Najaka, S. S. (2006) 'School-based crime prevention', in L. W. Sherman, D. P. Farrington, B. C. Welsh and D. L.

MacKenzie (eds) *Evidence-based Crime Prevention*, revised edition (New York: Routledge).

Greenberg, M. T. and Kusche, C. A. (2002) *Promoting Alternative Thinking Strategies: Blueprint for Violence Prevention*, 2nd edition (Boulder: University of Colorado).

Greenberg, M. T., Kusche, C. A., Cook, E. T. and Quamma, J. P. (1995) 'Promoting emotional competence in school-aged children: The effects of the PATHS curriculum', *Development and Psychopathology*, 7:1, pp. 117–36.

Greenwood, P. W. (2006) *Changing Lives: Delinquency Prevention as Crime-control Policy* (Chicago: University of Chicago Press).

Greenwood, P. W., Karoly, L. A., Everingham, S. S., Houbé, J., Kilburn, M. R., Rydell, C. P., Sanders, M. and Chiesa, J. (2001) 'Estimating the costs and benefits of early childhood interventions: Nurse home visits and the Perry Preschool', in B. C. Welsh, D. P. Farrington and L. W. Sherman (eds) *Costs and Benefits of Preventing Crime* (Boulder, CO: Westview Press).

Grossman, J. B. and Tierney, J. P. (1998) 'Does mentoring work? An impact study of Big Brothers Big Sisters program', *Evaluation Review*, 22:3, pp. 403–26.

Hallfors, D., Cho, H., Livert, D. and Kadushin, C. (2002) 'Fighting back against substance abuse: Are community coalitions winning?', *American Journal of Preventive Medicine*, 23:4, pp. 237–45.

Harachi, T. W., Hawkins, J. D., Catalano, R. F., LaFazia, A. M., Smith, B. H. and Arthur, M. W. (2003) 'Evidence-based community decision making for prevention: Two case studies of Communities That Care', *Japanese Journal of Sociological Criminology*, 28, pp. 26–37.

Harrell, A., Cavanaugh, S., Harmon, M. A., Koper, C. S. and Sridharan, S. (1997) *Evaluation of the Children at Risk Program: Results one year after the end of the program. Research in brief* (Washington, DC: The Urban Institute).

Harrell, A., Cavanaugh, S. and Sridharan, S. (1999) *Evaluation of the Children at Risk Program: Results one year after the end of the program. Research in brief* (Washington, DC: National Institute of Justice).

Hawkins, J. D., Brown, E. C., Oesterle, S., Arthur, M. W., Abbott, R. D. and Catalano, R. F. (2008) 'Early effects of Communities That Care on targeted risks and initiation of delinquent behavior and substance use', *Journal of Adolescent Health*, 43:1, pp. 15–22.

Hawkins, J. D., Catalano, R. F. Jr. and Associates. (1992) *Communities That Care: Action for Drug Abuse Prevention*, 1st edition (San Francisco: Jossey-Bass).

Hawkins, J. D., Catalano, R. F. and Arthur, M. W. (2002) 'Promoting science-based prevention in communities', *Addictive Behaviors*, 27:6, pp. 951–76.

Hawkins, J. D., Catalano, R. F., Kosterman, R., Abbott, R. and Hill, K. G. (1999) 'Preventing adolescent health-risk behaviors by strengthening protection during childhood', *Archives of Pediatrics and Adolescent Medicine*, 153:3, pp. 226–34.

Hawkins, J. D., Oesterle, S., Brown, E. C., Arthur, M. W., Abbott, R. D., Fagan, A. A. and Catalano, R.F. (2009) 'Results of a type 2 translational research trial to prevent adolescent drug use and delinquency: A test of Communities That Care', *Archives of Pediatrics and Adolescent Medicine*, 163:9, pp. 789–98.

Hawkins, J. D., Smith, B. H., Hill, K. G., Kosterman, R., Catalano, R. F. and Abbott, R. D. (2007) 'Promoting social development and preventing health and behavior problems during the elementary grades: Results from the Seattle Social Development Project', *Victims and Offenders*, 2:2, pp. 161–81.

Henggeler, S. W. (1998) *Blueprints for Violence Prevention: Multisystemic Therapy* (Boulder: Centre for the Study and Prevention of Violence).

High/Scope UK (2009) *The Work of High/Scope UK*, available at: www.high-scope.org.uk/about_highscope/ [accessed on 25 November 2009].

Hope, T. (1995) 'Community crime prevention', in M. Tonry and D. P. Farrington (eds) *Building a Safer Society: Strategic Approaches to Crime Prevention*, Vol. 19 (Chicago: University of Chicago Press).

Howell, J. C. (1995) *Guide for Implementing the Comprehensive Strategy for Serious, Violent, and Chronic Juvenile Offenders* (Washington, D.C.: U.S. Department of Justice, Office of Juvenile Justice and Delinquency Prevention).

Howell, J. C. (2009) *Preventing and Reducing Juvenile Delinquency: A Comprehensive Framework*, 2nd edition (Thousand Oaks, CA: Sage).

Huang, B., Kosterman, R., Catalano, R. F., Hawkins, J. D., and Abbott, R. D. (2001) 'Modeling mediation in the etiology of violent behavior and adolescence: A test of the social development model', *Criminology*, 39:1, pp. 75–107.

Hutchings, J., Gardner, F., Bywater, T., Daley, D., Whitaker, C., Jones, K., Eames, C. and Edwards, R.T. (2007) 'Parenting intervention in Sure Start services for children at risk of developing conduct disorder: pragmatic randomised controlled trial', *BMJ*, 334:7595, p. 678.

Jolliffe, D. and Farrington, D. P. (2008) *The Influence of Mentoring on Reoffending*, (Stockholm, Sweden: National Council for Crime Prevention).

Jones, M. B. and Offord, D. R. (1989) 'Reduction of antisocial behavior in poor children by nonschool skill-development', *Journal of Child Psychology and Psychiatry and Allied Disciplines*, 30:5, pp. 737–50.

Kaplan, R. M. (2000) 'Two pathways to prevention', *American Psychologist*, 55:4, pp. 382–96.

Karoly, L. A., Greenwood, P. W., Everingham, S. S., Hoube, J., Kilburn, M. R., Rydell, C. P., Sanders, M. and Chiesa, J. (1998) *Investing in Our Children: What we know and don't know about the costs and benefits of early childhood interventions* (Santa Monica, CA: Rand Corporation).

Kazdin, A. E. (1997) 'Parent management training: evidence, outcomes, and issues', *Journal of the American Academy of Child and Adolescent Psychiatry*, 36:10, pp. 1349–56.

Klein, N. C., Alexander, J. F. and Parsons, B. V. (1977) 'Impact of family systems intervention on recidivism and sibling delinquency: A model of primary prevention and program evaluation', *Journal of Consulting and Clinical Psychology*, 45:3, pp. 469–74.

Kling, J. R., Ludwig, J. O. and Katz, L. F. (2005) 'Neighborhood effects on crime for female and male youth: Evidence from a randomized housing voucher experiment', *Quarterly Journal of Economics*, 20, pp. 87–130.

LaLonde, R. J. (2003) 'Employment and training programs', in R. A. Moffitt (ed.) *Means-tested Transfer Programs in the United States* (Chicago: University of Chicago Press).

Lipsey, M. W. and Wilson, D. B. (2001) *Practical Meta-analysis* (Thousand Oaks, CA: Sage).

Littell, J. H., Popa, M. and Forsythe, B. (2005) 'Multisystematic therapy for social, emotional, and behavioral problems in youth aged 10–17', *The Cochrane Database of Systematic Reviews*, 4.

Lonczak, H. S., Huang, B., Catalano, R. F., Hawkins, J. D., Hill, K. G., Abbott, R. D., Ryan, J.A.M. and Kosterman, R. (2001) 'The social predictors of adolescent alcohol misuse: A test of the Social Development Model', *Journal of Studies on Alcohol*, 62:2, pp. 179–89.

Lösel, F. and Beelmann, A. (2003) 'Effects of child skills training in preventing antisocial behavior: A systematic review of randomized evaluations', *Annals of the American Academy of Political and Social Science*, 587, pp. 84–109.

Lösel, F. and Beelmann, A. (2006) 'Child social skills training', in B.C. Welsh and D.P. Farrington (eds) *Preventing Crime: What Works for Children, Offenders, Victims, and Places* (New York: Springer).

Mason, W. A., Kosterman, R., Hawkins, J. D., Haggerty, K. P. and Spoth, R. L. (2003) 'Reducing adolescents' growth in substance use and delinquency: Randomized trial effects of a preventive parent-training intervention', *Prevention Science*, 4:3, pp. 203–312.

McCord, J. (1978) 'A thirty-year follow-up of treatment effects', *American Psychologist*, 33:3, pp. 284–9.

McCord, J. (2003) 'Cures that harm: Unanticipated outcomes of crime prevention programs', *Annals of the American Academy of Political and Social Science*, 587, pp. 16–30.

McCord, J., Widom, C. S. and Crowell, N. A. (eds) (2001) *Juvenile Crime, Juvenile Justice* (Washington, DC: National Academy Press).

National Academy for Parenting Practitioners (2009) *SAFE (the Study of Adolescents' Family Experiences)*, available at: www.parentingacademy.org/research/safe.aspx [accessed on 12 December 2009].

O'Connell, M. E., Boat, T. and Warner, K. E. (2009) *Preventing Mental, Emotional, and Behavioral Disorders among Young People: Progress and Possibilities* (Washington, DC: National Academies Press).

Offord, D. R., Kraemer, H. C., Kazdin, A. E., Jensen, P. S. and Harrington, R. (1998) 'Lowering the burden of suffering from child psychiatric disorder: Trade-offs among clinical, targeted, and universal interventions', *Journal of the American Academy of Child and Adolescent Psychiatry*, 37:7, pp. 686–94.

Ogden, T. and Hagen, K. A. (2006) 'Multisystemic therapy of serious behavior problems in youth: Sustainability of therapy effectiveness two years after intake', *Child and Adolescent Mental Health*, 11:3, pp. 142–9.

Olds, D. L. (2002) 'Prenatal and infancy home visiting by nurses: from randomized trials to community replication', *Prevention Science*, 3:3, pp. 153–72.

Olds, D. L. (2007) 'Preventing crime with prenatal and infancy support of parents: The Nurse-Family Partnership', *Victims and Offenders*, 2:2, pp. 205–25.

Olds, D. L., Eckenrode, J., Henderson, C. R., Jr., Kitzman, H., Powers, J., Cole, R., Sidora, K., Morris, P., Pettitt, L. M. and Luckey, D. (1997) 'Long-term effects of home visitation on maternal life course and child abuse and neglect: Fifteen-year follow-up of a randomized trial', *Journal of the American Medical Association*, 278:8, pp. 637–43.

Olds, D. L., Henderson, C. R., Jr., Chamberlin, R. and Tatelbaum, R. (1986) 'Preventing child abuse and neglect: a randomized trial of nurse home visitation', *Pediatrics*, 78:1, pp. 65–78.

Olds, D. L., Henderson, C. R., Jr., Cole, R., Eckenrode, J., Kitzman, H., Luckey, D. et al. (1998) 'Long-term effects of nurse home visitation on children's criminal and antisocial behavior: 15-year follow-up of a randomized controlled trial', *Journal of the American Medical Association*, 280:14, pp. 1238–44.

Olds, D. L., Henderson, C. R., Jr., Phelps, C., Kitzman, H. and Hanks, C. (1993) 'Effect of prenatal and infancy nurse home visitation on government spending', *Medical Care*, 31: 2, pp. 155–74.

Patterson, G. R. (1982) *A Social Learning Approach: Vol. 3. Coercive Family Process* (Eugene, OR: Castalia).

Perry, C. L., Klepp, K.-I. and Sillers, C. (1989) 'Community-wide strategies for cardiovascular health: The Minnesota Heart Health Programme youth programme', *Health Education and Research*, 4, pp. 87–101.

Petrosino, A., Turpin-Petrosino, C. and Buehler, J. (2006) 'Scared Straight and other juvenile awareness programs', in B. C. Welsh and D. P. Farrington (eds) *Preventing Crime. What Works for Children, Offenders, Victims, and Places* (Dordrecht, The Netherlands: Springer).

Piquero, A. R., Farrington, D. P., Welsh, B. C., Tremblay, R. and Jennings, W. G. (2009) 'Effects of early family/parent training programs on antisocial behavior and delinquency', *Journal of Experimental Criminology*, 5:2, pp. 83–120.

Reynolds, A. J., Temple, J. A. and Ou, S.-R. (2003) 'School-based early intervention and child well-being in the Chicago Longitudinal Study', *Child Welfare Journal*, 82:5, pp. 633–56.

Reynolds, A. J., Temple, J. A., Robertson, D. L. and Mann, E. A. (2001) 'Long-term effects of an early childhood intervention on educational achievement and juvenile arrest: A 15-year follow-up of low-income children in public schools', *Journal of the American Medical Association*, 285:18, pp. 2339–46.

Roberts, R. (2007) 'A new approach to meeting the needs of looked after children experiencing difficulties: The Multidimensional Treatment Foster Care in England Project', *ACAMH Occasional Papers No 26. Fostering, Adoption and Alternative Care*, pp. 59–68.

Rosenbaum, D. P. (1988) 'Community crime prevention: A review and synthesis of the literature', *Justice Quarterly*, 5, pp. 323–95.

Roussos, S. T. and Fawcett, S. B. (2000) 'A review of collaborative partnerships as a strategy for improving community health', *Annual Review of Public Health*, 21, pp. 369–402.

Rutter, M., Giller, H. and Hagell, A. (1998) *Antisocial Behavior by Young People* (Cambridge: Cambridge University Press).

Sainsbury Centre for Mental Health (2009) *The Chance of a Lifetime* (London: Sainsbury Centre for Mental Health).

Sanders, M. R. (1999) 'Triple P-Positive Parenting Program: towards an empirically validated multilevel parenting and family support strategy for the prevention of behavior and emotional problems in children', *Clinical Child and Family Psychology Review*, 2:2, pp. 71–90.

Sanders, M. R., Markie-Dadds, C., Tully, L. A. and Bor, W. (2000) 'The Triple P-Positive Parenting Program: A comparison of enhanced, standard, and self-directed behavioral family intervention for parents of children with early onset conduct problems', *Journal of Consulting and Clinical Psychology*, 68: 4, pp. 624–40.

Sanders, M. R., Markie-Dadds, C. and Turner, K. M. (2003) *Theoretical, Scientific and Clinical Foundations of the Triple-P Positive Parenting Program: A population approach to the promotion of parenting competence. Parenting Practice and Research Monograph No 1* (Parenting and Family Support Centre, University of Queensland).

Schochet, P. Z., Burghardt, J. and McConnell, S. (2008) 'Does Job Corps work? Impact findings from the National Job Corps Study', *American Economic Review*, 98, pp. 1864–86.

Schweinhart, L. J., Barnes, H. V. and Weikart, D. P. (1993) *Significant Benefits: The High/Scope Perry Preschool Study through Age 27* (Ypsilanti, MI: High/Scope).

Schweinhart, L. J., Montie, J., Zongping, X., Barnett, W. S., Belfield, C. R. and Nores, M. (2005) *Lifetime Effects: The High/Scope Perry Preschool Study through Age 40* (Ypsilanti, MI: High/Scope Press).

Schweinhart, L. J. and Weikart, D. P. (1980) *Young Children Grow Up: The Effects of the Perry Preschool Programme on Youths through Age 15* (Ypsilanti, MI: High/Scope Press).

Scott, S., O'Connor, T. and Futh, A. (2006) *What Makes Parenting Programmes Work in Disadvantaged Areas? The PALS trial* (York: Joseph Rowntree Foundation).

Scott, S., Spender, Q., Doolan, M., Jacobs, B. and Aspland, H. (2001) 'Multicentre controlled trial of parenting groups for childhood antisocial behaviour in clinical practice', *BMJ*, 323: 7306, pp. 194–8.

Sexton, T. L. and Alexander, J. F. (2003) 'Functional Family Therapy: A mature clinical model for working with at-risk adolescents and their families', in T. L. Sexton, G. R. Weeks and M. S. Robbins (eds) *The Handbook of Family Therapy* (New York: Taylor and Francis).

Shiner, M., Young, T., Newburn, T. and Groben, S. (2004) *Mentoring Disaffected Young People: an Evaluation of Mentoring Plus* (York: Joseph Rowntree Foundation).

Sundell, K. (2009) 'The transportability of US evidence-based programs to other social systems', *Campbell Collaboration Colloquium*, Oslo, May 2009.

Sundell, K., Hansson, K., Löfholm, C. A., Olsson, T., Gustle, L.-H. and Kadesjö, C. (2008) 'The transportability of multisystemic therapy to Sweden: Short-term results from a randomized trial of conduct-disordered youths', *Journal of Family Psychology*, 22:4, pp. 550–60.

Sutton, C., Utting, D. and Farrington, D. P. (2004) *Support from the Start* (London: Department for Education and Skills).

The Social Research Unit. (2009) *Practising what Practice Preaches*, available at: www.dartington.org.uk/development [accessed on 8 December 2009].

Timmons-Mitchell, J., Bender, M. B., Kishna, M. A. and Mitchell, C. C. (2006) 'An independent effectiveness trial of multisystemic therapy with juvenile justice youth', *Journal of Clinical Child and Adolescent Psychology*, 35:2, pp. 227–36.

Tobler, N. S. (1986) 'Meta-analysis of 143 adolescent drug prevention programs: Quantitative outcome results of program participants compared to a control or comparison group', *Journal of Drug Issues*, 16:4, pp. 537–67.

Tobler, N. S., Lessard, T., Marshall, D., Ochshorn, P. and Roona, M. (1999) 'Effectiveness of school-based drug prevention programs for marijuana use', *School Psychology International*, 20:1, pp. 105–37.

Tremblay, R. E. and Craig, W. M. (1995) 'Developmental crime prevention', in M. Tonry and D. P. Farrington (eds) *Building a Safer Society: Strategic Approaches to Crime Prevention*, Vol. 19 (Chicago: University of Chicago Press).

U.S. General Accountability Office (2003) *Youth Illicit Drug Use Prevention: DARE Long-Term Evaluations and Federal Efforts to Identify Effective Programs. Report GAO-03-172R* (Washington, DC: Author).

Utting, D. and Langman, J. (eds) (2005) *A Guide to Promising Approaches*, 2nd edition (London: Communities That Care).

Utting, D., Monteiro, H. and Ghate, D. (2007) *Interventions for Children at Risk of Developing Antisocial Personality Disorder. Report to the Department of Health and Prime Minister's Strategy Unit* (London: Policy Research Bureau).

van Lier, P., Vitaro, F. and Eisner, M. (2007) 'Preventing aggressive and violent behavior: Using prevention programs to study the role of peer dynamics in maladjustment problems', *European Journal on Criminal Policy and Research*, 13, pp. 277–96.

Wandersman, A. and Florin, P. (2003) 'Community interventions and effective prevention', *American Psychologist*, 58:6–7, pp. 441–8.

Wasserman, G. A. and Miller, L. S. (1998) 'The prevention of serious and violent juvenile offending', in R. Loeber and D. P. Farrington (eds) *Serious and Violent Juvenile Offenders: Risk Factors and Successful Interventions* (Thousand Oaks, CA: Sage).

Webster-Stratton, C. (1984) 'Randomized trial of two parent-training programs for families with conduct-disordered children', *Journal of Consulting and Clinical Psychology*, 52:4, pp. 666–78.

Webster-Stratton, C. (1998) 'Preventing conduct problems in Head Start children: Strengthening parenting competencies', *Journal of Consulting and Clinical Psychology*, 66:5, pp. 715–30.

Webster-Stratton, C. and Taylor, T. (2001) 'Nipping early risk factors in the bud: Preventing substance abuse, delinquency, and violence in adolescence through interventions targeted at young children (0 to 8 Years)', *Prevention Science*, 2:3, pp. 165–92.

Weiss, C. H., Murphy-Graham, E., Petrosino, A. and Gandhi, A. G. (2008) 'The fairy godmother – and her warts: Making the dream of evidence-based policy come true', *American Journal of Evaluation*, 29:1, pp. 29–47.

Welsh, B. C., Sullivan, C. J. and Olds, D. L. (2010) 'When early crime prevention goes to scale: A new look at the evidence', *Prevention Science*, 11:2, pp. 115–25.

Widom, C. S. (1989) 'The cycle of violence', *Science*, 244: 4901, pp. 160–6.

Wilson, D. B., Gottfredson, D. C. and Najaka, S. S. (2001) 'School-based prevention of problem behaviors: A meta-analysis', *Journal of Quantitative Criminology*, 17:3, pp. 247–72.

Wilson, D. B. and MacKenzie, D. L. (2006) 'Boot camps', in B. C. Welsh and D. P. Farrington (eds) *Preventing Crime. What Works for Children, Offenders, Victims, and Places* (Dordrecht, The Netherlands: Springer).

Yin, R. K., Kaftarian, S. J., Yu, P. and Jansen, M. A. (1997) 'Outcomes from CSAP's Community Partnership Program: Findings from the National Cross-Site Evaluation', *Evaluation and Program Planning*, 20:3, pp. 345–55.

Zakocs, R. C. and Edwards, E. M. (2006) 'What explains community coalition effectiveness? A review of the literature', *American Journal of Preventive Medicine*, 30:4, pp. 351–61.

Chapter 8

Families and parenting*

Barbara Maughan and Frances Gardner

From the earliest days of criminological enquiry, family factors have been central to explanatory models of youth crime. Empirical studies on the effects of 'broken homes' began as early as the 1920s (Wells and Rankin 1991), and today, searches of electronic databases identify literally thousands of reports examining links between family structure, family functioning, styles of parenting and youth crime. This huge body of research has established beyond doubt that delinquency is more common in some family forms than in others, and shows systematic links with styles of parenting and patterns of family life. Research on parenting has contributed directly to the development of some of the best-supported interventions for childhood conduct problems, and much public and policy debate turns on the findings of family-related research.

This chapter focuses on two main aspects of this large literature. First, we draw together evidence on the extent to which variations in family structure and functioning contribute to *individual differences* in young people's risk of involvement in antisocial behaviour and crime. This is in a sense the 'traditional' approach to family influences underlying the great majority of criminological and developmental research: how far do family factors contribute to variations in individuals' risk of offending within a particular sample or historical era? But as other chapters in this volume make clear, this is by no means the only causal question of interest. Between the 1950s and the 1990s, *overall* levels of youth offending rose sharply, at a time when many aspects of family life were also undergoing major change: divorce rates rose, cohabitation, single parenthood and step-families all became more common, and family constellations became

*We are grateful to Emily Williamson for help in compiling the demographic trend data, and to Sandra Woodhouse for help in preparing the manuscript. BM is supported by the Medical Research Council.

247

less stable and more fluid than in the past. Not surprisingly, the coincidence of the two sets of trends has led many commentators to conclude that these changes in family life caused – or at least contributed to – rising levels of youth crime. The second aim of this chapter is to valuate those claims. We summarize evidence on key trends in family demographics between the 1950s and the early 2000s; outline the more limited evidence on changes in parenting; and explore how far it is indeed plausible to conclude that family-related changes contributed to the rise in levels of youth crime.

Interpreting family-related research on youth crime

Michael Rutter (Chapter 5 this volume) provides an overview of the key issues involved in identifying causal influences on young people's behaviour. Two aspects of that discussion are particularly relevant here. First, many different causal pathways contribute to risk for offending, and many different risk factors – some individual, others 'contextual' – are likely to be involved. As a result, family-based risks will almost always be just one element in a more complex nexus of factors that increase or decrease risk of involvement in crime. In some instances, *combinations* of those factors may carry quite different implications: some styles of parenting, for example, may be associated with an increased risk of behaviour problems for young people living in crime-prone neighbour-hoods, or those with delinquent friends, but have little or no impact in the absence of these other potential risks. As a result, we need to view findings on family influences alongside knowledge of other contributors to young people's behaviour problems, and be wary of assuming that growing up in family type X, or experiencing parenting style Y, will always, under all circumstances, have similar implications.

Implicitly if not explicitly, most studies of family factors and delin-quency set out to identify *causal* influences on youth crime. As Michael Rutter outlines (Chapter 5, this volume), however, that is far from an easy task. Several rather different factors can complicate interpretation of findings (Maughan 2001; British Academy 2010). First, both family structures and styles of parenting co-vary with numerous other influences on youth offending. Many socio-demographic indicators vary systemati-cally across family structures, and many characteristics of parents – their age, their educational backgrounds and indeed their own propensities for antisocial behaviour – affect the types of relationships they enter, and the styles of parenting they provide. Where then do the key influences on young people's outcomes lie? To isolate the role of family factors, we need studies that take account of these other (confounding) influences, either through the use of statistical controls (the most usual approach), or through the more complex design approaches that Michael Rutter outlines. Because many of the individual characteristics of interest here are partly heritable, genetically informative designs (studies of adoptees, for example, where parents and children differ in their genetic backgrounds) may be important in differentiating truly 'environmental' influences from those where effects are also likely to involve some element of genetic mediation.

Second, children influence, as well as being influenced by, those around them; the temperamentally difficult child may 'evoke' more negative parenting than his or her more placid counterpart, and the irritable adolescent may frustrate all but the most determined parents' efforts at displaying warmth. Bidirectional influences of this kind have been documented in the literature for many years, and clearly form an important part of the causal picture (Pettit and Arsiwalla 2008). In one-off, cross-sectional surveys, however, we cannot tell who is influencing whom: longitudinal data, or results from intervention studies, are essential to tease these questions out. Third, youth offending and the childhood behaviour problems that often precede it are far from homogeneous. As discussed in more detail in Chapter 3, although much delinquency involves relatively 'occasional' offenders, all studies also consistently identify small groups that show prolific – and often very long-term – histories of crime. Family-based risks may be more salient for some of these young people than for others. Moffitt (1993), for example, has argued that the combination of adverse temperamental characteristics and particular styles of early parenting may be key risk factors for early-onset offending, while peer and other influences are more central to delinquency that is confined mainly to the teens. Though by no means all research studies are able to make these distinctions, where they can, we are likely to gain a more nuanced and realistic picture of family effects.

Finally, we should add a note on terminology and on the scope of this chapter. Although youth crime is primarily an adolescent phenomenon, behaviour problems that increase risk for offending can clearly begin much earlier in childhood, and family-related influences on these behaviours have also been reported from the earliest stages of development. As a result, we draw on evidence from studies of family factors and younger children's behaviour problems as well as on those that focus more specifically on the teenage years. Evidence on these earlier life-stages (and on related non-delinquent behaviours in teens) comes from a range of disciplines: developmental psychology, child mental health research, behavioural genetic studies, and others. Inevitably, these disciplines use differing terminologies (and somewhat differing definitions) to index the behaviours they seek to understand: conduct disorder, disruptive behaviour, externalizing problems, and – following a long-established tradition in the social and biological sciences – 'antisocial behaviour'. Consistent with our sources, we follow that tradition here. This means that we use the term 'antisocial behaviour' to refer to a broad spectrum of disruptive and difficult behaviours, including but in no way confined to those that are illegal, rather than in the narrower sense of 'unwanted' (and usually relatively public) behaviours implied in more recent political discourse.

With these issues in mind, we turn to the more detailed evidence on links between family factors and youth crime. Like many past commentators, we distinguish between family structures (differentiated, for example, in terms of single or two-parent family status, or parents' marital histories), and the influences of family relationships and styles of parenting.

Family structure and delinquency

Probably the most widely-investigated family correlate of delinquency in the criminological literature is 'broken homes'. Consistently, across different historical eras and study settings, young people from disrupted family backgrounds have been found to be at some increased risk of involvement in crime. Reviewing this literature in the early 1990s, Wells and Rankin (1991) concluded that the prevalence of overall delinquency was typically some 10–15 per cent higher for young people in non-intact than in intact homes. Rodgers and Pryor (1998), reviewing outcomes of divorce, reached a similar conclusion: in general, risks of delinquency were roughly doubled for children from disrupted families, with results remarkably consistent over time and place. Findings from the Cambridge Study in Delinquent Development (the premier long-term UK longitudinal study of risk for youth crime) paint a similar picture. In this 1950s-born cohort of inner-city boys, teenagers from permanently disrupted families (around 18 per cent of the sample) were at a roughly twofold increased risk of both self-reported delinquency and officially recorded juvenile crime. This study has tracked participants into middle adulthood. Although contrasts between men from disrupted and stable family backgrounds were less marked at this stage, even in adulthood conviction rates showed some continuing associations with childhood family disruption (Juby and Farrington 2001).

The robustness of these associations is striking, though it is also important to bear in mind that they reflect *average* figures, and point to relatively modest effects. Most studies find that outcomes show important variability within as well as between family types, so that despite overall group differences, most young people from non-intact families will not become involved in offending, and many in intact families will. In addition, taken alone, these results tell us nothing about *why* family disruption is associated with delinquency – a point we return to later in the discussion. Finally, many 'classic' criminological studies of broken homes were undertaken many years ago, in an era when rates of family

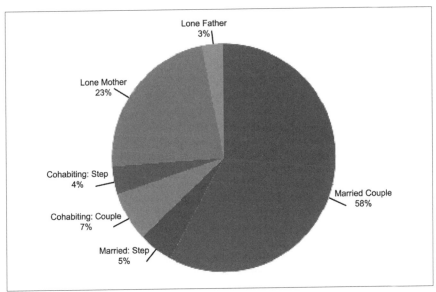

Figure 8.1 Dependent children in different family types: 2001 UK Census

breakdown were low, and a simple 'intact' vs 'non-intact' dichotomy captured the main variation in family forms. Today, that situation has altered radically. One recent US study identified 13 different family types in a contemporary adolescent cohort (Apel and Kaukinen 2008), and data from the 2001 Census reflect a similarly complex pattern in the UK (see Figure 8.1). In the Britain of the early twenty-first century, only just over half of dependent children lived in 'traditional' married couple families, and a further 7 per cent in cohabiting couple households. Around a quarter lived with a single parent (very predominantly their mother), and approaching 10 per cent were in step-families, roughly evenly divided between those where parents were married and those where they were cohabiting. In addition, family types varied systematically across cultural and ethnic groups, with single parent households more common in African Caribbean families, and children of Asian heritage more likely to be growing up with two married parents than their white counterparts (White 2002).

The emergence of these new family forms has resulted from the convergence of a range of demographic changes that have occurred since the end of the Second World War. We illustrate some of the most central of these trends below; fuller details are available in several recent syntheses (see e.g. Cabinet Office 2008; Office for National Statistics 2007a). In addition to data on marriage, cohabitation and divorce, we note trends in two other aspects of family demographics that show consistent links with delinquency: family size (where young people from large families

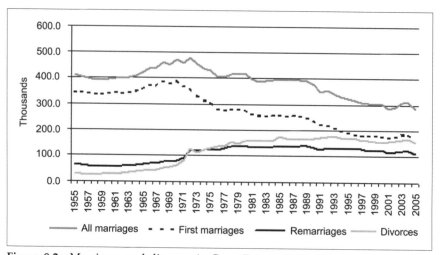

Figure 8.2 Marriages and divorces in Great Britain, 1955–2006

Sources: Office for National Statistics; General Register Office for Scotland; Northern Ireland Statistics and Research Agency.

have typically been found to be at increased risk of offending (Rutter *et al.* 1998)), and maternal age, where children of very young mothers are vulnerable to a range of adverse developmental outcomes including antisocial behaviour and crime (Moffitt 2002).

Family formation and dissolution: demographic trends

Figure 8.2 shows trends in two of the most basic indicators of family formation and dissolution: rates of marriage and divorce. Numbers of first marriages rose between the mid 1950s and the early 1970s, but have fallen steadily since that time; the remarriage rate rose across the 1970s, but has remained relatively stable since. As a result, overall rates of marriage have shown a marked decline since the 1970s. Especially across the late 1960s and the 1970s, these changing patterns of entry into marriage were accompanied by marked increases in rates of divorce. In 1973, the ratio of divorces to marriages was 25:100; by 2005, that figure had more than doubled, to 55:100. Not all divorces, of course, are between partners with children; as Figure 8.3 shows, however, the numbers of children involved in divorce followed similar trends, more than doubling across the 1970s, and showing a further peak in the early 1990s.

A third key change in the post-war years was the rise in rates of non-marital cohabitation. In the 1950s, only 2 per cent of couples lived together before marriage; by the late 1990s, that figure had risen to 75 per cent (Haskey 2005). About three in five first cohabitations now turn into

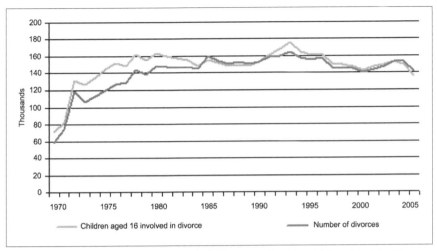

Figure 8.3 Number of divorces and children aged under 16 involved in divorce, England and Wales
Source: ONS Focus on Children.

marriages, but cohabiting unions themselves are less stable than marriages: recent estimates suggest that less than a fifth of cohabiting unions survive for five years, and fewer than one in ten survive for ten years or more (Ermisch and Francesconi 2000).

Inevitably, these changes have affected the types of couple relationships into which children are born. Figure 8.4 shows trends in the overall birth rate since 1950, and in the numbers of births occurring inside and outside marriage. In the 1970s, around 10 per cent of births occurred outside marriage; by the early 2000s, that figure had risen to 40 per cent. Much of this increase reflects a rise in the numbers of births jointly registered to cohabiting couples; indeed, the numbers of 'solely registered' births declined somewhat over the same period. The impact of these changes continues to influence children's family situations up to the present day. Between 1998 and 2008, for example, the number of children living in married couple families fell by 1.0 million (a fall of 7 per cent), while the numbers living with cohabiting couples and lone parents increased by 0.6 and 0.1 million respectively. The overall fall in the birth rate also affected average family size, especially in couple families. In the early 1970s, over 40 per cent of children lived in sibling groups of three or more children; by 2007, that figure had dropped to 28 per cent.

Taken together, these trends have contributed to an increase in both the diversity and the fluidity of contemporary family forms. When parents divorce or separate, most children spend periods in a single parent household; later, many become part of new step ('reconstituted' or

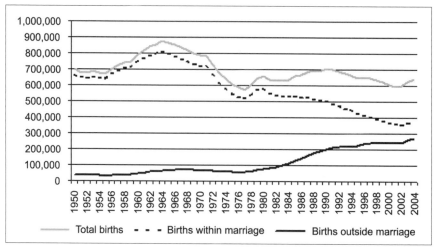

Figure 8.4 Births in England and Wales by parents' marital status, 1950–2004

Sources: Office for National Statistics; General Register Office for Scotland; Northern Ireland Statistics and Research Agency.

'blended') families. In 2006, around 1 in 4 dependent children lived in lone parent households, a rise from 1 in 14 in the early 1970s (Office for National Statistics 2007b). Consistent data on step-families have only been collected more recently; studies suggest, however, that they too are a fast-growing family form (Ferri and Smith 2003).

Related trends

Alongside these trends, changes have also taken place in series of related factors (themselves well-established correlates of risk for delinquency) that co-vary with family type. Among the most important of these are parental age and family economic circumstances.

As Figure 8.5 shows, women's mean ages at marriage fell across the 1950s and 1960s, but have risen steadily thereafter. Paralleling these trends, ages at first births have also risen; between 1971 and 2006, for example, married women's average age at the birth of their first child rose by over six years, from 23.9 to 30.2 years. As Figure 8.5 also shows, ages at first birth vary systematically with marital status. Since the early 1970s unmarried women have had their first child earlier than their married counterparts; by the early 2000s, the gap in ages at first birth amounted to some three years. As a result, the age profiles of parents also vary consistently by family type (Figure 8.6). In general, cohabiting couple families are much younger than married couples, while lone mothers tend to be some ten years younger than lone fathers. Mirroring these overall trends, the proportion of births to teenage mothers (often regarded as an

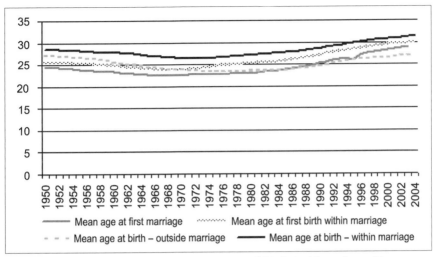

Figure 8.5 Women's mean age at marriage and birth inside and outside marriage, UK 1950–2004

Sources: Office for National Statistics; General Register Office for Scotland; Northern Ireland Statistics and Research Agency.

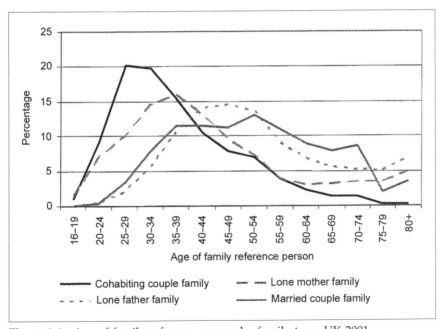

Figure 8.6 Age of family reference person by family type, UK 2001

Sources: Focus on Families, Office for National Statistics, Census 2001, General Household Survey (GHS), Office for National Statistics; Census 2001, General Register Office for Scotland; Census 2001, Northern Ireland Statistics and Research Agency

255

especially high-risk group in relation to behaviour problems in offspring) rose across the early post-war years, to a peak of over 10 per cent of all live births in the early 1970s. Since that time it has fallen back to around 7 per cent (see Chapter 2 for further details).

A variety of factors – changing social norms, women's increased participation in the labour market, the availability of contraception and abortion, and changes in the legislative framework surrounding family breakdown – have all contributed to these trends. The expansion of educational opportunities for women also played a key part. In the 1950s and 60s, for example, it was more educated women who first led the moves towards cohabitation, while mean ages at motherhood have increased more steeply for women with higher educational levels than their less qualified counterparts.

Finally, as discussed in more detail in Chapter 2, although average household incomes doubled in real terms between the early 1970s and the early 2000s, not all family types benefited equally from these trends. In particular, single parent families (already economically disadvantaged in the 1960s and 70s) have become markedly more disadvantaged relative to couple families since that time.

Many of these trends are interrelated. As a result, today's young people are not only growing up in more fluid and varied family settings than in the past, but those settings vary systematically in terms of parental characteristics and key socio-demographic indicators. Table 8.1 gives a flavour of these differences, showing a profile of the circumstances of UK 11–15-year-olds in 'traditional' two-parent households, single parent families and reconstituted or step families at the turn of the millennium. The data are taken from results pooled across two large-scale, nationally-representative surveys of child and adolescent mental health undertaken by the Office for National Statistics in 1999 (Meltzer *et al.* 2000) and 2004 (Green *et al.* 2005). As a group, young people in single-parent families were strikingly disadvantaged by contrast with those in both 'traditional' two-parent and step families in terms of family income, housing tenure and neighbourhood conditions. Mothers in both single-parent and step families tended to be younger than those in 'traditional' two-parent households, and were also less well qualified. In addition, the table includes data on two other indicators likely to have implications for young people's developmental outcomes: levels of maternal psychological distress, as measured by scores on the General Health Questionnaire (Goldberg and Williams 1998), and exposure to adverse life events (such as serious illnesses, accidents or financial difficulties) during the lifetime of the child. Once again, young people in single-parent and reconstituted families were markedly more likely to face stressors of this kind than their peers in stable two-parent homes.

Taken together, these findings underscore two key issues. First, from the perspective of understanding individual differences in youth crime,

Table 8.1 Family type and correlated factors: 1999 and 2004 ONS studies, 11–15-year-olds

	Family type		
	'Traditional' (n = 5010)	Single parent (n = 1926)	Reconstituted (n = 987)
Maternal characteristics			
Age at birth of child (mean, years)	28.4	26.3	25.0
% teen mothers	2.9	10.4	11.7
% no qualifications	19.3	32.8	25.2
Maternal distress (GHQ score [mean])	1.54	2.68	2.08
Material/social circumstances			
% lowest income quintile	6.1	55.3	10.1
% rented housing	15.9	40.3	29.4
% 'hard pressed' neighbourhood (2004 only)	15.5	40.3	29.4
Psychosocial adversity			
% > =3 adverse life events	7.3	32.1	29.0

Sources: 1999 and 2004 ONS Child Mental Health Surveys.

they suggest that contemporary discussions of family structure need to be more nuanced than in the past, and take account of a much wider range of family forms. Second, as Table 8.1 makes clear, variations in family type are inextricably linked with variations in a range of other socio-demographic and psychosocial factors that themselves show clear links with youth crime; as a result, focusing on family structures alone is almost certainly to over-simplify a much more complex reality. We turn now to findings from more recent studies that are beginning to take these differing factors into account.

Individual differences in offending: contemporary studies of family structure and adolescent behaviour

One of the most detailed analyses of contemporary family structures and adolescent behaviour problems has been reported by Apel and Kaukinen (2008). These authors used data on over 8,000 adolescents surveyed in the US National Longitudinal Study of Youth 1997 to construct a complex indictor of family structure differentiated both in terms of the presence of biological parents(s) and more detailed aspects of family form. This classification made it possible to identify outcomes for young people in relatively 'new' family types (including, for example, those living with both biological parents but where the *family* was blended because one or other parent had children from a past relationship); and to assess the impact of parents' marital status across all family types.

At the most general level, the results confirmed findings from much past research. As a group, young people living with both biological parents had the lowest rates of antisocial behaviour, while youth in all 'non-intact' families had higher rates; indeed, the average 16 per cent increase in antisocial behaviour for adolescents in non-intact families closely mirrored estimates of the effects of family disruption from much past research. At a more detailed level, however, the findings highlighted a number of other effects. First, there was considerable heterogeneity within the 'intact' family category, with young people in blended families reporting higher rates of antisocial activities than those in nuclear families, and the small group whose parents were cohabiting scoring higher again. Controls for an extensive series of potential confounds (including housing and material circumstances, maternal age, parental strictness and support-iveness, school performance, peer affiliations and past antisocial behaviour) attenuated these effects, but failed to eliminate them entirely. Among young people living with one biological parent, although those in single parent households were at increased risk by contrast with adolescents in intact families, those living with step-parents, or where the biological parent was cohabiting with an unrelated partner, were if anything at slightly higher risk; once again, statistical controls for socio-economic and other confounds accounted for some but not all of these differences.

These pointers that parental cohabitation and 'blended' families may be associated with adverse outcomes for children are echoed in a number of other US reports. Though UK evidence is less extensive, at least in relation to step-families, some similar patterns have also begun to be identified here. Findings from longitudinal analyses of the UK Offending, Crime and Justice Survey (OCJS, a self-report study of offending carried out between 2003 and 2006) showed that while single-parent family status reduced the likelihood of young people following a delinquency/drug free trajectory by six percentage points, the effects of upbringing by a mother and stepfather were considerably more marked (Hales et al. 2009); the 1998/9 Youth Lifestyles Survey also noted higher rates of self-report offending among young people in single-parent and step-families (Flood-Page et al. 2000). In the Child Mental Health surveys reported in Table 8.1, levels of parent-rated conduct problems were significantly higher among teenagers in both single-parent and step-family households than those in two-parent families, but did not differ between those two family types. UK evidence on cohabitation is more limited, and those pointers that are available suggest that effects may be less marked than in the US; Ford et al. (2004), for example, found no difference in rates of psychiatric disorder (including conduct disorder) between young people in married and cohabiting couple families in the 1999 Child Mental Health Survey. We must await results from future studies of UK samples to confirm and extend these findings.

Interpreting links between family demographics and offending

What mechanisms lie behind these associations? In general, more detailed studies of the links between 'broken homes' and delinquency have suggested that the key risks lie in the adverse effects of exposure to family discord, and the cascade of other difficulties and disruptions that often follows parental separation and divorce (see e.g., Rodgers and Pryor 1998; Rutter *et al.* 1998; Lansford 2009). Parental loss per se appears not to be the key feature: children who lose a parent through death, for example, are at no increased risk of antisocial behaviour, while those in discordant but intact families are (see e.g., Juby and Farrington 2001). In addition, the effects of divorce are similar for adopted and biological children, ruling out selection effects based on parental characteristics or genetic mediation (Amato and Cheadle 2008; Burt *et al.* 2008). Divorce is now widely recognized as a process, rather than a discrete event: relationships between parents are often poor long before a breakdown takes place, and may continue to be so long afterwards. Partnership breakdowns are often associated with increases in parental distress, which may themselves affect parent-child relationships and parents' capacity to respond to children's needs. In addition, some families will face house moves, disrupting children's schooling and friendship networks, and the great majority will face increased financial pressures. Cumulating (and often interacting) risks of this kind may all play a part in influencing young people's development when parents separate or divorce.

Post-separation, different family constellations may be associated with differing patterns of risk. Single parenthood is often a transitional state, later followed by involvement in new family forms. Chapple (2009) recently undertook a meta-analysis of child outcome in single-parent families drawing on studies from a range of OECD countries. Effects on broadly defined 'externalizing' outcomes (including conduct disorder, delinquency and other indices of disruptive behaviour problems) were somewhat higher than for other child outcomes, but in statistical terms would still be regarded as small. In addition, effects varied markedly across countries (and were typically lower in non-US than in US studies), underscoring the need for caution in generalizing findings across cultures, at least in terms of family structure. Though single-parent families are much more commonly headed by mothers than by fathers, parent gender may also be important: the role of father absence has attracted much attention, but in addition, both UK (Juby and Farrington 2001) and US (Apel and Kaukinen 2008) studies report higher rates of delinquency/ antisocial behaviour among young people in father- rather than mother-headed single-parent homes.

As we have seen, single-parent families frequently face severe economic and material disadvantages, and young and less well-educated mothers are over-represented in this group. How far are the adverse effects of single parenthood attributable to these associated disadvantages? Studies differ somewhat in their answers here, but there are at least some pointers that much of the increased risk for antisocial behaviour among young people in single-parent households can be attributed to these and other correlated risks. Fergusson *et al.* (2007), for example, studying the long-term impact of single parenthood on early adult criminality in a 1970s-born New Zealand cohort, found that initially significant differences between study members from single parent and other family backgrounds were reduced to non-significance by controls for a composite measure of family problems and parental criminality. In the UK samples reported on in Table 8.1, initially significant differences between young people in single parent and two-parent households on parent ratings of conduct problems were entirely eliminated by controls for family income and housing tenure; by contrast, differences between adolescents in step-families and those in stable two-parent homes remained significant when all of the factors listed in Table 8.1 were controlled. Though there may be some residual differences between single and two-parent families that are not easily explained by other factors, Fergusson *et al.* (2007) concluded that from a policy perspective, a focus on the functioning of the family may be more important than a count of the number of parents in the home.

As we have seen, some evidence also suggests that despite living in two-parent households, young people in step-families may also be at some increased risk of delinquency and antisocial behaviour; in addition, a variety of studies suggest that these effects may be more marked for teenagers than for younger children. To an extent, these differences appear to be associated with (and sometimes largely attributable to) the effects of family transitions (Manning and Lamb 2003). The great majority of children in step-families will inevitably have faced a number of family changes, and cohabiting parents appear to have less stable relationship histories than their married counterparts. Gibson-Davis (2008) outlined three contrasting theoretical models that might account for differing outcomes in these groups: (i) structural factors (whereby, for example, marriage may carry economic and emotional advantages that increase parenting effectiveness); (ii) evolutionary accounts, whereby adults are less motivated to invest in non-biologically-related offspring; and (iii) selection effects, whereby adults who marry differ from those who cohabit in personal characteristics that in turn affect their parenting. Empirical tests of these differing possibilities are limited at this stage; findings from the Fragile Families and Child Wellbeing Survey (a longitudinal US study of young children), however, suggest that for mothers, selection effects were the most likely explanation for family type variations, but that other factors impacted the parenting of fathers in different family constellations (Guzzo and Lee 2008). Once again, we must await more detailed studies of this kind in UK samples, and of older children and adolescents, to assess how far these conclusions are more generally applicable. Finally, we note one other important gap in current research. Although, as outlined earlier, family structures vary in important ways between ethnic groups in the UK, so far as we are aware no studies have as yet examined the implications of these differences for ethnic group variations in offending.

Family structure and time trends in youth offending

Given these consistent links between family structure and variations in youth offending, it is no surprise that the major changes in family demographics outlined earlier in this chapter have also been canvassed as possible drivers of the post-war rise in overall levels of youth crime. What is perhaps more surprising is the dearth of studies that have directly attempted to test this out. Much of the work on understanding historical changes in crime trends has involved explanations at an aggregate level (see e.g. Blumstein and Wallman 2000), comparing overall trends in offending with trends in other potential 'explanatory' factors. The limitations of this approach – and in particular, the difficulties of moving from aggregate-level data to inferences about individuals (the 'ecological fallacy') – have been highlighted for many years (Robinson 1950). Even when aggregate data on trends in one factor (such as family structure) follow an apparently similar trajectory to those in another (such as youth offending), we must be cautious in inferring causal links between the two. Where interpretations of aggregate data can be less ambiguous, of course, is when adolescent outcomes and potential risk factors follow *different* historical trends: if rates of risk factor X fell over a period when youth offending was rising, for example, we could feel more confident that risk factor X was unlikely to be involved.

With these cautions in mind, are there any conclusions that we can safely draw from a comparison of aggregate trends in youth offending and in family demographics in the years since the Second World War? As outlined in Chapter 3, levels of youth offending showed a long-term rise up to the mid 1990s, but then began to fall. The period marked by rising rates of youth crime thus coincided with a time when divorce rates were rising, and when single parenthood, cohabitation and blended families were also becoming more common. In that sense, then, there might be some grounds for considering that changes in family demographics could, at least in principle, be implicated in changing levels of youth crime. As we have seen, however, other family factors associated with offending have shown different – and potentially countervailing – trends: in particular, mothers' age at first childbirth has risen, and families today are generally smaller than in the past. Though the net effects of these differing changes are difficult to assess, it would clearly be unwise to assume that all demographic trends have pressed in a consistently 'negative' direction. In addition, the *meaning* of these varying family factors may change as they become more or less common (Collishaw *et al.* 2007). It has been widely assumed, for example, that the negative effects of divorce will have attenuated as parental separation has became more common, and less stigmatizing (though empirical evidence is not entirely consistent with this view, see e.g. Amato 2001), and there is growing evidence that large family size may have quite different (and much less marked) implications for delinquency in contemporary cohorts than in the past (see e.g. Hales *et al.* 2009). Finally, any account based on aggregate data must incorporate recent falls, as well as earlier rises, in levels of youth crime. Although divorce rates stabilized in the early 1980s, other family-related changes continued well beyond that time – so that while some family trends might plausibly be related to the initial *rise* in youth offending, they seem much more difficult to square with the subsequent *fall* in crime occurring from the mid 1990s onwards.

Ideally, studies based on individually-linked data on adolescent behaviour and family structure in different cohorts are needed to resolve these issues. So far as we are aware, only one such study has been reported to date. Using data on parent-rated conduct problems from three large-scale, nationally-representative samples of teenagers studied in 1974, 1986 and 1999, Collishaw *et al.* (2004) found that levels of adolescent conduct problems rose significantly and systematically across this 25-year period – a period that clearly overlaps with at least part of the documented rise in rates of youth crime. In their first report, these authors noted that trends in conduct problems were similar for young people from different social backgrounds and family types. In a second report (Collishaw *et al.* 2007), they set out to examine associations with family type in more detail. As expected, the proportions of teenagers in intact two-parent families fell across the three study samples (from 85 per cent in 1974 to 65 per cent in 1999), and the proportions in single and step-parent families increased. Despite these changes, living in a single parent family was associated with a very similar increased risk of conduct problems in all three cohorts (with odds ratios varying between 1.8 to 2.1), while the odds associated with living in a step-family decreased, from 3.0 in the earliest cohort to 1.7 in the most recent. Assessed jointly, changes in the proportions of young people growing up in these different family settings across the last quarter of the twentieth century were estimated to account for a modest 9 per cent of the observed increase in rates of adolescent conduct problems.

At first blush, these conclusions might seem puzzling: how could differences in family structure be associated with risk for behaviour problems *within* each study cohort, yet changes in the prevalence of those structures account for so little variation in changing levels of behaviour problems over time? As it turns out, contrasts of this kind are not uncommon. Quite different factors, for example, have contributed to the overall rise in alcohol consumption in recent decades from those that influence individuals' risk for lighter or heavier drinking within any given historical era. Though evidence on links between changing trends in family structure and in offending is clearly more limited than we would like, our tentative conclusion at this stage is that it may well constitute another example of this kind. Variations in family structure – in particular, factors associated with family breakdown, and more recently with 'blended' families – do indeed show consistent links with individual variations in risk for youth crime. By contrast, the major *changes* in family structure and stability that have occurred over recent decades seem much more modestly implicated in rising levels of antisocial behaviour (which are also likely to have been influenced by the myriad other changes affecting young people's lives over the same period (see e.g. Rutter and Smith 1995)) – and clearly cannot account for recent falls in overall levels of youth crime.

Parenting influences

We turn now to more 'proximal' aspects of family influence, and in particular to the role of parenting. It is clear from several decades of longitudinal research in many countries that parenting has a strong influence on individual differences in antisocial behaviour and offending. Numerous authoritative reviews have now synthesized findings from this extensive body of research (see e.g. Dishion and Patterson 2006; Loeber and Stouthamer-Loeber 1986; Wells and Rankin 1991; Patterson *et al.* 1992; Rutter *et al.* 1998; Youth Justice Board 2005; Hoeve *et al.* 2009). In this section we focus on parenting styles, behaviours and skills, that is, on the ways in which parents interact on a day-to-day (and even minute-to-minute) basis with their offspring. In this sense, 'parenting' is distinguished both from the wider environment provided by parents and from parental characteristics, such as their mental health or offending history – though both of these types of factors clearly influence parenting and parent-child relationships.

In discussing research findings in this area it is important to consider the range of ways in which parenting can be assessed. These include self-report (either by parent or youth questionnaires), more detailed semi-structured interviews, and direct observational methods. Direct observations can be conducted in natural settings such as the home, or in more contrived settings, such as a clinic or laboratory, and are often considered the 'gold standard' for measuring parenting behaviours (see

Gardner 2000 for a review), although validity will of course depend on the purpose of the assessment. It is important to note at the outset that the type of method used to assess parenting is likely to influence the strength of associations with youth outcomes reported in different studies. Such associations may be particularly strong when there is a high degree of method overlap between reporting of parenting and reporting of antisocial behaviour (Dishion *et al.* 1999), such as for example, when the parent is the sole reporter (common in studies of young children), or when the young person reports on both their own behaviour and that of their parent (common in adolescent research). This problem can be minimized by using independent measures of one variable (such as police records for youth outcomes), or independent observations of parenting. Responses on self-report measures of parenting (and especially questionnaires) are likely to be influenced by factors such as mood and social desirability, making it important to exercise caution in interpreting data based only on self-report. Although method overlap and the related problem of reliance on self reports are common limitations of many studies in the field, it is worth noting that much of what we know about parenting influences on problem behaviour has been confirmed using observational data.

Although there is a complex interplay between multiple biological and social contributors to problem behaviour (see Rutter, Chapter 5, this volume), there may nevertheless be good reasons for asking about the strength of the evidence for the causal role of a particular factor such as parenting. First, parenting can be seen a 'final common pathway', that mediates the effects of more distal influences on child outcomes such as family structure, poverty (Conger *et al.* 1994) and parental mental illness (Kim-Cohen *et al.* 2006). Second, since we know a good deal about how to modify parenting (see Chapter 6, this volume), then the policy implications of research in this field are substantial. Third, we know from intervention trials that the beneficial effects of modifying parenting apply across a wide range of family types (Baydar *et al.* 2003; Gardnerl *et al.* 2009, 2010), across ethnic groups and countries (Eshel *et al.* 2006; Reid *et al.* 2001; Scott *et al.* 2001) and across child characteristics, including boys and girls (Ollendick *et al.* 2008; Sonuga-Barke *et al.* 2001; CPPRG 2002).

It has been argued that we can be more confident about the causal role of a particular factor when there is converging evidence from both longitudinal and experimental designs (Bryant 1990), especially those that test for mechanisms mediating the effects of complex interventions (Rutter 2005). For some aspects of parenting, such evidence exists. Thus, in addition to a corpus of longitudinal studies (Hoeve *et al.* 2008; Loeber and Stouthamer-Loeber 1986) there are many randomized controlled trials showing that programmes for teaching parents child management skills are effective in reducing antisocial behaviour in both childhood and adolescence (for systematic reviews, see Barlow and Stewart-Brown 2000; Dretzke *et al.* 2005; Woolfenden *et al.* 2001). Moreover, that parenting skill *per se* is a key active ingredient of successful intervention has been shown by several studies of mediating mechanisms within randomized trials (Dishion *et al.* 2003, 2008; Martinez and Forgatch 2001; Gardner *et al.* 2006, 2010). At first sight, it might seem self evident that parenting skill is critical for child outcomes – and indeed most parenting interventions assume that this is so (see e.g. Hutchings *et al.* 2004). However, it is also possible that in practice, parenting interventions could exert their effects via alternative or additional mechanisms, such as enhancing parents' mood, improving their confidence or providing social support. Thus, it is important for understanding causal mechanisms to test out these competing possibilities (Gardner *et al.* 2006; Weersing and Weisz 2002).

As we shall see, there is a substantial body of research, based on a range of research designs, measurement sources and contexts, suggesting that parenting qualities do play a causal role in the onset and maintenance of problem behaviour in children and young people (Baumrind 1991; Loeber and Stouthamer-Loeber 1986; Pettit *et al.* 1997, 2001; Gardner *et al.* 2006, 2007; Patterson *et al.* 1992). The influence of parenting begins early in life, and appears to continue into adolescence (Dishion *et al.* 2003; Dodge and Pettit 2003, Farrington 1995; Hill 2002), with adolescent outcomes influenced by current as well as by earlier parenting (Steinberg and Silk 2002; Woolfenden *et al.* 2001). Some have claimed that parenting practices may account for as much as 30 per cent of the variation in youth conduct problem outcome (Patterson 2002; Patterson *et al.* 1992) – although one recent review put the figure at a more modest 11 per cent (for delinquency: Hoeve *et al.* 2009). These significant effects nevertheless leave a good deal of room for other influences, both environmental and genetic (see Rutter, Chapter 5, this volume), an issue we return to later. For policy and practice decisions, however, the important issue may not be the (moderate) size of parenting effects on children's development, but the effects on child behaviour found in carefully controlled trials of parenting interventions.

It is also important to consider whether parenting influences vary with child and family charactersitics. Broadly speaking, there appear to be similar parenting influences on girls and boys (see e.g. Moffitt *et al.* 2001), although it should be noted that there have been fewer studies of antisocial behaviour in girls than in boys, and that many of those that have included young people of both genders have not examined gender differences in the effects of parenting (Kroneman *et al.* 2009). In a similar way, the *aspects* of parenting implicated in risk for more and less severe types of offending, or in early and later onset groups, seem likely to have much in common, though young people with more severe histories of problem behaviour may also have faced more extended, severe or complex family difficulties. We noted earlier that some parenting interventions appear to be effective across a range of ethnic groups and regions of the world; however, as we shall see, a more complex picture emerges from basic research on ethnicity and harsh parenting. UK studies (e.g. Armstrong *et al.* 2005) suggest there may be some ethnic differences in extent of parental monitoring and supervision, but there has been little work in the UK to date linking parenting to antisocial outcomes in different ethnic groups.

We turn now to examining which facets of parenting are important, and at which developmental stages. Successful parenting involves a myriad skills and qualities that vary across age, culture and social context. Nevertheless, most models of parenting (Barber *et al.* 2005; Baumrind 1991; Steinberg and Silk 2002) are in agreement in highlighting two central dimensions: first, a positive dimension related to levels of involvement and responsiveness (warmth, availability, positive engagement, and support) and second, a dimension related to facets of behavioural control (discipline, expectations, monitoring, and behaviour management) which, at its extreme, may be expressed as harsh or punitive parenting and frequent conflict, which in turn may border on physical maltreatment. We follow this broad framework here, focusing on i) parental involvement and warmth and ii) parental discipline, monitoring and control. The evidence we draw on comes from studies conducted in a range of western countries, including both the UK and the US; broadly speaking, the findings appear to be consistent across countries.

Positive parenting: warmth and involvement

Attachment theory has been important in drawing our attention to the crucial role of early parent–child interactions, especially the role of early warmth and sensitivity, in building relationships that have both short and long-term benefits for children's development and for preventing mental health problems. A number of studies have investigated the role of early positive parenting, such as levels of warmth, supportive behaviour, and shared activities in the development of conduct problems in childhood (Gardner *et al.* 2003, 2007; Rothbaum and Weisz 1994) and adolescence (Hoeve *et al.* 2009; Pettit *et al.* 2001; Steinberg and Silk 2002). For example, UK studies using direct observations in the home, or time diaries, to measure parenting, have shown that time spent in early parent–child positive activities, such as joint play and conversation, are linked to lower levels of child problem behaviour (Gardner 1994; Gardner *et al.* 2003; Galboda-Liyanage *et al.* 2003). Unsurprisingly perhaps, since there are strong continuities between child and adolescent problem behaviours, longitudinal studies have also found predictions from early parental involvement to fewer conduct problems in adolescence (Ary *et al.* 1999; Patterson *et al.* 1992; Pettit *et al.* 1997), independent of social class and gender. Parental warmth and responsiveness are similarly linked to fewer problem behaviours in childhood and adolescence (Rothbaum and Weisz 1994; Steinberg and Silk 2002), and are targets for change in successful interventions. Hoeve *et al.*'s (2009) meta-analysis, which attempted to synthesize findings across 160 studies of the relationship between parenting and delinquency, found an average effect size of .23 for positive parenting. Interestingly, there were no differences in the strength of this relationship in longitudinal and cross-sectional studies – implying that both early and current parenting are consistently linked to adolescent problem behaviour. On the other hand, when they examined the effect of age on this association, in cross-sectional studies only (which made up the majority, 70 per cent, of the studies reviewed), they found that the association between parenting and delinquency was stronger in younger than in older adolescents.

As well as building a healthy context for development via the parent–child relationship, positive parenting strategies may also serve more directly to prevent problem behaviour from occurring, for example at times of day that are 'high risk' for toddler boredom and tantrums. This facet of parenting may be thought of as 'proactive', or anticipatory (Dishion *et al.* 2008; Gardner *et al.* 1999, 2007; Pettit *et al.* 2001; Rutter 2001). Longitudinal studies, based on observing proactive parenting in the home, suggest that parents are able to help prevent problem behaviour across early childhood by structuring the child's time effectively with attention and activities (Gardner *et al.* 2003), and by using strategies such as turning a boring task into a game, or giving clear rules and incentives before misbehaviour occurs (Gardner *et al.* 1999). Based on parent interviews, Pettit *et al.*'s (2001) study suggest there may also be longer-term effects of early proactive parenting into adolescence.

Mediation analyses show that changes in 'positive parenting' – including warmth, praise, involvement, and proactive strategies – together help account for improvements in problem behaviour following intervention, at least in younger children (Dishion *et al.* 2008; Gardner *et al.* 2006, 2010 in press; Martinez and Forgatch 2001). Some studies have tested competing mechanisms of change: two randomized trials of the Webster-Stratton programme in community settings in the UK (Gardner *et al.* 2006, 2010 in press), for example, found that change in positive but not in harsh parenting mediated change in conduct problems. Gardner *et al.*'s (2006) trial also found that parents' sense of competence improved as result of intervention, and accordingly the authors went on to test whether this also served as a mediator of change. However, it did not, suggesting that alterations in parenting skills and behaviour may be more important in driving intervention change than change in parents' confidence about their parenting.

Most of this literature is based on studies of mothers; however, UK cohort studies (among other sources) attest to the importance of father involvement (Flouri 2005), although there have been fewer longitudinal studies using direct observation of father behaviour, and none to our knowledge which examines mediators of intervention change in fathers.

Parental control

For most families, issues of discipline and control first emerge in the early toddler years, when children become more active, mobile and unsafe, and begin more frequently to oppose their parents' demands. These 'oppositional' outbursts commonly lead into episodes of parent–child conflict, which often include toddler aggression and tantrums. This developmental transition to more frequent and intense conflict and problem behaviour marks the period of the 'terrible twos' (Shaw *et al.* 2000). Although this is a normal stage of development, it is also a time when longer-term helpful or unhelpful patterns of conflict prevention and resolution can develop, depending on how parents manage these behaviours. Patterson *et al.* (1992), for example, describe a 'coercive family process' whereby child problem behaviour comes to be learned and over-learned during conflict, via processes of modelling and mutual reinforcement by parent and child. Often the key process encouraging the development of problem behaviour is negative reinforcement, whereby the parent becomes angry, but then gives in to the child's noisy demands in order to buy short-term peace and quiet (Gardner 1989; Dishion and Patterson 2006).

A key feature of effective parenting interventions (see Chapter 6, this volume) is to help parents become aware of their own coercive cycles and learn alternative strategies that avoid anger and capitulation to tantrums. Typically, these 'limit-setting' techniques are taught only after first building up skills for positive interactions, given their importance for child development, as discussed earlier (Webster-Stratton 1998). Developmental transitions such as emerging toddlerhood may be particularly promising times to engage parents in preventive interventions, as parents may be more receptive to change when meeting new challenges, such as the onset of normal tantrums (Gardner and Shaw 2008; Shaw *et al.* 2006). Similar principles and skills are used in parenting interventions with older children and teenagers – based on building good communication, monitoring the child's behaviour, using calm, consistent limit setting, and devising reasonable consequences for both appropriate and undesirable behaviour (Dishion and Kavanagh 2003).

Harsh parenting lies at one end of a spectrum of parental control and discipline, shading at the extreme into physical abuse (Patterson *et al.* 1992). Harsh parenting includes use of physical discipline, as well as hostile verbal and vocal acts such as yelling, shouting and threatening, and insulting or humiliating the child. The line between harsh and abusive parenting is not easy to draw, as any social worker knows, and this applies both to physical and emotional abuse. This judgement is complicated further by the fact that beliefs and laws about physical disciplining of children vary across and within cultures, and across time. There are strong links between the frequency and level of physical punishment, and child problem behaviour (Fergusson and Lynskey 1997;

Gershoff 2002; Farrington 1995) although the strength of this correlation appears to vary by cultural group (Deater-Deckard *et al*. 1996; Lansford *et al*. 2005) – no doubt at least partly because cultural differences in norms for punishment affect the reasons why parents punish, and the meaning of such acts for children.

The potential causal importance of parental control strategies, both harsh and constructive, is underscored by findings from longitudinal studies, and by analyses of mediator effects in intervention trials. Constructive forms of parental discipline – including clarity of expectations and consistent use of incentives and consequences – are linked to lower levels of problem behaviour in children and adolescents (Patterson *et al*. 1992), as is proactive use of discipline (Gardner *et al*. 1999; Pettit *et al*. 1997). The links between harsh parenting and child problem behaviour are well documented; in a recent meta-analysis, Hoeve *et al*. (2009) found somewhat stronger predictions from harsh, rejecting parenting to delinquent outcomes than from either monitoring or positive, supportive parenting. There have been few studies of change in discipline techniques as mediators of intervention change, although one study found that reductions in harsh parenting, as well as improvements in positive parenting, mediated the effects of a parenting intervention on child problem behaviour outcomes (Brotman *et al*. 2009).

Notwithstanding definitional difficulties, more extreme harsh parenting such as physical maltreatment (sometimes defined as assaults resulting in physical marking or harm) is sadly a relatively common experience for a sizeable minority of children. A nationally representative survey of young adults conducted by the National Society for the Prevention of Cruelty to Children in 1999 (Cawson *et al*. 2000) found that around 20 per cent had experienced one or more forms of physical violence during childhood by a parent or carer, with 7 per cent defined as experiencing serious physical abuse. Physical abuse is one of the strongest predictors of a range of child and adult psychiatric disorders, including increased likelihood of conduct problems, substance abuse and suicidality (e.g. Fergusson and Lynskey 1997; Schuck and Widom 2001). Research on prevalence, consequences, risk factors and interventions for child abuse have been brought together in several recent systematic reviews (e.g. Barlow *et al*. 2006; and in a recent Lancet series (Gilbert *et al*. 2009a, 2009b; MacMillan *et al*. 2009).

Finally, we turn to a facet of parental control that becomes more important in late childhood and adolescence, namely parental monitoring of young people's activities and whereabouts when the parent is not there. Although by this definition monitoring only becomes important at an age when children are allowed unsupervised time, it is plausible that monitoring, which is largely a preventive, rather than reactive, form of discipline, has its developmental origins in early proactive parenting (Dishion and McMahon 1998; Gardner *et al*. 2007). This style of parenting involves careful monitoring of the young child around the house, in order to be aware of the child's needs, and to anticipate troublesome situations.

Parental monitoring has long been shown to be an important correlate of adolescent conduct problems (see e.g. Dishion and McMahon 1998; Hoeve *et al.* 2009). Evidence from both longitudinal studies and randomized intervention trials suggests that parental monitoring has direct and indirect effects on future adolescent conduct problems, substance use and affiliation with delinquent peers (Farrington 1995; Loeber and Stouthamer-Loeber 1986; Patterson *et al.* 1992; Dishion *et al.* 2003). In addition, research has shown that many parents of boys at high risk for antisocial behaviour *reduced* their levels of monitoring and guidance as their children reached adolescence. This process appeared especially marked for parents of youth with deviant peers. Parental disengagement contributed to what might be termed 'premature adolescent autonomy', and to heightened risks for later adolescent substance use and antisocial behaviour (Dishion *et al.* 2004). Family interventions targeted at maintaining parental monitoring as high-risk youth reach adolescence have beneficial effects in relation to later risk for substance use and, furthermore, there is evidence that change in parental monitoring is a key mechanism mediating intervention outcome (Dishion *et al.* 2003). Some studies have found that levels of monitoring vary by family type, with lower levels of monitoring in lone-parent (Astone and McLanahan 1991), and step- (Kim, Hetherington and Reiss 1999) families. At the same time, it has been argued that the effectiveness and importance of parental monitoring also depend on the characteristics of the adolescent and the neighbourhood. For example, Stattin and Kerr (2000) have argued that the construct of monitoring depends as much on adolescents' willingness to disclose, as it does on parents' skill at tracking their offspring, and thus reflects a bidirectional process. In addition, there is also some evidence that monitoring has a greater protective effect on youth antisocial outcomes in families where both parents work (Jacobsen and Crockett 2000), and that higher levels of monitoring may be required to achieve the same beneficial outcomes in high-risk neighbourhoods (Forehand *et al.* 1997).

Parenting interventions and causes of antisocial behaviour

Parenting interventions have been remarkably well tested, in randomized trials, in many settings and countries, for both prevention and treatment, and appear to be effective in reducing problem behaviour in childhood and in adolescence. There are new efforts to roll out and further test these interventions when transformed into real world services (Hutchings *et al.* 2007) and even when 'taken to scale', permeating whole populations (Prinz *et al.* 2009). This evidence is covered in Chapter 6 (on prevention) in this volume, and in other recent reviews (Dretzke *et al.* 2005; Piquero *et al.* 2008). We have referred in the present chapter frequently to intervention studies (including mediation analyses) as they are a valuable part of the causal evidence for the effects of parenting on child antisocial behaviour, in combination with longitudinal designs. Recent genetic evidence, based on the study of differences between genetically identical twins, provides further compelling evidence for the role of parenting as a true environmental influence effect on child problem behaviour (Bowes *et al.* 2009; Viding *et al.* 2009) Together, these contrasting sources of evidence (Rutter 2005) provide a powerful case for the role of parenting.

It was stressed earlier, however, that despite its clear causal role, parenting nevertheless only accounts for a modest part of the variation in antisocial behaviour, leaving much room for other social and biological (including genetic) influences. Intervention studies are also beginning to help us understand more about the complex interplay between these factors (Wikstrom and Loeber 2000). Thus, although we have cited evidence to show that parenting interventions can be effective across a wide range of children and families, they are not effective with all. It is helpful for causal theory building, and also for practice and policy, to identify which family and child characteristics moderate the effects of parenting influences, such that some children (and parents) are more or less susceptible to parenting influences (Belsky *et al.* 2007), good and bad, than others. For example, recent longitudinal and intervention studies suggest that children with a certain genetic polymorphism appear to respond more strongly both to poor parenting (Bakermans-Kranenburg and Van IJzendoorn 2007), and to improvements in parenting, following a parenting intervention (Bakermans-Kranenburg *et al.* 2008) than others. In addition, some studies have found that children with high levels of callous-unemotional traits are less responsive to parenting influence (Hawes and Dadds 2005; Wootton *et al.* 1997; Viding *et al.* 2009), although others have not (Frick *et al.* 2003). These studies have been conducted mainly using parent self-report measures of harsh and controlling parenting, and need replicating and extending to include observational data, and importantly, to incorporate positive dimensions of parenting. Callous-unemotional children are predicted to be less sensitive to punishment, and instead to have a more reward-oriented response style (Frick and Viding 2009); as a result, they may be relatively more responsive to positive, rewarding parenting (and hence to interventions based on these strategies), than to attempts at control (such as 'time out' (Hawes and Dadds 2005)). Future research in these areas will be important both in helping us understand more about underlying reasons for variations in response to parenting programmes, and in developing more tailored approaches suited to the needs of specific sub-groups of children.

Parenting and time trends in youth offending

In the final sections of this chapter we return to the question of time trends in offending, and explore whether changes in parenting and parent-child relationships over the second half of the twentieth century could have contributed to rising levels of youth crime. Concerns over perceived 'declines' in the quality of family life and parenting figure prominently in both public and policy debate (see e.g. Ambert 2007; Margo and Dixon 2006; DfES 2006), and it is widely assumed that factors such as rising levels of family breakdown and increases in parents' working hours have placed strains on parents' time commitment to their children, and possibly on their capacity to respond to children's needs. Given the strong evidence that both parental involvement and appropriate levels of control and discipline are associated with lower levels of conduct problems at the individual level, 'declines' in those aspects of parenting might well be expected to show an impact on overall levels of youth crime.

How far does the research evidence bear out these concerns? With colleagues, we recently undertook a review of time trends in parenting and their associations with adolescent problem behaviours (Gardner, Collishaw *et al.* 2009; Nuffield Foundation 2009). So far as we are aware, this review provides the most comprehensive account of trends in parenting currently available, and we draw briefly on its findings here. Its first main conclusion was a surprising, and in some ways a sobering one: despite widespread public perceptions of changes in family life and parenting in recent decades, reliable evidence on such changes is extremely sparse. This is not, of course, because of any general lack of research on parenting; as we have seen, this has been a major focus of interest for developmentalists, interventionists and criminologists for many years. Instead, the key difficulty lies in the lack of *comparable* data on samples studied at different points in time. In the case of trends in family structures, time-trend data are relatively easy to construct on the basis of regularly-gathered, publicly available statistics. In the case of parenting, no such sources exist. Repeated data on social *attitudes* to child-rearing are quite widely available – but data on changes in the day-to-day realities of family life are much more limited. Much of the research on parenting discussed earlier in this chapter is based on (relatively) small sample sizes, and uses intensive approaches to data-gathering that would be impractical to apply in the large-scale, representative samples needed for time-trend research. As a result, with a few notable exceptions, current evidence on time trends in parenting is derived from studies using a much more 'broad brush' approach, and focuses on indicators that are at best only indirect markers of the constructs of real interest.

Time trends in parental involvement and responsiveness

Beginning with indicators of parental involvement, the Gardner review was unable to identify any direct studies of time trends in parental warmth or responsiveness to children. Instead, it drew together evidence on factors that might at least provide opportunities for parental involvement: trends in broadly defined patterns of parental 'time use' with children, and in more specific activities such as reading with young children and the frequency of family meals.

Parental time spent with children

Surveys of adults' time use have been used to study the impact of social change on family life for many years. Though not specifically designed to capture specific aspects of parenting, surveys of this kind give at least some beginning insights into the contexts for parents' involvement with their children, and the impact of factors such as increases in parents' working hours or changes in family composition on parent–child activities over time. Although the *quantity* of time spent with children is only a weak proxy for the *quality* of parenting, there is nonetheless some evidence for an association between the two (Zuzanek 2001). Methodological limitations on time-use data have been much discussed (Bianchi *et al.* 2006; Gauthier *et al.* 2004). Set against these disadvantages, however, time use studies have the important strengths of being based on large, representative samples and providing repeated measures, some spanning several decades. In addition, as we shall see, many findings show remarkable consistency across cultures, increasing confidence in the picture of adult time use that they paint.

Studies based on nationally representative UK time use surveys (see e.g Fisher *et al.* 1999) have reported steady increases in parents' childcare time (as a main activity) from 1960s to the 1990s, and data from the US and other countries show a broadly similar picture (Casper and Bianchi 2002). Gauthier *et al.* (2004) analysed time-use data for two-parent families from 16 different countries, and concluded that there had been broadly similar trends towards increasing time spent with children from the 1960s to 2000 across all the countries studied. These trends were similar for employed and non-employed mothers; interestingly, despite large differences between these groups in time spent in paid work, employed and non-employed mothers differed little in the time they reported spending with children. Trends for fathers have tended to be steeper than those for mothers; Sayer *et al.* (2004), for example, found dramatic increases in fathers' time spent with children, with a doubling of reported time spent between 1985 and 1998.

What lies behind these somewhat unexpected trends? Several rather different factors have been proposed. First, the increasing availability of time-saving household appliances has meant that time spent in house-work has markedly decreased. Second, for both men and women, the reproductive trends towards later childbearing and smaller family size outlined earlier in this chapter have been bound up with changing cultural norms that place increased emphasis on parents' investment in the social and cognitive development of their children, and underscore fathers' direct involvement in caregiving roles (Bianchi *et al.* 2006). And third, though mothers are indeed more likely to return to work earlier than in the past, there is evidence that parents make extra time to spend with children by engaging in more multitasking and 'squeezing' of other activities, and by devoting more leisure time to child- rather than adult-centred activities (Bianchi *et al.* 2006).

Reading with children and family meals

In addition to these general data on parents' time spent with children, the Gardner review reported evidence on trends in two more specific parent–child activities: parents' reading with young children, and joint family meals. Though these are still relatively indirect indicators of parental involvement, both do show associations with children's behavioural adjustment (see e.g. Guo *et al.* 2008). In relation to reading, both published data and new analyses supported the general picture of increasing parental engagement with children emerging from time diary studies. The proportions of parents reporting regular reading with their children rose steadily across samples studied in the 1960s and 70s, and continued to rise thereafter; in addition, more detailed analyses of cohorts studied in 1975 and 2005 suggested that although parental reading remained strongly socially patterned even in the more recent cohort, gaps between social groups and family types had narrowed over time. Findings on family meals – an issue of concern to social commentators for many years – painted a somewhat less optimistic picture. Though trend data were limited, several different sources pointed to reductions in shared family meals over time. In general, however, the changes involved were relatively modest, and few studies provided information on the quality of family interactions during mealtimes, likely to be central to interpreting effects of any overall trends. Given the marked changes in the ethnic composition of the child population in the UK in recent decades, the earlier cohorts represented in studies of family activities were inevitably predominantly white. As a result, very little is known about the extent to which changes in parental involvement and family activities have been echoed in all ethnic groups. Recent evidence (Maynard and Harding 2010) suggests, however, that this may be an important consideration: young people in minority groups report higher levels of involvement in family outings and visits than their white counterparts, and the frequency of family meals also varies systematically across ethnic groups.

Parental responsiveness: young people's views

The most detailed data on young people's perceptions of changes in parental responsiveness come from a purposively designed study of time trends (the Youth Trends study, Collishaw *et al.* submitted; Nuffield Foundation 2009). This study built on exactly similar questions asked of representative samples of UK teenagers studied 20 years apart, in 1986 and 2006. Like the other findings reviewed thus far, the results gave little evidence of any general decline in levels of parental involvement. Young people's ratings of their parents' interest in them and their ideas showed no change between the two study cohorts, and proportions of 'quality time' spent with parents increased.

Trends in parental control and monitoring

Turning to issues of parental monitoring and control, it is clear that social attitudes to these issues have changed over time in important ways. In Britain as elsewhere, evidence from attitude surveys suggests that child-rearing values have shown a long-term shift from an emphasis on obedience to one of valuing greater autonomy in the young (see e.g. Alwin 1990; Smith and Farrington 2004). As discussed in Chapter 2, the path from childhood to adulthood has changed radically in recent years; as part of those changes, young people now expect greater freedom in the use of their time than in the past, and a larger role in decision-making within the family. In addition, attitude surveys have documented an almost universal decline in acceptance of the physical punishment of children (see e.g. Finklehor and Jones 2006), reflected in bans or restrictions on the use of physical punishment in schools in many countries.

How far are these attitudinal and societal changes reflected in more direct data on monitoring and control in families? In relation to young children at least, some aspects of parental monitoring appear to have become closer in recent years: there has been a marked decline, for example, in the numbers of primary-school children walking to school alone (Sonkin *et al.* 2006; Department for Transport 2007), reflecting increased parental concerns about road safety and stranger danger (Gill 2007). For parents of teenagers, parallel concerns may well have grown in relation to factors such as peer delinquency, drug use, and knife crime, and also contributed to closer monitoring over time. In practice, however, the Gardner review was unable to identify any published studies of trends in parental monitoring of young people, nor in styles of parental punishment. The Youth Trends study (Collishaw *et al.*, submitted) compared young people's reports on these issues collected from samples studied in 1986 and 2006. The results pointed to increases over time in parents' monitoring of teenagers' out-of-home activities, and in the proportions of young people who regularly told their parents where they were going, and what they planned to do. In addition, parental expectations were higher in the more recent cohort, and indicators of parental strictness and discipline had increased.

Time trends in parenting: overview and conclusions

Despite widespread public concern over 'declines' in the quality of parenting, the first main conclusion to emerge from this brief review is how little hard evidence on trends in key aspects of parenting has actually been collated. Some at least of the reasons for this lack are not hard to seek: detailed studies of parenting are demanding, and most research (very properly) focuses on attempting to answer new questions rather than repeating studies conducted in the past. The result, however, is that there are major gaps in our understanding of the ways in which parents' involvement with their children and control of their activities may have changed in recent decades. In addition, such evidence as is available points in a somewhat unexpected direction. Where demographic trends might lead us to expect reductions in the time parents spend with children, consistent findings from many countries suggest just the reverse; where public attitudes increasingly favour granting autonomy and independence to the young, the limited empirical evidence suggests that in some areas at least, parental monitoring has increased.

Given the limitations of the data available on trends in parenting – both in terms of the volume of relevant research, and the rather indirect nature of much of the material that does exist – the conclusions we can draw from these findings must be tentative at best. To the extent that they are indicative of underlying trends in those aspects of parenting known to be most important for youth offending, however, we must conclude that current evidence provides little support for 'declines' in parenting that could account for increases in youth crime.

Conclusions

Variations in family structures and in parenting have long been known to be associated with variations in risk for youth crime. In terms of understanding *individual differences* in offending, recent evidence has both underscored and expanded on the lessons learned about these associations in the past. Family breakdown was among the earliest-identified correlates of youth offending. Recent evidence suggests that, despite massive changes in patterns of family life in recent years, the discord, disruption and disadvantage that all too often accompany parental separation can still carry negative implications for children, by no means always offset by involvement in new 'blended' families. Estimates suggest that overall, these effects are relatively modest, and that the reasons underlying them are complex, including both the socio-economic and the psychosocial stresses that often follow family transitions as much as the nature of family forms *per se*.

The extensive research on more detailed aspects of parenting leaves little doubt that it plays a key role in the complex of influences, individual and environmental, that go to shape young people's behaviour. Longitudinal studies, along with evidence from intervention designs, have confirmed cross-sectional findings that two main aspects of parenting form the key elements here: positive parenting, centring on parental involvement and warmth, and appropriate strategies for management and control. These influences start early in childhood, and persist to adolescence; most importantly, alongside evidence that they contribute to the onset and maintenance of behaviour problems, they have also proved highly effective targets for intervention.

These individually-based associations have, not surprisingly, led many commentators to assume that changes in the family may also have contributed to changing *levels* of youth crime. Since the 1950s, the demographics of family life have undoubtedly changed dramatically: rates of divorce rose markedly between the 1960s and 1980s, and the proportions of children growing up in single-parent and step-families have continued to increase. Cohabitation – in general, a less stable partnership form than marriage – has also become more common. At the same time, women's involvement in the labour market increased, ages at first childbirth rose, and families in general became smaller in size. These differing trends show complex inter-relationships, often complicated by variations in socio-economic circumstances; as a result, we must be wary of drawing simplistic conclusions about their likely effects. In practice, reliable evidence on links between trends in family demographics and trends in adolescent behaviour problems is limited, and points to very modest effects at most. Evidence on trends in parenting is yet more constrained; such pointers as are available, however, give no support to assumptions of 'declines' in the quality of parenting in recent decades. As a result, while family factors are clearly implicated in individual differences in youth offending, current evidence suggests that we may need to look elsewhere to understand trends – both rising and falling – in overall levels of youth crime.

References

Alwin, D. (1990) 'Cohort replacement and changes in parental socialization values', *Journal of Marriage and the Family*, 52, pp. 347–60.

Ambert, A. (2007) *Contemporary Family Trends. The rise in the number of children and adolescents who exhibit problem behaviors: Multiple causes* (Ottawa: Vanier Institute of the Family).

Amato, P. R. (2001) 'Children of divorce in the 1990s: An update of the Amato and Keith (1991) meta-analysis', *Journal of Family Psychology*, 15: 3, pp. 355–70.

Amato, P. R. and Cheadle, J. E. (2008) 'Parental divorce, marital conflict and children's behavior problems: A comparison of adopted and biological children', *Social Forces*, 86:3, pp. 1139–61.

Apel, R. and Kaukinen, C. (2008) 'On the relationship between family structure and antisocial behaviour: Parental cohabitation and blended households', *Criminology*, 46:1, pp. 35–70.

Armstrong, D., Hine, J., Hacking, S., Armaos, R., Jones, R., Klessinger, N. and France. A. (2005) *Children, Risk and Crime: the On Track Youth Lifestyles Surveys. Home Office Research Study 278* (London: Home Office).

Ary, D., Duncan, T., Biglan, A., Metzler, C., Noell, J. and Smolkowski, K. (1999) 'Development of adolescent problem behavior', *Journal of Abnormal Child Psychology*, 27, pp. 141–50.

Astone, N.M. and McLanahan, S. (1991) 'Family structure, parental practices and high school completion', *American Sociological Review*, 56, pp. 309–20.

Bakermans-Kranenburg, M. J. and Van IJzendoorn, M. H. (2007) 'Genetic vulnerability or differential susceptibility in child development: The case of attachment', *Journal of Child Psychology and Psychiatry*, 48, pp. 1160–73.

Bakermans-Kranenburg, M., Van IJzendoorn, M., Pijlman, F., Mesman, J. and Juffer, F. (2008) 'Experimental evidence for differential susceptibility: Dopamine D4 receptor polymorphism (DRD4 VNTR) moderates intervention effects on toddlers' externalizing behavior in a randomized controlled trial', *Developmental Psychology*, 44, pp. 293–300.

Barber, B., Stolz, H. and Olsen, J. (2005) 'Parental support, psychological control, and behavioral control: assessing relevance across time, culture, and method', *Monographs of the Society for Research in Child Development*, 70, pp. 1–137.

Barlow, J. and Stewart-Brown, S. (2000) 'Review article: Behavior problems and parent-training programs', *Journal of Developmental and Behavioral Pediatrics*, 21:5, pp. 356–70.

Barlow, J., Johnston, I., Kendrick, D., Polnay, L. and Stewart-Brown, S. (2006) 'Systematic review of the effectiveness of parenting programmes in treating abusive parenting', *Cochrane Database of Systematic Reviews*, 3, pp. 1–20.

Baumrind, D. (1991) 'The influence of parenting style on adolescent competence and substance use', *The Journal of Early Adolescence*, 11, pp. 56–95.

Baydar, N., Reid, M.J. and Webster-Stratton, C. (2003) 'The role of mental health factors and program engagement in the effectiveness of a preventive parenting program for Head Start mothers', *Child Development*, 74, p. 1433–53.

Belsky, J., Bakermans-Kranenburg, M.J. and van IJzendoorn, M.H. (2007) 'For better and for worse: Differential susceptibility to environmental influences', *Current Directions in Psychological Science*, 16:6, pp. 300–4.

Bianchi, S., Robinson, J. and Milkie, M. (2006) *The Changing Rhythms of American Family Life* (New York: Russell Sage).

Blumstein A. and Wallman, J. (2000) *The Crime Drop in America* (Cambridge: Cambridge University Press).

Bowes, L., Arseneault, L., Maughan, B., Taylor, A., Caspi, A. and Moffitt, T.E. (2009) 'School, neighborhood, and family factors are associated with children's bullying involvement: A nationally representative longitudinal study' *Journal of the American Academy of Child and Adolescent Psychiatry*, 48:5, pp. 545–53.

British Academy (2010) *Social Science and Family Policies* (London: British Academy Policy Centre).

Brotman, L.M., O'Neal, C.R., Huang, K.Y., Gouley, K.K., Rosenfelt, A. and Shrout, P. (2009) 'An experimental test of parenting practices as mediators of preschool physical aggression', *The Journal of Child Psychology and Psychiatry*, 50:3, pp. 235–45.

Bryant, P. (1990) 'Empirical evidence for causes in development' in G. Butterworth and P. Bryant (eds) *Causes of Development: Interdisciplinary Perspectives* (Hemel Hempstead: Harvester Wheatsheaf), pp. 33–45.

Burt, S.A., Barnes, A.R., Mcgue, M. and Iacono, W.G. (2008) 'Parental divorce and adolescent delinquency: ruling out the impact of common genes', *Developmental Psychology*, 44:6, pp. 1668–77.

Cabinet Office (2008) *Families in Britain: An Evidence Paper* (London: Cabinet Office).

Casper, L. and Bianchi, S. (2002) *Continuity and Change in the American Family*. (New York: Sage).

Cawson, P., Wattam, C., Brooker, S. and Kelly, G. (2000) *Child Maltreatment in the United Kingdom: a Study of the Prevalence of Abuse and Neglect* (London: NSPCC).

Chapple, S. (2009) *Child Well-being and Sole-parent Family Structure in the OECD: An analysis*, OECD Social, Employment and Migration Working Papers No 86 (Paris: Organization for Economic Co-operation and Development).

Collishaw, S., Gardner, F., Maughan, B., Scott, J. and Pickles, A. (submitted) 'Historical change in parenting of adolescents: Can it explain the rise in youth problem behavior?'

Collishaw, S., Goodman, R., Pickles, A. and Maughan, B. (2007) 'Modelling the contribution of changes in family life to time trends in adolescent conduct problems', *Social Science and Medicine*, 65: 12, pp. 2576–87.

Collishaw, S., Maughan, B., Goodman, R. and Pickles, A. (2004) 'Time trends in adolescent mental health', *Journal of Child Psychology and Psychiatry*, 45, pp. 1350–62.

Conduct Problems Prevention Research Group (2002) 'Predictor variables associated with positive Fast Track outcomes at end of third grade', *Journal of Abnormal Child Psychology*, 30, pp. 19–36.

Conger, R.D., Ge, X., Elder, G.H., Lorenz, F.O. and Simons, R.L. (1994) 'Economic stress, coercive family process, and developmental problems of adolescents', *Child Development*, 65, pp. 541–61.

Deater-Deckard, K., Dodge, K.A., Bates, J.E. and Pettit, G.S. (1996) 'Physical discipline among African American and European American mothers: links to children's externalising behaviours', *Developmental Psychology*, 32, pp. 1065–72.

Department for Education and Skills (2006) *Every Child Matters* (London: Department for Education and Skills).

Department for Transport (2007) *National Travel Survey, 2007* (London: Department for Transport).

Dishion, T. and Kavanagh, K. (2003) *Intervening in Adolescent Problem Behavior: A Family-centered Approach* (New York: Guilford Press).

Dishion, T.J., Li, F., Spracklen, K.M., Brown, G. and Haas, E. (1999) 'Measurement of parenting practices in research on adolescent problem behavior: A multi-method and multitrait analysis' in R. S. Ashery (ed.), *Research Meeting on Drug Abuse Prevention through Family Interventions*, NIDA Research Monograph No. 177 (Washington DC: U.S. Government Printing Office), pp. 260–93.

Dishion, T. and McMahon, R. (1998) 'Parental monitoring and prevention of child and adolescent problem behavior: A conceptual and empirical formulation', *Clinical Child and Family Psychology Review*, 1, pp. 61–75.

Dishion, T., Nelson, S. and Bullock, B. (2004) 'Premature adolescent autonomy: parent disengagement and deviant peer process in the amplification of problem behaviour', *Journal of Adolescence*, 27, pp. 515–30.

Dishion, T., Nelson, S. and Kavanagh, K. (2003) 'The family check-up with high-risk young adolescents: preventing early-onset substance use by parent monitoring', *Behavior Therapy*, 34, pp. 553–71.

Dishion, T.J. and Patterson, G.R. (2006) 'The development and ecology of antisocial behavior' in D. Cicchetti and D.J. Cohen (eds) *Developmental Psychopathology. Vol. 3: Risk, Disorder, and Adaptation* (New York: Wiley), pp. 503–41.

Dishion, T.J., Shaw, D.S., Connell, A., Wilson, M., Gardner, F. and Weaver, C. (2008) 'The Family Check Up with high-risk families with toddlers: Outcomes on positive parenting and early problem behavior', in press, *Child Development*.

Dodge, K.A. and Pettit, G.S. (2003) 'A biopsychosocial model of the development of chronic conduct problems in adolescence', *Developmental Psychology*, 39:2, pp. 349–71.

Dretzke, J., Frew, E., Davenport, C., Barlow, J., Stewart-Brown, S., Sandercock, J., Bayliss, S., Raftery, J., Hyde, C. and Taylor, R. (2005) 'The effectiveness and cost-effectiveness of parent training/education programmes for the treatment of conduct disorder, including oppositional defiant disorder, in children', *Health Technology Assessment*, 9.

Ermisch, J. and Francesconi, M. (2000) 'Cohabitation in Great Britain: Not for long, but here to stay', *Journal of the Royal Statistical Society, Series A*, 163:2, pp. 153–71.

Eshel, N., Daelmans, B., Mello, M.C. and Martines, J. (2006) 'Responsive parenting: interventions and outcomes', *Bulletin of the World Health Organisation*, 84:12, pp. 991–8.

Farrington, D. (1995) 'The development of offending and antisocial behaviour from childhood: key findings from the Cambridge Study of Delinquent Development', *Journal of Child Psychology and Psychiatry*, 36, pp. 929–64.

Fergusson, D.M., Boden, J.M. and Horwood, L.J. (2007) 'Exposure to single parenthood in childhood and later mental health, educational, economic and criminal behaviour outcomes', *Archives of General Psychiatry*, 64:9, pp. 1089–95.

Fergusson, D. and Lynskey, M. (1997) 'Physical punishment/maltreatment during childhood and adjustment in young adulthood', *Child Abuse and Neglect*, 21, pp. 617–30.

Ferri, E. and Smith, K. (2003) 'Family Life' in E. Ferri, J. Bynner and M. Wadsworth (eds) *Changing Britain, Changing Lives, Three Generations at the Turn of the Century* (London: Institute of Education).

Finklehor, D. and Jones, L. (2006) 'Why have child maltreatment and child victimization declined?' *Journal of Social Issues*, 62, pp. 685–716.

Fisher, K. McCulloch, A. and Gershuny, J. (1999) *British Fathers and Children: A Report for Channel 4 Dispatches* (University of Essex: Institute for Social and Economic Research).

Flood-Page, C., Campbell, S., Harrington, V. and Miller, J. (2000) *Youth Crime: Findings from the 1998/99 Youth Lifestyles Survey. Home Office Research Study 209* (London: Home Office).

Flouri, E. (2005) *Fathering and Child Outcomes* (Chichester: Wiley).

Ford, T., Goodman, R. and Meltzer, H. (2004) 'The relative importance of child, family, school and neighbourhood correlates of childhood psychiatric disorder', *Social Psychiatry and Psychiatric Epidemiology, 34*, pp. 487–96.

Forehand, R., Miller, K.S., Dutra, R. and Chance, M.W. (1997) 'Role of parenting in adolescent deviant behavior: replication across and within two ethnic groups', *Journal of Consulting and Clinical Psychology*, 65, pp. 1036–41.

Frick, P.J. and Viding, E.M. (2009) 'Antisocial behavior from a developmental psychopathology perspective', *Development and Psychopathology*, 21, pp. 1111–31.

Frick, P.J., Kimonis, E.R., Dandreaux, D.M. and Farell, J.M. (2003) 'The four year stability of psychopathic traits in non-referred youth', *Behavioural Sciences and the Law*, 21, pp. 713–36.

Galboda-Liyanage, K., Prince, M. and Scott, S. (2003) 'Mother-child joint activity and behaviour problems of pre-school children', *Journal of Child Psychology and Psychiatry*, 44, pp. 1037–48.

Gardner, F. (1989) 'Inconsistent parenting: Is there evidence for a link with children's conduct problems?' *Journal of Abnormal Child Psychology*, 17, pp. 223–33.

Gardner, F. (1994) 'The quality of joint activity between mothers and their children with behaviour problems', *Journal of Child Psychology and Psychiatry*, 35, pp. 935–48.

Gardner, F. (2000) 'Methodological issues in the direct observation of parent-child interaction: do observational findings reflect the natural behavior of participants?' *Clinical Child and Family Psychology Review*, 3, pp. 185–99.

Gardner, F. and Shaw, D. (2008) 'Behavioral problems of infancy and preschool children (0–5)', in M. Rutter, D. Bishop, D. Pine, S. Scott, J. Stevenson, E. Taylor and A. Thapar (eds) *Rutter's Child and Adolescent Psychiatry*, 5th edition (Oxford: Blackwell).

Gardner, F., Burton, J. and Klimes, I. (2006) 'Randomised controlled trial of a parenting intervention in the voluntary sector for reducing child conduct problems: outcomes and mechanisms of change', *Journal of Child Psychology and Psychiatry*, 47, pp. 1123–32.

Gardner, F., Collishaw, S., Maughan, B. and Scott, J. (2009) 'Has parenting changed over recent decades? Can changes in parenting explain the rise in adolescent problem behaviour?' Working paper submitted to the Nuffield Foundation.

Gardner, F., Connell, A., Trentacosta, C., Shaw, D., Dishion, T. and Wilson, M. (2009) 'Moderators of outcome in a brief family-centred intervention for preventing early problem behaviour', *Journal of Consulting and Clinical Psychology*, 77, pp. 543–53.

Gardner, F., Hutchings, J., Bywater, T. and Whitaker, C. (2010) 'Who benefits and how does it work? Moderators and mediators of outcomes in a randomised trial of parenting interventions in multiple 'Sure Start' services', in press, *Journal of Clinical Child and Adolescent Psychology*.

Gardner, F. Shaw, D., Dishion, T., Burton, J. and Supplee, L. (2007) 'Randomized trial of a family-centred approach to preventing conduct problems: Linking changes in proactive parenting to boys' disruptive behaviour in early childhood', *Journal of Family Psychology*, 21, pp. 398–406.

Gardner, F., Sonuga-Barke, E. and Sayal, K. (1999) 'Parents anticipating misbehaviour: An observational study of strategies parents use to prevent conflict with behaviour problem children', *Journal of Child Psychology and Psychiatry*, 40, pp. 1185–96.

Gardner, F., Ward, S., Burton, J. and Wilson, C. (2003) 'Joint play and the early development of conduct problems in children: a longitudinal observational study of pre-schoolers', *Social Development*, 12, pp. 361–79.

Gauthier, A. H., Smeeding, T. M. and Furstenberg, F. (2004) 'Are parents investing less time in children? Trends in selected industrialized countries', *24th General Conference of the International Union for the Scientific Study of Population* (Salvador-Bahia, Brazil: Blackwell Publishing Inc).

Gershoff, E. (2002) 'Corporal punishment by parents and associated child behaviors and experiences: A meta-analytic and theoretical review', *Psychological Bulletin*, 128, pp. 539–79.

Gibson-Davis, C. M. (2008) 'Family structure effects on maternal and paternal parenting in low income families', *Journal of Marriage and Family*, 70, pp. 452–65.

Gilbert, R., Kemp, A., Thorburn, J., Sidebotham, P., Radford, L., Glaser, D. and MacMillan, H. (2009a) 'Recognising and responding to child maltreatment', *The Lancet*, 373, pp. 167–80.

Gilbert, R., Widom, C.S, Browne, K., Fergusson, D., Webb, E. and Janson, S. (2009b) 'Burden and consequences of child maltreatment in high-income countries', *The Lancet*, 373: 9657, pp. 68–81.

Gill, T. (2007) *No Fear: Growing Up in a Risk Averse Society* (Calouste Gulbenkian Foundation).

Goldberg, G. and Williams, P. (1998) *A User's Guide to the General Health Questionnaire* (Windsor: NFER_Nelson).

Green. H., McGinnity, A., Meltzer, H., Ford, T. and Goodman, R. (2005) *Mental Health of Children and Young People in Great Britain* (Office for National Statistics. Hampshire: Palgrave Macmillan).

Guo, G., Roettger, M.E. and Cai, T. (2008) 'The integration of genetic propensities into social-control models of delinquency and violence among male youths', *American Sociological Review*, 73, pp. 543–68.

Guzzo, K. and Lee, H. (2008) 'Couple relationship status and patterns in early parenting practices', *Journal of Marriage and Family*, 70, pp. 44–61.

Hales, J., Nevill, C., Pudney, S. and Tipping, S. (2009) *Longitudinal Analysis of the Offending, Crime and Justice Survey 2003–06. Research Report 19.* (London: Home Office).

Haskey, J. (2005) 'Living arrangements in contemporary Britain: Having a partner who usually lives elsewhere and Living Apart Together (LAT)', *Population Trends*, 122, pp. 35–45.

Hawes, D.J. and Dadds, M.R. (2005) 'The treatment of conduct problems in children with callous-unemotional traits', *Journal of Consulting and Clinical Psychology*, 73, pp. 737–41.

Hill, J. (2002) 'Biological, psychological and social processes in the conduct disorders', *Journal of Child Psychology and Psychiatry*, 43, pp. 133–64.

Hoeve, M., Blokland, A., Dubus, J.S., Loeber, R., Gerris, J.R. and van der Laan, P.H. (2008) 'Trajectories of delinquency and parenting styles', *Journal of Abnormal Child Psychology*, 36:2, pp. 223–35.

Hoeve, M., Dubas, J.S., Eichelsheim, V.I., van der Laan, P.H., Smeenk, W. and Gerris, J.R.M. (2009) 'The relationship between parenting and delinquency: a meta-analysis', *Journal of Abnormal Child Psychology*, 37:6, pp. 749–75.

Hutchings, J., Bywater, T., Daley, D., Gardner, F., Whitaker, C., Jones, K., Eames, C. and Edwards, R. T. (2007) 'Parenting intervention in Sure Start services for children at risk of developing conduct disorder: pragmatic randomised controlled trial', *British Medical Journal*, 334, pp. 678–85.

Hutchings, J., Lane, E. and Gardner, F. (2004) Making evidence-based intervention work in D. Farrington, C. Sutton and D. Utting (eds) *Support from the Start: Working with Young Children and their Families to Reduce the Risks of Crime and Antisocial Behaviour* (London: DFES).

Jacobson, K. and Crockett L. (2000) 'Parental monitoring and adolescent adjustment: An ecological perspective', *Journal of Research on Adolescence*, 10, pp. 65–97.

Juby, H. and Farrington, D. P. (2001) 'Disentangling the link between disrupted families and delinquency', *British Journal of Criminology*, 41:1, pp. 22–40.

Kim, J., Hetherington, E. and Reiss, D. (1999) 'Associations among family relationships, antisocial peers, and adolescents' externalizing behaviors: Gender and family type differences', *Child Development*, 70, pp. 1209–30.

Kim-Cohen, J., Caspi, A., Rutter, M., Tomas, M P. and Moffitt, T.E. (2006) 'The caregiving environments provided to children by depressed mothers with or without an antisocial history', *American Journal of Psychiatry*, 163:6, pp. 1009–18.

Kroneman, L.M., Loeber, R., Hipwell, A.E. and Koot, H.M. (2009) 'Girls' disruptive behavior and its relationship to family functioning: A review', *Journal of Child and Family Studies*, 18, pp. 259–73.

Lansford, J.E. (2009) 'Parental divorce and children's adjustment', *Perspectives on Psychological Science*, 4, pp. 140–52.

Lansford, J.E, Chang, L., Dodge, K.A., Malone, P.S., Oburu, P., Palmérus, K., Bacchini, D., Pastorelli, C., Bombi, A.S., Zelli, A., Tapanya, S., Chaudhary, N., Deater-Deckard, K., Manke, B. and Quinn, N. (2005) 'Cultural normativeness as a moderator of the link between physical discipline and children's adjustment: A comparison of China, India, Italy, Kenya, Philippines, and Thailand', *Child Development*, 76, pp. 1234–46.

Loeber, R. and Stouthamer-Loeber, M. (1986) 'Family factors as correlates and predictors of juvenile conduct problems and delinquency' in N. Morris and M. Tonry (eds) *Crime and Justice: An Annual Review of Research, Vol 7* (Chicago: University of Chicago Press), pp. 29–149.

MacMillan, H.L., Wathen, C.N., Barlow, J., Fergusson, D.M., Leventhal, J.M. and Taussig, H.N. (2009) 'Child Maltreatment 3: Interventions to prevent child maltreatment and associated impairment', *Lancet*, 373: 9659, pp. 250–66.

Manning, W. and Lamb, K. A. (2003) 'Adolescent well-being in cohabiting, married, and single-parent families', *Journal of Marriage and the Family*, 65:4, pp. 876–93.

Margo, J. and Dixon, M. (2006) *Freedom's Orphans: Raising Youth in a Changing World* (London: Institute for Public Policy Research).

Martinez, C. and Forgatch, M. (2001) 'Preventing problems with boys' noncompliance: Effects of a parent training intervention for divorcing mothers', *Journal of Consulting and Clinical Psychology*, 69, pp. 416–28.

Maughan, B. (2001) 'Conduct disorder in context' in J. Hill and B. Maughan (eds) *Conduct Disorders in Childhood and Adolescence* (Cambridge: Cambridge University Press), pp. 169–201.

Maynard, M.J. and Harding, S. (2010) 'Ethnic differences in psychological well-being in adolescence in the context of time spent in family activities', *Social Psychiatry and Psychiatric Epidemiology*, 45, pp. 115–23.

Meltzer, H., Gatward, R., Goodman, R. and Ford, T. (2000) *The Mental Health of Children and Adolescents in Great Britain* (Office for National Statistics. HMSO).

Moffitt, T.E. (1993) 'Adolescence-limited and life-course-persistent antisocial-behavior – a developmental taxonomy', *Psychological Review*, 100:4, pp. 674–701.

Moffitt, T. E. and E Risk Study Team (2002) 'Teen-aged mothers in contemporary Britain', *Journal of Child Psychology and Psychiatry*, 43:6, pp. 727–42.

Moffitt, T.E., Caspi, A., Rutter, M. and Silva, P.A. (2001) *Sex Differences in Antisocial Behaviour* (Cambridge: Cambridge University Press).

Nuffield Foundation (2009) *Time Trends in Parenting and Outcomes for Young People* (London: The Nuffield Foundation).

Office for National Statistics (a) *Marriages and divorces 1961–1999: Social Trends 31.* Office for National Statistics [Online]. Available at: http://www.statistics.gov.uk/StatBase/ssdataset.asp?vlnk=3451a ndMore=Y [Accessed 19 January 2010]

Office for National Statistics (b). *Live births: 1838–2004, occurrence within/outside marriage and sex.* Office for National Statistics [Online]. Available at: http://www.statistics.gov.uk/STATBASE/xsdataset.asp?vlnk=3805andMore=Y [Accessed 19 January 2010]

Office for National Statistics (c). *Births: 1938–2004, mean age of women at marriage and at live birth.* Office for National Statistics [Online]. Available at: http://www.statistics.gov.uk/STATBASE/xsdataset.asp?vlnk=4179andMore=Y. [accessed 19 January 2010]

Office for National Statistics (d). *Focus on Children*, Office for National Statistics [Online]. Available at: http://www.statistics.gov.uk/focuson/children/default.asp [accessed on 19 January 2010]

Office for National Statistics (e). *Population Trends 122 – Winter 2005*, Office for National Statistics [Online]. Available at: http://www.statistics.gov.uk/downloads/theme_population/PopTrends122v1.pdf [accessed on 19 January 2010]

Office for National Statistics (2007a) *Social Trends 37.* Office for National Statistics/Palgrave MacMillan; Basingstoke, Hampshire.

Office for National Statistics (2007b) *Focus on Families* (Hampshire: Palgrave Macmillan).

Office for National Statistics (2009) *Social Trends 39.* Office for National Statistics/Palgrave MacMillan; Basingstoke, Hampshire.

Ollendick, T.H., Jarrett, M.A., Grills-Taquechel, A.E., Hovey, L.D. and Wolff, J.C. (2008) 'Comorbidity as a predictor and moderator of treatment outcome in youth with anxiety, affective, attention deficit/hyperactivity disorder, and oppositional/conduct disorders', *Clinical Psychology Review*, 28, pp. 1447–71.

Patterson, G. (2002) 'The early development of coercive family process' in J. Reid G.R. Patterson and J. Snyder (eds) *Antisocial Behavior in Children and Adolescents* (Washington DC: APA), pp. 25–44.

Patterson, G., Reid, J. and Dishion, T. (1992) *Antisocial Boys* (Eugene, OR: Castalia).

Pettit, G. S. and Arsiwalla, D. D. (2008) 'Commentary on special section on "Bidirectional Parent-Child Relationships": The continuing evolution of dynamic, transactional models of parenting and youth behavior problems', *Journal of Abnormal Child Psychology*, 36:5, pp. 711–18.

Pettit, G.S., Bates, J.E. and Dodge, K.A. (1997) 'Supportive parenting, ecological context, and children's adjustment: A seven-year longitudinal study', *Child Development*, 68, pp. 908–23.

Pettit, G.S., Laird, R., Dodge, K., Bates, J. and Criss, M. (2001) 'Antecedents and behavior-problem outcomes of parental monitoring and psychological control in early adolescence', *Child Development*, 72, pp. 583–98.

Piquero, A.R., Farrington, D.P., Welsh, B.C., Tremblay, R.E. and Jennings, W. (2008) *Effects of Early Family/ Parent Training Programmes on Antisocial Behaviour and Delinquency*, Campbell Systematic Reviews, available at: www.campbellcollaboration.org

Prinz, R.J., Sanders, M.R., Shapiro, C.J., Whitaker, D.J. and Lutzker, J.R. (2009) 'Population-based prevention of child maltreatment: The U.S. Triple P System Population Trial', *Prevention Science*, 10, pp. 1–12.

Reid, M., Webster-Stratton, C. and Beauchaine, T. (2001) 'Parent training in HeadStart: a comparison of program response among African-American, Asian-American, Caucasian, and Hispanic mothers', *Prevention Science*, 2, pp. 209–27.

Robinson, W.S. (1950) 'Ecological correlations and the behavior of individuals', *American Sociological Review*, 15, pp. 351–7.

Rodgers, B. and Pryor, J. (1998) *Divorce and Separation: The Outcomes for Children* (York: Joseph Rowntree Foundation).

Rothbaum, F. and Weisz, J. R. (1994) 'Parental caregiving and child externalizing behavior in nonclinical samples: A meta-analysis', *Psychological Bulletin*, 116, pp. 55–74.

Rutter, M. (2001) 'Conduct disorder: future direction: An afterword', in J. Hill and B. Maughan (eds) *Conduct Disorders in Childhood and Adolescence* (Cambridge: Cambridge University Press).

Rutter, M. (2005) 'Environmentally mediated risks for psychopathology: Research strategies and findings', *Journal of the American Academy of Child and Adolescent Psychiatry*, 44, pp. 3–18.

Rutter, M., and Smith, D.J. (1995) *Psychosocial Disorders in Young People: Time Trends and Their Causes* (Chichester: Wiley).

Rutter, M. R., Giller, H. and Hagell, A. (1998) *Antisocial Behaviour by Young People* (New York: Cambridge University Press).

Sayer, L., Gauthier, A. and Furstenberg, F. (2004) 'Educational differences in parents' time with children: Cross-national variations', *Journal of Marriage and the Family*, 66, pp. 1152–69.

Schuck, A. M. and Widom, C. S. (2001) 'Childhood victimization and alcohol symptoms in females: Causal inferences and hypothesized mediators', *Child Abuse and Neglect*, 25, pp. 1069–92.

Scott, S., Spender, Q., Doolan, M., Jacobs, B. and Aspland, H. (2001) 'Multicentre controlled trial of parenting groups for childhood antisocial behaviour in clinical practice', *British Medical Journal*, 323, pp. 194–7.

Shaw, D., Bell, R. and Gilliom, M. (2000) 'A truly early-starter model of antisocial behavior revisited', *Clinical Child and Family Psychology Review*, 3, pp. 155–72.

Shaw, D.S., Dishion, T.J., Supplee, L., Gardner, F. and Arnds, K. (2006) 'A family-centered approach to the prevention of early-onset antisocial behavior: Two-year effects of the family check-up in early childhood', *Journal of Consulting and Clinical Psychology*, 74, pp. 1–9.

Smith, C. and Farrington, D. (2004) 'Continuities in antisocial behavior and parenting across three generations', *Journal of Child Psychology and Psychiatry*, 45, pp. 230–48.

Sonkin, B., Edwards, P., Roberts, I. and Green, J. (2006) 'Walking, cycling and transport safety: an analysis of child road deaths', *Journal of the Royal Society of Medicine*, 99, pp. 402–5.

Sonuga-Barke, E.J., Daley, D., Thompson, M., Laver-Bradbury, C., Weeks, A. (2001) 'Parent-based therapies for Attention Deficit/Hyperactivity Disorder: A randomised controlled trial with a community sample', *Journal of the American Academy of Child and Adolescent Psychiatry*, 40, pp. 402–8.

Stattin, H. and Kerr, M. (2000) 'Parent monitoring: A reinterpretation', *Child Development*, 71: 4, pp. 1072–85.

Steinberg, L. and Silk, J. (2002) 'Parenting adolescents', in M. J. Bornstein (ed.) *Handbook of Parenting*, 2nd edition, *Vol. 1 Children and Parenting* (Mahwah, NJ: Erlbaum), pp 103–35.

Viding, E., Fontaine, N.M.G., Oliver, B.R. and Plomin, R. (2009) 'Negative parental discipline, conduct problems and callous-unemotional traits: monozygotic twin differences study', *British Journal of Psychiatry*, 10, pp. 414–19.

Webster-Stratton, C. (1998) 'Preventing conduct problems in Head Start children: strengthening parenting competencies', *Journal of Consulting and Clinical Psychology*, 66, pp. 715–30.

Weersing, R. V. and Weisz, J. (2002) 'Mechanisms of action in youth psychotherapy', *Journal of Child Psychology and Psychiatry*, 43, pp. 3–29.

Wells, L. E. and Rankin, J. (1991) 'Families and delinquency: A meta-analysis of the impact of broken homes', *Social Problems*, 38:1, pp. 71–93.

White, A. (2002) *Social Focus in Brief: Ethnicity 2002* (London: Office for National Statistics).

Wikström, P. H. and Loeber, R. (2000) 'Do disadvantaged neighborhoods cause well-adjusted children to become adolescent delinquents? A study of male juvenile serious offending, individual risk and protective factors, and neighborhood context', *Criminology*, 38, pp. 1109–11.

Woolfenden, S.R., Williams, K. and Peat, J. (2001) 'Family and parenting interventions in children and adolescents with conduct disorder and delinquency aged 10–17', *Cochrane Database of Systematic Reviews* 2001, Issue 2. Art. No: CD003015, available at: www.mrw.interscience.wiley.com/cochrane/clsysrev/articles/CD003015/frame.html

Wootton, J.M., Frick, P.J., Shelton, K.K. and Silverthorn, P. (1997) 'Ineffective parenting and childhood conduct problems: the moderating role of callous-unemotional traits', *Journal of Consulting and Clinical Psychology*, 65, pp. 301–8.

Youth Justice Board (2005) *Risk and Protective Factors* (London: Youth Justice Board).

Zuzanek, J. (2001) 'Parenting time: Enough or too little?' *Isuma*, 2, pp. 125–33.

Chapter 9

Models of youth justice

Lesley McAra

The brief given to the author of this chapter was to: (i) explore the principles that underpin youth justice systems; (ii) examine key differences between youth justice systems internationally; and (iii) identify a small number of distinct ideal models that serve to crystallize the main policy options.

This brief, however, presents a number of challenges. Debates about youth justice have traditionally been framed by the competing imperatives of the justice versus welfare approaches (Hazell 2008). However, as I aim to demonstrate, this is a somewhat over-simplified understanding of the myriad principles shaping both policy discourse in contemporary western societies and the core imperatives that underpin international conventions (such as the Beijing Rules 1985). Furthermore, youth justice systems are complex architectural phenomena and the variant principles which underpin policies do not always translate into institutional infrastructure in straightforward ways – with a multiplicity of processes, procedures and programmes aimed at delivering, in some instances, rather similar outcomes (contrast, for example, the expert welfare committee in Finland with the welfare oriented lay panel in Scotland, see below), or similar modes of infrastructure being aimed at rather disparate outcomes (as, for example, the more punitive court-based system in, Colorado USA contrasted with the more protectionist one in Belgium, see respectively Huizinga *et al.* 2003; Put and Walgrave 2006).

A further challenge, particularly, in terms of 'crystallizing' policy options, is that variant systems have evolved in quite specific spatial and temporal locations. What role does this external context (political, cultural, economic) play in shaping the evolving institutional and discursive frameworks of youth justice? To what extent does it facilitate or impede the transplantation of policy from jurisdiction to jurisdiction? How far does it impact on the capacity of institutions and actors to reform?

Moreover, while a particular system may adhere to a strong set of guiding principles, these principles may be skewed or subverted by the working practices and cultures of the various agencies which act as gatekeepers to and/or colonize the systems themselves. To what extent and under what conditions do tensions arise between the overall systemic aims and objectives, and the cultural practices of key agencies/agents? What is the practical impact on the client base (namely young offenders) of such tensions and how might they be avoided?

In addressing these challenges, the chapter is divided into three parts. Part 1 explores the evolving theoretical/philosophical frameworks around which debates on youth justice have been conducted; examines the range of outcomes which (singly or in combination) extant youth justice systems seek to achieve (the 'telos' of youth justice); and briefly overviews the key components of international norms and conventions. Part 2 explores in more detail variant models of youth justice (in terms of institutional infrastructure), in the course of which some of the key differences between systems internationally will be highlighted. Part 3 explores the links between system and context and the problems that this may pose for policy reform. The chapter concludes with a review of the policy implications.[1]

I. The principles of youth justice

Arguably all youth justice systems (in developed countries) are required to fulfil two potentially competing objectives:

(i) firstly to help troubled young people to change, develop and overcome their problems – to provide a turning point in their lives;

(ii) secondly to deliver a firm, prompt and appropriate response to youth offending – a response which offers the best means of protecting the public when necessary.

Reconciling these objectives is particularly problematic in the case of young people who seriously and persistently offend. Although posing a threat to others, they are themselves fragile and vulnerable victims and in need of protection and support (Smith and Ecob 2007; McAra and McVie 2010). Balancing the needs of such offenders with the needs of society, as a consequence, involves both moral and political choices.

This section examines four paradigms which, arguably, have come to dominate youth justice discourse: just deserts; welfare; restoration; and 'actuarialism'. Each of these paradigms offers a different solution to the problem of balancing the needs of the vulnerable offender with the needs of society. Indeed, by deconstructing these paradigms, we begin to interrogate the core assumptions about the nature of personhood and the relationship between the citizen, the community and the state which inhere in current policy.

Key paradigms

The just deserts paradigm is predicated on a view of the child primarily as a rights bearer and rights claimant whose autonomy, privacy and entitlement to due process is required to be respected. For children over the age of criminal responsibility, offending is understood to be a product of rational choice. Indeed children who come into conflict with the law are expected to take responsibility for their behaviour and its consequences. Under a just deserts model the aim of intervention is to deter and to punish, such that the child will weigh up the risks of certain punishment against the potential rewards of crime and find the latter wanting (the offender in this context functions as a 'flawed consumer'). The desert model is predicated on 'classicist' principles (Beccaria 1963; Bentham 1973): whilst advocating that there should be proportionality between the deed and the punishment, the model also argues for parsimony in punishment (the least restrictive sanction commensurate with the seriousness of the act). A core objective of the desert model is to be didactic (with the citizen being a key 'audience' of punishment) and this, in turn, is predicated on a contractual relationship between the state and the individual citizen.[2]

In contrast, the welfare model constructs the child primarily as a bearer of entitlements: the child is a person to whom duties are owed by the state and indeed by the wider community. Offending is understood as stemming from deeper-seated needs and the child is not considered fully responsible for their actions. Childhood is thus construed as a protected phase of development, by the end of which full capacity is reached. According to a welfare model the aim of intervention is to diagnose/treat and to rescue/rehabilitate, with expert input from social work, psychiatry and education. Programmes require to be proportionate to level of need presented and thus indeterminate forms of intervention are often valorized. According to a welfarist model, early, preventative intervention is best delivered through universal social, education and health services rather than criminal justice. Principal objectives of welfarism are to be nurturing and transformative. Underscored by philanthropic sensibilities, welfarism valorizes a model of development in which the child is construed as lying at the heart of a supportive family, and the family lying at the heart of a supportive community (McAra and McVie 2010).

In respect of the restorative paradigm, personhood is understood as being shaped directly by the community and cultural context (Zehr and Mika 1998). Children have both positive entitlements and rights. Offenders are perceived as rational individuals who have the capacity to take

Table 9.1 Youth justice paradigms

	Just deserts	Welfare	Restorative	Actuarial
Personhood	Child as rights bearer	Child as bearer of entitlements	Child as bearer of entitlements and rights	Child qualified bearer of rights
	Individuals constitutionally self-interested	Individuals a product of experience	Individuals constitutionally good	Individuals potentially bad
	Offender as rational and responsible	Offender as non-rational, irresponsible	Offender as rational and responsible	Offender as dangerous
Social relations	Core relationship: contractual, state vs. individual citizen	Core relationships: nested model of state, community family, child	Core relationships: inclusive; child, victim and community	Core relationship: adversarial; community vs. potential offender
	Didactic	Transformative	Integrationist	Protective
	Audience: Citizens	Audience: Offender and family	Audience: Community and victims	Audience: Public
	Sensibility: Retribution	Sensibility: Philanthropy	Sensibility: Connection	Sensibility: Fear
Intervention	Aim to deter and punish	Aim to diagnose and to rescue	Aim to support victims, to restore harm, to reconnect child to community, to build more cohesive peaceful community	Aim to diminish current and future risk, safeguard victims and the wider community
	Proportionality to deeds, parsimony	Proportionality to needs	Proportionality to harm caused	Proportionality to risk

responsibility for their behaviour and recognize/acknowledge the suffering they have caused. Under a restorative paradigm the aim of intervention is to support victims, restore the harm caused and reconnect the child offender to the community. An important outcome of the restorative process is, thereby, the construction of a peaceful and cohesive community. The principal actors and audiences for intervention are communities and victims (not the state); the core objective being integration.

Finally, the actuarial model views the child, first and foremost, in terms of his or her inherent capacity for wrong-doing, and aims to tackle this. Offenders are conceived as a threat to social order and the child's 'needs' are constructed as evidence of risk. Interventions are therefore carefully calibrated in proportion to risk posed (and thus can be indeterminate in nature where the offender is perceived as highly dangerous), the aim being to safeguard society and prevent future victimization. Expert involvement is crucial to the assessment of risk. Early preventive intervention requires careful targeting, with criminal justice workers being key to this process. In this context, offenders become a commodity to be assessed, packaged and then (in extreme cases) warehoused. The principal audience for actuarial interventions is the broader public, with protection and reassurance (to overcome public fears) being core objectives.

The links between normative debates and international conventions

How then should we decide amongst these competing paradigms? Is there a fundamental moral order, a universal set of values against which we can critically assess these paradigms? Or are value systems fundamentally under-girded by cultural or political specificity?

The international conventions relating to justice for children, developed over the last decades of the twentieth century by the United Nations (UN), have attempted to construct a cosmopolitan touchstone against which the policy and practice of individual jurisdictions can be measured. These conventions include: the UN Convention on the Rights of the Child (1989); the UN Standard Minimum Rules for the Administration of Juvenile Justice (the Beijing Rules 1985); the UN Directing Principles for the Prevention of Juvenile Delinquency (the Riyadh Guidelines 1990); and the UN Rules for the Protection of Juveniles Deprived of their Liberty (the Havana Rules 1990).

Somewhat ironically these conventions are, themselves, beset by tensions, in particular between just deserts and welfarist imperatives (Put and Walgrave 2006). This is exemplified, in particular, by the Beijing Rules. Juvenile justice institutions are charged with the requirement to meet the needs of the child, protect his or her basic rights *at the same time* as meeting the needs of society. According to the rules, interventions should be both parsimonious (with a core emphasis on prevention, diversion or community-based programmes, with institutional care being used as an intervention of last resort) and proportionate to the seriousness of the offence *as well as* proportionate to the circumstances of the offender (with an overriding emphasis on the provision of care, protection, education and vocational skills). Procedures should protect the rights of the child (including the right to privacy), promote participation (including that of parents) and decisions should be in the best interests of the child.

Little guidance is given within the Beijing Rules, as to how the balance between each of these imperatives can be achieved. Indeed the rules acknowledge, that in terms of implementation, cognisance needs to be paid to the 'economic, social and cultural conditions prevailing in each Member state' (Rule 1.5), with the implication that there may be widespread variation as to how 'needs' and 'parsimony' are interpreted.

The links between normative debates and youth justice policy

As indicated in other chapters within this volume, elements of each of the above four paradigms are embedded in almost all western systems to a lesser or greater extent, including UK jurisdictions. For example within England, restorative interventions (such as the referral order) rub shoulders with preventive interventions predicated on a risk factor paradigm; and responsibilization strategies (such as the abolition of *doli incapax* in 1998) rub shoulders with more welfarist measures as, for example, the intensive fostering option within youth rehabilitation orders (see Muncie and Goldson 2006). Similarly within Scotland, a range of competing principles have now been grafted onto the existing welfarist model of juvenile justice as exemplified by the punitive dimensions of the antisocial behaviour agenda pre 2007, the mushrooming of reparation and mediation schemes within and the incursion of the risk factor/actuarial paradigm into policy on early intervention post 2007 (McAra and McVie 2010).

A charge that might be levelled at youth justice systems more generally is their fundamental incoherence and indeed ambivalence towards the children who come within their ambit. Offenders are *simultaneously* conceived as autonomous (as per the desert model) and over-determined (by context and circumstance, as per the welfarist model); as potentially evil (in extreme versions of the actuarial model) and penitent (in the restorative model); as commodity (in the actuarial model) and flawed consumer (in the desert model); as being outsiders (in the actuarial and restorative justice models) and insiders (in the welfarist model).

Does such incoherence matter? In normative terms, a system may be in danger of losing its legitimacy when its underlying principles are in contradiction. Interventions proportionate to risk or proportionate to need might be viewed as highly unjust by a children's rights protagonist who valorized interventions proportionate to deeds and parsimony in punishment. Similarly, interventions based primarily on punishment or deterrence would be conceived as fundamentally unjust according to a welfarist perspective, as well as antithetical to community cohesion by some advocates of restorative justice. Moreover, given the range of competing conceptions of the offender which abound within contemporary policy, one can see how the formal regulatory framework of youth justice would fail to function effectively as a moral compass for young people (to mix metaphors, if the youth justice system were a parent, it would be assessed as being a fairly inconsistent one!).

However, as a political strategy, the complex framework of youth justice has the *potential* to be highly effective (a point which will returned to later in the chapter). Rather like total policing whereby community and military style policing help to legitimate each other, so too do interventions which lie on either side of the above dyads become mutually legitimating. Thus welfarist interventions which conceive the child as over-determined may gain acceptability precisely because the system is undergirded by more punitive interventions requiring the child to take responsibility; the corollary of this being that the harshness of certain modes of sanctioning may become more acceptable precisely because 'softer' more inclusive interventions also exist. Together these dyads form a carapace of control over young people: a consequence of the pragmatic approach which policy-makers have taken in recent years to normativity in matters relating to youth justice.

2: The architecture of youth justice

The architecture of contemporary youth justice is a complex one. One of the few points of commonality amongst systems of juvenile justice in the developed world is their bifurcatory nature: all systems allow the cases of children (who have reached the age of criminal responsibility) to be dealt with according to an adult court model if they have committed very serious offences (such as homicide or rape) (see Hazell 2008 for an overview). That aside, individual systems exhibit major variation in terms of both structure and core personnel.

A key differentiating feature is whether the system deals with both child offenders and those in need of care and protection (a generic system) or whether it deals only with offenders (a specialist system). A further differentiating feature is whether the system has a court-based structure or whether it places a 'non-judicial' body at the heart of decision-making (such as a tribunal). Within court-based structures there are variations between family courts, specialist youth courts and modified versions of adult courts. Court-based structures can also be differentiated between those which operate inquisitorial, participatory or adversarial procedures. Within youth justice systems which have developed 'non-judicial' based structures there are variations between those which involve lay persons in decision-making and those which involve only experts (e.g. social workers); and within lay-based structures themselves, there are variations between those which involve specially trained members of the public (whose involvement will continue for many years) and those which involve families and victims in particular cases (as, for example, in family group conferencing).

Many commentaries on youth justice link the paradigms discussed in Part 1 above to specific forms of institutional infrastructure: for example, welfarism is often associated with indeterminate interventions set in train by the decisions of a non-judicial body such as a tribunal or welfare committee; by contrast the just deserts paradigm is said to valorize court-based structures and determinate forms of intervention (Winterdyk 2002; Hazell 2008). While the above paradigms do predispose themselves to certain institutional infrastructures, arguably there is no necessary *causal* relationship between principle and architecture. For example it is possible to deliver welfare interventions via a court-based model; similarly due process and privacy rights can be delivered using a tribunal system. Importantly a distinction requires to be made between the processing of cases (including modes of determining appropriate disposals/interventions) and the characteristics of the subsequent disposals/interventions themselves. Thus, although family group conferencing is one mode of delivering restorative justice, it is possible to incorporate restorative interventions into a youth justice system via a court-based model (as for example in England in respect of referral or reparation orders (Crawford and Newburn 2003)).

England currently operates a 'specialist youth court model' of justice (following the formal separation of the care and justice systems for children as a result of arrangements introduced by the Children Act 1989), the core architecture of which is set out in Table 9.2. As indicated in the table, the age of criminal responsibility is currently age 10. Below this age, specialist youth offending teams (who are also involved in the provision of services and support to child offenders from age 10) can be involved in the oversight of children whose behaviour or circumstances indicate that they are at risk of being involved in offending in the future. Youngsters involved in offending from age 10 to 17 are normally dealt with in the Youth Court (staffed by magistrates) but can be dealt with in the Crown court in cases of extreme seriousness. Court processes (in both the Youth and Crown Court) are adversarial in nature although, in the light of the European Court of Human Rights rulings,[3] modifications required to be made in the Crown Court to ensure that children properly understand proceedings.

In this section of the chapter, I am going to explore four models of youth justice (also set out in Table 9.2) which differ in significant ways from the institutional infrastructure in England. These four models are derived from the systems in Scotland, Finland, Belgium and New Zealand. These

Table 9.2 The architecture of youth justice

England/Wales	**Under 10** Youth offending team (prevention)	**10–17** Youth court. Crown court if serious case		**18+** CJ system
Generic youth court (exemplar: Belgium)	**Under 16** Youth court deals with welfare and offending	**16–17** Youth court. But transfer possible to 'Extended Youth Court' using adult criminal code		**18+** CJ system Youth measures can be extended to age 23
Lay tribunal (exemplar: Scotland)	**Under 8** Lay tribunal deals with welfare	**8–15** Lay tribunal CJ system if serious case	**16–17** CJ system but can remit to lay tribunal	**18+** CJ system
Welfare committee (exemplar: Finland)	**Under 15** Welfare committee	**15–20** CJ system modified with special youth measures and possible remit to welfare committee		**21+** CJ system
Conferencing + age-graded court system (exemplar: New Zealand)	**Under 10** Family group conference and family court	**10–14** Family group conference and family court CJ transfer if serious	**15–17** Family group conference and youth court CJ transfer if serious	**18+** CJ system

jurisdictions have been selected as they capture succinctly the major variations evident across youth justice systems (outlined above) and thus function effectively as 'quasi-ideal' typical models against which to interrogate the English model. The bold lines in the table indicate the age of criminal responsibility in each jurisdiction and the grey lines indicate the point of exit from the tutelage of juvenile justice institutions and/or interventions.

Generic youth court model

Under a generic court model, the same institutional infrastructure deals with both children in need of care and protection and child offenders. The youth court is staffed by specialist juvenile judges and supported by a specialist youth court social service. During the investigative phase, the prosecutor deals with matters relating to the facts of the offence whilst the judge takes charge of the social examination into the child's circumstances, family context and behaviour and makes decisions on any provisional measures (such as placement in foster care or other mode of residential care) (Put and Walgrave 2006). Measures available to the court are intended first and foremost to be protective and educative (including secure forms of care) and there is no differentiation in the types of measure available for offenders and care and protection cases. The best interests of the child should be paramount in any decisions made. Belgium is a key exemplar of this model of youth justice.

In Belgium, the youth court deals with youngsters up to the age of 18, the age of criminal responsibility. Importantly, the youth court judge continues involvement with a case post-sentencing. All measures are subject to review on a regular basis and can be extended beyond the age of majority, up until the age of 23. The youth judge is also required to visit, at least twice a year, any child who has been placed in a 'public institution' (a form of secure care) (Christiaens and Nuytiens 2009).

It is important to note that Belgium, notwithstanding its welfarist ambitions, operates a twin-track system which has recently undergone some modifications. Prior to 2006 it was possible to divert cases to the adult criminal justice system from age 16 to 17 where the youth court judge felt that existing measures would not provide for the rehabilitation of the offender. (Under this arrangement, all measures available for adults could be used for children, including life sentences, and prison sentences would be served in an adult prison.) In practice very few cases were ever transferred (around 3 per cent of cases in any one year, according to research by Vanneste *et al.* 2001). The Youth Protection Act 2006 (which should have been implemented in full by 2009) set out new criteria and procedures regarding such 'transfers'. The criteria included the seriousness of the offence and/or that the child had experience of at least one previous youth court measure. Cases are now transferred to an Extended

Youth Court presided over by two juvenile judges and one judge of the Correctional Court. As in the past, the Extended Youth Court applies the rules of adult criminal law but an upper limit has been placed on imprisonment (of 30 years) and offenders sentenced to periods of custody are to serve their sentences in special youth detention centres (see Christiaens and Nuytiens 2009 for extended discussion of the new measures).

Welfare committee and age-graded court system

An alternative model (common in Scandinavian countries) is a welfare committee combined with a modified adult court system. All children who come to the attention of the authorities for 'offending' below the age of criminal responsibility (which is generally in the mid-teenage years) are dealt with by the child welfare system (where decisions are based on the best interests of the child). Beyond this age, youngsters are dealt with in the criminal courts and according to the adult criminal code. However, the system is age-graded, with a range of special youth measures, limitations on the use of custody and potential to remit cases back to the welfare committee where children are exceptionally needy. Finland is a key exemplar of this model of youth justice.

Within Finland the age of criminal responsibility is currently set at age 15. Modified adult procedures are available for youngsters aged between 15–20 and welfare measures (via the welfare committee) can also be extended up to age 20 (see Lappi-Seppälä 2006). Special measures for youths include supervision connected with a 'conditional sentence' for a maximum of two years (somewhat akin to a suspended sentence) and the Juvenile Punishment Order (the latter of which has been characterized by Lappi-Seppälä as premised on a mixture of neo-classicist and rehabilitative principles). Importantly, distinctions are made between the 15–17 and 18–20-year-old age groups. Diversion from prosecution is most often used for the 15–17-year-old age group and prison sentences ('unconditional sentences') are only used in exceptional circumstances (for example in the cases of homicide, aggravated robbery and drug offences). No youngster under the age of 18 can be given life imprisonment. Where a 15–17-year-old is placed under supervision in a community setting by the courts, services may be provided by social work or private volunteers. By contrast 18–20-year-olds will generally be supervised by the probation service. Finally, there are no dedicated prisons for the 'young adult' age group (15+) but youngsters will serve their sentences in special wards within extant institutions (Lappi-Seppälä 2006).

Lay tribunal

A third quasi-ideal typical model is the lay tribunal. As with the generic court model, the lay tribunal deals with child offenders and those in need of care and protection. The best interests of the child is the paramount principle along with minimal intervention where possible (parsimony). A characteristic feature of this model is the separation of the judgement of evidence from the disposition of a case. The former lies in the hands of a 'reporter' whose principal task is to investigate referrals and decide if there is a prima facie case that one of the statutory grounds of referral to the system has been met and that the child is in need of compulsory measures of care. The principal task of the lay tribunal is to consider the measures to be applied. Before a tribunal can take place both the child and his/her parents have to accept the grounds for referral (in the case of an offender there has to be an admission of guilt). If the grounds are disputed, the case is referred to the courts for a proof hearing. At the tribunal the child and his or her parents will be present, along with a social work specialist and any other relevant expert. Decisions will be taken by a lay panel (three adults, drawn from a wider committee of specially trained members of the community). The process is intended to be consensual and participatory with all decisions taken in the best interests of the child. Measures available to the tribunal are residential or non-residential supervision requirements under the tutelage of social work. Scotland is a key exemplar of this model of youth justice.

Within Scotland the children's hearing system normally deals with children on care and protection grounds from birth up to age 15 inclusive and with child offenders from age 8 (the age of criminal responsibility) to 15. However interventions are subject to review and can be extended up to age 18. While decision making should be in the 'best interests' of the child, there is now a caveat that those presenting a risk to self and/or others can be exempt from this principle (McAra 2006).

The majority of 16 and 17-year-olds in Scotland are dealt with in the adult criminal courts. There are no special measures for this age group although any 'young adult' sentenced to custody will serve their sentence in a young offenders' institution (there is one dedicated institution for males and one dedicated house in the main prison for women in Scotland, at Corntonvale). The courts do have the power (little used) to remit such cases back to the children's hearing for advice or disposal (and must remit for advice if the child is still subject to a supervision requirement) (McAra 2006).

Importantly, in spite of its strong welfarist foundations, Scotland too operates a twin-track system. The Crown reserves the right to prosecute the most serious cases in the criminal courts from age 8 onwards. In practice very few such cases are dealt with in this way (around 140 each year and a high proportion of these are remitted back to the hearing system for disposal (McAra 2006)). For children under the age of 12, any prosecution requires the Lord Advocate's[4] express permission.

Conferencing and age-graded court system

The final ideal type places family group conferencing at the heart of the youth justice process and combines this with a family court (for younger children who are either in need of care and protection or who offend) and a specialist youth court (for offenders only in the mid teenage years). This model of justice has been developed in New Zealand (although modified versions of it can be found in other jurisdictions, for example Northern Ireland).

The current system in New Zealand is framed by the Children, Young Persons and their Families Act 1989. A core aim of that Act was to involve families in the youth justice process, and to consider the wishes, and obtain the support, of the child. Criminal proceedings should not be used if alternative measures are possible and thus there is a major emphasis on diversion. Children should be kept in the community as far as possible, there should be parsimony in sanctioning and any intervention should promote juvenile development and have regard for victims (Bradley *et al.* 2006).

Within New Zealand, the age of criminal responsibility is 10 years old. Where a court appearance is necessary (see below), children between the ages of 10 and 13 inclusive are dealt with in the Family Court (which also deals with children in need of care and protection). Those aged between 14 and 17 will be referred to a specialist youth court for offenders only. From age 18 onwards offenders are dealt with in the adult system.

Family group conferencing is integrated into the system at a number of different stages. For example a family group conference can be held at the pre-charge stage and depending on the outcome might result in diversion away from the formal system. A conference can also be held at the pre-sentence stage (in cases where the child accepts guilt), and the youth court will then determine whether any action plan developed via the conference constitutes a sufficient sanction. Plans arising from conferences might include apology, some form of reparation, unpaid work of benefit to the community and/or participation in a counselling programme. Youngsters who deny the charges will be dealt with in court (according to an adversarial process).

As with other jurisdictions, New Zealand also operates a bifurcated system. The most severe sanction available to the family and youth courts is to record a conviction and transfer the case to the District or High Court for sentence. For such cases the full range of adult sentences is available. For youngsters up to the age of 15 any custodial term will be spent in a youth justice residence. However, from age 15 onwards, youngsters will serve a custodial sentence in an adult prison. Special wings are available for those under the age of 17. Importantly there are no specialist wings available for girls, so they always have to mix with adult female prisoners.

Assessing the architecture

What are the benefits of these variant models? What are their pitfalls? Limitations of space mean that it is not possible to give a detailed assessment of each individual model; instead some key points of controversy will be highlighted as related to various dimensions of the architecture itself and the impact on young people.

Age of entry and exit

As indicated in Table 9.2, there are major variations in the models in respect of the age at which young people enter and exit the youth justice system and variations with regard to the age of criminal responsibility (which is not always coterminous with the age of entry into the youth justice domain, as for example in Belgium).[5] While international conventions are clear in respect of the 'limits' of childhood (namely age 18, as per the UN Convention on the Rights of Child), they are typically fudged in respect of lower limits with regard to the age of criminal responsibility. Thus article 4(1) of the Beijing Rules states:

> In those legal systems recognizing the concept of the age of criminal responsibility for juveniles, the beginning of that age shall not be fixed at too low an age level, bearing in mind the facts of emotional, mental and intellectual maturity.

However, the commentary on the rules also states there is likely to be some relationship between responsibility for behaviour and other 'social rights and responsibilities' such as the age at which matrimony is permitted.

A common trend within jurisdictions, cross-nationally, is for the age of criminal responsibility to rise over time (Hazell 2008) and this is almost certainly linked to shifting perceptions of childhood. In the nineteenth century, separate institutions for dealing with young offenders often emerged in a piecemeal fashion as childhood gradually began to be consolidated as a separate phase requiring special protection (Aries 1973; Smelser 1959).[6] Over the course of the twentieth century childhood itself became more stretched and there was a corresponding extension in the period during which the transition to adulthood occurred (see Chapter 2).

A key exception to the common trend (of a rising age of criminal responsibility) has been the UK. Age 10 was set as the age of criminal responsibility in England/Wales[7] in 1963 (a rise from age 8) and in Scotland[8] age 8 was established as far back as 1937. The low age is somewhat out of kilter with the broader historical and cultural shifts in respect of childhood just described. In many spheres of life children and young people are treated as immature, dependent and in need of nurturing and support and yet at the same time, they are required to be responsible for their criminal behaviour (and can be dealt with via the same institutional processes as adults). Importantly, research evidence confirms that the most serious and persistent child offenders are amongst the most vulnerable young people across the UK. Such children are the least supported and least nurtured of all youngsters. They suffer disproportionately high levels of victimization and are faced with a high intensity of social adversity (including poverty, family crises and school exclusion or drop-out) (see Smith and Ecob 2007; McAra and McVie 2010). Indeed, the very youngsters who are assumed to have the capacity to take responsibility for their behaviour are precisely those who have the least capacity to do so.

Participation

International conventions place a high value on the participation of young people in formal processes – not only is there a requirement that youngsters in conflict with the law fully understand procedures, but the voice of the child must be heard in such procedures (article 12(2) of the UN Convention on the Rights of the Child; and rule 14(2) of the Beijing Rules).

While much of the architecture, described above, functions primarily as a means of 'processing' child offenders (in other words it is a means of determining which particular measures should be applied), it is important not to underestimate the impact which such processing has on the youngsters who come within its purview. Each stage in decision-making can be viewed as a form of 'intervention' in its own right. Youngsters' perceptions as to whether they are being fairly or unfairly treated, and the extent to which their voice is heard, are likely to shape their views on the legitimacy of measures which are subsequently applied. This in turn may have longer-term consequences in terms of compliance (see Jones 2006; Bottoms 2001).

The mode and extent of participation will of course be shaped by the very architecture of the system itself. Adversarial court processes limit the child's voice to evidential concerns. Feelings, attitudes and beliefs are secondary to the demands of case construction. The child becomes an object to be interrogated, his or her participation is thereby confined to an elucidation of the facts of the case.

Within more inquisitorial systems, the principal decision-makers are more closely involved in the investigatory phase. While the trial itself is aimed at uncovering truth (and thereby determining guilt or innocence), the court has prior knowledge of the broader context of the alleged offending behaviour. An inquisitorial model thereby allows for greater interaction between the judge and the accused than is possible in an adversarial process. As research on therapeutic jurisprudence has shown, the greater the interaction between the agents of justice and the offender, the more positive the impact on subsequent behaviour (McIvor 2009).

Other models of youth justice have the potential to be more participatory than court-based systems. An explicit aim of the tribunal model, set out above, is to be inclusive and consensual. The tribunal is intended to allow discussion about the context of offending, with involvement of both the child and his or her caregivers alongside the lay panel and other relevant experts. In practice, however, such tribunals are not as participatory as might be claimed or as might be desirable. Hallet *et al.* (1998), for example, found that in the Scottish children's hearing system, children and their parents often felt inhibited and that proceedings were dominated by social work.

Family group conferences (FGCs) provide a different model of participation. While adherents of conferencing hold an almost evangelical view of its benefits, some evaluations in the context of New Zealand suggest that large numbers of victims do not attend and where they do attend, often do not feel that they have been involved in the decision-making process (Maxwell 2004). As Bradley *et al.* note 'the emphasis on the informal aspects of the FGC process tend to ignore the reality of who is in charge of the principal mechanisms of the system, namely the police, youth justice coordinators, and social workers . . .' (2006: 91). Again, as with Scotland, there have been concerns as to whether professionals dominate the system.

Due process and parsimony

Core benefits claimed for the court-based models of youth justice are the procedural guarantees that are generally offered (in respect of due process and respect for the rights of the accused) and the use of fixed-term sentences (see Hazell 2008). But do such models necessarily offer better procedural safeguards in practice than more informal modes of justice?

Research on the system in England has consistently highlighted ways in which working practices of agencies and individuals colonizing the system (including the judiciary) undermine procedural safeguards, as highlighted in the monitoring reports of the United Nations Committee on the Rights of the Child (see Muncie 2008 for an overview) and in more recent research by May *et al.* (2010) on the ways in which ethnic minority groups have suffered discriminatory treatment. Moreover the vagaries of case construction and the quality of lawyers on offer may not always work to protect the rights of the accused and have been the subject of much debate (see Morris 2002).

In jurisdictions which involve alternative, more informal processes to criminal courts, critics claim that there can be pressures to admit to offences and that sometimes the evidence is not adequately tested. There are also concerns about net-widening (that informal measures may bring a wider range of youngsters under the tutelage of agencies, youngsters who might have been diverted away under more formal arrangements). Research evidence is somewhat thin on the ground as regards these claims. In respect of net-widening, Maxwell and Morris (1993) found no evidence of this in their research on family group conferencing in New Zealand. Indeed they found that compared with matched controls within the courts, the youngsters received less incursive penalties.

A further criticism of non-court models is their capacity to institute long-term (sometimes indeterminate) intervention, disproportionate to the seriousness of the offence which triggered the intervention in the first place. As was noted, in jurisdictions such as Scotland, supervision requirements can be continued and extended up until the age of criminal majority. However, research has found that this rarely happens in practice. In Scotland, the majority of supervision requirements last for around one year and are generally terminated at age 15 (McAra 2006). As the focus of intervention in many non-court models of justice is the needs of the child, then longer-term and more intensive modes of intervention may well be warranted.

Importantly, the use of fixed-term sentences in court-based models does not necessarily result in greater parsimony. Arguably the revolving door of repeat short sentences of detention (evident in jurisdictions such as England, see Goldson 2002) means that, contra the principle of parsimony, many young offenders are effectively serving a life sentence by instalments (McAra and McVie 2010).

Building community solidarity and meeting the needs of society

A number of the quasi-ideal models involve the community in the justice process (via the lay panel or conferencing). Does community involvement meet the needs of society and help strengthen social bonds in ways which court-based models cannot?

The notion of community that abounds in much youth (and adult) justice policy cross-nationally is generally regarded as an unqualified good. However, as a concept, it is often ill-defined and used in somewhat conflicting ways (community being conceived simultaneously as a mode, site and effect of governance). In practice, communities defined by geographical space are often highly fragmented and diverse, bundled together by accident of location. Communities defined by some form of identity/emotional attachment may transcend local boundaries – but these are often riven with internal factions, and problems remain in respect of which groups or individuals constitute their legitimate representatives (Hughes 2004). Unsurprisingly then, research on lay involvement in youth justice has generally found that volunteers are not wholly representative of the 'communities' in which they are located. For example, within Scotland, panels have been dominated by the white middle class, particularly in the early years of the children's hearing system and there have been major concerns that panels attempt to inflict middle-class notions of morality on a socially distant client group (McAra 2006).

Restorative justice has been used successfully in post-conflict societies as a mechanism through which to build a more cohesive society through the recognition of victim suffering (as for example in South Africa and Northern Ireland). Its use in jurisdictions such as New Zealand has aimed to install a greater degree of cultural sensitivity and social inclusion into modes of dispute resolution (see Morris 2002). Where such procedures work well, there may be a greater sense of justice by, on and for the community. Indeed the very use of conferencing in this context may serve to empower communities and help cement a sense of collective identity.

Impact of system contact: facilitating desistance from offending

Finally in this section, which model of youth justice best facilitates desistance from offending?

One of the challenges in assessing the variant models is that there is very little research on the impact of youth justice systems, qua systems, on young people and the communities within which they live. Much research on youth crime and justice in a UK context has focused on programme evaluation and/or offers an assessment of the impact of individual elements of the youth justice process. Rather less research has explored the broader and possibly cumulative impact of the youth justice process as a whole (McAra and McVie 2010).

There is, however, a growing body of international comparative research based on data from longitudinal studies, which suggests that contact with any youth justice system (irrespective of its architecture and core values) and experience of more severe forms of sanctioning, in particular, are as likely to result in enhanced as diminished offending risk (see Sherman *et al.* 1998; Klein 1986). Taken to its extremes this research would suggest (in a manner akin to labelling theory) that contact with the youth justice system is inherently criminogenic.

Amongst the most powerful evidence of the negative consequences of system contact is that from a comparative study undertaken by Huizinga *et al.* (2003). Drawing on data from two longitudinal projects (one sited in Bremen, Germany and the other in Denver, USA), the authors found that arrests and sanctions had only a limited impact on offending, resulting for the most part in the maintenance or increase in the previous level of offending (with increases being more likely in the case of the individuals given the most severe sanctions). The similarity in outcomes is particularly striking given the very different ethos of the youth justice system in Germany (more lenient, focused on diversion) from that of Denver (more punitive, propels offenders quickly into court, limited diversion). The authors conclude that it may not be the severity or otherwise of the sanctions on offer which is significant in terms of tackling offending, but rather the 'simple certainty of response' (2003: 5).

The conclusions of this research have found further support in evidence from the Edinburgh Study of Youth Transitions and Crime (McAra and McVie 2007). McAra and McVie (2005, 2007) found that selection effects were operating at three stages of the system (police charging, referral to the reporter and referral to a children's hearing) in a way that ensured that certain categories of young people – 'the usual suspects' – were propelled into a repeat cycle of referral into the children's hearing system, whereas other equally serious offenders escaped the attention of formal agencies altogether. The deeper young people who were identified as the usual suspects penetrated the youth justice system, the more likely it was that their pattern of desistance from involvement in serious offending was *inhibited* (McAra and McVie 2007). The research concludes that one of the keys to tackling serious and persistent offending and facilitating desistance lies in a maximum diversion approach: an approach which is supportive of more informal modes of dispute resolution.

3. Youth justice in context

Youth justice systems have never been solely devoted to reducing youth crime. They also convey a range of complex messages with regard to citizenship, individual autonomy and the boundaries of community morality (as indicated in Part 1 above). This section explores the ways in which both the evolving architecture and core messages of youth justice systems are closely entwined with the social, political and cultural contexts within which they are located. It draws on policy developments in four of the jurisdictions which formed the basis of the ideal typical models presented in Part 2 (England, Scotland, New Zealand and Finland as summarized in Table 9.3) and assesses the implications in respect of reform.

England and Scotland

Over the past 30 years, the youth justice systems in England and Scotland have undergone two major phases of development which are strongly interlinked with the evolving nature of civic culture both north and south of the border.

Two phases of policy development

In phase one (which lasted from the early 1970s until the mid 1990s), there was major divergence between the systems in respect of principles and architecture. In Scotland this phase saw the full flowering of welfare values in youth justice, with the implementation of the children's hearing system in 1971, predicated on the Kilbrandon philosophy.[9] By contrast in England over the 1970s there was a major retreat from welfarist principles, as key provisions of the welfare-orientated Children and Young Persons Act 1969 were not implemented (including mandatory care proceedings for the under-14s instead of prosecution and planned restrictions on magistrates' powers to use custody (Newburn 1997). Indeed the 1970s saw a major *increase* in custody for young offenders in England and a shift in the balance of power within the system away from social work (which had previously been dominant) in favour of the judiciary (Cavadino and Dignan 2007). During the 1980s a more complex set of values began to frame English juvenile justice. On the one hand, the punitive edge continued, in the wake of the election of the Thatcher government, with greater emphasis on the 'short, sharp, shock'. On the other hand, practitioners challenged these values from below, introducing a form of systems management aimed at diverting youngsters out of the system, or minimizing levels of intervention (Newburn 1997). However, systems management was largely abandoned in the early 1990s, with a further lurch towards greater punitiveness. This was given particular impetus with the tragic murder of James Bulger by two 10-year-old boys in 1993; an event which led the then prime minister to declare that society should 'condemn a little more and understand a little less'.

In phase two, from the late 1990s until around 2007, there was a degree of convergence between England and Scotland. This convergence was evident primarily in respect of the evolving principles of youth justice, although some minor architectural modifications were made in Scotland (specifically the pilot youth courts, see below) which drew inspiration from England.

During the second phase, both jurisdictions embraced the lexicon of new public management. As with other areas of public policy, strategic planning, national standards, target setting, efficiency, effectiveness, monitoring and evaluating became key watch words in youth justice. Public protection, risk management and effective, evidence-based practice framed youth justice interventions. There was also a gradual elision between the social exclusion, crime prevention and criminal justice policy frameworks. Rights talk permeated each system, a process given particular momentum by the incorporation of the European Convention on Human Rights into domestic law. Furthermore both systems became equally in thrall to the promises held out by restorative justice (as exemplified by the mushrooming of victim offender mediation schemes, conferencing and police restorative cautioning initiatives), with victims attaining stakeholder status in each jurisdiction. Finally a key policy aim in both jurisdictions was to reduce persistent offending and tackle antisocial behaviour and both jurisdictions legislated to enable the use of civil orders to tackle low-level crime and disorder (antisocial behaviour orders and parenting orders). Youth courts for 16 and 17-year-old offenders were also piloted in Scotland.

Relationship between policy development and civic culture

What then are the links between the two phases and civic culture? During phase one, England experienced what Hall (1979) has termed the 'great moving right show'. Structural pressures linked to late modernity led to a breakdown in the post-war consensus on issues such as welfare, the economy and crime. This resulted in a major political realignment, with skilled working-class voters shifting allegiance from predominantly traditional Labour party politics to new conservatism and a rightwards drift for members of the middle classes who became increasingly disenchanted with high taxes, stop/start economic policy, and the 'undeserving' beneficiaries of the welfare state. Clear blue water emerged between the major political parties within the UK as the Conservative party (elected to office in 1979) abandoned its traditional one-nation, paternalistic ethos, with a firm commitment to neo-liberal economic policy. As a consequence 'authoritarian populism' began to dominate at both a civic and political level, becoming a source of both identity and pride for certain key groups (see Hall *et al.* 1978). In this turbulent context, penal welfare values (which had dominated youth justice up until the 1970s) rapidly lost cultural anchorage.

During phase two, from the late 1990s onwards in England, political polarization initially diminished. The Labour party had undergone a process of modernization, ditching its more radical left-wing elements and shifting to occupy the centre-right ground. The New Labour government of 1997 placed social inclusion, urban regeneration and social justice at the heart of its agenda at the same time as trying to win the support of floating voters with promises of rigorous economic management and being tough on crime. The promises of 1997, however, slowly turned into disillusionment and civic culture within England underwent a process of increased fragmentation. Major schisms arose over issues such as the war in Iraq, asylum seekers and terrorist suspects, immigration and race relations. There were also debates over the nature of English identity and Britishness (Clarke 2008). All of this took place against the backdrop of increased moral panic and popular fears (around crime and disorder, threats posed by religious extremists, food scares, worries about global pandemics etc.). This context paved the way for a more complex and contradictory penal framework to gain anchorage within England; one in which inclusionary imperatives (linked to restoration, prevention and rehabilitation) jostled with more exclusionary and punitive imperatives, with the latter once more increasingly trumping the former (see Muncie and Goldson 2006; Moore 2008).

Table 9.3 Key developments in youth justice

	England	Scotland	New Zealand	Finland
1970s	*Environment* • Macro-economic and social transformation • Increased political polarization • Civic culture rightwards movement	*Environment* • Macro-economic and social transformation • Increased political tension (constitutional crisis) • Civic culture welfarist, Scottish identity as 'other-to-England'	*Environment* • Political cohesion, State as extension of family, open and transparent • Civic culture, 'Better Britain'	*Environment* • Political cohesion • Civic culture, egalitarian, welfarist
	→			
1980s	*Internal culture* • Policy networks increased fragmentation (power struggle) • Punitive (top down and wins through) • Systems management plus residual welfarism (bottom up and loses out)	*Internal culture* • Policy networks strong coherence • Penal-welfare values →	*Internal culture* • Policy networks strong coherence • Penal-welfare values → *Environment* • Macro-economic and social transformation, economic crisis, emigration and deregulation • Civic culture, conflicted values, heterogeneity	*Internal culture* • Policy networks strong coherence • welfarist plus 'humane neo-classicism' →
	→			

1990s

Environment
- Exponential growth in trans/supra-national institutional forms and pressures
- Full impact of globalization
- Cosmopolitanism
- 9/11; 7/7

- Diminished political polarization (the third way?)
- Civic culture (attempts to remobilize communities and embrace multi-culturalism: increased schisms?)
- The 'politics of fear'

Internal culture
- Policy networks: increased coherence?
- Hyper-institutionalization
- Punitive, managerialist, restorative, preventative, rehabilitative

→

2000s

Environment
- Exponential growth in trans/supra-national institutional forms and pressures
- Full impact of globalization
- Cosmopolitanism
- 9/11, 7/7

- Resolution of constitutional crisis (the devolved settlement)
- Civic culture (drift?)
- Political capacity building in context of devolution
- The 'politics of fear'

Internal culture
- Policy networks increased fragmentation and struggles for power
- Hyper-institutionalization
- Punitive, managerialist, restorative and preventative
- Penal-welfare values losing out

Internal culture
- Policy networks increased, fragmentation
- Punitive, managerialist, restorative

Turning to Scotland, one of the reasons why the youth justice system was able to sustain a commitment to welfarism from the 1970s until the mid 1990s (during phase one) was because of the distinctive nature of Scottish civic and political culture (with its greater emphasis on communitarian values, public provision of welfare and mutual support) (see Paterson 1994; McAra 2005). This culture provided a conceptual locus within which penal welfare values could thrive, in the context of an increasingly contested political arena (with a major disjuncture emerging between identity politics in Scotland and the increasingly strident right-wing ideologies of the Thatcher and Major governments at Westminster).

In the period after devolution (late 1990s and 2000s), youth justice institutions found it increasingly difficult to achieve such cultural anchorage. Arguably civic culture in Scotland went into a period of drift. Politics became far less polarized and there was greater ideological congruence between the Labour/Liberal democratic coalition governments in Scotland and the Blairite New Labour government at Westminster. This served to weaken a sense of political identity in Scotland based on 'other-to-England', with a concomitant weakening of the purchase of welfarism as a principal framework around which debates on youth justice took place. A 'conceptual space' opened up for other, more visceral, penal discourses to leach in during phase two, as ministers increasingly looked south of the border for inspiration.

New Zealand and Finland

The strong inter-relationship between youth justice and civic culture is also evident within both New Zealand and Finland.

(i) Two phases of youth justice in New Zealand

As with England and Scotland, developments in youth justice in New Zealand between the 1970s and 2000s fall into two major phases (although the timing of these phases was slightly different).

During the 1970s, welfare values dominated youth justice as exemplified by arrangements introduced by the Children and Young Persons Act 1974. The Act stated that the best interests of the child should be the paramount consideration in decision-making; it formalized diversion arrangements for child offenders and instituted separate proceedings for child (under-14s) and juvenile offenders (14–17-year-olds) (Bradley et al. 2006).

Over this time frame, there was a high level of political and civic cohesion in New Zealand, based around the concept of 'Better Britain'.[10] Pratt (2006) in particular, has highlighted the way in which New Zealand characterized itself as a country of 'joiners', with a mushrooming of intermediate institutions in the public sphere, providing a focal point for community solidarity.

However, in the 1980s there was a massive transformation in civic and political culture fuelled by economic crisis (government debt spiralled over this period and there was increased emigration of young people) and the subsequent importation of neo-liberal policies (instituted, somewhat ironically, by a Labour government and reinforced by national [centre-right] governments). As Pratt (2006) notes, New Zealand went from a highly-regulated society to a deregulated one almost overnight. One of the fallouts from these transformations was that society become more heterogeneous and pluralist, accompanied by increasingly vocal claims of the Maori first peoples for equality (Pratt and Clark 2005).

Pratt (2006) has written of the paradoxes of New Zealand culture: that even in days of 'Better Britain', there was a dark side to culture – with inclusiveness for some being sustained at the cost of excluding others. Similarly, after the economic crisis of the 1980s he writes about the conflicted nature of New Zealand society which valorized at one and the same time greater choice but also desired conformity; valorized indulgence and also frugality; and pushed for a meritocracy in the context of older egalitarian values. The fragmentation of older civic values and the range of competing imperatives which framed New Zealand's evolving sense of cultural identity both undergirded and gave impetus to a more conflicted youth justice agenda.

Major change in youth justice came initially with the implementation of the Children, Young Persons and their Families Act 1989 (described in Part 2 above) which introduced family group conferencing into the youth justice process. However, there was also a punitive turn in political and policy rhetoric, with a new political consensus emerging over the turn of the century around a tough law and order agenda. This was exemplified by a series of populist movements lobbying for harsher sentences (as for example the Sensible Sentencing Trust) and campaigns (especially amongst the centre–right parties) to lower the age of criminal responsibility and to restore shame as a central element in juvenile justice (Pratt and Clark 2005; Bradley et al. 2006).

Cultural and penal stability in Finland

In contrast to the other jurisdictions under review, the Finnish youth justice system has exhibited rather less volatility over the past 30 years.

The institutional infrastructure described in Part 2 above was introduced over the course of the 1930s and 1940s in Finland. Welfarism has thus traditionally framed interventions for the under-15s and, more recently, a form of what Lappi-Seppälä (2006) has termed 'neo-classical humanitarianism' has framed interventions for the 15–20-year-old age group. Importantly, reforms made to the system in the 1970s were aimed primarily at decarceration (attempting to reduce imprisonment rates for the over-15s and transforming the nature of residential care for the under-15s) and tackling concerns about involuntary institutional treatment, rather than fundamentally altering its core precepts.

Social democratic and egalitarian values have been a core characteristic of Finnish society, in which, traditionally, there has been limited class differentiation. Finnish society has thus been marked by its cohesiveness and lack of political polarization. While there has been a strong tradition of local (self) governance (contributing to community solidarity), at the same time the populace has generally taken a positive view of the state, as the benign provider of services and support. Education is particularly valorized as is the role of experts in youth justice (see Pratt 2008; Lappi-Seppälä 2006). This cultural backdrop has provided a context in which welfare and more humanitarian values could thrive: the relative stability of civic culture providing anchorage for a sustained commitment to child well-being.

Implications for policy reform

The relationship between youth justice and its immediate 'environment' has important implications regarding the capacity of systems to reform. The examples set out above indicate that welfarist policies are more sustainable in jurisdictions where there is social cohesion and where civic culture is stable and framed by a strong sense of communitarian and/or social democratic values (as for example in Scotland up until the late 1990s and in Finland over a much longer term). By contrast, more punitive and conflicted rhetoric emerges in the context of social and political turbulence. Such rhetoric is fed by, and in turn feeds upon, the increased anxieties and insecurities produced by rapid social, political and economic change (as occurred in England from the 1970s onwards and in New Zealand from the 1980s onwards).

The examples also suggest that particular policy narratives make sense under very specific conditions: thus within New Zealand, family group conferencing gained its justification as a means of reconstructing a 'lost' sense of civic and cultural identity in the course of the late 1980s and early 1990s; within England a punitive rhetoric gained enhanced legitimacy in the aftermath of the murder of James Bulger in the early–mid 1990s.

Taken together the developments in each of the jurisdictions suggest that the capacity of governments (or, indeed, individuals or agencies) to effect youth justice reform is likely to be constrained by the broader cultural context within which the particular system is located. Changes made to the principles or architecture of youth justice require to be protected from any broader cultural imperatives which may conspire to undermine their effectiveness. This in turn requires reformers to look beyond the youth justice system and take cognisance of the facilitators and inhibitors of transformation within the cultural environment itself.

Conclusion: crystallizing the policy options

A central tension which besets extant systems of youth justice is the requirement to meet the needs of the troubled and vulnerable young offender at the same time as meeting the needs of society. The aim of any reform, first and foremost, should be to reconcile such tensions.

As indicated in Part 2, research tells us that compliance is facilitated where young offenders perceive decision-making to be legitimate, and this, in turn, is facilitated by structures which enhance their participation. Research also tells us that diversion from formal measures impacts positively on offending. The same research highlights the vulnerabilities and social adversities which beset the lives of serious and persistent young offenders, indicating that broader social and educational measures have an important role to play in the reduction of youth crime (as much, if not more so, than the formal youth justice system itself).

Reducing youth crime and dealing promptly with its manifestations will do much both to protect the public and meet the needs of victims in the short and long term. In respect of the principles and architecture of youth justice such ambition, arguably, will be best effected by paradigms which emphasize the need to build positive connections between the child, their family and the community (such as the welfarist or restorative paradigms) and by a model of justice which draws offenders and their parents/caregivers into discussion and dialogue. The latter suggests that more informal, non-judicial modes of case processing will be particularly helpful (as for example the lay-tribunal or conferencing models).

Efforts at policy reform never begin with a *tabula rasa*. The capacity for transformation will always be constrained, to a lesser or greater extent, by the broader social, cultural and political environment within which a system is located. In the context of the UK and specifically England, this environment has facilitated the emergence of a conflicted policy framework: some elements are underpinned by a desire to promote social inclusion, to reintegrate and to enhance citizenship (as exemplified by much of the community safety agenda); other elements, by contrast, are aimed at exclusion, dispersal and punishment (as exemplified by core aspects of the antisocial behaviour agenda). Importantly, as noted in Part 1, each of the inclusionary and exclusionary imperatives has functioned to legitimize the other. Reform will be crucially dependent on challenging and uncoupling this co-dependency, allowing more inclusionary dynamics to flourish without the backstop of punitiveness. In the context of the insecurities and anxieties associated with late modernity, this will require a bolder vision on the part of the reformer: a vision which makes public education a key priority; a vision which recognizes that community solidarity (however difficult to achieve) has an important role to play in empowering families and generating trust; and a vision which rises above the political pragmatism so evident in contemporary youth justice policy, and engages once more in normative debate about our duties towards the most vulnerable and needy.

Notes

1 Within this chapter reference is made to England rather than England *and Wales* in recognition of the degree of divergence which has occurred between the jurisdictions in respect of policy over the course of the 2000s (see McAra 2005).

2 Under social contract theory, individuals give up some of their freedom so that the state can enforce laws in the interests of the common good. The state in return must protect the common good and not interfere with the rights and liberties of the individual. The lives of citizens are consequently regulated by the 'rule of law' and the state gains legitimacy through its capacity to guarantee security and safety for its citizens within its territorial boundaries (see Vold *et al.* 2002 for an overview).

3 *T.* v *UK ECHR*, application no. 24724/94; *V.* v. *UK ECHR*, application no. 24888/94 16 December 1999.

4 The Lord Advocate is the head of the Scottish Prosecution Service.

5 Indeed the variation in these quasi-ideal models is also mirrored worldwide, where the age of criminal responsibility ranges from as low as 6 in Mexico to 18 in Belgium, and the age of criminal majority from age 12 in Singapore to age 25 in China (Hazel 2008).

6 Aires contends that during the middle ages as soon as children reached about age 7 (shortly after they were fully weaned from their mothers) they were treated as adults. From the seventeenth century onward the period of childhood gradually extended and was increasingly separated from adulthood (see Aries 1973).

7 Change was enabled by the Children and Young Persons Act 1963.

8 Change was established by the Children and Young Persons (Scotland) Act 1937.

9 The Kilbrandon philosophy was named after the chair of the committee set up in the 1960s to review the extant Scottish juvenile justice system. The recommendations of the committee formed the basis of the Social Work (Scotland) Act 1968 which, in turn, set in train the children's hearing system. According to the Kilbrandon philosophy, deeds are symptomatic of problems in the normal up-bringing process or broader social malaise, interventions should be based on a social educational model of care, with best interests to be paramount in decision-making (McAra 2006).

10 The concept of 'Better Britain' signifies New Zealand's claim to have warmer weather and to be a friendlier and more open society (see Pratt 2006 for further discussion).

References

Aries, P. (1973) *Centuries of Childhood* (Harmondsworth: Penguin).

Beccaria, C. (1963), *On Crimes and Punishments*, translated, with an introduction, by H. Paolucci (Indianapolis: Bobbs-Merrill).

Bentham, J. (1973) *An Introduction to the Principles of Morals and Legislation* (New York: Hafner Press). First published in 1780.

Bottoms, A (2001) 'Compliance and Community Penalties', in A. Bottoms, L. Gelsthorpe, and S. Rex (eds) *Community Penalties: Change and Challenges* (Cullompton: Willan Publishing), pp. 87–116.

Bradley, T., Tauri, J. and Walters, R. (2006), 'Demythologising Youth Justice in Aotearoa/New Zealand', in J. Muncie and B. Goldson (eds) *Comparative Youth Justice* (London: Sage), pp. 79–95.

Cavadino, M. and Dignan, J. (2007) *The Penal System: An Introduction*, 4th edition, (London: Sage).

Christiaens, J. and Nuytiens, A. (2009) 'Transfer of Juvenile Offenders to the Adult Court in Belgium: Critical Reflections on the Reform of a Moderate Practice', *Youth Justice*, 9: 2, pp. 131–42.

Clarke, J. (2008) 'Still Policing the Crisis?', *Crime, Media, Culture*, 4:1, pp. 123–9.

Crawford, A. and Newburn, T. (eds) (2003). *Youth Offending and Restorative Justice: Implementing Reform in Youth Justice* (Cullompton: Willan Publishing).

Goldson, B. (2002) 'New Punitiveness: The Politics of Child Incarceration' in J. Muncie, G. Hughes and E. McLaughlin (eds) *Youth Justice: Critical Readings* (London: Sage), pp. 386–400.

Hall, S. (1979) 'The Great Moving Right Show', *Marxism Today*, 23, pp. 14–20.

Hall, S., Clarke, J., Critcher, C., Jefferson, T. and Roberts, B. (1978) *Policing the Crisis: Mugging, the State and Law and Order* (London: Macmillan).

Hallet, C., Murray, C., Jamieson, J. and Veitch, B. (1998) *The Evaluation of the Children's Hearings in Scotland, Volume 1 'Deciding in Children's Interests'* (Edinburgh: The Scottish Office Central Research Unit).

Hazell, N. (2008) *Cross-national Comparison of Youth Justice* (London: Youth Justice Board).

Hughes, G. (2004) 'Straddling Adaptation and Denial: Crime and Disorder Reduction Partnerships in England and Wales', *Cambrian Law Review*, 25, pp. 1–23.

Huizinga, D., Schumann, K., Ehret, B. and Elliot, A. (2003) *The Effects of Juvenile Justice Processing on Subsequent Delinquent and Criminal Behaviour: A Cross-National Study* (Washington: final report to the National Institute of Justice).

Jones, R. (2006) 'Architecture, Criminal Justice and Control', in S. Armstrong and L. McAra (eds) *Perspectives on Punishment: The Contours of Control* (Oxford: Oxford University Press), pp. 175–96.

Klein, M. (1986) 'Labelling Theory and Delinquency Policy – An Empirical Test', *Criminal Justice and Behaviour*, 13, pp. 47–79.

Lappi-Seppälä, T. (2006) 'Finland: A Model of Tolerance?', in J. Muncie and B. Goldson (eds) *Comparative Youth Justice* (London: Sage), pp. 177–95.

Maxwell, G. (2004) 'Youth Justice: A Research Perspective', *Social Work Now*, 28: August, pp 4–10.

Maxwell, G. and Morris, A. (1993) *Families, Justice and Culture: Youth Justice in New Zealand* (Wellington, New Zealand: Social Policy Agency and Institute of Criminology).

May, T., Gyateng, T. and Hough, M. (2010) *Differential Treatment in the Youth Justice System: Equality and Human Rights Commission Research Report 50* (London: Institute for Criminal Policy Research, King's College London).

McAra, L., (2005) 'Modelling Penal Transformation', *Punishment and Society*, 7:3, pp. 277–302.

McAra, L. (2006) 'Welfare in Crisis? Youth Justice in Scotland', in J. Muncie and B. Goldson (eds) *Comparative Youth Justice* (London: Sage), pp. 127–45.

McAra, L. and McVie, S. (2010) 'Youth Crime and Justice: Key Messages from the Edinburgh Study of Youth Transitions and Crime', *Criminology and Criminal Justice* 10: 3, pp. 179–209.

McAra, L. and McVie, S. (2007) 'Youth Justice? The Impact of Agency Contact on Desistance from Offending', *European Journal of Criminology*, 4: 3, pp. 315–45.

McAra, L. and McVie, S. (2005) 'The Usual Suspects? Street-life, Young Offenders and the Police', *Criminal Justice*, 5:1, pp. 5–35.

McIvor, G. (2009) 'Therapeutic Jurisprudence and Procedural Justice in Scottish Drug Courts', *Criminology and Criminal Justice*, 9:1 pp. 29–49.

Moore, S. (2008) 'Neighbourhood Policing and the Punitive Community', *Crime Prevention and Community Safety*, 10, pp. 190–202.

Morris, A. (2002) 'Critiquing the Critics: A Brief Response to Critics of Restorative Justice', *British Journal of Criminology*, 42: 3, pp. 596–615.

Muncie, J. (2008) 'The Punitive Turn in Juvenile Justice: Cultures of Control and Rights Compliance in Western Europe and the USA', *Youth Justice*, 8:2, pp. 107–21.

Muncie, J. and Goldson, B. (2006) 'England and Wales: the New Correctionalism', in J. Muncie and B. Goldson (eds) *Comparative Youth Justice* (London: Sage), pp. 34–47.

Newburn, T. (1997) 'Youth, Crime and Justice', in M. Maguire, R. Morgan and R. Reiner (eds) *The Oxford Handbook of Criminology*, 2nd edition (Oxford: Clarendon), pp. 613–60.

Paterson, L. (1994) *The Autonomy of Modern Scotland* (Edinburgh: Edinburgh University Press).

Pratt, J. (2006) 'The Dark Side of Paradise: Explaining New Zealand's History of High Imprisonment', *British Journal of Criminology*, 46: 4, pp. 541–60.

Pratt, J. (2008) 'Scandinavian Exceptionalism in an Era of Penal Excess', *British Journal of Criminology*, 48:2, pp. 119–37.

Pratt, J. and Clark, M. (2005) 'Penal Populism in New Zealand', *Punishment and Society*, 7:3, pp. 303–22.

Put, J. and Walgrave, L.(2006) 'Belgium: From Protection towards Accountability', in J. Muncie and B. Goldson (eds) *Comparative Youth Justice* (London: Sage), pp. 111–26.

Sherman, L.W., Gottfredson, D.C., Mackenzie, D., Ecj, J., Reuter, P. and Bushway, S.D (1998) *Preventing Crime: What Works, What Doesn't, What's Promising, Research Brief, National Institute of Justice* (Washington D.C.: US Department of Justice, Office of Justice Programmes).

Smelser, N. (1959) *Social Change in the Industrial Revolution* (London: Routledge and Kegan Paul).

Smith, D.J. and Ecob, R. (2007) 'An Investigation into Causal Links between Victimization and Offending in Adolescents', *British Journal of Sociology*, 58:4, pp. 633–59.

Vanneste, C., Amrani, L., Mintet, J. and Neyt, N. (2001), *Les Décisions Prises par les Magistrats du Parquet et les Juges de la Jeunesse à l'Égard des Mineurs Délinquants* (Brussels: Institut National de Criminalistique et de Criminologie).

Vold, G., Bernard, T. and Snipes, J. (2002) *Theoretical Criminology* (Oxford: Oxford University Press).

Walgrave, L. (2004) 'Restoration in Youth Justice', in M. Tonry and A. Doob (eds) *Youth Crime and Youth Justice* (Chicago: University of Chicago Press), pp. 543–98.

Winterdyk, J. (2002) 'Introduction', *Juvenile Justice Systems: International Perspectives*, 2nd edition (Toronto, Canada: Canadian Scholars' Press), pp. xi–xl.

Zehr, H. and Mika, H. (1998) 'Fundamental Concepts of Restorative Justice', *Contemporary Justice Review*, 1, pp. 47–55.

Chapter 10

Youth justice reform in Canada: reducing use of courts and custody without increasing youth crime[*]

Nicholas Bala, Peter J. Carrington and Julian V. Roberts

Until the early 1990s, youth offending was a largely 'non-partisan issue' in Canada. The Young Offenders Act (YOA),[1] which came into force in 1984, was passed with the unanimous consent of parliament. However, while the reported youth crime rate peaked in the early 1990s, since then controversy over the appropriate responses to youth offending has markedly increased in Canada.

The YOA marked a significant departure from the informal, welfare-oriented approach of the earlier Juvenile Delinquents Act[2] which had been in effect since 1908; the YOA placed greater emphasis on accountability of youth and as well as on their legal rights, and established a uniform national age jurisdiction for youth court of 12 through to the 18th birthday. While conservative politicians criticized the YOA for being 'soft on youth crime,' there were also concerns that under the YOA use of courts and custody rose, and by the early years of the millennium Canada had one of the lowest rates of youth diversion and highest rates of youth custody in the world.[3] In response to these very different concerns, the then Liberal government enacted the Youth Criminal Justice Act (YCJA),[4]

[*] This chapter draws heavily on: Bala, Carrington and Roberts, 'Evaluating the Youth Criminal Justice Act after five years – a qualified success' (April 2009) 51(2) *Canadian Journal of Criminology and Criminal Justice* 131–168. The authors wish to acknowledge that the statistics reported here are derived from public-use datasets distributed by Statistics Canada. We acknowledge the assistance with access to data provided by Donna Calverley, Rebecca Kong, and Anthony Matarazzo of the Canadian Centre for Justice Statistics. The opinions expressed here are those of the authors and do not represent the views of Statistics Canada.

which came into force in 2003. The YCJA was a political compromise, attempting to address continuing public anxiety about a relatively small number of highly publicized cases involving the most violent youth offenders, while also responding to the growing concerns of juvenile justice professionals, advocates for youth, and academic critics about the large numbers of less serious adolescent offenders being processed through the courts and committed to custody. The YCJA has resulted in significant decreases in the use of youth courts and youth custody in Canada, without any corresponding increase in rates of reported youth crime. However, the Supreme Court of Canada has ruled unconstitutional one of the most significant provisions directed at the most serious offenders, one that created 'presumptive offences' for which there was an onus on a youth to justify why an adult sentence should not be imposed.

This chapter provides a brief summary of the principal provisions of the YCJA and reviews data on the first five years of implementation of the statute. The major focus is on diversion from court, the use of custody and youth crime trends. It should be noted, however, that the YCJA has extensive provisions to protect the legal rights of youth (including ensuring that young persons have access to legal counsel), to protect the privacy of youth and prohibit publication of identifying information, and to encourage parental involvement in the youth court process (although parents cannot be held accountable under the Act for offences committed by their children).[5]

As an important introductory point, the responsibility for enacting criminal laws in Canada, including the YCJA, rests with the federal government. However, the provinces and territories are responsible for, and assume the expenses of provision of services for young offenders, including police, probation, legal services for youth, and prosecution, community and correctional services. Since the YCJA came into force, the rate of custody use has dropped quite significantly, and a number of youth custody facilities in Canada have been closed. This has saved provincial governments a considerable amount of spending on custody, some of which has been redirected to community-based programmes for youth.

Reducing use of courts and custody

The YOA provided relatively little direction to police and prosecutors about when to divert cases from the courts, and gave much discretion to judges in sentencing youth. This lack of direction contributed to wide variations in the application of Act, and to a gradual increase in the rates of use of courts and custody during the 1990s as political pressures to respond to youth crime increased. The YCJA, while a complex statute, provides much more structure for the exercise of discretion by police,

319

prosecutors and judges, and articulates clearer principles about the importance of using community-based responses to youth crime.

Preamble and principles

The preamble to the YCJA makes clear the intent of parliament that Canada should 'have a youth criminal justice system that reserves its most serious interventions for the most serious cases and reduces the over-reliance on incarceration for non-violent young persons'. The Act also has a 'Declaration of Principle' (s. 3) which affirms that the criminal justice system for youths 'must be separate from that of adults'. The Declaration establishes the overall purpose of Canada's youth justice system, with s. 3(1)(a) stating that:

> the youth criminal justice system is intended to
> (i) prevent crime by addressing the circumstances underlying a young person's offending behaviour,
> (ii) rehabilitate young persons who commit offences and reintegrate them into society, and
> (iii) ensure that a young person is subject to meaningful consequences for his or her offence, in order to promote the long-term protection of the public.

Thus rehabilitation is as important as preventing crime and imposing meaningful consequences on young offenders. Further, the *long-term protection* of the public is seen as the *consequence* of rehabilitation and accountability, rather than as an independent objective of the youth justice system. This statement directs judges to impose sentences that facilitate the rehabilitation of young offenders, rather than custodial sentences that will merely punish or incapacitate them.

The Declaration of Principle of the YCJA articulates a set of principles for responding to youthful offenders that places the greatest emphasis on the proportionality of the response, with s.3(1)(c) emphasizing that 'fair and proportionate' accountability is *the* central principle for responding to youth offending. The Principles recognize, however, that youth should have limited accountability in comparison to adults, 'consistent with the greater dependency of young persons and their reduced level of maturity'. Judicial concerns about heightened vulnerability and limited accountability of adolescents are illustrated by the Supreme Court's 2008 decision in *R vs D.B.*[6] which held unconstitutional provisions of the YCJA that create a presumption of adult sentencing for the most serious offences; that decision is more fully discussed below.

Diversion from youth court by extrajudicial measures

The YCJA encourages the diversion of cases from youth court, providing for both 'extrajudicial measures' and 'extrajudicial sanctions'. 'Extrajudicial sanctions' are non-court community-based programmes through which police and Crown prosecutors may refer apprehended youth instead of charging them; these programmes may involve family group conferencing with victim and offender, direct restitution or community service, or may require a youth to attend counselling. Youth sent to these programmes must accept responsibility for their acts, but do not receive a youth court record for their participation, although if they reoffend, their prior participation in extrajudicial sanctions may be a factor in how they are subsequently dealt with. The concept of 'extrajudicial measures' includes formal programmes of extrajudicial sanctions, as well as oral warnings or written cautions issued by the police, or having the police officer 'take no further measures' other than discussing the situation with the youth and perhaps the parents.

The Act clearly is intended to reduce the number of youths appearing in youth court, particularly first-time offenders and juveniles accused of minor offences, providing that a police officer apprehending a youth believed to have committed an offence 'shall' consider whether to invoke an extrajudicial measure rather than commencing judicial proceedings (s.6). The Act affirms the importance of diversion, recognizing in s. 4(a) that: 'extrajudicial measures are often the most appropriate and effective way to address youth crime'. The Act also specifies that extrajudicial measures may be used more than once for a youthful offender (s. 4(d)). Although there is no reliable data on the use of extrajudicial measures for a second time with a youthful offender, it is apparent that there is considerable variation in police practice in this regard. Many officers and prosecutors will only give a youth 'one chance' with diversion. A recent survey of police and other justice system professionals suggests that police in Quebec have the greatest willingness to use extrajudicial measures on two or more occasions with a single youth (DeGusti *et al.* 2009); the relatively low police charging rate in that province also suggests that there is a greater willingness to make repeated use of extrajudicial measures in Quebec, and reserve the youth court process for the most serious or frequent offenders. Quebec has long had the most child welfare-oriented approach to youth justice in Canada, and has the closest links between its child welfare and youth justice systems.

The YCJA encourages police and prosecutors to make greater use of diversionary programmes, but it also makes it clear that the decision of police and prosecutors to lay charges and send a matter to youth court rather than divert a case is not subject to judicial review (ss.3(1)(d)(i) and 6(2)). Although a judge may informally signal that a case should be diverted, or may impose the very mild sentence of a reprimand for a case that should have been diverted, the success of the diversionary provisions of the YCJA is dependent on the attitudes and policies of police and prosecutors, as well as the availability of community-based alternatives to youth court. While there is substantial variation across Canada in provincial policies and in local community programmes, extrajudicial sanctions programmes have been established throughout the country, and in many places these programmes have a restorative justice philosophy and may deal with minor violent offences – for example, by victim-offender reconciliation meetings that may result in an apology to the victim, restitution, and perhaps counselling for the offender (Bala 2003b). The introduction of the YCJA was accompanied by transitional federal government funding to encourage the provinces (which are responsible for the provision of youth justice services and the implementation of the Act), to establish more community-based programmes for responding to youth offending. In addition, prior to the YCJA coming into force, the federal government funded professional educational initiatives directed at police and prosecutors; these programmes were intended to encourage the use of community-based responses to youth offending.

The YCJA has clearly resulted in a significant decline in the number of youth charged by police, and an increase in the use of various methods of police diversion. Figure 10.1 shows the changes from 1986 to 2007 in the rates per 100,000 of youth who were charged[7] and who were diverted by police. In 2003, the year that the YCJA came into effect, the rate of youth charged by police dropped by 18 per cent from the previous year – from 4,490 per 100,000 to 3,690 – and the rate of diverted youth increased by a similar amount. For the first time since youth justice statistics have been collected in Canada, more apprehended youth were diverted by police than were charged.[8] Since 2003, the rates of youth charged and diverted have remained almost constant, and show no signs of returning to their pre-YCJA levels.

Figure 10.1 also shows that the rate per 100,000 of youth identified by police as chargeable – referred to here as the 'police-reported youth crime rate' – has changed very little since the YCJA came into effect in 2003. Although it peaked in the early 1990s, it was almost constant from 2001 to 2007 at about 8,000 per 100,000: the same level as in the mid 1980s. The essentially unchanged level of reported youth crime before and after 2003 has two major implications. First, it suggests that the YCJA has not resulted in an increase in youth crime rates.[9] Second, since the per capita rate of youth apprehended by police did not change, changes in per capita rates of court cases or custodial populations following the introduction of the YCJA must be due to changes in the functioning of the youth justice system.

Another way of considering the change in police practices is to examine the charge ratio, or percentage of chargeable youth who were charged, which indicates the relative degree to which police are clearing cases by laying a charge rather than by alternatives to charging. This indicator declined gently from 1991 to 2002. In 2003, the first year that the YCJA was in effect, it dropped substantially from 57 per cent to 45 per cent charged: a relative decline of 21 per cent in one year. While regional

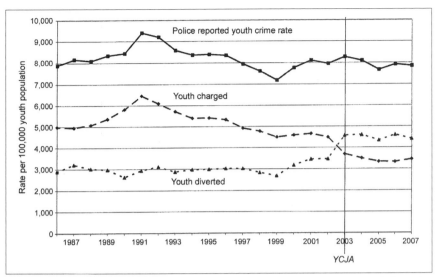

Figure 10.1 Rates of reported youth crime, youth charged and diverted, Canada, 1986–2007

Source: Statistics Canada, Canadian Centre for Justice Studies, *Uniform Crime Reporting Survey*.

variation in police charging rates has persisted, under the YCJA it has declined. In 2002, the youth charge rate ranged from 37 per cent in British Columbia to 70 per cent in Ontario, a rate that was nearly twice as high. By 2007, the highest charge ratio was still in Ontario, at 49 per cent, and lowest in British Columbia at 33 per cent, but the highest rate was only about 1.5 times greater than the lowest. Thus the YCJA has not only caused a substantial increase in the use of alternatives to charging, but also appears to have triggered a considerable reduction in regional differences in the use of alternatives to charging.

Restrictions on use of pre-trial detention

In more serious cases, the Crown prosecutor may seek the detention of the youth pending trial (remand custody). Under the YOA there were concerns that some youths were being detained before trial in situations in which an adult would be released, for example in cases where a judge was concerned that a homeless youth or juvenile prostitute might be at risk of harm if not detained. The YCJA has provisions intended to reduce the use of remand custody.

Section 29(1) of the YCJA specifies that pre-trial detention shall *not* be used as a 'substitute for appropriate child protection, mental health or other social measures'. Section 28 of the *YCJA* makes it clear that a youth should only be detained *before* sentencing in circumstances in which an

323

adult could be detained, generally on the primary grounds of ensuring attendance in court, or on secondary grounds if detention is 'necessary for the protection or safety of the public', because there is a 'substantial likelihood' of offending or witness intimidation (s.515(10) Criminal Code). Further, s. 29(2) of the YCJA creates a rebuttable presumption that detention on the secondary grounds, for the protection or safety of the public, should only occur if the youth could receive a custodial sentence under the YCJA. If a youth court judge has child welfare concerns about a youth appearing before the court, s. 35 of the YCJA allows the judge to refer the youth to a local child welfare agency for assessment; although the youth justice process is not discontinued, in these cases the primary intervention in the life of the adolescent may be through child welfare. There is no data on the extent to which s. 35 is being used, but it would appear that in most places there is little or no use of this provision, as it only gives judges an opportunity to 'refer' cases for child welfare assessment, and not to order the agency to be involved. The province where there would seem to be the greatest use of this provision is Quebec, where the child welfare and youth justice systems are most closely related (DeGusti *et al.* 2009).

It is difficult to accurately assess the impact of the YCJA on national rates of youth in pre-trial remand custody, because data are not available for Ontario prior to 2003/04 – and Ontario accounts for almost half the national total number of young persons in remand custody in Canada. However, with this limitation in mind, Figure 10.2 provides a picture of changes over time.

There was a decrease in 2003/04 in the use of remand custody, the first year that the YCJA was in effect, but it was preceded by similar decreases in a number of prior years, and was followed by substantial increases in 2006/07 and 2007/08. The average rate of youth in remand custody in 2007/08 (36 per 100,000) was the same as in 2000/01. Thus, on a national level, the YCJA has not had an impact on the use of pre-trial remand, and regional variations persist and in some cases are increasing. In 2007/08, on a per capita basis, more than five times as many youth were in pre-trial remand custody in the Prairies region as in Quebec.

Despite the fact that the provisions of the YCJA were intended to restrict the use of both pre-trial detention (remand) and post-adjudication custody, the Act has only had a significant impact on custody, but effectively none on pre-trial detention. A number of different explanations have been offered for this difference (Department of Justice 2007)[10] and it is likely that there are several factors involved. One may be that the provisions restricting use of custody are significantly more detailed, and in some situations absolutely preclude the use of custody, whereas the provisions around use of pre-trial detention merely create presumptions and continue to give judicial officers discretion. Another factor may be that in many places in Canada initial decisions about pre-trial detention

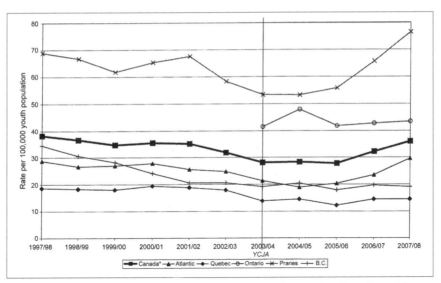

Figure 10.2 Average daily rates of youth in remand custody, Canada and by region

Source: Statistics Canada, Canadian Centre for Justice Statistics, *Corrections Key Indicators Report*, Table 251-0008.

Note: The 'Canada' series omits Ontario and Nunavut, due to missing data.

are made by lay justices of the peace, while sentencing decisions are only made by legally trained judges; although detention decisions are subject to review by a legally trained judge, this review process can be cumbersome, and the lack of legal training of initial decision-makers may affect the extent to which the new Act has had an effect on prior practice.

Another pre-trial issue is that often youth who are arrested are initially released on bail by the police or the court, but subject to restrictive conditions that are not related to the risk of their reoffending or the administration of justice. For example, parents may request that term of release include a curfew, a requirement that 'house rules' are to be followed and that the youth attend school. Youths may breach these conditions and then find themselves in court facing 'administration of justice' charges, for which there may be a greater likelihood of detention. There is considerable concern about the imposition of terms of release that are not directly related to the risk of reoffending (e.g. non-association with co-accused) or the administration of justice (e.g. non-contact with alleged victims or witnesses) and the effect of this on remand rates.

Whatever the explanation, with the use of post-adjudication custody dropping quite dramatically under the YCJA and remand being relatively unaffected, it would appear that a significant number of youths are in effect serving custodial sentences on a 'pre-adjudication' basis. At the sentencing hearing, the youth court judge may decide that any expectations for custody are satisfied by 'time already served' in pre-adjudication detention, but may add a period of probationary conditions and supervision in the community.

There are significant concerns about the continued high rate of pre-trial remand custody. There is generally less rehabilitative programming available in remand facilities and conditions may be harsher than in custody facilities. Further, because of the sudden and unplanned removal of a youth from his community and family that results from remand, youth tend to find this a more disruptive experience than being placed in custody. It has been suggested that there could be further legislative reforms to reduce the use of remands by providing more detailed legislative guidance and placing clearer restrictions on the use of remand, as well as restricting conditions for release (Department of Justice 2007). There could also be programmatic changes, such as extending the use of community-based bail supervision programmes for youth; these programmes have only been established in a few centres, but they have had some success in supervising and supporting youth on remand, increasing the likelihood of their attending court as required, and decreasing the risk of their offending or violating terms of release while on remand.

Purpose and principles of sentencing

The YCJA articulates the *purpose* of sentencing in youth court, and then sets out *specific principles* of youth sentencing. Section 38(1) states that: 'The purpose of [youth court] sentencing ... is to hold a young person accountable for an offence through the imposition of just sanctions that have meaningful consequences for the young person and that promote his or her rehabilitation and reintegration'.

The omission of any reference to deterrence in the YCJA statement of sentencing purpose may well have contributed to lowering the number of custodial sentences imposed in youth court (Cesaroni and Bala 2008). The absence of reference to deterrence in the YCJA, in contrast to the Criminal Code which governs adult sentencing, suggests that general and specific deterrence are not to be considered appropriate goals for sentencing young offenders. In 2006 the Supreme Court of Canada, in *R vs B.W.P.*,[11] upheld a trial decision that emphasized the importance of rehabilitation in sentencing a youth found guilty of manslaughter. The Court discussed the role of deterrence in sentencing, observing that for adults 'general deterrence is factored in the determination of the sentence, the offender is punished more severely, not because he or she deserves it, but because the court decides to send a message to others who may be inclined to engage in similar criminal activity'. The Supreme Court recognized that under the previous statute, the YOA, general deterrence had been a legitimate objective in sentencing youths, albeit to a lesser extent than for adults. The Court accepted, however, that the YCJA established 'a new sentencing regime' for young offenders in Canada. Justice Charron wrote that the Act:[12]

> sets out a detailed and complete code for sentencing young persons under which terms it is not open to the youth sentencing judge to impose a punishment for the purpose of warning, not the young person, but others against engaging in criminal conduct. Hence, general deterrence is not a principle of youth sentencing under the present regime.

The Supreme Court also recognized that while neither general nor specific deterrence should be objectives of sentencing in youth court, the fact that a youth is to be held accountable in youth court undoubtedly has 'the effect of deterring the young person and others from committing crimes'.

The YCJA provides a detailed set of sentencing principles for judges to apply. Two of these principles include the concept of restraint with respect to imprisonment: thus s. 38(2)(d) states that 'all available sanctions other than custody that are reasonable in the circumstances must be considered'. Further, s. 38(2)(e) requires that, subject to the requirement that sentences are to be proportionate to the offence, 'the sentence must be the least restrictive sentence that is capable of achieving the purpose [of sentencing]'. Another provision of the YCJA (s. 38(2)(a)) places a limit on the severity of sentencing in youth court: the sentence must not result in a punishment that is more severe than the punishment that an adult offender convicted of the same offence in similar circumstances would receive. This principle reflects the more general statement in the Declaration of Principle in the YCJA that the youth justice system is premised on 'fair and proportionate accountability that is consistent with the greater dependency of young persons and their reduced level of maturity'. Having provided youth court judges with these general, restrictive sentencing principles, the legislation then prescribes specific criteria that have to be met before a young offender can be committed to custody.

Restrictions on the use of custody

Under the YOA, a judge could not commit a young offender to custody unless the court considered 'a committal to custody to be necessary for the protection of society having regard to the seriousness of the offence and the circumstances in which it was committed, and having regards to the needs and circumstances of the young person' (s.24(1)). This vague provision offered little real guidance as to when youths should be imprisoned. As a result of this and other similarly vague provisions in the YOA, adolescent custody rates in Canada under that Act were amongst the highest in the world, with some judges using youth custody to achieve child welfare objectives, others to deter youth offending, and others to achieve accountability.

At the adult level in Canada there are still no specific offence-based criteria that must be met before an adult offender is imprisoned. In contrast, the provisions relating to the imposition of a custodial sentence in youth court in the YCJA are far more directive and restrictive, with s. 39(1) establishing four 'gateways'[13] to youth custody:

> A youth justice court shall not commit a person to custody . . . unless
> (a) the young person has committed a violent offence; [or]
> (b) the young person has failed to comply with non-custodial sentences; [or]
> (c) the young person has committed an . . . offence for which an adult would be liable to imprisonment for a term of more than two years and has a history that indicates a pattern of findings of guilt . . . or
> (d) in exceptional cases where the young person has committed an indictable offence, the aggravating circumstances of the offence are such that the imposition of a non-custodial sentence would be inconsistent with the purpose and principles [of youth sentencing] set out in section 38.

Thus there are only four circumstances in which a young offender may be committed to custody. Significantly, in its first sentencing decision under the YCJA, the Supreme Court in *R. vs C.D.* held that s. 39(1) should be 'narrowly construed', emphasizing that this provision should be interpreted in a manner that is consistent with the intent of the Act, as set out in the preamble, in a way that restricts the use of youth custody.[14] The Supreme Court held that the offence of dangerous driving, involving a high speed police chase of a youth in a stolen vehicle, was not a 'violent offence', as it did not involve actual bodily harm or the intent to cause harm; accordingly a youth found guilty of this offence could not receive a custodial sentence, even though his offence potentially endangered the public; as there was no proof of intent to harm and no harm actually resulted, it was not a 'violent offence'.

Section 39 has resulted in a substantial reduction in the use of custody since under the YOA there were significant numbers of young offenders who were imprisoned but who fell outside any of the four conditions now prescribed by the YCJA. It is noteworthy that s. 39(1)(b) provides that a youth can receive a custodial sentence for breach of probation or some other community-based sentence *only* if the youth has breached a previous community-based sentence; that is, a breach of a first probationary sentence cannot result in a custodial sentence. Further, apart from exceptional circumstances or where a youth has previously failed to comply with non-custodial sentences, a non-violent offence can result in a custodial sentence only if the offence is reasonably serious (i.e. an offence for which the maximum adult sentence is greater than two years) *and* there is a 'history that indicates a pattern of findings of guilt' (s. 39(1)(c)). In 2008, the Supreme Court again emphasized the need to narrowly construe the sentencing provisions of the Act, ruling that this provision generally requires a minimum of three prior judicial findings of guilt.[15]

If the case before a youth court satisfies one of the four conditions listed in s. 39(1), a number of other custody-related principles must still be considered before a court can imprison the young offender. The first restriction constitutes a clear reminder to judges in s. 39(2) of the principle of restraint with respect to the use of custody, even if one of the conditions of s. 39(1) is satisfied:

> if [one of the criteria for custody] apply, a youth justice court *shall not impose a custodial sentence* ... unless the court has considered all alternatives to custody raised at the sentencing hearing that are reasonable in the circumstances, and determined that there is not a reasonable alternative, or combination of alternatives, that is in accordance with the purpose and principles [of sentencing at the youth court level] [emphasis added].

A second principle to be observed before a custodial sentence is imposed is designed to discourage judges from escalating the severity of the sentence in response to subsequent offending. Having imposed an alternative to custody for one offence, some judges may 'up-tariff' and impose a custodial sentence if a youth reappears before the court, reasoning that the first sentence was insufficiently severe to discourage the offender. Section 39(4) attempts to constrain this judicial practice, providing that: 'The previous imposition of a particular non-custodial sentence on a young person does not preclude a youth justice court from imposing the same or any other non-custodial sentence for another offence'. While this provision does not prohibit judges from following the 'step principle' logic at sentencing, the provision means that the same alternative sanction may be imposed on consecutive occasions. A third principle that restricts the use of custody is more clearly binding on youth court judges, with s. 39(5) explicitly stating that a youth court 'shall not' use custody as a substitute for a child protection, mental health or other social measure. Under the YOA, a common justification for imposing a custodial sentence on troubled adolescents was that the judge could see no other way of providing the necessary social intervention for an adolescent at risk. Under the YCJA this justification for the imposition of custody is prohibited, though as noted a youth may be referred by the court to child welfare services.

Finally, a youth court is obliged, prior to imposing custody, to consider a pre-sentence report prepared by a probation officer, as well as any sentencing proposal made by the young offender or his or her counsel. The YCJA also permits a judge to convene a conference or refer a case to a community-based conference before imposing a sentence. This step might facilitate receiving advice from family or community members, or could allow for a victim–offender meeting before sentencing (s. 41).

Section 39(9) requires youth court judges who impose a term of custody to provide reasons why 'it has determined that a non-custodial sentence is not adequate' to achieve the purpose of sentencing ascribed to the youth court system. This is yet another provision of the YCJA that creates an impediment to the imposition of a custodial term in youth court.

New community-based sentences

In order to encourage judges to sentence fewer youths to custody, the YCJA created a number of new community-based sanctions that are intended to provide youth with more supervision and support in the community. Some of these new sentences, like the attendance centre orders and intensive supervision and support, may only be imposed if a representative of provincial youth corrections services agrees. Although efforts have been made to establish such services in all provinces, some provincial governments have been slow to establish such community-based programmes. In particular, intensive supervision and support orders have been used most in British Columbia, where the government has provided the most resources for this programme.

The most significant new community-based sentence is the 'deferred custody and supervision order' (DCSO), which can be imposed by the court even without special programming being introduced by a provincial government. This sentence allows the court to permit the youth to remain in the community for the duration of the order, subject to supervision by probation officers. In the event of an 'apprehended' or actual breach of the terms of the supervision order, the youth may be immediately placed in custody by probation staff without the prior necessity of another court hearing, although subject to a later youth court hearing to determine whether the youth should remain in custody for the balance of the sentence or again be released, perhaps on modified conditions. This sentence can be imposed for a period of up to six months, and only if the youth has *not* committed a 'serious violent offence'. The DCSO is only to be imposed if the court concludes that a custodial sentence should be imposed. This new sanction represents the last opportunity for the court to spare the offender committal to custody, with the youth on a 'much shorter leash' than probation, and it has been used quite frequently. On a national level, DCSOs are imposed at a rate of 3 DCSOs to every 17 custody orders (Thomas 2008). These orders should only be made for youth who would otherwise received a custody sentence, suggesting that about 3 out of 20 or 15 per cent of youth who would have otherwise received a custodial sentence receive a deferred custody sentence and remain in the community. An unknown proportion of those youth who receive the deferred custody sentence are subsequently apprehended for violations of the conditions of their release and placed in custody.

Custody and community supervision

As under the YOA, the maximum custodial sentence that may be imposed under the YCJA is three years, except for murder for which it is ten years.[16] Under the YOA, juveniles sentenced to custody generally remained in an institution until the end of the sentence, unless a judicial review modified the sentence. Under the YOA there was no conditional release mechanism (such as parole) for juvenile prisoners (though correctional authorities could make some use of temporary absence passes to release a young prisoner into the community). In practice, judicial review under the YOA was cumbersome to arrange and did not regularly occur.

Under the YCJA, all custodial sentences are composed of custodial and community supervision phases. The community phase has been introduced to provide more supervision and support for youth in the period immediately following release, when the youth faces the challenge of readjustment and there is a high risk of reoffending. The YCJA instructs judges not to take account of the fact that a portion of the 'custody sentence' will be served in the community under supervision (s.39(8)). For all but the most serious offences, the first two-thirds of the sentence is served in custody and the last third under supervision in the community. For the most serious offences, there is judicial discretion about how to divide the total sentence between custody and community supervision, and for all custodial sentences there is the possibility of judicial review to allow early release or continued detention after the presumptive release date. Further, for all but the longest sentences, a period of supervision under probation may follow the completion of the sentence of custody and supervision.

The introduction of this new type of custodial sentence did not in itself reduce the number of young offenders committed to custody, but it did reduce the average number of young persons in custody on any given day by reducing the average length of time spent in custody.

The YCJA also introduced the sentence of intensive rehabilitative custody and supervision order (IRCS). The IRCS order allows a court to confine a youth to a mental health facility, or to approve an individual plan that includes confinement and treatment, though it does not allow for involuntary medical treatment (e.g. drug therapy). This sentence may only be imposed on a juvenile offender who has committed one of a small number of very serious offences *and* who is suffering from a mental or psychological disorder. As a result of the statutory restrictions on their

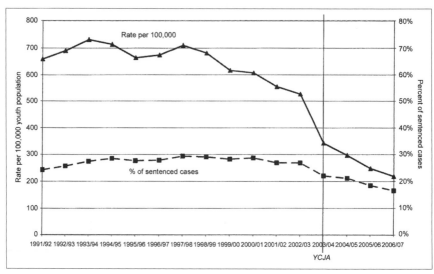

Figure 10.3 Rates and proportions of custodial sentences in youth court, 1991/92–2006/07

Source: Statistics Canada, Canadian Centre for Justice Statistics, *Youth Court Survey* and *Integrated Criminal Court Survey*.

use, very few of these orders have been made. Only 16 of these orders were recorded by Statistics Canada in the first four years of the YCJA, although the data are unavailable for some provinces.

Figure 10.3 shows changes over time in the use of custodial sentences in youth court, as indicated by two statistics. The rates per 100,000 show the number of custodial sentences standardized by youth population, and reflect changes in the number of cases coming to youth court, in the proportion of cases with a finding of guilt, and in sentencing patterns. The proportions of sentenced cases show the use of custodial sentences, standardized by the total number of sentences handed down, and reflect only changes in custodial sentencing itself. Both indicators show a drop after the YCJA came into force in 2003/04.

The per capita rate of custodial sentences dropped by 35 per cent in 2003/04, and by a further 36 per cent over the following three years. These substantial reductions reflect both the decrease in the proportion of custodial sentences handed down and the decrease in the volume of cases coming to youth court. As a result, the rate of custodial sentences handed down in youth court in 2006/07 (219 per 100,000) was less than half of the rate in 2002/03 (526 per 100,000).

The proportion of sentenced cases receiving a custodial disposition dropped from 27 per cent in 2002/03 to 22 per cent in 2003/04 – a drop of just under one-fifth in one year, and dropped further in subsequent years so that in 2006/07 only 17 per cent of sentenced youth court cases resulted in a custodial sentence. This drop in the proportion of sentenced cases receiving a custodial sentence is significant. The reduction in the numbers of youth charged by police was – consistent with the provisions of the YCJA – concentrated in less serious offences (Carrington and Schulenberg 2008). Therefore the cases reaching court are, on average, more serious than under the YOA; the observed reduction in the proportion of custodial sentences is strong evidence for the effectiveness of the provisions of the YCJA that restrict the use of custodial sentences.

While the use of custodial sentences has decreased substantially in all regions of Canada under the YCJA, there continues to be substantial variation among regions, with Quebec continuing to have the lowest rate of youth court cases receiving a custodial sentence, a rate about one-half that in Ontario, the province with the highest rate.

With decreasing numbers of youth sentenced to custody, as shown in Figure 10.4, the average daily rate of youth in sentenced custody also decreased dramatically after the YCJA came into force: by 43 per cent in 2003/04 and a further 37 per cent over the following four years. By 2007/08, the average daily rate of youth in sentenced custody (38 per 100,000) was only 35 per cent of the rate in 2002/03 (108 per 100,000). In contrast, the average daily rate of youth in remand custody does not appear to have been affected by the YCJA. As a result of the continuing decrease in the number of youth in sentenced custody, the proportion accounted for by remand of all youth in custodial facilities had increased from 25 per cent in 2002/03 to 47 per cent in 2007/08. The average daily

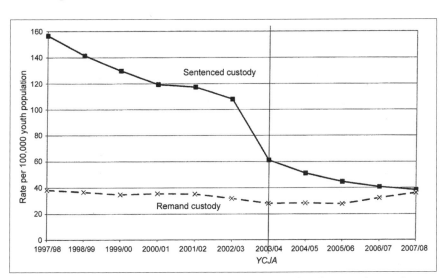

Figure 10.4 Average daily rates of youth in sentenced and remand custody, Canada

Source: Statistics Canada, Canadian Centre for Justice Statistics, *Corrections Key Indicators Report*, Table 251-0008.

number of youth in remand custody in Canada in 2007/08 was 1,009 – slightly more than the 990 youth in sentenced custody.

While the YCJA has dramatically reduced rates of youth in sentenced custody, it has not had an impact on regional variation. Over the past ten years, British Columbia and Quebec have had similar low rates, and the Atlantic and Prairie regions have had similarly high rates, approximately 2.5 to 3 times as high as British Columbia and Quebec. In Ontario, rates of youth in sentenced custody were similar to those of the Atlantic and Prairie regions before the YCJA came into effect, and have been closer to those in British Columbia and Quebec since then.

Sentencing young offenders as adults

While much of the YCJA is intended to reduce the use of courts and custody for less serious young offenders, the YCJA also included provisions to facilitate sentencing of the most serious youthful offenders as adults. The YCJA changed the process from that under the YOA, by abolishing the pre-adjudication transfer hearing that could result in a trial in adult court and adult sentencing. The YCJA provides that the decision about whether to impose an adult sentence is to be made at a post-adjudication hearing, just prior to sentencing. Abolishing the pre-trial transfer hearing expedites the process for making a decision about adult sentencing. Further, the YCJA adopted the concept of the 'presumptive offence'; if a youth 14 years or older was found guilty of murder, attempted murder, manslaughter, aggravated assault or a third 'serious violent offence', the YCJA had a presumption that an adult sentence would be imposed.[17]

In its 2008 decision in *R. vs D.B.* the Supreme Court of Canada ruled that it is a violation of the 'principles of fundamental justice' and s. 7 of the Canadian Charter of Rights and Freedoms to have presumptive offences for youth offenders. The Court accepted that it is a principle of fundamental justice that young people are entitled to a *presumption* of 'diminished moral blameworthiness or culpability'. This reflects their age compared with adults, their heightened vulnerability, relative immaturity and a reduced capacity for moral judgment. A presumption of an adult sentence is inconsistent with the principle of fundamental justice that young people are entitled to a presumption of diminished moral culpability. The Court made it clear that the Charter of Rights does not preclude imposing an adult sentence on a young person, as the seriousness of the offence and the threat to society posed by the youth may require an adult sentence.[18] However, the Charter requires that the Crown must always justify imposing an adult sentence on a youth.

If an adult sentence is imposed, a young person is usually still placed in a youth custody facility, with provisions for transfer to an adult facility upon reaching the age of 18. If a person who was a youth at the time of the offence receives an adult sentence for murder, there is the same mandatory life sentence as for an adult, but the court will set eligibility for parole at an earlier date than an adult being sentenced for the same offence, reflecting the limited accountability of even those youth convicted and sentenced as adults for the most serious offences.

There are no reliable data on adult sentencing of youth under the YCJA. However, the reported case law makes clear that adult sentences are rarely imposed, and only for the cases involving the most serious offences, and then only for youth who have a history of violence and who seem unlikely to be rehabilitated by a youth sentence.

Conclusions

With the substantial decline in the use of youth courts and custody, it is clear that police, prosecutors, probation officers and judges have generally applied the YCJA in a way that has resulted in more use of diversion and community-based alternatives to custody. The clear statements of principle and the directive provisions of the Act have had an effect, as have decisions of the Supreme Court of Canada, which have consistently taken a 'narrow' approach to the use of custody. The extensive professional education programmes prior to the implementation of the Act, funded and supported by the federal government, are also likely have had an impact on the attitudes of justice system professionals. While there is no national data on the attitudes of professionals towards youth crime and the YCJA, one study in Alberta suggests a significant degree of support by police and probation officers for philosophy of the new Act, though wide variation in attitudes within these groups and continuing concerns about lack of resources as well as concerns about specific provisions of the Act (DeGusti 2008). In this study, youth probation officers were generally more supportive of the diversionary and rehabilitative aspects of the Act than police, though police officers appreciated their increased discretion about charging and the relatively expeditious resolution of cases through the use of extrajudicial measures.

Although the YCJA has clearly resulted in a decline in the use of courts and custody for youthful offenders in Canada, in cases involving more serious offences or youths with lengthy records who have not responded to community-based options, youth courts have generally continued to impose custodial sentences. Furthermore, while the presumption for adult sentencing for the most serious youth offenders has been ruled unconstitutional, adult sentences are still imposed in a small number of cases involving very violent youth, where the Crown satisfies the youth court that this is an appropriate sentence.

Without increasing recorded youth crime rates, the YCJA has resulted in a very significant reduction in the use of courts and custody for adolescent offenders in Canada, and hence allowed for a significant reduction in spending on youth courts and custody facilities, generally accompanied by shifting resources to community-based programmes. On the other hand, the large regional variations in the use of custody and remand have not been eliminated under the YCJA.

Despite the success of YCJA in achieving its principal objective, youth justice issues remain controversial in Canada. The minority Conservative government still has a 'get tough on crime agenda', which includes proposals for amendments to the YCJA. While the Canadian public is not facing more youth crime than a generation ago, there is still a high level of public concern about the issue. This may be a result of significantly increased media attention on violent youth crime (Sprott 1998; Roberts *et al.* 2007) and may perhaps even reflect a subtle form of racial stereotyping, as a disproportionate number of youthful offenders in Canada are members of minority groups. Further, while youth crime has not significantly increased, youth culture has changed. Adolescents in general spend less time with adults, including their parents, than a generation ago, and have a less respectful attitude towards adults and legal authority, increasing the sense of alienation that growing numbers of adults feel towards teenagers today (Bibby 2001; Hersch 1998).

In June 2008, Conservative Prime Minister Stephen Harper denounced Canada's approach to handling young offenders as 'an unmitigated failure', in that it did not 'hold young lawbreakers responsible for their behaviour and . . . make them accountable to their victims and society'.[19] The Conservative Party's October 2008 election platform advocated adding deterrence and denunciation as youth sentencing objectives, and went on to propose 'automatic, stiffer sentences for persons 14 and older convicted of serious and violent crimes', as well as provisions that would allow increased publication of the names of serious youthful offenders. Interestingly, while there is some public support for 'toughening' the law, the other political parties rejected the Conservative approach to youth offending during the 2008 election campaign.[20] In March 2010, the minority Conservative government introduced Bill C-4[21] to amend the YCJA, but the Minister of Justice indicated that the proposals were more of a 'fine tuning' than a 'complete overhaul'[22] of the Act. It would appear that the Conservatives believe that raising youth crime issues 'plays well to their base,' especially during an election, but they do not seem intent on changing the law in a way that would dramatically increase the use of courts and custody for Canadian youth.

Some provisions in Bill C-4 will tend to increase the use of custody, such as proposals to add denunciation and specific deterrence as sentencing principles, and the redefinition of 'violent offence' to include an offence that 'endangers the life or safety of another person by creating a substantial likelihood of causing bodily harm'. However, reflecting the

2008 Supreme Court decision in *R v D.B,.* which ruled unconstitutional 'presumptive' adult sentencing for adolescents, Bill C-4 does not change the adult sentencing provisions. Further, the situations where publication of the identity of a youth could be publicized will only be slightly expanded. Some of the provisions of Bill C-4 may actually result in fewer youths being placed in pre-trial remand detention, by restricting such placement to cases where a youth is charged with a 'serious offence'(where the maximum adult sentence would be five years or more) and there are concerns about commission of a further serious offence or non-attendance in court.

At time of writing (April 2010), the exact nature and timing of amendments to the YCJA are not known. Experience with the YOA and YCJA clearly suggest that if legislative changes result in a significant increase in the use of courts and custody for youth, this would impose serious human costs on youth and their families, and substantial financial costs on provincial correctional authorities, but without reducing rates of youth crime. Ultimately the effect of any legislative changes will depend on how they are interpreted and applied by judges. It is to be hoped that they recognize that sending significantly more youth into custody would increase the cost of the youth justice services without increasing public safety.

Appendix: recent reports and inquiries into youth crime and justice in Canada

Public concerns about youth offending have resulted in three major reports in the past few years by provincial agencies or commissions. These reports analysed different problems in the youth justice system, reviewed research literature and made recommendations for reform.

A retired Nova Scotia Supreme Court Justice conducted a public inquiry in that province and in 2006 issued a report about a case where a youth with a history of auto theft and high speed police chases was released on bail; two days later the youth stole another car and was again involved in police chase, this one resulting in the tragic death of another motorist. Nunn's report (Nunn 2006) included recommendations for legislative reform and changes in provincial policy, in particular with respect to pre-trial detention and prevention of offending by youths with learning disabilities.

In Ontario, Canada's largest province, there have been growing concerns about youth and gang violence, especially in Toronto, one of the most racially diverse cities in the world. Two highly respected individuals, a former Chief Justice of the province and a former speaker of the provincial legislature, were asked to study the causes of youth violence, and make recommendations for addressing them. Roy McMurtry and

Alvin Curling (2008) issued a five-volume report which included a detailed literature review as well as research on the administration of youth justice in the province. Significant themes of the report included the effects on rates of youth violence of excessive policing, lack of community supports and the alienation of minority youth. The report's recommendations were focused on changes in policing, education and social supports, as well as better coordination within the youth justice system.

The British Columbia Representative for Children and Youth (2009) issued a detailed retrospective cohort study of involvement in the youth justice system of all youth in the province born in 1986 and in school at the age 12 years (over 50,000 youth). A major focus of the study was upon the high rates of youth justice system involvement of children in the child welfare system. Child welfare wards were much more likely to be arrested and placed in custody; they were more likely to be involved in the youth justice system than to graduate from high school. This report devotes particular attention to the problems faced by Aboriginal youth. The report included recommendations for changes in child welfare system, some aimed at early childhood but others at adolescents, as well as proposing changes in the youth justice and education systems.

Notes

1 Young Offenders Act, R.S.C 1985, c. Y–1, enacted as S.C. 1980–81–82–83, c. 110.
2 Juvenile Delinquents Act, enacted as S.C. 1908, c. 40; subject to minor amendments over the years, finally as Juvenile Delinquents Act, R.S.C. 1970, c. J–3.
3 Canada, *Youth Justice Renewal Strategy* (Ottawa: Department of Justice 2002); and Doob and Sprott (2004).
4 *Youth Criminal Justice Act*, S.C. 2002, c. 1, in force 1 April 2003.
5 For a much more detailed discussion of youth justice in Canada, see Bala (2003a) and Bala and Anand (2009).
6 2008 SCC 25.
7 In three provinces police recommend charges, but there is then pre-charge screening by a Crown prosecutor, who may decide not to charge; in those three provinces, the numbers of youth 'charged' include youth who were the subject of a police recommendation to charge, but were screened by the Crown.
8 See Carrington and Schulenberg (2008) for a more detailed analysis of the change in police charging practices in 2003; they show that the change in 2003 took place during the second quarter, after the YCJA came into force on 1 April 2003.
9 In the absence of national time series data on criminal victimizations perpetrated by youth or on self-reported youth crime in Canada, the police-reported youth crime rate is the only indicator of the level of youth crime available for studying trends over time. In theory, it is possible youth crime increased after the YCJA came into effect, but that this was not reflected in the police data, either because the public reduced their reporting of youth

crime to the police, which seems very unlikely, or because the police reduced the recording of chargeable youths who were not charged. This also seems unlikely. If anything, the legislation provided an incentive to police to increase the recording of youth cleared extra-judicially, as this would demonstrate police compliance with the intent of the legislation that the proportion of extrajudicial clearances be increased.

10 For further discussion and recommendations of issues concerning pre-trial youth detention, see Nunn (2006).

11 [2006] S.C.J. 27.

12 [2006] S.C.J. 27, at para. 4.

13 The term 'gateway' is commonly used amongst justice system professionals, and was adopted by the Supreme Court of Canada in *R. vs C.D.*, [2005] 3 S.C.R. 668, 2005 SCC 78.

14 *R. vs C.D.*, [2005] 3 S.C.R. 668, 2005 SCC 78.

15 *R vs S.A.C.* 2008 SCC 47.

16 As discussed more fully below, it is also possible for a youth court to impose a longer adult sentence for the most serious offences, though this rarely occurs.

17 Since 1995 the *YOA* also had a 'presumptive offence' provision, but it only applied to young persons 16 and older, and the list of offences did not include the 'third serious violent offence.'

18 See e.g., *R vs A.O.*, [2007] O.J. 800 (C.A.).

19 Canwest News Service, reporting on a speech given by the Prime Minister to the Canadian Crime Victims Foundation in Vaughan, Ontario (Canwest 2008).

20 Canadian Broadcasting Corporation, 'Conservatives vow to toughen youth justice act', www.cbc.ca posted Sept. 22, 2008.

21 Bill C-4, 40th Parliament – 3rd Session, 1st Reading, 15 March 2010.

22 Canwest News Service, 'Tories won't overhaul youth crime law: Fine-tuning only' 29 January 2010.

References

Bala, N. (2003a) *Youth Criminal Justice Law* (Toronto: Irwin Law).

Bala, N. (2003b) 'Diversion, Conferencing, and Extrajudicial Measures for Adolescent Offenders', *Alberta Law Review*, 40, pp. 991–1027.

Bala, N. and Anand, S. (2009) *Youth Criminal Justice Law*, 2nd edition (Toronto: Irwin Law).

Bala, N., Carrington, P.J. and Roberts, J.V. (2009) 'Evaluating the Youth Criminal Justice Act After Five Years – A Qualified Success', *Canadian Journal of Criminology and Criminal Justice*, 51(2) pp. 131–68.

Bibby, R.W. (2001) *Canada's Teens: Today, Yesterday, and Tomorrow* (Toronto, ON: Stoddart).

British Columbia Representative for Children and Youth/ Office of the Provincial Health Officer (2009) *Kids, Crime and Care – Health and Well-Being of Children in Care: Youth Justice Experiences and Outcomes* (British Columbia: Representative for Children and Youth/ Office of the Provincial Health Officer) available at: http://www.rcybc.ca/Images/PDFs/Reports/Youth%20Justice%20Joint %20Rpt%20FINAL%20.pdf

Carrington, P. and Schulenberg, J. (2008) 'Structuring police discretion: The effect on referrals to youth court', *Criminal Justice Policy Review*, 19, pp. 349–67.

Cesaroni, C. and Bala, N. (2008) 'Deterrence as a Principle of Youth Sentencing: No effect on youth, but a significant effect on judges', *Queen's Law Journal*, 39, pp. 447–81.

DeGusti, B. (2008) *The Impact of the Youth Criminal Justice Act on Case Flow in Alberta and System Response in Calgary* (Calgary, AB: Canadian Research Institute for Law and the Family).

DeGusti, B., MacRae, L., Vallée, M., Caputo, T. and Hornick, J.P. May (2009) *Best Practices for Chronic/Persistent Young Offenders* (Calgary, Canadian Research Institute for Law and the Family).

Department of Justice Canada (2002) *Youth Justice Renewal Strategy* (Ottawa: Department of Justice).

Department of Justice Canada (2007) *Pre-Trial Detention Under The Youth Criminal Justice Act: A Consultation Paper* (Ottawa: Department of Justice Canada).

Doob, A.N. and Sprott, J. 'Changing Models of Youth Justice in Canada', in M. Tonry and A.N. Doob (eds), *Youth Crime and Youth Justice: Comparative and Cross-National Perspectives*, 31 Crime and Justice (Chicago: University of Chicago Press, 2004).

Hersch, P. (1998) *A Tribe Apart: A Journey into the Heart of American Adolescence* (New York: Ballantine Books).

McMurtry, R. and Curling, A. (2008) *The Review of the Roots of Youth Violence* (Toronto: Queens Printer), available at: http://www.rootsofyouthviolence.on.ca/english/aboutus.asp

Nunn, M. (2006) *Spiralling out of Control: Lessons Learned From a Boy in Trouble*, Report of the Nunn Commission of Inquiry (Nova Scotia: Nunn Commission of Inquiry), available at: http://gov.ns.ca/just/nunn_commission/_docs/Report_Nunn_Final.pdf

Roberts, J., Crutcher, N. and Verbrugge, P. (2007) 'Public Attitudes to Sentencing in Canada: Exploring Recent Findings', *Canadian Journal of Criminology and Criminal Justice*, 49, pp. 75–107.

Sprott, J. (1998) 'Understanding Public Opposition to a Separate Youth Justice System', *Crime & Delinquency*, 44, pp. 399–411.

Thomas, J. (2008) 'Youth court statistics, 2006/2007', *Juristat*, 28:4, p. 1.

Chapter 11

Public opinion, politics and the response to youth crime

Trevor Jones

The general aim of this chapter is to consider the political possibilities for a significant change in the direction of policy responses to youth crime and antisocial behaviour in England and Wales. More specifically, it aims to assess the feasibility, given the prevailing conditions of popular and political debate about crime and punishment, of a shift away from 'populist punitive' responses in youth justice policy and towards more balanced evidence-led approaches. The discussion is based on the premise that in most respects, the political constraints on progressive developments in the specific field of youth justice are similar to those regarding penal policy as a whole. Rather than consider the strengths and limitations of particular policy approaches, the aim is to explore the factors shaping policy-making and the possibilities of a changed approach. The discussion starts from certain key assumptions: (1) youth justice policy in England and Wales (as with penal policy as a whole) has shifted in a decisively punitive direction in recent decades; (1) these punitive shifts have been driven more by populist political concerns than by a pragmatic assessment of the available evidence; and (2) the resulting policy outcomes have been generally undesirable.

The chapter attempts to address three sets of questions, each of which corresponds to a substantive section.

- What is the evidence about public attitudes to crime and punishment in general, and youth crime and youth justice in particular? Is public opinion about crime as punitive as it first appears?

- What factors shape both punitive public/political opinion and the shift towards harsh penal policies? Why are politicians more likely in some polities than others to be drawn to expressive, populist responses to youth crime rather than more rational 'evidence-led' approaches?

- What are the political prospects for a radically changed approach in England and Wales? What *should* be the role of public opinion and of other sources of influence in shaping youth justice policy?

1. Public opinion on (youth) crime and punishment

A punitive public

A central theme within academic discussions of penal policy in recent years has concerned the 'punitive turn' in penal policy across a number of countries that has its roots in the decline of faith in penal welfarism from the 1970s onwards (Garland 2001). An important part of this story concerns increasingly emotive and politicized debates about crime and punishment associated with a significant hardening of public attitudes about offenders, characterized by Bottoms (1995: 40) as 'populist punitiveness'. In the last few years the picture of a global shift towards punitive penal policies has been challenged and qualified by an emerging body of comparative work that highlights striking contrasts in approaches to penal policy between developed nations (Cavadino and Dignan 2005; Tonry 2007). Still, there is a consensus that criminal justice policies have become notably more punitive in England and Wales than in other western democracies (bar the USA). These shifts towards punitiveness have also been visible, perhaps particularly so, in the development of policy on youth crime and antisocial behaviour, which has often been justified – implicitly or explicitly – by appealing to an assumed popular majority of support for more punishment.[1]

There is certainly plenty of evidence for the existence of punitive attitudes amongst the public with regard to crime and punishment in general. Much of this research is based on quantitative surveys of public opinion. Whilst a detailed review of the specific findings of the various studies is not necessary here, a number of clear general themes emerge from a reading of this literature.[2]

- Public opinion surveys in a number of countries – but particularly in the UK, USA and Australia – indicate a growth in the proportion of surveyed people expressing more punitive views towards offenders from the 1970s onwards.

- Levels of public knowledge about crime are low. For example, views about overall crime levels, their rate and direction of change, and views about the prevalence of more serious forms of crime are all in stark contrast to the picture provided by evidence from victimization surveys and official statistics. Relatively high proportions of the public report that they think crime has been rising during the past decade when the BCS shows that overall victimization has been falling sharply. High proportions of respondents to opinion surveys overestimate substantially the proportion of total crime accounted for by serious and violent offences.

- The survey evidence indicates low levels of knowledge about the institutions and processes of the criminal justice system. For example, relatively few respondents in surveys demonstrate knowledge about the range of options open to the courts in dealing with offenders.

- These low levels of knowledge are no barrier to the expression of strong opinions about the effectiveness of criminal justice agencies. Low levels of confidence in the criminal justice system are expressed, with particularly low levels of stated trust for the performance of the courts in sentencing offenders.

- Overly-lenient sentences are a popular perceived cause of higher levels of crime overall, suggesting a general belief in the utilitarian functions of punishment.

- There also appears to be a strong popular attachment to the notion of retribution and just deserts as general justifications for the punishment of offenders.

- Cross-national surveys suggest that public opinion about crime in some countries is consistently more punitive than in others. The UK stands out amongst all European countries as demonstrating the most punitive attitudes to punishment.

Research focusing on youth crime and justice shows generally similar patterns of public attitudes, although there are some notable differences. Roberts (2004) provides a useful summary of international evidence about attitudes to youth crime (although, as he points out, this mainly focuses upon Anglophone common law countries). A range of opinion poll and survey evidence indicates a high level public concern about youth crime. However, as with crime in general, Roberts (2004) suggests that there is a striking degree of public ignorance about 'the real story' of youth crime. This includes a widespread belief that youth offending is rising (in the face of empirical evidence that suggests the opposite), a marked tendency to overestimate the volume of serious crime committed by young people, an inflated estimate of the risk from young offenders of particular types of violent crime, and a firm belief that the vast majority of young offenders are highly likely to reoffend (Roberts 2004: 500–3). In another parallel to the research on public opinion about crime and punishment in general, studies indicate very low levels of knowledge about and trust in the institutions and processes of youth justice. Low proportions of respondents to surveys report that they feel the youth justice system is doing a good job, and stated confidence in the youth justice system is often lower than the (low) levels expressed in other parts of the criminal justice system. At the same time, relatively few respondents are able to demonstrate any detailed knowledge of institutions of youth justice or the sentencing options available to the courts. High proportions of respondents to surveys indicate beliefs that excessive leniency in the sentencing of offenders are a key cause of offending. So far, then, the patterns are similar or identical to public views about adult offending. However, there is some survey evidence that public opinion does recognize the age of young offenders as a possible mitigating factor that reduces their culpability, though this recognition tends to disappear when cases of serious violent crime are considered. With regard to non-violent offending, there seems to be simultaneous support for both punishment and prevention, and more support for the principle of rehabilitation of young offenders. In line with the research on crime and punishment in general, there is a strong correlation between low levels of knowledge (as stated in surveys) and more punitive opinions about appropriate ways of dealing with young offenders.

The most extensive research on public opinion and youth justice in England and Wales is the study by Hough and Roberts (2004). This reports the first nationally representative public opinion survey focused explicitly upon youth crime and justice in England and Wales. Lack of knowledge about youth crime trends was shown by the fact that three-quarters of those surveyed believed the numbers of young offenders had increased in recent years, whereas the actual numbers of young offenders dealt with by the police had been falling during the two years prior to the survey. There was a tendency to overestimate the proportion of youth crime accounted for by violent offences, and to overestimate the prevalence of repeat offending by young offenders. Levels of knowledge about the youth justice system were low. For example, only about a quarter of those surveyed had heard of Youth Offending Teams. These low levels of knowledge were paralleled by low levels of stated confidence, with only about one in ten respondents stating that the youth justice system did a good job. There was a general belief that lenient sentencing was an important cause of crime, which applied as much to youth as to adult offenders.

On the basis of opinion poll and survey evidence, then, there is considerable evidence for support for punitive responses to offending (whether by adults or, in a slightly more equivocal way, by young people). This, according to Roberts (2004), explains the attraction for politicians of trumpeting harsh and punitive policies to deal with offenders. To do otherwise would be to commit electoral suicide. This state of affairs is perpetuated by the ongoing obsession – reflected in both media focus and government funding of research into public attitudes – with blunt measures of public attitudes to crime in the form of opinion polls. Hough and Roberts (2002b) are critical of these trends, not least because they argue that the broad-brush description of public attitudes from opinion polls needs to be qualified by more detailed and nuanced examinations of public perceptions and views. More subtle and intensive research, they argue, calls into question widely held assumptions about the straightforward punitiveness of public opinion.

From public opinion to public judgment

Politicians of all hues have justified 'get tough' shifts in criminal justice – including (perhaps especially) in youth justice – with reference to the majority of the electorate who express punitive views in public opinion polls. However, in recent years alternative methods of examining public opinion have suggested that public views on crime and punishment may be much more complex than they first appear (Sparks 2000). It has been suggested by a number of authors that quantitative survey questions about crime and punishment actually elicit punitive responses. If participants in a survey are asked if they think that judges are too lenient, or whether the death penalty should be introduced for premeditated murder, then it is not surprising that many respond in the affirmative. Opinion polls may be based upon a statistically representative sample of the population, but too often the form of question asked pushes respondents into selecting quick responses whether or not they have the required knowledge upon which to base their answers (Green 2006). People tend to answer survey questions about crime and punishment based on the 'worst case scenario' rather than the typical criminal case (Roberts 2004). The term 'young offender' brings to mind visions of the most shocking cases and people frame their answers accordingly. As Hutton (2005) argues, public attitudes to punishment 'are, at least in part, an artefact of the methodology used to uncover them'.

An important theme in the recent work on public attitudes to punishment has been to challenge the notion of an undifferentiated 'punitive' majority, and posit that public opinion about crime and offenders is more complex and nuanced than opinion polls suggest. The basis of this approach involves distinguishing between public 'opinion' and public 'judgement'. The former can be summarized as the relatively unrefined 'top of the head' responses to simple survey questions that characterize much opinion poll research. The latter can be defined as 'the state of highly developed public opinion that exists once people have engaged an issue, considered it from all sides, understood the choices that it leads to, and accepted the full consequences of the choices they make' (Yankelovich 1991, quoted in Green 2006). Public judgement emerges when respondents are given more information about the context of what they are being asked, details of particular cases rather than broad general questions, and given the opportunity to reflect and discuss the complexities of an issue. As a growing body of research now shows, when methods of measuring public opinion are developed to include more information provision and the opportunity for more reasoned deliberation, a very different picture of 'public opinion' emerges. Roberts (2004) goes so far as to describe this as the 'real story' about public opinion.

The 'survey effect' has been observed across a range of studies, including some of the ones mentioned above. For example, in terms of opinion about crime and offending in general, the responses to general survey questions about sentencing show many people responding that judges are too lenient. When the same people are provided with details of real cases and asked to select an appropriate sentence themselves, the sentences chosen by the public are similar to, or more lenient than, those actually given by sentencers (Hough and Roberts 1998; Hough and Park 2002). This contrast arises because it is relatively easy to be punitive when considering appropriate sentences in the abstract, without any information about the circumstances of the particular offence or offender, and because of the tendency to respond to general questions about sentencing by envisaging the atypical 'worst possible' cases. Hutton (2005) – who used a range of qualitative research methods including focus groups and deliberative polling, including the possibility for information provision and reflection, found that public attitudes to crime and punishment are far from fixed in a punitive mode, but are much more complex, contradictory, and malleable than the picture presented by opinion polls. Similarly, Green (2006) suggests that 'deliberative polling' offers the potential for accurately recording the complexity of public opinion about crime. This involves the selection of a statistically representative random sample of the public who are then provided with the incentives and opportunities to engage in-depth with a particular topic before coming to an informed judgment. Such groups are provided with detailed briefing materials, convene for a few days during which they have an opportunity to listen to presentations giving more in-depth information about the topic under consideration, and the chance to discuss and deliberate with each other about their views. Such approaches allow citizens to develop their views within the context of various alternative 'frameworks', whereas in standard opinion polls, as in the press and in exchanges with 'the man in the pub', the dominant discourses are normally free of contextual information about the particular case, and therefore tend to be abstract, ideological, and emotional.

These deliberative methods have been applied to research on attitudes towards youth crime and appropriate responses to young offenders. Hough and Roberts (2002b) and Roberts (2004) already showed that even in their responses to generic survey-style questions, representative samples of the general public tend to be more equivocal in their views about young offenders than is the case with regard to adults. Their survey evidence did suggest that with regard to non-violent offences at least, there is a general acceptance that an offender's youth may be a mitigating factor and reduce the level of culpability in a particular case. Nevertheless, punitive responses to general questions about youth crime remain salient in survey research. However, when respondents are asked to select a particular sentence for a specific case for which contextual information is provided (for example, about the offender's social circumstances or expressions of remorse), the chosen sentences become more moderate. Informing the respondents that a young offender had taken some steps towards reparation for the offence had a particularly powerful effect, with fewer respondents choosing custody in such cases (Roberts and Hough 2005). Similarly, because only low proportions of the public have any knowledge of the alternative sanctions available, they tend to associate punishment in a relatively straightforward way with custody. When provided with information about a range of options available, fewer people chose custody. Finally, when comparing the actual sentence in a particular case with the one that respondents thought the courts would impose it is clear that members of the public tend to underestimate the severity of the sentencing of young offenders, just as they do in answers to more general questions. Overall, then, Roberts and Hough conclude that 'despite their critical reaction to the youth courts, the British public is far from uniformly punitive towards young offenders' (2005: 228).

Policy implications: educating politicians and the public

This 'rationalist' approach to public opinion research on crime has a number of clear implications. First, there is a need to educate politicians and sentencers that assumptions about the 'punitive public' are questionable. Political assumptions about the likely negative electoral consequences of a calmer and more progressive policy approach are not necessarily correct. Second, there needs to be much more and better provision of public information about 'the real picture' of crime and punishment. If the general public realise that overall crime risk is low and falling, that serious and violent crimes are relatively rare, and that harsh penal policies do not reduce crime, then this will lead to a moderation of public views about punishment. Third, there should be less official emphasis on large scale 'top of the head' public opinion surveys, and more investment in the forms of 'deliberative polling' discussed by Green (2006), Hough and Park (2002) and others. For example, Green (2006) proposes that deliberative polls become a 'standard feature' of consultation processes prior to criminal justice white papers, that such polls on a few specific issues are conducted as part of each sweep of the British Crime Survey, that ad hoc deliberative polls are established following high profile incidents such as the killing of James Bulger, and that the

Home Office (and/or perhaps now the Ministry of Justice) provide funding for the training of facilitators with expertise in such methods. In a similar vein, Roberts (2004) suggests a relatively straightforward three point plan for challenging political drift towards punitive responses to youth crime. First, educate the public about the 'real' nature of youth crime. Second, increase the volume and extent of in-depth research into public opinion (of the kind described above) and encourage research that attempts to measure the opinions of 'informed' samples of the public. Third, researchers need to engage with the politicians and policy-makers who drive punitive policy responses and demonstrate to them the error of their thinking about the punitive electorate (2004: 527–34). This kind of thinking has informed a range of developments. For example, the 'Rethinking Crime and Punishment' research programme funded between 2001 and 2004 by the Esmée Fairbairn Foundation funded over 50 projects with the broad aim of increasing public understanding of, and involvement in, criminal justice (Esmée Fairbairn Foundation 2004).

These arguments are important in a number of ways. They provide a corrective to widely held assumptions about the inevitability of uniformly punitive public views about crime and punishment. And it is difficult to view as anything other than laudable proposals to improve political and public debate via more deliberative and informed discussions of crime and justice. However, these policy prescriptions do have some limitations, particularly if they are presented as the central plank of a strategy to transform the politics of punishment. A key problem with these approaches is that they beg the question, if public responses are not, in fact, generally punitive, then why have politicians had so much success in selling avowedly punitive policies? Whilst it is clearly the case that 'public opinion' is, to a degree, a construction of the method used to measure it, this is as much a criticism of the validity of more deliberative methods as it is of survey questionnaires. As Hutton (2005) himself points out, the opinions expressed in public opinion surveys are no less 'real' than those expressed in more deliberative forums, such as citizens' juries or panels. From the perspective of those on the political right, the moderated views that are the outcome of deliberative research methods reflect the influence placed upon respondents by researchers who have an interest in eliciting a more liberal set of responses. Why are the results obtained from 'deliberative' methods (methods that allow for a much greater uncontrolled input from the researcher) superior to the first thoughts that people give in answer to survey questions? After all, immediate first thoughts may well betray more of 'true' responses than do considered opinions. It is clear that public views about crime (and other key issues of the day) are more complex than they appear in opinion polls. This is probably because judgements about what to do about crime spring from conflicting principles based on a mixture of mentalities and emotions, as well as 'rational' reflection and consideration. Everyone holds these incompatible principles to some extent, and can find themselves in a state of personal conflict if required to develop their views in more detail. The rationalist assumptions underpinning these kinds of approaches suggest an over-simplified relationship between knowledge provision and attitudes.

The considerable literature on fear of crime demonstrates that public attitudes about crime and punishment have little to do with any 'factual' assessment of crime risks. Insecurity and anxiousness about crime, and punitive attitudes towards offenders, are associated with complex emotional feelings about social change, or about broader economic or social insecurity. Provision of better information about crime will do little to address these deeper concerns. It is likely that most people have a repertoire of attitudes and modes of behaviour and can switch into one or another depending on the context. Context and social pressure act as cues in deciding what behaviours (and stated attitudes) are appropriate at a particular time. Returning to the research outlined above, when Roberts and Hough (2005) (for example) provide more information about individual cases, this could be seen as providing the contextual cues (or social pressure) that nudge respondents into adopting a different mode of discourse for the time being. Importantly, this is not to say that the more punitive public opinions will not resurface when the context is different (eg. in the voting booth). Although the impact of deliberative methods on people's immediate stated attitudes appears to be clear from the above research, what is less clear is how enduring these changes in stated attitude are over time and across different contexts, and, crucially, how these views correspond with actual voting behaviour.

Although it is certainly the case that this research has demonstrated that people's views are malleable – at least in the short term – what is striking about the public opinion research is the marked persistence of punitive views in numerous such surveys since the 1970s. The leading researchers in this field acknowledge this apparent hardening of attitudes as a significant shift from earlier periods (Roberts 2004). Another factor that causes problems for the 'educating the public' approach concerns the importance of symbolic politics in contemporary discourse about crime. The incentive to make political appeal to the heart rather than the head within the arena of crime control appears to be linked with deeper social and cultural shifts, as well as to the institutional characteristics of particular forms of democracy, which will be considered in the next section. The assumed political effectiveness of 'playing to the gallery' by the deployment of crime control symbols does not seem to be based on false premises, in so far as it actually appears to work rather well. It can be argued that 'public opinion' will always trump 'public judgment' when it actually matters. Even though the provision of information and opportunities for deliberation do appear to facilitate a more considered and moderate public judgement on crime matters, ultimately it may be public opinion 'from the top of the head' that counts when push comes to shove – in the voting booth.

2. The political attraction of punitive policies

Whether or not public opinion about crime and punishment is in fact more equivocal than has been generally assumed, there is no doubt that both main political parties in Britain have found harsh penal rhetoric increasingly attractive in recent decades. This rhetoric has also made itself felt in concrete penal policies. Although punitive public attitudes – at least on some measurements – are an important part of the story, they are perhaps not the primary explanation. A strong urge to avoid the accusation of being 'soft on crime' has been a central feature of competitive party politics in the UK and USA for many years now. However, the notion that politicians simply respond to a punitive public avoids more fundamental questions about developments in contemporary societies that render punitive policies more politically attractive. In particular, there is an influential body of work that suggests that deeper structural forces are at work to shape both public attitudes *and* political responses to crime. This work has important implications for the possibilities of a changed political landscape in penal policy and youth justice.

Structuralist explanations

An important strand of thinking within structuralist explanations suggests that shifts in political economy have driven western industrial nations towards more punitive approaches to crime and punishment. For example, Nils Christie (2000) explored global penal expansion during the latter part of the twentieth century. In his view, changes in social organization in capitalist societies have led both to a decline of informal social controls and to an increased tendency to report incidents as crimes. The public thirst for tougher punishment has been encouraged by a generalized sense of insecurity associated with structural and cultural developments in capitalist societies. In particular, the 'commodification' of crime control has fuelled the expansion of prison populations. Christie argues that penal policy in many industrialized countries is increasingly shaped by the 'prison-industrial complex', a coalition of commercial penal and industrial interests that profit from penal expansion. On this account, the ongoing expansion of incarceration and penal systems in general are the 'natural outgrowth of our type of society, not an exception to it' (2000: 178). Another influential radical structuralist account has been developed by Loïc Wacquant, whose explanation of expanding incarceration rates and other forms of penal harshness in the USA focuses on the function that such policies perform for the operation of capitalist production (Wacquant 2001). He argues forcefully that European nations, although trailing behind the USA at the moment in their use of imprisonment, are bending to the pressures of global capitalism that drive Europe as well as America down the route of penal expansionism.

A variation on the structuralist theme is the highly influential account of penal change provided by David Garland (1996, 2000, 2001), who charts the emergence of a 'culture of control' in the UK and USA during the latter part of the twentieth century (Garland 2001). Garland argues that the style and substance of penal policy in the UK and USA have become increasingly similar in recent years. This is explained by fundamental shifts of social structures and cultural configurations applicable, to a greater or lesser degree, across many 'late modern' capitalist societies. Garland argues that, in both the USA and UK, two kinds of contrasting policy strategy have been introduced. The first type involves the introduction of pragmatic 'adaptive' approaches to crime and disorder, such as the introduction of private sector management techniques to the criminal justice systems; the promotion of management reforms; privatization and contracting out; performance measurement; diversion from the criminal justice system; the pragmatic redefinition of the goals of criminal justice agencies; and the 'responsibilization' of a range of private, voluntary and community agents in the field of crime control. The second kind of strategy involves the simultaneous adoption of policies of 'denial' and 'acting out'. In both the US and the UK, governments, having limited instruments for effective action in the crime control arena, have responded by adopting primarily expressive penal policies, the object of which is 'to denounce the crime and reassure the public' (2001: 133) rather than to reduce levels of crime. Whilst these contrasting strategies are in tension, they are also related in a number of important ways. For example, the technical and managerial discourse about crime that is associated with the former strategy is profoundly unsatisfying to the public, and fans the flames of more expressive and emotional penal rhetoric.

For the current purposes, these accounts offer gloomy answers to questions about possibilities for change, because harsher penal policies have such deep roots in contemporary social and economic systems. With regard to the more radical structural analyses, it is difficult to hold out real hope for any meaningful reform in the absence of a radically changed form of capitalism, or the birth of a new economic and social order altogether. Garland's account provides little more in terms of hope for a progressive shift in penal policy. Despite his acceptance that '[p]olitics and policy always involve choice and decision-making and the possibility of acting otherwise' (2001: 139), the broader focus of his argument downplays the importance of political agency as a shaper of policy outcomes. The political choices that have been made were tightly constrained by deeper changes in social structures and cultural sensibilities. The analysis suggests implicitly that the nature and direction of penal change are almost inevitable, and that we are trapped in an 'iron cage' of the control culture whose bars will constrain us for the foreseeable future. These arguments have been subject to criticism in view of their dystopian implications and deterministic flavour (Zedner 2002).[3] Zedner argues that Garland's account is normatively flawed by its fatalistic implications about the almost certain futility of programmes for positive penal policy change. The empirical validity of Garland's approach has also been questioned, both in terms of the lack of appreciation of the complexity of penal developments, even within the UK and USA, and its implicit assumption that these penal developments are generalized across many other nations (Young 2003). As will be discussed in a later section, comparative research has challenged the notion of a straightforward global convergence of harsher penal policies (Tonry 2007).

The public policy process

Whilst the 'empirical particulars' (Garland 2001) of the policy-making process are not the focus of structuralist accounts, it is worth making brief reference to a large political science literature that looks in detail at the ways in which public policies are formulated, shaped and implemented. Such work can provide important insights into the factors influencing why certain policies and not others come to be adopted by decision-makers, and what happens to these policies in the process of implementation. To this end, researchers have attempted to analyse the nature of policy networks, identify the key players in the policy process, the resources upon which they draw and the types of relationships between them. Relations between the different parties within policy networks are characterized by 'power dependence' (Stoker 1998). Since policy actors have access to different types and levels of resources – financial, political, legal or administrative – the policy process is characterized by negotiation and bargaining among a myriad bodies, both state and non-state. An important theme within this literature concerns the strategies adopted by policy actors and the impact of these factors on agenda-setting and policy outcomes. Whilst there is not the space for a detailed consideration of this work, the clear message for current purposes concerns the fundamental unpredictability of the policy process, and the importance of political agency and institutional context. Although it is clear that policies are developed within a wider social, economic and political context, these wider factors constrain rather than determine political outcomes. To influence policy requires focused activities on many levels, bearing not only on the decision-making stage, but also setting the context for agenda-setting ('pre-decisions') and problem definition, briefing the actors in the legislative process, and following through to implementation through detailed regulation, court decisions, and other concrete aspects of policy. Policy outcomes are further negotiated via the activities of practitioners and 'street-level' bureaucrats.

One model which pays due attention to the complex and fluid nature of the policy process, yet provides a systematic approach to its analysis, is offered by John Kingdon (1995). He identifies three distinct 'process streams' that operate within the system for making public policy. The 'problem stream' is the process of generating problems that come to the attention of policy-makers. The 'policy stream' involves generating policy ideas and proposals. Finally, the 'political stream' is characterized by a range of contextual variables such as the outcome of elections, shifts in popular opinion, interest group campaigns and so on. Kingdon argues that although they usually operate more-or-less independently of one another, the three streams converge at critical times whereby 'solutions become joined to problems and both of them are joined to favourable political forces' (1995: 20). On occasion, 'policy windows' (in the form of opportunities for promotion of particular proposals or conceptions of a problem) are opened by developments in the political stream (such as elections, political scandals, or international crises) or the emergence of particularly compelling problems. These windows provide openings for 'policy entrepreneurs' to promote favoured proposals and/or highlight particular problems. The key defining characteristic of policy entrepreneurs 'is their willingness to invest their resources – time, energy, reputation, and sometimes money – in the hope of future return' (1995: 122). Policy entrepreneurs work to facilitate the linking of problems and proposed solutions to the political stream. Their success depends upon their ability to respond quickly to these windows of opportunity before other solutions become favoured. Whilst the skill of the policy entrepreneur is an important element, there is also a substantial element of happenstance involved. Central to this model, therefore, is the recognition of the contingent nature of policy, highlighting the often unanticipated nature of policy formation and outcome. This approach suggests that significant developments in policy are most likely when problems, policy proposals and politics are linked together into a clear package. It also clearly reinserts the notion of political agency into considerations of policy change.

Politicians promote harsh penal policies for a variety of reasons, many of which have little to do with crime and everything to do with strategic political advantage. The promotion of a tough 'law and order' image was one of the core bases for the reinvention – and subsequent electoral success – of the Democratic Party in the USA and the Labour Party in the UK during the 1990s. The hardening of criminal justice and youth justice policies in England and Wales from the early 1990s has been linked to strategic decisions of the then Conservative Government in response to pressure from a Labour Opposition appealing to the electorate on the basis of its relatively new 'law and order' credentials (Downes and

Morgan 2007; Newburn 2007). Harsh penal policies and the associated rhetoric of politicians are – likely as not – as much a cause of punitive public opinions as a consequence of them. A growing body of research evidence has demonstrated that public opinion about crime and punishment is led by politicians rather than vice versa. Looking back towards the shift towards more punitive law and order policies in the USA during the 1970s, it has been shown that shifts in official political discourse on crime and punishment actually pre-dated the growth of punitive public attitudes as measured by opinion polls (Beckett 1997). It must follow that politicians – at best – have mistaken assumptions about the existence of a punitive majority that end up being self-fulfilling, or – at worst – act cynically in deploying crime control rhetoric in order to win elections with little regard for the instrumental effectiveness of their policies.

The importance of political agency at lower levels in the policy-making system tends to be neglected by structuralist accounts, leading them to exaggerate the punitiveness of penal policy in particular jurisdictions, according to a number of critiques. Recent accounts of youth justice policy in the UK, for example, describe a complex field that combines expressive and politicized responses with a set of more pragmatic and preventive interventions alongside an ongoing commitment to traditional welfare-based rehabilitative policies (Bottoms and Dignan 2004; Goldson and Hughes 2010). As Tonry (2007) has argued, even in those countries that have experienced a general shift to harsher penal policies, in most cases this has been moderated by the activities of professionals and practitioners who resist the intended outcomes of punitive policies, and/or other policy changes that are more progressively-oriented. Pollitt's (2001) analysis of different levels of policy – talk, decisions and action – is helpful here. The punitive shift is most apparent at the level of policy 'talk' – political rhetoric and symbolic politics. However, this rhetoric is not always entirely translated into policy 'decisions' (concrete manifestations of policy such as legislation, legal rulings, institutional reforms, or formal policy directives). There can be an even more complex mixture at the level of policy 'action', in terms of the day-to-day implementation of policies by street-level bureaucrats (see Jones and Newburn 2007 for an analysis of these ideas in the field of criminal justice policy). Thus, the intended outcomes of harsh policies trumpeted by vote-hungry politicians can be mediated, reshaped or resisted altogether by policy-makers and practitioners at lower levels of the policy process.[4]

This provides some counterbalance to the notion of the unrestrained rush towards punitive policy, but the lessons for current purposes are rather limited. Although piecemeal resistance to the negative aspects of national policies may be surprisingly effective, this is something quite different from bringing about a comprehensive and significant shift in policy approach at the national level. Nevertheless, it remains helpful to be reminded that policy can be influenced at different points in the system, as well as perhaps providing a cautionary note about the problems of implementation that are faced by any general policy programmes, of whatever stripe. It also reminds us that even in centralized polities, where policy directions from the centre are more difficult to oppose, resistance to particular national policy trends can still be effective. With regard to the UK, it is important not to overstate the centralized nature of crime control policy. Although not the focus of this chapter, the Scottish youth justice system (and criminal justice system more broadly) has contrasted in important ways with that operating south of the border (Bottoms and Dignan 2004; McAra and McVie 2010). In a similar way, the youth justice arrangements of Northern Ireland have taken on distinctive forms from those in other parts of the UK, both before and after formal devolution (Goldson and Hughes 2010). In England and Wales, criminal justice and youth justice remain *de jure* non-devolved issues. Thus, as Tonry (2007: 26) observes '[i]f the government of the day chooses to act illiberally and to politicize criminal justice policy, there are no competing governmental power centres to stop it'. Yet even within the current devolution settlement, distinctive approaches to youth justice have been emerging in Wales (Edwards and Hughes 2008, 2009) where the trend of policy is towards a more inclusive approach to youth offending than in England, one that is focused on social rather than criminal justice. Drakeford (2010) demonstrates how distinctive policy approaches in the Welsh context are related to the *de facto* embedding of youth justice policies within a broader range of public services, many of which have been formally devolved to the Welsh Assembly Government. The possibility of formal devolution of youth justice powers to Wales is under consideration at the time of writing, after the recent submission of a report on this subject to the Welsh Assembly Government (Drakeford 2010). Thus, even within apparently centralized polities, there are possibilities for the emergence of distinctive policies in the field of youth justice. We will return to this point in the final section of the chapter.

Cross-national comparative research on penal policy trends

The striking evidence from cross-national comparative consideration of penal trends – and similarly trends in youth justice system (Tonry 2004a) – suggests that the thesis of a general shift towards punitive penal policies has been overstated. The shift that is most visible in the UK and USA seems to have been resisted in many other countries (Tonry 2007). Although there remains a lack of detailed cross-national comparative research, an emergent body of literature provides some important clues about what factors may explain this. In particular, Cavadino and Dignan (2005) have used quantitative and qualitative data to compare levels of penal 'severity' across nations. They provide a typology of families of nations distinguished according to their political economy, based on an index of political, institutional, social and economic variables. They found that there are strong associations[5] between levels of penal severity and the characteristics of different types of political-economic organization. In particular, 'neo-liberal' countries (such as the UK, USA, Australia and New Zealand) are notably harsher in their penal policies than 'conservative corporatist' countries (e.g. France, Germany), 'social democratic' nations (Sweden, Finland) and the country characterized as 'oriental corporatist' (Japan). This kind of analysis is developed by various other authors who identify particular features of the political economy and social organization of different democratic countries as key to understanding the development of more or less harsh and politicized approaches to penal policy (Lacey 2007; Tonry 2007; Green 2007). What emerges from this analysis is the interconnectedness of national cultural dispositions, political institutions and aspects of social and economic organization: all these appear to interact so as to predispose nations to greater or lesser punitiveness in penal policy. Of course, it is of little comfort to those who would change the politics of youth crime in England and Wales to hear that things are different in Norway or Germany. The key aim here is to consider what practical lessons for England and Wales can be learned from those countries following a different route in their approach to youth crime/penal policy. Analysis of the comparative literature suggests the following factors as key shapers of the nature of penal politics in different national contexts.

Economic and social policy approaches

There appears to be a growing consensus amongst informed commentators that the general approach to economic and social policy that has dominated in the UK for the last three decades is an important part of the explanation for the nature of penal politics in England and Wales. Lacey (2007) considers possible explanations for the striking correlations between 'neo-liberal' political economic organization (or 'liberal market economies' (LMEs)) and measures of severity in penal policy, when compared with corporatist/social democratic countries (generalized as 'coordinated market economies' (CMEs)). Tonry's (2007) analysis of 'risk factors' draws similar general conclusions. LMEs have a greater cultural attachment to individualism, and a policy stance that favours deregulation, competition and free markets, and in particular, labour market 'flexibility'. These countries tend to have more limited and restrictive social welfare policies, and greater levels of social and economic inequality. CMEs, by contrast, exhibit less concern about improving labour market flexibility, with the approach to social and economic policy based on long-term investment in high skills manufacturing, reflected in greater government and employer spending on education and training. Such countries adopt a more coordinated approach to economic policy that brings employers, labour and government together to negotiate over key issues of economic management.[6]

Political institutions

Another important explanatory variable highlighted by cross-national comparative research concerns the particular approach to democracy and the institutional manifestation of these ideas in different countries. A number of authors have drawn on the the distinction – outlined originally by Lijphart – between 'competititive' and 'consensus' political systems (Tonry 2007; Green 2007). The former kind of political system – prevalent in Anglophone, common law countries such the UK – is characterized by adversarial two-party politics and first-past-the-post electoral systems that almost always result in single party government. The political system is designed to produce strong government, such that small swings in aggregate voter preferences can lead to major changes in government majorities. Coalition government is rare and political party discipline is strong. The end result is an extremely strong hand for the executive, such that Quintin Hogg (1976), a distinguished politician and political commentator, called the UK an 'elective dictatorship'. The office of UK Prime Minister has during recent decades accrued increasing *de facto* powers, provoking debates about the shift away from 'cabinet government' and towards 'prime ministerial diktat'. The presidential styles of two dominant prime ministers since 1945 – Margaret Thatcher and Tony Blair – have underlined and entrenched such trends. The evidence currently being provided to the Iraq Inquiry underlines the striking *de facto* and *de jure* power of a British prime minister, supported by a parliamentary majority, to push through contentious policies in the face of massive public opposition. This is not to argue that the system lacks checks and balances, for it is subject to lobbying by special interests and pressure groups, and to blockages and delays. But compared with the systems in other European countries, the British system is more likely to produce clear governmental programmes for the electorate to choose between. Once a government is in power with a large majority in parliament, the electorate can do little to resist a determined executive. This feeds into a particular political culture, in which politics is a zero/sum game. The aim of the opposition is to criticize and undermine the government of the day, with the occasional exception such as the field of national security policy. Adversarial politics provide incentives for politicians to inspire or exploit emotive populist discussions of policy, perhaps most vividly illustrated in the field of crime politics. Lacey (2007) argues that in such a 'winner takes all' political system there is the need to appeal to the 'median voter', the representative of that body of floating voters who are crucial to the outcome of elections. The deployment of expressive symbolism to attract these voters proves difficult for political parties to resist, particularly with regard to emotive issues surrounding crime and punishment. Thus, this distinctive set of political institutions and associated practices makes its mark on criminal justice and penal policy-making.

The role of expert elites in policy-making

A crucial development within the Anglo-American model of democracy is the declining prestige of 'elite' expertise in policy-making, and the growing influence of popular sentiment (Tonry 2007). Experts are not completely squeezed out of the system, but their influence is increasingly challenged by a populist discourse that reflects an apparently growing distrust of experts, be they social scientists or criminal justice professionals. The general collapse of faith in penal experts was an important part of Garland's (2001) analysis, and is reflected more broadly in falls in levels of public trust in a range of political and democratic institutions. The temptation for governments to play an avowedly populist hand both reflects and strengthens these shifts. Green (2007) demonstrates this in his analysis of the political and media discourse that followed the killing of the toddler James Bulger by other children in England in 1993, and a similar child-on-child killing in Norway one year later. There were striking contrasts between the political and media responses to each of the respective killings. In Norway, there was less press coverage overall, and the story remained at the forefront of media debate for a much shorter time. Discussion in the Norwegian press was more pragmatic and less emotional, and – crucially – the opinions of experts such as child psychologists and social workers were given prominent coverage. In Britain, by contrast, in the course of the media frenzy following the Bulger killing, the story continued to be front page news for far longer,[7] and the tone of press discussion was highly condemnatory and emotional. The views of experts were either not reported or, on the rare occasions that they were mentioned, subject to ridicule. Tonry (2007) sees this downplaying of expertise as a key distinguishing feature of the more populist conceptions of democracy that pertain in the USA and UK, as compared with other European systems.

Expert influence did not always struggle to compete with media-led populist opinion on crime in England and Wales. Prior to the 1970s, the system of policy-making was a relatively closed one, and the 'expert' views of officials dominated decision-making. Although those days are long gone, there remains a lively debate about the possibilities for research-led policy-making on crime control in the UK. Following their election victory in 1997, the Labour Government expressed a commitment to evidence-led policy-making manifested in the launch of the Crime Reduction Programme from 1999. The aim of the programme was to gather, disseminate and deploy social scientific research-based knowledge about the effectiveness of criminal justice and policing interventions. Initially, the programme was planned to last for ten years, but it ran into problems and was ended prematurely in 2002. Few projects eventually developed as planned, and the programme concluded with a remarkable absence of useful research findings or substantive outcomes. This experiment in research-led policy therefore came to an end in confusion and acrimony, with accusations and counter accusations between the research community and policy world of political manipulation of findings on one side and the inadequacies of academic research on the other (Maguire 2004; Hope 2004). In many ways, this episode reflected a long-standing problem of effective engagement between policy and research. As Maguire (2004: 226) noted, 'most researchers and policy-makers ultimately inhabit different worlds which differ significantly in terms of aims, values, and interests'. In particular, the need for politicians and policy-makers to appear authoritative, to demonstrate success (ideally in easily-digestible quantitative terms), and most important, to produce results within the timescales set by the political cycle, can make for difficult relations with academic experts. Maguire's conclusion was that evidence-led policy-making needs to be conceived in a more modest way as an iterative process, rather than structured as 'one-off' large-scale programmes.

The research community finds itself in a difficult position with regard to influencing crime policy, and a number of responses are possible. From the viewpoint of 'critical' criminologists, it is impossible to untangle research and politics. On this view, to undertake government-funded research – at best – is to be restricted to politically safe and intellectually uninteresting issues. At worst, it involves being willingly co-opted into providing scientific credibility for the state's repressive approaches to social control. On the other hand, an increasingly vocal 'crime science' promotes the possibilities for criminology providing objective and scientifically valid answers to the policy-makers' question 'what works?' (Sherman 2009). Whereas crime science policy entrepreneurs have had some success in promoting their ideas to policy-makers – who quite naturally are attracted to offers of certainty and predictability from research findings – this approach has been the source of significant controversy amongst academic criminologists (Hope 2009). The prospects for a meaningful engagement of research and crime policy still seem rather distant. However, there are positive signs, for example in the recent focus on the need for a 'public criminology' (Loader and Sparks forthcoming) including outward-looking intellectual projects that seek to make a positive difference on the world of crime and control. Adam Edwards and James Sheptycki (2009) have advocated the development of empirically grounded and methodologically eclectic criminological research that can engage meaningfully with major policy questions of the day, and challenge the current privileging of the folk wisdom of popular opinion. This 'Third Wave' criminology makes a vigorous case for the value of expert social scientific input into policy formulation, as opposed to the accounts of other political and moral actors (Edwards and Sheptycki 2009). Such an approach has much to commend it, and particularly in the simultaneous avoidance of the 'impossiblism' of much critical criminology, and the methodological tunnel vision and often dubious promises of crime science.

This call for a more self-conscious advocacy of the value of social scientific knowledge to policy development comes at a time when populist democratic experiments in 'community engagement' are actively promoting a valorizing of 'popular opinion' over other sources of knowledge about crime and punishment. A key example of this is provided by Louise Casey, the former head of the government's 'Respect' taskforce, in the foreword to her report to the Cabinet Office, *Engaging Communities in Fighting Crime*:

> Most of all I would urge policy makers, professionals, lobby groups and law makers to take note of one thing – the public are not daft. They know what's wrong, they know what's right, and they know what they want on crime and justice. And it's time action was taken on their terms. (2008: 4)[8]

The news media

Media reporting of crime and punishment are often singled out as key explanations for hostile political and popular opinions about crime and punishment. Roberts (2004), for example, identifies the extent and nature of media reporting about crime as a vital factor in shaping punitive public attitudes. As Pople and Smith (Chapter 3) discuss, there is strong evidence that consumption of particular forms of news media is associated with greater levels of anxiety about crime and with poorer levels of knowledge about actual trends and patterns of offending. British Crime Survey data, for example, show that readers of tabloid newspapers are substantially more likely to worry about burglary and violent crime than readers of broadsheet newspapers, and also much more likely to think that crime levels have increased. A number of distinctive features of the UK media market increase the probability of emotive and exaggerated reporting of crime when compared with some other European countries. For example, the highly competitive nature of the UK popular press market – with most newspapers being sold from news-stands and shops (rather than via subscription, as in Norway) – gives newspapers incentives to produce lurid headlines and leading stories, in order to grab the attention of the passing punter. The UK newspaper media is dominated by a few large and powerful corporations with their own political as well as business agendas. The political importance of the tabloid press was a key factor shaping Tony Blair's appointment of a former political editor of the *Daily*

Mirror as his press secretary. Although other countries have tabloid newspapers and are far from immune to febrile press discussions of crime and offenders, these factors make the UK press particularly distinctive. Whilst crime stories have always formed a staple part of news media reporting, with all the attendant distortions and exaggerations, the increasing political importance of tabloid newspapers has been a vital part of UK crime politics in recent years. A number of pressures push the popular press towards more punitive discussions of crime and punishment. The fact that most newspapers have explicitly conservative leanings has a clear ideological influence on the reporting of law and order issues. Probably more important, though, are the general features of the news-making process and particular institutional features of the news market that make highly emotive and sensationalist reporting of crime almost inevitable (Reiner 2007). Newspapers need to sell copies, and shocking stories that focus on violent and/or sexual crimes are a proven and effective method of doing this.

Cultural values

A number of authors suggest that different penal cultures (and cultures more generally) are an important part of the explanation for tendencies towards or against harsh penal policies. Tonry (2007), in his risk factor analysis suggests, for example, that the presence of 'Anglo-Saxon' political cultures is associated with a greater probability of adopting harsh penal approaches, whereas the presence of francophone culture has the opposite effect. Melossi (2001) relates the striking differences over time between penal systems in the USA and in Italy to contrasting cultural attitudes associated with Protestant and Catholic traditions. A number of explanations of the nature of penal policies in the USA highlight distinctive features of the USA as key factors. For example, Whitman (2003) presents an analysis of US penality that draws upon a combination of cultural and institutional explanations. He contrasts the penal histories of France and Germany with that of the USA, and contrasts the relatively strong tradition of state bureaucracy in Germany and France with the much more limited and distrusted state apparatus in the USA. Whitman argues that in the more hierarchical and class-divided France and Germany, where forms of punishment were related to social status, the modern period saw a conscious process of 'levelling-up' in punishment. This involved a gradual improvement of the treatment of prisoners, who were all eventually accorded a degree of respect and moderate treatment. By contrast, in the more egalitarian USA, a strong element of degradation in punishment remains. Whitman also sees political institutions as an important part of the explanation, with particular reference to the relative insulation of penal policy-making from popular sentiment in France and Germany. In these and other continental European countries, criminal justice decision-making is strongly influenced by professional cadres of trained bureaucrats, compared with the strong ideology of popular democracy in the USA. Zimring (2003) links the persistence of capital punishment in the USA (in stark contrast with European nations) to long-established historical traditions and distinctive cultural traits that are particularly associated with parts of the USA (what he terms 'the vigilante tradition').

Can the harsher penal approach of England and Wales be explained in a similar way by reference to particular 'cultural' characteristics? Tonry (2004b) argues that until the early 1990s penal policy in the UK had more in common with other Western European nations than with the USA. However, since this time there has been a growing tendency for British policy to emulate that in parts of the USA. Much of this is linked to the Labour Party's changed position on crime and punishment, but Tonry believes that these policy outcomes were made more likely by three peculiarly British cultural characteristics. First, he argues that British people have become peculiarly risk-averse with respect to crime. This is partly because of government's emphasis on crime prevention in recent decades, which has had the unintended effect of exacerbating fear of crime. Second, in common with Whitman (2003), he suggests that the British have developed a cultural taste for the 'debasement' of offenders. Finally, he argues that people in Britain have a more acute sense of 'self righteousness and punitiveness' about offenders than exists in other European countries (Tonry 2004b: 55–66).

At a broad level of comparison, cultural explanations of differing national approaches to penal policy do seem to have some purchase. However, it is difficult to test such arguments empirically, due to the difficulty in finding valid measures of 'cultural dispositions'. Furthermore, we should beware of advancing over-generalized notions of 'national' cultural characteristics – for example concerning an 'English and Welsh' culture of punitiveness – that overlooks evidence of contrasting cultures of control at the regional and local levels. For example, there are clear variations in youth justice approaches both within and between England and Wales that bring into question generalizations about 'national' cultures (Goldson and Hughes 2010).

3. Changing direction: assessing the political possibilities

In the light of this discussion, is it feasible to change the direction of youth justice policy, and how could this be brought about? Can we imagine how a calmer and more evidence-led approach to policy-making in this field might emerge? In this final section, the first part considers the broad contextual factors associated with populist politics that limit the room for manoeuvre in policy-making. The second part focuses on particular aspects of current circumstances that may offer openings, however modest, for a more progressive shift in policy-making in England and Wales.

Contextual factors

The more radical structuralist accounts of penal change suggest that a clear shift in the nature and substance of penal policy in the near future is very unlikely, and would require revolutionary change in the global economic system, along with associated political and social transformations. Other structuralist accounts, such as that of Garland (2001), have similarly pessimistic implications: they suggest that change in the broad thrust of penal policy would require a fundamental shift in deeper economic, social and cultural conditions that confine the policy choices within quite narrow constraints. However, as we have seen, a considerable body of comparative research suggests that things could be different here in Britain because they are different in other advanced economies with some form of democratic politics. Nevertheless, the above review of factors associated with harsher approaches to penal policy still suggests there are formidable obstacles in the way of reform. A dramatic shift of direction in youth justice policy (or in crime policy more generally) would run counter to recent political trajectories and would push against several intractable features of our political system.

It is difficult to see any major shifts in the key contextual factors that are closely associated with the nature of crime politics in England and Wales. Even the most optimistic social democrat would probably admit that any significant change in approach towards a substantially more inclusive and coordinated social and economic policy – in effect, a sudden conversion of the UK to the European 'social model' – is unlikely to happen in the near future. Indeed, the general drift of social and economic policy is in the opposite direction. Despite the temporary return to a brand of Keynesian demand management during the global financial crisis, the magnitude of the current budget deficit means that the UK is facing a period of austerity. Whatever the outcome of the next election, we certainly face substantial cuts in public expenditure, including a retreat from the real increases in social welfare expenditure that have occurred under recent Labour administrations.

Similarly, it is hard to see any substantial changes in the political institutional variables that are strongly associated with our particular form of crime politics, at least in the near future. The one significant exception to this argument concerns the possibilities of electoral reform, which has recently reappeared at the edges of the political agenda. Should replacement of the 'first-past-the-post' electoral system by a form of proportional representation (PR) actually come about, this would be of longer-term relevance in perhaps signalling a retreat from adversarial, two-party politics in the UK. There is at least the possibility that electoral reform could become a bargaining tool in the case of a hung parliament, with the Liberal Democrats holding the balance of power. At the time of writing (March 2010) the 2010 General Election is being presented as one of the most unpredictable for many years, and the outcome of a minority government or even a coalition remains a distinct possibility.[9] The Liberal Democrats have remained lukewarm in response to recent reports of the prime minister's 'deathbed conversion' to electoral reform (Toynbee 2009). But this would be unlikely to remain their position in circumstances – such as a hung parliament – where they might have real bargaining power. However, the nature of the electoral system is but one of a range of linked institutional and cultural factors that shape our current brand of penal politics, and on its own would be unlikely to change the adversarial nature of our system in the short or medium term.[10]

It is more difficult to assess the possibilities of a dramatic shift in the nature of the news media in the UK. The current style and substance of UK press discussion of crime is shaped primarily by features of the news market that are particular to Britain, that operate alongside what seem to be perennial features of the news-making process everywhere. Whilst it is difficult to see any major change in the reporting of youth crime in the UK tabloid press in the immediate future, it may be that the growth of new media technologies has at least the potential to change things. Some writers have argued that new forms of electronic media are having a rather marginal impact on the political process (Bimber 2001). In contrast, other authors have emphasized the positive potential of new internet technologies, arguing that the growth of the new electronic media may transform the nature of political participation, improving access to information and bringing about a more informed and balanced public discussion of major public policy issues (Tolbert and McNeal 2003). On another viewpoint, some authors have raised warnings about potential negative consequences of new information technologies, which may bring about a 'thin citizenship' in which more significant forms of political participation are increasingly replaced by superficial web-based expressions of preference (Howard 2003). It remains very difficult to predict how these developments will play themselves out in the politics of crime in the UK. We might speculate that the democratizing potential of the internet could come to challenge some of the enduring features of the UK news market, such as its concentration in the hands of a few multi-national companies and its overt ideological biases. Against this, shrinking circulation related to the increasing availability of online news media may result, at least in the immediate term, in an even more fiercely competitive news media market, and further increase the pressure to present attention-grabbing and emotive news stories. It remains difficult to imagine any radical attempt to change direction on youth justice policy away from a punitive trajectory, at least in the medium term, that would not face hostile press opposition.

All these factors are tied up with a broader notion of differing political (and penal) 'cultures'. To the extent that national cultures can be shown to exist (and this is difficult), changing the 'culture' of a nation does not look like a realistic possibility except in the very long term. The likelihood is that any attempts to change the direction of youth justice policy will need to work within the prevailing cultural climate for the foreseeable future.

The potential for change

The various features of the social, economic and political structure that have been reviewed, along with associated political and penal cultures, place severe constraints on what can be done to change the youth justice system. These structural and cultural conditions may change as a consequence of tectonic shifts in the global or national economy or in technologies, or as a direct result of government actions. In any case, any such changes are hard to predict, and may not make youth justice any easier. In the meantime, attempts to shift the direction of penal policy have to work within the known constraints of the present social, economic and political structures and the associated cultures. Within those constraints, what are the realistic possibilities for change? We focus on two ideas with potential for development: the scope for reasserting the authority of expertise and establishing it on an independent footing; and the opportunity for finding policy windows, small at first, that can be used to open up debate and to find leverage for larger changes.

Reasserting expertise

There seems to be a strong consensus among commentators that populist influence in criminal justice and youth justice policy-making in the competitive electoral system of England and Wales has an unhealthy impact on policy outcomes. Indeed, as Lacey (2007) notes, more direct forms of democracy are associated with a reduced likelihood of policy outcomes that accord with 'liberal democratic' expectations; that is, policies based on a desire to be 'reintegrative and inclusionary' (2007: 8). As she puts it:

> And here we encounter one of the most troubling empirical para-
> doxes of contemporary democratic criminal justice. For the fact is
> that, in many countries, criminal justice policy has been driven in an
> exclusionary direction with – perhaps even because of – popular, and
> hence literally democratic, support. (2007: 8)

A number of critics of the populist trends in penal policy in this jurisdiction have compared penal policy-making in England and Wales unfavourably with some other European countries. A key part of this argument relates to the higher degree of insulation of policy-making from popular opinion. This devolution of relatively high levels of decision-making to non-partisan 'experts' is presented as a positive feature of these systems of democracy (Lacey 2007; Green 2007). And yet, when it comes to a consideration of the formerly 'closed' system of criminal justice policy-making that operated in England and Wales prior to the 1970s, some liberal commentators appear to be uneasy, on grounds of both general principle and practicality.

Loader (2006) argues that to attempt to insulate policy-making from wider public influences would be 'profoundly antidemocratic'. But there is nothing inherently 'antidemocratic' about attempting to insulate decision-making processes – within reason – from popular sentiment (Tonry 2007). This is only necessarily the case if one conceives of democracy in a particular way: as a method for ensuring citizen participation in decision-making and responsiveness to partisan political bodies. There is a strong association with these more direct models of popular democracy and punitive and ineffective penal outcomes, as the story of 'three strikes' sentencing in California demonstrates (Zimring *et al.* 2001; Jones and Newburn 2006). Democracy can be seen as a set of principles or values, of which responsiveness and citizen participation are an important part, but alongside other values such as equity, protection of minority rights, effective use of public resources, and the distribution of power (Jones *et al.* 1995). Different democratic traditions place different weights on the various values, with some continental European countries placing relatively greater emphasis on, for example, the distribution of power, equity, and effectiveness as compared with the more 'direct' democratic values of citizen participation and responsiveness. The insulation of decision-making power from populist influences is a quite deliberate element in the design of these systems. That this feature does not tend to be castigated as antidemocratic[11] by British penal commentators is mainly because the policy outcomes in these countries are deemed to be considerably more palatable than those in the UK. As Tonry (2007) points out, in most countries, professional and expert opinions are seen as quite legitimate sources of authority in criminal justice policy-making. Indeed, one of the key reasons for creating a criminal justice bureaucracy was to distance important decisions from the sway of emotion and vengeance. The professional autonomy of senior criminal justice professionals is an important and enduring element of British constitutional tradition. Indeed, the policy-making autonomy of chief constables and the doctrine of judicial independence have in recent years been an important source of resistance to politically-driven illiberal ('antidemocratic' on Lacey's earlier definition) policies such as 'zero tolerance' and 'three strikes' (Jones and Newburn 2007). It is important, therefore, to recognize that different institutional forms of democracy balance the various democratic values in different ways, and one overall approach is not necessarily more or less 'democratic' than another.

The re-insulation of penal policy can also be challenged on practical grounds. Green (2006) argues that such an approach would be politically unacceptable, and would have negative outcomes in the longer term. The risk would be that an increasingly alienated public responded to their exclusion from decision-making elites by becoming more frustrated and punitive in their demands. Greenberg (2002) makes some similar arguments in relation to the USA. In some parts of the USA, he argues, an attempt to move back to a more expert-dominated system is unlikely to work, because 'where political systems are competitive, and freedom of speech and a free press are maintained, philosopher kings cannot easily rule through noble lies' (2002: 244). Because of the salience of crime and punishment in popular and political debates (unlike economic policy, for example), in Greenberg's view it would be extremely difficult to insulate criminal justice from democratic pressures in polities where such independence is not already part of the political system. In England and Wales, however, a greater degree of professional independence has remained a central – if increasingly challenged – part of the penal system. This tradition suggests that conscious attempts to re-distribute the balance of democratic values – away from certain forms of popular sentiment and towards accepting the authority of expert opinion – may not be as culturally jarring in the UK as they would be in the more populist states of the USA. As noted earlier, there is a much more established constitutional tradition of professional independence in the fields of sentencing and policing than exists in any part of the USA. There is also a degree of political and public acceptance of the deliberate insulation of decision-making in certain fields, such as economic management and medicine, from the direct influence of popular opinion. Although there are from time to time high-profile controversies, non-partisan institutions taking key decisions based on expert advice rather than political expedient are well established. Interestingly, Zimring et al.'s (2001) analysis of the development of three strikes sentencing in California led them to similar conclusions about punishment and democracy. They used the example of the Federal Reserve Board – a non-partisan expert body that sets interest rates – to demonstrate how the principle of insulating decisions from popular sentiment has been accepted in some areas of public policy. They argue that sentencing should also be taken out of politics and given instead to expert independent Commissions with a brief to produce fair, rational and consistent policies. The Sentencing Advisory Panel and the Sentencing Guidelines Council in England and Wales, created during a period of populist pressure, are a precedent for the creation of non-partisan expert bodies in the criminal justice field.

Lacey (2007) proposes that an important precondition of a more progressive shift in penal policy would be a self-conscious effort by the major parties to voluntarily take the (party) politics out of criminal justice decision-making. She argues, in effect, for a mutual cessation of political hostilities in the field of criminal justice and crime control, based on an appeal to reason. Although accepting that this would be difficult, she cites a number of reasons for thinking it is not out of the question: that all parties stand to lose from an irrational and expensive penal policy, that all parties are vulnerable to political attack on law and order, and that there are other aspects of public policy, such as matters pertaining to national security, where bipartisan consensus can and does occur. Such an approach would involve the establishment of a Royal Commission to undertake a full review of penal policy, and make recommendations for the introduction of new non-partisan and expert institutions to which key decisions on penal policy would be devolved. There are recent precedents for the establishment of forums based on expert representation and/or bipartisan consensus. Lacey refers to the creation of the Monetary Policy Committee of the Bank of England, to which the new Labour administration devolved decisions about interest rate levels in 1997. More recently, Gordon Brown has established cross-party 'task forces' in various spheres of policy. These new approaches are in addition, of course, to the now well-established bipartisan inputs of the Select Committee system of the House of Commons. However welcome such developments are, it is difficult to see how they can challenge the strong imperatives of competitive party democracy when push comes to shove. Ultimately, Lacey's proposals would mean asking politicians to voluntarily lay down some of their most potent weapons in the electoral battles ahead, and it is difficult to see this happening, such is the entrenched nature of crime politics in this country. Of course, we should not overlook the important institutions that already exist to facilitate the influence of expert evidence over policy decisions. The Youth Justice Board already plays an important part in commissioning applied research on effective practice and disseminating its findings to practitioners (see Stephenson *et al.* 2007). However, the highly politicized nature of criminal justice (and youth justice) policy means that balanced assessments of the available evidence are always vulnerable to being swept aside by the forces of political expediency.[12] But there are policy spheres which remain the focus of intense political controversy, and yet which have managed to develop institutions that provide a greater degree of insulation from crude populist pressures and wider avenues for expert input than currently exist within the field of youth justice.

The sphere of health policy, for example, may provide a useful model for the development of similar approaches in the field of youth justice. The National Institute for Health and Clinical Excellence (NICE) was established in 1999 (originally as the National Centre for Clinical Excellence). NICE was intended initially to remove decisions about treatment from the 'postcode lottery', whereby the availability of particular treatments and drugs varied between local National Health Service Trust areas. NICE publishes guidelines for the NHS regarding the use of health technologies (including new and established drugs and medical interventions), guidance on clinical practice (i.e. best practice in the care of patients with particular health conditions), and guidelines on public health promotion and disease prevention. NICE guidelines are formulated by expert committees based on research evidence. There have been suggestions from a number of criminologists, particularly those within the tradition of crime science, that this model of objective evidence-led policy-making provides a way forward for criminal justice and penal policy. A 'National Centre for Youth Justice Excellence', along similar lines to the proposals of Wilcox and Hirschfield (2007) would apply the principles underlying NICE to the youth justice field. It would, for example, provide clear research-based guidelines for prevention and intervention with young offenders. In fact, the NICE model has been cited for developments already established within the field of crime control, such as the National Centre for Policing Excellence, which was set up in 1998.

Whilst the creation of some expert research body to inform key decisions on youth justice policy makes sense, a major problem is found in the critiques of crime science outlined earlier. The application of a straightforward clinical research model to interventions in complex social fields such as policing, offender management, or youth justice, is problematic in a number of ways. In particular, the difficulties in achieving a consensus about valid methodological approaches and clear research findings are magnified. Even within the ostensibly more certain field of clinical research, of course, methodological and political controversies can call into doubt the notion of expert consensus. Although one of the key aims of NICE was to provide a non-partisan expert body to take key decisions, it has been increasingly involved in controversy in recent years. Some of these controversies have arisen because of the inevitable tension between healthcare decisions in individual cases, and national policies and resource allocation. In addition, there have been suggestions that NICE decisions are also subject to lobbying by special interests, not least powerful pharmaceutical companies keen to promote their own drugs (House of Commons Health Committee 2008). However, notwithstanding the controversies and problems that NICE has faced, the principles upon which the NICE model is based do seem to offer some way forward in providing a more credible and effective buffer between the vicissitudes of popular opinion on youth crime, and the decisions of key policy-makers in the field. Consideration of this approach within the field of crime and penal policy is not new, of course. It has been suggested by a number of commentators that criminal justice and penal policy might develop analogous institutions for the impartial decisions about 'best practice' based on the best available research (Shepherd 2007; Sherman 2009). To date, these suggestions about the creation of non-partisan expert bodies to inform policies in the fields of criminal justice and penal policy are most closely associated with a particular take – and a controversial one

369

– on 'what counts' in terms of criminological research (Sherman 2009). However, whilst fundamental disagreements remain about standards of evidence and methodological approaches, many social scientists would surely support consideration being given to the creation of expert institutions that are insulated, to a degree, from the political process, so long as these institutions were compatible with the requirements of public accountability. Such institutions could, in theory, commission research that drew upon a range of methodological traditions. This could include, where appropriate, the lessons of quantitative experimental criminology, but also draw upon other kinds of methodological approach that can give rise to credible and compelling evidence. As Goldson (2010) argues, despite the noise associated with methodological and ideological divisions in research community, there is a significant degree of social scientific consensus about core features of the youth crime problem and the possible policy responses to it that would meet the requirements of effectiveness and justice. This corpus of knowledge has in recent decades had very limited influence over actual policy decisions. In addition to commissioning direct research on youth crime and justice, deliberative forms of research on public opinions on youth justice could be undertaken, based on the proposal of Green (2006) outlined earlier. These sources of evidence could then be used to inform decision-making and the formulation of implementation guidelines, and to provide a more robust challenge to crude populist pressures. Whatever the existing problems with promoting evidence-based policy, the case needs to be made for basing policy more directly on the 'contributory expertise' of social scientists (Edwards and Sheptycki 2009), rather than upon 'top of the head' public opinion or cynical political opportunism.

Policy windows

Empirical political science studies have shown us that it is important not to overestimate the degree of coherence and predictability of the policy-making process. Whilst this essentially serendipitous nature of the policy process can of course work to frustrate attempts to radically change policy (as well as actions to continue down a well-trodden path), it does have some practical lessons for those concerned with promoting a change in direction. The work of John Kingdon outlined earlier demonstrates that whilst the broader contextual factors that constitute the 'political stream' – including those contextual factors outlined above – are an important factor in policy change, they are not the only factors nor even are they always the most important. Whilst it is difficult to engineer the appearance of 'policy windows', a clear lesson of empirical studies of crime control policy-making in recent years is to ensure that the policy prescriptions are being promoted in such a way as to take advantage of any windows that may arise, at the same time as working on the more long-term project of bringing about broader changes in the political stream (for example, via the public information approach outlined above, or attempts to influence press debate by engaging more skilfully with the news media).

What is certain is that 'policy windows' will open in the period following the next general election. Even if the election results in a majority government, this will involve an initial period during which new ministers are taking up their cabinet portfolios and are searching for particular policy initiatives with which to make their mark. A coalition government – or minority government dependent on parliamentary support from the smaller parties – presents a wider range of potential policy windows. These windows provide opportunities to sell policy programmes, preferably attached to pressing political problems, to key decision makers. Given that the pressing political problem of the day concerns the economy, one effective line of promotion could emphasize costs and efficiency (as much as any moral arguments). As Drakeford (2010) points out in his analysis of youth justice policy in Wales, the more welfare-oriented approach to youth crime policy adopted by the Welsh Assembly Government is related to a broader ideological/moral position, but crucially also appeals to considerations of 'enlightened self-interest' these spring from an understanding at senior political levels about the expensive and counter-productive nature of many punitive youth justice interventions. In parallel with Lacey's (2007) arguments about penal policy in general, it seems that the period immediately following the formation of a new government would be an opportune time to attempt to demonstrate to ministers that some current policy options – such as the incarceration of children – are both costly and ineffective and that credible alternatives can be offered. In another way, whilst the contextual political obstacles to radical shifts in youth justice (and penal policy) remain forbidding, certain aspects of the UK democratic tradition make radical, and unpopular, policy shifts more possible than in the 'consensus-based' systems of continental Europe. As research on policy-making in the Netherlands has shown, whilst consensus and negotiation (along with the input of expert opinion) may be strengths of the Dutch model, important limitations include a built-in 'institutional conservatism' and a strong tendency to resist radical change (Jones 1995). Indeed, it has been suggested in connection with the Netherlands that the tradition of devolving policy decisions to expert commissions is one method of effectively neutralizing radical proposals.[13] In brief, if the Commission wishes to propose changes that are both radical and vulnerable to populist opposition, the chances of bringing these into being – though modest – are probably greater than were the political system characterized by the checks and balances and tradition of compromise that is prevalent in many continental European countries.

This relates to another helpful notion provided by the work of Kingdon, that of the policy entrepreneur. Under most circumstances, influencing

policy requires considerable entrepreneurial activity. As the above discussion of evidence-based policy demonstrates, it is a recurrent frustration
of criminological researchers that that their research findings do not reach
and influence key stakeholders. However, a consideration of the politics
of crime control policy-making over recent years shows that policy
entrepreneurs played a key role in the promotion of ideas such as 'zero
tolerance' and 'three strikes' (Jones and Newburn 2007; Newburn and
Jones 2007). One particularly effective form of policy entrepreneurship
was 'elite networking': working directly with those whose job it is to
attempt to influence policy such as think tanks and pressure groups. It
also provided means for two other forms of elite networking – direct work
with practitioners and use of the media – both of which arguably play a
vital role in the promotion of ideas. Without overstating the influence of
policy entrepreneurs as straightforward authors of policy change (in that
many of these proposals had good fit with prevailing political conditions),
it would be unwise to overlook the contribution made by energetic and
politically astute policy agents.[14] In addition, a relatively simple and
plausible policy narrative increases the likelihood that particular ideas
will take hold and, once they do, will remain influential. Clearly, in order
to have an impact on public policy it is not sufficient to simply have a
powerful narrative. There needs to be a 'policy window' that provides
opportunities in the context of a favourable constellation of political
forces, linked to key problems arising on the agenda of politicians/policy-
makers and various solutions that are currently being offered. These
windows of opportunity provide space for advocates of particular ideas
and approaches, but it still remains for such people to take advantage of
them.

Thus, although in many ways, the policy narratives behind some of the
more punitive policy shifts have been 'of their time' in terms of having
certain consonance with prevailing social and political conditions, the
influence of such narratives was by no means inevitable. The agency of
key individuals and organizations possessing a significant degree of
political acumen and practical advocacy skills has played a major part in
the story of the wider influence of these ideas. Although paradoxical in
some ways, this story does provide some positive lessons for those who
seek to influence policy in the opposite direction.

A final point relates to the earlier discussion about variations in local
cultures of control, and policy windows that may emerge in relation to the
decentralization of policy-making within the UK. Interesting divergences
between youth justice policy in the devolved polities of Wales, Scotland
and Northern Ireland have been widely noted (Drakeford 2010; Goldson
and Hughes 2010; McAra and McVie 2010).[15] Whilst the first aim of the
ambitious policy entrepreneur is to exert influence at the apparent apex
of political power to obtain political commitment to a radical shift at the
highest level, devolution has clearly provided other points in the system

for the exertion of effective political influence. As already noted, even within the current devolution settlement in which youth justice policy remains a Whitehall responsibility, policy approaches in Wales have already diverged in some important ways from those in England, and in a direction which is more in keeping with the general approaches that the Commission is likely to advocate. If formal devolution of youth justice policy to the Welsh Assembly Government is adopted, this would provide a very significant policy window, even if only in one of the polities of the UK. Similar policy windows may open should there be a genuine decentralization of public policy-making away from the national level to regional and local levels in England. Even in the absence of any significant regional devolution in England, considerable variation in the practical implementation of youth justice policies has been noted (Burney 2009). It may be that more substantial shifts in policy in devolved polities such as Wales could act as a lever of influence to bring about policy change in regions of England. At present, there is only limited autonomy in different regions of England to develop distinctive local approaches. However, there have been some significant political signals from both major parties that a more decentralized approach to policy-making in England – across a range of public policy areas – may be on the cards. For example, in 2009, the Government introduced the Total Place initiative, part of the Treasury's Operational Efficiency Programme that aims to explore ways of maintaining public service levels in the face of substantial public sector expenditure cuts, via improving 'joined up' approaches at the local level to bring about efficiency savings. A key part of this programme, currently being piloted in a number of areas in England, involves the decentralization of a range of public services. The Conservative Party has increasingly championed decentralization of policy-making powers across a variety of spheres to the local level, and in late 2009 published a Green Paper to this effect (Conservative Party 2009). Independently of these national discussions about the possibilities of localization in public services, the Youth Justice Board has reportedly been considering a degree of budgetary devolution to the local level, which may also provide some small policy windows for the promotion of alternative approaches.

To conclude, whilst the realization of radical top down policy change at the level of England and Wales might be the ideal aim, the earlier analysis of the formidable contextual constraints suggests that this will remain extremely difficult to achieve. There may, however, be a more realistic prospect of promoting change at lower points in the system, at least in the medium term. It might be hoped that a series of modest and incremental changes might eventually gather momentum from the 'bottom up', providing exemplars of effective policy change at the local and regional level, and eventually contributing to a broader shift in policy across the board. This is not to argue that attempts to bring about change at the national (England and Wales) level should be abandoned. Rather, it is to propose a degree of realism about such an ambition and to suggest that policy promotion should also be undertaken at the regional and local level. This should include systematic attempts at policy entrepreneurship in the devolved polities of the United Kingdom, as well as in regional areas of England where there is already evidence of some space for the development of distinctive local approaches. If the current political fashion for the promotion of localism proves to be more than just rhetoric, such spaces may well be set to grow in the near future.

Notes

1 Tonry (2007) rightly cautions against assuming a clear and straightforward meaning to 'punitiveness'. In the UK, as in other countries, policies to deal with crime and offenders, including youth offenders, have included a shifting mixture of approaches, only some of which can be accurately labelled as punitive (Ramsay 2008; Bottoms and Dignan 2004). However, there is wide consensus that the balance has shifted significantly towards harsher 'expressive' law and order policies in recent decades.

2 See for example, Cullen *et al.* (2000); Hough and Roberts (1998); Hough and Roberts (2002); Roberts *et al.* (2002); Mayhew and van Kesteren (2002).

3 Garland subsequently developed his theories further in response to such criticisms (Garland 2005).

4 Consider the effective judicial undermining of 'two' and 'three strikes' laws in the UK (Jones and Newburn 2006); the resistance to actuarial risk management methods apparent amongst front line probation staff (Kemshall and Maguire 2001); and the general arguments of Cheliotis (2006) regarding the political agency of criminal justice practitioners in resisting the 'iron cage' of the new penology.

5 These associations are not shown to be statistically significant. It would be difficult – perhaps impossible – to demonstrate a statistical relationship given the inevitably small number of observations, each nation counting as a single unit.

6 Not all liberal commentators share Lacey's (2007) and Tonry's (2007) admiration for the political and economic arrangements of continental European systems as compared with the Anglo-American tradition. See for example Freedland (1998) for a robust advocacy of US democratic principles compared with European traditions.

7 At the time of writing the Bulger case has re-emerged as a focus of national media attention with the announcement that Jon Venables (one of the two individuals convicted of the murder of James Bulger and subsequently released on licence) has been recalled to prison for alleged serious offences. This has led to controversy about the appropriateness of public release of information about the accusations against Venables, prior to any parole hearing or court case. It also demonstrates the continued salience of the Bulger case in public debates about youth crime.

8 This embrace of populist conceptions of democratic input to policy-making is not restricted to the Labour Party. The Conservatives have expressed support,

for example, for increased local electoral control over policing modelled on local policing in the USA.

9 In the event, the outcome of the General Election of May 2010 was a hung Parliament with the Liberal Democrats holding the balance of power. The resulting coalition agreement between the Conservatives and the Liberal Democrats included a commitment to a referendum on electoral reform.

10 Indeed, the experience of New Zealand suggests that the introduction of PR into an otherwise largely unchanged liberal competitive political system can actually have the effect of making crime politics more punitive, in part because it increases the potential for influence of single issue minority parties (Pratt and Clark 2005).

11 A number of other features of the 'consensus model' of democracy could be criticized as 'antidemocratic' including: the uncertain relationship between electoral outcomes and the political complexion of the government, the disproportionate power in the system that can be given to parties with a small minority of the vote (sometimes including extremist parties), the lack of a clear choice for voters between party programmes, and the inherent risk of weak or unstable coalition governments.

12 The dominance of political expediency over expert opinion under the current arrangements has been demonstrated, for example, by the replacement of the former Chair of the Youth Justice Board, Professor Rod Morgan, and the more recent sacking of the former Chairman of the Advisory Council on the Misuse of Drugs, Professor David Nutt.

13 Similar arguments have been made with regard to the deployment of Royal Commissions in the UK (see Maguire and Morris 1994).

14 It should be remembered that when some of the leading neo-liberal think tanks were first established in the UK, many of their ideas were completely out of kilter with the prevailing consensus about social and economic policy. Indeed, even during the first Thatcher administration, when Peter Young of the Adam Smith Institute authored a pamphlet promoting the idea of private prisons, Young himself felt that the idea was so far off the political agenda as to be considered a 'bit of a joke' (quoted in Jones and Newburn 2007).

15 Examination of developments in the other smaller jurisdictions of the British Isles also provides examples of innovative interventions in the field of youth crime that moves away from a purely punitive trajectory. For example, the Criminal Justice (Children and Juvenile Court Reform) (Bailiwick of Guernsey) Law 2008 introduced "Child, Youth and Community Tribunals", based in part on the welfare-oriented elements of the Scottish system (Janet Gaggs, personal communication).

References

Beckett, K. (1997) *Making Crime Pay: Law and Order in Contemporary American Politics* (New York: Oxford University Press).

Bimber, B. (2001) 'Information and Political Engagement in America: The Search for Effects of Information Technology at the Individual Level', *Political Research Quarterly*, 54:1, pp. 53–67.

Bottoms, A. (1995) 'The Philosophy and Politics of Punishment and Sentencing', in C. Clarkson and R. Morgan (eds) *The Politics of Sentencing Reform* (Oxford: Oxford University Press), pp. 17–49.

Bottoms, A. and Dignan, J. (2004) 'Youth Justice in Great Britain', in M. Tonry (ed.) *Youth Crime and Youth Justice: Comparative and Cross National Perspectives, Crime and Justice: A Review of Research*, volume 31 (Chicago: University of Chicago Press), pp. 21–184.

Burney, E. (2009) *Making People Behave: Anti-Social Behaviour, Politics and Policy*, 2nd edition (Cullompton: Willan Publishing).

Casey, L. (2008) *Engaging Communities in Fighting Crime* (London: Cabinet Office).

Cavadino, M. and Dignan, J. (2005) *Penal Systems: A Comparative Approach* (London: Sage).

Cheliotis, L. (2006) 'How Iron is the Iron Cage of New Penology? The Role of Human Agency in the Implementation of Criminal Justice Policy'. *Punishment and Society*, 8:3, pp. 313–40.

Christie, N. (2000) *Crime Control as Industry* (London: Routledge).

Conservative Party (2009) *Control Shift: Returning Power to Local Communities*, Responsibility Agenda, Policy Green Paper No. 9 (London: Conservative Party).

Cullen, F., Fisher, B. and Applegate, B. (2000) 'Public Opinion about Punishment and Corrections', in M. Tonry (ed.) *Crime and Justice: A Review of Research*, volume 27, pp. 1–79 (Chicago: University of Chicago Press).

Downes, D. and Morgan, R. (2007) 'No Turning Back: The Politics of Law and Order into the Millennium', in M, Maguire, R. Morgan and R. Reiner (eds) *The Oxford Handbook of Criminology*, 4th edition, pp. 201–40 (Oxford: Oxford University Press).

Drakeford, M. (2010) Devolution and Youth Justice in Wales. *Criminology and Criminal Justice*, pp. 137–54.

Edwards, A. and Hughes, G. (2008) 'Resilient Fabians? Anti-social behaviour and community safety work in Wales', in P. Squires (ed.) *ASBO Nation: The Criminalization of Nuisance* (Bristol: Policy Press), pp. 57–72.

Edwards, A. and Hughes, G. (2009) 'The Preventive Turn and the Promotion of Safer Communities in England and Wales: Political Inventiveness and Governmental Instabilities', in A. Crawford (ed.) *Crime Prevention Policies in Comparative Perspective* (Cullompton: Willan Publishing), pp. 62–85.

Edwards, A and Sheptycki, J. (2009) 'Third Wave Criminology: Guns, Crime and Social Order', *Criminology and Criminal Justice*, 9:3, pp. 379–97.

Esmée Fairbairn Foundation (2004) *Rethinking Crime and Punishment: The Report* (London: Esmée Fairbairn Foundation).

Freedland, J. (1998) *Bring Home the Revolution: How Britain Can Live the American Dream* (London: Fourth Estate).

Garland, D. (1996) 'The Limits of the Sovereign State: Strategies of Crime Control in Contemporary Society', *British Journal of Criminology*, 36:4, pp. 445–71.

Garland, D. (2000) 'The Culture of High Crime Societies: Some Preconditions of Recent "Law and Order" Policies', *British Journal of Criminology*, 40:3, pp. 347–75.

Garland, D. (2001) *The Culture of Control* (Oxford: Oxford University Press).

Garland, D. (2005) 'Beyond the Culture of Control', in M. Matravers (ed.) *Managing Modernity: Politics and the Culture of Control* (London: Routledge).

Goldson, B. (2010) 'The Sleep of (Criminological) Reason: Knowledge-Policy Rupture and New Labour's Youth Justice Legacy', *Criminology and Criminal Justice*, 10:2, pp. 155–78.

Goldson, B. and Hughes, G. (2010) 'Sociological Criminology and Youth Justice: Comparative Policy Analysis and Academic Intervention', *Criminology and Criminal Justice*, 10:2, pp. 211–30.

Green, D. (2006) 'Public Opinion Versus Public Judgment on Crime: Correcting the "Comedy of Errors"', *British Journal of Criminology* 46:1, pp. 131–54.

Green, D. (2007) 'Comparing Penal Cultures: Child-on-Child Homicide in England and Norway', in M. Tonry, M. (ed.) *Crime, Punishment and Politics in Comparative Perspective. Crime and Justice: A Review of Research*, volume 36 (Chicago: University of Chicago Press), pp. 591–643.

Greenberg, D. (2002) 'Striking Out in Democracy', *Punishment and Society* 4:2, pp. 237–52.

Hogg, Q. (1976) 'Elective Dictatorship', BBC London: The Richard Dimbleby Lecture, 14 October 1976.

Hope, T. (2004) 'Pretend it Works: Evidence and Governance in the Evaluation of the Reducing Burglary Initiative', *Criminal Justice* 4:3, pp. 287–308.

Hope, T. (2009) 'The Illusion of Control: A Response to Professor Sherman', *Criminology and Criminal Justice*, 9:2, pp. 125–34.

Hough, M. and Roberts, J. (1998) *Attitudes to Punishment: Findings from the British Crime Survey*, Home Office Research Study No. 179 (London: Home Office).

Hough, M. and Park, A. (2002) 'How Malleable are Attitudes to Crime and Punishment? Findings from a British Deliberative Poll', in J. Roberts and M. Hough (eds) *Changing Attitudes to Punishment: Public Opinion, Crime and Justice* (Cullompton: Willan Publishing), pp. 163–83.

Hough, M. and Roberts, J. V. (2004) *Youth Crime and Youth Justice: Public Opinion in England and Wales*, Criminal Policy Monograph (Bristol: Policy Press).

House of Commons Health Committee (2008) *National Institute for Health and Clinical Excellence*, First Report of Session 2007/8 (London: The Stationery Office Limited).

Howard, P. (2003) 'Digitizing the Social Contract: Producing American Political Culture in the Age of New Media', *The Communication Review*, 6:3, pp. 213–45.

Hutton, N. (2005) 'Beyond Populist Punitiveness?', *Punishment and Society* 7:3, pp. 243–58.

Jones, T. (1995) *Policing and Democracy in the Netherlands* (London: Policy Studies Institute).

Jones, T., Newburn, T. and Smith, D.J. (1996) 'Policing and the Idea of Democracy', *British Journal of Criminology*, 36:2, pp. 182–98.

Jones, T. and Newburn, T. (2006) '"Three Strikes and You're Out": Exploring Symbol and Substance in American and British Crime Control Politics', *British Journal of Criminology*, 46:5, pp. 781–802.

Jones, T. and Newburn, T. (2007) *Policy Transfer and Criminal Justice: Exploring US Influence over British Crime Control Policy* (Buckingham: Open University Press).

Kemshall, H. and Maguire, M. (2001) 'Public Protection, Partnership and Risk Penality: The Multi Agency Risk Management of Sexual and Violent Offenders', *Punishment and Society* 3:2, pp. 237–64.

Kingdon, J. (1995) *Agendas, Alternatives and Public Policies*, 2nd edition (New York: Harper Collins).

Lacey, N. (2007) *The Prisoners' Dilemma: Political Economy and Punishment in Contemporary Democracies* (Cambridge: Cambridge University Press).

Loader, I. (2006) 'Fall of the Platonic Guardians: Liberalism, Criminology and Political Responses to Crime in England and Wales', *British Journal of Criminology*, 46:4, pp. 561–86.

Loader, I. and Sparks, R. (forthcoming) *Public Criminology? Criminological Politics in the 21st Century* (London: Routledge).

Maguire, M. and Norris, C. (1994) 'Police Investigations: Practice and Malpractice', *Journal of Law and Society*, 21:1, pp. 72–84.

Maguire, M. (2004) 'The Crime Reduction Programme in England and Wales: Reflections on the Vision and on the Reality', *Criminal Justice* 4:3, pp. 213–37.

Mayhew, P. and van Kesteren, J. (2002) 'Cross National Attitudes to Punishment', in J. Roberts and M. Hough (eds) *Changing Attitudes to Punishment: Public Opinion, Crime and Justice* (Cullompton: Willan Publishing), pp. 63–92.

McAra, L. and McVie, S. (2010) 'Youth Crime and Justice: Key Messages from the Edinburgh Study of Youth Transitions and Crime', *Criminology and Criminal Justice* 10:2, pp. 179–209.

Melossi, D. (2001) 'The Cultural Embeddedness of Social Control: Reflections on the Comparison of Italian and North American Cultures Concerning Punishment', *Theoretical Criminology* 5:4, pp. 403–24.

Newburn, T. (2007) '"Tough on Crime": Penal Policy in England and Wales', in M. Tonry, M. (ed.) *Crime, Punishment and Politics in Comparative Perspective. Crime and Justice: A Review of Research*, volume 36 (Chicago: University of Chicago Press), pp. 1–48.

Newburn, T. and Jones, T. (2007) 'Symbolizing Crime Control: Reflections on Zero Tolerance', *Theoretical Criminology*, 11:2, pp. 221–43.

Pollitt, C. (2001) 'Convergence: The Useful Myth?', *Public Administration* 79:4, pp. 933–47.

Pratt, J. and Clark, M. (2005) 'Penal Populism in New Zealand', *Punishment and Society*, 7:3, pp. 303–22.

Ramsay, P. (2008) 'The Theory of Vulnerable Autonomy and the Legitimacy of the Civil Preventative Order', in B. McSherry, A. Norrie and S. Bronitt (eds) *Regulating Deviance: The Redirection of Criminalization and the Futures of Criminal Law*, pp. 109–40 (Oxford: Hart Publishing).

Reiner, R. (2007) 'Media-Made Criminality: The Representation of Crime in the Mass Media', in M. Maguire, R. Morgan and R. Reiner (eds) *The Oxford Handbook of Criminology*, 4th edition, pp. 302–37 (Oxford: Oxford University Press).

Roberts, J. (2004) 'Public Opinion and Youth Justice', in M. Tonry (ed.) *Youth Crime and Youth Justice: Comparative and Cross National Perspectives. Crime and Justice: A Review of Research*, volume 31. (Chicago: University of Chicago Press), pp. 495–542.

Roberts, J., Stalans, L., Indermaur, D. and Hough, M. (2002) *Penal Populism and Public Opinion: Findings from Five Countries* (New York: Oxford University Press).

Roberts, J. and Hough, M. (2002a) (eds) *Changing Attitudes to Punishment: Public Opinion, Crime and Justice* (Cullompton: Willan Publishing).

Roberts, J. and Hough, M. (2002b) 'Public Attitudes to Punishment: The Context', in J. Roberts and M. Hough (eds) *Changing Attitudes to Punishment: Public Opinion, Crime and Justice*, pp. 1–14 (Cullompton: Willan Publishing).

Roberts, J. and Hough, M. (2005) Sentencing Young Offenders: Public Opinion in England and Wales, *Criminal Justice*, 5:3, pp. 211–32.

Shepherd, J. (2007) 'The Production and Management of Evidence for Public Service Reform', *Evidence and Policy*, 3:2, pp. 231–51.

Sherman, L. (2009) 'Evidence and Liberty: The Promise of Experimental Criminology', *Criminology and Criminal Justice*, 9:1, pp. 5–28.

Sparks, R. (2000) 'The Media and Penal Politics', *Punishment and Society* 12:1, pp. 98–105.

Stephenson, M., Giller, H. and Brown, S. (2007) *Effective Practice in Youth Justice* (Cullompton: Willan Publishing).

Stoker, G. (1998) (ed.) *The New Politics of British Local Governance* (Basingstoke: Macmillan).

Tolbert, C. and McNeal, R. (2003) 'Unravelling the Effects of the Internet on Political Participation', *Political Research Quarterly*, 56:2, pp. 175–85.

Tonry, M. (2004a) (ed.) *Youth Crime and Youth Justice: Comparative and Cross National Perspectives. Crime and Justice: A Review of Research*, volume 31 (Chicago: University of Chicago Press).

Tonry, M. (2004b) *Punishment and Politics: Evidence and Emulation in the Making of English Crime Control Policy* (Cullompton: Willan Publishing).

Tonry, M. (2007) 'Determinants of Penal Policies', in M. Tonry (ed.) *Crime, Punishment and Politics in Comparative Perspective*, Crime and Justice: A Review of Research, volume 36 (Chicago: University of Chicago Press), pp. 1–48.

Toynbee, P. (2009) 'A Deathbed Conversion Will Do: It's Now or Never for PR', *The Guardian*, 22 December.

Young, J. (2003) 'Searching for a New Criminology of Everyday Life: A Review of "The Culture of Control"', *British Journal of Criminology* 43:1, pp. 228–43.

Wacquant, L. (2001) 'Deadly Symbiosis: When Ghetto and Prison Meet and Mesh', *Punishment and Society* 3:1, pp. 95–134.

Whitman, J. (2003) *Harsh Justice: Criminal Punishment and the Widening Divide Between America and Europe* (New York: Oxford University Press).

Wilcox, A. and Hirschfield, A. (2007) *A Framework for Deriving Policy Implications from Research. Project Report*, University of Huddersfield (unpublished). Available at: http://eprints.hud.ac.uk/5841/1/WilcoxFramework.pdf

Zedner, L. (2002) 'Dangers of Dystopias in Penal Theory', *Oxford Journal of Legal Studies*, 22:2, pp. 341–66.

Zimring, F. (2003) *The Contradictions of American Capital Punishment* (New York: Oxford University Press).

Zimring, F., Hawkins, G. and Kamin, S. (2001) *Punishment and Democracy: Three Strikes and You're Out in California* (New York: Oxford University Press).

Chapter 12

Key reforms: principles, costs, benefits, politics[*]

David J. Smith

The failures of our present responses to youth crime and antisocial behaviour are deep-rooted and far-reaching. Change will not happen overnight, but we may be approaching a unique moment when an opening appears in the battlements, and the process of change can begin. For reasons that are only partly understood, the long-established drop in crime has at last been reflected in a sharp decline in youth custody. This falling 'market' will soon highlight the need to reconsider plans for youth custodial institutions and buildings. In the aftermath of the 2010 general election, crime and justice are unlikely to be the focus of party competition. Expenditure on youth justice in England and Wales – already high by international standards – rose by 45 per cent in six years from 2000. The fiscal crisis will impose cuts on public expenditure whichever party is in power, while any alternative to the present high rate of youth custody would be cheaper and would offer better value for money.

The detailed evidence and analysis set out in the preceding chapters are the starting point for the development of plans for reform. The Commission's blueprint is set out in its Report. Here we review in broad terms how the facts and analysis point towards a few key reforms that could transform the youth justice system and shift resources from punishment to prevention.

*With thanks to Larissa Pople, who made a substantial contribution to this chapter by collecting and evaluating the information on costs and benefits that is summarized in the second last section; and to Paul Johnson, who contributed to the costs and benefits section and commented on the text as a whole.

Failures of the current system

Our problems with youth justice arise from inescapable tensions between different objectives. As Lesley McAra explains in Chapter 9, youth justice systems are required both 'to help troubled young people to change, develop and overcome their problems' and 'to deliver a firm, prompt and appropriate response to offending' as a means of protecting the public. These objectives potentially conflict, and reconciling them 'is particularly problematic in the case of young people who persistently and seriously offend'. As a result of this tension, in the history of the English system there has been a contest and an oscillation between punishment and welfare, and between deterrence and rehabilitation. These tensions are accommodated in different ways in different systems, but the way they are contained within the system in England and Wales is singularly incoherent. As suggested by McAra, this incoherence or ambiguity may be a useful political strategy, but it results in a level of ineffectiveness that cannot be sustained for much longer. That is especially because the principal actors within the system lose confidence in what they are doing and lack of self-confidence is reflected in lack of public confidence.

The following specific failures have been detailed in earlier chapters:

- a high rate of reconviction – three out of four young offenders sentenced to custody are reconvicted within a year (see Chapter 4);

- the system tends to go on prosecuting the same large numbers of young offenders even when crime is falling substantially (see Chapter 3);

- the system targets the poor, the disadvantaged, and certain ethnic minorities (see Chapter 3);

- the system targets 'the usual suspects' and processes the same offenders again and again, without touching other more advantaged young offenders (see Chapter 3);

- the high rate of youth custody – much higher than in comparable European countries – is ineffective, expensive, and harmful (see Chapter 4, and also Chapter 6 on the negative effects of imprisonment);

- custodial institutions for young offenders vary widely in costs and quality, but many are in unsuitable buildings and locations, and provide inadequate opportunities for young offenders to change and develop (see Chapter 4);

- arrangements for resettlement of offenders on release from custody are patchy (see Chapter 4);

- the parallel and competing system for dealing with antisocial behaviour can stigmatize young people for normal behaviour, and breaches of civil orders can lead to long periods of custody, which constitutes a threat to human rights (see Chapter 5);

- court proceedings are rarely intelligible to young offenders (see Chapter 4);

- the courts cannot follow through to ensure that community-based sanctions are properly implemented (see Chapter 4);

- aspects of the system breach international conventions (see Chapter 4) although as McAra points out in Chapter 9, these conventions themselves are beset by tensions between punishment and welfare;

- although many proven prevention programmes are being implemented, local communities lack the means of organizing prevention in their areas (see Chapter 7).

Since 1997 the government has introduced a vast number of reforms in an effort to improve the performance of the youth justice system. John Graham's assessment in Chapter 4 is that in terms of the government's own managerial targets, 'performance is at best mixed (albeit with some encouraging signs of improvement in the last year or so)'. Judged against broader values and objectives – Does the system reflect fairness and equity? Does it comply with international obligations? Does it deliver social justice? – Graham concludes that it fails. To quote one example, recent youth justice 'reforms' 'have increasingly targeted *younger* children, not only through the abolition of *doli incapax*, but through lowering the age at which secure remands and custodial disposals can be applied'. More than one-third of 12–14-year-olds who are incarcerated are not persistent offenders and have not committed a serious offence (Glover and Hibbert 2009). Again, the number of girls who are convicted and the number sentenced to custody have greatly increased, despite no evidence of any change in self-reported rates of offending; also, girls are being convicted at a younger age even though the average age at which girls start to commit offences has remained constant (Phillips and Chamberlain 2006).

The context of reform

The time is ripe for reform especially because crime has been falling since 1994, so that the system, during a period of transformation, would be under less pressure than in the recent past. Combining the evidence from recorded crime statistics and the British Crime Survey, Chapter 3 shows that there was a sustained, strong rise in crime from 1950 to 1994, a reversal of this long-term trend in the mid 1990s, and a fall thereafter. Although violent crime as a whole has fallen at a slower rate than property crime, serious violent crimes have probably declined in the

2000s, and knife crimes and gun homicides have declined since the mid 1990s. Probably trends in youth crime are much the same as trends in overall crime, although there was an unexplained upward trend in *convictions* of young people for violence, reaching a peak in 2005/6.

Although crime has substantially declined in fact, three-quarters of respondents in the latest British Crime Survey thought it had risen in the past two years. As set out in Chapter 3, there is strong evidence that these paradoxical views are fed by competitive political debate, which heightens perceptions and plays on anxieties, and by popular newspapers and other mass media. Yet the structure of public opinion is multi-layered. Views about national levels of crime are most influenced by political debate as filtered through the media, whereas perceptions of crime in the neighbourhood are more strongly influenced by personal observation and experience. Hence, people are far less likely to think that crime has increased in their own neighbourhood than nationally, and *anxiety* about crime has steadily declined even though people judge (at the cognitive level) that crime has increased nationally. Although politicians, egged on by the media, have led people to believe that crime is rising, personal experiences, perceptions and feelings tell a different story. Hence, there may be a reservoir of potential support to be tapped by astute politicians promoting more progressive policies.

Since the Second World War there have been fundamental changes in the nature of youth as the pattern of transitions from childhood to adulthood has been transformed. These changes help to explain why there is a growing tendency to see young people as a threat. They also imply that the youth justice system must adapt to the changing character and needs of its clientele. The developmental path leading from childhood to adulthood has become much longer because puberty and sexual activity come earlier whereas work, leaving home, cohabitation, marriage and childbearing all come later than before. These changes are so significant that some writers describe a phase of 'emerging adulthood' when there is a moratorium on social roles and commitments. Young people have become a more conspicuous and identifiable group, spending most of their time with people around their own age, and displaying distinctive, sometimes spectacular, youth cultures. These have been given an added impetus by the development of youth markets for products that are then used as markers of identity, with the result that young people need to have these products in order to 'be someone'. Such an identifiable and separate group can readily become the focus of fear and stigmatization. At the same time, the extension of youth heightens the tension between a firm response to crime and a response appropriate to an offender's level of maturity. Responding appropriately has also become more difficult because young people have become less rooted in local attachments to family and neighbourhood, and more connected (through electronic means) to people and organizations all over the place.

Since 1980, these changes in the nature of youth have been framed by striking increases in inequality both at the bottom and at the top of the income distribution (see Chapter 2). A group of unqualified young people became more conspicuously different from the increasing majority with some sort of qualification, and the social ties and social capital of this group declined steeply. This particular group may become the focus of both prevention and rehabilitation, even if offending among the great majority of young people continues to decline. As outlined in Chapter 6, poverty and disadvantage are indirect causes of offending, through their effect on the family, and as shown in Chapter 3, they are strongly related to whether young people become entangled with the criminal justice system. Also, there is evidence that income inequality is associated with higher offending in society at large (see Chapters 2 and 6).

The family is central to an understanding of youth offending and to programmes for preventing and responding to it. As detailed in Chapter 8, despite massive changes in patterns of family life in recent years, the discord, disruption and disadvantage that often accompany parental separation increase the chances that children will offend, although the effects are not large. Positive parenting that expresses emotional warmth, and appropriate strategies for management and control, have an important influence on the later development of behaviour through childhood and into adolescence. Interventions that aim to influence parenting behaviour are among the most successful (see Chapter 7). Although family structures have changed dramatically since 1960 and although families have become much more unstable, there is no evidence that these changes have been accompanied by an overall decline in the quality of parenting. There is little or no evidence that changes in family structures are among the causes of the post-war rise in youth crime.

Research going back as long as a hundred years has shown that various 'risk factors' are associated with an increased probability that a young person will become involved in offending, but more recent research has been able to go further and to establish some of the causes of offending. Two advances are important in establishing causes. The strongest projects use longitudinal designs in which the same individuals are followed up for several years, so that cause and effect can be clearly separated in time. Also, the best designs are now sensitive to genetic influences, so that for example the similarity of parents' and children's behaviour because of genetic inheritance can be separated from the influence of parenting on the child's later development. As set out in Chapter 6, research using these and other strong methods has confirmed that family discord is a true cause of later offending in children. Poverty is an indirect cause of youth offending through its effect on the family: it is much harder to be a good parent in poor and crowded housing, in a run-down and disorderly neighbourhood where other children are badly behaved, with little money for food and clothes, and with little time and energy left over after a full day's work while struggling to cope with demands at home. Lack of work opportunities is a cause of offending: the same individuals offend less often during periods of employment than when they are out of work, a fact that reinforces the importance of programmes to help offenders leaving prison to resettle in the community. Similarly, gang membership is a true cause of offending, because young people offend more often during periods when they are gang members than at other times. Research summarized in Chapters 1 and 6 indicates that imprisonment is crimi-nogenic – it is a cause of further offending among those who are imprisoned rather than a method of reforming them. Although alcohol and drugs are probably not prime causes of offending, in the presence of other causes they make offending more likely. It is probably no accident that the rise in consumption of alcohol and drugs by young people coincided with the rise in youth crime in the post-war period, although a causal relationship has not been strictly established. The rise in crime was probably also related to the growth of criminal opportunities.

Over the past 20 years or so it has been firmly established that there are important genetic influences on offending. There is no 'gene for crime' but there are genetic influences on certain behavioural disorders, such as attention deficit and hyperactivity, which are in turn causes of criminal offending in young people. Also, certain aspects of brain functioning, and certain cognitive factors, such as poor ability to think and plan ahead, are associated with antisocial behaviour (see Chapter 6). These findings make a 'punishment model' of youth justice seem all the more inappropriate.

Finally, as amply illustrated in Chapter 7, many programmes aiming to prevent offending in young people have been shown to work and to deliver good value for money.

Key reforms

Lesley McAra, in Chapter 9, explains that youth justice systems in all developed countries 'are required to fulfil two potentially competing objectives:

(a) first, to help troubled young people to change, develop and overcome their problems – to provide a turning point in their lives;
(b) second, to deliver a firm, prompt and appropriate response to youth offending – a response which offers the best means of protecting the public when necessary.'

The first of these objectives chimes with the principle, in the Scottish system, that the welfare of the child is paramount.[1] Under (a) it is recognized that the young person has committed a criminal offence, but youth offending is assumed to arise out of trouble and difficulty, and the emphasis is explicitly on dealing with the underlying problems and supporting a process of personal change and development. How can we resolve the tension between this welfare principle and the second objective, 'to deliver a firm, prompt and appropriate response to youth offending'?

The essential first step is to disavow punishment as a proper aim of the youth justice system, because punishment deliberately aims to do damage. The principle that the young offender's welfare is paramount means that the central aim is to give young people the chance to choose a better way of life and to encourage and support a process of positive change. Such a welfare principle is inescapably in conflict with the principle of punishment. Reasonable punishment is closely allied to the principle of retribution, which has the great advantage that it restricts punishment to cases where an offence has been proved and limits it to what is proportionate to the offence. On the other hand, the principle of retribution also makes it clear that punishment has to be damaging. The offence itself is damaging to individuals and to communal ties. The idea of punishment is that equal or proportionate damage should be done to the offender. Aiming to harm the offender – as punishment does, by its nature – must always conflict with the principle that the welfare of the young offender is paramount.

Of these two it is the welfare principle rather than the principle of punishment that must be retained, because it is unjust and ultimately self-defeating to treat children and adolescents as if they were mature and fully responsible adults. Yet a reformed youth justice system will still be something quite different from a system for providing education or social care. Although the welfare principle should be paramount, it cannot be the only principle of a system that aims to deliver justice rather than social support. It is important to retain the objective of delivering 'a firm, prompt and appropriate response to youth offending' while insisting that this response must not be punitive: it must not set out to cause pain, harm or distress to young offenders, or to damage their life chances. It should be a system of *justice* (not social work) which nevertheless promotes the welfare of offenders. In other words, there should be a fundamental shift towards justice and away from punishment. Is it possible to find an interpretation of justice that is consistent with promoting the welfare of young offenders, without any compromises? The best hope is through adopting restorative justice principles.

One of the essential features of restorative justice is that it aims to hold offenders to account and make them recognize the harm they have done. By setting up a dialogue between offender and victim, together with others (such as family members) who have a stake or were affected by the crime, restorative conferences can bring young offenders to a vivid realization of the consequences of their actions. Such a realization is a moment of reconnection with other people, in sharp contrast to punishment, which is an act of exclusion and a moment of rupture.

The concept of restoration is analogous to retribution, since both are in different ways intended to be a proportionate response to the crime. The essential difference is that the proportionate repayment is destructive in the case of punishment but constructive in the case of restoration. In both cases, there are problems in deciding what counts as proportionate since often the harm caused by the crime and what can be done to repay it cannot be measured on the same scale. Also, the cost of the crime may easily be more than the offender can repay. But as proved by experience of restorative justice in many countries including Northern Ireland, these problems can be overcome.

The central conclusion that emerges from the systematic review of evidence in the preceding 11 chapters is that restorative justice should become the core of the youth justice system. There are three reasons for thinking that a system based on restorative justice principles could be at least as effective as the present system in controlling youth crime.

1. Restorative justice is a tougher way of holding young offenders to account than most of the sentences that are currently handed out by the Youth Court. It can include any and all of the community-based measures that now form part of Referral Orders. It can be delivered at least as promptly as the measures within current sentences. The difference lies in the rationale underlying the measures and – crucially – in the way that the young offender engages with the victim and with others concerned.

2. From the evidence reviewed in Chapter 1, there is little or no evidence that punitive systems are more successful in controlling crime than less punitive ones. A functioning criminal justice system is an important precondition for controlling crime. But marginal changes in the number of offenders that are punished have small effects, at most, on the amount of crime, and these effects are achieved by taking offenders out of circulation (in custody) rather than through deterrence. Despite a large volume of research, there is no consistent evidence that more severe sanctions reduce crime compared with less severe ones. On balance the evidence suggests that the experience of imprisonment tends to increase reoffending. Also, as explained in Chapter 2, a wide range of societal changes probably have more influence than the youth justice system on the level of youth crime.

3. A growing body of evidence from a number of countries shows that sentences based on restorative justice principles can often be more effective than conventional sentences in changing offenders' behaviour (Sherman and Strang 2007). Also, evaluations of three restorative justice schemes in England are showing promising results (Shapland et al. 2008).

For all of these reasons, it is unlikely that a fundamental shift towards restorative justice within the youth justice system would lead to a rise in youth crime. It is more likely that restorative justice would help to reduce youth crime, because it avoids some of the perverse effects of a more punitive system, and helps to reintegrate young offenders into normal society.

The Commission's Report, together with the separate report of the tribunals project, discuss alternative, more detailed models for reform. Here we sketch the main features of these reforms in broad outline.

1. Reduce the number of court cases

As explained earlier, the number of cases going to court tends to remain stable even when the volume of youth offending goes down. The large number of court cases is damaging for several reasons.

- A prime objective is to respond promptly and firmly to youth offending, but despite the best efforts at streamlining, the court process is inherently prone to delays.

- The court process has to be formal and in some respects impersonal, in order to meet the requirements of justice and to protect human rights in an adversarial system. Young people find the formal court process hard to understand and often feel alienated from it. Although the courts can improve the way they communicate with young offenders, there will always be difficulties that spring from the essential nature of the process.

- Large numbers of court cases tend to translate into large numbers in custody.

- The court process is very expensive, so that almost any alternative is likely to be better value for money.

In Chapter 4, Graham describes the extraordinary 'diversionary interlude' in the 1980s when the numbers of convictions and custodial sentences were greatly reduced, before the reversal of policy in the early 1990s. There is no desire to return to the policies of the 1980s, especially because they led to a political rebound. What is needed instead is a steady, sustainable move towards reducing the number of court cases. What the experience of the 1980s shows, however, is that the numbers of court cases can be reduced even without major legislation. The most important factor seems to be a clearly understood policy that is reflected in the culture of all of the actors within the system.

There are three major stages at which matters can be resolved without going to court.

(a) As set out in Chapter 2, for the most part unwanted behaviour is informally controlled by schools, families, employers, minor officials, shopkeepers, neighbours, and so on. Moreover, the specialists who are dedicated to law enforcement – the police and the courts – rely on the backing of a network of informal controls. The first step is to encourage individuals, groups and organizations to deal with youth behaviour they do not like through challenge, discussion, and negotiation, rather than by reporting it to the police. That means tipping the balance towards an informal resolution, where possible, and away from quickly invoking an external bureaucracy.

(b) A long-established feature of the system is that offenders who admit the offence can be cautioned instead of being prosecuted. Policy on cautions has oscillated wildly over the past 20 years. During the 'diversionary interlude' of the 1980s, there was a large increase in the number of formal cautions issued by the prosecutor: for example, the proportion of 14–16-year-old boys cautioned for indictable offences doubled between 1980 and 1990 (see Chapter 4). There was probably also a large increase in the number of informal cautions issued by the police (see Chapter 4, endnote 3). Practitioners favoured the practice of cautioning the same offender on subsequent occasions for a second or third offence (repeat cautioning). In 2004, the Home Office ended the practice of repeat cautioning and handed the decision to caution in all cases to the police, leading to a steep decline in cautions and a steep rise in prosecutions. In 1998 this non-statutory cautioning system was replaced with a new statutory final warning scheme, which allows young offenders no more than two chances – a reprimand and a final warning – before they are referred to court. Reprimands are generally used for first-time minor offenders, whereas final warnings usually trigger the Youth Offending Team (YOT) to prepare a programme of interventions. Much more recently, in 2008, the Youth Crime Action Plan announced a 'triage' system for diverting some young offenders from prosecution. This scheme is currently[2] being piloted in 69 YOT areas. YOT workers are embedded in police stations, where they carry out assessments of young people brought in and switch some of them from arrest to a programme of early intervention. The latest episode in this tangled tale is the most promising one. Policy should build on and extend the 'triage' scheme which promises to be a sustainable method of reducing the numbers being prosecuted, because there is systematic selection by specialist staff of cases to be diverted, and because diversion is firmly tied to provision of early prevention programmes.

(c) For cases that do result in a criminal charge, a major reform of the process is required. Where the young person admits to the offence, if it is not a very serious one, the prosecutor should be required to offer a restorative conference as an alternative to taking the case to court. Experience in Northern Ireland suggests that young offenders will accept that offer in the great majority of cases. The response to the offence will then be delivered more promptly and at smaller cost than if the case had gone to court. As explained below, the full range of interventions can be made available at this stage through the restorative conference mechanism.

2. Reduce the number of young people in custody

A sustainable policy of avoiding prosecution where possible ((1) above) will create a momentum towards reducing the numbers of custodial sentences, but in time it could be complemented by a reversal of statutory changes that have extended custody to younger offenders (aged 12–14), extended sentence lengths for all young offenders, and extended powers to remand young offenders in custody awaiting trial (see Chapter 4). In particular, detention and training orders, introduced in 2000, have been widely used by magistrates in their shortest form (two months in custody plus four months training in the community) although there is widespread agreement among practitioners that nothing can be achieved during a short period of custody. As Graham states (Chapter 4, p. 117), 'It is difficult to reconcile the ratcheting-up of penal policy with the introduction of targets to reduce the number of young offenders remanded and sentenced to custody'. A recent, encouraging development was the publication of overarching principles for the sentencing of young offenders by the Sentencing Guidelines Council (2009). Graham (p. 121) considers that these principles, 'if followed, could substantially alter the sentencing of young offenders and potentially the ethos of the youth justice system'. Pending statutory change, dissemination of these principles backed by unambiguous government support could have an important effect.

3. Restorative conferences

Through reparation orders, introduced in 1998, the government made a start towards building restorative justice into the system. That was extended by the introduction of the referral order in 1999. As a consequence, most first-time young offenders pleading guilty are referred to a Youth Offender Panel run by volunteers. The panel brings victims, offenders and families together to agree a contract that addresses the victim's needs and ensures offenders face up to the consequences of their behaviour. Central to the reforms that are under consideration is a development and strengthening of these moves towards restorative justice. Restorative conferences would become the normal method of dealing with young offenders, as they already are in Northern Ireland. As specified in (1) above, they would be used by the Crown Prosecution Service as an alternative to prosecution, where the offence is admitted. Also, they would become the normal sentence on conviction for the vast majority of offences committed by young people aged 10–17.

(a) For the vast majority of offences, excluding the most serious ones, the court would be required to offer a restorative conference as the sentence. A conference would be offered regardless of the plea (guilty or not guilty). Offenders must be allowed to decline a conference (the most likely course if they continue to maintain their innocence on conviction) in which case the court would have to determine another sentence after receiving social inquiry reports.

(b) At present, restorative programmes in England and Wales are run by Youth Offending Panels consisting of volunteers. On the basis of the experience in Northern Ireland, the new restorative conferences should be run by professional facilitators recruited and trained to perform this role and no other. From the latest available statistics, victims are present at 74 per cent of the restorative conferences in Northern Ireland, a considerably higher proportion than for similar schemes in other countries. The use of professional facilitators who are well trained and highly persistent is the key reason why this high participation rate has been achieved.

(c) Once the court has prescribed a restorative conference on conviction, the facilitator should meet separately with each of the parties involved (the victim, the offender, their family members, the police officer in the case, the social worker) to develop a restorative justice programme that is acceptable. The facilitator should then return to the court within a time limit (four weeks in Northern Ireland) to present the plan, which the court may either accept or modify. The facilitator should then manage the execution of the programme within the time limit prescribed (never more than 12 months in Northern Ireland).

(d) The programme can encompass a wide range of measures and interventions. Some of these (such as a written apology, making good damage) will aim to make good the harm done. Others (such as help in withdrawing from drugs or alcohol, anger management courses) will aim to help the offender overcome faults and disabilities that led to the offending behaviour. The programme can include interventions with the offender's family (such as parenting courses).

(e) The facilitator reports back to the court to state whether or not the programme was completed within the timetable. If it was not completed, the court has powers to take further action.

Experience in Northern Ireland shows that young offenders engage much more closely with restorative justice programmes of this kind than with standard community-based sanctions. The programmes are also satisfying to the majority of victims.

4. Try all cases (10–17-year-olds) in the youth court

At present, serious cases involving defendants aged 10–17 can be transferred to the Crown Court, as happened in the trial of two 10-year-old boys for the murder of James Bulger in 1993. Transfer to the Crown Court of child defendants amounts to the denial of a fair trial under European law, and it attracts destructive and punitive attention from the media. The European Court of Human Rights was highly critical of the transfer of the defendants in the James Bulger case. In a review commissioned by the government, Lord Justice Auld recommended that all defendants aged 10–17 should in future be dealt with in the youth court. This recommendation has not been implemented, and in 2008, 3,600 young people under the age of 18 were tried in the Crown Court. As part of the present package of measures, it is important that Lord Justice Auld's recommendation should finally be implemented, for four reasons among many. First, the youth court should in future have a high level of specialist knowledge and experience of dealing with young offenders that the Crown Court cannot have. Secondly, young offenders must find it extremely difficult to participate effectively in adult court proceedings. Thirdly, transfer to the Crown Court is incompatible with making restorative justice the core of the youth justice system. Fourthly, it conveys a powerful symbolic message that the authorities aim to punish young offenders, a message that is incompatible with the principles which, we argue, should be the foundation of youth justice.

5. Raise the level of specialist expertise in the youth court

At present most youth courts are presided by a panel of three lay magistrates, although a much smaller number, mostly in London and Birmingham, are presided by a district judge sitting alone, who is a professional lawyer. Both district judges and magistrates receive some specialist training for work in the youth court, but this is not extensive. There is scope for substantially increasing the level of specialist expertise. In Northern Ireland, a new cadre of district judges who sit only in the youth court has been created, and every panel consists of a professional district judge and two lay magistrates. That arrangement works well, and it seems a desirable model because it combines professional expertise with input from people belonging to local communities. A court with a highly trained professional on the panel is likely to deal with business more quickly and efficiently than a lay panel. All members of youth court panels should receive substantial specialist training. This becomes easier to achieve as more of the work devolves on specialist district judges.

Specialist training would also be required for restorative conference facilitators. New courses would need to be created including modules that are suitable for various actors in the system (judges, magistrates, facilitators, members of youth offending teams) and specialized modules for specific actors (such as judges and magistrates). Training would need to develop interpersonal skills (especially in communicating with young people), intellectual skills (for example, how to evaluate evidence about the effectiveness of interventions), and knowledge (about the youth justice system and broader prevention programmes).

6. Integrate children's welfare services with offender management

In the Scottish system, all matters concerning children's welfare are handled by the same (lay) panel that organizes the response to children's offending. In England and Wales, by contrast, the Children Act 1989 separated proceedings for children in need of care and protection from those accused of committing crimes. Children in need of care are dealt with in the family proceedings courts although of course they are often the same as the children accused of offences in the youth courts. Given that the principle of separating the two systems is entrenched, special efforts should be made to integrate children's welfare services with responses to youth offending through the justice system. Children's Trusts have the task of coordinating all of the local services concerned with children's welfare, so one option would be to create close links between restorative conference facilitators and Children's Trusts. Making use of these links, facilitators would need to have the capacity to involve social workers and relevant health service staff in the conference and to make use of a full range of programmes and interventions managed by different branches of local government, the NHS, and other services.

7. Limit ASBOs to non-criminal matters

Britain is highly unusual among developed nations in having separate legislation to deal with 'antisocial behaviour' as distinct from crime. It is of course hard to believe that there is a special problem of 'antisocial behaviour' in Britain that is not paralleled elsewhere. Instead, policy on antisocial behaviour in Britain has developed over the past dozen years out of a particular form of political competition allied to the formal properties of a youth justice system ripe for reform. Where the standard youth justice system is perceived to be clumsy, over-formal, long-winded and ineffective, there is a strong impetus to supplement it with something more flexible. But there are serious disadvantages with creating a parallel system, as set out in Chapter 5. Most important, it may become an alternative route to custody, which may become a short cut.[3] Because it is not fully integrated with the rest, this add-on module may not express the principles that will animate a reformed youth justice system.

In practice, many of the behaviours dealt with through ASBOs are criminal, although minor (in a few cases, they may even be quite serious). In some cases, a pattern of repetition makes behaviours that seem individually trivial much more serious, and worth responding to as crimes. As the youth justice system becomes more flexible and responsive, with restorative principles at its core, it becomes capable of delivering an appropriate response to antisocial behaviour that has criminal elements. The response to criminal antisocial behaviour should therefore be transferred to the reformed youth courts, and it should be framed in the categories of the criminal law. This approach ensures that there is a serious response to serious antisocial behaviour with the safeguards provided by criminal procedure.

Non-criminal antisocial behaviour should then be mainly dealt with through the existing Acceptable Behaviour Contracts, but there may be a role for the lay youth offending panels in framing and overseeing these contracts. This would be a way of helping local people to engage with and challenge the problematic behaviour of young people.

8. Reshape custodial institutions

As the numbers of young offenders in custody are reduced, so the nature of remaining custodial institutions must change. They will house mainly young people with serious behavioural problems and needing specialist care and education. The present Young Offenders Institutions – essentially prisons – will need to be phased out, with the Secure Children's Homes and Secure Training Centres being adapted to meet the needs of the young people sent to them, who will tend to be deeply troubled. The favourable staff to young person ratios in these smaller institutions would need to be maintained, and their emphasis on rehabilitation and reintegration would need to be developed further. There may be scope for creating academies for young offenders that serve both the custodial population and the much larger body of young offenders prescribed training as part of a restorative justice programme.

9. Switch resources to prevention

Chapter 7 gives many examples of programmes to prevent young people from developing patterns of criminal behaviour as they grow up. Using high standards of evidence, all of the cited programmes have been shown to reduce criminal conduct later in life. There are examples of successful programmes at different stages – in infancy, in childhood and in adolescence – and successful examples of universal programmes, ones targeted on disadvantaged neighbourhoods, and others on disadvantaged individuals or families. As outlined below, the benefits of successful prevention typically outweigh the costs by a considerable margin, although of course the benefits are realized a number of years later, when a different government will be in power. In the long run there will be major benefits from reducing custody and switching resources to prevention.

Nearly all prevention programmes produce a range of benefits. For example, the High/Scope Perry Preschool Project carried out in Ypsilanti, Michigan, reduced offending but also increased educational attainment, employment prospects, and income (see Chapter 7). This represents both an opportunity and a problem. There is the opportunity to produce benefits in many different areas of policy from a single investment. The problem is that several different government departments, and budgets, stand to gain from the same programme, so it is not clear which department should take the lead and how much each should contribute. Reduction of the numbers in custody would be enough to fund a significant share of a range of prevention programmes, but mainstream departments such as health and the Department of Children, Schools and Families should also play an active role and pay a large share of the cost.

Bringing about reform

Whatever they may say in public, politicians and practitioners of various persuasions recognize the failures of the response to youth crime and would like to see reforms, but they do not see a way of bringing it about. As set out in Chapter 11, the obstacles to change are formidable. For the political parties, tough criminal justice policies are like an addictive drug. Having discovered that punitive rhetoric helps to win elections, and having overcome earlier inhibitions and taboos about using it, they find it hard to give up for fear of being exposed as weak and out of touch with popular feeling. As explained by Trevor Jones in Chapter 11, public opinion is certainly complex. People have a repertoire of partly inconsistent attitudes and opinions about crime and justice. Generalized views about what is happening in the country at large are strongly influenced by information – more often misinformation – in the media and by the tone of political debate, so that people can firmly believe that crime is rising when in fact it has been falling for 15 years (see Chapter 3). Perceptions of what is happening nearer at hand, in the neighbourhood, are more strongly influenced by personal observation, experience, and hearsay. Again, views from the top of the head about how convicted criminals should be sentenced tend to be punitive, but given time to consider contextual information about a particular case, people choose similar sentences to the ones handed down by the courts, although they typically believe the courts are far more lenient than they actually are. Because of the complexity of these views and the many influences on them, it is not clear that better provision of information about crime and justice will change anything very much. Since the same people have multiple opinions, politicians and the media hold decisive power, even if they do not know how to wield it. Whether or not a policy is supported crucially depends on how it is presented and whether it is contested. Short of a truce between the parties, however, there is always the danger of a race to the bottom in criminal justice policy. How can this be avoided?

It seems unlikely that a single masterstroke can transform the political landscape in the field of youth justice, in the way that the politics of economic management was transformed by transferring decisions on the interest rate to the Monetary Policy Committee in 1997. Certainly it is desirable to shelter decisions about youth justice from the heat of political competition, but there is no one fix that will perform the feat: it can best be done in small steps by building on existing nodes of influence that are independent of politics. Over time, the general drift of policy should be to reassert the authority of experts and of evidence-based analysis. The tradition of insulating certain decisions from politics is well established in medicine: the National Institute for Health and Clinical Excellence (NICE) publishes guidelines on drugs and interventions that are to be made available and on clinical practice to be followed, as well as on measures to promote public health and prevention of disease. Evidence about what works in youth justice may not yet be as well founded as in medicine, and may be more closely entangled with values, ethics and ideologies; all the more reason, then, for a move towards generating more good evidence and placing greater reliance on it. The Centre for Excellence and Outcomes in Children and Young People's Services, funded by the Department of Children, Schools and Families, is a similar example in the field of child development. The professional autonomy of senior criminal justice professionals – especially chief constables and judges – is an enduring element of the British tradition, and the best strategy is to build on it. Examples of independent bodies that articulate professional, evidence-based standards are the National Centre for Policing Excellence, the Sentencing Advisory Panel, and the Sentencing Guidelines Council. Although as yet such bodies lack the weight and scale of NICE in the medical field, they could be the start of a tradition on which governments can build.

The nine policy initiatives set out earlier add up to a major change in the aims and balance of the youth justice system, as well as in detailed arrangements. The process of policy change does not unfold in a rational and coherent manner, so developments are hard to predict. It would be foolish to prescribe how the changes can be brought about. It will probably take a number of years. In England and Wales it is possible that a single, large package of reforms could be introduced, as happened in Scotland. There, ten years elapsed between the establishment of Lord Kilbrandon's working party and the implementation of its proposals.[4] What is more likely is that reformers – or policy entrepreneurs – can take advantage of windows of opportunity to change particular features of the system, while at the same time working on the long-term project of making broader changes in the political stream. As Jones makes clear in Chapter 11, although there has been a very marked shift towards more punitive policies over the past 25 years in some developed countries – the US and Britain, especially – the change is not by any means a universal feature of late modern polities. As explained in Chapter 10, Canada is an important example of a country that shares many features with the US, but has introduced statutory changes that substantially reduced youth custody without any increase in levels of youth crime. Michael Tonry (2007) has argued that there are features of the British scene – the market for popular newspapers and the structure of political competition, in particular – that make it especially difficult to resist the drift towards self-defeating punitivism. Nevertheless, there may be a conjunction of events that opens a window to policy entrepreneurs, and the policy process may be able to go on from there.

In gathering the critical mass to power change, it is important to mobilize advocates within the existing structures, such as like-minded chief constables, prison governors, judges and magistrates. As new structures are established they create new cadres of professionals with a belief and a stake in core values and practices such as those of restorative justice. Professional conference facilitators and specialist youth judges, with their extensive training and specialist knowledge, would be natural advocates of a new practice and culture of youth justice.

An important strategy for bringing about change is devolution of power to the local level. Currently all three types of custodial institution for young offenders are funded by the Youth Justice Board, and custody accounted for 63 per cent of its budget in 2007/8. Local Youth Offending Teams are jointly funded by the Youth Justice Board, the police, the health service, probation, and (the largest share) out of the local authority budgets for education and social services. Currently under discussion is a plan to transfer the budget for youth custody to local authorities, which would give them an incentive to transfer expenditure from (costly) custodial institutions to cheaper and more cost-effective prevention programmes. A useful strategy for bringing about change might be to hand more power over budgets to local people, so that they take ownership of local policies. People close to the ground are unlikely to continue for long with punitive policies that are ineffective, damaging, and expensive, whereas politicians playing to the gallery at the national level have a much greater incentive to do so.

Devolution to the local level is essential for the development of crime prevention programmes in particular. As set out in Chapter 7, Communities That Care is a proven model for developing and managing effective programmes for preventing young people from becoming offenders. Essential to this approach is that local people take ownership of these programmes, and the structures that will allow this to happen need to be created. Probably this can best be done by building on and adapting two existing multi-agency structures at the local level: the Children's Trusts, and the Crime Prevention Panels. The new local crime prevention organizations will then need to dispose of their own budgets made up from contributions from various sources, as in the case of Youth Offending Teams.

Devolution of decision-making, budgets, and management of prevention and custody to the local level will also create a larger body of people with experience and knowledge of the system who will become some of the key advocates for progressive change.

Costs and benefits

The current system of youth justice, covering the costs of policing, the Youth Justice Board, Youth Offending Teams and a wide range of other services covering both prevention and dealing with youth crime, is expensive. The great majority of the costs are swallowed up by policing and dealing with young people once they enter the system, though, as we shall see, putting numbers on total cost with any confidence is remarkably difficult. Spending on prevention is very low by comparison.

Two questions arise with respect to the proposals being made. First, what would their costs be to the Exchequer in comparison with the current system? Second, how would the long-term benefits compare? Because we are not even able to access good information on the current costs of the system, it is not possible to answer either of these questions definitively. However, we do know that allowing large numbers of young people to enter the youth justice system, with many being punished, is both very costly and highly ineffective. Reforms which reduce the numbers going down this route will save money. And we know that a number of preventive programmes can be highly cost effective. So as long as a reduced use of the criminal justice system is reflected in lower resources being spent on it – itself a potential challenge – and preventive programmes are well targeted, it is likely that changes of the kind we propose could both save public money and result in better outcomes.

Here we are able to collate the existing evidence on the cost of the current system and point out in broad terms the effectiveness of prevention strategies. More work is undoubtedly possible and needed in this area though, in particular to allow comparisons to be made across a range of possible policies on a consistent basis. There is enough evidence to show that reform proposals should be developed and costed in detail. The costs and benefits of reform cannot be accurately evaluated at this stage for several reasons:

- a preliminary survey of official data reveals major gaps that make it impossible to produce a reasonably accurate estimate of the present costs of responding to youth crime;

- there are widely varying estimates of the costs of some elements of the present system, notably youth offender institutions;

- some proposals (e.g. youth conferencing, specialist district judges, reshaped custodial institutions) can only be spelt out in detail and costed after extensive consultation;

- there is information about the costs and benefits of certain specific prevention programmes, but not about all;

- the transitional costs of moving to different systems cannot be estimated far in advance.

According to HM Treasury statistics, total expenditure on public order and safety in 2008/9 in England and Wales was £24.6 billion, comprising £14.2 billion on police; £6.2 billion on courts; £4.0 billion on prisons; and £0.2 billion on other public order and safety. This total is the same as expenditure on children and families (£24.6 billion) but much smaller than education (£72.6 billion) or health (£96.8 billion). However, identifying within the total expenditure on public order and safety the amount spent on young people is more or less impossible. Certain elements can be clearly identified. The current costs of community sentences and prison are relatively straightforward to calculate as they are paid for by the Youth Justice Board (YJB) and Youth Offending Teams (YOTs). In 2008/9, secure accommodation cost the YJB £313 million, while a further £23 million was spent on education and training for young people in custody. Supervision in the community and related programmes, if we equate that to YOTs and other YJB-run programmes, cost £351 million, while a further £43 million was spent by the YJB on central services.

The other major elements to be considered are police, legal aid, the Crown Prosecution Service and courts. A series of Home Office research projects have tried to estimate the economic and social costs of crime (Dubourg et al. 2005), showing separate figures for different elements of the cost, and for different crime categories. The methods used are not spelt out in detail, and the results seem to leave major elements of the costs of public services unaccounted for.[5] For the time being, we are therefore obliged to adopt a rough and ready method. Official figures show that about one-fifth of all arrests, cautions and convictions are of under-18-year-olds. We therefore start by assuming that about one-fifth of the total time and resources of the police, the courts, legal aid and the Crown Prosecution Service is attributable to young people. On this basis, we arrive at the estimates shown in Table 12.1. Unfortunately, these estimates are highly unsatisfactory. In particular, the estimates for legal aid, the

Table 12.1 Crude estimates of the cost of criminal justice services in response to youth crime, England and Wales 2008/9

	Estimate (millions)	How estimated
Police	£2,839	20% of total public spending on police
Legal aid	£227	20% of total public spending on the Criminal Defence Service
Crown Prosecution Service	£127	20% of total public spending on the Crown Prosecution Service
Courts	£127	20% of total public spending on the criminal courts
Youth Offending Teams	£351	Supervision, special programmes
Youth Justice Board central costs	£43	Education and training, central administration
Youth custody	£336	Costs of youth custody (three types of institution) as funded by Youth Justice Board, including education and training
Total	£4,050	

Crown Prosecution Service and the courts are probably too high, since the proportion of cases involving serious offences is considerably lower for younger than for older defendants.[6] In the case of the police, there is a conceptual problem, since much of what they do is not a direct response to crime, but it can be argued that everything (or nearly everything) that they do should be at least indirectly related to crime or public safety. Yet when the level of crime goes down, as it has since 1994, this does not inevitably lead to a reduction in the size or cost of the police service.[7]

These estimates are extremely unsatisfactory, and in planning reforms to youth justice services it will be important first to obtain much better financial information than is currently available. On the pessimistic side, these estimates illustrate the enormous cost of the police service in relation to the rest of the system. That is a problem because the size and cost of the police service seems to be extremely unresponsive to changes in the amount of police business. Even if we could reduce the number of young people being dealt with by the police, that would not necessarily lead to a reduction in police costs, and if there were any such reduction, it would only be many years later. On the optimistic side, reducing the number of court cases and the use of custody could produce significant savings relatively quickly.[8] More detailed planning and much better information are needed before the size of such savings can be estimated.

The confused state of existing information can be illustrated by considering the costs of youth custody. Of the £305.7m spent on youth custody in 2007/8

- £212.5m was allocated to the 2,951 places provided by the 17 Young Offenders Institutions (averaging £72,009 per place);

- £47m to the 301 places provided by four secure training centres (averaging £156,246 per place);

- £46.2m to the 218 places provided by 14 local authority secure children's homes (averaging £211,747 per place).

On the face of it, then, a place at a Young Offenders Institution (effectively a prison for young offenders) is two to three times less costly than a place at a secure training centre or a secure children's home (both are much smaller units providing more intensive care, education and training). These differences are usually explained in terms of staff-to-offender ratios, which have been estimated to be as low as 1:2 in secure training centres and secure children's homes and as high as 1:25 in Young Offenders Institutions (National Audit Office 2004). Secure training centres were also built more recently, thus incurring higher capital costs. However, a recent proposal for a pilot Young Offenders Academy in east London that looked at the costs of the secure estate found that the costs of places at Young Offenders Institutions had been substantially understated. The true per capita cost was estimated to be around £100,000 (Foyer Federation forthcoming). The authors argued that the figures quoted by the Youth Justice Board probably do not include 'all the costs incurred by national and regional management on administration, premises, insurance, staff pensions, depreciation, land, capital and other central expenditure'. This requires further investigation, but illustrates that estimation of the costs of the most central elements of youth justice services remains in doubt.

One of the key reforms suggested above, along with reducing the numbers in custody, is to close the Young Offenders Institutions and use smaller institutions, along the lines of secure training centres and secure children's homes, to house the much smaller numbers of young people remaining in custody. Although there is confusion about the true costs, it is clear enough that the cost per place is considerably higher at the smaller institutions with more favourable staff-to-inmate ratios. The reform can probably be funded – with further savings – by reducing the numbers in custody, but a reasonable question is whether the additional benefits from using the smaller institutions outweigh the additional costs per place. It is impossible to answer this question from the information available, and it will always be very difficult. Although reconviction rates can be quoted (see Chapter 3) they are not a reliable guide to the benefits of the three types of institution. That is because they do not adequately control for the systematic differences in the characteristics of young offenders sent to the three types of institution, and because they do not follow them up for long enough afterwards. Also, the smaller institutions provide a range of benefits that are not captured by reconviction rates. Given much better information, the proposal for a shift to smaller secure units could usefully be evaluated by a cost benefit analysis, but a decision on this and other matters needs to be taken long before such an analysis can be made available.

Estimating expenditure on youth crime prevention is hard because many different programmes contribute, ranging from large, universal ones, such as Sure Start, which produce a wide range of benefits, to smaller ones that are focused specifically on youth offending. The Department of Children, Schools and Families (DCSF) has recently brought together figures from various sources to produce the following estimates. Overall, resources are heavily weighted towards large and universal prevention programmes such as children's centres and extended schools (£1.7 billion) and other wider programmes including Connexions (information, advice and support for young people, £270 million), improving participation in positive activities for young people (£320 million), and an estimated £140 million for pupil referral units (education for young people excluded from school). Excluding these large programmes, DCSF estimate that £230 million is spent on a wide range of smaller interventions that at least contribute to preventing youth offending, within which around £160 million is spent annually on programmes

Table 12.2 Programmes whose main remit is to reduce youth crime: England and Wales, 2009/10

Programme	Resources (£millions)	Type
YCAP Think Family funding	2.1	System reform
YCAP Family Intervention Projects	18.7	Family-centred
Operation Stay Safe	1.7	Area-based
Street Teams	6.4	Area-based
After school patrols	3.1	Area-based
Triage in custody suites	3.7	System reform
Intensive Intervention Projects	4.0	Targeted at-risk
Challenge and Support Projects	3.9	Targeted at-risk
Youth Capital Fund Plus	22.5	Diversionary
Safer Schools Partnerships	23.0	Schools
Tackling knives/Gangs Action Programme	7.5	Enforcement
Youth Inclusion Programme	24.0	Targeted at-risk
Youth Inclusion and Support Panels	24.0	Targeted at-risk
YOT Parenting Programmes	6.0	Parenting
YOT innovative schemes	1.8	Targeted at-risk
Intensive Fostering	6.0	Targeted at-risk
Extended Schools Guns and Gangs	2.0	Schools
Total	160.4	

Source: DCSF.

whose main remit is to reduce youth crime. The latter programmes that focus on crime prevention are listed in Table 12.2.

From these figures, the total value of prevention programmes that focus on youth crime, at £160m, is just under half the cost of youth custody, at £336m. A key proposal for reform, arising out of the evidence assembled in this book, is that expenditure should be switched to prevention. There have been a number of attempts to assess in monetary terms the benefits and costs of specific programmes to prevent youth crime, most of them based on US data (Scott *et al.* 2001; Welsh and Farrington 2005; Greenwood *et al.* 1998; Aos *et al.* 2001, 2006). As set out in Chapter 7, a considerable number of programmes, using a range of different ap-proaches, have been shown to produce useful effects, yet only a small number of those that have been shown to work or to be promising in evaluations with an experimental or a quasi-experimental design (i.e. using a randomized controlled trial or a control group) have also performed cost-benefit analyses. We therefore know rather little about the economic costs and benefits of programmes to prevent offending, especial-ly programmes in the UK.

There is strong evidence from the US that early intervention with children in the nursery-school years and their mothers, especially when targeting high-risk groups, is effective in raising life chances in a variety of ways, including reducing the chances of arrest and conviction. Three programmes in particular have been shown to have very favourable cost/benefit ratios: the Nurse–Family Partnership Project (Olds *et al.* 1993; Karoly *et al.* 1998; Aos *et al.* 2001); the High/Scope Perry Pre-School Project (Barnett 1993; Karoly *et al.* 1998; Aos *et al.* 2001); and the Participate and Learn Skills Programme (Jones and Offord 1989).

Steve Aos and colleagues (2006) systematically reviewed 212 evalu-ations of programmes for young offenders in the criminal justice system, and 14 evaluations of prevention programmes with measures of crime reduction effects. Most of the programmes were conducted in the US. For some of the programmes, the analysis is based on numerous evaluations. All evaluations had comparison groups, and most had enough informa-tion to support a detailed cost-benefit analysis. Prevention programmes having a very favourable cost/benefit ratio were two mentioned already above: nurse-family partnerships, and pre-kindergarten education for children in low-income families (primarily the High/Scope Perry Pre-school Project). Four prevention programmes targeting the high school years produced measurable but considerably smaller benefits than the early years programmes. These included the Seattle Social Development Project, a programme giving financial aid to students to encourage them to graduate from high school, a programme to guide career choices, and parent–child interaction therapy. There was much more evidence about programmes targeting young people in the criminal justice system. A number of these showed very favourable cost/benefit ratios. Cost-effective programmes included: multidimensional treatment for young people in foster care; projects to divert adolescents from the criminal justice system (strongly relevant to one of the key reforms suggested above); family integrated transitions; functional family therapy on probation; multisystemic therapy (currently on trial at various locations in England and Wales, see Chapter 7); aggression replacement training; juvenile sex offender treatment; and restorative justice for low-risk offenders.

In line with the evidence summarized in Chapter 7, these findings show that switching resources from custody to early prevention and to personal change programmes for offenders is likely to be very cost effective. An essential feature of this policy, however, is that it should be evidence-led. The existing evidence base, most of it coming from the US, should be used to select the best programmes, and as they are implemented in England and Wales, these programmes should be evaluated using robust research methods. In that way the stock of useful programmes and evidence about how they work in Britain can be gradually built up.

Next steps

There is a formidable body of evidence that points to the need for reform of the systems for preventing and responding to youth crime and antisocial behaviour. This book aims to draw together the best evidence and to indicate key reforms in outline. In its report, the Commission sets out its more detailed recommendations against the background of the evidence presented here. Of course, the social scientific evidence is sadly lacking in many areas, but at any given time decisions have to be taken on the basis of the best available evidence, and life cannot stand still waiting for science to catch up. If there is support for a set of key reforms in outline, the next step is to develop more detailed plans in consultation with the actors within the youth justice system. The aim should be to use trusted, established, and familiar centres of power and influence within the existing systems as the base from which to develop and adapt.

Notes

1 However, the Scottish system covers all matters concerning children, whether or not they involve offending by the child. Here McAra is applying the 'welfare principle' to systems, like the one in England and Wales, that only deal with youth offending.
2 March 2010.
3 Glover and Hibbert (2009) found that 22 per cent of 12–14-year-olds in custody had been locked up for breach of an ASBO or a community order.
4 In Scotland, the working party under the chairmanship of Lord Kilbrandon was established in 1961; its report, which proposed the Scottish Children's

Hearing system, was published in 1964; its recommendations were largely implemented by the Social Work (Scotland) Act 1968, which came into force in 1971.

5   The largest element of expenditure is on the police. In a conference presentation Dubourg (private communication) stated that crime incidents accounted for 30 per cent of police time, non-crime incidents for 14 per cent and other activities for 56 per cent. In the costing model, other activities were treated as an overhead and their costs re-distributed between dealing with crime and non-crime incidents. In this model, therefore, crime incidents should account for 68 per cent of police costs ($=30/30+14$). In fact, the total costs of dealing with crime, as estimated by this model, add up to much less than 68 per cent of total police costs.

6   In response to a parliamentary question on 28 February 1997, the Lord Chancellor's Department stated that the total gross cost of legal aid in respect of juvenile cases heard in the youth court during 1995/6 was £16.8 million. Although relating to a much earlier year, this suggests that the estimate for legal aid in Table 12.1 is much too high, probably because young defendants tend to plead guilty and not to be represented.

7   Of course, an increase in police numbers (and therefore cost) could be among the causes of a decline in crime, but relevant research suggests that police numbers are not of central importance in driving crime rates. Trends from 1994 demonstrate that governments do not quickly adjust the police budget to reflect the amount of police business, as reflected in the crime rate. This suggests that it may be difficult in practice to switch government spending from one part of the criminal justice system to another.

8   Spending on custody seems to respond quickly to changes in demand. For example, spending on youth custody increased between 2000/1 and 2007/8 in line with the rise in the number of children sentenced and remanded to custody.

References

Aos, S., Miller, M., Drake, E. (2006) *Evidence-Based Public Policy Options to Reduce Future Prison Construction, Criminal Justice Costs and Crime Rates* (Olympia, WA: Washington State Institute for Public Policy).

Aos, S., Phipps, P., Barnoski, R. and Lieb, R. (2001) *The Comparative Costs and Benefits of Programs to Reduce Crime* (Olympia, WA: Washington State Institute for Public Policy).

Audit Commission (2004) *Youth Justice 2004: A review of the reformed youth justice system* (London: Audit Commission).

Barnett, W.S. (1993) 'Benefit-cost analysis of preschool education: Findings from a twenty-five year follow-up' *American Journal of Orthopsychiatry* 63(4), pp. 500–8.

Barnett, W.S. (1993) 'Economic evaluation of home visiting programs', *The Future of Children* 3(3), pp. 93–112.

Dubourg, R., Hamed, J. and Thorns, J. (2005) *The Economic and Social Costs of Crime Against Individuals and Huseholds 2003/04*, Home Office On-Line Report 30/05 (London: Home Office).

Foyer Federation (forthcoming) *Young Offenders Academy: Stage 2 Final Report* (London: the Foyer Federation).

Greenwood, P., Model, K, Rydell, P. and Chiesa, J. (1998) *Diverting Children from a Life of Crime: Measuring Costs and Benefits* (Rand Corporation: Rand Monograph Report).

Glover, J. and Hibbert, P. (2009) *Locking Up or Giving Up: Why Custody Thresholds for Teenagers aged 12, 13 and 14 Need to be Raised* (Ilford: Barnardo's). http://www.barnardos.org.uk/locking_up_or_giving_up_august_2009.pdf

Jones, M.B. and D.R. Offord. (1989) 'Reduction of antisocial behavior in poor children by nonschool skill-development', *Journal of Child Psychology and Psychiatry* 30(5), pp. 737–50.

Karoly, L. (1998) 'Inventing in our children: What we know and don't know about the costs and benefits of early childhood intervention' (RAND Report MR-898-TCWF).

Olds, D.L., C.R. Henderson, Jr., C. Phelps, H. Kitzman, and C. Hanks. (1993). 'Effect of prenatal and infancy nurse home visitation on government spending', *Medical Care* 31(2), pp. 155–74.

Phillips, C. and Chamberlain, V. (2006) *Mori five year report: an analysis of youth justice data* (London: YJB).

Scott, S., Knapp, M., Henderson, J. and Maughan, B. (2001) 'Financial cost of social exclusion: follow-up study of antisocial children into adulthood', *British Medical Journal* 323: pp. 191–xxx.

Shapland, J., Atkinson, A., Atkinson, H., Dignan, J., Edwards, L., Hibbert, J., Howes, M., Johnstone, J., Robinson, G. and Sorsby, A. (2008) *Does Restorative Justice Affect Reconviction? The Fourth Report from the Evaluation of Three Schemes* (London: Ministry of Justice).

Sherman, L. W. and Strang, H. (2007) *Restorative Justice: The Evidence* (London: The Smith Institute).

Tonry, M. (2007) 'Determinants of Penal Policies' in M. Tonry (ed.) *Crime, Punishment, and Politics in Comparative Perspective: Crime and Justice, A Review of Research* Vol. 36, pp. 1–48 (Chicago: University of Chicago Press).

Welsh, B. and Farrington, D. (2005) 'Economic Costs and Benefits of Early Intervention' in C. Sutton, D. Utting and D. Farrington (eds) *Support from the Start: Working with Young Children and their Families to Reduce the Risks of Crime and Anti-social Behaviour* (London: DfES).

Index

Added to a page number 'f' denotes a figure, 't' denotes a table and 'n' denotes notes.